Barron's

巴朗SAT

1600（第6版）

Barron's SAT 1600 (6th edition)

[美] 卡尔内瓦莱（Linda Carnevale）
特科尔斯基（Roselyn Teukolsky） 编著

世界图书出版公司
北京·广州·上海·西安

图书在版编目（CIP）数据

Barron's巴朗SAT1600：第6版 = Barron's SAT 1600, 6th: 英文 / (美) 卡尔内瓦莱（Linda Carnevale），（美）特科尔斯基（Roselyn Teukolsky）编著. —影印本. —北京：世界图书出版有限公司北京分公司，2018.12
ISBN 978-7-5192-5143-7

Ⅰ. ①B… Ⅱ. ①卡… ②特… Ⅲ. ①英语—高等学校—入学考试—美国—自学参考资料 Ⅳ. ①H310.41

中国版本图书馆CIP数据核字（2018）第216478号

书　　名	Barron's巴朗SAT1600（第6版） BARRON'S BALANG SAT 1600（DI 6 BAN）
编　　著	[美] 卡尔内瓦莱（Linda Garnevale）　[美] 特科尔斯基（Roselyn Teukolsky）
责任编辑	夏　丹
出版发行	世界图书出版有限公司北京分公司
地　　址	北京市东城区朝内大街137号
邮　　编	100010
电　　话	010-64038355（发行）　64033507（总编室）
网　　址	http://www.wpcbj.com.cn
邮　　箱	wpcbjst@vip.163.com
销　　售	新华书店
印　　刷	三河市国英印务有限公司
开　　本	880 mm × 1230 mm　1/16
印　　张	31
字　　数	744千字
版　　次	2018年12月第1版
印　　次	2018年12月第1次印刷
版权登记	01-2018-6088
国际书号	ISBN 978-7-5192-5143-7
定　　价	89.00元

目 录

CONTENTS

ACKNOWLEDGMENTS 致谢

We owe thanks to many people who helped in the creation of this book.

We are grateful to our editors, Linda Turner and Samantha Karasik for their unflagging patience and advice. We would also like to thank Wayne Barr for his guidance and the production staff at Barron's for their work in making the book happen. Special thanks to our production manager, Lucille Schneider, and exceptional copyeditor, April Martinez. Thanks also to the evaluators of the manuscript, who came up with some excellent suggestions for improvement.

We had some invaluable help from our students. Garrett Tate, Ali Mehravari, and Rachel Zax painstakingly combed through the math section of the book looking for errors. They were unstinting in offering advice and suggestions. A special thank-you to Andrea B. Goetz, Dana Jean, Brian Tashman, and Jean Benz, skillful writers who generously took the time to write under deadline pressure and who allowed their exemplary essays to be featured in this book. We extend much appreciation to all of our students who helped us to understand the intricacies and challenges of this test from their points of view.

Thank you to Fred Deppe, Helen Perl, and Karen Seifert at Ithaca High School for sharing the latest math textbooks. Thank you to Steven Levy for his enthusiastic contribution to the vocabulary exercise that debuted in the second edition. Warm regards to our former colleagues at Cold Spring Harbor High School and Ithaca High School.

This book could not have happened without the understanding and support of family members and the kind words of encouragement from friends. With much appreciation to Laura March, whose support and guidance from the inception of this project have been invaluable. And a special thank-you to Brenda Cooper for her daily messages of encouragement. Much gratitude to our husbands, who were devoted partners in this project from the beginning, Sandro Carnevale and Saul Teukolsky. Hugs to our children, Phillip, Andrew, and Luca Carnevale, and Rachel and Lauren Teukolsky, and Josh Adams. We dedicate this book to them.

Linda Carnevale
Old Brookville, NY

Roselyn Teukolsky
Ithaca, NY
August 2017

WELCOME TO THE 1600 CLUB
欢迎来到1600分俱乐部

If the words SAT 1600 CLUB are calling your name, then you are a top student, a strong reader, and a motivated, serious test taker. You are ready for the big leagues, and you don't have time for piddling advice such as "Focus on what you're reading," "Use your calculator for long division," or "Clear your mind before you start the grammar section." You want select, inspired strategies that can make a difference to your score.

As you work through this book, focus on the strategies given for each question type. We want you to have it all: the basics *and* beyond. We leave no stone unturned as we share with you a multitude of tips and techniques that have enabled us to achieve perfect scores in our respective areas of expertise. You *can* realize your personal best score!

The math and verbal coaching in this book is thorough, multifaceted, and effective. Wherever possible, we offer alternative approaches to answering questions. We let you in on the do's and don'ts of smart test taking. If you score 700 or above on each of the sections of the updated SAT, you will enter the ranks of the top 5 percent of students, the 1600 Club.

THE UPDATED SAT TEST 新版SAT考试

The 1600 Club is up to speed on the updated SAT test.

Over the last couple of years, the SAT test has changed in a big way. If you are a member of the 1600 Club, you will

- Review the rigorous high school course work that forms the basis for the kinds of questions tested.
- Be prepared to learn fewer, more important topics in depth.
- Show skill in analyzing data presented in graphs and tables.
- Practice questions that require you to read, analyze, and comprehend challenging texts.
- Focus on your school work, rather than relying on tricks.
- Incorporate graphical data into information from reading passages.
- Decode meanings of words and how they're used in context.
- Recognize grammar, usage, diction, and syntax used in long reading passages.
- Analyze effective techniques of essay writing.
- Hone your core abilities in math to solve problems in context.
- Learn all the math categories and sharpen your skills in the areas of algebra that are emphasized in the current test.

- Review your course work on data analysis and statistics.
- Polish key topics in advanced algebra.
- Be aware of those additional topics for the math test, like trigonometry.
- Become skilled in using your graphing calculator.

WHO IS THIS BOOK FOR? 此书为谁而写？

This book is for *you* since you aspire to achieve a perfect score on the SAT. With consistent use of this book as part of your plan of study, you could achieve more than you think you're capable of! Week after week, read through the strategies and work hard on the practice exercises. Visualize yourself approaching the ranks of the top 5 percent of test takers. We have every confidence in you. You can do it!

WHAT SETS THIS BOOK APART FROM THE REST? 此书有何与众不同之处？

The majority of test takers can get the easier questions right—the level 1 and 2 questions. A good many can also do well on the level 3's, which are of medium difficulty. However, to achieve a score that stands out to the Ivy Leagues and the scholarship committees, you have to crack a good number of the harder, level 4 and 5, questions. Analysis of the math part of the SAT shows that, on average, 25 percent of all questions are ranked as hard—the level 4 and level 5 questions. More interestingly, a test taker who gets every level 1, 2, and 3 question correct, but misses every level 4 and 5, can max out only at a 650 score. For where you want to go and for what you want to achieve, a 650 split may not cut it.

Think of this book as a push to the finish line. Let's strive to get you as close to an 800 as possible on each of the two sections. For the verbal parts, original strategy acronyms help you to answer questions on the reading test and to write a high-scoring essay. For the tricky math questions, some "nonclassroom" strategies show you how to achieve surprisingly fast and successful results. With practice you will start to recognize which strategies apply to particular questions.

The Online Test 在线测试

In addition to the practice test in Part 5, this book also comes with an online test that can be accessed on your computer, smartphone, or tablet. The online test is a complete sample SAT test with Reading, Writing and Language, and Math sections, as well as an optional Essay section, as they appear on the actual SAT exam. Detailed answers and explanations are provided for every question.

To access the online test, go to: *barronsbooks.com/TP/SAT/1600/*

WHAT EXACTLY IS ON THE SAT? SAT究竟考什么？

The SAT test is 3 hours long, or 3 hours plus 50 minutes if you do the optional essay.

There are three sections:

1. Evidence-Based Reading and Writing
    - Reading Test
    - Writing and Language Test

2. Math
   - No-Calculator Section
   - Calculator Section
3. Essay (optional)

Score Reporting 分数报告

Score Reporting: The scale range is 400–1600:

200–800 for Evidence-Based Reading and Writing
200–800 for Math
2–8 on each of three traits for the Essay

Time 时间

Time: 180 minutes without essay, 230 minutes with essay
Reading: 65 minutes for 52 questions or tasks
Writing and Language: 35 minutes for 44 questions
Essay: 50 minutes for 1 task
Math: 80 minutes for 58 questions

You have your work cut out for you!

Mathematics Section—Worth 800 Points 数学：800分

- 80 minutes
- 25-minute no calculator section, 20 questions
- 55-minute calculator section, 38 questions
- Multiple-choice questions in which you select the answer from four choices
- Grid-in questions in which you provide the answer in a small grid
- Two related extended reasoning questions to which you provide grid-in answers

Evidence-Based Reading and Writing Section—Worth 800 Points 基于证据的阅读和写作：800分

Reading Test

- 65 minutes
- 52 questions
- 4 single passages and one pair of passages
- (500–750 words per passage or paired set of passages)

Writing and Language Test

- 35 minutes
- 44 questions
- 4 passages (400–450 words per passage)

An Essay (optional)

- 50 minutes to write an essay based on one passage 650–750 words long
- Scoring aspects: Reading, Analysis, and Writing (sub-score of 2–8 per aspect)

Graph/Table-Related Questions 图表题

As of March 2016, the SAT features questions on the Reading Test, as well as on the Writing and Language Test, that require students to reference visual data representations. These depictions of data can appear in a variety of formats, including tables, charts, bar graphs, line graphs, and even pie charts. To simplify, in the explanation that follows, we will refer to these graphical depictions simply as "graphs."

Reading and interpreting graphs is a skill that can be strengthened with practice. One approach is to "sidebar" and annotate the information that answers these questions. To do so, use the following steps:

Step 1: Determine what information the graph displays. What are the information labels for the ***x*-axis** and the ***y*-axis**? What **duration of time** is depicted in the graph? How many **types of data** points appear? Ask yourself: Where are the zeros? Be aware that the axes on the graph may not start at zero.

Step 2: Consider the graph's **title** and **subtitle**, if provided.

Step 3: Read any **footnotes** that may appear beneath the graph.

Step 4: Determine whether a **legend** or a **key** accompanies the graph. If so, what information does it contain?

Step 5: Realize that if a **dotted line** appears within a line graph it indicates the mean (average) in terms of the data displayed.

Step 6: Read the **source information** that typically appears beneath the graph. It usually starts with "Adapted from…" Perspective, context, and insight can be gleaned from the source of the graph as well as from its copyright date.

Step 7: Finally, determine what **conclusions** can be accurately drawn from this graph.

Just as it is wise and effective to annotate reading passages, it is equally important to annotate graphs and charts using the surrounding white space. Astute test-takers annotate graphs and their corresponding information, including titles, legends, axes, labels, source notes, and footnotes. In addition, you can annotate by underscoring, circling, or drawing an asterisk near information you feel is most important and relevant to the questions you are asked to answer.

1600 CLUB ICONS 1600分俱乐部图标

As you work through this book, you will spot several icons, each of which provides you with a helpful test-taking tip.

Active Pencil  铅笔

Whenever you see the ***Active Pencil*** icon, expect a recommendation showing you how to use your sharpened pencil as a test-taking tool. Smart test takers stay on top of their tasks by writing as they think. This gives them an edge and helps them to keep focused.

Time Saver  计时器

Look for the ***Time Saver*** icon to get tips on how to enhance your test-taking speed, without losing accuracy. High scorers know that time is of the essence on the SAT.

Calculator  计算器

Look for the ***Calculator*** icon for alternative solutions to some of the math problems. Judicious use of your calculator can save you time and effort on several questions.

The 1600 Club knows what to expect on the SAT test.

GET IN THE GAME 备考

Acing the SAT has much to do with getting in the game. Think of it this way: When a goalkeeper shows up at a 5-hour soccer tournament, she is equipped and ready, with a mindset toward winning. She has her cleats, shin guards, goalie gloves, padded goalie shorts, and a goalkeeper's jersey. She is also equipped with at least two water bottles, a sports drink, and energy-sustaining snacks. She is ready for the task.

When you show up on the SAT test day, will you be geared up and ready? The night before, pack each of the following items in a small tote bag, and bring them to the test. Use this checklist to make sure you're good to go:

1600 Club Test-Day Checklist
1600分俱乐部推荐考试当天所带物品清单

- ❑ Your admission ticket
- ❑ Proper ID, with a current, recognizable photo, such as a driver's license or student ID card
- ❑ At least two sharpened #2 pencils
- ❑ A hand-held pencil sharpener, in case the one available to you is defunct
- ❑ A graphing calculator (preferable) or scientific calculator

- ❑ An extra set of fresh batteries; we've heard too many sad stories about batteries that go dead
- ❑ A water bottle
- ❑ A couple of energy-sustaining snacks
- ❑ A small package of tissues
- ❑ Cough drops, in case you start to cough or your throat becomes dry

A special note about cell phones. Use of cell phones, iPods, iPads, or any other tablet device is not allowed within the SAT test centers. If your device makes noise, or you're seen using a device, including during breaks, you may be dismissed immediately, your scores may be canceled, and your device may be confiscated and not returned to you.

The bottom line: Be smart and leave your phone at home on test day!

Make sure that you're bright-eyed and alert on the day of the test. Get a good night's sleep, and save the late-night partying for another weekend.

The 1600 Club is always prepared and leaves nothing to chance.

STUDY GUIDES 学习指导

Beginning on page 7, we have included two sample study guides that provide goals for you to work toward depending upon how much time you have left before the test. The first study guide will prepare you to review the Evidence-Based Reading, Evidence-Based Writing and Language, and Essay sections of the SAT, while the second study guide will prepare you to review the Mathematics section of the SAT. The last column in each guide provides chapters from this book that you should refer to in order to check off each goal.

Evidence-Based Reading, Evidence-Based Writing and Language, and Essay Study Guide

基于证据的阅读、基于证据的写作和语言，以及论文写作指导

Time Left Before the Test	Goals	Chapters from This Book
8 weeks	Learn the basics of the SAT by reading "Welcome to the 1600 Club." Then begin your review by studying the "1600 Club Reading Strategies." ❑ Learn the "1600 Club Global Reading Strategies" and the "Reading Secret Formula." ❑ Study the "High Scorer's Strategy Acronym." ❑ Work through the "Practice Reading Questions" and be sure to review the answer explanations!	Welcome to the 1600 Club Chapter 1: 1600 Club Reading Strategies Chapter 2: Practice Reading Questions
7 weeks	Prepare for the Evidence-Based Writing and Language Test. ❑ Familiarize yourself with the "Grammar Counting" technique. ❑ Learn how to identify verb errors, pronoun errors, faulty idioms, faulty parallelisms, and diction errors. ❑ Study how to avoid misplaced modifiers, when to use adjectives versus when to use adverbs, and how to spot plural-singular inconsistencies, redundancies, and wordiness. ❑ Review the sections on faulty comparisons, run-ons, comma splices, and fragments, and learn how to avoid them in your own writing.	Chapter 3: English Grammar and Usage

Time Left Before the Test	Goals	Chapters from This Book
6 weeks	Sharpen your skills with the "Practice Writing and Language Questions," which cover two passage genres: humanities and careers. ❑ Learn how to answer questions that involve bar graphs, like the ones that correspond to Passage 2 in this section. ❑ Remember to carefully read through the answer explanations, which are important instructional tools for test preparation.	Chapter 4: Practice Writing and Language Questions
5 weeks	Although the essay is an optional part of the SAT, it will still be to your benefit to familiarize yourself with the tools for writing a well-constructed essay, because these tools will help you in college and beyond. ❑ Study the "1600 Club Comprehensive Strategies." ❑ Review the section that teaches you how to "Take Inventory of the Author's Use of Evidence, Reasoning, and Stylistic Elements." ❑ Learn how to create a "Timing Plan" so that you can pace yourself as you write your essay. ❑ Study some of the most important essay-writing strategies, including the sections entitled "Engage Your Reader," "Edit, Using the 1600 Club Checklist," "Support Your Thesis with Examples," and "Sentence and Vocabulary Variety." ❑ Learn how to assess your writing and how to maintain your voice throughout your essay.	Chapter 5: Writing the 50-Minute Essay

Time Left Before the Test	Goals	Chapters from This Book
	❑ Review how to "Eliminate SMOG" from your writing (SMOG includes spelling errors, mechanical errors, overuse, and grammatical errors). ❑ Pay close attention to the "Essay Scoring Guide" so that you know exactly what the test graders will be looking for in your essay.	
4 weeks	Anticipate what to expect on the essay by familiarizing yourself with the "Sample Source Texts." ❑ Try writing an essay, or maybe two! Ask a teacher, parent, or skilled writer to review your essay and provide constructive feedback.	Chapter 6: Sample Source Texts
3 weeks	Once you've reviewed the "Sample Source Texts" from Chapter 6, review the sample advanced responses that would score well. Follow this up by strengthening your verbal skills with the section on "Upper-Level Vocabulary Building." Study each of the following closely: ❑ "1600 Club Vocabulary Immersion" ❑ "Four-Letter-Word List for Club Members" ❑ "Upper-Level Word Lists for Club Members" ❑ "Exercise: Choose the Correct Synonym" Make flash cards for the vocabulary words that are new to you or challenging for you.	Appendix: Sample Source Text Advanced Responses (Chapter 6) Appendix: Upper-Level Vocabulary Building

Time Left Before the Test	Goals	Chapters from This Book
2 weeks	Take the SAT Practice Test available online (see the inside front cover of this book for details). ❑ Try the whole test in the time allotted. ❑ Identify your areas of weakness. (Every question refers to a section in this book.) ❑ Review the relevant sections in this book that you still need to brush up on.	Online SAT Practice Test
1 week	Take the SAT Practice Test in Part 5 of this book. Work toward the goals described above. Be sure to review your areas of weakness.	Part 5: SAT Practice Test
1 day	Create flash cards of important grammar rules, timing tips, strategy acronyms, and vocabulary words. Review any final areas that you need a quick refresher on!	All sections of this book

Mathematics Study Guide 数学学习指导

Time Left Before the Test	Goals	Chapters from This Book
8 weeks	Dip your toe in with some sample questions and techniques. ❑ Learn the "Gridding-in Rules." ❑ Study the "How to Use the Graphing Calculator" section with your calculator in hand. ❑ Practice the "Tips for the SAT Math Sections."	Chapter 7: Getting Started Chapter 8: Strategies for Solving SAT Math Problems

Time Left Before the Test	Goals	Chapters from This Book
7 weeks	Study numbers, probability, sequences, basic geometry, and problems in context. ❑ Pay particular attention to "Sequences Involving Exponential Growth." ❑ "Special Right Triangles" occur in many SAT Math problems. Learn the lengths! ❑ "Areas and Perimeters" must be reviewed carefully. ❑ The "Coordinate Geometry" formulas must also be at your fingertips. ❑ Practice those word problems. Make a sketch for each setup.	Chapter 9: 1600 Club Background Topics Chapter 10: Problems in Context
6 weeks	Review functions, linear functions, and linear equations and inequalities. These are crucial topics on the SAT. Therefore, be sure to brush up on: ❑ slope ❑ the equation of a line ❑ linear equations and inequalities ❑ the linear function as a model	Chapter 11: Heart of Algebra
5 weeks	Go over percents and statistics, which are popular topics on the SAT. ❑ Review percents! ❑ Study the "Strategies for Reading Simple Graphs." (There will be lots of them on the No-Calculator section of the test.) ❑ The "Centers of Data" (mean, median, and mode) will show up in many questions, so know them well! ❑ Review the sections on "Standard Deviation," "Scatterplots," and "Line of Best Fit."	Chapter 12: Problem Solving and Data Analysis

Time Left Before the Test	Goals	Chapters from This Book
4 weeks	Study advanced algebra, including quadratic functions, all equations, transformations, and composition of functions. This is the major part of your high school algebra, and it will feature prominently on the Mathematics section of the SAT. Pay special attention to: ❑ the quadratic function ❑ quadratic equations and inequalities ❑ equations with rational expressions ❑ modeling quadratic functions	Chapter 13: Passport to Advanced Math
3 weeks	Review solid geometry, circle geometry, trigonometry, and complex numbers. There will be a few questions on these topics. To get a perfect score: ❑ Know how to apply the formulas for prisms, cylinders, cones, and pyramids. ❑ Learn the Circle facts, including the "Equation of a Circle in the Plane." ❑ In the Trigonometry section, pay special attention to "Radians and Arc Length" and learn about the Cofunction Identity. ❑ Review the definition and simplification of "Complex Numbers."	Chapter 14: Additional Topics in Math
2 weeks	Take the SAT Practice Test available online (see the inside front cover of this book for details). ❑ Try the whole test in the time allotted. ❑ Identify your areas of weakness. (Every question refers to a section in this book.) ❑ Review the relevant sections in this book that you still need to brush up on.	Online SAT Practice Test

Time Left Before the Test	Goals	Chapters from This Book
1 week	Take the SAT Practice Test in Part 5 of this book. Work toward the goals previously described. Be sure to review your areas of weakness.	Part 5: SAT Practice Test
1 day	Create an index card of facts and formulas. Review any final areas that you need a quick refresher on!	All sections of this book

Be sure to visit *barronsbooks.com/TP/SAT/1600/*
to take the online practice test!

第一部分 PART 1

THE EVIDENCE-BASED READING TEST 基于证据的阅读测试

In the Reading Test, you will have four passages and one set of paired passages to read on a variety of topics. Topics include United States literature, world literature, history, social studies, and science. Still other questions will test your reasoning skills as you analyze the passages based on their science or history content. Passages will vary and range in length from 500 to 750 words per passage. You will have ten to twelve questions to answer based on each reading passage.

The types of questions you will be asked are numerous but basically fall into the following categories.

■ An Emphasis on Words Used in Context

Unequivocally, there is an inextricable link between vocabulary and reading comprehension. With a rich, deep, and expansive vocabulary, you are more likely to absorb what you read accurately and fully. In addition, you can more readily discern the meanings of words in various contexts and usages. Vocabulary's vital role should not be underestimated, particularly when text is rich, multilayered, and complex.

The updated SAT will focus on Tier Two words, which are words that have "high-utility" across a wide range of disciplines as they are used in written texts. Unlike Tier One words, which are primarily conversational, Tier Two words are used more often in mature writing. Unlike Tier Three words, which tend to be limited to a specific concentration and are relatively rare in their written text frequency, Tier Two words appear frequently in high-quality and mature texts. Beyond simply knowing a word's definition, you will be asked to demonstrate an in-depth competency with the various meanings of words that will necessitate gleaning subtleties of meaning through context.

■ An Emphasis on Command of Evidence

The SAT Reading Test requires you not only to glean relevant details and information from a text but also, in some cases, to identify the particular segment or segments of the passage that best serve as the evidence for the conclusions you determine. In other words, you are expected to interpret text and validate your interpretations by citing the best textual support. Support can be taken from the passage itself or from accompanying graphics, such as diagrams, charts, and tables.

The updated SAT Evidence-Based Reading Test will require you to analyze bar graphs, charts, and tables.

■ The Inclusion of Informational Graphics

On the SAT Reading Test, two passages will most likely include one or two graphics (charts, bar graphs, diagrams, illustrations, or tables) that convey information and/or data related to the given passages. You will be asked to interpret the information demonstrated in one or more graphics and/or asked to accurately incorporate that information with information provided in the text.

第一章 Chapter 1

1600 CLUB READING STRATEGIES 1600分俱乐部阅读策略

Hunting and gathering, listening . . . these are skills that humankind has been practicing since the dawn of time. To some extent, they're built into our genetic code—innate, inherent, intrinsic—you get the idea. How hard can they be? Ask a caveman. No, really, here's how these skills apply to critical reading at the long-passage level.

Here are two analogies to mull over that pertain to critical reading:

1. *Critical reading is like hunting and gathering*—hunting, that is, for context clues.
2. *Critical reading is like listening very carefully*—listening (in your mind) to what the author is saying.

1600 Club Global Strategies 1600分俱乐部总体策略

HUNTING AND GATHERING 寻找与搜集信息

Context clues come in several forms: groupings of words that are scattered through the text, a phrase, or, simply, a significant word. Each word an author uses means something. The author's choice of words offers clues as to his or her meaning, point of view, mood, and attitude. To answer reading questions accurately, you have to sniff out and scope out the context clues in the passage or the relevant information in accompanying graphs and tables.

PASSAGE EVIDENCE 段落中的证据

There is no guesswork in critical reading and no "maybe this answer works." There is no place for personal conjecture or creativity. Do not "read into" anything. You're probably a cerebral type, so you may be prone to do just that, but resist. Do the work required to get the right answers: gather the evidence! In addition to collecting specific words that function as context clues, gather phrases and sentences that support a particular answer choice. These items are called passage evidence.

"Evidence" refers to words, phrases, sentences, and graphical information that support the best answer choice.

1600 Club Coaching: *High scorers "listen" very carefully as they read.*

LISTENING 聆听

Listen (in your mind) so carefully that you get a full sense of the author's viewpoints and attitudes. Listen so carefully that you can, in a sense, paraphrase what he or she is saying without injecting your opinions or any other outside information. Listen clearly, resisting the impulse to call upon what you've learned from your textbooks or from educational television programming. Even the Discovery and History channels will not help you here.

Think of it this way. The author, lying on the couch, is telling a story, and you are sitting in a leather swivel chair, notebook in hand, listening carefully to everything he or she is saying. You are even taking mental notes in addition to written ones. This patient-therapist model represents the kind of careful listening you need to succeed when working on critical reading at the long-passage level.

More Coaching: *High scorers are loyal to what is expressed in the passage. They never select answers that distort or stray from what is said by the author.*

Be such a good listener that you can paraphrase just what the author has said. Immerse yourself in the author's perspective, and—above all—do not think for yourself. Independent thinking, or thinking too deeply, can get you in trouble on the SAT.

READING SECRET FORMULA 阅读的秘密公式

The critical reading secret formula is a global strategy that you can use as you read paragraphs, long passages, or paired passages.

✻ Critical Reading Secret Formula = Read + React + Interact *plus* Visualize ✻

When you read, you're in charge. You should put yourself into an active reading mode. Don't let the author's words run over your head like rainwater. You must absorb what is said; in other words, you need to become an *active reader*. The formula above is your recipe for active reading. If you employ these steps as you read, you will be in a strong position to absorb and recall all the points that the author puts forth.

Evidence-based reading on the SAT is a far cry from reading for pleasure. On this test, have you ever seen an action-packed passage on basketball? The latest fashions? The greatest gaming systems? Snowboarding a black diamond ski slope? No! In case you haven't noticed, the College Board does not go out of its way to make the reading passages interesting. Rarely or never will you find a reading passage on snowboarding, mountain biking, baseball, or the raddest malls.

Former critical reading topics have included: black American fiction and the romance novel, nuclear reactors and particle accelerators, emigrating from Poland to Canada, ancient Athens as a model of democracy, the mating habits of red-winged blackbirds, and a Chinese-American grappling with her cultural identity. Reading rather dry, often convoluted passages on such topics requires discipline. Psyche yourself up to get into the passages and to follow the active reading formula as a way to discipline yourself as you read. Here's the high scorer's reading credo: *I'll get the passage; it won't get me.*

1600 Club Coaching: *High scorers abandon their personal theories of the world and get into the author's head instead.*

Read 阅读

As you read, get into the author's head. See the world through the author's eyes, no matter how strange his or her "world view" may seem to you. Abandon any feelings, biases, and reasoning that you associate with the topic; read the passage with your mind as a clean slate. As you read, etch the author's point of view and vision onto your mental slate so that passage evidence is available for you to call upon later.

React, Using ABS 做出反应，用上ABS

Reading is not about having words, like raindrops, run over your head. It's about absorbing the words and letting them impact you. As you read, react to what you're reading! Obviously you cannot talk aloud; the proctor might think you're losing it! But a dialogue should be going on *in your head*—a dialogue between you and what the author is saying in the passage. Using your active pencil, you may even want to jot down marginal notes or symbols next to paragraphs that indicate your reactions. For example: *Great idea!* or **Unreal!** or ?? or !! or VERY SAD or *Brave!* or ☹ or ☺ or ✱, as the passage moves you. See the Gallery of Symbols on page 20.

Let ABS (**A**bbreviations, **B**rief Notations, **S**ymbols) remind you of a few pencil-to-paper ways in which you may react to a passage as you read. To put ABS into practice, start off by requiring yourself to write one or more ABS notations, as explained below, for every paragraph that you read. Try jotting down ABS notations in the margins as you work through practice passages, and see if ABS helps you to connect with greater clarity to the contents of the passages.

With practice, you may find that you only need to write ABS notations for every second or third paragraph that you read. Experiment with ABS and see what works most effectively for you.

"A" Stands for Annotate, using Abbreviations "A"代表缩写

You can write, in abbreviated form, your reactions to what you are reading. Instead of writing "role reversal between mother and daughter," simply annotate in the margins *mthr-dghtr RR*. Instead of writing "nostalgic for his younger days," write *nstgc-youth*. Instead of "very bitter relationship break-up," *bttr bk-up*. You get the idea. The key is to write your reactions in an abbreviated form so that it is quick and won't clutter up the margins and obscure the passage that you will—no doubt—need to refer back to. Practice reacting and annotating the text in abbreviated form as you work through the practice exercises and tests in this book and online.

"B" Stands for Brief Notations "B"代表短注释

Brief notations are basically the same as abbreviations, yet they serve as an additional reminder to keep your written reactions *brief* and simple. Brief notations may or may not be abbreviated, but they should be brief: one or two words at most! If you must write more than that, then abbreviations should kick in!

Examples of brief notations that might appear in the margins of critical reading passages include: *conflict, truce, money, intrigue, fallacy, harmful rumor, equal rights, adaptation, cultural value*, and so on. These one- or two-word marginal memos will come in handy as you navigate the passage, for the second time, as you look for details and evidence to support the best answer choice. Your marginal notes will serve as reminder "messages" for you, helping you to keep track of all that you have read and how the information is laid out in the passage.

"S" Stands for Symbols "S" 代表符号

If you like doodling and drawing, using symbols to respond to the reading will suit you well. We've touched upon symbols, but the potential for symbols is virtually limitless. Develop your own repertory of symbols that you can use to express your feedback and response to the various reading passages on the SAT. Consider the "Critical Reading Gallery of Symbols" below:

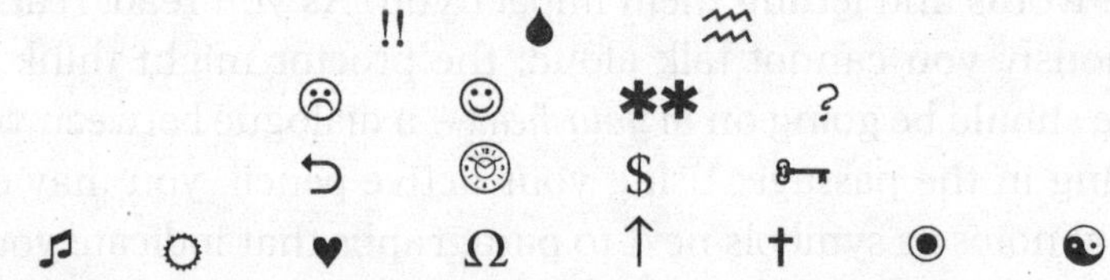

Be creative. Think outside the box! Which symbols might you use in addition to the ones presented in the Symbol Gallery above?

To get a six-pack, you must work your abs. To get as close to an 800 as possible, add ABS to your critical reading strategy repertoire.

Talk to yourself: "That's an odd way of looking at tree bark" or "I wonder what it would be like to have broad, colorful shoulder patches like the black raven."

Ask yourself: "Why would this dude want to study extraterrestrial radio static? How could he take such a risk and contradict all the current data?"

Silently ponder: "Who knew that certain cultures communicate through the fruit they serve?" or "Is this author gently poking fun, or is he being downright sarcastic?"

REACTING while reading will make you a more effective reader. You will absorb more and remember more.

Interact 交互反应

Try to connect with the passage on some level. Interacting while reading will help you to retain what is being discussed. Relate the passage to yourself. Again, get an internal dialogue going. For example:

> **"I wouldn't want to leave my hometown either."**
> **"I know what it's like to feel as though my identity has many aspects."**
> **"I never realized that deserts could be cold."**
> **"I never thought of a bat as a flying mouse!"**
> **"If I were an investigative journalist, I'd also be skeptical about my information sources."**

Again, don't let the words run over your head like rainwater.

Visualize 形象化

Your mind's eye is very powerful. Put it to work for you as you read the critical reading passages. For many of us, vision is our predominant learning modality. If the passage is about a midwestern prairie, visualize the countryside as delineated by the author. In your mind's eye, paint pictures of the rustic bridges, the serene landscape, and the tall yellow daffodils that the author describes.

If the passage is about a New England town meeting, visualize the details that the author mentions. Can you see the assembled townspeople? Can you imagine what they're talking about? Can you picture the inside of the quaint church where the New Englanders have convened?

If the passage is about a futuristic museum design, imagine the building's interior and exterior just as the author depicts them. Use your imagination to bring the cold steel to life. See the sharp angles of the futuristic building. Imagine the ebony and scarlet color combination the author describes.

Leisure reading can occur while you're at the beach watching the surf. Leisure reading can occur while you're eating pizza. You can even read a good book while catching the sports highlights on TV. Pleasure reading and critical reading on the SAT, however, are a world apart. When the passages are long, esoteric, and sometimes downright boring, reading comprehension requires focused attention and smart strategies.

1600 Club Strategies 1600分俱乐部策略

Strategy 1: **R**ead passages piece by piece.

Strategy 2: **E**xtract the main idea from the passage.

Strategy 3: **A**nswer line-reference and sidebar questions first.

Strategy 4: **D**elve into higher-order thinking questions.

Strategy 5: **I**dentify the author's mood, tone, and purpose as you read.

Strategy 6: **N**arrow in on the *best* answer choice. Never omit.

Strategy 7: **G**lobal questions should be answered at the very end.

STRATEGY 1: READ PASSAGES PIECE BY PIECE
策略1：分块阅读长段落

How to read the passage, that is the question. Should I read the entire passage? Should I read just the first third? Should I read just the beginning and the end? Should I read the questions and then go back to the passage to hunt for answers? Most students are in a quandary about how to approach the critical reading sections.

You're smart, a high achiever, so it's unlikely that you'll have any trouble reading the entire passage—piece by piece. What does a "piece" of the passage look like? That's up to you. For some, a "piece" is a paragraph or two. For others, a "piece" is a half or a third of the passage. Experiment with reading "pieces" at a time, and you'll discover what works for you. Read so that you can maintain your concentration. After you read each piece, turn to the questions and answer the ones based on that piece. Working in this way keeps you focused and prevents you from getting befuddled by taking in too much information at a time.

Breaking a passage into "pieces" is one way to downsize a potentially daunting task. You are probably a strong and avid reader; nevertheless, breaking a long passage

Reading Passages
Do not read the entire passage at once.
Likewise, don't answer all the questions in one spurt.
Instead, follow a strategic and pragmatic process or "modus operandi."

into pieces gives you an edge by helping you to stay focused as you read and to answer the questions that correspond to each piece. High scorers know there is no real advantage to reading a passage in one spurt. In fact, if you read the entire thing in one gulp (all 80 lines, let's say), then, when you have to deal with questions based on the first couple of paragraphs, you will end up wasting time rereading those early parts of the passage. The early paragraphs will no longer be fresh in your mind after you've slogged through 80 lines or more.

As illustrated below, a "piece" is usually a paragraph or two. (Your first piece should always include the introductory, italicized "blurb" that precedes the passage.) You are self-directed and motivated, so decide what works best for you. The dotted lines show where this passage might be downsized into manageable pieces.

Version 1—Illustrates reading a science passage in five pieces
版本1——分五部分阅读长段落
(for the prudent reader who wants to stay *very* focused)

This passage is taken from Charles Darwin's 1872 book, The Expression of the Emotions in Man and Animals.

Dotted lines show where passage can be cut into pieces.

No doubt as long as man and all other animals are viewed as independent creations, an effectual stop is put to our natural desire to investigate as far as possible the causes of Expression. By this doctrine, anything and everything can be equally well explained; and it has proved as pernicious with respect to Expression as to every other branch of natural history. With mankind some expressions, such as the bristling of the hair under the influence of extreme terror, or the uncovering of the teeth under that of furious rage, can hardly be understood, except on the belief that man once existed in a much lower and animal-like condition. The community of certain expressions in distinct though allied species, as in the movements of the same facial muscles during laughter by man and by various monkeys, is rendered somewhat more intelligible, if we believe in their descent from a common progenitor. He who admits on general grounds that the structure and habits of all animals have been gradually evolved, will look at the whole subject of Expression in a new and interesting light.

The study of Expression is difficult, owing to the movements being often extremely slight, and of a fleeting nature. A difference may be clearly perceived, and yet it may be impossible, at least I have found it so, to state in what the difference consists. When we witness any deep emotion, our sympathy is so strongly excited, that close observation is forgotten or rendered almost impossible; of which fact I have had many curious proofs. Our imagination is another and still more serious source of error; for if from the nature of the circumstances we expect to see any expression, we readily imagine its presence. Notwithstanding Dr. Duchenne's great experience, he for a long time fancied, as he states, that several muscles contracted under certain emotions, whereas he ultimately convinced himself that the movement was confined to a single muscle.

In order to acquire as good a foundation as possible, and to ascertain, independently of common opinion, how far particular movements of the features and gestures are really expressive of certain states of the mind, I have found the following means the most serviceable. In the first place, to observe infants; for they exhibit many emotions, as Sir C. Bell remarks, "with extraordinary force"; whereas, in after life, some of our expressions "cease to have the pure and simple source from which they spring in infancy."[18]

Dotted lines show how you may read this long passage in manageable chunks.

In the second place, it occurred to me that the insane ought to be studied, as they are liable to the strongest passions, and give uncontrolled vent to them. I had, myself, no opportunity of doing this, so I applied to Dr. Maudsley and received from him an introduction to Dr. J. Crichton-Browne, who has charge of an immense asylum near Wakefield, and who, as I found, had already attended to the subject. This excellent observer has with unwearied kindness sent me copious notes and descriptions, with valuable suggestions on many points; and I can hardly over-estimate the value of his assistance. I owe also, to the kindness of Mr. Patrick Nicol, of the Sussex Lunatic Asylum, interesting statements on two or three points.

Thirdly Dr. Duchenne galvanized, as we have already seen, certain muscles in the face of an old man, whose skin was little sensitive, and thus produced various expressions which were photographed on a large scale. It fortunately occurred to me to show several of the best plates, without a word of explanation, to above twenty educated persons of various ages and both sexes, asking them, in each case, by what emotion or feeling the old man was supposed to be agitated; and I recorded their answers in the words which they used. Several of the expressions were instantly recognized by almost everyone, though described in not exactly the same terms; and these may, I think, be relied on as truthful, and will hereafter be specified. On the other hand, the most widely different judgments were pronounced in regard to some of them. This exhibition was of use in another way, by convincing me how easily we may be misguided by our imagination; for when I first looked through Dr. Duchenne's photographs, reading at the same time the text, and thus learning what was intended, I was struck with admiration at the truthfulness of all, with only a few exceptions. Nevertheless, if I had examined them without any explanation, no doubt I should have been as much perplexed, in some cases, as other persons have been.

Annotate passages as you read. Circle and underline key points and terms so that you can refer back to them more easily when answering the questions.

Version 2—Illustrates reading the passage in three pieces
版本2 ——分三部分阅读长段落
(for the more voracious reader who can sustain concentration with longer pieces)

This passage is taken from Charles Darwin's 1872 book, The Expression of the Emotions in Man and Animals.

No doubt as long as man and all other animals are viewed as independent creations, an effectual stop is put to our natural desire to investigate as far as possible the causes of Expression. By this doctrine, anything and everything can be equally well explained; and it has proved as pernicious with respect to Expression as to every other branch of natural history. With mankind some expressions, such as the bristling of the hair under the influence of extreme terror, or the uncovering of the teeth under that of furious rage, can hardly be understood, except on the belief that man once existed in a much lower and animal-like condition. The community of certain expressions in distinct though allied species, as in the movements of the same facial muscles during laughter by man and by various monkeys, is rendered somewhat more intelligible, if we believe in their descent from a common progenitor. He who admits on general grounds that the structure and habits of all animals have been gradually evolved, will look at the whole subject of Expression in a new and interesting light.

Reading in pieces keeps you ***focused.*** *Reading with* ***concentration*** *keeps you aware of what is stated or implied in the passage.*

The study of Expression is difficult, owing to the movements being often extremely slight, and of a fleeting nature. A difference may be clearly perceived, and yet it may be impossible, at least I have found it so, to state in what the difference consists. When we witness any deep emotion, our sympathy is so strongly excited, that close observation is forgotten or rendered almost impossible; of which fact I have had many curious proofs. Our imagination is another and still more serious source of error; for if from the nature of the circumstances we expect to see any expression, we readily imagine its presence. Notwithstanding Dr. Duchenne's great experience, he for a long time fancied, as he states, that several muscles contracted under certain emotions, whereas he ultimately convinced himself that the movement was confined to a single muscle.

In order to acquire as good a foundation as possible, and to ascertain, independently of common opinion, how far particular movements of the features and gestures are really expressive of certain states of the mind, I have found the following means the most serviceable. In the first place, to observe infants; for they exhibit many emotions, as Sir C. Bell remarks, "with extraordinary force"; whereas, in after life, some of our expressions "cease to have the pure and simple source from which they spring in infancy."[18]

In the second place, it occurred to me that the insane ought to be studied, as they are liable to the strongest passions, and give uncontrolled vent to them. I had, myself, no opportunity of doing this, so I applied to Dr. Maudsley and received from him an introduction to Dr. J. Crichton-Browne, who has charge of an immense asylum near Wakefield, and who, as I found, had already attended to the subject. This excellent observer has with unwearied kindness sent me copious notes and descriptions, with valuable suggestions on many points; and I can hardly over-estimate the value of his assistance. I owe also, to the kindness of Mr. Patrick Nicol, of the Sussex Lunatic Asylum, interesting statements on two or three points.

Thirdly Dr. Duchenne galvanized, as we have already seen, certain muscles in the face of an old man, whose skin was little sensitive, and thus produced various expressions which were photographed on a large scale. It fortunately occurred to me to show several of the best plates, without a word of explanation, to above twenty educated persons of various ages and both sexes, asking them, in each case, by what emotion or feeling the old man was supposed to be agitated; and I recorded their answers in the words which they used. Several of the expressions were instantly recognized by almost everyone, though described in not exactly the same terms; and these may, I think, be relied on as truthful, and will hereafter be specified. On the other hand, the most widely different judgments were pronounced in regard to some of them. This exhibition was of use in another way, by convincing me how easily we may be misguided by our imagination; for when I first looked through Dr. Duchenne's photographs, reading at the same time the text, and thus learning what was intended, I was struck with admiration at the truthfulness of all, with only a few exceptions. Nevertheless, if I had examined them without any explanation, no doubt I should have been as much perplexed, in some cases, as other persons have been.

Divide and Conquer 划分并各个击破

"Divide and conquer" is another name for reading strategy 1: reading in pieces. Divide and conquer is generally defined as a political strategy in which a powerful entity breaks up large concentrations of power into chunks that individually have less power than the one implementing the strategy.

Apply the divide and conquer premise to long reading passages and paired passages by "chopping up" the reading passages into paragraphs. Read one paragraph at a time; then "jump out" of the passage to answer questions that correspond to that paragraph. Unlike the ACT, whose reading comprehension questions tend to come from random parts of the passage, the SAT usually presents questions in the order of the material presented, making the divide and conquer technique particularly effective.

Sip, Don't Slurp 默读，不要出声

Now you have seen two ways of reading a long passage *in pieces*. Do you see how the "pieces" method can help you to feel in better control of a lengthy passage? The 1600 Club knows the value of "sip, don't slurp" when it comes to digesting the passage. There's really no advantage to reading a long passage in one big, gurgling gulp.

"Sip, don't slurp" brings to mind another point. Sip carefully the parts of the passage that you mark with sidebars or line references (see page 30), for you are guaranteed to have questions that pertain to these parts. Just because a portion of the passage has no sidebars or line references, however, doesn't mean you should skip over it.

Skim, Don't Skip 浏览，不要跳读

As mentioned above, there will always be portions of the passage that do not contain either sidebars or line references. These "unmarked" portions can be as small as a few lines or as large as a few paragraphs. No matter the case, skim, don't skip. The fact that these parts are not referenced doesn't mean you shouldn't read them. You don't need to scrutinize them painstakingly, but you should skim them, or "speed read" through these unmarked portions. Remember: you need to understand overarching aspects of the passage such as main idea, author's tone, and author's purpose in order to answer global questions (see Strategy 7).

Skimming parts of the passage is a time saver, but you have to be wise about when to skim and when to really focus.

Be Savvy About Sidebars (Refer to page 30)
理解补充材料（参考第30页）

- When sidebars are short (3 lines or fewer) You should scrutinize the lines; the passage evidence is likely to be subtle.
- When sidebars are long (4 lines or more) You should skim the lines to find the validating information that you need in order to select the right answer.
- When sidebars are nonexistent You should skim these parts; don't skip them altogether!

The Blurb—Know the Author/Know the Topic
简介——理解作者、主题

Make sure the first "piece" that you read is the blurb that introduces the passage. As Strategy 2 tells you (page 30), the blurb is one place that is likely to contain the main idea of the passage. There's another reason, though, why the blurb is important and should not be overlooked: more often than not, it names the author of the passage. This tidbit of information can be helpful when you are answering certain questions. Also, knowing the author helps to develop a point of view as you read. Therefore, as you read the italicized blurb, ask yourself, "Who is the author?" For authors who have written passages in the College Board practice book, you might ask: Is this author

- a physicist or a botanist?
- a German composer or a Korean-American poet?

- a Colonial American dramatist or a Colombian novelist?
- a doctor specializing in neurological disorders?
- a scholar of African-American culture?
- a critic of modern architecture or a historian?

Knowing the author establishes a mind-set and focus, and gives you a valuable edge as you embark on the passage reading.

1600 Club Coaching: *Extract important information from the blurb that precedes each reading passage. Pertinent information includes "Who's the author?", "What's the topic?", and "What's the setting (geographical location and time period)?".*

Outline Reading Approach 概要阅读法

If timing is a concern, try Outline Reading. If you have self-tested and timed yourself several times, and still can't get through the reading passages (even if taken piece by piece), try this middle-ground approach.

Checklist: Outline Reading in Greater Detail 清单：详细阅读大纲

- Before reading the passage, refrain from doing the following:
  Do not read the questions first. Time sapper.
  Do not attempt to memorize the questions before reading the passage. Time sapper.
  Do not read or skim the sets of four answer choices first. Also a time sapper.
  Do not attempt to remember a series of seven to twelve reading questions. *Big time sapper.*
- Skim the questions for numbers (numbers pop!) and quickly mark the passage with line references and sidebars accordingly.
- Skim the introductory material. Underline the main focus of the passage(s).
- Carefully and actively (*read + react + interact + visualize*) read the introductory paragraph. If this paragraph is unusually short, read the next paragraph as well for good measure. It is particularly important to absorb the ideas expressed in opening paragraphs.
- Read the first two sentences (topic sentence and one more for good measure) of each body paragraph. Skim or skip (depending on your pacing as a test taker) the rest of each body paragraph. If you have not marked a particular body paragraph with line references and sidebars, you may be able to skip it. Give it a try!
- Trust your judgment. Read short body paragraphs ("bite-size" paragraphs) in their entirety. Read long paragraphs with this time-saving approach: read the first two sentences, skim the middle, read the last sentence.
- Carefully and actively read the concluding paragraph.
- It is prudent to revisit the passage for most questions: reread generously around line references, reread sidebars, and skim pertinent parts of the passage . . . as you hunt for context clues and textual evidence.

Try Outline Reading to see if it works for you. This may be more important than ever, now that *all* questions on the SAT are passage based.

Outline Reading is effective because this method provides you with an overall sense of the passage and a framework for how the information is laid out. Below is an example of how outline reading works. The bold parts are the parts that you should read with focus and concentration. The nonbold parts you can read in a more hasty, superficial fashion, *slowing down wherever there are sidebars or line references.* Remember: you should *still* be reading piece by piece (a paragraph or two at a time, for example) and answering related questions after reading each piece.

*Carefully read the **blurb** that appears at the top of the passage, and attentively read the **introductory paragraph**.*

***This passage is taken from Charles Darwin's 1872 book,* The Expression of the Emotions in Man and Animals.**

No doubt as long as man and all other animals are viewed as independent creations, an effectual stop is put to our natural desire to investigate as far as possible the causes of Expression. By this doctrine, anything and everything can be equally well explained; and it has proved as pernicious with respect to Expression as to every other branch of natural history. With mankind some expressions, such as the bristling of the hair under the influence of extreme terror, or the uncovering of the teeth under that of furious rage, can hardly be understood, except on the belief that man once existed in a much lower and animal-like condition. The community of certain expressions in distinct though allied species, as in the movements of the same facial muscles during laughter by man and by various monkeys, is rendered somewhat more intelligible, if we believe in their descent from a common progenitor. He who admits on general grounds that the structure and habits of all animals have been gradually evolved, will look at the whole subject of Expression in a new and interesting light.

Peruse the topic sentence of every body paragraph.

Read the last sentence of particularly long body paragraphs.

The study of Expression is difficult, owing to the movements being often extremely slight, and of a fleeting nature. A difference may be clearly perceived, and yet it may be impossible, at least I have found it so, to state in what the difference consists. When we witness any deep emotion, our sympathy is so strongly excited, that close observation is forgotten or rendered almost impossible; of which fact I have had many curious proofs. Our imagination is another and still more serious source of error; for if from the nature of the circumstances we expect to see any expression, we readily imagine its presence. **Notwithstanding Dr. Duchenne's great experience, he for a long time fancied, as he states, that several muscles contracted under certain emotions, whereas he ultimately convinced himself that the movement was confined to a single muscle.**

In order to acquire as good a foundation as possible, and to ascertain, independently of common opinion, how far particular movements of the features and gestures are really expressive of certain states of the mind, I have found the following means the most serviceable. In the first place, to observe infants; for they exhibit many emotions, as Sir C. Bell remarks, "with extraordinary force"; whereas, in after life, some of our expressions "cease to have the pure and simple source from which they spring in infancy."[18]

Read the topic sentence of every body paragraph.

In the second place, it occurred to me that the insane ought to be studied, as they are liable to the strongest passions, and give uncontrolled vent to them. I had, myself, no opportunity of doing this, so I applied to Dr. Maudsley and received from him an introduction to Dr. J. Crichton-Browne, who has charge of an immense asylum near Wakefield, and who, as I found, had already attended to the subject. This excellent observer has with unwearied kindness sent me copious notes and descriptions, with valuable suggestions on many points; and I can hardly overestimate the value of his assistance. I owe also, to the kindness of Mr. Patrick Nicol, of the Sussex Lunatic Asylum, interesting statements on two or three points.

Read the topic sentence of every body paragraph.

Thirdly Dr. Duchenne galvanized, as we have already seen, certain muscles in the face of an old man, whose skin was little sensitive, and thus produced various expressions which were photographed on a large scale. It fortunately occurred to me to show several of the best plates, without a word of explanation, to above twenty educated persons of various ages and both sexes, asking them, in each case, by what emotion or feeling the old man was supposed to be agitated; and I recorded their answers in the words which they used. Several of the expressions were instantly recognized by almost everyone, though described in not exactly the same terms; and these may, I think, be relied on as truthful, and will hereafter be specified. On the other hand, the most widely different judgments were pronounced in regard to some of them. This exhibition was of use in another way, by convincing me how easily we may be misguided by our imagination; for when I first looked through Dr. Duchenne's photographs, reading at the same time the text, and thus learning what was intended, I was struck with admiration at the truthfulness of all, with only a few exceptions. Nevertheless, if I had examined them without any explanation, no doubt I should have been as much perplexed, in some cases, as other persons have been.

Attentively read the concluding paragraph in full.

Long and dry reading passages can be daunting and confusing, even for AP English or AP European History students. If you are a voracious and avid reader, you may be inclined to read the passage in halves or thirds—or even to read the entire thing in a single gulp. Determining what a "piece" of the passage means is a matter of personal style and preference. Experiment to discover what works best for you as you navigate the reading passage.

STRATEGY 2: EXTRACT THE MAIN IDEA FROM THE PASSAGE 策略2：从段落中提取中心思想

1600 Club Coaching: *Maintain a focused rhythm of concentration as you work through the SAT. Train yourself to block out distractions.*

Read with your eye peeled for the main idea. Cultivate this habit as you practice reading passages. Knowing the main idea is very helpful in answering questions involving the author's main purpose, the best title for the passage, and the author's point of view. Having a handle on the main idea is also helpful when it comes to answering a "mouthful" of a question such as this: "With which of the following statements would the author most likely agree/disagree?"

Know where to find the main idea.

More often than not, you can find the main idea in one *or more* of these three places:

1. The blurb (introductory material that precedes the passage)
2. The thesis (usually the last line of the first paragraph)
3. Somewhere in the concluding paragraph (usually at the end)

Outline reading should have familiarized you with these three imperative areas of the passage.

Once you feel you have hit on the main idea of the passage, use your pencil to underline it or jot a bold asterisk (*) nearby in the margin. Your pencil markings will help you later when you must answer a main idea, primary purpose, or any type of "global" question (question that pertains to the whole passage) later on.

STRATEGY 3: ANSWER LINE-REFERENCE AND SIDEBAR QUESTIONS FIRST 策略3：首先解答参考题目和补充题目

1600 Club Coaching: *Contrary to popular opinion, while there's little value to* ***reading*** *the questions beforehand, there's great value to* ***skimming*** *the questions ahead of time to locate line references and* ***marking*** *the passage accordingly.*

Let's review our critical reading process so far:

Strategy 1 told you that you're not going to read the entire passage in one big chunk. You read in "pieces." Thank goodness!

Strategy 2 told you the three places where you are most likely to find the main idea.

Now, **Strategy 3** is very important: *Before you begin reading the passage piece by piece,* you should skim the questions for *line numbers* and mark the text accordingly. Numbers within questions signal that you are going to be asked about a specific area of the text. According to the line numbers given in the questions, you should mark the passage with "sidebars" and "line references." When you do practice tests, mark the passage in this manner. Once you get the hang of this strategy, it takes only a small amount of time and will save you time later as you refer to the passage to find the evidence that supports the best answer.

The passage below illustrates two ***line references*** (lines 4 and 13), and a ***sidebar*** that spans lines 10–14. These line references and sidebars correlate with questions that are asked, based on the Darwin reading passage (reproduced below), such as the following: In line 4, "this doctrine" most closely refers to. As a general rule, line references are rather brief: a word, a phrase, or just a line or two of text. Sidebars are longer, usually spanning three lines or more. Keep sidebars simple; a roughly drawn vertical line is all that is required. This is how text marked with sidebars and line references might look:

> No doubt as long as man and all other animals are viewed as independent creations, an effectual stop is put to our natural desire to investigate as far as possible the causes of Expression. By this doctrine *(line reference)*, anything and everything can be equally well explained; and it has proved as pernicious with respect to Expression as to every other branch of natural history. With mankind some expressions, such as the bristling of the hair under the influence of extreme terror, or the uncovering of the teeth under that of furious rage, can hardly be understood, except on the belief *(sidebar)* that man once existed in a much lower and animal-like condition. The community of certain expressions in distinct though allied species, as in the movements of the same facial muscles during laughter by man and by various monkeys, is rendered somewhat more intelligible *(line reference)*, if we believe in their descent from a common progenitor. He who admits on general grounds that the structure and habits of all animals have been gradually evolved, will look at the whole subject of Expression in a new and interesting light.

1600 Club Coaching: *The correct answer to a hard* ***words-in-context*** *question is often the word's lesser known secondary or tertiary meaning.*

Do you ever wonder how carefully you should read the passages?

This isn't driver's education, but think of your text markings as "road signs" and let them guide you as you read. You can read the parts of the passage *without* sidebars and line references in a more cursory or superficial fashion. (See Outline Reading Approach, pages 27–30.)

The sidebars and line references with which you have marked the passage are road signs that tell you precisely where to slow down and pay close attention because you know there will be questions relating to those areas of the text. Your text markings (sidebars and line references) will guide you in creating a rhythm as you read through the passage.

In the example above, lines 10–14 are particularly important; there will not only be a question pertinent to those five lines as a unit, but also a question about the word *intelligible*, which appears in line 13. Remember: you must consider the line references within their context: "5 lines up and 5 lines down" is a good rule of thumb to follow. If no context clue can be found and no light is shed on the question by using "5 lines up and 5 lines down," consider a broader context, "6 lines up and 6 lines down" or "7 lines up and 7 lines down," until you find passage evidence that validates an answer choice.

Words-in-Context Questions 词汇题

Hard words-in-context questions can be very challenging. They may appear straightforward, but analysis of model tests shows that words-in-context questions are often ranked as *hard*. On hard questions, the "regular meaning" of the word that comes most readily to mind is most likely *not* the correct answer. More often, the meaning of the word *in context* is its lesser used meaning, even its secondary or tertiary meaning (for example, "pretender" for one who claims a throne; "charged" for inspired; "classic" for well known; "halting" for limping; "credit" for believe; and "crush" for a crowd of people). The preceding examples were all taken from practice SATs published by the College Board.

Word meanings rely heavily on context; it's worthless to answer a word-in-context question without going back to the passage to read at *and around* that line.

Words-in-Context Questions

Regular, More Predictable Meaning of Word

Unusual In-Context Meaning of Word

Consider how varying contexts can lend different meanings to words like *synthesis*, *dedicated*, and *dynamic*.

Sharpening Skills—Words in Context 加强技巧——文中的词汇

Picture some hypothetical passage (bet you've never been asked to do that before). Suppose that you are asked the meaning of "happy" as used in line 52. You should read the word within a sizable context. (Remember: "5 lines up, 5 lines down" is a good rule of thumb.) At the very least, you should start by reading lines 50–54. You see how the word is used: "a *happy* circumstance." Now look at the answer choices:

(A) spontaneous (B) joyful (C) unexpected (D) lucky

If you hadn't read the word in the context of the passage, you would probably pick one of the "regular" meanings, such as *joyful*. But if the context of the passage reveals that the circumstances arose from sheer good fortune, then the answer is (D), *lucky*.

Answer the more straightforward, line-reference questions first. Then answer the higher-order inference questions that typically take more time.

No matter its difficulty level, each correctly answered question earns you a point.

Sharpening Skills—Secondary and Tertiary Meanings of Words 加强技巧—— 词汇的第二和第三种意义

The College Board sometimes features unlikely or lesser-known definitions of words. This can make sentence completion and critical reading questions particularly tricky and hard. For example, "consequences" may be positive (+) or negative (–) in connotation, depending on context. Although many of us have a negative association for the term "consequences," in the following answer choice, the context of the paragraph reveals that these "consequences" were *positive* in nature and effect: (C) Harriet's bold redesign had far-reaching *consequences*.

Correct Answer	What Test Takers Might Think the Word Means	What the Word Means Within Context of the Passage*	Question Difficulty
conviction	being charged with a crime; jail sentence	strongly held personal belief	hard
crush	pulverize; orange soda; boy-girl affection	crowd of people Context Clue: "mob"	hard
discriminating	prejudiced	selective	hard
halt	stop	to stop and start Context Clue: "limping gait" Note: gait is a manner of walking.	hard
hail	rain down balls of ice; praise	welcome	hard
treacherous	dangerous	disloyal	hard

*Examples in this chart are from questions appearing on actual SATs.

Sharpening Skills—Pay Attention to Prefixes 加强技巧——关注前缀

Noticing and underlining prefixes is important, no matter what type of question you are answering. Whether you are working on a line-reference question, a sidebar question, or a words-in-context question, avoid careless errors by underlining prefixes within the reading comprehension questions and answer choices. This simple pen-to-paper strategy will clarify meaning so you can answer questions more accurately by avoiding careless errors.

If an answer choice contains the word *inflexible*, students, in haste, often misread it as *flexible* and therefore erroneously (wrongly, inaccurately) pick that choice. Consider the question and answer choice that follow.

In both passages, the author suggests that the mannerisms of "those at war" (line 59) were greatly influenced by

(C) the agency's inadequate control over the radio media

In answer choice C, the prefix *in-* is the two-letter disqualifier! The prefix makes the entire answer choice incorrect. Now that's tricky!

To avoid careless comprehension errors, use your Active Pencil to underline prefixes as in the words below.

desensitize
disagree
immaterial
inaccuracy
inconsequential
inflexible
misinterpret
unorthodox

STRATEGY 4: DELVE INTO HIGHER-ORDER THINKING QUESTIONS 策略4：钻研深度理解类题目

Pace yourself by answering higher-order thinking questions (time-sapping doozies) *after* you have answered the "directed" questions for which you have marked sidebars and line references. Higher-order questions can be recognized by their use of words and phrases such as *infer, suggests, implies, it can be concluded that, it seems that, most closely means.*

Once you've done your outline reading and have answered the more straightforward line-reference questions, you are ready to tackle these harder questions. Always embed these questions in a broad context so that you get a fuller sense of the author's message and point of view. For example, if a test question asks what you can infer from the phrase "loftier yet understated" in line 34, you should read broadly around this phrase. On a harder question like this one, you should read *at least* from about line 29 to line 39 to get a solid sense of the phrase in its context.

Inference questions require higher-order thinking skills, a sort of synthesis between what is stated and what you can glean as insight. Inference demands a sort of reading between the lines, a mining for something that's beneath surface-level information. Challenge yourself to go below the words and into the "subtext." Inference questions require you to draw conclusions by reasoning beyond given facts.

Skipping Hard Questions Responsibly 难题放后面

If you find that you're spending too much time grappling with an inference question, skip it for the time being. Try the global questions first, and return to the tough ones later.

The 1600 Club knows not to spend too much time grappling with any one question. It also knows how to temporarily skip and later return to questions responsibly.

Skipping questions sounds carefree, like skipping rope when you were a child. Feeling nostalgic? In fact, skipping questions comes with two responsibilities:

Skipping Questions: *The 1600 Club knows how to skip questions responsibly, without ending up in a quagmire.*

1. Remember to return to the question. Boldly circle the entire question in your test booklet, providing yourself with a conspicuous reminder that this question is being saved for later.
2. Remember to pay attention to how you grid in the bubble sheet. This may sound like a petty caveat, but many unfortunate students have skipped a question here or there, forgotten to skip the corresponding line of "bubbles" on the answer sheet, filled in the wrong ovals, and ended up with a bubbling-in debacle that had them erasing furiously and wasting precious time!

Yes, skipping this or that question and saving it for later sounds innocuous, but beware!

The 1600 Club takes skipping seriously and knows how to handle it without incurring a bubble-sheet nightmare.

STRATEGY 5: IDENTIFY THE AUTHOR'S MOOD, TONE, AND PURPOSE AS YOU READ
策略5：阅读的时候，留意作者的情绪、语气和意图

- You're a sensitive reader, and you get that the author wishes he were a kid again, but do you get that he is creating a mood that is *nostalgic* or *reminiscent?*
- You're a sharp reader, and you get that the author, a competitive scientist, is belittling his contemporaries, but do you get that his tone is *deprecatory* or *disparaging?*
- You're an insightful reader, and you get that the author regrets his hurtful actions, but do you get that the mood conveyed is *contrite* or *penitent?*
- You easily pick up on subtle context clues, and you get that the author is angry, but do you get that he is expressing a mood that is *indignant* or *belligerent?*

More often than not, the problem is not that you don't get the author's tone or mood—it's that you may not know the word that describes what you are sensing. Challenge yourself to learn this additional tier of vocabulary. As you read the passages, be aware of expressions of tone and mood so that you'll be prepared to answer related questions. The vocabulary lists given below are rich and varied but by no means exhaustive.

Vocabulary Coaching: *The 1600 Club gets an edge on critical reading questions by becoming familiar with the meanings and subtle distinctions of the vocabularies of tone and mood.*

The Vocabulary of Tone 语气方面的词汇

Admonishing—*warning*
Aloof—*detached*
Apologetic—*being sorry; admitting fault*
Assertive—*strongly stating*
Cautious—*hesitant*
Confrontational—*argumentative*
Contrite—*remorseful*
Cynical—*seeing worst in people*
Defensive—*protecting one's point of view*
Derisive—*ridiculing*
Empathetic—*having feeling for others*
Emphatic—*stressing one's points*
Entreating—*begging, pleading*
Explanatory—*explaining*
Inquisitive—*asking questions*
Nostalgic—*remembering the past*
Penitent—*remorseful*
Reflective—*remembering the past*
Sardonic—*sarcastic*
Scathing—*harsh*
Scholarly—*intellectual, cerebral*
Sensationalistic—*exaggerating emotions*
Skeptical—*doubtful*
Tentative—*hesitant*
Understated—*mildly suggested; unstressed*
Wry—*bitter or ironic*

Make flash cards for the vocabulary words that you find unfamiliar or challenging.

The Vocabulary of Mood 情绪方面的词汇

Amusement—*humor*
Bemusement—*puzzlement*
Detachment—*lack of concern*
Disdain—*scorn*
Disparagement—*belittlement*
Indignation—*anger*
Irony—*incongruity*
Mockery—*derision; insincere imitation*
Objectivity—*realism; factualism; having no opinion*
Optimism—*positive thinking*
Pessimism—*negative thinking*
Smugness—*self-satisfaction; complacency*
Somber—*sullen, gloomy*

Top scorers avoid extreme answer choices for tone and mood. In general, authors want to come across as level-headed and reasonable, not as off their rockers. It is highly unlikely for the mood or tone of a passage to be:

☒ scathingly critical	☒ downright outraged
☒ impenetrably scholarly	☒ painfully distrustful
☒ feverishly indignant	☒ unbearably arrogant

Use your pencil and PET (Process of Elimination Technique) to cross off answer choices that are extreme. By so doing, you will narrow in on the correct answer.

STRATEGY 6: NARROW IN ON THE *BEST* ANSWER CHOICE
策略6：圈定最佳选项

Narrow in on the best answer choice by using the good old, tried-and-true process of elimination. First, cross off answer choices that are not supported in any way, shape, or form by the passage. These are "fluff" answer choices that are not confirmed by something, somewhere, that the author says. Also, avoid picking answers just because they *appear* fair, reasonable, true, or intelligent.

Narrowing in on the best answer choice has everything to do with *first* knowing precisely what the question is asking. Use your Active Pencil to underline key words in the question itself. This discipline will keep you focused on what you are supposed to answer.

Once you're clear on what the question is asking, you can see more clearly which answer choices are incorrect and which could work.

Sharpening Skills—Key Words 加强技巧——关键词

Underline the key word or words in the following questions. The key words should signal precisely what you are supposed to answer.

1. With which of the following statements would the Passage 2 author most likely disagree?
2. The example in the final paragraph serves to illustrate which of the following sentiments?
3. Which of the following personal endeavors most closely contradicts the author's public statements?
4. The form of the author's argument is best described as . . .
5. Which of the following detracts least from the author's perspective on telecommuting?

Key Words—Answers 关键词——答案

Some subjectivity and subtlety are involved in underscoring key words. This answer key illustrates possible ways of underlining key words in each question.

1. With which of the following statements would the Passage 2 author most likely disagree?

2. The example in the final paragraph serves to illustrate which of the following sentiments?
3. Which of the following personal endeavors most closely contradicts the author's public statements?
4. The form of the author's argument is best described as . . .
5. Which of the following detracts least from the author's perspective on telecommuting?

High scorers use this acid test: Has the author written something that confirms all aspects of the answer I have chosen? If you can't find the evidence in the passage, then cross off that answer choice—it's incorrect.

When reading a critical reading question, high scorers take very seriously the words "According to the author," "The author suggests," and "The author mentions." They know that they must select an answer that is substantiated, somewhere in the text, by what the author has written. "According to the author," for instance, does not mean any of the following:

1600 Club Coaching:
Take "According to the author" very seriously.

- According to your personal opinion or perspective
- According to your conjecture
- According to your gut feeling or common sense
- According to your parents, teachers, relatives, coaches, or advisors
- According to your assumptions
- According to your creativity or imagination
- According to your speculation or conjecture (opinion or guess)

High scorers never accept or select *partially correct* answer choices. Even *one word* that is not validated somewhere in the passage can discredit an entire answer choice.

If an answer choice is the best, it's *all* right, each and every word of it. Don't settle for partially correct answers. Remember: second-best or partially correct answers do not receive partial credit on the SAT.

As mentioned previously, be sure to winnow out extreme answer choices, which are melodramatic or excessive. For example, it's unlikely that an author's mood would be "downright disgusted" or "superbly elated."

Cross off answers that you know don't work. Don't underestimate PET—the Process of Elimination Technique, as it moves you closer to the right answer and simplifies your task.

Decisive crossing off prevents you from being distracted by unlikely answer choices and keeps you focused on finding the *best* answer choice.

~~(A) Fluff answer~~
~~(B) Fluff answer~~
(C) Runner-up or second-best answer
(D) Best answer!

Once you're down to two answer choices, your cerebral wheels really have to start turning. What do you do now? First, go back to the pertinent part of the passage and seek out context clues that validate one answer over the other. Second, scrutinize the answer choices. If a mere one word is "off" or inaccurate, that answer choice is invalid.

The more you practice finding validating proof in the passage, the more adept you will become at distinguishing the second-best from the best answer. When they're down to two answer choices, 1600 Clubbers never resort to *eeny, meeny, miny, mo.* Neither should you.

Reading Technique: The Rule of Thirds 阅读技巧：三分法则

A unique reading strategy, the Reading Rule of Thirds helps you narrow in on the *best* answer choices instead of picking "false positives," "traps," and "decoys" that diminish your critical reading score. It helps you decide which answers to pick when you are down to two choices. Typically, the majority of test takers can cross off two choices with relative ease, finding themselves down to two answer choices. With more skimming and rereading of the pertinent parts of the passage, many test takers are able to then eliminate an additional answer choice.

Now they find themselves "down-to-two," pencil hovering over choice B and choice D . . . debating whether choice D or choice B is best. We all know that uncomfortable position, making us feel uneasy, even a little queasy. We've done a lot of hard work: we've read the question carefully, we've reread a broad context around the references line(s), and we feel confident about the two choices we have eliminated. Yet, two answer choices remain! Now our wheels start grinding. We're feeling indecisive. They both look good. Which to choose? Rule of Thirds to the rescue!

The Rule of Thirds Is an Active Pencil Technique

三分法则是一种自动铅笔法

Use your Active Pencil to divide your remaining answer choices into *thirds* by making two quick and simple backslash lines. Next, scrutinize each third to make sure it is completely valid and substantiated (confirmed, verified) by what is stated or implied in the passage.

The College Board test makers are tricky. More often than not, a "decoy" answer choice seems to work quite well. However, this choice is the runner-up. The runner-up choice is incorrect, a "false positive," usually because of *one* disqualifying word or phrase. In fact, there are decoy answer choices that are $\frac{4}{5}$ths correct, $\frac{8}{9}$ths correct, $\frac{10}{11}$ths correct, and so on. That's how tricky test questions can be. Reading Rule of Thirds to the rescue!

Try also reading backward. Reading backward forces you to closely consider and scrutinize all the parts of the answer choice. Though this technique might at first seem odd, it works. This technique forces you to read and consider each and every word. Try reading the answer choices backward to see if this unique strategy works for you. Of course, reading backward is always followed by reading the answer choice forward.

Consider this question and corresponding answer choice:

The author enumerates (lists) "marketing, product banning, and measures taken against disingenuous (dishonest, deceitful) businesses" in lines 38–40 in order to

(C) Unequivocally verify that recent college graduates altered the procedures of the corporate business world through their actions

Rule of Thirds:

✘ ✔

(C) *Unequivocally verify* that recent college graduates / altered the procedures of

✔

the corporate business world / through their actions

"Unequivocally verify" is the disqualifying phrase. It is too strong and definitive of a verbal phrase, based on passage evidence. The passage does not *unequivocally (undoubtedly, absolutely) verify (prove, confirm)* that the graduates changed corporate America.

Rule of Thirds Backward:

✔ ✔

(A) through their actions . . . altered the procedures of the corporate business

✘

world . . . *unequivocally verify* that recent college graduates

Time Saver: When reading questions start with *Which of the following, if true,* or *Which of the following, if available,* you can assume that the choices are "given" as true or available. Knowing this obliterates (eliminates) the time that you might otherwise take trying to determine which choices are true or available.

Consider this sample hard question in which key words and potentially hard words are italicized:

Which of the following, if *true,* would *debunk* (contradict) the *legitimacy* (soundness, authority) of the author's assumption about the effect of technological innovations *enumerated* (listed, itemized) in lines 73–82?

Rule of Thirds:

✔ ✔ ✔

(D) The townspeople had always / regarded new technology as threatening / and potentially damaging to human relationships.

In this case, the Rule of Thirds helps us to focus on and validate each and every third of the answer choice. Use your Active Pencil to put a check mark (✔) above each third for which you find support in the passage.

Rule of Thirds Backward:

✔ ✔ ✔

(D) and potentially damaging to human relationships . . . regarded new technology as threatening . . . The townspeople had always

READ ANSWER CHOICES BACKWARD To help you focus on each and every word within the answer choice, read the answer choices backward. Read backward in segments or in groups of phrases like this:

Reading backward, choice (A) *was annoyed that she permitted Willa to infuriate him in public*, becomes:

✘ ✔ ✔ ✔

(A) *in public . . . to infuriate him . . . she permitted Willa . . . was annoyed that*

With close examination, "public" is revealed as the single disqualifying word that makes this choice incorrect. That's tricky! When we revisit the passage's introductory material, we find that it says, "During a family barbeque . . .," which may likely be held at home and, therefore, not necessarily in *public*.

STRATEGY 7: GLOBAL QUESTIONS SHOULD BE ANSWERED AT THE VERY END 策略7：最后解答总括性题目

Global questions are those that focus on the overarching ideas, themes, or purpose of the passage. In other words, they are based on the whole passage. You should save these questions until the end, after you have digested the passage as a whole. Be aware that global questions may appear anywhere in the lineup of critical reading questions. Even if the very first question is global—and often it is—you should save it until the end.

Global questions are predictable, so you should always keep them in mind when you read a passage. There's no need to peruse the critical reading questions ahead of time. Usually, the questions fall into two categories: line reference/sidebar and global.

Examples of Global Questions

- Based on what is stated in the passage, the author's main purpose is . . .
- Which of the following provides the best title?
- The author's attitude toward the individual discussed is primarily one of . . .
- The author's overall tone is best described as . . .
- Based on what is expressed in the passage, the author would most likely agree/disagree with which of the following statements?
- The mood conveyed by the author is primarily one of . . .
- Which of the following statements, if true, would most strongly undermine the author's point of view?

Remember Those Globals!! 别忘了做总括性题目！

Even the brightest students sometimes *forget* to answer the global, overarching questions on the SAT. Here's why: the test taker encounters a global question in the very first question on the passage. She then sees another global shortly after the first one. She knows that she should save them until the end, so she skips them, planning to return to them at a later time. But after answering all of the remaining questions, she simply forgets about those two globals! (Of course, since our test taker is very bright, she most likely would have answered the questions correctly.)

As the adage says, out of sight, out of mind.

How can you remember those global questions? Suppose you discover that questions 1 and 4 are global. Here's how to remember to return to them: at the very end of the series of questions, write 1 and 4 to remind yourself. This basic strategy can preclude your sacrificing points because of overlooking a few questions.

Also, boldly circle the global questions right on your test booklet. Do not simply circle the question *number*; boldly and broadly circle the entire question, including the four answer choices. This sweeping circle will provide you with a conspicuous reminder to return to those questions when you're ready.

Use your pencil to boldly circle questions to which you want to return later. In the critical reading sections, for example, circle global questions, which are based on the reading passage as a *whole*. In math sections, circle hard questions on which you need more thought. Your circles should be bold, dark, and sweeping. Bold circles are conspicuous (in your face!); you are unlikely to miss them and to forget to go back to those questions!

Paired-Passage and Global Questions 配对段落和总括性题目

On paired-passage reading, two passages are juxtaposed for the sake of comparison and contrast. Your task is to read each one and get a sense of their differences and similarities. To answer global questions about double passages, you should ask yourself these questions as you read through the second passage:

- Are the passages more similar to, or more different from, each other?
- Do the authors see eye to eye on the issue at hand?
- Are the authors supporting or undermining each other?
- Do the authors have similar tones or moods, or are they quite different?

You're an insightful reader. Often you can begin to answer these questions after reading the first paragraph or two of Passage 2.

ADDITIONAL STRATEGIES FOR READING SAT PASSAGES
SAT段落阅读的其他策略

To Read or Not to Read the Questions First—That Is the Perennial Decision 是否先读题——这是一个长期的疑虑

When it comes to critical reading, whether or not to read the questions first is truly a matter of preference. Try both ways to see which works best for you. For many test takers, reading the questions before the passage is a waste of time. You will have to read the questions carefully later anyway.

As Strategy 3 of the READING acronym (answer line-reference and sidebar questions first) indicates, you should skim the questions for line-number references. Numerals stand out, so they are easy to spot without actually reading the question. Skimming for numbers and marking the text can be done very quickly and really helps you as you read, since you have a "road map" of the parts on which questions are based. Marking the text for ten questions usually takes only 25 to 35 seconds. Try it and see for yourself.

As for the rest of the questions, test designers do not typically reinvent the wheel when it comes to the types of questions they ask. For this reason, beyond skimming for line numbers, scrutinizing the remaining questions is not practical. Instead, acquaint yourself with and anticipate frequently asked question types as you read. In this way, you'll be more prepared and better able to answer them quickly and easily. Frequently asked questions include:

- Author's mood, tone, or attitude?
- Primary purpose of passage?
- Best title?
- Form and structure of passage?
- Words–in–context questions?
- Statement with which the author would be most likely to agree or disagree?

Read and Heed Key Words in the Questions and Answer Choices 阅读并留意题目与选项中的关键词

Traditional key words include: *all, except, least, most, not, never, often, rarely, usually*. Both traditional and more subtle key words are underlined in the examples that follow. Some examples illustrate pivotal words in the question only; others illustrate key words in the question *as well as* in the correct answer. Medium and hard refer to the question's level of difficulty. Revealingly, none of the questions below are easy in difficulty. Keep your eyes peeled for and underline key words in questions and answer choices. Examples illustrate hard question formats.

HARD QUESTION STRUCTURE: The author of Passage 2 would probably agree with which of the following assertions about the explanation of *The Lost Horizon* offered in Passage 1 ?

ANSWER: It is not representative of the way *The Lost Horizon* is typically discussed in English classrooms.

HARD QUESTION STRUCTURE: Which of the following, if true, would most directly disprove what "Astronomers initially conjectured" (line 22)?

ANSWER: People do not tend to speculate about extraterrestrial life when they look up into the skies at night, marveling at the constellations and shifting light. (The negating adjective *not* makes all the difference. Underline key words.)

HARD QUESTION FORMAT: The example in lines 14–17 primarily suggests that . . .

ANSWER: Palmer's insights into natural disposition were not apparent in his daily life. (Once again, the correct answer contains the key word *not*.)

HARD QUESTION STRUCTURE: Which of the following, if true, would undermine the veracity of the author's assumption about the consequences of urbanization discussed in lines 45–57? (*Undermine* often appears within reading comprehension questions and answer choices. It means to weaken, sap the energy of; also, to contradict, belie.)

ANSWER: Residents have always considered industry and urbanization as desirable. (Use your Active Pencil to underline the key word in the correct answer choice: *always*.)

HARD QUESTION FORMAT: In line 62, the phrase "distressing pleasure" suggests that Yolanda's enjoyment is tempered by . . . (Key word, *tempered*, means lessened, alleviated the severity of.)

HARD QUESTION STRUCTURE: Which of the following situations, if true, would be most analogous to the dilemma presented in the passage?

No Line References and Not a Global Question! What Now?

没有直接对应的参考信息，不是总括性问题！怎么办?

If you are asked about something specific in the passage and no line reference is given, skim the question for a key term that centers in on what information the question is seeking. Whenever possible, let the key term be a proper noun since proper nouns are capitalized and therefore easier to find in the passage. Skimming the passage for dates, whenever relevant, is a good idea too since numbers also stand out. Once you've found your key term, read around it to find the context clue that points to the best answer choice.

When a question does not provide line references, astute students skim the question for key terms, underline them, and then hunt them down in the passage.

To illustrate this time saver, key terms are underscored in the following questions:

1. Which of the following was the most significant aspect of Mendel's research on peas and inherited traits? (Skim passage for Mendel.)
2. In which two ways are minerals different from the other elements that are mentioned? (Skim passage for minerals.)
3. When the family emigrated from Poland in 1732, which emotion was predominant among the three siblings? (Skim for both Poland and 1732.)

You now have a disciplined, step-by-step, and thorough method to follow for reading critically. Now that you know what to do, let's iron out what you *should not* do in terms of "smart" answering on the evidence-based reading sections.

READING NO-NO'S 阅读题解题禁忌

- **No** guesswork*
- **No** answering based on your outside reading or knowledge
- **No** answering based on your opinions or beliefs
- **No** "reading into" the passage, or reading beyond what the author is actually saying
- **No** selecting answers just because you think they're probably true
- **No** selecting answers just because they appear reasonable
- **No** random guessing, without first trying hard to eliminate as many answer choices as you can (applies to all sections)

*A note about guesswork: Even when you've narrowed down the answer choices to two—(B) or (D), let's say—you still should not guess. Instead, the high scorer returns to the pertinent part(s) of the passage and rereads for context clues and other evidence that validate one answer, (B) or (D), over the other.

The bottom line for 1600 Club critical reading: Select only answers that are substantiated by words, phrases, or sentences in the italicized blurb or the passage. In other words, an answer choice must be based on passage evidence only! As previously pointed out, sometimes context clues are several lines away (either up ↑ or down ↓) from the line referenced by a question. Likewise, sometimes passage evidence and clues are outside the sidebar indicated by the question. For example, if the sidebar indicates lines 34–37, the context clue that confirms the correct answer could appear in lines 30 and 31 or lines 39 and 40.

SUMMARY: HIGH SCORER'S STRATEGY ACRONYM 总结：高分得主的应试策略缩写

- Has anyone ever told you that your "learning style" is predominantly visual?
- Do you have a photographic memory?
- Have acrostics or acronyms helped you to remember processes or information in the past?
- When you learn, do you find yourself drawn to diagrams, charts, and other visual cues?

If so, then consider the seven strategies listed below for critical reading as spelling the word "READING." Here is the high scorer's acronym:

R	**ead** longer passages piece by piece.
E	**xtract** the main idea from the passage.
A	**nswer** line-reference questions first.
D	**elve** into higher-order-thinking questions last.
I	**dentify** the author's mood, tone, and purpose as you read.
N	**arrow** in on the *best* answer choice.
G	**lobal or holistic** questions should be answered at the very end.

If you're a visual learner, on test day one or more of the boldfaced words listed will pop into your mind, prompting you to remember a strategy approach for reading and answering questions on long passages.

PRACTICE TEST QUESTIONS 练习测试题

Note: The directions in this book are not verbatim repetitions of directions on actual College Board tests, but these directions tell you what you need to know.

Passage 1: U.S. Literature

Directions: Read the passage below, and then answer the questions that follow. The correct response may be stated outright or merely suggested in the passage.

The following is an excerpt from American author F. Scott Fitzgerald's 1922 novel The Beautiful and Damned.

At eleven he had a horror of death. Within six impressionable years his parents had died and his grandmother had faded off almost imperceptibly, until, for the first time since her marriage, her person held for one day an unquestioned supremacy over her own drawing room. So to Anthony life was a struggle against death that waited at every corner. It was as a concession to his hypochondriac imagination that he formed the habit of reading in bed—it soothed him. He read until he was tired and often fell asleep with the lights still on.

His favorite diversion until he was fourteen was his stamp collection; enormous, as nearly exhaustive as a boy's could be—his grandfather considered fatuously that it was teaching him geography. So Anthony kept up a correspondence with a half dozen "Stamp and Coin" companies and it was rare that the mail failed to bring him new stamp-books or packages of glittering approval sheets—there was a mysterious fascination in transferring his acquisitions interminably from one book to another. His stamps were his greatest happiness and he bestowed impatient frowns on any one who interrupted him at play with them; they devoured his allowance every month, and he lay awake at night musing untiringly on their variety and many-colored splendor.

At sixteen he had lived almost entirely within himself, an inarticulate boy, thoroughly un-American, and politely bewildered by his contemporaries. The two preceding years had been spent in Europe with a private tutor, who persuaded him that Harvard was the thing; it would "open doors," it would be a tremendous tonic, it would give him innumerable self-sacrificing and devoted friends. So he went to Harvard—there was no other logical thing to be done with him.

1. It can be inferred from lines 2–5 that Anthony's grandmother
   (A) was not much into housekeeping
   (B) haunted her grandson unmercifully
   (C) was directly responsible for her grandson's hypochondria
   (D) played a submissive role during her married life

2. The form and structure of this passage are best described as
   (A) scattered flashbacks
   (B) present to past chronology
   (C) chronological biography
   (D) concrete examples followed by general statements

3. In line 11, "exhaustive" most nearly means
   (A) tiring
   (B) irritating
   (C) fatiguing
   (D) extensive

4. Which best describes Anthony's attitude toward those who disrupt him while he is engaged in activities related to his stamp collecting (lines 18 and 19)?
   (A) solicitous
   (B) contemptuous
   (C) nonchalant
   (D) aloof

Passage 2: Science

Directions: Read the passage below, and then answer the questions that follow. The correct response may be stated outright or merely suggested in the passage.

This passage is taken from Charles Darwin's natural science writings, The Expression of the Emotions in Man and Animals.

No doubt as long as man and all other animals are viewed as independent creations, an effectual stop is put to our natural desire to investigate as far as possible the causes of Expression. By this doctrine, anything and everything can be equally well explained; and it has proved as pernicious with respect to Expression as to every other branch of natural history. With mankind some expressions, such as the bristling of the hair under the influence of extreme terror, or the uncovering of the teeth under that of furious rage, can hardly be understood, except on the belief that man once existed in a much lower and animal-like condition. The community of certain expressions in distinct though allied species, as in the movements of the same facial muscles during laughter by man and by various monkeys, is rendered somewhat more intelligible, if we believe in their descent from a common progenitor. He who admits on general grounds that the structure and habits of all animals have been gradually evolved, will look at the whole subject of Expression in a new and interesting light.

The study of Expression is difficult, owing to the movements being often extremely slight, and of a fleeting nature. A difference may be clearly perceived, and yet it may be impossible, at least I have found it so, to state in what the difference consists. When we witness any deep emotion, our sympathy is so strongly excited, that close observation is forgotten or rendered almost impossible; of which fact I have had many curious proofs. Our imagination is another and still more serious source of error; for if from the nature of the circumstances we expect to see any expression, we readily imagine its presence. Notwithstanding Dr. Duchenne's great experience, he for a long time fancied, as he states, that several muscles contracted under certain emotions, whereas he ultimately convinced himself that the movement was confined to a single muscle.

In order to acquire as good a foundation as possible, and to ascertain, independently of common opinion, how far particular movements of the features and gestures are really expressive of certain states of the mind, I have found the following means the most serviceable. In the first place, to observe infants; for they exhibit many emotions, as Sir C. Bell remarks, "with extraordinary force"; whereas, in after life, some of our expressions "cease to have the pure and simple source from which they spring in infancy."

Active Reading Strategy
Be sure to annotate the passage to accurately absorb key points, the author's craft, and the passage's overall meaning and purpose.

In the second place, it occurred to me that the insane ought to be studied, as they are liable to the strongest passions, and give uncontrolled vent to them. I had, myself, no opportunity of doing this, so I applied to Dr. Maudsley and received from him an introduction to Dr. J. Crichton-Browne, who has charge of an immense asylum near Wakefield, and who, as I found, had already attended to the subject. This excellent observer has with unwearied kindness sent me copious notes and descriptions, with valuable suggestions on many points; and I can hardly over-estimate the value of his assistance. I owe also, to the kindness of Mr. Patrick Nicol, of the Sussex Lunatic Asylum, interesting statements on two or three points.

Thirdly Dr. Duchenne galvanized, as we have already seen, certain muscles in the face of an old man, whose skin was little sensitive, and thus produced various expressions which were photographed on a large scale. It fortunately occurred to me to show several of the best plates, without a word of explanation, to above twenty educated persons of various ages and both sexes, asking them, in each case, by what emotion or feeling the old man was supposed to be agitated; and I recorded their answers in the words which they used. Several of the expressions were instantly recognized by almost everyone, though described in not exactly the same terms; and these may, I think, be relied on as truthful, and will hereafter be specified. On the other hand, the most widely different judgments were pronounced in regard to some of them. This exhibition was of use in another way, by convincing me how easily we may be misguided by our imagination; for when I first looked through Dr. Duchenne's photographs, reading at the same time the text, and thus learning what was intended, I was struck with admiration at the truthfulness of all, with only a few exceptions. Nevertheless, if I had examined them without any explanation, no doubt I should have been as much perplexed, in some cases, as other persons have been.

1. It can be inferred from the beginning of the opening paragraph that with regard to "this doctrine" (line 4) the author feels

(A) inherently drawn
(B) curiously engaged
(C) belligerently vexed
(D) emphatically opposed

On the updated SAT, words-in-context questions will tend to feature Tier Two or more accessible vocabulary words, unlike the more arcane words on previous SAT exams.

2. In line 13, "intelligible" most nearly means

(A) vociferous
(B) insightful
(C) understandable
(D) intelligent

3. Lines 18–24 suggest that Darwin would most likely disagree with which of the following statements?

(A) The subtle distinctions between an expression of discouragement and one of disappointment are easily noted.
(B) Humans can become absorbed in the emotions of others.
(C) Changes in facial expressions are faint rather than pronounced.
(D) Sometimes it's hard to notice whether another was feeling anxious or was simply eager.

4. In line 37, "after life" most nearly means

(A) spiritual life
(B) life after death
(C) a more conscientious life
(D) a time later in life

5. Darwin portrays Dr. J. Crichton-Browne primarily as

(A) a lurid and egocentric individual
(B) a debunker of widespread misconceptions
(C) an intellectual inferior
(D) an invaluable and supportive colleague

6. The structure of the second half of the passage is best described as

(A) a listing of random vignettes
(B) a series of three suggestions for case studies
(C) assessments of statistical values
(D) haphazard, romanticized musings

7. In the final paragraph, the author suggests that various people's interpretations of the photographs taken of "the face of an old man" (line 52) are

(A) ludicrous
(B) unpredictable
(C) subjective
(D) inconsequential

Plug the word into the full *sentence to determine its closest meaning.*

8. In context, "galvanized" (line 51) most closely means

(A) surged
(B) electrified
(C) solidified
(D) incited

Answers and Explanations 答案与解析

Passage 1

1. D **3.** D
2. C **4.** B

1. **(D)** This is a hard interpretation question. Reread lines 2–5 carefully, trying to "downsize" them by paraphrasing them in your own words. The significant lines are "his grandmother had faded off almost imperceptibly, until, for the first time since her marriage, her person held for one day an unquestioned supremacy over her own drawing room." To paraphrase: Almost without notice his grandma had become lifeless; then one day—for the first time since she became a married woman—she became the dominant person in her bedroom (or something similar; paraphrasing is a subjective process). This passage is not about housekeeping or haunting her grandson, so (A) and (B) are incorrect. Neither is it suggested that grandma has caused Anthony's hypochondria; (C) is out. The best answer is (D).

2. **(C)** This is a question on structure and form of passage. Skim the passage, paying close attention to transitional language between paragraphs. This exercise can help you get a sense of the passage's overall organization. Choice (B), *present to past chronology*, is tempting since time order is significant; this passage, however, goes in the reverse, past to present. Choice (C), *chronological biography*, is the best choice since paragraph 1 is about Anthony at age eleven; paragraph 2, at age fourteen, and paragraph 3, at age sixteen. Time order is chronological; this passage is a biography because it tells about the boy's life.

3. **(D)** This is a word-in-context question. Consider the word within its context, looking for clues to its precise meaning: "his stamp collection; enormous, as nearly exhaustive as a boy's could be." *Exhaustive* is an adjective that modifies *stamp collection*. The context clue for the meaning of *exhaustive* is *enormous*, the word that precedes it. The best answer is (D), *extensive*.

4. **(B)** This is a global question on Anthony's attitude. Use sidebars, looking for clues about the author's attitude: "His stamps were his greatest happiness and he bestowed impatient frowns on any one who interrupted him at play with them." The context clue that illustrates the boy's attitude is underlined. The best answer is (B), *contemptuous*, which means scornful. This boy, a stamps aficionado, had *impatient frowns* for any philistine who disrupted him while engaged in his leisure pursuit. To answer correctly, you need to have a handle on the words in the answer choices. Here's a quick rundown: *solicitous* (A) means showing concern for others; *nonchalant* (C) means casual or carefree; *aloof* (D) means distant or uninterested.

Passage 2

1. D	**4.** D	**7.** C
2. C	**5.** D	**8.** D
3. A	**6.** B	

1. **(D)** This is a hard inference question signaled by "inferred." Embed "this doctrine" in context by rereading lines 1–6, then seek out context clues that indicate how the author feels about the doctrine explained in the opening lines. Lines 4–6 indicate that the author finds the doctrine to be "pernicious" (very harmful): "By this doctrine, anything and everything can be equally well explained; and it has proved as pernicious with respect to Expression as to every other branch of natural history." Therefore, the answer is (D), *emphatically opposed.* (C), *belligerently vexed,* can be eliminated as an extreme choice. Also eliminate (A) and (B), since they indicate that the author is in agreement with the doctrine.

2. **(C)** This is a word-in-context question. Embed "intelligible," an adjective, in its broader context, lines 11–17: "The community of certain expressions in distinct though allied species, as in the movements of the same facial muscles during laughter by man and by various monkeys, is rendered somewhat more intelligible, if we believe in their descent from a common progenitor. He who admits on general grounds that the structure and habits of all animals have been gradually evolved, will look at the whole subject of Expression in a new and interesting light." Try to paraphrase the tricky parts, expressing them in your own words, something like this: The group of different expressions in separate but related species...becomes more intelligible if we believe that the species come from a common ancestor. As you can see, a strong vocabulary greatly assists with paraphrasing. (A), *Vociferous,* means loud and therefore does not work in this sentence. (B), *insightful,* is not the answer even though you might pick this if you carelessly misread "intelligible" in line 13 as "intelligent." Choice (D), *intelligent* is a tricky decoy since it starts with the same six letters as "intelligible." The correct answer is (C), *understandable.*

3. **(A)** This is an inference question based on a seven-line sidebar (lines 18–24). Be sure to notice a key word in the question, "disagree." In the question, the word "suggest" indicates that this is a hard, inference-level question. Read over the lengthy section of the second paragraph, lines 18–24:

> The study of Expression is difficult, owing to the movements
> being often extremely slight, and of a fleeting nature.
> A difference may be clearly perceived, and yet it may be impossible,
> at least I have found it so, to state in what the difference consists.
> When we witness any deep emotion, our sympathy is so strongly
> excited, that close observation is forgotten or rendered
> almost impossible; of which fact I have had many curious proofs.

Determine four statements with which Darwin agrees; the odd man out is your answer! Consider (A), *The subtle distinctions between an expression of discouragement and one of disappointment are easily noted.* Since Darwin says, "The study of

Expression is difficult and it may be impossible to ...state in what the difference consists," this must be the statement he would disagree with. Choice (A) is the answer. With this same passage evidence in mind, Darwin must agree with (D), *Sometimes it's hard to notice whether another was feeling anxious or was simply eager*. Let's be certain we can eliminate the remaining answers. (B), *Humans can become absorbed in the emotions of others*: Darwin agrees, since he writes "When we witness any deep emotion, our sympathy is so strongly excited. . . ." Choice (C), *Changes in facial expressions are faint rather than pronounced*, is a statement Darwin would support since he writes "the movement being often extremely slight, and of a fleeting nature."

4. **(D)** This is a phrase-in-context question. Embed the given expression in a wide enough context (lines 32–39) so that you can ascertain its meaning within the passage: "In order to acquire as good a foundation as possible, and to ascertain, independently of common opinion, how far particular movements of the features and gestures are really expressive of certain states of the mind, I have found the following means the most serviceable. In the first place, to observe infants; for they exhibit many emotions, as Sir C. Bell remarks, 'with extraordinary force'; whereas, in after life, some of our expressions 'cease to have the pure and simple source from which they spring in infancy.'"

Since the life in line 37 refers to that of infants, the "after life" would offer contrast. The correct answer is (D), *a time later in life*. The idea is that infants are more expressive, through their features and gestures, than older individuals. Notice that line 38 says that we are not as "pure and simple" as we were during our infancy. We can surmise that *later in life*, as things become more complicated, we become less naïve. This change doesn't necessarily occur in old age, *late in life*, but would take place as we mature. Choice (C), *a more conscientious life*, would not necessarily be in contrast to the life of an infant, who may or may not have a "conscience," depending upon one's definition. There is no clear evidence that "after life" refers to either (A), *spiritual life*, or (B), *life after death*.

5. **(D)** This is a characterization question. Spot the key term, "Dr. J. Crichton-Browne," and skim around it for details that illustrate this character. The passage says, "This excellent observer has with unwearied kindness sent me copious notes and descriptions, with valuable suggestions on many points; and I can hardly over-estimate the value of his assistance." This is a positive appraisal of Dr. J. Crichton-Browne, so let's cross off the negatives—goodbye to (A), (B), and (C). Did you know that a "debunker" proves false or contradicts established beliefs and/or customs? The answer is (D).

6. **(B)** This is a question on passage structure. If you didn't pick up on the organizational structure while you were reading, go back to the second half of the passage and skim to get a sense of how it's "built." Notice "In the *first place* . . . observe infants" (line 36), followed by "In the *second place*, it occurred to me that the insane ought to be studied" (lines 40–41), and finally, "*Thirdly* Dr. Duchenne galvanized, as we have already seen, certain muscles in the face of an old man" (lines 51–52). Therefore, the answer is (B), a series of three suggestions for case studies. The passage evidence just laid out is not (A), *a listing of random vignettes*, since the concepts presented are not random, but rather are related ideas about whom to study. Also, the word *vignettes* is highly visual and descriptive, which this listing is not. Choice (C) is out since statistics are nowhere to be found. Also, there are no *romanticized musings* in the latter half of this passage, so eliminate (D).

7. **(C)** This is an inference question based on subtle descriptions. Skim through the final paragraph, looking for clues about how the author describes "various people's interpretations" of the enlarged photos of the old man's face. The last paragraph is chunky; you shouldn't simply rely on your memory or take a guess. As always, your answer should be based on the acid test: *according to the author.* The onus is on you to find something in the last paragraph that validates one of the answer choices. Have you found the pertinent part of the paragraph? Here it is, with context clues underlined:

> Several of the expressions were instantly recognized by almost everyone, though described in not exactly the same terms; . . .
> . . . the most widely different judgments were pronounced in regard to some of them. . . .
> . . . how easily we may be misguided by our imagination.

It sounds as though the participants had diverse ways of describing the photos and "widely different judgments," and their imaginations influenced their interpretations. Now that you have found the evidence, which is the best answer? (A), *ludicrous*, is out since the author is not mocking or downright dismissing the interpretations of the observers. (B) and (D) are not validated; here nothing says that the interpretations were *unpredictable* or *inconsequential* (trivial). The answer is (C), *subjective*.

8. **(D)** This is a word-in-context question. Be open to the multifarious meanings of "galvanized," an action verb. To illustrate the importance of open-mindedness when it comes to words-in-context questions, let's consider three possible meanings for galvanize: (1) to apply an electric current, (2) to excite someone into doing something, and (3) to coat metal with a topping of zinc. Now contemplate the word in its context: "Thirdly Dr. Duchenne galvanized, as we have already seen, certain muscles in the face of an old man, whose skin was little sensitive, and thus produced various expressions which were photographed on a large scale." Choices (A) and (B), *surged* and *electrified*, relate to the first meaning of galvanize but do not fit this context. If the old man's face were (C) *solidified*, no expressions could be detected; cross off this choice with your active pencil. The correct answer is (D), *incited* (roused, stirred up).

VERY HARD READING PASSAGES 特别难的阅读段落

A recipe for making peanut butter s'mores or the ultimate chocolate chip cookie would be more fun, but let's talk about the recipe for a very hard critical reading passage.

Recipe for a very hard evidence-based passage = stuffy + convoluted + cryptic + theoretical + abstruse = the passage you are about to read.

Read in digestible pieces, and hold on tight (stay focused).

PRACTICE TEST QUESTIONS 练习测试题

> **Directions:** Read the passage below, and then answer the questions that follow. The correct response may be stated outright or merely suggested in the passage.

The following passage is excerpted from philosopher Immanuel Kant's The Metaphysical Elements of Ethics, *first published in 1780.*

If there exists on any subject a philosophy (that is, a system of rational knowledge based on concepts), then there must also be for this philosophy a system of pure rational concepts, independent of any condition of intuition, in other words, a metaphysic. It may be asked whether metaphysical elements are required also for every practical philosophy, which is the doctrine of duties, and therefore also for Ethics, in order to be able to present it as a true science (systematically), not merely as an aggregate of separate doctrines (fragmentarily). As regards pure jurisprudence, no one will question this requirement; for it concerns only what is formal in the elective will, which has to be limited in its external relations according to laws of freedom; without regarding any end which is the matter of this will. Here, therefore, deontology is a mere scientific doctrine (*doctrina scientiae*).

Now in this philosophy (of ethics) it seems contrary to the idea of it that we should go back to metaphysical elements in order to make the notion of duty purified from everything empirical (from every feeling) a motive of action. For what sort of notion can we form of the mighty power and Herculean strength which would be sufficient to overcome the vice-breeding inclinations, if Virtue is to borrow her "arms from the armory of metaphysics," which is a matter of speculation that only few men can handle?

Hence all ethical teaching in lecture rooms, pulpits, and popular books, when it is decked out with fragments of metaphysics, becomes ridiculous. But it is not, therefore, useless, much less ridiculous, to trace in metaphysics the first principles of ethics; for it is only as a philosopher that anyone can reach the first principles of this conception of duty, otherwise we could not look for either certainty or purity in the ethical teaching. To rely for this reason on a certain feeling which, on account of the effect expected from it, is called moral, may, perhaps, even satisfy the popular teacher, provided he desires as the criterion of a moral duty to consider the problem: "If everyone in every case made your maxim the universal law, how could this law be consistent with itself?" But if it were merely feeling that made it our duty to take this principle as a criterion, then this would not be dictated by reason, but only adopted instinctively and therefore blindly.

But in fact, whatever men imagine, no moral principle is based on any feeling, but such a principle is really nothing else than an obscurely conceived metaphysic which inheres in every man's reasoning faculty; as the teacher will easily find who tries to catechize his pupils in the Socratic method about the imperative of duty and its application to the moral judgment of his actions. The mode of stating it need not be always metaphysical, and the language need not necessarily be scholastic, unless the pupil is to be trained to be a philosopher. But the thought must go back to the elements of metaphysics, without which we cannot expect any certainty or purity, or even motive power in ethics.

1. According to the author, all of the following would be antithetical to "a metaphysic" (line 5) EXCEPT

(A) an individual's visceral sense
(B) a pure certitude
(C) man's free will
(D) an intended outcome

2. In the first paragraph of the passage, the author does which of the following?

I. Defines a term
II. Cites an expert
III. Gives the Latin name for a term
IV. Explains the distinction between two terms

(A) I only
(B) II only
(C) I and II only
(D) I, III, and IV only

3. Lines 21–25, "For what sort of notion . . . few men can handle?" can be described as

(A) a hyperbole that accents the disparity between male and female inner strengths
(B) an alliterative description of philosophical ideas
(C) an extended metaphor that contrasts good and evil
(D) a rhetorical question that contains both a mythological allusion and a personification of a human attribute

4. In context, the expression "decked out" in line 27 most closely means

(A) detailed and described
(B) bedecked with ornaments
(C) dressed up and bejeweled
(D) combated vehemently

5. In line 41, "dictated" most nearly means

(A) divulged
(B) ordained
(C) avowed
(D) determined

6. What can you infer about the assumption the author is making in lines 50–53, "The mode of stating it need not be always . . . be trained to be a philosopher"?

(A) The majority of students will become befuddled by a high level of pedagogic, philosophical instruction.
(B) Only for the student who plans to become a practicing philosopher is an erudite and intellectual level of training required.
(C) Today's philosophical teaching is, regrettably, over the heads of most average students.
(D) A pupil's inner state of morality greatly affects the way he conducts himself during a Socratic seminar.

Answers and Explanations 答案与解析

1. B	**3.** D	**5.** D
2. D	**4.** A	**6.** A

1. **(B)** This is a hard all/except question, requiring you to know that *antithetical* means "opposite to." Scope out context clues up/down/around line 5 that indicate what a metaphysic is. The context clue is "a system of pure rational concepts, independent of (excluding) any condition of intuition," so (A), (C), and (D) are all out since they involve an aspect of intuition, which you can think of as perception or insight. Active Pencil! These choices involve something other than "pure rational concepts." The only exception is (B), which is the correct answer. Like roman-numeral-list questions, ALL/EXCEPT questions tend to be time-consuming.

2. **(D)** This is a hard, time-consuming roman-numeral-list question. Peruse paragraph 1 to find examples of each of the items in the roman numeral list. Place a check mark next to each item you find so that you can keep track of what you have located in paragraph 1. You don't want to waste precious time finding more than one example!
I. The author defines "philosophy" in line 1 and "metaphysic" in line 5.
II. No expert or authority is quoted.
III. The Latin term *doctrina scientiae* appears in line 16.
IV. The author explains the difference between "a true science" and "an aggregate of separate doctrines" in lines 9 and 10.
The correct answer is (D).

3. **(D)** This is a hard interpretation question. Reread the lines quoted in the question carefully, and try to "downsize" them by paraphrasing in your own words. Choice (A) might appear true, but it is actually a false-positive, an only-partly-true decoy answer. The idea of *hyperbole* (great exaggeration) is touched upon (*mighty power and Herculean strength*), but this answer choice should be tossed out since nowhere in the lines quoted is the difference stressed between the inner strengths of male and female. Alliteration requires the repetition of an initial consonant sound, as in "**r**edolent **r**ed **r**oses." No alliteration occurs, so cross off (B). A metaphor is a direct comparison without *like* or *as*, for example, "Love is a red rose." No metaphor appears in lines 21–25; eliminate (C). The correct answer is (D). A *rhetorical question* is asked simply for effect. The mythological allusion (reference) is to Hercules, and Virtue is personified in the passage, for she is "to borrow her arms."

4. **(A)** This is a hard expression-in-context question. Reread the sentence in which "decked out" appears. Seek out clues to elucidate its meaning. This question is particularly hard because of the vocabulary in the answer choices: *bedecked, bejeweled,* and *filigree*. These words may present obstacles or, at the least, cause some hesitation. The author is saying that, when Ethics is taught in classrooms, teachers tend to "deck it out" or dress it up with items of information that relate to metaphysics. But he does not mean dressed up literally, so (B) and (C) are out. (D) does not make sense since teachers in their right minds do not simultaneously include something in their teaching and oppose it passionately. The answer is (A).

5. **(D)** This is a hard vocabulary word-in-context question. Reread carefully the sentence in which "dictated" appears to get a sense of the word's context. Predict a substitute for the word. Carefully select the closest answer choice. Choice (A) is out since *divulged* usually means revealed secret information. Choice (B) is out also, since the connotation of *ordained* has to do with an individual being formally assigned priestly or holy orders. *Avowed* doesn't quite fit, so cross out (C). The answer is (D).

6. **(A)** This is a hard inference and assumption question. The answer choices are long and heavy-weight, making this question even more challenging. Reread the sidebar: "The mode of stating it need not be always metaphysical, and the language need not necessarily be scholastic, unless the pupil is to be trained to be a philosopher," trying to pick up an underlying message put forth by the author. Choice (B) is close, but the author is not directly stating that only students who want to become philosophers require *erudite* (scholarly) training. Choice (C) is out since no statement is made about *most average students.* Choice (D), according to common sense, is probably true, yet no evidence in the passage speaks to pupils' morality. The answer is (A) since lines 50–53 imply that without training (in philosophy), the pupil would not comprehend explanations coached in metaphysical/scholastic terms. *Befuddled* means confused.

PRACTICE TEST QUESTIONS/PAIRED PASSAGES
练习测试题/配对段落题目

Directions: The questions that follow the two passages in this section relate to the contents of both and to their relationship. The correct response may be stated outright or merely suggested.

The following two passages, which are excerpted from the works of two well-known social thinkers, are about slavery in America. Passage 1 is taken from Henry David Thoreau's Slavery in Massachusetts. *Passage 2 is excerpted from Booker T. Washington's autobiography,* Up From Slavery.

Passage 1

Much has been said about American slavery, but I think that we do not even yet realize what slavery is. If I were seriously to propose to Congress to make mankind into sausages, I have no doubt that most of the members would smile at my proposition, and if any believed me to be in earnest, they would think that I proposed something much worse than Congress had ever done. But if any of them will tell me that to make a man into a sausage would be much worse—would be any worse—than to make him into a slave—than it was to enact the Fugitive Slave Law—I will accuse him of foolishness, of intellectual incapacity, of making a distinction without a difference. The one is just as sensible a proposition as the other.

Divide and Conquer the Passage
The dotted lines indicate how you might go about reading this passage piece by piece. At each break, consider which questions (if any) you can answer while that piece is fresh in your mind.

I hear a good deal said about trampling this law under foot. Why, one need not go out of his way to do that. This law rises not to the level of the head or the reason; its natural habitat is in the dirt. It was born and bred, and has its life, only in the dust and mire, on a level with the feet; and he who walks with freedom, and does not with Hindoo mercy avoid treading on every venomous reptile, will inevitably tread on it, and so trample it under foot—and Webster, its maker, with it, like the dirt-bug and its ball.

Recent events will be valuable as a criticism on the administration of justice in our midst, or, rather, as showing what are the true resources of justice in any community. It has come to this, that the friends of liberty, the friends of the slave, have shuddered when they have understood that his fate was left to the legal tribunals of the country to be decided. Free men have no faith that justice will be awarded in such a case. The judge may decide this way or that; it is a kind of accident, at best. It is evident that he is not a competent authority in so important a case. It is no time, then, to be judging according to his precedents, but to establish a precedent for the future. I would much rather trust to the sentiment of the people. In their vote you would get something of some value, at least, however small; but in the other case, only the trammeled judgment of an individual, of no significance, be it which way it might.

It is to some extent fatal to the courts, when the people are compelled to go behind them. I do not wish to believe that the courts were made for fair weather, and for very civil cases merely; but think of leaving it to any court in the land to decide whether more than three millions of people, in this case a sixth part of a nation, have a right to be freemen or not! But it has been left to the courts of justice, so called—to the Supreme Court of the land—and, as you all know, recognizing no authority but the Constitution, it has decided that the three millions are and shall continue to be slaves.

Passage 2

I was born a slave on a plantation in Franklin County, Virginia. I am not quite sure of the exact place or exact date of my birth, but at any rate I suspect I must have been born somewhere and at some time. As nearly as I have been able to learn, I was born near a cross-roads post-office called Hale's Ford, and the year was 1858 or 1859. I do not know the month or the day. The earliest impressions I can now recall are of the plantation and the slave quarters—the latter being the part of the plantation where the slaves had their cabins.

Of my ancestry I know almost nothing. In the slave quarters, and even later, I heard whispered conversations among the colored people of the tortures which the slaves, including, no doubt, my ancestors on my mother's side, suffered in the middle passage of the slave ship while being conveyed from Africa to America. I have been unsuccessful in securing any information that would throw any accurate light upon the history of my family beyond my mother. She, I remember, had a half-brother and a half-sister. In the days of slavery not very much attention was given to family history and family records—that is, black family records. My mother, I suppose, attracted the attention of a purchaser who was afterward my owner and hers. Her addition to the slave family attracted about as much attention as the purchase of a new horse or cow. Of my father I know even less than of my mother. I do not even know his name. I have heard reports to the effect that he was a white man who lived on one of the near-by plantations. Whoever he was, I never heard of his taking the least interest in me or providing in any way for my rearing. But I do not find especial fault with him. He was simply another unfortunate victim of the institution which the Nation unhappily had engrafted upon it at that time.

So far as I can now recall, the first knowledge that I got of the fact that we were slaves, and that freedom of the slaves was being discussed, was early one morning before day, when I was awakened by my mother kneeling over her children and fervently praying that Lincoln and his armies might be successful, and that one day she and her children might be free. In this connection I have never been able to understand how the slaves throughout the South, completely ignorant as were the masses so far as books or newspapers were concerned, were able to keep themselves so accurately and completely informed about the great National questions that were agitating the country. From the time that Garrison, Lovejoy, and others began to agitate for freedom, the slaves throughout the South kept in close touch with the progress of the movement. Though I was a mere child during the preparation for the Civil War and during the war itself, I now recall the many late-at-night whispered discussions that I heard my mother and the other slaves on the plantation indulge in. These discussions showed that they understood the situation, and that they kept themselves informed of events by what was termed the "grape-vine" telegraph.

During the campaign when Lincoln was first a candidate for the Presidency, the slaves on our far-off plantation, miles from any railroad or large city or daily newspaper, knew what the issues involved were. When war was begun between the North and the South, every slave on our plantation felt and knew that, though other issues were discussed, the primal one was that of slavery. Even the most ignorant members of my race on the remote plantations felt in their hearts, with a certainty that admitted of no doubt, that the freedom of the slaves would be the one great result of the war, if the northern armies conquered. Every success of the Federal armies and every defeat of the Confederate forces was watched with the keenest and most intense interest. Often the slaves got knowledge of the results of great battles before the white people received it. This news was usually gotten from the colored man who was sent to the post-office for the mail. In our case the post-office was about three miles from the plantation, and the mail came once or twice a week. The man who was sent to the office would linger about the place long enough to get the drift of the conversation from the group of white people who naturally congregated there, after receiving their mail, to discuss the latest news. The mail-carrier on his way back to our master's house would as naturally retail the news that he had secured among the slaves, and in this way they often heard of important events before the white people at the "big house," as the master's house was called.

Coaching—Paired Passages
Read the passages piece by piece, answering pertinent questions as you go. Answer Passage 1 only questions first. Then answer Passage 2 only questions. Lastly, answer questions that involve both passages: the holistic or global questions.

1. In Passage 1 it can be inferred that the Congressional members "would smile" (line 5) for which of the following reasons?

(A) They believe that the author's proposed intention is ludicrous.
(B) They are making an effort to conceal their inner scorn toward the author.
(C) They are sealing the author's proposition with a smile as a way of demonstrating their consent.
(D) They are mocking the author's demeanor and his point of view.

2. According to the Passage 1 author, "making a distinction without a difference" (lines 12–13) can be characterized as all of the following EXCEPT

(A) an admirable and judicious trait
(B) a line of argument that Thoreau finds offensive and nearly absurd
(C) a reasoning process that results from mental obtuseness
(D) a way of thinking that reflects mental ineptness

3. Thoreau does which of the following in paragraph 2 of Passage 1?

I. Personifies that which is inanimate and intangible
II. Relates a bit of hearsay
III. Explains nature's connection to lawmaking
IV. Contradicts an established fallacy

(A) I only
(B) I and II only
(C) I and IV only
(D) III only

4. In Passage 1, which of the following most accurately explains why the friends of the slaves "shuddered" (line 30)?

(A) The slaves' friends were fearful that they too might become indentured servants one day.
(B) The slaves' friends internalized the cold and stern emotions of slaveholders and slavery advocates.
(C) The slaves' friends visibly trembled under the crushing leadership of crooked judges and juries.
(D) The slaves' friends realized that the future of slavery was in the hands of a legal body.

5. In line 38, "precedents" most nearly means

(A) retired judges
(B) predecessors
(C) legal rivals
(D) prior legal decisions

6. In lines 49–50, the author's inclusion of the phrase "a sixth part of a nation" serves mainly to

(A) demonstrate his mathematical prowess
(B) heighten people's understanding of the staggering ratio of slave owners to slaves
(C) underscore the considerable number of slaves as a sizable segment of the population
(D) show his ability to manipulate ratios and statistics

7. The first paragraph of Passage 2 reveals which of the following about Booker T. Washington's impressions of his early life?

(A) The situation of his birth and early upbringing are perceived as both distasteful and disdainful.
(B) The circumstances surrounding his birth and early upbringing are opaque and ambiguous.
(C) Despite his efforts, he has learned only very disturbing tidbits about his birth and early youth.
(D) He knows little about his birth because his interest level on this topic was surprisingly very low.

8. According to Passage 2, how is the slaves' knowledge of Lincoln's campaign as discussed in lines 108–111 most accurately explained?

I. The mother "fervently praying" (lines 91–92)
II. The "middle passage of the slave ship" (line 70)
III. The "grape-vine telegraph" (line 107)
IV. The "mail-carrier" (line 128)

(A) I only
(B) II only
(C) II and III
(D) III and IV only

9. In view of their contextual meanings in both passages, the term "sausages" (line 4, Passage 1) and the term "horse or cow" (line 80, Passage 2) serve mainly to

(A) accentuate the difference between the value of processed foods and that of natural livestock
(B) create a ludicrous set of images in order to diminish the graveness of the topic of slavery
(C) reference popular examples of food and property that were traded during the 1800s
(D) illustrate the dehumanizing and demeaning aspects of the institution of slavery

10. The attitude toward slavery held by the passage authors and the attitude toward slavery held by Congress (Passage 1, paragraph 1) are, respectively, best described as

(A) the former attitude is apathetic; the latter is pedantic
(B) the former attitude is resigned; the latter is skeptical
(C) the former attitude is regretful; the latter is matter of fact
(D) the former attitude is mocking; the latter is irreverent

11. On the issue of slavery in America, which of the following best describes the perspectives of these two authors?

(A) Thoreau is a social observer and philosopher who is ardently opposed to slavery; Washington has actually experienced slavery.
(B) Thoreau covertly advocates slavery; Washington overtly opposes slavery.
(C) Thoreau dislikes all slavery leaders; Washington dislikes only slave owners who "erased" his personal history.
(D) Thoreau is a detached historian; Washington is also detached and is numb from an overabundance of personal trauma.

Answers and Explanations 答案与解析

1. A	**5.** D	**9.** D
2. A	**6.** C	**10.** C
3. B	**7.** B	**11.** A
4. D	**8.** D	

1600 Club Coaching: *Reading these answer explanations thoroughly is an excellent test preparation strategy.*

1. **(A)** This is a hard inference question. Consider "would smile" in its broader context for clues about why members of Congress smiled. From "if any believed me to be in earnest," we can understand that Congress would think the author was jesting and, therefore, would not take his proposition seriously. They would react to this nonsensical or *ludicrous* idea with a smile; (A) is the answer. There are no context clues to support (B), *conceal their inner scorn;* (C), *demonstrating their consent;* or (D), *mocking the author's demeanor,* that is, his behavior and conduct.

2. **(A)** This is a tricky all/except question. Find clues to the meaning and the relevance in context of "making a distinction without a difference." Context clues in the vicinity of this phrase include "foolishness" and "intellectual incapacity" (line 12). All choices except (A) reflect these clues, so (A) is the correct answer. Potentially challenging vocabulary in the answer choices include *judicious* (fair and just), *obtuseness* (vacuity, stupidity), and *ineptness* (lack of skill.)

3. **(B)** This is a hard roman-numeral-list question. Just like ALL/EXCEPT questions, roman-numeral-list questions are time-consuming to answer, requiring a good deal of passage revisiting and reviewing.
I. The Fugitive Slave Law (referred to as "this law" in line 15) is personified: the context clues are *"its natural habitat"* and *"It was born and bred."* (lines 18 and 19);
II. "Hearsay" is rumor. Context clue to support II is "I hear a good deal said about . . ." (line 15)
III and IV. No textual evidence.
The answer is (B).

4. **(D)** This is a tricky explanation for a word-in-context question. Skim up and down and around the word "shuddered" to get clues about precisely why the friends of slaves shuddered. Not (A), since there's no evidence that they feared becoming slaves themselves. Not (B), since there's no mention of *cold and stern emotions*. Not (C), because there's no mention of *crooked juries or judges*. The correct answer is (D) since it is the closest paraphrasing of "the friends of the slave, have <u>shuddered</u> when they have understood that his fate was left to the legal tribunals [courts] of the country to be decided. Free men have no faith that justice will be awarded in such a case" (lines 30–34).

5. **(D)** This is a word-in-context question. Reread the complete sentence that contains "precedents," and predict what the word means. No doubt, you recognize the prefix *pre-*, so you know you need an answer that relates to *before*. The answer choices are challenging, though, because (A), (B), and (D) all relate to *before* in one way or another. The broad context of the word (reproduced below) shows that precedents have something to do with how judges have decided cases. But (A), *retired judges;* (B), *predecessors;* and (C), *legal rivals* have more to do with persons and less to do with (D), *prior legal decisions,* which is the answer. Notice that "precedents" is preceded by the possessive pronoun "his," clarifying that precedents are prior decisions of the judge. Choice (D) makes the most sense.

> . . . the friends of the slave, have shuddered when they have understood that his fate was left to the legal tribunals of the country to be decided. Free men have no faith that justice will be awarded in such a case. The judge may decide this way or that; it is a kind of accident, at best. It is evident that he is not a competent authority in so important a case. It is no time, then, to be judging according to his precedents, but to establish a precedent for the future. I would much rather trust to the sentiment of the people. In their vote you would get something of some value, at least, however small; but in the other case, only the trammeled judgment of an individual, of no significance, be it which way it might.

Sometimes, as in this case, tough word-in-context questions require you to reread and reconsider a broad context in order to settle on the meaning that makes most sense.

6. **(C)** This is a purpose question. Reread "a sixth part of a nation" in context to get a sense of the main purpose it serves. The italic blurb that precedes the passage tells you that the author is Thoreau, who was "a social thinker," not a mathematician or physicist; therefore, there's no reason for him to (A) *demonstrate his mathematical prowess* or (D) *show his ability to manipulate ratios and statistics.* The phrase does not indicate a *ratio of slave owners to slaves,* so (B) is out. The most sensible answer is (C).

7. **(B)** This is a getting the gist of a paragraph question. Skimming the paragraph for details about Booker T. Washington's birth and early life reveals that few, if any, solid details are known. In fact, everything from the place of his birth to the date of his birth is vague and sketchy. The answer is (B). You're sharp, but perhaps *opaque* (dark, obscure) and *ambiguous* (unclear; vague) are potentially challenging words that appear in this answer choice. Choice (A) is unsupported because there's no evidence to support a description of his birth and his upbringing as *distasteful and disdainful.* Likewise, there's no proof that the author's interest in his birth is *very low,* so (D) is out. Choice (C) is off since the unknowns about his youth are not confirmed as *disturbing.*

8. **(D)** This is a time-consuming roman-numeral-list question. To ace this demanding question, diligently skim the four line references given in items I–IV. A quick overview of lines 91–92 and line 70 will reveal that I and II have nothing to do with information about the Lincoln campaign being passed on orally from one slave to another. Skim around lines 107 and 128, however, and you'll readily pick up on how *the grape-vine telegraph* and the *mail carrier* were both conduits of political information. The correct answer is (D). You need to work quickly on list questions, so you don't lose time.

9. **(D)** This is a tricky decoding-of-terms question that involves both passages. Delve back into the passages and read up, down, and around each of the very visual terms, "sausages" and "horse or cow." You're sharp, so you'll see that these terms are symbolic or figurative, rather than literal, in their meanings. Considering the contexts of these terms, you find nothing about the *value* (monetary or otherwise) of *processed foods and that of natural livestock*, so cross (A) off with your active pencil and move on! You're savvy enough to understand that sausages and horses/cows are mentioned for more than comic relief, so (B) is out. This passage isn't about the marketplace of the 1800s, so bye-bye (C). The answer is (D); certainly, thinking of a human being as a sausage, horse, or cow is *dehumanizing* and *demeaning* that individual.

10. **(C)** This is a challenging question on paired passages and their authors' attitudes. Questions on attitude, mood, or tone require you to have absorbed the overall sense and feel of the passages so that you can answer questions, such as this one, that require you to consider the passages on a holistic level. The Passage 1 author is writing on the topic of American slavery, so how could he be *apathetic*? Choice (A) is out. Also, the Passage 1 author is neither *resigned* (accepting) when it comes to slavery nor *mocking*; he obviously considers slavery to be a serious issue worth writing about. Cross off (B) and (D). The correct answer is (C).

11. **(A)** This is a paired-passage perspectives question—yikes! Reflect on all of the reading and rereading and thinking you have done so far on this passage. You should be in tip-top shape to probe into this paired-passage point-of-view question. It is not true that Thoreau *advocates slavery*, covertly or openly. He opposes it, so cross off (B). Choice (C), Thoreau *dislikes all slavery leaders*; *Washington dislikes only slave owners who have "erased" his personal history*. Neither author is *detached*; each has an opinion and strong feeling toward the topic of slavery, so (C) and (D) are invalid. The correct answer is (A). The evidence: The italic blurb identifies Thoreau as a "social thinker." It is clear that Washington has experienced slavery because he uses the first-person point of view, "I," to relate his experiences.

CONDENSED "READ SMART" STRATEGIES "READ SMART" 策略

R: Read, React, Reread 阅读，反应，重读

Read the passage through thoughtfully. Try to visualize and bring to life what you are reading.

Read actively: circle, underline, visualize, make notes in the margins, define pronouns (*it, that, those, there, them,* etc.) as you read so that you read with clarity and accuracy. Defining pronouns will ensure that you don't lose track of the concepts, people, places, or objects that were previously mentioned.

React to what you are reading so that what you read makes an impact on you and sticks.

React dramatically so that you are more likely to remember the ideas, images, and information given in the passage.

Reread any parts of the passage that you want to absorb more fully.

Reread the questions themselves so that you are clear about precisely what the question is asking.

E: Engage, Extract 结合，提炼

Engage with the author's statements, as you try to understand his points and viewpoints. Engage by underlining and/or circling key points as well as adjectives that serve to depict the author's viewpoint on the topics, people, places, and ideas about which he is writing.

Extract basic but vital information such as author's message, main ideas, overarching lines of reasoning, and purpose(s) in writing the passage.

A: Annotate, Absorb 注释，理解

Annotate as you read, as many passages are at a high level of textual difficulty. Make it a habit to annotate by jotting comments in the marginal spaces provided in your test booklet. You can annotate in a variety of ways, such as using symbols. (See the Gallery of Symbols on page 20.) The main rule of thumb is to keep your notes brief; a word, a couple of words, or a short phrase written in abbreviated form should suffice.

Absorb the undertones that are expressed in the passage, such as the author's mood or tone. This mindset of being on the lookout for tone and mood can help when answering the questions next.

D: Do's and Don'ts 要做的和不要做的

Do read all introductory material that may be provided.

Do read all titles and labels and all informational graphics that may accompany the passage.

Do circle and underline key terms, phrases, and concepts as you read. Jot an asterisk (*) next to key concepts or in the margins alongside key portions of the passage. This way, you can find these terms and sections more easily later.

Don't use your outside knowledge or life experience to answer questions: use only information that is stated or implied in the accompanying passage or passages.

Don't omit any questions. There is no penalty for an incorrect answer.

Don't make assumptions about how the author feels. Find the passage evidence first.

第二章 Chapter 2

PRACTICE READING QUESTIONS 阅读练习题

Now that you have studied strategy approaches to effective reading, try some practice questions. This chapter contains multiple-choice questions similar to those you are likely to encounter on the updated SAT Reading Test. Reading test questions will be based on passages that address the following three broad content areas: United States and world literature, history and social studies, and science. The passage content will be apportioned at 20 percent, 40 percent, and 40 percent, respectively, across those three categories of reading subjects. As on the formal model SAT, correct answers are based on what is stated or implied in the accompanying passages; outside knowledge and personal opinion are not applicable. Take note that one of the history passages will be—or is very likely to be—an excerpt from a text that explores topics that make up the "Great Global Conversation" (culturally important and engaging texts exploring issues that affect political and civic life) or a United States-based founding document, such as the Declaration of Independence, the U.S. Constitution, the Articles of Confederation, or the Gettysburg Address.

The following passages and questions are abridged, as they are intended to provide a sampling for practice across most of the reading content areas that will appear on the SAT. Actual passages will be longer (500 to 750 words per passage or per paired set of passages), and 10 to 12 questions will accompany each reading passage or paired set.

LITERATURE 文学作品

Note: On the actual test, literature excerpts will come from both contemporary and classic works by authors working in the United States or around the world.

Content: U.S. Literature / Prose Fiction

Focus: Students must read and understand a passage that is prose fiction.

Remember to use a pen or pencil to annotate the text as you read!

Questions 1–4 are based on the following paired passages.

Directions: The questions that follow the two passages in this section relate to the content of both and to their relationship. The correct response may be stated outright in the passages or merely suggested.

The first passage is excerpted from Out of Doors—California and Oregon, *by J. A. Graves; the second, from* At the Earth's Core, *a work of fiction by Edgar Rice Burroughs.*

Passage 1

In the pasture were swales of damp land, literally overgrown with wild blackberry bushes. They bore prolific crops of long, black, juicy berries, far superior to the tame berries, and they were almost entirely free from seeds. Many a time have I temporarily bankrupted my stomach on hot blackberry roll, with good, rich sauce. The country fairly teemed with game. Quail and rabbit were with us all the time. Doves came by the thousands in the early summer and departed in the fall. In winter the wild ducks and geese were more than abundant. In the spring wild pigeons visited us in great numbers. There was one old oak tree which was a favorite resting-place with them. Sheltered by some live oak bushes, I was always enabled to sneak up and kill many of them out of this tree.

Passage 2

We must have traveled several miles through the dark and dismal wood when we came suddenly upon a dense village built high among the branches of the trees. As we approached it my escort broke into wild shouting which was immediately answered from within, and a moment later a swarm of creatures of the same strange race as those who had captured me poured out to meet us. Again I was the center of a wildly chattering horde. I was pulled this way and that. Pinched, pounded, and thumped until I was black and blue, yet I do not think that their treatment was dictated by either cruelty or malice—I was a curiosity, a freak, a new plaything, and their childish minds required the added evidence of all their senses to back up the testimony of their eyes.

1. In context, "tame" (line 4) most likely refers to blackberries that are

(A) orderly and cultivated
(B) docile and untainted
(C) easier to pick and tastier to eat
(D) domesticated and demure

2. Which most accurately describes the sentiments that the Passage 1 author has toward the "old oak tree" and "oak bushes" (lines 12 and 13) with respect to the sentiments that the Passage 2 author has toward the "wood" (line 16)?

(A) Passage 1 author feels a sense of ownership and affectation; Passage 2 author, of self-protection.
(B) Passage 1 author feels a sense of nostalgia and whimsy; Passage 2 author, of scathing hostility.
(C) Passage 1 author feels a sense of comfort and cover; Passage 2 author, of foreboding and gloom.
(D) Neither author feels a personal connection to these natural elements.

3. According to Passage 2 as a whole, the author uses the phrase "poured out" (line 21) to convey which of the following regarding the "creatures" in line 20?

(A) They are an unruly and belligerent bunch intent on doing the narrator serious harm.
(B) They pile around the narrator because of their enthusiastic curiosity about him.
(C) They are primitive, yet intelligent.
(D) Their effusive emotions cause them to be disorderly and impulsive.

4. In line 25, "dictated" most nearly means

(A) ordained
(B) tyrannized
(C) prescribed
(D) determined

Answers and Explanations 答案与解析

1. A **3.** B
2. C **4.** D

1. **(A)** This is a subtle word-in-context question. Carefully read up, down, and around line 4 to get a sense of this word in its context. "Tame" most closely refers to blackberries that are, according to the narrator, inferior to the ones described in the previous line 2 as "overgrown," "wild," and "prolific." The best antithetical description of the tame berries is (A), *orderly and cultivated.* There is no evidence to validate the other choices.

2. **(C)** This is a question comparing/contrasting similar elements that appear in both passages. In each passage, read closely around the three line references to glean a sense of the authors' feelings toward these elements of nature. Pertinent parts:

(Passage 1)

There was one old oak tree which was a favorite resting-place with them. Sheltered by some live oak bushes, I was always enabled to sneak up and kill many of them out of this tree.

(Passage 2)

dark and dismal wood

With these significant parts in focus, you can readily see from the underlined context clues that the best answer is (C): *Passage 1 author feels a sense of comfort and cover; Passage 2 author, of foreboding and gloom.* For (A), *ownership* could work, but *affectation* could not (unless, of course, you misread this word as *affection*). For (B), *nostalgia* could work, but not *whimsy*. You should make it a habit to avoid an extreme answer such as *scathing hostility*. Choice (D) is out since the woods are significant to both authors.

3. **(B)** Meaning of a verb phrase in context. Read at, up, down, and around this line reference to get a sense of the subtler implications of the phrase "poured out." Who are the "creatures"? Focus on the pertinent part to recall who the creatures are and why they "poured out." Pertinent part:

later a swarm of *creatures* of the same strange race as those who had captured me *poured out* to meet us. Again I was the center of a wildly chattering horde. I was pulled this way and that. Pinched, pounded, and thumped until I was black and blue, yet I do not think that their treatment was dictated by either cruelty or malice—I was a curiosity, a freak, a new plaything, and their childish minds required the added evidence of all *their senses to back up the testimony of their eyes.*

To paraphrase these lines, a bunch of creatures came running out to meet the narrator and his friend. The creatures surrounded the narrator, talking loudly and grabbing at him because of their curiosity, which stemmed from their childish and inquisitive minds. The answer cannot be (A) since the passage states "I do not think that their treatment was dictated by either cruelty or malice" (lines 24–26). Choice (C) is out since no statement implies that the creatures are *intelligent.* Choice (D) is also out; yes, their emotions are effusively displayed, but the creatures are not portrayed as *impulsive*. The answer is (B).

4. **(D)** This is a word-in-context question. Consider this verb in the larger context in which it is used: "I do not think that their treatment was dictated by either cruelty or malice." Choice (A) is out, since *ordained* connotes an appointment to a religious order. Choice (B), *tyrannized,* is too strong to fit this context. Choice (C), *prescribed,* relates to a written order, as one for medicine. The *best* answer is (D).

HISTORY/SOCIAL STUDIES 历史／社会研究

Note: On the test, the history/social studies excerpts will include portions of United States-based founding documents and/or texts that contribute to what the College Board refers to as the "Great Global Conversation"—engaging and cultural/historical works that address issues at the center of civic and political life. Topics explored may also include topics in the social sciences, including anthropology, communication studies, economics, education, human geography, law, linguistics, political science, psychology, and sociology (and their subfields).

Passage 1

CONTENT: Social Studies

FOCUS: Students must read and understand a passage and any accompanying graphic on a social studies–related topic.

Remember to use a pen or pencil to annotate the text as you read!

Questions 1–3 are based on the following passage.

Author Lori Benzoni is the Pediatric Program Manager of the Department of Pediatrics at Winthrop University Hospital. Her health-related articles are featured in Children's Hospital Magazine *and the nationwide online periodical* ABLEnews.com, *which caters to the disabled.*

The Link Between Poverty and Obesity

Obesity is a serious health concern for children and adolescents. The proliferation of this disease is on the rise. According to the CDC, Centers for Disease Control, obesity increased from 5 to 10.4% between 2007–2008 in 2- to 5-year-olds and from 6.5 to 19.6% among 6- to 11-year-olds. (CDC, 2008) Among adolescents, obesity increased from 5 to 18.1 during that same period. (CDC, 2008) Obesity results when a child consumes more calories than the child uses. There are various factors that can be contributing to this increase such as genetics, behavior, lifestyle, and environmental.

Unfortunately we cannot control what genes we acquire from our parents. Genetic factors alone can play a role in specific cases of obesity. This factor has been traced back to the Pima Indians who have "an unusually high rate of obesity." (Science Daily, 2007) The obesity is thought to be linked to thrifty metabolism that allows them to metabolize food more efficiently in times when little was available but causes problems when food is in abundance. Studies are looking away from genetics now and into the other factors contributing to obesity because genetic characteristics of the human population has not changed in the last three decades, but the prevalence of obesity tripled among school-aged children during that time. (CDC, 2008)

Behavioral factors such as energy intake and physical activity play a role in obesity as well. For energy intake, children are more likely to consume sugar-sweetened beverages than meals. Participating in physical activity is another factor that has decreased over the years. The activities children find fun these days are the ones that promote a sedentary behavior. These activities include computers, video games, and handheld devices. Environmental factors are a major contribution to obesity. It is not only the home environment but schools, child care, peers' homes, and the community as a whole. Having the healthy choices in the refrigerator and cabinets at home only enable the child to attain such foods; although, once the child leaves the home, he or she is open to making choices or someone else is making them on their behalf. Access to proper food choices can be challenging and expensive.

Households without money to buy enough food often have to rely on cheaper, high calorie foods to cope with limited money for food. "Families try to maximize caloric intake for each dollar spent, which can lead to over consumption of calories and a less healthful diet." (FRAC, 2006) This quote exemplifies the ultimate link between poverty and obesity. There are many ways that we can implement a healthier regimen for our children. Educating them is the first and easiest way to give them information about healthy eating and how fast foods damage their body. Fast food restaurants have been starting to offer apples and salads as a side rather than fries and these are the small things that make a difference! I truly do not believe we can change the food system that we currently have due to the amount of steps it would require, but implementing a better selection of low priced choices for families is needed. Schools should ask for funding for healthy meals that can be given to the children who are coming from low income families. At least by doing this, the child will receive a least two good meals during the day. In the study by Gutin, it states that "School based obesity prevention programs are likely to be a cost effective use of public funds." (2008) I believe that if parents were able to give a small donation to the schools, they will be spending less on preparing food for their children that may be of high caloric content, and they would know that their children will receive fresh, healthy breakfasts and lunches at school.

(2006). Obesity and Hunger. *FRAC*. Retrieved on December 18, 2010 from *www.frac.org/html/hunger_in_the_us/hunger&obesity.*

(2007). Genetics Has a Key Role in Obesity. *Science Daily*. Retrieved on December 18, 2010 from *www.sciencedaily.com/releases/2007/10/071016074958.*

(2008). Childhood Overweight and Obesity. *CDC: Centers for Disease Control and Prevention.* Retrieved on December 18, 2010 from *www.cdc.gov/obesity/childhood/.*

Wang, L., Gutin, B., Barbeau, P., Moore, J. & Hanes, J. (2008).Cost-Effectiveness of a School Based Obesity Prevention Program. *Journal of School Health*, (78), pages 619–624.

1. Which correlation is most effectively substantiated based on the data outlined in paragraph 1?

(A) More mature populations exhibit a slower rate of rise in obesity levels.
(B) For younger children, obesity rates rise less dramatically than for the older groups.
(C) There is an inverse relationship between age and obesity.
(D) Environmental factors contribute most significantly to the rate of obesity within a given age group.

2. As used in lines 13–16 (*The obesity is thought to be linked to thrifty metabolism that allows them to metabolize food more efficiently in times when little was available but causes problems when food is in abundance*), the term "thrifty" most nearly means

(A) careful.
(B) malicious.
(C) frugal.
(D) deceptive.

3. All of the following are cited as impediments to countering obesity EXCEPT

(A) the cost of nutritious, high-quality foods.
(B) a decline in fitness activity.
(C) sedentary pastimes.
(D) making choices for oneself.

Passage 2

CONTENT: Social Studies

FOCUS: Students must read and understand a passage and any accompanying graphic on a contemporary social studies–related topic.

Questions 4–7 are based on the following passage.

Excerpted from the Brooklyn Journal of International Law *(Volume 39, 2014), this note, "Greece's Not-so-warm Welcome to Unaccompanied Minors: Reforming EU Law to Prevent the Illegal Treatment of Migrant Children in Greece" was written by Victoria Galante, J.D.*

Greece's Not-so-warm Welcome to Unaccompanied Minors

This Note proposes an amendment to the current law governing Greece's treatment and care of unaccompanied migrant children. It argues that the European Union (EU) must share in the responsibility for Greece's noncompliance with its treaty obligations and amend its laws in ways that both compel and facilitate Greece's compliance. Part I of this Note provides background on the problem of Greece's detention of unaccompanied minors, explaining why they arrive unaccompanied and why they flee to Greece. Part I also discusses Greece's international law obligations under two multilateral treaties to which Greece is a party—the CRC (U.N. Convention on the Rights of the Child and the ECHR (European Convention on Human Rights). Part II explains how Greece is currently violating its treaty obligations, highlighting the 2011 case of *M.S.S. v. Belgium & Greece* and explaining the role EU's Dublin II regulations play in Greek detention conditions. Part III proposes a two-part solution to Greece's violations of the CRC and the ECHR. First, the Note proposes the elimination of all conflicts of interest in the care of unaccompanied minors entering Greece. Second, it calls for the EU's actual execution of the "best interests of the child" principle through the prohibition of child detention and a mandate for alternatives that are sensitive to children's vulnerability and foster a sense of trust. Finally, the Note concludes with final recommendation for both the EU and Greece.

4. The stance taken in this excerpt is best described as that of

(A) an uninformed observer relying on third-person accounts.
(B) an authority delineating an historical perspective.
(C) a politician striving for neutrality.
(D) an advocate seeking improved conditions.

5. Which choice provides the best evidence for the answer to the previous question?

(A) Lines 2–4 ("It . . . noncompliance") It argues that the European Union (EU) must share in the responsibility for Greece's noncompliance.
(B) Lines 6–8 ("this Note . . . Greece") This Note provides background on the problem of Greece's detention of unaccompanied minors, explaining why they arrive unaccompanied and why they flee to Greece.
(C) Lines 13–14 ("explaining . . . conditions") These lines explain the role EU's Dublin II regulations play in Greek detention conditions.
(D) Lines 18–21 ("calls for . . . trust") These lines call for the EU's actual execution of the "best interests of the child" principle through the prohibition of child detention and a mandate for alternatives that are sensitive to children's vulnerability and foster a sense of trust.

6. The main rhetorical effect of the series of three phrases in lines 6–15 ("provides background . . . explains how Greece . . . violating . . . proposes a two-part solution") is to

(A) delineate the purpose behind the writing of the Note, based on Galante's viewpoint.
(B) impugn, most notably, Greece and its involvement with the children's care.
(C) express that Galante thinks the proposed amendment (line 1) is likely to fail in three precise ways.
(D) propose a multistep course of action for ameliorating the treatment of these migrant children.

7. As used in line 18, "actual" most nearly means

(A) unabashed.
(B) legitimate.
(C) real.
(D) preordained.

Answers and Explanations 答案与解析

1. B **3.** D **5.** D **7.** C
2. C **4.** D **6.** A

Passage 1: The Link Between Poverty and Obesity

1. **(B)** Understanding relationships is central to this question, which requires students to absorb and synthesize information and ideas. *Correlation*, which means a direct relationship or association, is a key word in the question. Based on the empirical evidence (percentages, date ranges, age spans) provided in paragraph one ("According to the CDC . . . during that same period."), the most substantiated (supported by evidence) answer choice is (B), *For younger children, obesity rates rise less dramatically than for the older groups*. The remaining choices—(A), (C), and (D)—lack precise line evidence to unequivocally validate them. Choice (A), *More mature populations exhibit a slower rate of rise in obesity levels*, is not confirmed by the text; neither are choices (C), *There is an inverse relationship between age and obesity*, and (D), *Environmental factors contribute most significantly to the rate of obesity within a given age group*. Take choice (D), for example. The article does not stress, in either an implied or directly stated manner, environmental factors as primary cause of obesity.

2. **(C)** This is a classic word-in-context vocabulary question that requires students to select the best meaning of the word as it applies to the context as seamlessly and as precisely as possible. Reread lines 13–16, *The obesity is thought to be linked to <u>thrifty</u> metabolism that allows them to metabolize food more efficiently in times when little was available but causes problems when food is in abundance*. Choices (A) *careful*, (B) *malicious*, and (D) *deceptive* would make poor diction (word choice) options, as their meanings are not well-suited to the sentence as a whole. The most fitting answer is (C) *frugal*, which pertains to using time, money, resources (or, in this case, energy and calories) wisely and even sparingly.

3. **(D)** This tricky ALL/EXCEPT question features two potentially hard (challenging at least) vocabulary words in the question itself: *impediments* (obstacles, blocks, factors that impede or obstruct progress) and *countering* (counteracting, working against, mitigating in some contexts). Be sure to notice these key words and consider them carefully. Choice (A) is cited as an *impediment* in the vicinity of lines 34–37. Choices (B), *a decline in fitness activity*, and (C), *sedentary pastimes*, are also evidenced by the text as obstacles to countering obesity in lines 23–26. The best answer is choice (D), *making choices for oneself*, as the second half of paragraph 3 expresses that individuals who choose beverages and foods wisely can prevent or ward off obesity.

Passage 2: Greece's Not-so-warm Welcome to Unaccompanied Minors

4. **(D)** This question requires students to glean the overarching rhetorical stance of the author (which is understood as the author's standpoint, attitude, or position on the topic). The best answer is (D), *an advocate seeking improved condition*. An advocate is a proponent or supporter of a cause. Based on the content of lines 18–21: *it* [this Note] *calls for the EU's actual execution of the 'best interests of the*

child' principle . . . a sense of trust." choice (D) is the best answer. Choice (A), *an uninformed observer relying on third-person accounts*, is not the best answer for two main reasons. First, the author comes across as being *informed* in several areas of the text. For example, she notes in line 1 "current law governing . . . ." and in lines 8–9 she asserts that she will later discuss Greece's "international law obligations under two multilateral treaties . . . ." Second, third-person accounts, or stories/narratives, are not referenced. Third-person accounts would involve the use of the personal pronouns *he, she, they,* or *them*, or the names of specific peoples and/or parties. Choice (B), *an authority delineating an historical perspective*, is not the best answer because, although one can reasonably consider our author an authority, as she is a published Juris Doctor proposing an amendment to law, this excerpt lacks a sense of a broad historical or chronological perspective on this issue and its long-term development. Choice (C), *a politician striving for neutrality*, is not the best answer because the text neither substantiates Galante as a politician nor describes Galante's stance as neutral (unbiased, lacking a definitive opinion). On the contrary, she comes across as having a resolute opinion about the issues she addresses.

5. **(D)** This question represents a two-part, evidence-based question set that was recently added to the SAT test. The best evidence to the previous question is provided by choice (D) because lines 18–21 ("calls for . . . trust") illustrate Galante's position as a passionate advocate for these migrant children. Choice (A) is not the best answer because lines 2–4 ("It . . . noncompliance") serve to describe the "amendment" mentioned in line 1. Thus, these lines do not serve as the best evidence for the answer to the previous question. Choice (B) is not the best answer because lines 6–8 ("this Note . . . Greece") inform the reader about a topic that will be addressed later in the Note so these lines do not serve as the best evidence for the answer to the previous question. Likewise, choice (C) is not the best answer because lines 13–14 ("explaining . . . conditions") elaborate on just one portion of the Note, Part II. These lines, thus, do not serve as the best evidence for the answer to the previous question.

6. **(A)** This question asks students to determine the overall rhetorical effect of three phrases, as they are used in the particular context of this social studies reading. Rhetorical effect pertains to the skillful use of language to create a particular effect on the reader and/or to persuade the reader. Choice (A), *delineate the purpose behind the writing of the Note, based on Galante's viewpoint*, is the best answer because, together, the action verbs *provides, explains,* and *proposes* indicate Galante's plan of action or trifold purpose in writing the Note. Choice (B), *impugn, most notably, Greece and its involvement with the children's care*, is not the best answer because *impugn* (to censure, to accuse) is a particularly harsh word, unsuitable given the overall scholarly tone of the Note. Choice (C), *express that Galante thinks the proposed amendment (line 1) is likely to fail in three precise ways*, is incorrect because the text does not substantiate Galante's notion that the amendment will fail or be futile. Choice (D), *propose a multistep course of action for ameliorating the treatment of these migrant children*, is also not the best answer because these lines represent a statement of purpose more than a process for ameliorating (improving, bettering) the way the children are treated.

7. **(C)** To answer this word-in-context question, revisit the lines in which *actual* is used: "... *[the Note] calls for the EU's* *__actual__* *execution of the 'best interests of the child' principle ....*" *Actual* is used as an adjective to modify *execution*, which in this context means the carrying out of a principle or standard. On the SAT, the College Board indicates that words-in-context questions will tend to ask more so about the more basic (often used, conversational) or Tier Two vocabulary words, such as *actual* or *dynamic*, and less so about little-used, esoteric words such as *retrenchment, sybarite, flotilla*, or *venality*. Choice (C), *real*, is the best answer. *Real* and *actual* are intimately related as adjectives and, in this usage, they are viable synonyms. In other words, the Note seeks *real* compliance—as opposed to adherence that is merely projected, possible, or likely—with the indicated principle (line 16) and as well as a mandate (line 18) in the children's best interest. Choice (A) is not the best answer because *unabashed* means unashamed or bold. Choice (B) is not the best answer because *legitimate* means compliant with the law, which is too forceful in this context. Choice (D) is not the best answer because *preordained* means predetermined or destined, which likewise neither fits nor flows semantically.

SCIENCE 科学

Note: On the SAT, science passages will explore both fundamental ideas as well as recent developments in the natural and physical sciences, including Earth science, astronomy, biology, chemistry, and physics (and their subfields).

Passage 1

CONTENT: Science

FOCUS: Students must read and understand a passage and any accompanying graphic on a science-related topic.

Questions 1–3 are based on the following passage.

Author Lori Martin is the Pediatric Coordinator at Winthrop University Hospital; Martin writes both online and print articles for ABLE *Newspaper.*

History of Hearing Devices

Communication is a key factor in our lives. The inability to communicate through speech can be extremely difficult to live with. Unfortunately there are those who cannot hear due to structural and physiological abnormalities. Cochlear implants can help these people to live normal and prosperous lives. This device was invented in 1970, by Professor Graeme Clark in Melbourne, Australia. As of the year 2007, twenty thousand deaf people have been implanted. The majority of those implanted are from "First World" nations such as the United States, Australia, Japan, and Western Europe (Christiansen, 2002). Before this was invented, parents used other ways of communicating with their children. Sign language or manual communication was the most prominent way of communication between parent and child starting from birth. The earlier the parents began signing, the faster the child was able to understand. This clever use of our hands is still utilized today with both implanted and deaf persons. As early as the 1800s devices have been invented to help deaf and hearing impaired persons. The first invention was of the Clarvox Lorgnette trumpet in France. This ear trumpet hung down from the ear and was strongly resonate to speech frequencies. The poorer the hearing loss the larger the trumpet would be made. Electronic hearing aids were the next in line around 1899. Alexander Graham Bell invented this device with the use of a carbon transmitter. This was strictly for telephone usage and for funneling sound to the ear. In 1977, hybrid hearing aids were invented. Hybrid technology offered digital features to raise or lower the amplifier of the hearing aid. It was a cordless, battery operated hearing aid with a separate hand held instrument that controlled sound. Several other types of hearing aids were invented and with each device capabilities increased and the size decreased. Since 2000, new hearing aids have been successful but not for those with truly profound hearing loss. This group should be evaluated for a cochlear implant.

1. The overall rhetorical purpose of this passage is to

(A) inform readers about the developments of hearing aids and related technology.
(B) dissuade readers from using handicap measures such as signing.
(C) discount the possibilities of full hearing loss remediation in the future.
(D) recount the rise and eventual decline of hearing aid popularity.

2. Given that more than one paragraph break would enhance the clarity and effectiveness of this passage, where would one new paragraph break make sense?

(A) After the word *implanted* in line 7
(B) After the word *children* in line 11
(C) Before the word *electronic* in line 20
(D) Before the word *hybrid* in line 23

3. According to the passage, one can infer that all of the following would be considered desirable features of a more advanced hearing aid EXCEPT

(A) the ability to allay severe hearing loss.
(B) small size.
(C) remote controlled.
(D) digital features.

Passage 2

CONTENT: Science

Questions 4–7 are based on the following passage.

This paragraph is taken from Personal Experience of a Physician, *written by John Ellis.*

Homoeopathy is strictly a scientific system of medicine. It is based upon a law of nature—"Similia similibus curantur," or the law that remedies will cure symptoms and diseases similar to those which they will cause when taken by healthy persons. It is wonderful with what care, skill, and perseverance the new *Materia Medica* has been developed, mostly by intelligent physicians, commencing with Hahnemann, taking the different remedies in varying doses, and carefully and patiently watching the symptoms that follow, and writing them down day after day; and then, when similar symptoms occur in case of disease, giving the remedies and carefully watching and writing down the results. Allopathic physicians, as a rule, have not the slightest conception of the vast amount of patient and persevering labor in this direction which has been done by physicians as well educated as they are, and most of whom have graduated in the same schools, who have devoted their lives to this work. Are not these facts worthy of the consideration of every physician in the world who desires the highest good of his fellow men?

4. Based on the information presented in this passage, you can infer that *Materia Medica* (line 5) most likely refers to

(A) a maternal approach to medicine.
(B) a medical tome that outlines therapeutic procedures for open-minded physicians.
(C) an international panel of well-reputed researchers in the field of homeopathy.
(D) the system and science of the novel homeopathic medicine.

5. In lines 6–10 and on the basis of the entire passage, "taking the different remedies . . . and writing down the results" conveys the idea that

(A) homeopathy is a painstaking and prudent process.
(B) Hahnemann was not simply diligent; he was obsessive-compulsive.
(C) the practice of allopathic physicians is much more laid back and inaccurate than that of homeopathic physicians.
(D) the skills required of an investigative journalist are similar to those required of a physician.

6. John Ellis implies that mankind can receive "the highest good" (lines 15–16) under which of the following conditions?

(A) Doctors begin "carefully watching and writing down the results" (line 10).
(B) Physicians, worldwide, make being "well educated" (line 13) their overarching goal.
(C) Doctors exercise "patient and persevering labor in this direction" (lines 11–12).
(D) Doctors inexorably dedicate themselves to "allopathic" (line 10) modes of medicine.

7. Author Ellis does all of the following in this scientific passage EXCEPT

(A) define a scientific term.
(B) name a pioneer in the field of homeopathy.
(C) include a specimen of Latin terminology.
(D) harshly condemn the practices of allopathic physicians.

Passage 3

CONTENT: Science

Questions 8–14 are based on the following passage.

THINK
Before reading further, do you have the roles of wasp and caterpillar straight?

A common wasp, *Copidosoma floridanum*, is a parasite. The female wasp lays one or two eggs inside the egg of the cabbage looper moth. As the host egg develops into a 2- to 3-inch-long caterpillar, each wasp egg develops into wasp embryos. A single wasp egg can produce more than 3000 genetically identical siblings, each about one-fifth of an inch long. Most of the larvae are maggotlike creatures that drink the caterpillar's blood. However, up to one-fourth of them grow into a different form, called soldiers. These soldiers develop slender, snakelike bodies and rasping jaws. Instead of drinking the blood of their hosts, they attack other wasp larvae and kill them.

The bloodsuckers that are not killed by the soldiers eventually begin to devour the organs of their host, become pupae, develop into adults, and fly away. The soldiers themselves cannot escape and die with the eviscerated husk of the caterpillar.

Two biologists discuss the purpose of the soldiers in the host.

Biologist 1

Much evidence suggests that soldiers exist to destroy the competition. Recall that thousands of wasps are all struggling for food inside a single host. A cabbage looper often plays host to larvae from several wasp mothers. It may even carry larvae from other species of wasps. Soldiers kill off unrelated wasps, thus allowing their siblings to have more food.

The soldiers themselves cannot reproduce. Yet by killing off competitors, they increase the odds that their genetically identical (nonsoldier) siblings will survive and have offspring.

It has been found that soldiers can tell the difference between their siblings and unrelated wasps. In one experiment, unrelated *Copidosoma* wasp eggs were injected into a cabbage looper that was already host to developed larvae. The intruders were almost always eliminated by the resident soldiers.

Biologist 2

The main purpose of the soldiers is to ensure that their sisters succeed. To this end, they kill off many of their brothers. When *Copidosoma* mothers lay two eggs in a host, one egg produces thousands of males and the other, thousands of females. The female soldiers will kill many of their brothers. This fratricide appears to be driven by evolution. Although the female soldiers are genetically identical to their sisters, they share only some of their genes with the males, which come from a separate egg. Thus, these soldiers get a bigger evolutionary benefit from the success of their sisters than from that of their brothers. A few males are more than enough to fertilize thousands of female wasps. Any extra males in the host are just unwanted competition for food.

It has been shown experimentally that female eggs produce more soldiers than male eggs do, which leads to the culling of more male wasps.

THINK
What, exactly, do the two biologists disagree about?

8. Based on the information in the passage, which of the following is an *incorrect* statement about the development of *Copidosoma* wasps?

(A) As the moth egg develops into a caterpillar, the wasp egg develops into thousands of wasp larvae, most of which drink the caterpillar's blood.
(B) Up to one-fourth of the wasp larvae become soldiers, whose job is to attack rival larvae.
(C) The bloodsucking wasp larvae that are not killed by the soldiers are in danger of being killed by rival bloodsucking larvae from other species.
(D) Wasps eventually fly away from the caterpillar, leaving the soldiers trapped inside to die.

9. According to the passage, what do wasp soldiers tend to do?

(A) Attack other soldiers
(B) Eat the organs of the host caterpillar
(C) Suck the blood of the host caterpillar
(D) Attack bloodsucking larvae

10. According to Biologist 2,

(A) female wasp soldiers are responsible for killing male wasp soldiers.
(B) female wasp soldiers are responsible for killing female wasp soldiers.
(C) female wasp soldiers are responsible for killing female bloodsuckers.
(D) female wasp soldiers are responsible for killing male bloodsuckers.

11. Biologists 1 and 2 would agree that

(A) the main purpose of the wasp soldiers is to eliminate wasps from other families.
(B) the main purpose of the wasp soldiers is to provide an evolutionary benefit for their species.
(C) the *Copidosoma* wasp and cabbage looper moth are mutually beneficial in each other's development.
(D) the male and female wasp soldiers compete with each other for food.

12. According to Biologist 1, Biologist 2 is wrong because he has overlooked which fact?

(A) Female soldiers are unable to reproduce.
(B) It has been shown that male soldiers do not attack other wasps.
(C) It has been experimentally established that soldiers kill off wasps from other species.
(D) It has been experimentally established that when a wasp lays two eggs in a host, more female eggs develop into soldiers than male eggs.

13. Suppose a subsequent experiment shows that wasp soldiers come in two different forms. Soldiers that develop early tend to attack their own families. Late-developing soldiers are more likely to attack other species of wasps. Whose theory would this experiment tend to confirm?

(A) Biologist 1 only
(B) Biologist 2 only
(C) Biologist 1 and Biologist 2
(D) Neither Biologist 1 nor Biologist 2

14. Which of the following studies would be likely to resolve the difference of opinion of the two biologists?

(A) Study the development of several generations of a different wasp species that also uses soldiers.
(B) Study mixed colonies of *Copidosoma* wasps and other wasp species. Document the development of *Copidosoma* wasps for several generations.
(C) Create a colony of only *Copidosoma* wasps and document their development for several generations.
(D) Study the development of several generations of at least two other species that depend on parasites for their development.

Answers and Explanations 答案与解析

1 A	5. A	9. D	13. C
2. C	6. C	10. D	14. B
3. A	7. D	11. B	
4. D	8. C	12. C	

Passage 1: History of Hearing Devices

1. **(A)** This holistic type question requires the student to determine and analyze the author's rhetorical purpose, her overarching purpose in writing this passage. Choice (A), *inform readers about the developments of hearing aids and related technology*, is the best answer because the passage is, overall, informative in its tone. Also hearing aids and their corresponding technology are dealt with throughout, further emphasizing Martin's purpose. Choice (B), *dissuade readers from using handicap measures such as signing*, is incorrect because Martin positively refers to signing in line 13 and calls it a "clever use of our hands" (line 14). Choice (C), *discount the possibilities of full hearing loss remediation in the future*, is not the best answer because the author does not come across as pessimistic, or negative thinking. Choice (D), *recount the rise and eventual decline of hearing aid popularity*, is incorrect because there is no passage evidence one can point to that attests to the decline of hearing aid popularity.

2. **(C)** This question requires students to analyze the text structure and organization as a whole. When working on this organization question, pay close attention to the words *after* and *before*. To consider the proposed paragraph placements accurately, use caret marks to indicate where the breaks would occur. Choice (C), *Before the word* electronic *in line 20*, is the best answer because at this point in the passage the author addresses the advent of the electronic hearing device. A new paragraph here would enhance the passage's organizational effectiveness and clarity, following a golden rule: new topic, new paragraph. Choice (A), *After the word* implanted *in line 7*, is not correct because a new paragraph here would create an abrupt break in the explanation of the development of the cochlear implant. Choice (B), *After the word* children *in line 11*, is not the best answer because this sentence is about alternative ways of communicating with hearing-challenged students; the next sentence elaborates on this by discussing sign language and manual communication (gesturing can fall under this category). Therefore, these sentences should not be split up. Finally, choice (D), *Before the word* hybrid *in line 23*, is incorrect because a new paragraph here would, likewise, awkwardly break up the flow of description, which in this case is about hybrid technology and hearing aids.

3. **(A)** This question requires the student to analyze claims in an all/except question format. These types of question can be challenging, as they tend to be time consuming. Find textual evidence that supports *three* of the features listed as "desirable." The remaining choice is the correct answer, as this is an all/except question. Choice (A), *the ability to allay severe hearing loss*, is the best answer because this feature is neither directly stated nor implied as an advantage, given the prospect

of an advanced hearing aid. Likewise, choice (C), *remote controlled*, is incorrect because this feature is described in and around line 24 and prefaced in a positive light with the phrase, "Hybrid technology offered . . . ." Given the preceding date of 1899, the hybrid hearing aids invented in 1977 would be considered more advanced. Choice (B) (*small size*) is also incorrect, as this advanced feature (small size) is positively referenced in the vicinity of lines 27–28: ". . . with each device capabilities increased and the size decreased." Likewise, Choice (D), *digital features*, is not the correct answer because digital features are mentioned as an enhancement offered by the hybrid hearing aid in line 24.

Passage 2: Personal Experience of a Physician

4. (D) This is an obscure (Latin) term-in-context question. As a disciplined critical reader, reread up, at, and around this term in order to glean its meaning in context. Pertinent part:

> It is wonderful with what care, skill, and perseverance the new *Materia Medica* has been developed, mostly by intelligent physicians, commencing with Hahnemann, taking the different remedies in varying doses, and carefully and patiently watching the symptoms that follow, and writing them down day after day; and then, when similar symptoms occur in case of disease, giving the remedies and carefully watching and writing down . . . .

Choice (A) is incorrect since *maternal* cannot be substantiated; nowhere is there mention of mothers, grandmothers, or the female touch. (B) is out since a "tome" (a big book or volume) is not "developed" (line 5) by a process, but is written by an author. Choice (C), *Materia Medica*, sounds lofty enough and appears very important with its two capital letters, but there's no evidence that this is a name of a group of international researchers. This answer choice would require a great deal of creativity on your part. (D) is the answer.

5. (A) This is a question that requires understanding the subtleties of part of the passage as it relates to the passage as a whole. Skim over the referenced lines, focusing on the purpose of this part of the passage in terms of the whole. Avoid (B) since it is an unsubstantiated, borderline-extreme answer. Perhaps allopathic practice is "more laid back," but no evidence is presented to support its being "inaccurate"; (C) is out. Active pencil! (D) is out since it's a jump (based on your conjecture)! The answer is (A) since the process, as described, is certainly meticulous ("painstaking") and careful ("prudent").

6. (C) This is a tough inference question that alludes to several terms and phrases used throughout the passage. Using line references where given, refer to the passage to see what answer choice would confirm mankind's receiving "the highest good." (A) "Carefully watching and writing down the results" is not all that's needed for doctors to bestow the "highest good" upon man. (B) Being "well educated" is not enough to enable physicians, whether allopathic or homeopathic, to transfer the "highest good" to men, especially since "well educated" (in context) refers to two types of medical education. (A) and (B) are out. You're using PET!

Choice (D) is out since "allopathic" medicine is presented as antithetical to homeopathic medicine. Active pencil! The answer is (C) since "in this direction" (line 12) refers to the direction of homeopathy, which is the system of medicine the author advocates.

7. **(D)** This is a time-consuming "all/except" question. Use your memory of what you've read and skim the passage, when you need to, to confirm three of the four answer choices. (A) Ellis defines a scientific term in lines 1 and 2. (B) Ellis names a homeopathy pioneer in line 6. (C) "Similia similibus curantur" (line 2) is a sampling of Latin terminology. The answer is (D).

Passage 3: Wasps

8. **(C)** All of the statements are confirmed in the passage except for choice (C). The bloodsucking larvae do not kill other larvae. Only the soldiers kill.

Get the answer immediately by glancing at the correct column when the question begins with "According to . . ."

9. **(D)** The soldiers attack only bloodsucking wasp larvae. Each of the other choices is wrong. Choice (A) is incorrect because soldiers are not attacked. They do not compete for food as there is a large supply of bloodsuckers for them to eat. In choice (B), only the bloodsuckers eventually eat the organs of the host. Choice (C) is incorrect because the soldiers eat other (bloodsucking) larvae. They do not compete with the bloodsuckers for food (host blood).

10. **(D)** According to Biologist 2, the female soldiers kill their bloodsucking brothers. Every other choice is incorrect. Choices (A) and (B) are incorrect because soldiers do not kill other soldiers. Choice (C) is incorrect because the female wasp soldiers help their sisters by killing off their bloodsucking brothers.

11. **(B)** In each of the theories, the actions of the soldiers tend to provide an advantage for the wasps within their own gene pool. According to Biologist 1, this advantage is provided when the soldiers attack larvae from other species and other mothers. According to Biologist 2, the advantage comes when sister soldiers, who are genetically identical to sister bloodsuckers, kill off their brothers with whom they are genetically different. The other choices may be downright incorrect, or they may be correct but not in the viewpoint of one of the biologists. Biologist 2 would disagree with choice (A) saying that the purpose of the soldiers is to eliminate male bloodsuckers from their own family. Choice (C) is wrong: The caterpillar derives no benefit from the wasps, which eventually cause its (the caterpillar's) death. Choice (D) is wrong because the soldiers do not compete for food—more than enough larvae are available for them to eat.

12. **(C)** Biologist 2 does not mention the fact that soldiers have been observed to kill larvae from other species. The other choices may be factually correct but not necessarily flaws in Biologist 2's theory. For choice (A), the fact that soldiers do not reproduce is not a factor in either theory. Choice (B) is not mentioned in the passage. Even if it were true, it would not be consistent with either theory. And the fact that the female egg produces more soldiers than the male egg, choice (D) would tend to *bolster* Biologist 2's theory.

13. (C) An experiment that showed that soldiers attack both other species and their own siblings would support both biologists' points of view. The purpose of the soldiers is the crux of their disagreement.

14. (B) In order to resolve questions about *Copidosoma* wasps, studies must be done *of these wasps.* Also, to confirm the viewpoint of Biologist 1, other species need to be included in this experiment. Thus, choice (B) is correct and choice (C) is wrong. Choice (A) is incorrect because although studying different wasp species may lend support for either theory, it would not be satisfactory in resolving the differences between Biologist 1 and Biologist 2 for *Copidosoma* wasps. The study in choice (D) would not be useful. The *Copidosoma* wasps do not depend on parasites for development. They themselves are the parasites! Note that this is an answer choice that you should eliminate immediately; no species depends on parasites to aid in their development. Parasites cause only harm.

第二部分 PART 2

THE EVIDENCE-BASED WRITING AND LANGUAGE TEST 基于证据的写作和语言测试

In the Writing and Language sections, students must recognize and correct various types of mechanical, grammar, diction, syntax, and usage errors as they appear within passages. Students will no longer be asked to analyze and identify errors in separate, isolated sentences. Students must choose the best of four alternatives to an underscored part of the passage, or choose "NO CHANGE" and the best of three remaining alternatives. Students will make decisions that make the language most effective in terms of, but not limited to, proper agreement, logical comparisons, pronoun usage, verb tense, and punctuation. Graphics are either taken from quality sources or created for the test itself. In their original form, passages are well written and grammatically sound.

Passage topics and themes may include any of the following: careers, history/social studies, the humanities, and science, with the core writing modes of argument, informative/explanatory text, and nonfiction narrative represented. Most typically, careers passages address trends, debates, and issues in major fields of work, such as health care or information technology. History/social studies passages discuss historical topics or topics in the social sciences, including anthropology, communication studies, economics, education, human geography, law, linguistics, political science, psychology, and sociology (and their subfields). Humanities passages explore subjects in the arts and literature. Science passages investigate concepts, discoveries, and research in the natural sciences, including Earth science, biology, chemistry, and physics (and their subfields).

This test requires students to answer questions based on extended contexts (passages and paired passages) rather than in isolation or in abridged (e.g., single-sentence, short-paragraph) contexts. Although some questions can be answered by referring to a single clause, phrase, or sentence, others require students to have an understanding of several sentences, one or more paragraphs, or the passage in its entirety. Questions may focus on a single word, a phrase, or a full sentence such as in the following example: Which choice most effectively establishes the main topic of the paragraph?

第三章 Chapter 3

ENGLISH GRAMMAR AND USAGE 英语语法与应用

Let's face it—for many students, grammar is an arcane and boring subject. How interesting are mismatched correlative conjunctions and misplaced participles? Some English teachers dislike teaching grammar because of students' facial expressions during lessons: "Now let's discuss comma usage as it relates to restrictive and nonrestrictive subordinating clauses." Yikes!

The good news: None of these questions requires you to draw intricate sentence diagrams or to label parts of speech, so wipe the sweat off your brow. More good news: You don't have to rewrite grammatically flawed sentences and transform them into grammatically flawless ones. In short, the English grammar and usage questions, as unappealing as they sound, are not *that* intense.

The not-so-good news: The objective grammar questions hold you to a high standard of proper written English. Don't fight it; go with it, even though the correct form may sometimes sound strange. To ace this portion of the test, psyche yourself to take pride in expressing the English language in a grammatically sound and pristine way. To approach a perfect score on the writing sections, you need to develop a high regard and sensitivity for the conventions of standard, written, grammatically correct English. Language that is considered conversational or colloquial does not fit the requirements of written English.

Unfortunately, our fast-paced world, with its text messaging and instant messaging, has desensitized many of us to what standard written English actually sounds like. We live in a world of quick chats and brief notes. We live in a world of verbal and written shorthand: *k, lol, g2g, brb, ttyl, sup, nvm, idk, . . .*

Now imagine your loving parent hovering over your laptop, asking, "*To whom* are you speaking?" or "Is that your user profile *in which* you listed your favorite music groups?" Now imagine your parent sitting down for a chat and saying, "I am disappointed in *your impatience* with your brother." You might ask yourself, "From *whence* did this person come?" Or maybe not. (Every italicized phrase or word is absolutely correct.) The point is, standard written English tends to be so butchered in everyday usage that it's hard to know whether certain grammatically correct phrases are actually right or wrong.

To make matters worse, for the most part, you can't rely on newscasters, politicians, and highly regarded talk-show hosts to model exemplary English usage. Multitudinous grammatical errors come across the television and radio airwaves every hour.

Remember: the SAT is about standard *written* English, not *spoken* English.

NEW WRITING STRATEGY! GRAMMAR COUNTING: 1, 2, 3
新的写作策略！语法计数：1，2，3

Grammar counts on the SAT. You have to answer 44 multiple-choice objective grammar questions, contributing to your overall score ranging on a scale from 200 to 800. Because your writing sample is scored holistically, the conventions of standard written English grammar and usage also count when you write your essay.

Count your way to a competitive multiple-choice writing score!

Grammar counting helps you recognize inconsistencies and agreement errors within sentences so that you can make the necessary corrections. As you read the sentences, conduct an internal dialogue of "counts."

As easy as *1, 2, 3* . . . Count subjects. Count nouns. Count people. Count pronouns. Use your Active Pencil to indicate the count. Jot down *1* for singular; jot down *2* for plural.

Illustrations of Grammar counting, using snippets from sentences that could appear in passages:

2 *1* *2*

. . . Gary and Lillian . . . conducted an extensive poll (about the spending habits) . . .

2 *2*

The poem's allusions and creative expressions . . . (Compound subject . . . that's *2*! If the poem itself is referenced, the singular pronoun "it" would agree, and singular verb forms would be required.)

1 *2*

. . . the consumption (of natural herbal remedies) . . . (Singular subject . . . that's *1*! If the remedies are referred back to, the count for resources is 2, indicating plural.)

2

. . . Governor Gary and Congresswoman Lillian . . . (That's *2* for two people! To agree with 2, a plural verb must follow. Likewise, Gary and Lillian would be referred back to using plural personal pronouns such as "they" and "them." The singular "it" would not agree.)

2 *2*

The chronological records (of artifact findings) . . . (That's a plural subject . . . indicated by *2* since the records are plural, plural pronouns such as "they" or "them" would be used to refer back to the records.)

To illustrate grammar counting, try to spot the error in these sentences:

2 *2*

If it is confirmed empirically, the hypotheses of Regina Vander and Randi Stiles
(A: it is; B: empirically)

2 *1* *2*

will be among the greatest progressive strides in science of the past several decades.
(C: will be; D: greatest)

Noticing that "hypotheses" is plural will help alert you to the inconsistency between "hypotheses" and the singular pronoun "it." Therefore, the correct answer is choice A.

1 *2*

The galloping speed (of both science and computer technology) have forced many

A

2 *2* *1* *2*

graduates to consider questions that formerly were the singular realm of sociologists.

B C D

The prepositional phrase modifies the subject, the main noun.

Noticing that the subject "speed" is singular will help alert you to the subject–verb agreement error between "speed" and "have." Therefore, the correct answer is choice A.

2 *1* *2*

The vivid orange and black wings (of the monarch butterfly) cautions predators that

A B

the creature is poisonous if consumed.

C D

Noticing that the subject "wings" is plural (indicated by *2*), you will more likely detect the subject–verb agreement error between "wings" and "cautions." Therefore, because of this agreement error, the correct answer is choice A.

TAKE CARE TO READ THE PARAGRAPHS VERY CAREFULLY 仔细阅读段落

This tip is important. Read through each paragraph to absorb its meaning. The new sentence version that you select must maintain this original meaning. A revision that sounds good or is attractively concise is not the correct answer if that version distorts the original meaning.

Also, reading and internalizing the meaning of the original can help you to detect overall sentence errors such as faulty comparison and lack of parallelism, which will be discussed later.

IDENTIFY, FIRST, ALL VERBS AND PRONOUNS THAT ARE UNDERLINED 首先判定画线动词和代词的意义

Pronoun and verb errors are among the most pervasive on the SAT. Be a savvy grammarian who works smart: examine verbs and pronouns first. If these check out, then start looking for other types of errors: faulty diction, lack of parallel form, and comma splices.

Once you've identified a verb, make sure that it is in the correct tense and form *and* is in agreement with the subject. Ask yourself:

Time Saver
First scrutinize verbs and pronouns in the sentence.

Keep your eye on them since a bevy of errors surround these parts of speech.

Working this way is time efficient.

Is the verb in the right tense?	**If not, there is an error in *verb tense*.**
Is the verb in the right form?	**If not, there is an error in *verb form*.**
Does the verb agree with the subject?	**If not, there is an error in *subject-verb agreement*.**

Also, be prudent about pronouns because multifarious (numerous and varied) errors involve these pesky little words: ambiguous pronouns, pronoun shifts, pronouns without antecedents, wrong pronoun case, misused pronouns. All of these errors will be addressed in detail later.

PAY CLOSE ATTENTION TO THE NONUNDERLINED PORTIONS OF THE PASSAGES 对段落中没画线的部分多加留意

This is one of the most effective tips for this section. Intuitively, test takers focus in very closely on the underlined portions of paragraphs. However, you need to focus as closely, *if not more closely,* on the nonunderlined portions. The reason: *Nonunderlined portions dictate the form of the underlined portions!*

Here are examples to illustrate this dynamic:

Nonunderlined Portions	Indications for Underlined Portions
In the early seventeenth century	**Need past tense**
Mia and her aunt Hillary	**Plural subject**
Either of the two pies	**Singular subject**
Either	**Need *or***
Not only	**Need *but* or *but also***
Next September	**Need future tense**
The young tennis enthusiasts	**Need plural pronouns: *they, them, their***
Neither of the candidates	**Need singular pronouns: *he, she, him, her, his, hers***
Swimming, jogging	**Need a parallel gerund; *fishing, hiking***

Naturally, you'll focus in on the underlined parts of sentences. It's the nonunderlined portions, however, that tell you how the underlined portions need to be, whether they should be changed somehow or remain as they are. Start noticing the form of the nonunderlined portions, and you will be better equipped to see whether or how the underlined portions should be rewritten.

HIERARCHY OF GRAMMAR GLITCHES 语法错误的等级

Do some aspects of English grammar sound like Greek (Swahili?) to you? Don't worry. This section covers every grammar glitch, one by one, with plenty of examples for each. After you study the examples, try the Sharpening Skills exercises to see how well you've grasped that particular error type. Think of the Hierarchy of Grammar Glitches as an overview of the test designers' pet peeves in regard to grammatical errors. As you can see, spelling and capitalization errors are not addressed.

One effective way to improve your writing and vocabulary is to read good books, good newspapers, and good periodicals. Specifically, read to improve your grammar skills. You'll be amazed at how much you can learn, in terms of writing mechanics and grammar, when you read with a mindset for grammar. For example, you can glean insight into how to use a semicolon and how to express logical comparisons. You can also pick up on parallel form and appropriate verb tenses. Try this focus next time you read; you can brush up on grammar and peruse a good book or news article at the same time. Multitasking—a beautiful thing!

Higher Frequency Errors

↑

Verb Errors
Pronoun Errors
Faulty Idioms
Faulty Parallelism
Diction Errors
Misplaced Modifiers
Adjective Versus Adverb Errors
Plural–Singular Inconsistency
Redundancy and Wordiness
Faulty Comparisons
Run-ons and Fragments
Less vs. Fewer

↓

Lower Frequency Errors

Let's review these grammatical topics, one by one:

Verb Errors 动词使用错误

Verb errors: wrong verb tense, wrong verb form, verb does not agree with subject

Chances are, you're an Honors English student or a student who typically achieves high Bs and As. In this case, you can readily spot the subject and verb of a sentence. You understand that the subject and verb work together. You also understand that singular subjects require singular verbs, which (unlike singular nouns) end in *s*. Yada-yada-yada . . . You know the basics.

Once you've spotted the verb, make sure that it is in the correct tense and form *and* in agreement with the subject.

Be vigilant about verbs because a multitude of errors surround these action and being words. Check out any underlined verbs first. Once you've found a verb, ask yourself these questions:

- **Is the verb in the right tense?**

  If not, there is an error in *verb tense*.
  Example: When we rode the chair lift to the top of the mountain, Julia *cries* out, "Here at last!" (*cried*)

- **Is the verb in the right form?**

  If not, there is an error in *verb form*.
  Example: Every morning, Joanna takes a walk to clear her mind, to tone her body, and *thinking* about the day ahead. (*to think*)

Time Saver
First check out verbs and pronouns in the sentence.

Keep your eye on them since a bevy of errors surround these parts of speech.

Working this way is time efficient.

- **Does the verb agree with the subject?**

  If not, there is an error in *subject–verb agreement*.
  Example: Around the track *runs* Sheila and Gus. (*run*)

To detect errors in subject–verb agreement, it is a good idea to "downsize" or simplify the sentence by crossing off prepositional phrases, appositives, and modifiers. The following examples illustrate downsizing. Read each sentence with only the words that are *not* crossed out. See how basic the downsized version sounds? A simpler sentence form allows you to detect subject–verb agreement errors more quickly.

Illustrations of Downsizing Sentences to Reveal the Simple Subject and Verb

1. Original version: Between the corner fruit market and Parkside Deli is the old-time barber shop that my dad took me to when I was a young boy.
   Downsized version: ~~Between the corner fruit market and Parkside Deli~~ is the ~~old-time~~ barber shop ~~that my dad took me to when I was a young boy~~.
   The subject and verb are in inverted order, yet they agree with each other. Both the subject and the verb are in singular form. (The barber shop *is.*)
2. Original version: The scenic pond that is surrounded by towering cypress trees were there ever since I can remember.
   Downsized version: The ~~scenic~~ pond ~~that is surrounded by towering cypress trees~~ were there ~~ever since I can remember.~~
   The subject and verb are in regular order, yet this sentence contains a subject–verb agreement error. The sentence should read *The pond <u>was</u> there.*
3. Original version: With its chilling sound track and mind-blowing special effects, "Raising Ducklings" are one of the zany movies that I will never forget.
   Downsized version: ~~With its chilling sound track and mind-blowing special effects,~~ "Raising Ducklings" are one ~~of the zany movies that I will never forget.~~
   This sentence contains a subject-verb agreement error. Despite the plural words *special effects and movies,* the sentence should read *"Raising Ducklings" <u>is</u> one . . .*
4. Original version: Before leaving Puerto Rico, Evan, an enthusiastic and brawny sixteen-year-old, wanted to rent a moped and take it for a ride along the scenic side streets.
   Downsized version: ~~Before leaving Puerto Rico,~~ Evan, ~~an enthusiastic and brawny sixteen-year-old,~~ wanted to rent a moped and take it ~~for a ride along the scenic side streets.~~
5. Original version: Alec, hardworking and charity-minded, readily accepted invitations to fundraising events and philanthropy dinners.
   Downsized version: Alec~~, hardworking and charity-minded, readily~~ accepted ~~invitations to fundraising events and philanthropy dinners.~~

Sharpening Skills—Verb Forms 加强技巧——动词形式

Using your ability to isolate the verb and the subject of a sentence, circle the verb error in each of the following sentences. Then write the correct form of the verb on the line provided. Detailed answer explanations follow.

1. Around the circus ring walks Miranda and her majestic white horses.

   ____

2. According to the band leader, neither the outdoor café nor the amphitheaters located outside the strip mall provides a good spot for the band to make its community debut. ________

3. The snowman, wearing a boldly striped hat and purple fleece gloves that stick out on his sides, is a whimsical addition to the backyard. ________

4. The purpose of the annual Career Night is illustrating the many professions that high school students may one day choose. ________

5. Before the Jansens left the lakeside cabin, they take a roll of group photos, capturing the natural beauty of this idyllic setting. ________

Verb Forms Answers 动词形式答案

1. Subject–verb agreement error; should be *walk* to agree with the plural subject *Miranda* and *horses.*

2. Subject–verb agreement error; what makes this especially hard is that the two subjects are linked by correlative conjunctions (*neither . . . nor*). In this case, the verb agrees with the latter subject; should be *provide* to agree with *amphitheaters.* What makes this question even more difficult is that the subjects and the verb are interrupted by the phrase *located outside the strip mall.* If a sentence has a compound subject (think of this as a "double subject" or two subjects joined together by a conjunction), the plural form of the verb should follow. For example, "Grilled chicken and a feta cheese omelet *are* Phillip's favorite post-workout meals." The compound subject (plural) is *Grilled chicken and a feta cheese omelet.*

3. Subject–verb agreement error; should be *adds* to agree with the subject, *snowman.* What makes this hard is that the subject and the verb are separated by the gerund phrase *wearing a boldly . . . his sides.*

4. Verb form error; should be the infinitive, *to illustrate*

5. Verb tense error; should be the past tense *took,* which is indicated by the introductory adverbial clause *Before the Jansens left the lakeside cabin.*

Pronoun Errors 代词使用错误

Pronoun errors: ambiguous pronouns; pronoun shifts; pronouns without antecedents; wrong pronoun case; misused pronouns

Be prudent about pronouns because multifarious (numerous and varied) errors involve these tricky words. After coping with verbs, high scorers check out underlined pronouns next. Study the box below to be sure you are familiar with singular and plural personal pronouns.

Singular Pronouns	Plural Pronouns
I, me	we, us
my, mine	our, ours
you, your, yours	you, your, yours
he, she, him, her	they, them
his, her, his, hers	their, theirs
it, its	

When you see a pronoun that is part of an underlined portion, ask yourself:

- **Does the pronoun agree in number and gender with its antecedent (word to which it refers)?**

  If not, there is an error in *pronoun agreement.*
  Example: A good skier is aware of *their* surroundings.
  (The singular noun *skier* takes the singular possessive *his.*)

- **Is the pronoun reference clear?**

  If not, there is an *ambiguous pronoun* error.
  Example: Tom and Phillip went on their annual hiking trip, even though *he* was suffering from a sprained ankle.
  (*He* is ambiguous since this pronoun can refer to either *Tom* or *Phillip.* Change *he* to *Tom* or *Phillip.*)

- **Has the pronoun point of view shifted?**

  If so, there is an error called *pronoun shift.*
  Example: You know you're in trouble when *one feels* butterflies racing in your stomach and chills crawling up your spine.
  (Since this sentence is written basically in the second-person *you,* to be grammatically consistent change *one feels* to *you feel.*)

- **Is the pronoun in the correct case, objective versus subjective?**

  If not, there is a *pronoun case* error.
  Example: Hank and Andrew offered their old scooters to my sister and *I,* but we politely refused.
  (Since the italic pronoun is the object of the prepositional phrase *to my sister and I,* change *I* to the objective case *me.*)

- **Does the pronoun appear in the predicate (verb) of the sentence, in the objective case?**

  If so, there is a *pronoun case* error.
  Example: I knew it was *her* who organized the surprise party.
  (Change *her* to the subjective pronoun case, *she*.)

Subjective-Case Pronouns (function as *subjects*)	**Objective-Case Pronouns** (function as *direct objects, indirect objects*, or *objects of prepositional phrases*)
I	me
we	us
he, she	him, her
you	you
they	them
who	whom

Know the W Pronouns

WHO	➔	**refers to a person**
		There is the gentleman *who* helped us change our flat tire.
WHAT	➔	**refers to an event or inanimate thing**
		***What* is that gigantic, green creature lurking beyond the fence?**
WHEN	➔	**refers to a date or time period**
		August 2007 is *when* he was born.
WHERE	➔	**refers to a place**
		The festival at the beach is *where* we met.
WHY	➔	**refers to a reason or cause**
		Please tell your brother *why* you wish to borrow his baseball mitt.

Faulty Idioms 习惯用语使用错误

People don't worry *over* their futures; they worry *about* their futures. One thing is not different *than* another thing; one thing is different *from* another thing. Connor does not excel *with* lacrosse; he excels *in* lacrosse. After waiting on line, visitors do not walk *in* the museum, they walk *into* the museum. Jenna has a sweet tooth; she doesn't have a preoccupation *on* dark chocolate, she has a preoccupation *with* dark chocolate.

You might think that *being* raised in an English-speaking home would suffice to prepare one to use idioms correctly in speaking and in writing. However, idiom errors are so rampant (television is a predominant culprit) that even the best students can stumble into the idiom trap.

The 1600 Club counters this problem by actively studying correct usage. One of the best ways is to learn common verb-preposition pairs, which are tested frequently in the Writing and Language portions of the SAT. When working on the identifying sentence errors section, pay close attention to prepositions that are underlined. The wrong preposition in a phrase produces an *idiom error*. As you know, prepositions are rather small words that show direction, location, or association: *to, toward, above, behind, onto, near, under, over, on, in, by, about, up, of, for, with*, and many more.

Sharpening Skills—Preposition Pairs 加强技巧——词组

Study the abridged list below of common verb-preposition pairs. Train your ear to *hear* which prepositions commonly follow which verbs.

Know These Verb–Preposition Pairs

accuse of	consist of	hope for
agree to/with/on	contribute to	inconsistent with
apologize for	cover with	insist on/upon
apply to/for	decide on/upon	participate in
approve of	depend on/upon	prevent from
believe in	dream about/of	protect from
care about/for	escape from	recover from
compare to/with	excuse for	regard as
complain about	forget about	release from
confide in	free from	succeed in
consistent with	hide from	wait for/on

FONY ABS Fony Abs

To connect items or ideas within a sentence, speakers and writers use connecting words called "conjunctions." To remember the most commonly used conjunctions, think of some body-conscious type flaunting a fake six-pack! Let FONY ABS be your silly mnemonic (memory-assisting device) for seven common conjunctions:

FONY = *for, or, nor, yet* ABS = *and, but, so*

Some learn these with the acronym, FANBOYS, but the list of conjunctions is the same.

Peanut Butter and Jelly 花生、黄油和果冻

To be a top scorer, you should know *not only* your FONY ABS *but also* your **correlative conjunctions**, hard-working pairs that go together like peanut butter and jelly. (Check out the correlative conjunctions that appear in the preceding sentence.) As pairs, correlatives hook up words, phrases, and clauses within a sentence. *Just as* some things go together, such as peanut butter and jelly, *so* correlative conjunctions work together in pairs. Know your correlative conjunctions. If you spot one in a sentence, look for its mate, which should also be in the sentence.

Grammar Coaching:
The 1600 Club knows correlative conjunction pairs cold.

These pairs are basic, easy to memorize, and pervasive on the multiple-choice grammar questions.

Memorize them.

neither . . . nor . . .
either . . . or . . .
not only . . . but also . . .
as . . . as . . .
just as . . . so . . .
both . . . and . . .
between . . . and . . .

Here are examples of how correlative pairs are used to connect items of information in sentences:

According to Aunt Lexi, **neither** raspberry pie **nor** chocolate-covered pretzels make a suitable dessert.

You can select **either** the blue trench coat **or** the beige tweed jacket.

In my opinion, you look **not only** fit **but also** radiant!

Since no one bothered to make a cozy fire, it is **as** cold in the log cabin **as** it is outdoors.

Just as quietly as he entered the room, **so** he left without a sound.

As you have learned, **both** steady concentration **and** a methodical approach can bring you into the ranks of the 1600 Club.

Memorize Some Idioms 记住一些习惯用语

The hardest (level 4 and level 5) grammar questions are often about idioms, language expressions of standard, written English. In everyday use, idioms are toyed with and denatured a bit, straying from their pure and eloquent form based on standard and proper, written English. Here are some examples: These examples are worthwhile to read, read aloud, read again, and remember:

A person is *regarded as* a hero . . . NOT *regarded to be* a hero.

Jack *prefers* hot dogs to hamburgers . . . NOT hot dogs *over* hamburgers and NOT hot dogs *more than* hamburgers.

Cardiovascular exercise is *necessary for* weight loss . . . NOT *necessary with* weight loss.

The Native American museum is the *only one of its kind* . . . NOT only *one of a kind.*

As intellectual beings, we *draw upon* resources . . . we do NOT *draw from* resources . . .

One person's idea of an enjoyable evening is often *different from* . . . NOT *opposite to* another person's sense of a pleasurable evening. (Note: In this sentence, *different than* cannot be used.)

Some birds are more *particular about* their nesting sites . . . NOT *particular in* their nesting sites.

The baseball pitcher *thought it wise* to wear a heart protector . . . NOT *thought it as wise* to wear a heart protector.

A neighbor may bring up an issue *with regard* to your boisterously barking dog . . . NOT *in regards to* your boisterously barking dog.

An unabridged list of common English idioms would be so extensive as to take up a bevy of pages. Search English idiomatic language on the Internet, and you will find numerous listings of common usage. Lists of English idioms provide good study material if idioms are challenging for you. Also, most grammar and composition textbooks contain lists of idioms; just check the table of contents.

Faulty Parallelism 平行结构使用错误

Cross off the one that doesn't belong:

grapes, filet mignon, cantaloupe

to enjoy music, to eat fine food, resting

tennis, football, sneakers

magazine editor, publishing, advertising copywriter

In standard written English, certain components of a sentence should be expressed in the same way. Keeping these parts similar is called "parallelism," or parallel form. Some English teachers refer to parallel forms as "overlapping diction." Without parallelism, clarity and logic within a sentence are compromised. Here's a tip-off for parallelism: a listing of items in a comma series appears in the sentence. Your job is to make sure that each member of the comma series is expressed in the same way. Although parallelism errors often occur within a comma series, they can occur if only two terms within a sentence are expressed in dissimilar ways. **Example:** Jenna looked forward to sleep-away camp mostly because she couldn't wait *to water-ski* and *hiking* the nature trails. The italicized terms are not parallel. To correct this error, change *hiking* to *to hike*.

Did you find the terms that don't belong in the box above? Answers: filet mignon, resting, sneakers, publishing. Use your ability to spot the odd-man-out in the the grammar questions on the SAT by making sure that items being compared or listed are parallel to one another.

Basic Examples of Parallelism

To get a sense of parallel form, consider these examples:

jogging, boating, and parasailing
(gerund, gerund, and gerund)

investigated, followed, and captured
(past-tense verb, past-tense verb, and past-tense verb)

to eat, to sleep, and to watch television
(infinitive, infinitive, and infinitive)

to find long sticks and to toast marshmallows
(infinitive-direct object and infinitive-direct object)

More Advanced Examples of Parallelism

barked loudly, growled angrily, and ran quickly
(past-tense verb-adverb, past-tense verb-adverb, and past-tense verb-adverb)

eating pizza, munching popcorn, and sipping soda
(gerund-object, gerund-object, and gerund-object)

Sharpening Skills—Parallel Form 加强技巧——排比形式

On the line provided, rewrite the part of the sentence that is not parallel to the other part or parts.

1. To increase your fitness level, you should not only stretch every day but also cardiovascular exercise.

____

2. Far from the ideal dinner guest, Gus would regularly belch, chew with his mouth open, and to pick his teeth at the dinner table.

____

3. Hillary's favorite pastimes include shopping at the mall, the latest movies, and instant-messaging her friends.

____

4. For birthdays and other special occasions, Petronella likes to give her brothers-in-law gloves, jewelry to her sisters, and electronic toys to her young sons.

____

5. For enthusiasts of the outdoors, either hiking or a bicycle—if done on a regular basis—can significantly increase one's cardiovascular endurance.

____

Parallel Form Answers 排比形式答案

1. *do* cardiovascular exercise
2. *pick* (delete *to* since the preceding verbs are not infinitives)
3. *seeing* the latest movies
4. *gloves to her brothers-in-law*
5. *bicycling*

Diction Errors 措辞使用错误

If a toddler throws a temper tantrum in front of the toy store, is he causing a "scenario" or a "scene" at the mall?

If you wish to bypass the quicksand pit, do you "circumnavigate" or "circumvent" it?

If you wish to tell your history teacher that you investigated myriad sources for your research paper, is it more appropriate to tell him that you did "exhaustive" or "exhausting" research?

Diction errors result from inappropriate word choice. When words are underlined in the identifying sentence errors section, be sensitive to their spellings and, therefore, their precise meanings. You need to consider, not whether a word is misspelled, but *how* it is spelled. (Spelling errors have historically been very rare on the SAT.) Spelling counts in the sense that you need to know which homophone appears in a sentence: *stationary* or *stationery*? *principle* or *principal*? *whether* or *weather*? *reign* or *rain*?

The acid test: Does the word sound "off"?

Ask yourself, "Is this the precise word that fits the context of this sentence?" If you think the word is "off," you may have spotted a diction error. Top scorers amass a strong and varied upper-level vocabulary. Top scorers are also sensitive to words that sound and/or look alike but have different meanings and usages. Study the lessons titled "Tricky Twins and Triplets" in Barron's *Hot Words for the SAT*. In these lessons, you will find words often confused, such as *indignant/indigenous/indigent*, *aesthetic/ascetic/atheistic*, and *coalesce/convalesce*. Knowing the precise meanings and spellings of words will help you spot diction errors on the SAT.

Sharpening Skills—Diction Errors 加强技巧——措辞使用错误

For each of the following sentences, circle either "No error" or "Diction error." The 1600 Club challenge: If you spot a diction error, replace the faulty word with a word that makes sense in the context.

1. Now that the clearance sale is over, I could kick myself; I should of bought the pool toys that were 75 percent off!

No error Diction error → Replace ______ with ______.

2. Andrew is taking antibiotics and trying his best to rest. Please do not exacerbate him with your taunting and teasing!

No error Diction error → Replace ______ with ______.

3. Despite our forgoing frivolous expenditures and unnecessary frills, we still cannot amass a sizable savings account.

No error Diction error → Replace ______ with ______.

4. To determine the duration of their stay at Snow Lodge Mountain, the Miltons took a family vote, deciding to prolong their stay from 7 days to 2 weeks instead of protracting it from 7 days to 5.

No error Diction error → Replace ______ with ______.

5. I'm tired of you feigning malaise; that's just your way of getting out of helping with the housework.

No error Diction error → Replace ______ with ______.

6. Hank, the fact is that the more I ascent to your demands, the more presumptuous you become with your requests.

No error Diction error → Replace ______ with ______.

7. Because of the author's concerns regarding her intellectual work being protected, the project editor ensured her repeatedly that her original work was copyright protected.

No error Diction error → Replace ______ with ______.

8. Because of a life-changing car accident, the young lady lost her short-term memory and was subsequently unable to sustain any new information.

No error Diction error → Replace ______ with ______.

9. Marcus is an assiduous student whose papers are always on time and whose test scores are among the highest; in fact, he is a model specimen of a conscious work ethic.

No error Diction error → Replace ______ with ______.

10. We are not exactly close friends, so why are you offended by me not inviting you to join us for dinner?

No error Diction error → Replace ______ with ______.

Diction Answers 措辞使用答案

1. Diction error → Replace *of* with *have.*
2. Diction error → Replace *exacerbate* with *exasperate.*
3. No error
4. Diction error → Replace *protracting* with *curtailing.*
5. Diction error → Replace *you* with *your.*
6. Diction error → Replace *ascent* with *assent.*
7. Diction error → *assured* fits this context better than *ensured.*
8. Diction error → Replace *sustain* with *retain.*
9. Diction error → Replace *conscious* with *conscientious.*
10. Diction error → Replace *me* with *my.*

Misplaced Modifiers 修饰语使用错误

To avoid ambiguity, modifying phrases need to be placed in close proximity to the word that they modify. Errors occur when modifiers are "misplaced," usually meaning that they are set apart from the noun or pronoun to which they refer.

The modifying phrases are italicized in the examples that follow. Notice how the meaning of the sentence changes when the modifying phrase and the word modified are in close proximity.

Who's hanging in the tree? Who's looking at whom?
***Hanging from the highest branch*, the man with binoculars eyed the monkey.**
***Hanging from the highest branch*, the monkey eyed the man with binoculars.**

Who's carefree, the girl or the shoreline?
Lola strolled along the Tappen Beach shoreline, *without a care in the world.*
***Without a care in the world*, Lola strolled along the Tappen Beach shoreline.**

Who's getting steamed?
Fresh vegetables are a vital component of a healthful diet. *To be cooked well*, Sheila steams her string beans and broccoli florets.

Who might get wet?
***Before reconfiguring plumbing pipes*, the main water valve in the house should be turned off.**

Who is running? Who dropped what?
Her cell phone fell out of her pocket and onto the street, chasing the *Labrador Retriever down the block.*

Who's rinsing?
Dental hygienists provide useful hints for your overall health. For example, *rinsing with mouthwash daily*, tooth decay can be prevented.

Adjective Versus Adverb Errors 形容词与副词使用错误

Those who help cheerful are more appreciated than those who help unwillingly.

Despite saying "no" constant to her pleading children, Mom is besieged with the same question over and over again.

Did you detect any grammatical errors in the sentences above? Each has an adjective/adverb error. Here are the corrected sentences:

Those who help *cheerfully* are more appreciated than those who help unwillingly.

Despite saying "no" *constantly* to her pleading children, Mom is besieged with the same question over and over again.

Sharpening Skills—Adjective/Adverb Errors
加强技巧——形容词/副词使用错误

Each sentence contains an adjective/adverb error. Replace the faulty adjective with the correct adverb.

1. Melvin, the shabby dressed man who walked his three shaggy dogs every day, rested with a cup of coffee at the corner of Forest Avenue and School Street.

2. Hank knows that, even though he did badly on his PSAT, he will perform more strong on the SAT.

3. Despite his sore calf muscle and sprained ankle, Augie performed miraculous in the 50-meter dash.

4. Comforting, Nanna Rose lulled baby Jean to sleep with a sonorous rendition of "Mary Had a Little Lamb."

5. We love you and miss you so much that we hope you return home quick!

Adjective/Adverb Answers 形容词/副词使用答案

1. *shabbily* dressed man
2. more *strongly*
3. performed *miraculously*
4. *Comfortingly*, Nanna Rose
5. return home *quickly*

Plural–Singular Inconsistency 单复数不一致

Can two children grow up and merge into one adult artist?
Can college classmates share the same GPA?

Reasonably, you know not. In the following sentences, however, these two logic-defying phenomena are not as easily spotted.

Mia and Maggie, the six-year-olds who attend the Museum Art School, dream of becoming a famous sculptor one day and sharing their own studio. (Can two young girls become one renowned sculptor? Change "a famous sculptor" to "famous sculptors.")

Popularity with the freshmen girls is not the only goal that Ralph and Rich share; these ambitious juniors also want to earn a GPA that will award them honor roll status. (Can two guys earn a single grade point average? Change "a GPA" to "GPAs.")

When sentences lack consistency between plural and singular components that go together, the resulting sentences are illogical. It's as if magic occurs in these unsound sentences.

Redundancy and Wordiness (Relatives of Flabby Phrasing)
句子冗余

Have you ever heard of the expression "beating a dead horse"?

Redundancy is like that: redundancy is saying the same thing over again, . . . or over again . . . and again.

The redundancy is boldfaced in this sentence:

Although he looks like a slugger, the guy at the plate **still** hasn't made contact with the ball **yet**.

You need one or the other, *yet* or *still*. Using both words is overkill. Wordiness is flabby writing that uses too many words to say something that can be expressed with brevity. Your mantra: "Concise is nice; wordy is out!" Keep this mantra in mind when you write your essay.

Sharpening Skills—Redundancy and Wordiness 加强技巧——句子冗余

Trim the fat in the following sentences by crossing off redundant and/or wordy expressions.

1. Ever since I was young, I wanted, from an early age, to pursue a career in either the performing arts or the fashion world.

2. Simultaneously talking on the telephone while writing a business letter is very challenging to do at the same time.

3. Although I sensed an atmosphere of instability, Ms. Hanna reassured me kindly and with gentle assurance that my senior position with the company was solid and secure.

4. All together, the dog barking, the television blaring, and the boys chattering created a crescendo of clamor that rivaled the roar of a hurricane itself, with all of these three noisy things happening at once.

5. Sluggishly walking from the couch to the dessert buffet, slow-moving Jim appeared less than enthusiastic to be at yet another holiday cocktail party even though he seemed to be enjoying a decadent walnut truffle.

6. Ravenous Harold ate both three croissants as well as two chunks of Fontina cheese.

7. The reason I was late is because my phone was on silent, and I didn't hear my alarm this morning.

Redundancy and Wordiness Answers 句子冗余答案

For each sentence, this answer key shows one way that you can eliminate redundancy and wordiness. These answers do not illustrate all possibilities.

1. Ever since I was young, I wanted~~, from an early age,~~ to pursue a career in either the performing arts or the fashion world.

2. ~~Simultaneously~~ talking on the telephone while writing a business letter is very challenging to do at the same time.

3. Although I sensed an atmosphere of instability, Ms. Hanna reassured me kindly ~~and with gentle assurance~~ that my senior position with the company was solid and secure.

4. All together, the dog barking, the television blaring, and the boys chattering created a crescendo of clamor that rivaled the roar of a hurricane itself, ~~with all of these three noisy things happening at once~~.

5. Sluggishly walking from the couch to the dessert buffet, ~~slow-moving~~ Jim appeared less than enthusiastic to be at yet another holiday cocktail party even though he seemed to be enjoying a decadent walnut truffle.

6. Ravenous Harold ate ~~both~~ three croissants as well as two chunks of Fontina cheese.

7. ~~The reason~~ I was late ~~is~~ because my phone was on silent, and I didn't hear my alarm this morning.

Faulty Comparisons 比较关系错误

Danny's off-road vehicle is cooler than Jackie.

Hannah's parents require more household chores than Mia and Ashton combined.

A summer getaway to Martha's Vineyard appeals more to Laura than Disney World.

Did you detect faulty logic in the sentences above? Each illustrates a faulty comparison.

Can an apple be sweeter than some other produce market? No! Can the lyrics of one musician be more sensitive than another musician? No! These comparisons do not make sense either. When you see that things are being compared, be sure that *like things are being compared:*

people compared to *people*

a *type of thing* compared to the *same type of thing*

an *activity* to another *activity*

Here's an equation to remember:

Faulty comparison = Faulty logic

Look at it this way: If you're amazed that one bird's beak is much shinier than another bird's beak, would you compare one bird to the other bird's beak, or would you compare one beak to the other beak? Obviously, the latter is correct. But if you're not concentrating when you read, you're apt to miss errors in faulty comparison.

Logic breaks down when dissimilar things are compared, as in the examples that follow.

Example 1

The yellow cockatiel's beak is much shinier than the grey cockatiel. (faulty comparison)
The yellow cockatiel's beak is much shinier than that of the grey cockatiel. (correct)
The yellow cockatiel's beak is much shinier than the grey cockatiel's. (also correct)

Example 2

By reading a bar graph that they found on an Internet site about nutrition, the curious couple discovered that the water content of a chestnut is similar to an apple. (faulty comparison)

By reading a bar graph that they found on an Internet site about nutrition, the curious couple discovered that the water content of a chestnut is similar to *that of* an apple. (correct)

By reading a bar graph that they found on an Internet site about nutrition, the curious couple discovered that a chestnut's water content is similar to an apple'*s*. (also correct)

Comparative Form	**Superlative Form**
Use to compare two things: *er* ending	Use to compare three or more things: *est* ending
Example: Of the two puppies, the small*er* one has the fuzzi*er* coat and the *more* playful disposition.	Example: Of the whole litter of pups, the small*est* one has the fuzzi*est* coat and the *most* playful disposition.
Taller, shorter, smarter, faster better, more	*Tallest, shortest, smartest, fastest best, most*

Let the 1600 Club's catchy mnemonic device work for you:
The *two*-letter ending *-er* is used to compare *two* items;
the *three*-letter ending *-est* is used to compare *three or more* items.

Sharpening Skills—Faulty Comparisons 加强技巧——比较关系错误

For each sentence, indicate whether there is a faulty comparison by circling "Error" or "No error."

1. A voracious nonfiction reader, Julian couldn't decide which of the four sports biographies he favored more. Error No error
2. The dark plaid wallpaper in the boys' bathroom is much more masculine than the powder room, which is conveniently situated off the kitchen. Error No error
3. Both on the playing field and off, Hugo's sportsmanship is far more admirable than that shown by Peter's. Error No error
4. Of all the Christmases she can remember, Julia decided that this past one was the greatest of them all in terms of the festivity and gratitude shown by her loved ones. Error No error

5. Hands down, the warm and mouth-watering cinnamon buns sold at Rosefeld Mall are much more scrumptious than Good Ole Bakery. Error No error

6. Full of comic humor and whimsy, Hank delightfully announced that his life is as inane and unpredictable as a circus clown. Error No error

7. Which roller coaster is the cooler one, Tricky Twister or Crazy Cyclone? Error No error

8. Hard Rock Hotel's waterslide or Portofino Bay Hotel—which slide do you think is the fastest? Error No error

Faulty Comparisons Answers 比较关系答案

1. Error; should be *he favored most.*
2. Error; should be *than the wallpaper in the powder room.*
3. Error; should be *than that shown by Peter.*
4. No error
5. Error; should be *than Good Ole Bakery's* or *those sold at Good Ole Bakery.*
6. Error; should be *that of a circus clown* or *a circus clown's.*
7. No error
8. Error; should be *Portofino Bay Hotel's*; *faster* should be used because only two slides are being compared.

Run-ons and Fragments 不分段和随意分段

Run-ons 不分段

For the improving sentences portion of the SAT, you will need to spot run-on sentences and, in each case, select the answer choice that most effectively eliminates the run-on. Also, for the essay portion of the SAT, you want your writing to be run-on-free! Most important, in your personal and professional life you want your written communications to be free of run-ons.

Attention, Grammar Gurus
Top scorers learn the hard and fast rules about how to use semicolons correctly.

Using shorthand notations, the chart below explains the basic rules of semicolon and comma use to punctuate compound sentences. There are many additional uses for semicolons and commas, but these are the ones that appear most frequently on the SAT.

Shorthand	Meaning	Run-ons	Sound Compound Sentences
IC	Independent Clause	IC , IC = comma splice	IC ; IC
		IC IC = fused sentence	IC, conjunction* IC

* FONY ABS

Here's the hard and fast rule for the types of run-ons that appear most frequently on the SAT: *The part of the sentence that precedes a semicolon must be an independent clause; the part of the sentence that follows the semicolon must also be independent.*

Fragments 随意分段

A dependent clause or a phrase on its own is a sentence fragment. Notice in the examples that follow that fragments can be short or long.

Because everybody else at the amusement park was wearing rain ponchos.
Nothing but silence.
Deciding to be the most prolific cartoonist who ever lived.

Sharpening Skills—Sentence Errors 加强技巧——句子错误

For each of the following, indicate on line *a* whether the item is a sentence, a fragment, or a run-on. 1600 Club members: for an added challenge, if the item is a fragment or a run-on, indicate on line *b* precisely what the sentence error is. If the item is a sound sentence, leave *b* blank.

1. Beyond the rustic post-and-beam fence and encroaching on the church parking lot that is just off of Glen Cove Road.

a. ________________ *b.* ________________________________

2. Justin likes the chocolate biscotti he also likes the cinnamon-pecan cookies.

a. ________________ *b.* ________________________________

3. Do you like the Mets, or do you like the Jets?

a. ________________ *b.* ________________________________

4. Early on weekday mornings, before she runs on her treadmill for 45 minutes, Beth meditates.

a. ________________ *b.* ________________________________

5. Without even looking back for a final glimpse of his aunt's puzzling facial expression.

a. ________________ *b.* ________________________________

6. Since Jeremy would not acknowledge his responsibility with regard to the impending debacle.

a. ________________ *b.* ________________________________

7. Because of Kurt's disrespectful tone, Myra would not look at him neither would Dave.

a. ________________ *b.* ________________________________

8. Dissillusioned, I left.

a. ________________ *b.* ________________________________

9. Hanging onto every word, an ancient talisman that originated in India.

a. ____________ *b.* ____________

10. Janice's humor was trenchant so was Doug's.

a. ____________ *b.* ____________

11. Without a word and without looking back, Frederick left the tranquil place where he had spent many afternoons composing earnest letters to his ex-girlfriend.

a. ____________ *b.* ____________

12. The sterling silver ring features an elaborate scroll design, it is named the Diva.

a. ____________ *b.* ____________

Sentence Errors Answers 句子错误答案

1. *a.* fragment
b. couple of phrases followed by an adjective clause
2. *a.* run-on
b. fused sentence (add semicolon after *biscotti*)
3. *a.* sentence (compound sentence)
4. *a.* sentence (complex sentence)
5. *a.* fragment
b. series of prepositional phrases
6. *a.* fragment
b. subordinate adverbial clause followed by prepositional phrases
7. *a.* run-on
b. fused sentence (add semicolon after *him*)
8. *a.* sentence (simple sentence)
9. *a.* fragment
b. gerund clause followed by a noun (*talisman*) modified by a subordinate adjective clause (*that originated in India*)
10. *a.* run-on
b. fused sentence (add semicolon after *trenchant*)
11. *a.* sentence (complex sentence)
12. *a.* run-on
b. comma splice (replace the comma with a semicolon to create a compound sentence)

Less vs. Fewer Less和Fewer

Use *fewer* when referring to people or things in the plural (e.g., motorcycles, iPads, ferrets, students, children). For example:

Today's youth are buying fewer motorcycles.
Fewer students are choosing to study math-related disciplines.
Fewer than twenty children develop the allergy before preschool.

Use *less* when referring to something that cannot be counted or does not have a plural (e.g., money, oxygen, youth, melody, wind). For example:

> **Office assistant is a more flexible job, but you will be paid less money.**
> **Drivers want to spend less time looking for parking.**
> **Unexpectedly, when the guitarist is on tour, he listens to less music.**

Less is also used with numbers when on their own and with expressions of time or measurement. For example:

> **Zahin's weight fell from 180 pounds to less than 165.**
> **Their business venture lasted less than three years.**
> **Merrick Manor is less than seven miles away from the boardwalk.**

A Final Note on Grammar and Usage Errors 关于语法和应用错误的最后注释

Just because something seems wrong doesn't mean that it is wrong. Sometimes hard questions feature sentences that contain words and/or phrases that sound or look wrong but are actually fine. Don't get trapped by these "false positives." The sentences that follow contain parts (italicized) that are likely to appear wrong to even the brightest students. Keep in mind that, just because you, your peers, and your teachers may not speak or write this way, the italicized parts are sound when it comes to standard written English.

> **Is this the picnic table *on which* you supposedly left your wallet?**
> (It may jar your ear, but *on which* is perfectly all right. Even though most people don't speak or write this way, the phrase is grammatically sound. In the real world of conversation, we would probably ask:
> Is this the picnic table where you supposedly left your wallet?
> (According to the conventions of standard written English, *where* is not used correctly here.)
> or:
> Is this the picnic table you supposedly left your wallet on?

> **This is the scene *in which* the tornado rips through the unsuspecting village.**
> Conversational English might go something like this:
> This is the scene where the tornado rips through the unsuspecting village.
> (According to the conventions of standard written English, *where* is not used correctly here.)

> ***Because* my purse had been stolen at the ballfield, I carried *neither* valuables *nor* sentimental items with me again.**
> (Maybe you were once told that a sentence may not start with *Because*. Provided that the sentence culminates in an independent clause, however, the sentence is grammatically acceptable.)

第四章 Chapter 4

PRACTICE WRITING AND LANGUAGE QUESTIONS 写作和语言测试练习题

Passage 1

CONTENT: Humanities

Questions 1–4 are based on the following passage.

On the updated SAT, 44 questions make up the Writing and Language section.

Despair and Inhumanity in the Film *Fargo*

Fargo is a riveting crime-drama movie set in Midwestern America that comically toys with the emotions and morals of ❶ its viewer. Not only does *Fargo* prove to be comically ironic, but this film also uses cutting edge directing to truly put the viewers at the creative mercy of the movie and its directors. The Coen brothers are the geniuses behind the creating of this picture. The social aspect of *Fargo* forces people to question the ethics, the morals, and the overall humanity of man. Some individuals might leave the movie theater questioning their best friend's motives and how genuine he or she may actually be. Only made in 1996, the brothers used myriad progressive techniques in the making of this film. *Fargo* artistically uses the brilliance of cutting edge ❷ cinematography: camera angles, positioning of objects, lighting, and dialogue. These effects emphasize despair and lack of humanity as the film's chief focuses.

Within the realm of shifting camera angles and viewpoints, there is a multitude of ways the Coen brothers strategically use such unique features to their advantage. A prime example of how the Coen brothers use intriguing camera angles is seen when the camera pans out over Jerry's car after he loses his investment opportunity. The camera

1. (A) NO CHANGE
   (B) their viewers.
   (C) their viewer.
   (D) it's dramatically inclined viewers.

2. (A) NO CHANGE
   (B) cinematography techniques such as camera angles,
   (C) cinematography camera angles,
   (D) cinematography; camera angles,

❸ is displaying the entire parking lot, which is barren, except for Jerry's car and his footsteps. This viewpoint not only shows the magnitude of the empty lot but also expresses Jerry's loneliness and desperation. The panoramic view ❹ provided by the audience's camera makes Jerry seem like a hopeless victim of his vast surroundings. Another way the Coen brothers use camera angles to translate a deeper message is seen in the beginning of the movie when the car steadily looms into view. This use of the camera lens dramatically shows how the directors desire that the viewer comprehend that nature is more powerful than man and how we are at its complete mercy.

3. (A) NO CHANGE
(B) while displaying
(C) displayed
(D) displays

4. (A) NO CHANGE
(B) the audience is provided for, by the camera
(C) the camera provides to its audience
(D) the camera providing to its' audience

On the updated SAT, there will be one passage on careers in the Writing and Language section.

Passage 2

CONTENT: Careers

Questions 1–6 are based on the following passage and its accompanying graphic.

Be sure to read all the language that accompanies every graph, including the title, subtitle (when provided), labels, and all footnotes or source notes.

Job Outlook for Physician Assistants

Percent Change in Employment, Projected 2012–2022

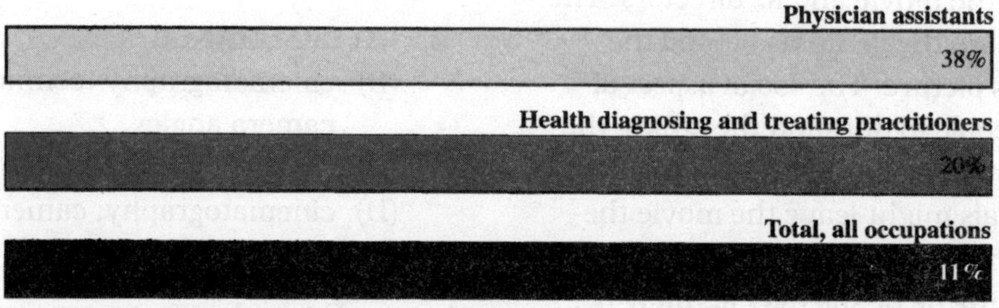

Note: All Occupations includes all occupations in the U.S. Economy.
Source: U.S. Bureau of Labor Statistics, Employment Projections program
Source: *http://www.bls.gov/ooh/healthcare*

Employment of physician assistants is projected to grow 38 percent from 2012 to 2022, ❶ much faster than the average for all occupations.

1. Which choice completes the sentence with the most accurate and specific information, based on the data represented in the graph?
(A) NO CHANGE
(B) more sluggishly, when compared to that of health diagnosing practitioners.
(C) nearly as fast as health practitioners in general.
(D) more than three times the rate of growth for all occupations in the U.S. economy.

Demand for healthcare services ❷ will be increasing because of the growing and aging population. More people means more need for healthcare specialists, and as the large baby-boom generation ages, it will require more healthcare. This, coupled with an increase in several chronic diseases such as diabetes, will ❸ drive the need for physician assistants to provide preventive care and treat those who are sick.

Physician assistants, who can perform many of the same services ❹ as doctors, are expected to have a larger role in giving routine care because they are more cost effective ❺ than being physicians. As more physicians retire or enter specialty areas of medicine, more physician assistants are expected to take on the role of primary care provider. Furthermore, the number of individuals who have access to primary care services will increase ❻ as a result of federal health insurance reform.

The role of physician assistants is expected to expand as states continue to allow assistants to do more procedures and as insurance companies expand their coverage of physician assistant services.

2. (A) NO CHANGE
(B) will have been increasing
(C) being increased
(D) will increase

3. In context, the word "drive" most closely means
(A) compel.
(B) constrain.
(C) coerce.
(D) control.

4. (A) NO CHANGE
(B) as doctors do
(C) as those performed by doctors
(D) as doctors'

5. (A) NO CHANGE
(B) then physicians.
(C) than are physicians.
(D) than physicians.

6. (A) NO CHANGE
(B) with accordance to
(C) as resulting from
(D) as a given because of

Data, as represented in tables or charts, are considered part of passage evidence on the SAT.

Concision, clarity, and consistency are all preferred grammatical conventions on the Writing and Language Test.

Answers and Explanations 答案与解析

Passage 1: Despair and Inhumanity in the Film *Fargo*

1. **(A)** In choice (A), *NO CHANGE*, the singular possessive pronoun "its" correctly refers back to the singular noun, "movie." Choices (B) and (C) are wrong because "their" is a plural possessive pronoun and does not agree with the singular antecedent, "movie." (D) is wrong because "it's" is a contraction that translates to "it is."

2. **(A)** In choice (A), *NO CHANGE*, a colon (:) correctly introduces a list (or, in some cases, an illustrative example). (B) (*cinematography techniques such as camera angles*), is unnecessarily redundant because it restates the word "techniques." (C) (*cinematography camera angles,*) is wrong because it lacks the required punctuation. (D) (*cinematography; camera angles,*) is incorrect because a semicolon (;) is used to separate two independent clauses and not to introduce a list.

3. **(D)** Choice (A), *NO CHANGE*, is wrong because there is no need to use a verb phrase, "is displaying." Choice (B) (*while displaying*) is both awkward and unnecessarily wordy. This test prefers concision. Choice (C) (*displayed*) is incorrect because this verb tense is inconsistent with the context. Consider the present tense verbs in the vicinity; in this case, consider the present tense verbs in the prior sentence: "use," "pans."

4. **(C)** The panoramic view *the camera provides to its audience* makes Jerry seem like a hopeless victim of his vast surroundings. Choice (B), *the audience is provided for, by the camera*, is wordy and encumbered with an unnecessary comma. Choice (D), *the camera providing to its' audience*, is wrong because it creates a sentence fragment and because "its'" is neither a possessive nor a contraction in the English language.

Passage 2: Job Outlook for Physician Assistants

1. **(D)** Choice (D) is correct because 38% is more than three times 11%, as the percentages are indicated in the informational graphic that accompanies this passage. Choice (A), *NO CHANGE*, is incorrect because *much faster* is not as specific as choice (D). Choice (B), *more sluggishly*, is wrong because sluggishly means slowly but the rate of growth for physician assistants is robust. Choice (C) is wrong because *nearly as fast as health practitioners* would be a rate of growth proximous to 20%.

2. **(D)** Choice (D), *will increase*, is correct because this verb phrase is correctly formatted in future tense. Choice (A), *NO CHANGE*, is incorrect because it lacks the concision (succinctness) of choice (D). Choice (B), *will have been increasing*, is excessively wordy, and choice (C), *being increased*, creates an awkward sentence fragment.

3. **(A)** In choice (A), *compel*, which means to *require* or, in some cases, *to force* is correct. Words-in-context questions must fit and flow most effectively in the given context. This is a diction question. You need to find the best word for the sentence in which it appears: *This, coupled with an increase in several chronic diseases such as*

diabetes, will drive the need for physician assistants to provide preventive care and treat those who are sick. Choice (B) does not fit because *constrain* means to *hold back* or *restrict*. Although (C), *coerce*, can work, it is somewhat strong given the meaning of the sentence. Finally, (D), *control*, neither fits nor flows in this context.

4. **(B)** Choice (B), *as doctors do*, creates a sound and balanced comparison. Choice (A), *NO CHANGE* ("as doctors,"), creates an illogical comparison because now the activity of someone is being compared to people, rather than the activities of those people. Choice (C), *as those performed by doctors*, is unnecessarily wordy and repetitive. This test prefers concision. Choice (D) is wrong because *as doctors'* introduces an illogical possessive.

5. **(D)** (*than physicians*) Choice (A), *NO CHANGE*, is incorrect because the verb *being* is awkward and extraneous. Likewise, the verb "are" in choice (C), *than are physicians*, is extraneous or unnecessary. Choice (B), *then physicians*, is wrong because the wrong form of the commonly confused then/than is used. In most contexts, "then" means next, later, or the following step in a process.

6. **(A)**, *NO CHANGE*. This phrase fits and flows in context: *Furthermore, the number of individuals who have access to primary care services will increase as a result of federal health insurance reform.* Choices (B), *with accordance to*, and (C), *as resulting from*, are awkward and cumbersome. Finally, choice (D), *as a given because of*, lacks the concision that this test prefers.

第三部分 PART 3

THE ESSAY 短文

On test day, the essay prompt that will be provided to you is basically the same from one test administration to the other. The College Board calls this feature "transparency," in that you, as a test taker, will know what to expect. Given this, you can prepare by developing your critical reading, analysis, and writing skills instead of trying to predict which kind of essay question (or essay prompt) might appear.

Furthermore, as the essay task focuses on a unique "source text" disclosed on test day, test takers must engage with the passage rather than rely on predrafted (in some cases) generic responses contemplated weeks before test day. Given these factors, the SAT essay task encourages meaningful composition that is closely connected with curriculum and instruction.

With regard to text complexity, essays will be geared toward the high school to college-bound reading level. They will tend to examine debates, trends, ideas, cutting-edge thinking, and the like in the sciences, art, civics, and cultural and political life with a wide range of relevance and interest. Passages will involve more complex, multisided, and "nuanced" debates instead of simple pro/con ones. The source texts will contain effective use of persuasive elements and strategies, logical reasoning, and the use of evidence.

Key points about the essay portion:

- Optional
- Given at end of the test
- Passage between 650 and 750 words
- Postsecondary institutions will decide whether or not to require the essay for admissions purposes.
- Essay results are reported separately; they are not part of the total 1600 score.
- Essay evaluation is based on three traits: reading (understanding the source/passage), analysis (analysis of the author's use of evidence, reason, and/or stylistic and persuasive elements, and/or features of the text of the student's own choosing), and writing (cohesiveness of the student's response as well as effective use of language).
- Each trait is scored on a scale of 1 to 4, for a total of 3 to 12 points; however, each score will be reported separately (e.g., 4-3-3).
- Two readers will evaluate the essay, and the two readers' marks will be combined for a total score; thus, a total score of 6 to 24 points is possible.

- Time allotted: 50 minutes. This represents your total time. You have 50 minutes in total to read through the essay (referred to as the source text) provided, gather your thoughts, jot down some notes or a rough outline (if you choose to do so), write, and do some basic editing of your essay.
- **Spelling counts.** Because the essays are graded holistically, all aspects of standard written English are taken into consideration, including spelling.
- **An essay that is off topic will not be evaluated.**

第五章 Chapter 5

WRITING THE 50-MINUTE ESSAY 50分钟短文写作

1600 Club Comprehensive Strategies 1600分俱乐部综合策略

Strategy 1:	Take inventory of the author's use of evidence, reasoning, and stylistic elements.
Strategy 2:	Have a timing plan: 10-35-5.
Strategy 3:	Engage your reader.
Strategy 4:	Edit, using the 1600 Club Checklist.
Strategy 5:	Support your thesis with examples.
Strategy 6:	Sentence and vocabulary variety
Strategy 7:	Assess what you have written.
Strategy 8:	Your voice

Writing is a life skill! You're motivated to do well in school and to perform brilliantly on your college entrance exams. Surely, you are also driven to do well in the vocation you eventually choose. Writing well is a lifelong skill that is pertinent to everyday living and to work situations. Psyche yourself to learn how to write well—not simply for the SAT, but also for your real life.

STRATEGY 1: TAKE INVENTORY OF THE AUTHOR'S USE OF EVIDENCE, REASONING, AND STYLISTIC ELEMENTS
策略1：弄清作者使用的证据、推理和风格元素

After you have read and absorbed the passage, you will be asked to consider, analyze, and discuss how the author uses

- Evidence, such as examples and facts, to support claims
- Reasoning to develop his thoughts and to connect his ideas and claims with evidence
- Rhetorical (stylistic) or persuasive features, such as diction (word choice) or appeals to emotion, to add power to his expressed ideas

You may also have to do one or both of the following as you develop a logical argument that is substantiated by supporting details and examples:

- Summarize the main idea and purpose of the source text
- Recognize flaws (that you may or may not detect) in the author's argument

Essay Coaching: *Insightfully explore **relevant examples** that develop and support a **coherent point of view**.*

*On the updated SAT, the essay is **optional**, but **strongly** recommended.*

You need to recognize, analyze, and clearly explain elements of the author's craft that are notably effective in the author's expression of his purpose and point of view.

STRATEGY 2: HAVE A TIMING PLAN: 10-35-5
策略2：合理安排时间10—35—5

A timing plan keeps you in control. Testing centers usually provide clocks or digital time displays in clear view. In some cases, proctors write the *start* time and the *stop* time on the blackboard and announce midway points so that you have a sense of how much time has elapsed and, more important, how much time you have left.

Essay Tip
Timing is key. Think 10-35-5.

You have 50 minutes to serve up a three-course meal: an appetizer (the introductory paragraph), a zesty entrée (at least two or three body paragraphs), and a memorable dessert (the concluding paragraph.)

The 1600 Club timing plan is **10-35-5**. This timing plan is a guide, so it is *flexible*. You, personally, may need only 9 minutes, for example, for stage 1; in this case, you will have an extra minute for stage 2.

Essay Practice and Timing 短文写作练习和时间分配

Schedule jam-packed?
No time to write the 50-minute essay?

Time Saver: Allot *half* the time (25 minutes) to write *half* an essay. Write about one single-spaced page, containing an introduction and one solid body paragraph. Next time you have another 25 minutes to spare, write the second half of your essay: about one single-spaced page, containing a second body paragraph and a conclusion. In general, write longer body paragraphs and relatively shorter introductory and concluding paragraphs.

Ask a parent, older sibling, trusted relative, teacher, or tutor to read and critique your essay so that you may benefit from some constructive feedback. With practice, rest assured that writing the essay will get easier and easier, particularly within the time constraints given.

The Essay—Stage 1: About 10 Minutes
短文阶段1：10分钟左右

Carefully read the writing **source text** that follows the initial directions. Brainstorm. Formulate your ideas. Brainstorm some more. If you have time, you can *roughly* sketch a lean "concept map" or "web." Or simply jot down a list of ideas (write words, phrases, and abbreviations, not complete sentences).

Time Saver
Jot down your brainstorming/prewriting notes in phrases and abbreviations.

Practice can make you a pro at spontaneous essay writing. Use Barron's big SAT preparation book to find sample source texts.

Fast-Forward Essay Writing 快速短文写作

Once you've worked through a good number of practice essays, you may want to try a fast-forward, time-saving approach: *read just the source text.* This approach may sound radical, but you may find that skipping over the initial directions gives you extra time to use on the actual composing and revising of your essay.

Time Saver
Do you consider yourself quick-minded and decisive? If so, try the "fast-forward" approach to get a jump-start on your essay writing.

The Essay—Stage 2: About 35 Minutes 短文阶段2：35分钟左右

Write. Write. Write. Don't sweat the small stuff now. Just get your ideas out of your head and onto the sheets of lined paper provided on your answer sheet. Let your thoughts flow. You're shooting for an exemplary 12 from each essay grader, so try to write a four- to six-paragraph essay that is well developed and clearly expressed. You should write an introductory paragraph, two to four body paragraphs, and a concluding paragraph.

If you have written two solid body paragraphs and see that you have time to write more, press on and add a third and possibly fourth body paragraph, for a total of five or six paragraphs. But don't add just for the sake of adding. Write more only if you have another insightful point to make or relevant example to discuss. Length matters less than quality; still, it is very unlikely that two paragraphs will earn you a high score on the essay.

The Essay—Stage 3: About 5 Minutes 短文阶段3：5分钟左右

Proofread and polish. (See the *1600 Club Checklist of Errors to Avoid,* page 132.) If there are changes that you wish to make, use single-line cross-outs for deletions. Do not litter your essay with sloppy scratch-offs and unsightly scribble-scrabble. A messy essay could be a turnoff to the evaluators.

Abridged Essay Practice 短文写作大纲

No doubt, you're superbusy: schoolwork, sports, college planning, part-time job, family, friends, volunteer work. . . . If a 50-minute block of uninterrupted time is an unimaginable luxury, you can practice essay writing in an abridged form. Cut the time allotted for writing the essay; give yourself 25 minutes to write two or three paragraphs. You can use one of these combinations:

25-Minute Combo

Example 1	*Example 2*
Write the appetizer and half the entrée:	Write the full entrée:
■ Introductory paragraph and body paragraphs 1 and 2	■ Two or three body paragraphs

Time Saver
Try "abridged essay practice" when you have a spare 10 minutes.

Know the Directions Cold 用心记住短文写作要求

Directions boxes both precede and follow the source text. Notice that no time is allotted in this timing plan for reading the directions that precede the source text. The reason is that you should *know* the directions cold ahead of time. The directions that follow the source text, the prompt, will be the same from test to test, except for the author's name and claim. Only the source text will change.

Know your essay directions. Read and study them now, making sure to include the finer details of the essay guidelines. Then, on test day, you can circumvent these lengthy directions, saving precious writing time.

Study the directions that follow now so that on test day you can skip them. These directions are not taken verbatim from an actual SAT, but they tell you everything you need to know.

Time Saver
Read and know these essay directions here and now so that on test day, you can skip them.

Directions: This is your opportunity to show that you can read and understand a passage and write an analysis of that passage. Be sure your essay demonstrates a clear and logical analysis of the passage, using precise language.

On the actual test, you will write your essay on the lines provided in your answer booklet; for now, write your essay on a lined paper. Remember to write or print legibly so that others can read what you've written.

You have <u>50 minutes</u> to read the passage and write a response to the prompt provided.

Essay Tip
Read between the lines: what they're telling you is that yes, to an extent, neatness counts.

As you read the passage below, consider how the author uses

- Evidence, such as examples and facts, to support claims.
- Reasoning to develop his thoughts and to connect his ideas and claims with evidence.
- Rhetorical (stylistic) or persuasive features, such as diction (word choice) or appeals to emotion, to add power to his expressed ideas.

Source text follows, followed by the prompt:

Write an essay in which you explain how the author presents and structures an argument to persuade his audience that the Dual Capacity framework supports student achievement. In your essay, analyze how the author uses one or more of the features listed above (or features of your own choice) to strengthen the logic and persuasiveness of his argument. Be sure that your analysis focuses on the most relevant elements of the passage.

Your essay should not explain whether you agree with the author's claims, but rather it should explain how the author builds an argument to persuade his audience.

Now that you are familiar with the essay directions, you should be able to answer the straightforward questions on the next page. If you're not sure of an answer, reread the preceding directions more carefully.

Sharpening Skills—Getting Essay Directions Down Pat
加强技巧——弄清短文写作要求

1. Does neatness of penmanship count?
   ☐ yes ☐ no ☐ not sure

2. Should I write in print or script?
   ☐ print ☐ script ☐ however I write more neatly

3. Should I write on every line, or should I double-space my essay?
   ☐ every line ☐ double space ☐ not sure

4. Should I write on the black lines of the essay paper that is provided, or should I indent, making wider margins?
   ☐ write on lines given ☐ indent ☐ not sure

5. If I run out of time before I've written my complete essay, will the evaluators read my "brainstorming" notes that I jotted down on the left or at the bottom of the Assignment page?
   ☐ yes ☐ no ☐ not sure

6. Should I use personal examples or nonpersonal examples, the latter being examples taken from my reading of literature, history books, science, or reputable newspapers and newsmagazines?
   ☐ personal ☐ nonpersonal ☐ either is fine

7. If I finish another writing skills or a critical reading section with time to spare, may I return to my essay to work on it?
   ☐ yes ☐ no ☐ not sure

Essay Directions Answers 短文写作要求释疑

1. *Yes*, neatness counts. You want your essay to be very legible.
2. *Print* and *script* are both fine. Use the form in which you write more neatly.
3. Write on *every line*.
4. *Write on lines given*. Essay evaluators will not think highly of gaping margins.
5. *No*, the evaluators will read only what is written on the lined paper provided.
6. In theory, *personal* and *nonpersonal* examples are both fine. But as a 1600 Clubber, you're eager to give this test everything you've got. Using examples from your reading could put a feather or two in your cap! The essay is your chance to tout your learning. Give yourself every possible advantage.
7. *No*, if you finish a section before the allotted time is up, you may go back and work on that section only.

STRATEGY 3: ENGAGE YOUR READER 策略3：吸引你的读者

Strong writers reel 'em in fast. Your introductory paragraph should be crisp, clear, and fairly brief. It should include a statement or two that relates to the topic. From there on, the introduction becomes focused on the topic itself. To keep things simple, plainly restate the given statement and tell whether you agree or disagree with it.

Essays in which the introductory paragraph was merely two or three sentences have been known to earn ratings of a 5 or 6. Introductions are simple and formulaic. The substance—the meat and potatoes—of your essay is made up of the body paragraphs.

Traditionally, the final sentence of the introductory paragraph is the thesis. Once the reader has read your thesis, there should be no question about your point of view.

STRATEGY 4: EDIT, USING THE 1600 CLUB CHECKLIST 策略4：校对，使用1600分俱乐部清单

Good writers know that editing is an ongoing process. Good writers know that editing can make the difference between writing that is clear and writing that is obfuscated (cloudy; opaque). As you write your sentences and paragraphs, scrutinize them with an editor's eye. The 1600 Club Checklist below helps you to be aware of the types of errors to avoid. You can edit and revise throughout the writing process, but it's smart to spend about 5 minutes more at the end in a more focused effort at improvement. Use these 5 minutes as your chance to show, for example, that you're competent with commas and adept with parallel form.

Okay—you can't do everything in 5 minutes (see Strategy 2). Still, you can achieve some polishing of your prose. Polishing involves more than crossing your *t*'s and dotting your *i*'s. For example, look for wordiness, repetition, and weak vocabulary. Also, as you edit your essay, make sure you haven't made any of the grammatical errors that the grammar portion of the SAT tests you on!

Good Writers Know It's Important to Also Be Good Editors 好的作者同时也是好的编辑

The checklist that follows is handy, but you can't take it with you—on test day, that is. Use it regularly as you proofread your essays for English and history classes. Eventually, the list will become second nature to you and will serve as a "mental editor's checklist" on test day.

1600 Club Checklist of Errors to Avoid

- Spelling errors
- Capitalization errors
- Punctuation errors: commas, semicolons, colons, apostrophes, quotation marks, end marks
- Verb errors: form, tense, agreement with subject
- Pronoun errors: form, agreement with antecedent, ambiguity
- Wordiness and superfluous language
- Redundancy
- Stale, repetitive vocabulary
- Lack of parallelism
- Double negatives
- Poor diction (word choice) and usage
- Lack of paragraph indentation
- Lack of coherence

Clean Editing 校对

Yes, in two concentrated minutes, you can add polish and clarity to your prose and bring your essay closer to that pristine score of 12. In editing, avoid sloppy crossouts and ink blots that make your essay look messy. Here are a few basic proofreading marks to give you that editor's edge and to keep your editing clean:

^ the caret, for inserting a letter, word, or phrase
* the asterisk, to show where long phrases or sentences should be added
— the clean, single-line crossout, to replace a word with the more effective word that you'll write neatly on top
¶ the paragraph symbol, to show where you want to indent
ℓ the delete symbol, to remove material; for example, a redundant word or expression. Remember: extraneous language is never preferable; economy of language is.

STRATEGY 5: SUPPORT YOUR THESIS WITH EXAMPLES
策略5：用事实论据支持论点

The "stuff" of your essay, the supporting examples, should be discussed in the body paragraphs. Three body paragraphs make for a very solid essay. You have to decide the length with which you are comfortable. Two well-supported body paragraphs can suffice and earn a perfect score.

To catapult your essay to a perfect 12, select examples that allow you to discuss the essay assignment in insightful ways. ***Insight*** is that special ingredient that moves "pretty good" essays closer to the level-12 ranks. Pertinent examples are ones that lend themselves to juicy and perceptive discussion of the topic. To a great extent: the more salient your examples, the stronger your insight.

Essay Coaching:
You aspire to achieve a perfect 12 on the essay. In addition to insightfully discussing your supporting examples, strive to fill all 46 lines of the essay paper provided. Every word should contribute to the development of pertinent examples; there should be no "filler."

Use This "Handy Reminder" to Write a Body Paragraph 段落主体写作

Think of your hand, with its five fingers, as a body paragraph. This may sound strange, but it is a visual mnemonic device. Hold your left hand in front of you, and pretend that it is one of the two or three body paragraphs that you should write on your SAT essay. This device is a great writing tool since your hand is always with you, a "handy reminder."

Your pinky represents a concise topic sentence that will begin a paragraph.

Your ring, middle, and pointer (index) fingers represent three body sentences that support your topic sentence. Body sentences should illustrate specific examples or details. As you write, be sure that each paragraph has unity. Do not go off on tangents. Do not digress from your topic. To keep yourself focused, frequently reread your topic sentence.

Essay Coaching:
Think of a body paragraph as your hand, with each finger representing one part of the paragraph structure.

Your thumb represents the closing sentence, which affirms or restates your point. To make things simple, you can reread your topic sentence and just tweak it a bit to come up with your closing sentence. This sentence, which is sometimes called the concluding sentence or the "clincher," can simply be a rephrasing of the topic sentence.

Your palm represents the unifying idea that gives coherence and focus to each body paragraph.

Give yourself a thumbs-up! You have written an organized and substantial body paragraph.

STRATEGY 6: SENTENCE AND VOCABULARY VARIETY
策略6：句型与词汇的多样化

Have you heard a CD "skip," playing the same part of a song over and over again? Well, that's how your essay will sound if all of your sentences are long, or if all of them are short. Don't put your reader to sleep. Refrain from writing sentences that are all more or less the same length.

Essay Coaching: *Strong writers use **vocabulary variety** to avoid sounding like broken records.*

*Strong writers spice up their essays with a handful of **upper-level vocabulary** words that fit and flow smoothly in context.*

Writing a good essay is a balancing act. You need some short sentences and some longer ones. Too much of one type makes the essay resemble either a choppy sea or a rambling, runaway train.

Vocabulary variety is also important. Too much of a good thing is not a good thing anymore. Too much use of the word *conflict* in your essay is boring. Too much use of the word *change* or *freedom* in your essay is boring. ZZZzzz . . .

Does the paragraph below sound like part of an essay that will impress the evaluators? Or does it sound like an essay that might irritate them or—horrors!—put them to sleep?

> *Change is good for everyone. Change is a dynamic force from which all can benefit. Without change, life would be an endless drone of the same old routine. Change separates thinkers from nonthinkers. Above all, change is the only way to ensure commercial development and the changing for the better of mankind. The future calls for change. Change is the key.*

Underline the key words that you might be tempted to overuse as you write your essay. The 1600 Club strives for rich, effective diction and vocabulary variety.

Boring! Some good ideas but boring just the same because the word *change,* like the figurative horse, is beaten to death. . . See the chart below for some other words the writer could have used in place of *change.*

Brainstorm other words that you can use to express these ideas. Varying your vocabulary will avoid repetition and redundancy in your writing. For example:

Key Words in Writing Topic That You're Tempted to Use Ad Nauseum	Alternative Words to Use So You Sound as Though You Have a Brain and So the Reader Does Not Fall Asleep
• Conflict	• strife, discord, struggle, dispute, friction
• Change	• development, evolution, transformation, modification, variation
• Freedom	• autonomy, independence, choice, free will, self-determination, liberty
• Wise	• sagacious, prudent, astute, keen-minded

Sharpening Skills—Vary Your Vocabulary 加强技巧——使用不同的词汇

Now it's your turn. Fill in the right-hand column of the chart below with at least three alternatives for each given word.

Key Words in Writing Topic That You Might Be Tempted to Use Ad Nauseum	Alternative Words to Use So You Sound as Though You Have a Brain and So the Essay Reader Does Not Fall Asleep
Power	
Inequity	
Kindness	
Competition	
Equality	
Collaboration	

STRATEGY 7: ASSESS WHAT YOU HAVE WRITTEN 策略7：评估你的写作

Writing is a recursive process, so you should frequently assess what you have written. Reread your output after every three sentences or so. In this way, you will refresh your memory in terms of the points you have made and the examples you have provided. Reading will also help you to avoid redundancy—a common plague in writing.

Writing is a recursive process. Going back over what you've written is a smart strategy for writing well.

Revision shouldn't just happen at the end. If, after every few sentences, you take a few seconds to reread and "re-see" what you have written, you will have an essay that flows more smoothly. Frequent assessment also eliminates wordiness. As you assess, you may even spot usage errors, spelling errors, or omission of words. Revising as you write also cuts down the time required to look over the essay in its entirety. Find a revision rhythm that works well for you.

Make sure that you have given the essay evaluators a hearty, three-course meal: appetizer (clear introductory paragraph), entrée (two or three well-supported body paragraphs), and dessert (a concluding paragraph). Even at this stage, you can add a sentence or two by using an asterisk and neatly writing the addition at the bottom of your essay.

STRATEGY 8: YOUR VOICE 策略8：写作的语态

Overly formal is undesirable. Although essays that use appropriate upper-level words like "erudite" or "convoluted" tend to score higher, be careful not to overdo it. Overcasual is taboo also. Your voice should be straightforward, reasonable, and persuasive. When in doubt, err on the side of being more conversational and natural, less formal.

Cut the fluff, slang, verbal clutter, and awkward, "put-on" vocabulary.

Fluff is out, too. Avoid phrases that say nothing: "in my opinion," "I believe that," "it is my truest estimation that," "to my way of thinking," "it seems only reasonable that," and so on. These phrases constitute "verbal clutter."

Quality, not quantity, is in.

What About Vocabulary? 词汇

You're determined to reach the ranks of the 1600 Club, so you're making a serious effort to learn high-frequency SAT words (like those in *Barron's Hot Words for the SAT*) and you're resolute about learning some harder, off-the-bell-curve words as well. (Study the word lists in the Appendix at the end of this book.)

Since you have an upper-level, mental word bank to call upon, challenge yourself to strengthen your essay with strong vocabulary words that you can use with *accuracy* and *comfort*. Avoid highfalutin words that mystify you when it comes to their precise definitions, spellings, and proper usages. If you use big words merely for the sake of adornment, your essay will come across as artificial, inflated, and unnatural.

A final note about the writing section . . .

As you know, two evaluators will read your essay. You want your essay to read clearly and smoothly. You don't want the readers to be distracted by mechanical and spelling errors. You don't want the readers to stumble over your errors. Careless errors—ones that you can easily eliminate in your editing—can leave a bad taste in the mouths of the readers, resulting in a lower score for you.

MORE 1600 CLUB STRATEGIES: ELIMINATE SMOG
更多1600分俱乐部策略：排除SMOG

Don't let **SMOG** cloud your essay!

What is **SMOG** ?

SMOG is an acronym that stands for **S**pelling, **M**echanics, **O**veruse, and **G**rammar. If you keep SMOG in mind as you write and edit, your essay will be clear and will reflect your command of the English language.

Spelling Errors 拼写错误

Spelling errors contribute to smog. It's true that misspelled words aren't the biggest deal when it comes to effective writing. Nevertheless, the fewer spelling errors in your essay, the more competent you will come across as a writer. At the present time, SAT essays are handwritten in pencil. You will not be typing your essay on a personal computer, so good old "spell check" will not be at your disposal.

To become a better speller, read more and pay close attention to the spellings of tricky words as you read. Make mental pictures of the tricky words that you encounter in good novels, newspapers, and textbooks. Reading and becoming a talented speller go hand-in-hand. No doubt, you're very busy, but look at this suggestion as multitasking and making the best use of your limited time.

Sharpening Skills—Spelling 加强技巧——拼写

The following is a list of twenty frequently used words that are spelling demons for many writers. Circle the correct spelling of each word.

1. accummulate	accumulate	acummulate
2. intresting	interesting	intaresting
3. successful	sucessful	succesfull
4. beautiful	beuatifull	beautyful
5. arguement	argeument	argument
6. beginning	beggining	begginning
7. therfor	therefore	theirfor
8. disagreement	disaggrement	disagreemint
9. ocurrence	ocurrance	occurrence
10. respectabel	respectable	respecttable
11. possibility	posibility	possabiluty
12. posessions	posetions	possessions
13. confrence	conference	conferrence
14. unnecessary	unneccessary	unneccesery
15. dissapointment	disappointment	disappointmint
16. sufficcient	sufficent	sufficient
17. delibratly	deliberratley	deliberately
18. acsessible	accesible	accessible
19. extraordinary	extraordinry	extrordinary
20. fullfilling	fulfiling	fulfilling

Spelling Drill Answers 拼写答案

1. accumulate	**8.** disagreement	**15.** disappointment
2. interesting	**9.** occurrence	**16.** sufficient
3. successful	**10.** respectable	**17.** deliberately
4. beautiful	**11.** possibility	**18.** accessible
5. argument	**12.** possessions	**19.** extraordinary
6. beginning	**13.** conference	**20.** fulfilling
7. therefore	**14.** unnecessary	

Mechanical Errors 标点符号使用错误

Mechanical errors contribute to smog. Some writers are comma-phobic, neglecting to insert commas where they belong. Other writers are comma-happy, sprinkling them here, there, and everywhere! A command of punctuation doesn't make you an awesome writer, but it does make you a writer who is proficient in one of the conventions of writing.

Lack and overuse of apostrophes, commas, and semicolons are examples of mechanical errors in punctuation. Other such errors involve end marks and quotation marks. Incorrect capitalization is another type of mechanical error.

Mechanical errors can adversely affect your writing. A misplaced comma or apostrophe may even significantly change the meaning of a sentence. Since you're probably a strong English student, the following drills will seem like child's play—a cinch! The point is, however, that even the best students are sometimes guilty of sloppy errors. Mechanical oversights can make a student come across as a "sleepy writer."

Sharpening Skills—Mechanics 加强技巧——使用标点符号

Don't be punctuation-phobic. Insert commas, apostrophes, and semicolons where they belong:

1. Before leaving for Florida Ms. Peach cleaned her house from top to bottom and tidied up her vegetable garden.

2. The post and beam fence blocks the childrens access to the forest beyond this is crucial since the woods are filled with poison ivy.

Insert capital letters, quotation marks, and end marks where they belong:

3. Have you read Edgar Allan Poe's gruesome and eerie short story titled the black cat

4. I am so excited to have memorized the names of the five great lakes: Huron, Ontario, Michigan, Erie, and Superior

Mechanics Drill Answers 使用标点符号答案

1. Before leaving for Florida, Ms. Peach cleaned her house from top to bottom and tidied up her vegetable garden.

2. The post and beam fence blocks the children's access to the forest beyond; this is crucial since the woods are filled with poison ivy.

3. Have you read Edgar Allan Poe's gruesome and eerie short story titled "The Black Cat"?

4. I am so excited to have memorized the names of the five great lakes: Huron, Ontario, Michigan, Erie, and Superior!

Overuse 过多空话

Overuse of "empty phrases" contributes to smog. Do you use "filler" when you write? "Filler" always gets a bad rap—just think of a hot dog. Do you write a lot without saying much? Yada-yada-yada. . . . Is your writing sluggish? Do you use "empty phrases" that slow down your essay?

Here are some examples of empty phrasing:

It is my opinion that . . .
It likely holds true that . . .
As it is often said . . .
I feel that . . .
It seems to me that . . .
I truly believe that . . .
For all intents and purposes . . .
It has been said that . . .

These kinds of phrases come across as hedging, giving your writing a spineless aura of uncertainty. Say what you want to say, and say it firmly, without equivocation.

Empty phrasing contributes to *smog*, making your ideas not only foggy but also flimsy.

Sharpening Skills—Eliminate Empty Phrasing 加强技巧——删除空话

Cross off the empty phrases in the paragraph below:

> For the most part, motivation comes from within. Each of us has the power and ability to put his or her thoughts into action. I believe that, for all intents and purposes, our innermost desires fuel our actions. By and large, external motivation is weak and short-lived. What we are told to do and what we witness are far less motivating than what our inner sense propels us to accomplish. When you want to change your intentions into actions, it is said that you should look within for the stimulus. You will find it deep within you, just waiting to take shape. This is truly what I believe.

Empty Phrasing Answers 删除空话答案

> ~~For the most part,~~ motivation comes from within. Each of us has the power and ability to put his or her thoughts into action. ~~I believe that, for all intents and purposes,~~ our innermost desires fuel our actions. ~~By and large,~~ external motivation is weak and short-lived. What we are told ~~to do~~ and what we witness are far less motivating than what our inner sense propels us to accomplish. When you want to change your intentions into actions, ~~it is said that~~ you should look within for the stimulus. You will find it deep within you, just waiting to take shape. ~~This is truly what I believe.~~

Here is the flab-free, succinct paragraph. Unlike the original paragraph, this one is lean and has a backbone.

> Motivation comes from within. Each of us has the power and ability to put his or her thoughts into action. Our innermost desires fuel our actions. External motivation is weak and short-lived. What we are told and what we witness are far less motivating than what our inner sense propels us to accomplish. When you want to change your intentions into actions, you should look within for the stimulus. You will find it deep within you, just waiting to take shape.

Grammatical Errors 语法错误

Grammatical errors contribute to smog. A fair portion of the SAT tests you on your ability to recognize and correct grammatical errors. It makes sense, then, that your essay should be as free of grammatical errors as possible. Turn to the Hierarchy of Grammar Glitches on page 98. Avoid these grammar glitches in your essay.

Sharpening Skills—Grammatical Errors 加强技巧——语法错误

Can you spot grammatical errors in the paragraph below? Use the "Grammar Error Bank" below to help you find four errors. The errors in the paragraph do not necessarily appear in the order in which they are listed in this box:

Grammar Error Bank

1. Subject-verb agreement error
2. Pronoun-antecedent agreement error
3. Ambiguous pronoun error: pronoun lacks a clear reference
4. Run-on (also known as comma splice)
5. Lack of parallelism

A backyard lawn is a wondrous place. It's a place to pitch a badminton net, it's a place to play bocci ball. You can even sunbathe there in a lounge chair when the sun is warm. If one desires, you can rake up piles of leaves in autumn and jump! You can collect pinecones in the yard and use them for crafts projects, scented fireplace crackle, or arranging natural centerpieces. A backyard, with its natural greenery and open spaces, offer a private place where the imagination can roam free.

Here is the paragraph, now free of grammatical errors.

A backyard lawn is a wondrous place. It's a place to pitch a badminton net, **and** it's a place to play bocci ball. You can even sunbathe there in a lounge chair when the sun is warm. If **you** desire, you can rake up piles of leaves in autumn and jump! You can collect pinecones in the yard and use them for crafts projects, scented fireplace crackle, or ~~arranging~~ natural centerpieces. A backyard, with its natural greenery and open spaces, **offers** a private place where the imagination can roam free.

SUMMARY: HIGH SCORER'S STRATEGY ACRONYM
总结：高分得主的应试策略缩写

- Do you like puzzles, acrostics, or anagrams?
- Do you like to remember things by making lists of items that spell out a word or name? In other words, do you find acronyms helpful?
- Do you like to picture things in your mind's eye?
- Do you daydream in detail or vivid color?

If so, visualize the "word picture" below. The initial letters of the eight strategies for writing an essay spell out "THE ESSAY."

T	**ake** inventory of the author's use of evidence, reasoning, and stylistic elements.
H	**ave** a timing plan: 10-35-5.
E	**ngage** your reader.
E	**dit**, using the 1600 Club Checklist.
S	**upport** your thesis with examples.
S	**entence** and vocabulary variety
A	**ssess** what you have written.
Y	**our** voice

ESSAY SCORING GUIDE 短文写作评分指南

The student's written response to the source text will be read and evaluated by two raters, or graders. Each grader will give 1 to 4 points each in these three categories: reading, analysis, and writing. Next, the raters' individual scores will be combined for a total of 2 to 8 points in each category.

In scoring the essay, graders will use the criteria indicated in the following rubric, which explains the characteristics shared by essays earning the same score point within each of the three categories, as indicated.

Score Point	Reading	Analysis	Writing
4	**Advanced:** The essay demonstrates thorough understanding of the source text. The essay shows an understanding of the source text's main idea(s) and of most important details and how they relate to one another. The essay is free of factual errors or interpretation with regard to the source text. The essay skillfully uses textual evidence (paraphrases, quotations, facts, or both), demonstrating a complete understanding of the text provided.	**Advanced:** The essay expresses an insightful analysis of the source text, demonstrating a sophisticated level of understanding of the text analysis. The essay offers a thorough and thoughtful evaluation of the author's use of reasoning, evidence, and/or stylistic and persuasive aspects, and/or feature(s) selected by the student. The response contains relevant, sufficient, and strategically chosen support for claim(s) or point(s) made. The essay focuses consistently on those features of the source text that are most notable and relevant to addressing the task.	**Advanced:** The essay is cohesive, demonstrating a highly effective command of and use of language. The essay includes a specific central claim. The response includes a skillful introduction and conclusion. The response demonstrates a deliberate and highly effective progression of ideas both within paragraphs and throughout the essay. The response has a wide variety in sentence structures. The response demonstrates a consistent use of precise word choice. The response maintains a formal style and objective tone. The essay reveals an effective and strong command of standard written English and is free, or virtually free, of grammatical and mechanical errors.

Score Point	Reading	Analysis	Writing
3	**Proficient:** The response shows a clear and effective understanding of the source text. The essay exhibits a clear understanding of the text's central idea(s) and important details. The response lacks substantive errors of fact and interpretation with respect to the source text provided. The response makes appropriate use of textual evidence (quotations, statistics, references, paraphrases, or both), demonstrating an understanding of the source text.	**Proficient:** The response offers an effective analysis of the source text provided and demonstrates an understanding of the analytical task. The essay skillfully evaluates the author's use of evidence, reasoning, and/or persuasive and stylistic/rhetorical elements, and/or feature(s) chosen by the student writer. The response contains pertinent and sufficient support for main claim(s) or point(s) made. The response focuses primarily on those features of the text that are most relevant to the essay writing task.	**Proficient:** The response is, for the most part, cohesive and demonstrates effective use and command of language. The essay includes a main or central claim or an implicit controlling idea. The response includes an effective introduction and conclusion. The essay demonstrates a logical flow and progression of ideas both within paragraphs and throughout the essay as a whole. The response has sentence variety. The essay demonstrates effective diction. The response maintains a formal style and objective tone. The response shows a good control of the conventions of standard written English and is free of significant errors that detract from the quality of writing.

Score Point	Reading	Analysis	Writing
2	**Partial:** The essay demonstrates some comprehension of the provided source text. The response shows an understanding of the text's central idea(s) but not of the relevant and important details. The response may contain errors of fact and/or interpretation with regard to the text. The essay makes restricted, minimal, and/or haphazard use of textual evidence (allusions, data, quotations, paraphrases, or both), demonstrating some understanding of the source text.	**Partial:** The response offers limited analysis of the source text and demonstrates only partial understanding of the analytical task. The response identifies and attempts to describe the author's use of evidence, logical reasoning, and/or stylistic and persuasive elements, and/or feature(s) of the student's own choosing, but merely asserts rather than explains their importance, or one or more aspects of the response's analysis are unwarranted based on the text. The response contains little or no support for claim(s) or point(s) made. The essay may be without a clear focus on features of the text that are most notable to addressing the task.	**Partial:** The response demonstrates little or no cohesion and limited skill in the use and control of language. The response may lack a clear premise (or central claim) or controlling idea, or the essay may digress from the claim or idea over the course of the written response. The response may include an ineffective introduction and/or conclusion. The response may demonstrate some progression of ideas within paragraphs but not throughout the response. The response has limited variety in sentence structures; sentence structures may be repetitive. The essay uses weak (general or vague) diction; word choice may be redundant. The response may deviate markedly from a standard (or formal type) of writing style and objective tone. The essay demonstrates a weak or limited control of mechanical and grammatical standards of written English and contains errors that detract from the effectiveness of the writing and may obscure understanding.

Score Point	Reading	Analysis	Writing
1	**Inadequate:** The response demonstrates little or no comprehension of the source text. The response fails to show an understanding of the text's central idea(s) and may include only details without reference to central idea(s). The response may contain numerous errors of fact and/or interpretation with regard to the text. The response makes little or no use of textual evidence (quotations, paraphrases, or both), demonstrating little or no understanding of the source text.	**Inadequate:** The response offers little or no analysis or ineffective analysis of the source text and demonstrates little or no understanding of the analytic task. The response identifies without explanation some aspects of the author's use of evidence, reasoning, and/or stylistic and persuasive (rhetorical) elements, and/or feature(s) of the student's choosing. Or numerous aspects of the response's analysis are unjustifiable based on the text. The response contains little or no support for claim(s) or point(s) made, or support is largely irrelevant. The response may lack focus on qualities and elements of the text that are relevant to addressing the task. Or the essay provides no apparent analysis (for example, it is primarily or exclusively summary).	**Inadequate:** The response demonstrates little or no cohesion and inadequate skill in the use and control of language. The response may lack a clear central claim or controlling idea. The response lacks a recognizable introduction and conclusion. The response does not have a discernible progression of ideas. The response lacks variety in sentence structures; sentence structures may be repetitive. The response demonstrates general and vague word choice; word choice may be awkward, poor, or ineffective. The essay may lack a style that is objective in tone and/or formal in its writing style. The response shows an inept or weak control of the conventions of standard written English and may contain several and various errors that weaken the quality of the essay.

第六章 Chapter 6

SAMPLE SOURCE TEXTS 范例文章

What follows are sample source texts that could be provided for student analysis on the essay portion of the SAT. The actual source text will not be revealed to test takers until test day. Familiarize yourself with the essay directions to give yourself a heads-up on test day.

Directions: This is your opportunity to show that you can read and understand a passage and write an analysis of that passage. Be sure your essay demonstrates a clear and logical analysis of the passage, using precise language.

On the actual test, you will write your essay on the lines provided in your answer booklet; for now, write your essay on a lined paper. Remember to write or print legibly so that others can read what you've written.

You have 50 minutes to read the essay and write a response to the prompt provided.

Source Text 1

As you read the passage below, consider how the author uses

- Evidence, such as examples and facts, to support claims.
- Reasoning to develop his thoughts and to connect his ideas and claims with evidence.
- Rhetorical (stylistic) or persuasive features, such as diction (word choice) or appeals to emotion, to add power to his expressed ideas.

Department of Education Releases New Parent and Community Engagement Framework

1 The fourth quarter of the school year is generally a time of preparation for schools and districts as they finalize next year's budget, student and teacher schedules, and professional development for the upcoming school year. During this time of preparation, it is important that schools and districts discuss ways that they can support parents and the community in helping students to achieve success.

Annotate the passage, underlining and circling examples of any persuasive devices that you can find.

2 To help in this work, the U.S. Department of Education is proud to release a framework for schools and the broader communities they serve to build parent and community engagement. Across the country, less than a quarter of residents are eighteen years old or younger, and all of us have a responsibility for helping our schools succeed. The Dual Capacity framework, a process used to teach school and district staff to effectively engage parents and for parents to work successfully with the schools to increase student achievement, provides a model that schools and districts can use to build the type of effective community engagement that will make schools the center of our communities.

3 An example of how the elements of the framework can lead to improved engagement is exhibited in my hometown of Baltimore. Baltimore City Public Schools worked to support 12,000 pre-kindergarten and kindergarten homes, and to engage families in home-based literacy practices. Each week students received a different bag filled with award-winning children's books, exposing children, on average, to more than 100 books per year. The book rotation also includes parent training and information on how to share books effectively to promote children's early literacy skills and nurture a love of learning. Through the program, families are also connected with their local public and school libraries. At the culmination of the program, children receive a permanent bag to keep and continue the practice of borrowing books and building a lifelong habit of reading.

4 For more information on the Dual Capacity Framework, as well as an introductory video from Secretary of Education Arne Duncan, please take some time and review our website at *www.ed.gov/family-and-community-engagement*. In the coming months, we will provide additional resources and information, so that schools, districts, communities, and parents can learn more about family and community engagement, as well as, share the wonderful work they are doing to build parent, school, and community capacity that supports all students.

Source: *www.ed.gov/blog/2014*, accessed June 7, 2015.

Write an essay in which you explain how the author presents and structures an argument to persuade his audience that the Dual Capacity Framework supports student achievement. In your essay, analyze how the author uses one or more of the features listed above (or features of your own choice) to strengthen the logic and persuasiveness of his argument. Be sure that your analysis focuses on the most relevant elements of the passage.

Your essay should not explain whether you agree with the author's claims, but rather it should explain how the author builds an argument to persuade his audience.

Source Text 2

As you read the passage below, consider how the author uses

- Evidence, such as examples and facts, to support claims.
- Reasoning to develop his thoughts and to connect his ideas and claims with evidence.
- Rhetorical (stylistic) or persuasive features, such as diction (word choice) or appeals to emotion, to add power to his expressed ideas.

Adapted from a recent online article, "Unlocking Our Nation's Wind Potential," published at energy.gov, this passage explores the possibility of making wind power a cost-effective energy source nationwide.

1 Wind is an important source of clean, affordable American energy. Wind power supplies nearly five percent of our nation's electricity demand across 39 states, and it's getting cheaper every year thanks to new strides in wind technology and policy. Since the 1980s, the cost of deploying wind energy has dropped by 90 percent. Meanwhile, further improvements are poised to make wind economical in every state.

2 An Energy Department report released today shows how the next generation of wind turbines could make reliable, cost-effective wind power a reality in all 50 states. Wind turbines harness energy in the wind that turns two or three propeller-like blades around a rotor. The rotor is connected to the main shaft, which spins a generator to create electricity. Wind turbines are mounted on a tower to capture the most energy. At 100 feet (thirty meters) or more above ground, they can take advantage of faster and less turbulent wind. Wind turbines can be used to produce electricity for a single home or building, or they can be connected to an electricity grid for more widespread electricity distribution.

3 The Energy Department report, Enabling Wind Power Nationwide, explains that advanced wind turbines with taller towers and longer blades will allow us to reach stronger, more consistent winds found high above the ground, unlocking wind energy's potential across an additional 700,000 square miles—roughly one-fifth of the land area of the United States.

4 These new taller wind towers are marvels of human ingenuity and engineering savvy. Developed by the Energy Department and industry partners, these technological wonders stand 110 to 140 meters tall in "hub height" (calculated at the center of the rotor), up to 1½ times the height of the Statue of Liberty. Their immense scale lets them take advantage of better wind resources, unobstructed by things like trees and buildings—and with blades longer than 60 meters, they can generate electricity more efficiently than ever before.

5 This is a big deal for wind power in America. Larger, more efficient wind turbines will create new opportunities for wind energy generation and job growth in places like the southeastern U.S., where wind speeds are generally low.

6 The combination of technological advances and additional wind energy deployments will continue to make wind power cheaper for millions of Americans, helping reduce greenhouse gas emissions as a part of our nation's robust clean energy portfolio. Our online Wind Vision Report explores how wind energy could support 600,000 American jobs and supply up to thirty-five percent of the nation's power by 2050.

7 What will the wind industry look like in the years ahead? New reports highlight a robust wind energy future. Additional wind generation will mean increasingly cost-effective, low-carbon electricity for millions of Americans. To learn more about next-generation wind technology, visit the Energy Department's Office of Energy Efficiency and Renewable Energy's Wind Program Research and Development website, where you can explore the future of wind in America with an interactive wind vision map. Related articles of interest include "Wind Vision: A New Era for Wind Power in the United States."

Source: *http://energy.gov/eere/articles/unlocking-our-nation-s-wind-potential.* Originally published May 19, 2015; accessed June 3, 2015.

Write an essay in which you explain how the author presents and structures an argument to persuade his audience that wind power technology can provide a robust, affordable energy to the United States. In your essay, analyze how the author uses one or more of the features listed above (or features of your own choice) to strengthen the logic and persuasiveness of his argument. Be sure that your analysis focuses on the most relevant elements of the passage.

Your essay should not explain whether you agree with the author's claims, but rather it should explain how the author builds an argument to persuade his audience.

Source Text 3

As you read the passage below, consider how the author uses

- Evidence, such as examples and facts, to support claims.
- Reasoning to develop his thoughts and to connect his ideas and claims with evidence.
- Rhetorical (stylistic) or persuasive features, such as diction (word choice) or appeals to emotion, to add power to his expressed ideas.

Adapted from an article on epa.gov, the following article provides EPA Administrator Gina McCarthy's statement on the historic Kigali Agreement. Be sure to read the text carefully and to annotate the document while taking an inventory of the author's most powerful, persuasive, and figurative devices.

Statement from EPA Administrator Gina McCarthy on Historic Kigali Agreement

1 This week, nearly 200 nations came together to take a historic step in combatting climate change. After years of hard work and difficult negotiations, a global commitment to protecting our planet brought us to this moment. Amending the Montreal Protocol will significantly phase down HFCs and avoid up to a half-degree centigrade of warming by the end of the century.

2 While we have seen many significant successes under President Obama's leadership in fighting climate change, this day will unquestionably be remembered as one of the most important in our effort to save the one planet we have. It is truly an exciting time for all of us who have worked so hard to achieve this new level of success, and as head of the U.S. delegation, I could not be more delighted with the outcome of the negotiations and our collective resolve. The prospects for the future of our planet are bright.

3 Protecting the air we breathe and slowing the effects of climate change are a core part of EPA's mission. And today, I am proud to say that we, alongside nearly every country on Earth, have taken another historic step in carrying out that mission by cutting down on the use of damaging hydrofluorocarbons, or HFCs.

4 Countries, including the United States, have long used HFCs to meet their refrigeration and air conditioning needs. These greenhouse gases can have warming impacts hundreds to thousands of times more potent than carbon dioxide. In a nutshell, these HFCs cool our homes and chill our food, but they are turning up the temperature of our planet.

5 And over the next several years, HFC use is expected to not only grow—but multiply. Their emissions are increasing by 10 to 15 percent on an annual basis globally. That's why, this week in Rwanda, world leaders took a giant leap forward by agreeing to a global phase-down of these harmful gases. As head of the U.S. delegation to the Meeting of the Parties to the Montreal Protocol, I met with leaders from around the world who share a commitment to protecting the planet and scaling down these harmful gases. Together, joined by Secretary of State John Kerry, we agreed to take action and get the job done. And that's exactly what we did.

6 The Montreal Protocol, a successful global environmental agreement, is already putting the world on track to heal the Earth's ozone layer by mid-century. And this week, 197 countries agreed on an ambitious amendment that will help protect Earth's climate by significantly reducing the consumption and production of HFCs.

7 By acting now, we're avoiding up to a full half a degree centigrade of warming by the end of the century. This is a big deal, because our scientists

say very clearly that we must keep our planet's temperature from rising 2 degrees above our normal temperature. And today's announcement brings us that much closer to avoiding that "point of no return."

8 We're also agreeing to devote more resources to finding and using safer, more climate-friendly alternatives. And we're building on the significant gains we've already made to protect ourselves and our children from the dangerous effects of climate change. At EPA, we're doing our part to cut down on HFCs here at home.

9 Just two weeks ago, we finalized two rules that will reduce the use and emissions of HFCs. The first—under our Significant New Alternatives Policy (SNAP) program—adds new alternatives to the list of acceptable substitutes for HFCs. It also sets deadlines to completely stop using HFCs in certain applications where safer alternatives are available. The second rule strengthens our current refrigerant management practices and extends them to include HFCs.

10 This week has truly been historic. Our global commitment to protecting our planet brought us to this moment. It's an exciting time for all of us who have worked so hard to get here. And while we have seen many significant successes under President Obama's leadership in tackling climate change, this day will be remembered as one of the most important. I was proud to represent the United States in Rwanda this week. There is no doubt in my mind that U.S. leadership was essential to reaching this agreement.

11 Yes, there will be challenges ahead. But the past week reminds us that when faced with clear science, when buoyed by the strong partnership of developed and developing countries working together, we can make great strides to protect the one planet we have.

Source: *www.epa.gov/newsreleases/statement-blog-epa-administrator-gina-mccarthy-historic-kigali-agreement*. Originally published October 15, 2016; accessed March 8, 2017.

Write an essay in which you explain how McCarthy structures and presents an argument to persuade her audience that combatting the ill effects of climate change is urgent. In your essay, analyze how the author uses one or more of the features listed above (or features and devices of your own choice) to strengthen the logic and persuasiveness of her argument. Be sure that your analysis focuses on the most relevant elements of the passage.

Your essay should not explain whether you agree with the author's claims, but rather it should explain how the author builds an argument to persuade her audience.

See page 459 for sample responses to all three source texts.

第四部分 PART 4

THE MATH SECTIONS 数学

GETTING STARTED

STRATEGIES FOR SOLVING SAT MATH PROBLEMS

1600 CLUB BACKGROUND TOPICS

PROBLEMS IN CONTEXT

HEART OF ALGEBRA

PROBLEM SOLVING AND DATA ANALYSIS

PASSPORT TO ADVANCED MATH

ADDITIONAL TOPICS IN MATH

第七章 Chapter 7

GETTING STARTED 开始

The SAT Math Test has changed in a big way. Grab on to your calculators and double down on your concentration in math and statistics classes because the updated SAT calls on all of your algebra skills, as well as your ability to analyze data in graphs and tables.

This book is aimed at students who aspire to a score of 1600—the 1600 Club. The fact that you are in this group means that you are good at math and can probably answer most of the SAT Math questions without too much exertion. To join the 1600 Club, however, you need to crack the new types of questions, as well as the more difficult questions at the end of the math sections. This part of the book provides strategies and practice for doing just that.

Before you even start the test, you can take steps to increase your chances of a perfect score.

1600 Club Strategies Before and During the Test
1600分俱乐部测试前和测试中策略

Strategy 1:	**S**tudy the basics and know each topic in this book.
Strategy 2:	**T**rain yourself on grid-ins. Learn the do's and don'ts.
Strategy 3:	**R**eview the formulas that precede the math sections.
Strategy 4:	**A**cquire awareness of question difficulty in the spectrum of questions.
Strategy 5:	**T**reat the test booklet as your own. Feel free to scribble in it.
Strategy 6:	**E**ducated guessing is a must if you don't know the answer.
Strategy 7:	**G**raphing calculators rule. Practice on the calculator you will use for the SAT.
Strategy 8:	**Y**es to learning all the types of questions!

MATH ON THE SAT SAT中的数学

Altogether there are 80 minutes of math on the SAT: a 55-minute section with 38 questions in which you are allowed—but not required—to use a calculator and one 25-minute section where no calculator is allowed. The questions are either multiple choice, where you select one of four answers, or grid-in, where you provide an answer in a small grid (more later).

Your total possible math score is 800. The College Board will report three subscores for your math test:

1. The Heart of Algebra
2. Problem Solving and Data Analysis
3. Passport to Advanced Math

The tricky brain-teaser, contest-type arithmetic questions of the past are gone. In a nutshell, here are what those categories (above) entail.

- The Heart of Algebra is an in-depth knowledge of linear equations and their applications (35 percent of the test).
- Problem Solving and Data Analysis involves ratios, percentages, and other quantitative relationships, as represented in graphs and tables (28 percent of the test).
- Passport to Advanced Math is the solution of problems by manipulating algebraic expressions or polynomials of second degree (or higher) (27 percent of the test).

There are some additional topics you'll be expected to know—geometry, trigonometry, volumes, etc. (10 percent of the test).

EASY VERSUS HARD QUESTIONS 简单题目与复杂题目

Here are some "bread and butter" questions, the type that 1600 students must get right, no *ifs, ands,* or *buts*. Try them.

Questions 题目

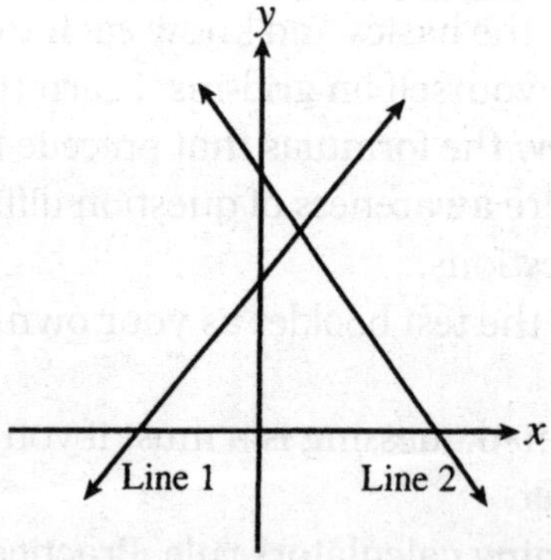

1. Consider two lines in the *xy*-plane, as shown above. If line 1 has equation $y = m_1x + b_1$, and line 2 has equation $y = m_2x + b_2$, which is a true statement?

(A) $m_1 < m_2$

(B) $b_1 < b_2$

(C) $b_2 < 0$

(D) $m_2 > 0$

2. Three friends start an international club that meets monthly. To increase membership, they decide that at the next meeting, each member will bring a friend, and at each subsequent meeting for the next 6 months, each member will bring a new member. For this plan, which of the following graphs, for $x > 0$, represents the number of members after x meetings?

(A)

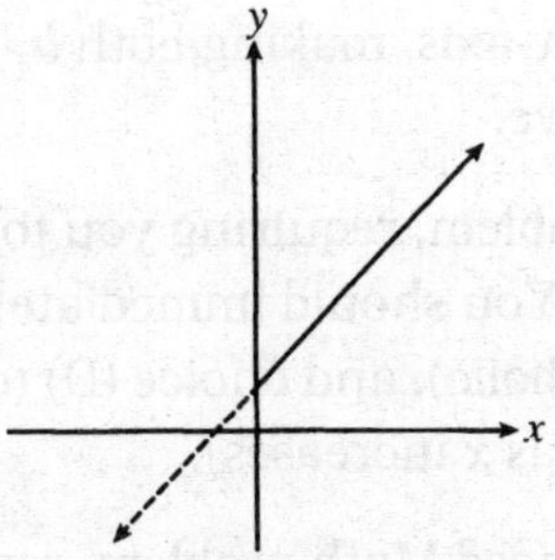

(C)

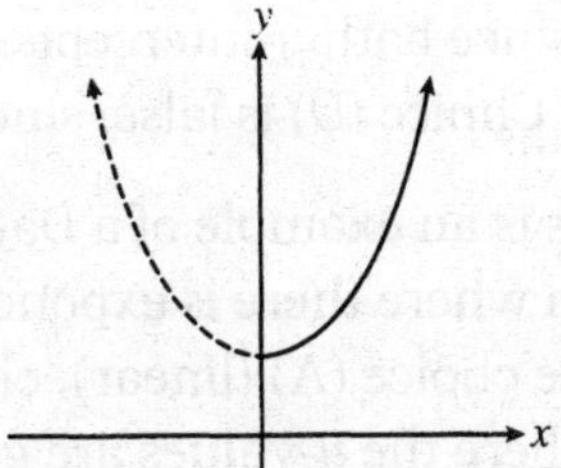

(B)

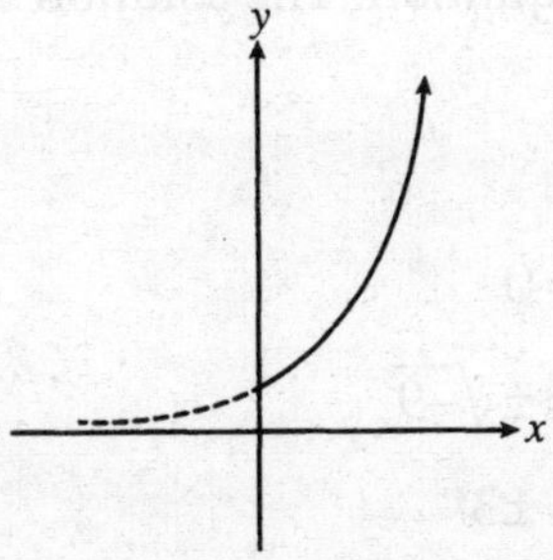

(D)

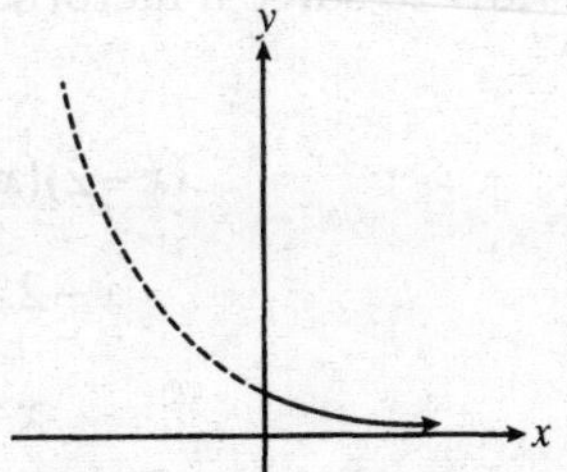

3. Which is true of the function $f(x) = (x - 2)(x^2 + 9)$?

(A) It has no real roots.
(B) It has 3 real roots.
(C) It has 1 real root and 2 complex roots.
(D) It has 3 complex roots.

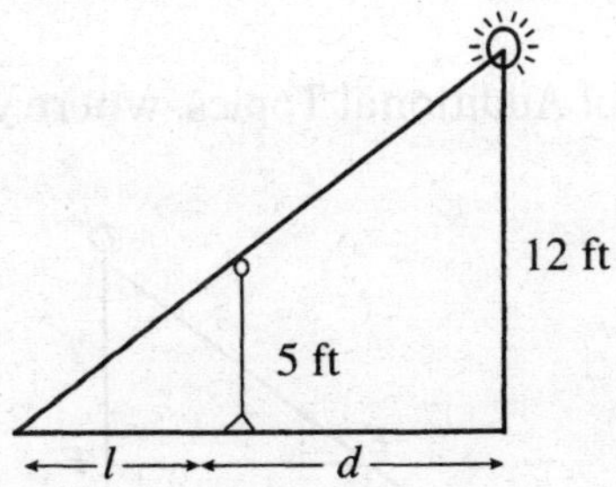

4. A woman 5 feet tall stands near a street lamp that is 12 feet tall, as shown in the figure above. Find a formula that expresses ℓ, the length of her shadow, in terms of d, her distance from the base of the lamp.

(A) $\ell = \frac{5}{12}d$

(B) $\ell = \frac{5}{13}d$

(C) $\ell = \frac{5}{7}d$

(D) $\ell = \frac{12}{13}d$

Solutions 解答

1. **(B)** This is an example of a Heart of Algebra problem, requiring you to know the graphical features of a linear equation. b_1 and b_2 are the y-intercepts of lines 1 and 2, respectively. Since line 1 cuts the y-axis at a lower point than line 2, $b_1 < b_2$. Choice (A) is false: m_1 and m_2 are the slopes of line 1 and line 2. Since line 1 has a positive slope and line 2 a negative slope, $m_1 > m_2$. Choice (C) is false, since both y-intercepts are above the x-axis, making both b_1 and b_2 positive. Choice (D) is false, since m_2 is negative.

2. **(B)** This is an example of a Data Analysis problem, requiring you to recognize a situation where there is exponential growth. You should immediately be able to eliminate choice (A) (linear), choice (C) (parabolic), and choice (D) (exponential *decay*, where the y-values are getting smaller as x increases).

3. **(C)** This is an example of a Passport to Advanced Math problem, requiring you to know how to solve a factored polynomial equation. The solution would be as follows:

$$(x-2)(x^2+9)=0$$

$$x-2=0 \text{ or } x^2+9=0$$

$$x=2 \text{ or } \quad x=\pm\sqrt{-9}$$

$$x=2 \text{ or } \quad x=\pm 3i$$

You shouldn't have to solve this equation to see that there are two complex roots. As soon as you get x^2 is equal to a negative number, you should understand that this will give two complex roots.

The 1600 Club tries to save time on every problem.

4. **(C)** This is an example of Additional Topics, where you should recognize similar triangles.

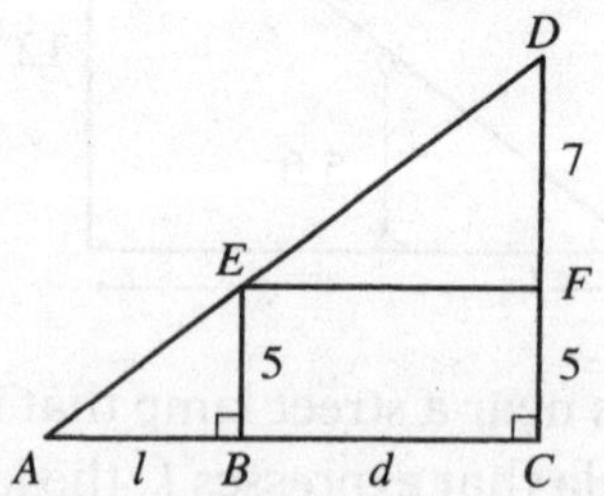

Refer to the diagram above.
Use the fact that $\triangle EAB$ is similar to $\triangle DEF$.

$$\therefore \frac{5}{\ell}=\frac{7}{d}$$

$$7\ell = 5d$$

$$\ell=\frac{5}{7}d$$

Alternatively, use the fact that $\triangle EAB$ is similar to $\triangle DAC$.

$$\therefore \frac{5}{\ell}=\frac{12}{\ell+d}$$

$$5(\ell+d)=12\ell$$

$$7\ell=5d$$

$$\ell=\frac{5}{7}d$$

What makes these questions easy is that each deals with one clearly defined topic that you should have mastered long ago. You can also get the answers without too much calculation, or maybe even solve them at a glance. The harder questions may dip into more than one topic or require more specialized knowledge or need more in-depth calculation.

Here are four questions that are similar to those above, but considerably harder. Try them!

Questions 题目

1. $16x=12\left(x+\frac{1}{6}\right)$

Jay V left his house at 2:00 P.M. and rode his bicycle down his street at a speed of 12 mph (miles per hour). When his friend Tamika arrived at his house at 2:10 P.M., Jay V's mother sent her off in Jay V's direction down the same street, and Tamika cycled after him at 16 mph. At what time did Tamika catch up with Jay V?

The equation above is used to solve this problem. What is the term $12\left(x+\frac{1}{6}\right)$ equal to?

(A) The time, in hours, Tamika took to catch up with Jay V
(B) The time, in hours, Jay V cycled before Tamika caught up with him
(C) The distance, in miles, traveled by Tamika
(D) The average speed, in miles per hour, of Tamika and Jay V

2. Let $f(x) = 2^{-x}$ and $g(x) = 4 \cdot 2^{-x}$. Which is true?

(A) $g(x) = f(x-2)$
(B) $g(x) = f(x+2)$
(C) $g(x) = f(x) - 2$
(D) $g(x) = f(x) + 2$

3. In a normal distribution of data, 68% of data values lie within 1 standard deviation of the mean, approximately 95% of data lie within 2 standard deviations of the mean, and 99.7% of data lie within 3 standard deviations of the mean. Suppose a set of data is normally distributed with a mean of 50 and standard deviation of 2. Approximately what percent of the data values are less than or equal to 46?

(A) 16
(B) 13.5
(C) 5
(D) 2.5

4. If $\cos \alpha = \sin \beta$, and $\alpha = \frac{5\pi}{6}$, which could be a value of β?

(A) $-\frac{\pi}{6}$

(B) $\frac{\pi}{6}$

(C) $-\frac{\pi}{3}$

(D) $\frac{\pi}{3}$

Solutions 解答

1. **(C)** This is a Heart of Algebra question, where a linear equation is used to model a context. Suppose x is the time, in hours, taken for Tamika to catch Jay V. Set up an equation using the facts that Jay V and Tamika covered the same distance, and that distance = speed × time.

$$\text{Tamika's distance} = \text{Jay V's distance}$$

$$16x = 12\left(x + \frac{1}{6}\right)$$

Note that Jay V's time in hours was $\left(x + \frac{1}{6}\right)$, where 10 minutes equals $\frac{1}{6}$ hours.

2. **(A)** This is a Heart of Algebra question, where you are expected to know $f(x)$ notation. Try each choice to see which one gives $g(x) = 4 \cdot 2^{-x}$. For choice (A):

$$\begin{aligned} f(x-2) &= 2^{-(x-2)} \\ &= 2^{2-x} \\ &= 2^2 \cdot 2^{-x} \\ &= 4 \cdot 2^{-x} = g(x) \quad \text{Yes!} \end{aligned}$$

3. (D) This is a Data Analysis question in which you're expected to know measures of central tendency and the meaning of "Normal distribution."

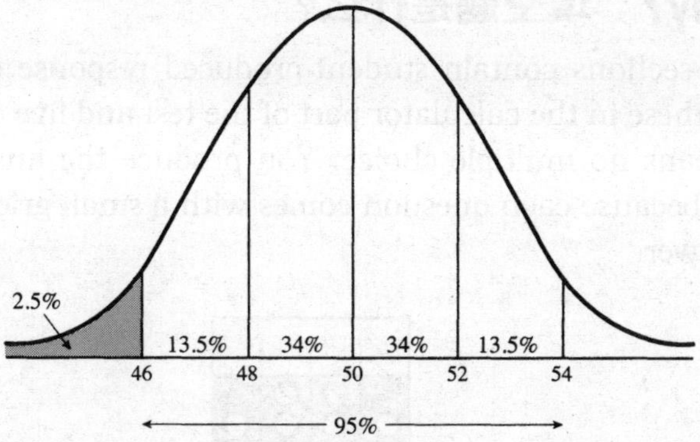

From the figure above, 5% of data values are less than 46 or greater than 54. Half of these are less than 46, namely, 2.5%.

4. (C) This is from Additional Topics, where you must know the trig functions, and, in particular, the cofunction relationship $\cos\theta = \sin\left(\frac{\pi}{2}-\theta\right)$.

$$\cos\frac{5\pi}{6} = \sin\left(\frac{\pi}{2}-\frac{5\pi}{6}\right)$$

$$= \sin\left(\frac{3\pi}{6}-\frac{5\pi}{6}\right)$$

$$= \sin\left(-\frac{2\pi}{6}\right)$$

$$= \sin\left(-\frac{\pi}{3}\right)$$

$$\therefore \beta = -\frac{\pi}{3}$$

GRID-INS 填空题

What Are They? 填空题是什么?

Both of the math sections contain student-produced response questions (grid-ins). There are eight of these in the calculator part of the test and five on the no-calculator part. A grid-in means no multiple choice. You produce the answer. The questions are called grid-ins because each question comes with a small grid, on which you will bubble in your answer.

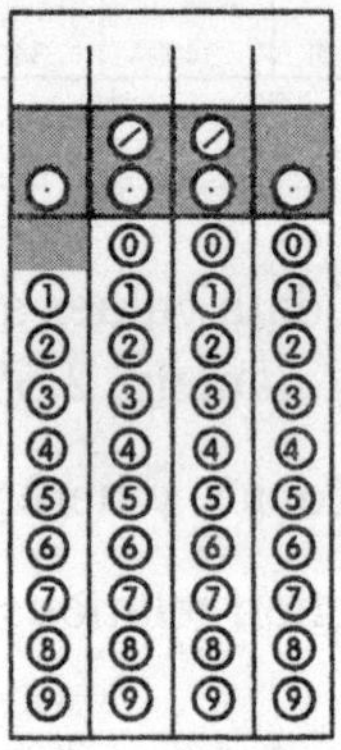

What the Answers Cannot Be 哪些不是答案

Notice on the grid above that the only symbols are the digits 0–9, the decimal point, and the slash. This means that the correct answer will never be negative, contain a variable, or contain a π or % symbol. Nor will the answer ever exceed 9999 or have a zero before the decimal point.

The top row is for you to enter your answer before gridding it in. Don't try to save time by omitting this step.

The 1600 Club avoids a careless mistake by writing the answer at the top of the grid.

Gridding-in Rules 填空题规则

The machine that scores your SAT test will only look at what you bubble in on the grid; so be sure you fill in the grid correctly.

- Stay left! Start your answer in the leftmost column of the grid. This ensures that you will always have room for your answer, and you won't lose precision in decimal answers.
- For each digit that you wrote in the top row, darken the corresponding oval.
- If you have a decimal answer between 0 and 1, for example .72885, don't start with zero. Start with the decimal point, and fill in as many digits as you can. You will get full credit for either .728 or .729. Since you don't need to round your answer, don't do it! Note that both .72 and .73 will be scored as incorrect. You must write as much of the answer as fits on the grid.

- If your answer is a fraction such as $\frac{12}{8}$, you can enter 12/8, 6/4, 3/2, or 1.5. Given that you don't need to reduce fractions, don't bother! What you may *not* do is bubble in your answer as a mixed number. For $1\frac{3}{2}$ you may not enter 11/2, which the machine will read as $\frac{11}{2}$.
- If you get a range of answers for a grid-in question, pick one and enter it. Often a question has more than one correct answer.

Question Difficulty 题目难度

The grid-in questions are at the end of each section of the test in increasing order of difficulty. This information is helpful to 1600 scorers. If the answer to the last question seems obvious to you at first glance, reread the question to spot what you're missing.

Scoring 得分

There is no penalty for a wrong answer, so guess if you can.

Final Tip 最后提示

Don't commit the crime of getting the answer right and the gridding-in wrong.

1600 Club members concentrate as if their lives depend on gridding-in their answers correctly.

Example 1

A soccer ball is kicked upward from ground level with an initial velocity of 52 feet per second. The function $h(t) = -16t^2 + 52t$ gives the ball's height, in feet, after t seconds. For how many seconds, to the nearest tenth of a second, is the ball at least 20 feet above the ground?

Solution: The answer is 2.4. This is a Passport to Advanced Math question, where you're expected to know the quadratic function.

Method I: Graphing Calculator

The function $h(t)$ is a quadratic function whose graph is a concave down parabola. You want to find the two values of t, t_1 and t_2, for which $h(t) = 20$, and then subtract them. The shaded region below shows where height h is greater than or equal to 20.

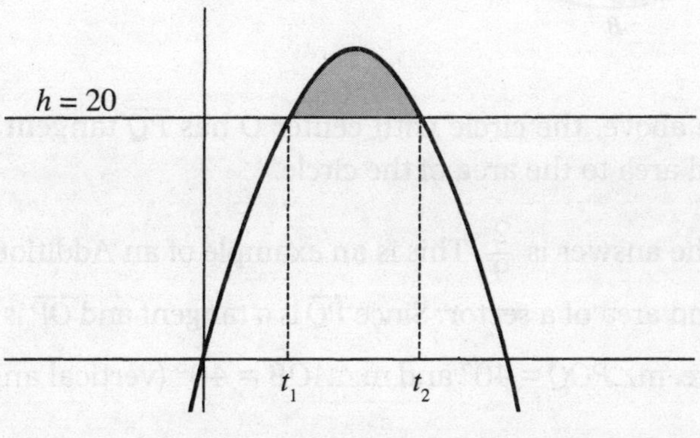

When you use the Intersect feature of the CALC menu to find t_1 and t_2, you should get the values .4457 and 2.804.

$$2.804 - .4457 \approx 2.4$$

Grid-in 2.4.

Method II: Quadratic Formula

You want to find the values of t for which $20 \geq -16t^2 + 52t$, namely, $4t^2 - 13t + 5 \geq 0$. Find the roots of $4t^2 - 13t + 5 = 0$:

$$t = \frac{-(-13) \pm \sqrt{(-13)^2 - (4)(4)(5)}}{2(4)}$$

$$= \frac{13 \pm \sqrt{89}}{8}$$

$$\approx 2.80 \text{ and } 0.45$$

Subtracting these values gives approximately 2.4.

Grid-in 2.4.

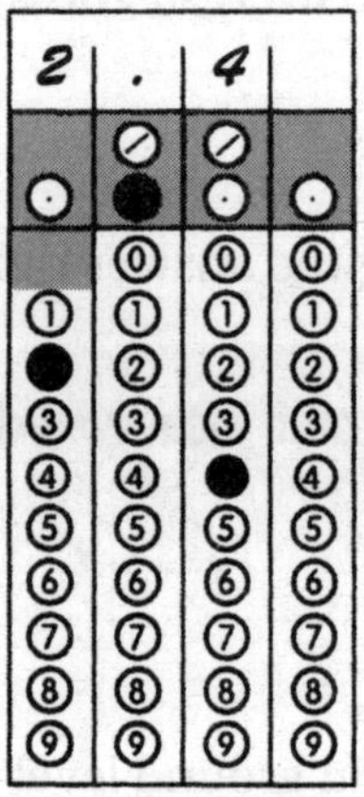

Example 2

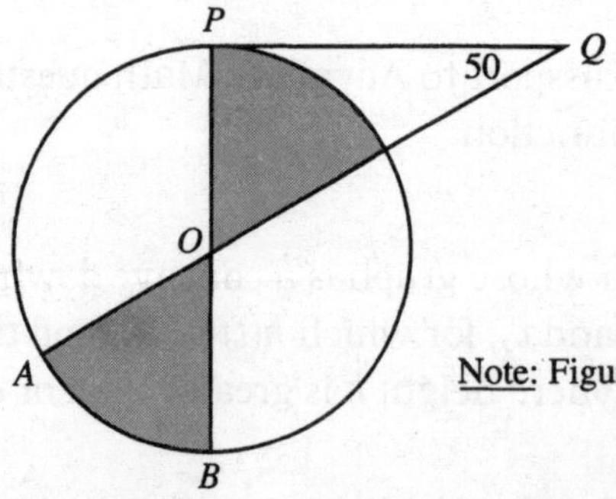

Note: Figure not drawn to scale.

In the figure above, the circle with center O has $\overline{PQ}$ tangent to it at P. Find the ratio of the shaded area to the area of the circle.

Solution: The answer is $\frac{2}{9}$. This is an example of an Additional Topic question: circle geometry and area of a sector. Since $\overline{PQ}$ is a tangent and $\overline{OP}$ is a radius, $\overline{PQ} \perp \overline{OP}$. Therefore, $m\angle POQ = 40°$ and $m\angle AOB = 40°$ (vertical angles are congruent). Each shaded sector is $\frac{40}{360} = \frac{1}{9}$ of the circle area. Therefore, the ratio of the shaded area to the area of the circle is $2\left(\frac{1}{9}\right) = \frac{2}{9}$.

Grid-in either 2/9 or .222.

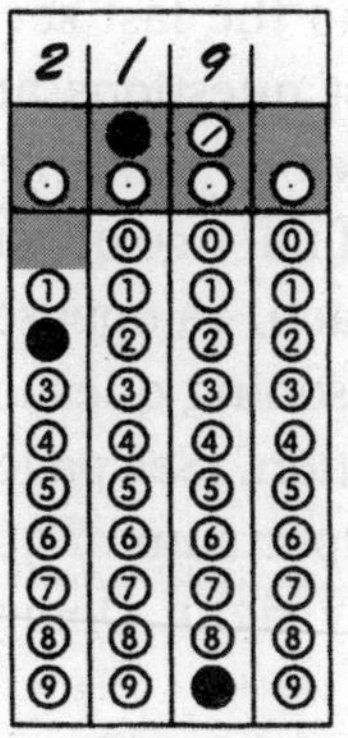

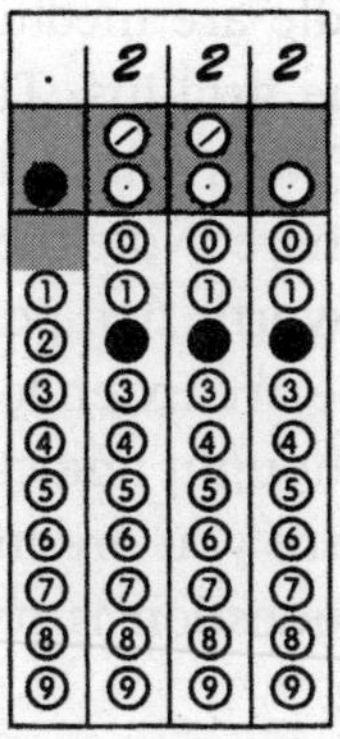

Example 3

The following table, from the U.S. Census Bureau, shows the median annual earnings in 1999 of workers with different levels of education.

Median Annual Earnings (Ages 21–64)

Level of Education	Median Annual Earnings ($)
Not a high school graduate	21,332
High school graduate	27,351
Some college	31,988
Bachelor's degree	42,877
Advanced degree	55,242

By what percent did the median annual earnings of a high school graduate (with no further education) exceed those of someone who was not a high school graduate?

Solution: The answer is 28.2. This is a Data Analysis question, where you must use data from a table to do a calculation. The table shows that for a high school graduate the median earning was $27,351, while for a nongraduate it was $21,332. The difference is $27{,}351 - 21{,}332 = 6019$. The percent by which this difference exceeds 21,332 is $\frac{6019}{21{,}332} \cdot 100 = 28.2$.

Grid-in 28.2.

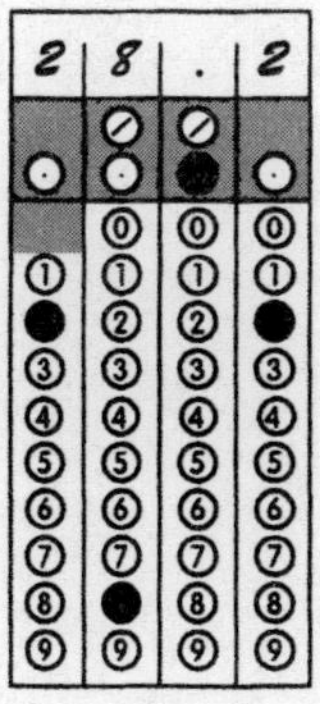

TIPS FOR THE SAT MATH SECTIONS SAT数学部分的提示

Question Difficulty 题目难度

The SAT Math questions in a given section get incrementally harder from start to finish. You may assume that the first few questions in the beginning are considered easy, those in the middle are medium, and the last several questions are hard. The same holds true for the grid-ins. The first questions are easy, the middle ones are medium, and the final few are hard. It therefore makes sense to start at question 1 and proceed in order from there. Note that the final two questions in the grid-in part of the calculator section are worth two points each, as opposed to the one-point questions that came before. These are Extended Reasoning questions that will almost certainly need a fair amount of thought and calculation. (See page 230.)

Keep track of where you are in the spectrum of questions. Picking an intuitive answer for an "easy" question is probably right. Doing so for a "hard" question is almost certainly wrong.

Don't get bogged down on any one question. Circle it in your booklet, and return to it if you have time.

The 1600 Club warms up on the easy questions, gathers steam on the medium ones, and leaves time to crack the hard ones at the end.

Guessing 猜测

There are no deductions for wrong answers! This means it pays to guess.

Be aware that to get an 800 score for math you need to answer just about every question correctly. Leaving more than one answer blank gives you no chance.

Suppose you're bogged down on one of the "hard" multiple-choice questions and just can't see a way to solve it. You can improve your guessing odds by eliminating any answer choice that seems obvious. Also eliminate an answer choice that contains a number given in the problem statement. These choices are distracters, meant to trap you.

If you must guess, don't dither. Guess and move on.

The Test Booklet 测试小册

The test booklet is yours, so use it! Cross off the wrong choices in the multiple-choice questions. Circle the questions you need to return to. Make diagrams where relevant. Write on the diagrams that are provided. (Don't waste time redrawing!)

After your booklet has been collected, no one will look in it again.

Your Answer Sheet 答题纸

The answer sheet, unlike the test booklet, is all important.

Since the scoring machine is very sensitive, beware of stray marks on your answer sheet. When you erase an answer, be sure to do it thoroughly.

Now consider the following nightmare scenario: You leave out a question, circle it in your answer booklet, and move on. You get so involved in the remaining problems that you fail to leave a blank on your answer sheet for the omitted question. *As a result, every subsequent answer is off by 1 in the grid.*

You are smart enough to understand what a disaster this would be. You must make sure that it doesn't happen.

One way of avoiding this problem is to transfer your answers in groups of five. Toward the end of the set, enter one at a time to guarantee that every question you answered gets bubbled on the answer sheet.

The 1600 Club really, really concentrates when filling in the answer sheet.

Calculators 计算器

You will need a graphing calculator for the calculator part of the SAT Math Test. You should bring the one you're comfortable with, the one you've been using in your math classes these past couple of years.

Please note that there are restrictions on the use of calculators. You are not allowed to use any of the following items as a calculator:

- Laptop or a portable/hand-held computer
- Calculator that has QWERTY (keyboard-like) keypad, uses an electrical outlet, makes noise, or has a paper tape
- Electronic writing pad or pen-input/stylus-driven device
- Pocket organizer
- Calculator function on a mobile phone

How to Use the Graphing Calculator 如何使用图表计算器

The discussion below refers to the TI-84 Plus graphing calculator. All graphing calculators, however, have similar features. Be sure to know your own calculator!

What follows is not a comprehensive manual. It assumes that you are familiar with your own graphing calculator and summarizes features that may be useful for the SAT. You probably know a lot more than what is presented here!

1. The [MODE] button shows all the default settings highlighted on the left. You should select Degree or Radian for the angle mode, depending on which is used in the question.

2. The "top" level of the calculator is where you will do arithmetic calculations and work with trig functions.

3. The [$y=$] button accesses the window where you will type the formulas for functions whose graphs you want to view. The functions must be in the form $y=$. For example, if you want to graph $2x-y=5$, you need to rewrite the equation as $y=2x-5$ before you can type it in. You must use the [X, T, θ, *n*] button for x and the [−] button for subtraction. The [(−)] button is for negation.

   Example: Here's how you would type in $y=-(x-4)^2$:

   [$y=$], [(−)], [(], [X, T, θ, *n*], [−], [4], [)], [x^2].

4. The [2nd] button allows you to access the "blue" functions. Thus, [2nd] [x^2] gets you the radical sign, $\sqrt{\ }$, since it appears in blue above the [x^2] button.

   Example: Here's how you would enter $y=\sqrt{2x-3}$:

   [$y=$], [2nd], [x^2], [2], [X, T, θ, *n*], [−], [3].

No closing parenthesis is required.

5. The [GRAPH] button gives you the graphing window, with both x- and y-axes ranging from −10 to 10. Your graph should appear.

6. The [WINDOW] button allows you to change the range of numbers on the x- and y-axes. Be sure to use the negation key, [(−)], for negative numbers.

7. The [TRACE] button allows you to use the right- and left-arrow keys to get values for points on the graph.

8. The [CALC] menu allows you to carry out some very useful operations after you've sketched a graph. Since [CALC] appears in blue above the [TRACE] button, you need [2nd] [TRACE]. Here's what the [CALC] menu allows:

   - value: Enter any x, and you'll get the corresponding y value.
   - zero: This gives a zero of the function, that is, an x-intercept of the graph. Use the left- and right-arrow keys to "bracket" the root. Just to the left of the root, hit [ENTER]. Then move just to the right, and hit [ENTER] twice. The graphing calculator will give you that x-intercept.

- minimum or maximum: This gives any minimum or maximum point on the graph. Again, you bracket the desired point. Get close to it on the left, [ENTER], get close to it on the right, [ENTER] twice, and the calculator will give you the coordinates of the desired point.
- intersect: This gives the intersection of two (or more) curves. Hit [ENTER] twice to select both graphs. When the calculator asks for a guess, move the cursor close to the point of intersection you want and hit [ENTER] again. The graphing calculator will give you that point of intersection.

9. The [MATH] menu allows you to get cubes, cube roots, and absolute values.

   Example: Find $\sqrt[3]{625}$. Go to the top level of the calculator. ([2nd] [MODE] is the way to [QUIT] and go there.) Then [MATH] [4] selects $\sqrt[3]{\ }$. Now type 625 [ENTER], and you get the answer, 8.549879733.

   Example: Graph $y = |x+4|$. [MATH] [NUM] abs gets you y = abs, and you can now enter $x + 4$.

10. To find statistical data about a list, for example the mean or standard deviation, etc., use [2nd] [LIST], then scroll across to [MATH]. When you select one of the categories, you'll be expected to enter the list in braces, so use [2nd] (to open the list and use [2nd]) to close it.

Some Final Tips 最后提示

The 1600 Club prepares ahead of time.

Here are some steps you should take to maximize your chances for success.

1. Before leaving home, put new batteries in your calculator and an extra set of fresh batteries in your pocket. Being a calculator wizard won't help if your batteries are dead.
2. At the start of a math section, don't use precious time studying the formulas at the top of the page. By the time you take the test, facts about special triangles, areas, volumes, and the Pythagorean theorem should be second nature to you.
3. Know the formulas in the appendix at the back of this book. Recognizing a situation that can be solved with a quick plug-in to a formula can save you time and effort.
4. At the start of the grid-in questions, don't waste time reading the extensive instructions for filling in the grids correctly. If you do all the grid-in questions in this book, the instructions will be second nature to you by the time you take the test.

第八章 Chapter 8

STRATEGIES FOR SOLVING SAT MATH PROBLEMS SAT数学部分解题策略

You've set your sights on an 800 for math, so it's a good bet that you can set up an equation and solve it with the best of them. If this is the solution that immediately strikes you, go for it. However, be aware that there are test-taking strategies—some of them unorthodox—that can lead to fast and accurate solutions, even for "difficult" problems.

1600 Club Strategies for Math Problems
1600分俱乐部数学题目策略

Strategy 1:	Pick good numbers for problems with percents or fractions.
Strategy 2:	Learn to plug-in answer choices, rather than solve the problem.
Strategy 3:	Use a graphing calculator for maximum or minimum problems.
Strategy 4:	Graphing calculators work for intersection of graphs.
Strategy 5:	Graphing calculators work for transformations.
Strategy 6:	Inequalities? A graphing calculator works here too!
Strategy 7:	Neat way to solve systems: substitution.
Strategy 8:	Good way to find shaded areas: subtraction.

PICK A NUMBER 选数字

What types of problems are candidates for this strategy?

- Problems involving variables rather than numbers
- Percent problems
- Problems with fractions
- Any problem for which your math teacher would suggest that you select variables and translate the English into algebra

Which numbers should you try?

- For percent problems, start with 100.
- For problems with fractions, start with the least common denominator (LCD) of all the fractions.
- If possible, pick simple integers, even if they're unrealistic in the context of the problem.

- Pick different numbers for different quantities.
- Don't choose a number in the problem statement. If you do, you may introduce a special case.

What is the technique? If there are variables in the answer choices, pick easy integer numbers (as mentioned above) for the variables. Find the answer to the problem using your numbers. Then plug your numbers into the answer choices, and see which choice gives you the answer that you got. Be sure to try all of the answer choices. If more than one choice gives the right answer, then you need to try other numbers.

Example 1

In a certain election, several students collected signatures to place a candidate on the ballot. Of these signatures, 25 percent were thrown out as invalid. Then a further 20 percent of those remaining were eliminated. What percent of the original number of signatures were left?

(A) 40% (B) 45% (C) 55% (D) 60%

Solution: (D) This is a percent problem, so start with 100 signatures. If 25 percent of 100 are thrown out, 75 are left. If 20 percent of 75 are thrown out, 60 are left. Therefore, 60 of the original 100 signatures, or 60 percent, are left.

Example 2 Grid-In

Three consecutive odd integers are such that three times the middle integer is 25 more than the sum of the smallest and largest. Find the largest of the integers.

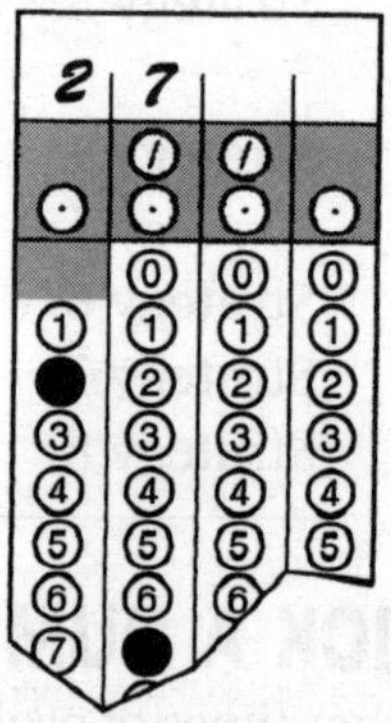

Solution: 27 If you pick the simplest set of consecutive odd integers, namely 1, 3, and 5, you can see at a glance that 3×3 is not 25 more than $1 + 5$. Notice that:

3(middle number) ≈ sum of the 3 numbers.

∴ 25 + (first + third) ≈ sum of the 3 numbers.

This suggests trying numbers in the twenties.

Try 21, 23, 25.

Is (3×23) 25 more than $21 + 25$; that is,
is 69 equal to $25 + (21 + 25) = 71$? No, but close!

Try 23, 25, 27.

$3 \times 25 = 75$, and $75 = 25 + (23 + 27)$. Yes!

Grid-in 27.

By the way, there's no rule that says you can't use algebra! Be sure to let x be the number you need to find, namely, the largest of the three odd integers. Then the consecutive odd numbers are $x - 4$, $x - 2$, and x. Now translate into math: "3 times the middle is 25 more than the sum of the smallest and largest":

$$3(x-2) = 25 + [(x-4) + x]$$

$$3x - 6 = 25 + 2x - 4$$

$$x = 27$$

Example 3

If $a=b^2c$, where $a\neq 0$ and $b\neq 0$, then $\frac{b}{c}=$

(A) $\frac{a}{b}$ (B) $\frac{a}{bc}$ (C) $\frac{a}{b^2c}$ (D) $\frac{a}{bc^2}$

Solution: (D) Suppose you pick $b=2$ and $c=3$. Then a must be 12, since $a=2^2(3)$. Therefore $\frac{b}{c}=\frac{2}{3}$. This is what you must get when you plug your values into the answer choices.

(A) $\frac{a}{b}=\frac{12}{2}=6$ No, not equal to $\frac{2}{3}$ (C) $\frac{a}{b^2c}=\frac{12}{12}=1$ No

(B) $\frac{a}{bc}=\frac{12}{6}=2$ No (D) $\frac{a}{bc^2}=\frac{12}{18}=\frac{2}{3}$ Yes!

Example 4

Mary has d dollars to spend and goes on a shopping spree. First she spends $\frac{2}{5}$ of her money on shoes. Then she spends $\frac{3}{4}$ of what's left on a few books.

Finally she buys a raffle ticket that costs $\frac{1}{3}$ of her remaining dollars.

What fraction of d is left?

(A) $\frac{1}{10}$ (B) $\frac{3}{20}$ (C) $\frac{1}{5}$ (D) $\frac{3}{10}$

Solution: (A) This is similar to the percent problem (Example 1), but now fractions are used. Pick the LCD of the fractions to replace d, the original number of dollars. The LCD of 3, 4, and 5 is 60.

$\frac{2}{5}$ of 60, that is, 24, is spent, leaving 36.

Then $\frac{3}{4}$ of 36, that is, 27, is spent, leaving 9.

Then $\frac{1}{3}$ of 9 that is, 3, is spent, leaving 6.

$\therefore \frac{6}{60}=\frac{1}{10}$ is the fraction of the original amount left.

Example 5

If x is not equal to 2 or –2, which is equivalent to $\frac{3x^2-8x+4}{x^2-4}$?

(A) $3-8x$ (B) $\frac{3x-2}{x+2}$ (C) $\frac{3x-2}{x-2}$ (D) $\frac{3x+2}{x+2}$

Solution: (B) You are given that x can be any number except 2 or –2. Nothing in the problem suggests that x can't be 0. Since 0 is an easy number to substitute, try it in the given fraction:

$$\frac{3x^2-8x+4}{x^2-4}=\frac{4}{-4}=-1$$

Now plug $x = 0$ into the answer choices to find which one equals –1.

(A) $3-8x=3$ No, not equal to –1

(B) $\frac{3x-2}{x+2}=-1$ Yes!

Again, if you're good at algebra, solve this problem algebraically by factoring the numerator and denominator and then canceling:

$$\frac{3x^2-8x+4}{x^2-4}=\frac{\cancel{(x-2)}(3x-2)}{\cancel{(x-2)}(x+2)}=\frac{3x-2}{x+2}$$

Example 6

A man has x dollars to be divided equally among p people. If n newcomers join the group, how many fewer dollars does each person get than each of the original people would have received?

(A) $\frac{xn}{p+n}$ (B) $\frac{x}{p+n}$ (C) $\frac{xn}{p^2+pn}$ (D) $\frac{-xn}{p^2+pn}$

Solution: (C) The key to doing this problem by plugging in numbers is to realize that x dollars will be divided among various numbers of people. Pick x to be a number with lots of factors: 36 is a good choice, and so is 20. Try $x = 20$, $p = 4$ (the original number of people), and $n = 6$ (the number of newcomers). When \$20 is divided by 4, each person gets \$5. When \$20 is divided by 6 + 4, each person gets \$2. The answer to the question is \$5 – \$2 = \$3. Now plug your numbers into the answer choices to see which one gives you 3.

(A) $\frac{xn}{p+n}=\frac{(20)(6)}{10}=12$ No

(B) $\frac{x}{p+n}=\frac{20}{10}=2$ No

(C) $\frac{xn}{p^2+pn}=\frac{(20)(6)}{16+24}=3$ Yes!

Note: **You can eliminate choice (D) without plugging in. The statement of the problem calls for a positive answer. You can see at a glance that the expression in (D) is negative.**

The algebraic solution of the problem is to say that p people would each get $\frac{x}{p}$ dollars, while $p + n$ people would each get $\frac{x}{p+n}$. The difference is:

$$\frac{x}{p}-\frac{x}{p+n}=\frac{x(p+n)-xp}{p(p+n)}=\frac{xn}{p^2+pn}$$

PLUG-IN 代入题

The plug-in strategy is a huge time-saver on the SAT. Instead of solving a problem from scratch and then optimistically searching for your answer among the choices, try plugging the values given in choices (A) through (D) into the problem to find the one that works. Remember: one of those choices is the correct answer! Your job is to use an efficient method to find it.

Plugging-in works whenever you're asked to find a specific numerical value, and you're given five numbers from which to choose. Since the answer choices are invariably arranged in increasing or decreasing order, starting with (B), a middle choice, sometimes saves time and effort. Even if (B) doesn't work, you may be able to see whether to try a higher or lower value. In that case, you'll be able to eliminate two more choices.

Example 7

Which is a solution to $(8^x)(2^4)=\left(\frac{1}{2}\right)^x$?

(A) −2 (B) −1 (C) $-\frac{1}{12}$ (D) 0

Solution: (B) A solution to the equation will give a true statement when you plug it in. Here, start by plugging in an easy number. Plugging in $-\frac{1}{12}$ is much harder than plugging in 0 or −1. Start with choice (D) and plug in 0, an easy number. Recall that $a^0 = 1$.

$$(8^0)(2^4) \stackrel{?}{=} \left(\frac{1}{2}\right)^0$$

$$(1)(16) \stackrel{?}{=} 1 \quad \text{False}$$

Try choice (B): plug in −1. Recall that $a^{-1}=\frac{1}{a}$ and $\left(\frac{1}{a}\right)^{-1}=a$.

$$(8^{-1})(2^4)\stackrel{?}{=}\left(\frac{1}{2}\right)^{-1}$$

$$\left(\frac{1}{8}\right)(16)\stackrel{?}{=}2 \quad \text{True!}$$

Again, there's no rule that says you can't use algebra if you know how to do it. The idea is to write everything with the same base, in this case 2:

$$(8^x)(2^4)=\left(\frac{1}{2}\right)^x$$

$$(2^3)^x 2^4=(2^{-1})^x$$

$$2^{3x}\cdot 2^4=2^{-x}$$

$$3x+4=-x$$

$$x=-1$$

Example 8

If $\frac{x^2-x-6}{x^2-4x+3}=\frac{4}{3}$, find x.

(A) −10 (B) −2 (C) 2 (D) 10

Solution: (D) Plug in choice (C), $x = 2$:

$$\frac{4-2-6}{4-8+3}\stackrel{?}{=}\frac{4}{3} \quad \text{No}$$

Try choice (D), $x = 10$:

$$\frac{100-10-6}{100-40+3}\stackrel{?}{=}\frac{4}{3} \quad \text{Yes!}$$

The method shown is a mindless way of solving the problem, but it has the virtue of always working. You can, however, use your knowledge of algebra and combine strategies to find the solution.

Notice that the trinomials in the given expression factor easily:

$$\frac{x^2-x-6}{x^2-4x+3}=\frac{(x-3)(x+2)}{(x-3)(x-1)}=\frac{x+2}{x-1}$$

Now plugging-in becomes a lot simpler, and you can quickly eyeball your way through the answer choices.

If you get as far as factoring and simplifying, solving the final equation becomes quite easy:

$$\frac{x+2}{x-1}=\frac{4}{3}$$

$$3x+6=4x-4 \quad \text{(Cross-multiply)}$$

$$x=10$$

The 1600 Club uses every tool in its toolkit.

Example 9

Line segment $\overline{AB}$ has midpoint (7, –1). If point A has coordinates (2, 6), then point B has coordinates

(A) $\left(\frac{9}{2}, \frac{5}{2}\right)$ (B) $\left(\frac{19}{2}, -\frac{9}{2}\right)$ (C) (12, –8) (D) (14, –8)

Solution: (C) Draw a picture. The coordinates of M, the midpoint of $\overline{AB}$, are given by:

$$\left(\frac{x_A+x_B}{2}, \frac{y_A+y_B}{2}\right)$$

Method I: Plug-In

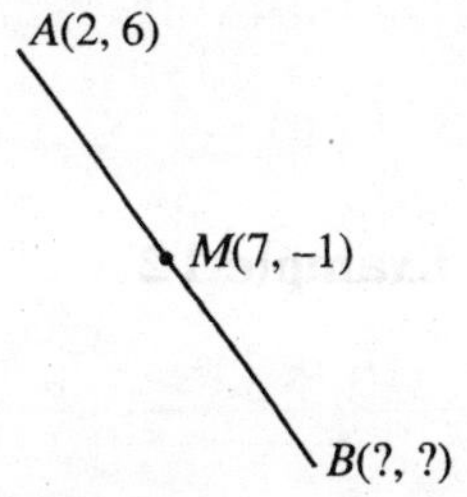

Notice that the average of the endpoints' x-coordinates is 7, and the average of the endpoints' y-coordinates is –1. Plug in the integer answer choices first.

(C): point B = (12, –8). Since A = (2, 6),

$$M=\left(\frac{12+2}{2}, \frac{-8+6}{2}\right)= (7, 1), \text{ the given midpoint.}$$

Method II: Slope

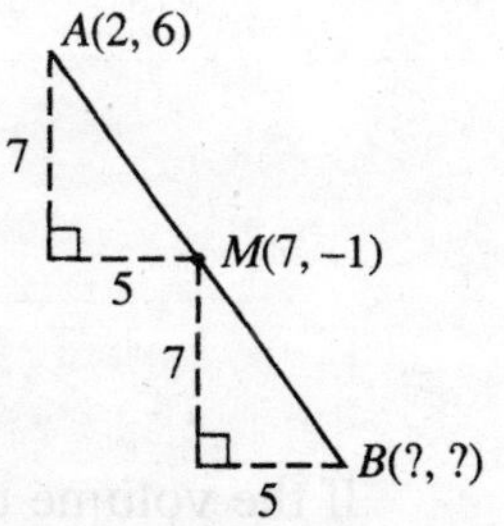

Notice that to get from point A (2, 6) to midpoint M (7, –1), the x-coordinate of A goes up 5 and the y-coordinate of A goes down 7:

$$2 + 5 = 7 \quad \text{and} \quad 6 - 7 = -1$$

The three points A, M, and B are collinear, and M is the midpoint of $\overline{AB}$.

Therefore, to get from M to B, the x-coordinate of M should go up 5, and the y-coordinate of M should go down 7:

$$7 + 5 = 12 \quad \text{and} \quad -1 - 7 = -8$$

Therefore, B is point (12, –8).

Example 10

The sides of a triangle are in the ratio 4:3:2. If the perimeter of the triangle is 792, what is the length of the smallest side?

(A) 176 (B) 200 (C) 264 (D) 352

Solution: (A) You're given a choice of four numbers, so try the plug-in strategy, starting with choice (B). If the smallest side is 200, the biggest side is double this length, or 400. The middle side is somewhere between these values. Even if you take a number only slightly larger than 200, you get a perimeter over 800—too big. Now you can also eliminate choices (C) and (D): 200 is too big, and 264 and 352 are even bigger! The answer must be choice (A).

This is a case where a direct solution is actually easier, if you see it. If the sides are in the ratio 4:3:2, then there are 9 "parts." If the perimeter is 792, each part is $792/9 = 88$. The smallest side is 2 parts, and $2 \times 88 = 176$.

Example 11

Ten pounds of mixed nuts contain 50 percent peanuts. How many pounds of peanuts must be added so that the final mixture has 60 percent peanuts?

(A) 2.5 (B) 5 (C) 6 (D) 10

Solution: (A) Try choice (C): 6 pounds of peanuts. The original 10-pound mixture contained 50 percent peanuts, or 5 pounds. Now you have 11 pounds of peanuts in a 16-pound mixture, more than 60 percent. This result automatically eliminates choice (D) as well. Try (A): adding 2.5 pounds of peanuts to 5 pounds gives 7.5 pounds of peanuts for a total of 12.5 pounds.

$$\frac{7.5}{12.5} = 0.6 = 60\% \quad \text{Yes!}$$

Example 12

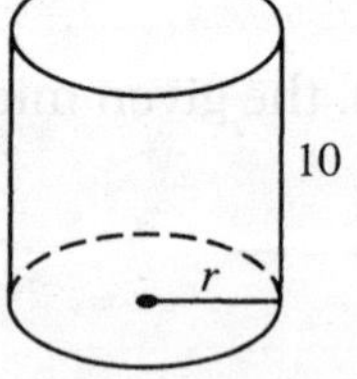

Note: Figure not drawn to scale.

If the volume of the cylinder shown above is $1{,}000\pi^3$, then the value of r, the radius of the base, is

(A) π (B) $\sqrt{10}$ (C) 10 (D) 10π

Solution: (D) The volume of a cylinder is:

$$V = (\text{area of base}) \times \text{height} = \pi r^2 h$$

Here, the height is 10, so $V = 10\pi r^2$. Set V equal to $1{,}000\pi r^3$ (given):

$$1{,}000\pi r^3 = 10\pi r^2$$

One of the answer choices is a value of r that makes the two sides equal. Don't blindly plug in $r = 10$, choice (C)! You can see that to end up with π^3 in the answer, you need to get two factors of π from r^2, so the answer must have a π. Try (D), $r = 10\pi$, which works.

THE GRAPHING CALCULATOR 图像计算器

Be aware that every time you push a calculator button, you're using valuable time. Still, there are several situations where you should consider a graphing calculator solution.

Identifying a Graph 确认图像

Suppose that you are given an equation and then asked about its graph. Sometimes the calculator can provide instant gratification.

Example 13

Which is the graph of $y = -(x-2)^2$?

(A)

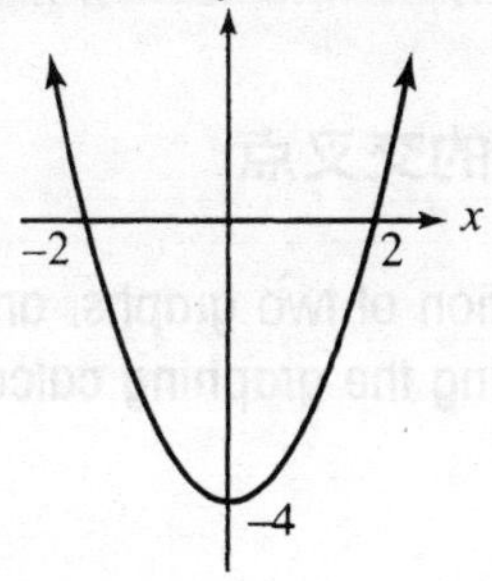

(B)

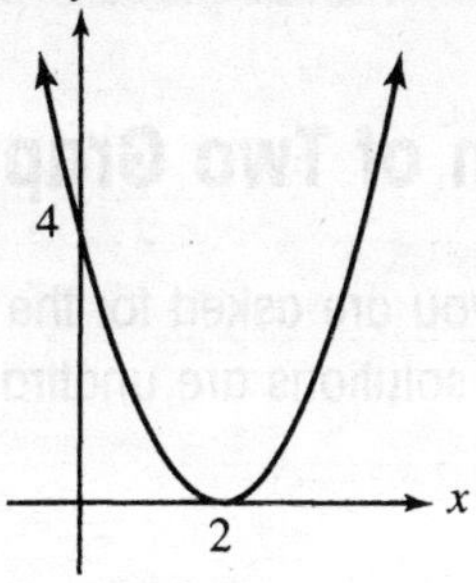

(C)

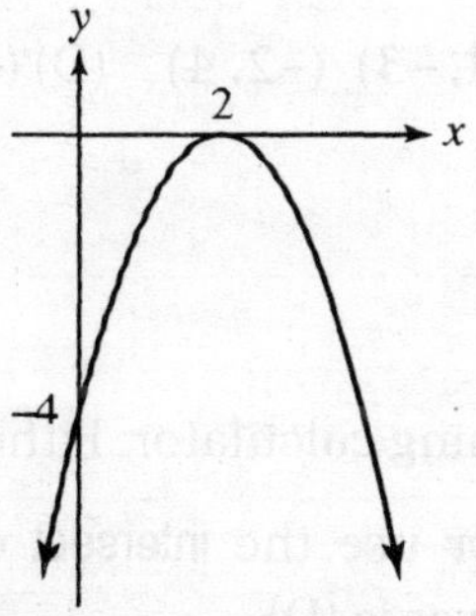

(D)

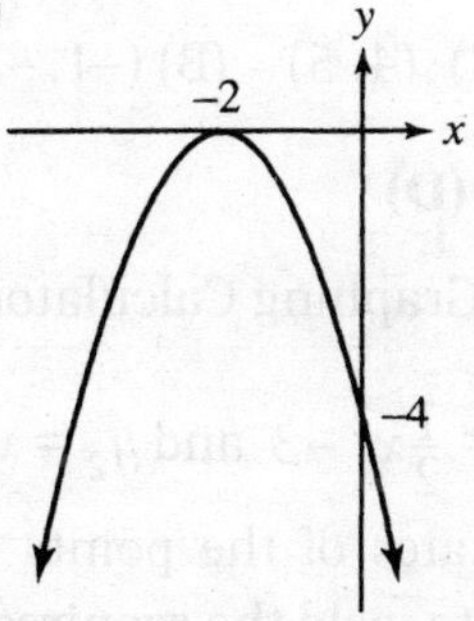

Solution: (C)

Method I: Graphing Calculator

Use the graphing calculator to sketch the graph of $y = -(x-2)^2$. The graphing window clearly shows a graph that matches choice (C)! End of story.

Of course, there are ways to solve this problem without a graphing calculator.

Method II: Logical Reasoning

Since the coefficient of x^2 is negative, the graph is concave down, eliminating choices (A) and (B). Also, since the constant term is –4, the y-intercept of the graph is –4, eliminating choice (B) (again!). Solving $-(x-2)^2 = 0$ yields $x = 2$ as a double root, eliminating choice (D). Therefore, the answer is (C).

Method III: Transformations

If $f(x) = -x^2$, the given equation, $y = -(x-2)^2$, represents $f(x-2)$. Then, as shown below, the graph of $f(x)$ is shifted 2 units to the right, resulting in choice (C).

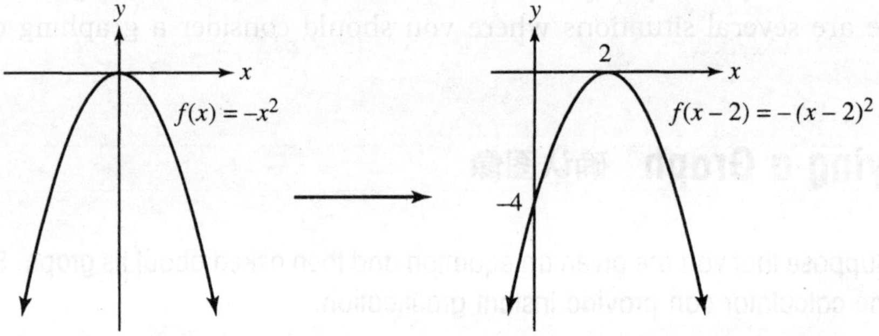

Be sure to check out the sections on "The Quadratic Function" and "Transformations" in Chapter 13.

Intersection of Two Graphs 两个图像的交叉点

When you are asked for the points of intersection of two graphs, and algebraic or plug-in solutions are unattractive, consider using the graphing calculator.

Example 14

Find the points at which the graphs of $y = \frac{1}{2}x^2 - 3$ and $y = x + 1$ intersect.

(A) (–2, –3) (4, 5) (B) (–1, –2) (5, 4) (C) (–4, –3) (–2, 4) (D) (–2, –1) (4, 5)

Solution: (D)

Method I: Graphing Calculator

Graph $y_1 = \frac{1}{2}x^2 - 3$ and $y_2 = x + 1$ on the graphing calculator. Either TRACE to get the coordinates of the points of intersection, or use the intersect option in the CALC menu to yield the required points. The answer is (D).

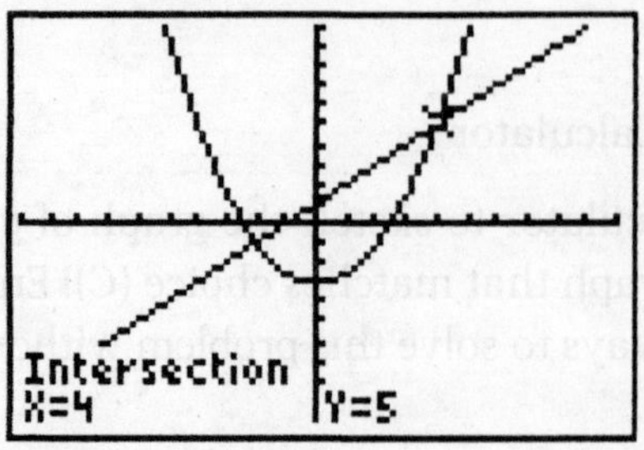

Again, you may prefer an algebraic or plug-in solution.

Method II: Algebra

Solve $y=\frac{1}{2}x^2-3$ and $y = x + 1$ simultaneously. Substitute $x + 1$ for y in the first equation:

$$x+1=\frac{1}{2}x^2-3$$

$$2x+2=x^2-6$$

$$x^2-2x-8=0$$

$$x=4 \text{ or } -2$$

Substituting $x = 4$ in $y = x + 1$ yields $y = 5$, and substituting $x = -2$ yields $y = -1$. Thus the coordinates where the graphs intersect are (–2, –1) and (4, 5), choice (D).

Method III: Plug-In

Since a point of intersection lies on both graphs, its coordinates must satisfy both equations. Go through each answer choice, plugging in the coordinates, until you find the points that satisfy both equations. If you start at choice (A), you find that you need to go all the way to choice (D):

$(-2, -1)$	$(4, 5)$
Plug into $y = \frac{1}{2}x^2 - 3$:	
$-1 = \frac{1}{2}(-2)^2\ 3$	$5 = \frac{1}{2}(4)^2\ 3$
$-1 = -1$ True	$5 = 8 - 3$ True
Plug into $y = x + 1$:	
$-1 = -2 + 1$ True	$5 = 4 + 1$ True

Transformations 变换

When you are given a transformation on a "mystery" function and can't remember the formula for the resulting graph, consider using the graphing calculator.

Example 15

The graph of $f(x)$ is shown below:

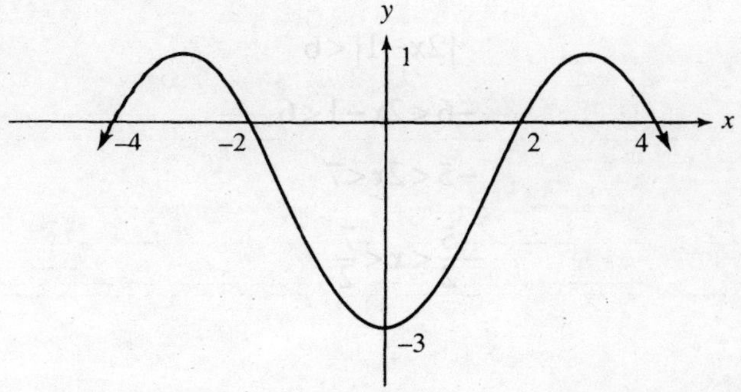

A transformation is applied that results in the following graph:

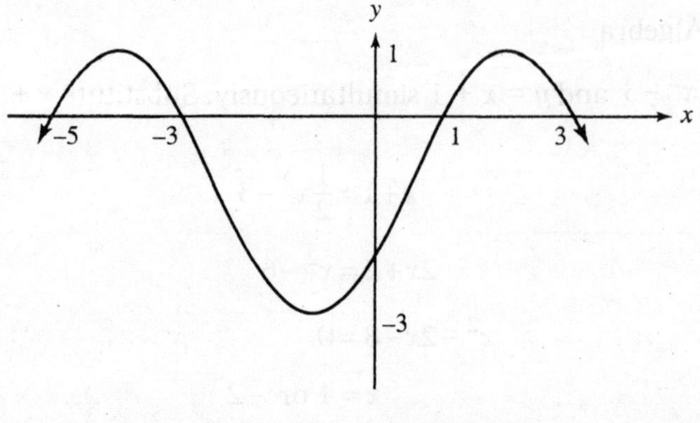

Which of the following functions describes this graph?

(A) $f(x-1)$ (B) $f(x+1)$ (C) $f(x)-1$ (D) $f(x)+1$

Solution: (B) Notice that the graph of $f(x)$ has been shifted 1 unit to the left, a move that always transforms $f(x)$ into $f(x+1)$. You should know this—but suppose you're not certain. A backup strategy is to graph an easy function like $y = x^2$ on the graphing calculator. Now graph $y = (x-1)^2$, which is $f(x-1)$, then $y = (x+1)^2$, which is $f(x+1)$, and so on, until you find the formula that shifts the graph of $y = x^2$ to the left.

Inequalities 不等式

You should consider using the graphing calculator in the solution of an inequality that seems tricky.

Example 16

The solution to the inequality $|2x-1| < 6$ is

(A) $x < -\frac{5}{2}$ or $x > \frac{7}{2}$

(B) $x < -\frac{7}{2}$ or $x > \frac{5}{2}$

(C) $-\frac{5}{2} < x < \frac{7}{2}$

(D) $-\frac{7}{2} < x < \frac{5}{2}$

Solution: (C)

Method I: Algebra

$$|2x-1| < 6$$

$$-6 < 2x-1 < 6$$

$$-5 < 2x < 7$$

$$-\frac{5}{2} < x < \frac{7}{2}$$

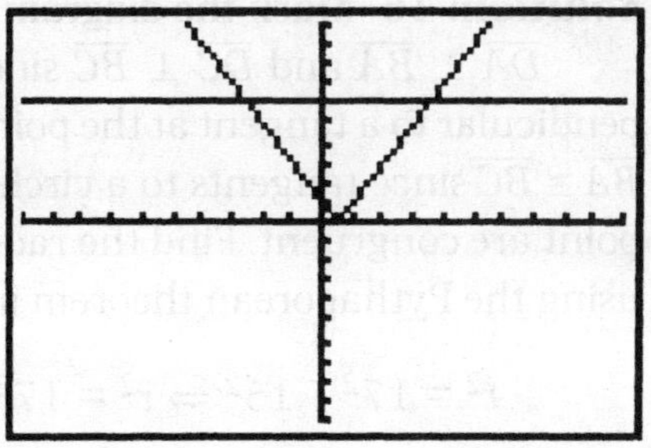

Method II: Graphing Calculator

Graph

$$y_1 = \text{abs}\,(2x - 1)$$
$$y_2 = 6$$

The question asks for x-values such that $y_1 < y_2$, namely, x-values such that the graph of y_1 is below the graph of y_2. A quick glance at the screen shows that this is true for the x-values in choice (C).

A final note:

The 1600 Club is familiar with a graphing calculator and knows when to use it, and when not to use it, to save time.

SOME ADDITIONAL TIPS 一些补充提示

Certain types of questions immediately suggest a place to start or a strategy to try.

Geometry 几何

In a geometry question where the figure is provided, mark in the test booklet all the given data and anything else you can deduce on the diagram. If necessary, add helpful line segments. When you find the answer, check that it seems reasonable if the diagram is drawn to scale: the answer can't be 7 if the longest segment in the diagram is 5.

Be warned: Many figures on the SAT are purposely not drawn to scale. (A note below the figure will state that the figure is not drawn to scale.) In such cases, any answer choice that appears reasonable is almost certainly wrong!

Example 17 Grid-In

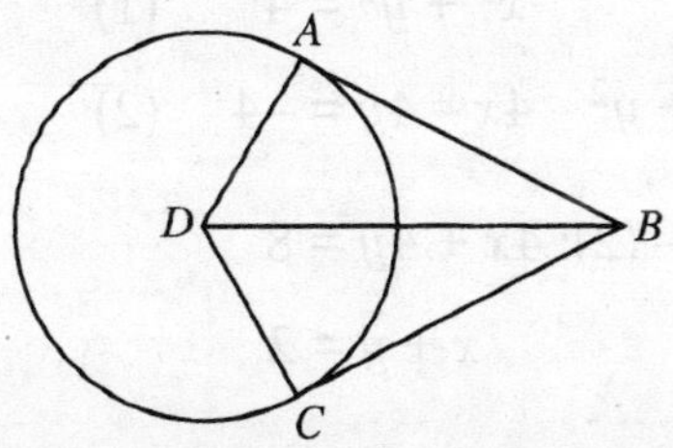

In the figure above, a circle with center D has tangents $\overline{BA}$ and $\overline{BC}$ at points A and C, respectively. If $\overline{BD}$ has length 17 and $\overline{BC}$ has length 15, find the perimeter of quadrilateral $ABCD$.

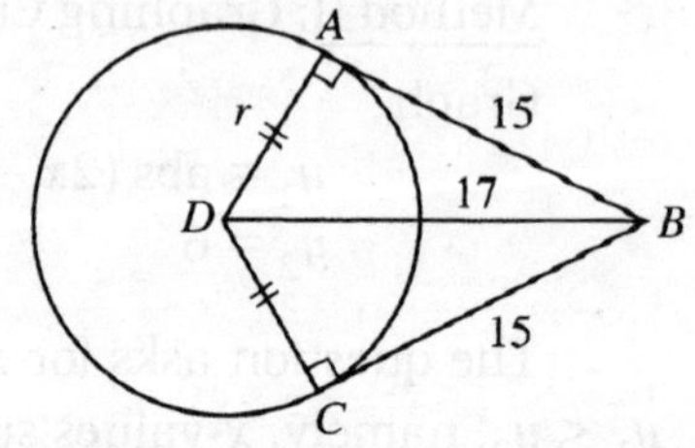

Solution: 46 Mark the diagram as shown.

$\overline{DA} \perp \overline{BA}$ and $\overline{DC} \perp \overline{BC}$ since a radius is perpendicular to a tangent at the point of contact. Also, $\overline{BA} \cong \overline{BC}$ since tangents to a circle from an external point are congruent. Find the radius of the circle by using the Pythagorean theorem in say, $\triangle ABD$:

$$r^2 = 17^2 - 15^2 \Rightarrow r^2 = 17^2 - 15^2 \Rightarrow r = 8$$

Then the perimeter of quadrilateral $ABCD$ is $2(15 + 8) = 46$. Notice that length 8 for the radius, approximately half of the length of $\overline{BC}$, looks reasonable on the diagram.

Grid-in 46.

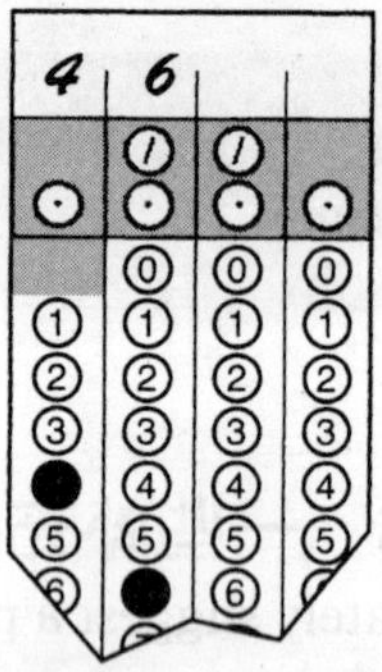

Combining Equations 组合方程式

If you're given two equations in x and y and are asked to find $x + y$, $x - y$, xy, or x/y, then add, subtract, multiply, or divide the given equations. The result may pleasantly surprise you.

Example 18

Given that $x^2 + y^2 = 4$ and $x^2 + y^2 - 4x - 4y = -4$, then $x + y =$

(A) 1 (B) 2 (C) 3 (D) 4

Solution: (B)

$$x^2 + y^2 = 4 \quad (1)$$

$$x^2 + y^2 - 4x - 4y = -4 \quad (2)$$

$$(1) - (2): 4x + 4y = 8$$

$$x + y = 2$$

Alternatively, since $x^2 + y^2 = 4$, replace $x^2 + y^2$ in equation (2) with 4:

$$4 - 4x - 4y = -4$$

$$4x + 4y = 8$$

$$x + y = 2$$

Shaded Areas 阴影面积

Subtract areas to find shaded regions.

Example 19

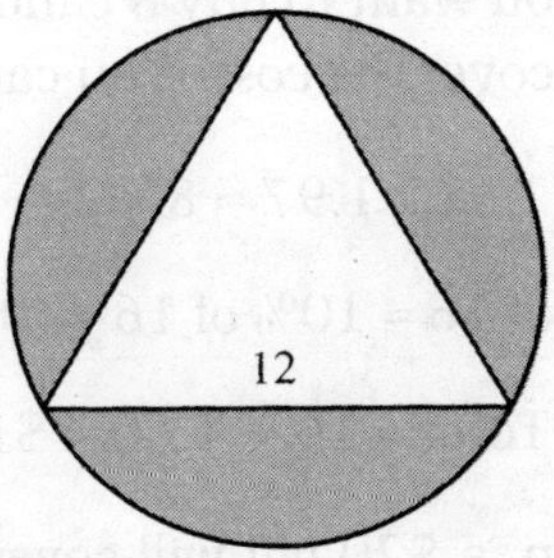

An equilateral triangle with side 12 is inscribed in a circle. Find the shaded area.

(A) $12\pi-36\sqrt{3}$ (B) $36\pi-48\sqrt{3}$ (C) $36\pi-36\sqrt{3}$ (D) $48\pi-36\sqrt{3}$

Solution: (D)

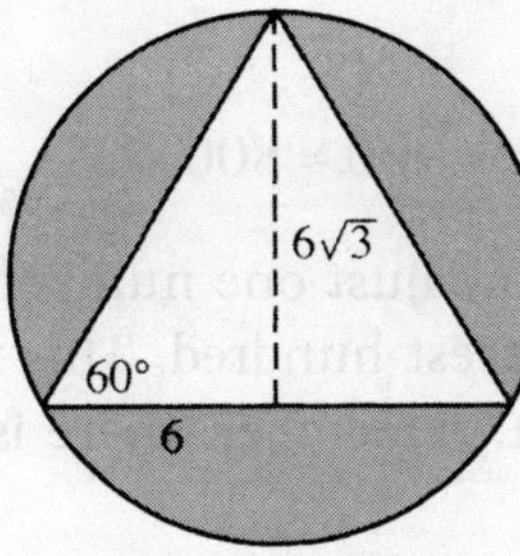

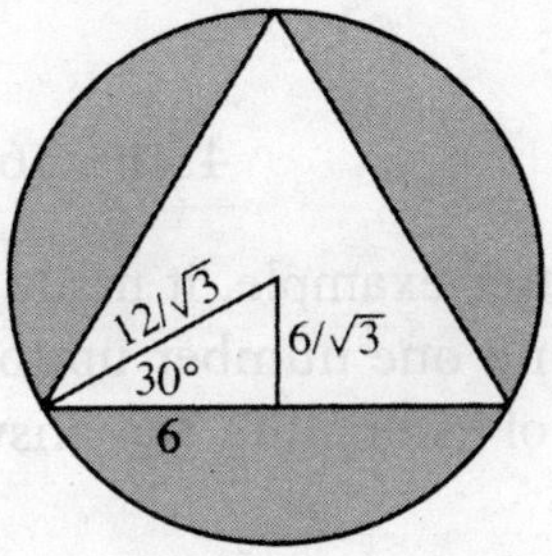

$$\text{Area of }\triangle=\left(\frac{1}{2}\right)(12)(6\sqrt{3})$$

$$=36\sqrt{3}$$

Radius of circle (○) $=\dfrac{12}{\sqrt{3}}$ (See diagram, above right.)

$$\therefore\ \text{Area of}\ \bigcirc=\pi\left(\frac{12}{\sqrt{3}}\right)^2$$

$$=48\pi$$

$$\therefore \text{Shaded area} = \bigcirc\ \text{area} - \triangle\ \text{area}$$

$$=48\pi-36\sqrt{3}$$

Estimation 估算

Estimation is finding a number that is close enough, but not exact. It's a great strategy to use if you're in a hurry, or if you just want an order of magnitude for your answer.

For example, suppose you want to buy 8 candy bars at \$1.97 each, plus 9% tax. Will a \$20 bill be enough to cover the cost? You can quickly estimate as follows:

$$8 \times 1.97 \approx 8 \times 2 = 16$$

$$\text{Tax: } 9\% \text{ of } 16 \approx 10\% \text{ of } 16 \approx (0.1)(16) = 1.60$$

$$\text{Total} \approx 16 + 1.60 \approx \$17.60$$

Based on this estimation, a \$20 bill will cover the cost. You can do this kind of calculation like lightning in your head. Pushing buttons on the calculator would take longer.

The main technique for estimating is to round numbers up or down to easier numbers and then to slightly adjust your answer. For example:

$$575 + 298 \approx 575 + 300 \approx 875$$

Similarly:

$$450 + 368 \approx 400 + 400 \approx 800$$

In the latter example, it made sense to adjust one number down to the nearest hundred and one number up to the nearest hundred. This may have been the quickest way of estimating the answer, but, remember, there is no "right way" of estimating.

For multiplication, the leftmost digit of a number has the greatest influence, so round accordingly:

$$4{,}392 \times 696 \approx 4{,}000 \times 700 \approx 2{,}800{,}000$$

On the Mathematics section of the SAT, it's often a good idea to try for a rough estimate of the answer, especially for the grid-in questions where there are no clues based on the answer choices. Sometimes a good estimate can give you a pretty good guess at the answer!

Example 20 Grid-In

The quantity 45% of 2.7×10^4 is rounded to the nearest thousand. The rounded answer can be expressed as $n \times 10^3$, where n is a positive integer. Find n.

Solution: 12 Note that 2.7×10^4 is $2.7 \times 10{,}000$. (10^4 is a 1 followed by 4 zeros.)

The expression 45% of 2.7×10^4, before rounding, is less than 50% of 27,000, which means less than half of 27,000. Less than half of 27,000 is less than 13,500. Therefore, guess that the rounded answer is 12,000, which can be expressed as 12×10^3.

The value of n would be 12.

A calculator solution yields: $(.45)(2.7)(10{,}000) = 12{,}150$

To the nearest thousand, the answer is 12,000, which is 12×10^3.

Grid-in 12.

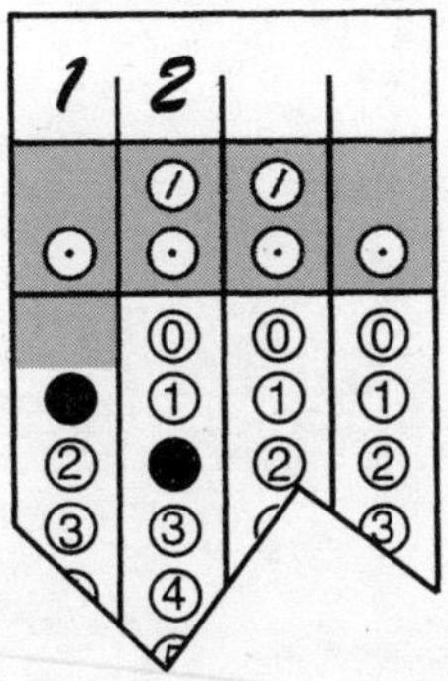

One final piece of advice: Every problem on the SAT is designed to be solved within a reasonable amount of time. If, after some thought, you can't come up with a reasonable way to tackle a problem, circle it in your test booklet and move on. Don't allow yourself to become bogged down in endless, futile calculation.

第九章 Chapter 9

1600 CLUB BACKGROUND TOPICS 1600分俱乐部题目

The SAT test assumes knowledge of each topic in this chapter. While you may not be asked a direct question on any one of these, you can be sure that many questions will require at least one of these topics as a first step in solving more complex problems.

If you're confident about these topics, skip ahead to the sample SAT questions at the end of the chapter.

1600 Club Background Topics
1600分俱乐部题目策略

Strategy 1:	**B**asic facts that you should know by now.
Strategy 2:	**A**bsolute value: the definition and solution of equations.
Strategy 3:	**C**oordinate geometry: distances, slopes, and equations.
Strategy 4:	**K**now how to find the probability of an event.
Strategy 5:	**G**eometric transformations, probability, and triangles.
Strategy 6:	**R**ational numbers, irrational numbers, squares, and square roots.
Strategy 7:	**O**dds and ends: counting, scientific notation, and sequences and series.
Strategy 8:	**U**nderstand exponential growth!
Strategy 9:	**N**umbers: know the basic sets.
Strategy 10:	**D**ifferent types of quadrilaterals and polygons: know their properties.

The 1600 Club has bread and butter topics at its fingertips.

NUMBERS 数

Sets of Numbers 数的集合

Many SAT questions involve nothing more than manipulation of numbers, yet these questions can be tricky. For starters, you need to be clear about which numbers belong to which sets.

Integers = {. . . , −4, −3, −2, −1, 0, 1, 2, 3, 4, . . .}
Nonnegative integers = {0, 1, 2, 3, 4, . . .}
Positive integers = {1, 2, 3, 4, . . .}
Negative integers = {−1, −2, −3, −4, . . .}
Even integers = {. . . , −4, −2, 0, 2, 4, . . .}
Odd integers = {. . . , −5, −3, −1, 1, 3, 5, . . .}

Consecutive Integers 连续整数

Consecutive integers are two or more integers that directly follow each other. For example, 10, 11, 12 are consecutive integers. If n is an even integer, then n, $n + 2$, $n + 4$ are *consecutive even integers*. Notice that if n is odd, then n, $n + 2$, $n + 4$ represent *consecutive odd integers*.

Factors and Multiples 因数和倍数

The *factors* of a positive integer n are the positive integers that can be divided into n without a remainder. For example, the factors of 18 are 1, 2, 3, 6, 9, 18.

The *multiples* of n are the positive integers that have n as a factor. For example, the multiples of 7 are 7, 14, 21, 28, 35, . . .

The *greatest common factor* or *greatest common divisor* of two integers is the largest integer that is a factor of both. The *least common multiple* of two integers is the smallest integer that is a multiple of both. For example, the greatest common factor of 12 and 30 is 6, whereas the least common multiple of 12 and 30 is 60.

Rational Numbers 有理数

The *set of rational numbers* is the set of all numbers that can be written as a fraction $\frac{a}{b}$, where a and b are integers and $b \neq 0$. Here are some examples of rational numbers:

$2 \left(\text{since } 2 = \frac{2}{1}\right)$

$0.68 \left(\text{since } 0.68 = \frac{68}{100}\right)$

$0.\overline{6} \left(\text{since } 0.\overline{6} = \frac{2}{3}\right)$

Notice that the *decimal equivalent* of a fraction can be obtained by dividing the numerator (top) by the denominator. Your calculator will do this for you in the blink of an eye. Your calculator can also find the fractional equivalent of a decimal. Type the decimal, or if you already have it displayed as the answer to a calculation, follow the decimal with MATH Frac ENTER, and you'll see the equivalent fraction displayed on the screen.

The 1600 Club knows that every integer, terminating decimal, and nonterminating repeating decimal is a rational number.

Squares and Square Roots 平方和平方根

Perfect squares pop up frequently on the SAT. Even though your calculator can help you here, you should recognize the first twenty perfect squares: 1, 4, 9, 16, 25, 36, 49, 64, 81, 100, 121, 144, 169, 196, 225, 256, 289, 324, 361, 400.

Every positive number has two *square roots*, a positive and a negative number. Thus the square root of 64 is 8 or –8. The symbol $\sqrt{64}$ represents the positive root, 8, while $-\sqrt{64}$ represents the negative root, –8. The solution to the equation $x^2 = 64$ is ± 8.

The 1600 Club does not forget the negative root when solving equations that require square roots on both sides.

Beware of questions that involve negative numbers, fractions, squares, and inequalities. These are a poisonous brew.

Example 1

If a and b are nonzero numbers such that $a < b$, which of the following must be true?

I. $\frac{1}{a} > \frac{1}{b}$

II. $a^2 < b^2$

III. $b^2 \geq 1$

(A) None (B) I only (C) II only (D) III only

Solution: (A) Look for a counterexample that shows each choice is false. Don't forget fractions and negative numbers!

I: $-2 < 2$ does not imply that $-\frac{1}{2} > \frac{1}{2}$.

II: $-2 < 1$ does not imply that $4 < 1$.

III: Let $b = \frac{1}{2}$. Notice that $b^2 = \frac{1}{4}$, which is less than 1.

The 1600 Club knows that a *single counterexample* shows that a statement is false.

COUNTING AND PROBABILITY 计算和概率

Counting 计算

To answer the question "How many ways can . . . ?" sounds simple: you just count. These problems, however, can be tricky.

The Basic Rule of Counting: If event 1 can happen in k different ways, and an independent event, event 2, can happen in m different ways, then the total number of ways in which both events can happen is km.

A typical problem is the "outfit" problem. If you have 3 pairs of jeans and 10 T-shirts, you have a choice of $3 \times 10 = 30$ different outfits, where an outfit consists of a pair of jeans and a T-shirt.

Note that the basic rule can be extended to more than two events. If, in addition to your jeans and T-shirts, you have 4 hats, the number of different possible outfits increases to $10 \times 3 \times 4 = 120$, where an outfit consists of a pair of jeans, a T-shirt, and a hat.

This is all you'll need to solve counting problems on the SAT test. However, knowing the formulas for permutations and combinations (in the following section) can lead to a speedier solution.

Permutations and Combinations 排列和组合

A *permutation* is the number of arrangements of n objects, where each different ordering of the objects counts as one permutation. The answer is $n!$ (n factorial). For example, how many arrangements are there of the letters E,X,A,M? Imagine having four slots:

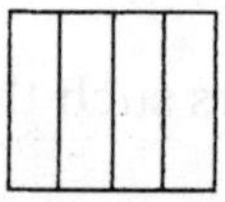

You have 4 choices for the first slot, 3 choices for the second slot, and 2 choices for the third slot. By the time you get to the fourth slot, there is no choice: just 1 letter is left. Therefore, the total number of arrangements is $4 \times 3 \times 2 \times 1 = 24$, which is equal to 4! It is important to understand that EXAM and MAXE, for example, are different permutations.

In general, the number of permutations of n items taken r at a time is given by the formula

$$_nP_r = \frac{n!}{(n-r)!}$$

Now consider the problem of calculating the number of 3-person committees that can be formed from 6 people who are willing to serve. There are $6 \times 5 \times 4$ ways of selecting 3 people. If the order of their selection, however, is irrelevant—for example, Mary-Tom-Nick is the same committee as Nick-Mary-Tom—you must divide by $3 \times 2 \times 1$ because each group of 3 people can be chosen in 6 different ways. When the order of choosing is not important, each arrangement is called a *combination.*

In general, the number of combinations of n items taken r at a time is given by the formula

$$_nC_r = \frac{n!}{(n-r)!r!} = \frac{_nP_r}{r!}$$

Probability 概率

Events 事件

Suppose that an experiment is performed. An *event* E is a set of particular outcomes of this experiment. If S is the set of all possible outcomes of the experiment, then E is a subset of S. For example, consider the experiment of flipping a fair coin and tossing a fair six-sided die. The set S of all possible outcomes is

$$S = \{H1, H2, H3, H4, H5, H6, T1, T2, T3, T4, T5, T6\}$$

Here are some events for the above experiment:

A = {Getting a prime number and tails} = {T2, T3, T5}
B = {Getting a head on the coin} = {H1, H2, H3, H4, H5, H6}
C = {Getting a 4 on the die} = {H4, T4}

Probability of an Event 事件发生的概率

The *probability* of an event E, $P(E)$, is given as follows: If E can occur in m ways out of a total of n equally likely ways, then

$$P(E) = \frac{m}{n} = \frac{\text{Number of outcomes in event } E}{\text{Total number of possible outcomes}}$$

For the coin/die experiment above, all 12 outcomes in set S are equally likely, so the probabilities of events A, B, and C (described above) are

$$P(A) = \frac{3}{12} = \frac{1}{4}, \quad P(B) = \frac{6}{12} = \frac{1}{2}, \quad P(C) = \frac{2}{12} = \frac{1}{6}$$

Note that:

- If event E is the empty set, it represents an *impossible event*, and $P(E) = 0$.
- If $E = S$, it represents a *certain event*, and $P(E) = 1$.
- Therefore, if E is a nonempty, nonequal subset of S, then $0 < P(E) < 1$.
- E', the *complement* of E, is the set containing all the elements of S that are not in E. Thus the probability that event E will *not* happen is given by $P(E') = 1 - P(E)$.
  In the coin/die experiment, the probability of getting a 4 on the die, $P(C)$, is $\frac{1}{6}$.
  The probability of *not* getting a 4 on the die = $P(C')$ = $1 - P(C) = 1 - \frac{1}{6} = \frac{5}{6}$.

Mutually Exclusive Events 互斥事件

In the coin/die experiment, recall that

A = {Getting a prime number and tails} = {T2, T3, T5}
B = {Getting a head on the coin} = {H1, H2, H3, H4, H5, H6}
C = {Getting a 4 on the die} = {H4, T4}

Events A and B are *mutually exclusive*. In other words, they cannot occur simultaneously in one run of the experiment. They are disjoint sets. To find the probability of getting tails with a prime number *or* heads on the coin, the probabilities are additive:

$$P(A \text{ or } B) = P(A \cup B) = P(A) + P(B)$$
$$= \frac{1}{4} + \frac{1}{2} = \frac{3}{4}$$

Contrast this with the problem of finding the probability of getting either a head on the coin (event B) or a 4 on the die (event C). Again you want to find $P(B \cup C)$. But in this case, events B and C are not mutually exclusive, since outcome H4 is in both events. The addition rule for finding the probability of B or C must be adjusted since the intersection of the two sets is nonempty: (You don't want to count the common element, H4, twice.)

$$P(B \cup C) = P(B) + P(C) - P(B \cap C)$$
$$= \frac{1}{2} + \frac{1}{6} - \frac{1}{12}$$
$$= \frac{7}{12}$$

Independent Events 独立事件

In the coin/die experiment, the probability of getting a head on the coin (event B) *and* a 4 on the die (event C) is given by the multiplication rule:

$$P(B \cap C) = P(B) \times P(C) = \left(\frac{1}{2}\right)\left(\frac{1}{6}\right) = \frac{1}{12}$$

Events B and C are *independent*. This statement should feel intuitively correct to you: $P(\{\text{Getting a 4 on the die}\})$ is independent of what happens on the coin toss.

In general: The probability that both A *and* B occur is given by

$$P(A \cap B) = P(A) \times P(B)$$

Event B is independent of event A if and only if the probability of event B is not influenced by whether A has or has not occurred. If $P(B)$ changes after A has occurred, then A and B are *dependent* events.

In this case $P(A \cap B) = P(A) \cdot P(B \mid A)$, where $P(B \mid A)$ means "the probability of B given that A has occurred."

Example 2

A small bag contains 4 white and 3 red marbles. Two marbles are randomly removed from the bag. Find the probability that a white marble is removed, followed by a red.

(A) $\frac{1}{7}$ (B) $\frac{2}{7}$ (C) $\frac{3}{7}$ (D) $\frac{4}{7}$

Solution: (B)

$$P(WR) = P(W) \cdot P(R \mid W)$$
$$= \frac{4}{7} \cdot \frac{1}{2}$$
$$= \frac{2}{7}$$

Notice that in a vacuum $P(W) = \frac{4}{7}$ and $P(R) = \frac{3}{7}$. But since "removing a white marble" and "removing a red marble" (without replacement) are dependent events, these probabilities must be adjusted if one of the events has already happened.

Example 3

A hat contains the integers 1 to 100, inclusive. If a number is drawn at random from the hat, what is the probability that a multiple of 5 or a multiple of 8 is drawn?

(A) $\frac{3}{5}$ (B) $\frac{33}{100}$ (C) $\frac{3}{10}$ (D) $\frac{31}{100}$

Solution: (C) The events in this experiment are

$A = \{\text{Getting a multiple of } 5\} = \{5, 10, 15, \ldots, 100\}$

$B = \{\text{Getting a multiple of } 8\} = \{8, 16, 24, \ldots, 96\}$

Method I: Find Number of Successful Outcomes

The total number of outcomes is 100, the number of integers that can be drawn. The "successful" outcomes are the numbers that are either multiples of 5 or multiples of 8.

Number of multiples of 5 = $\frac{100}{5}$ or 20

Number of multiples of 8 = $\frac{100}{8}$ or 12 (The remainder is irrelevant.)

But beware: The integers 40 and 80 are multiples of both 5 and 8. Don't count them twice! Thus the number of successful outcomes is $20 + 12 - 2 = 30$.

The required probability is $\frac{30}{100} = \frac{3}{10}$.

Method II: Find $P(A \text{ or } B)$

A and B are not mutually exclusive events, since each set contains 40 and 80.

$$\begin{aligned} P(A \text{ or } B) &= P(A \cup B) \\ &= P(A) + P(B) - P(A \cap B) \\ &= \frac{20}{100} + \frac{12}{100} - \frac{2}{100} \\ &= \frac{3}{10} \end{aligned}$$

Example 4

In a batch of 10 light bulbs, 2 are defective. If 3 of the bulbs are chosen at random, what is the probability that at least 1 of the chosen bulbs is defective?

(A) $\frac{8}{15}$ (B) $\frac{7}{15}$ (C) $\frac{3}{10}$ (D) $\frac{1}{4}$

Solution: (A)

A good way to save time here is to use the complement rule:

P(at least 1 bulb is defective) = 1 − P(none of the bulbs is defective).

In this way you need to deal with just one event: none of the 3 chosen bulbs is defective.

Method I: Find Number of Successful Outcomes

To find P (none of the 3 chosen bulbs is defective):

Total number of ways to pick 3 of the 10 bulbs = $\dfrac{(10)(9)(8)}{(3)(2)(1)} = 120$

(You need to divide by the number of arrangements of those 3 bulbs, since the order of picking them is irrelevant.)

There are $10 - 2 = 8$ nondefective bulbs.

Total number of ways to pick 3 nondefective bulbs = $\dfrac{(8)(7)(6)}{(3)(2)(1)} = 56$

$\therefore P$ (none of the bulbs is defective) = $\dfrac{56}{120} = \dfrac{7}{15}$

$$P(\text{at least 1 defective}) = 1 - P(\text{none defective})$$

$$= 1 - \frac{7}{15} = \frac{8}{15}$$

Method II: Tree Diagram

A tree diagram provides a snapshot of a multistage experiment. At each stage all possible outcomes are shown. Each "branch" of the tree represents one composite outcome of the completed experiment.

Below is a tree diagram for the light bulb problem. Think of the problem as a three-stage experiment in which each stage involves choosing 1 bulb. At each stage, either a defective bulb (D) or a nondefective bulb (N) is chosen.

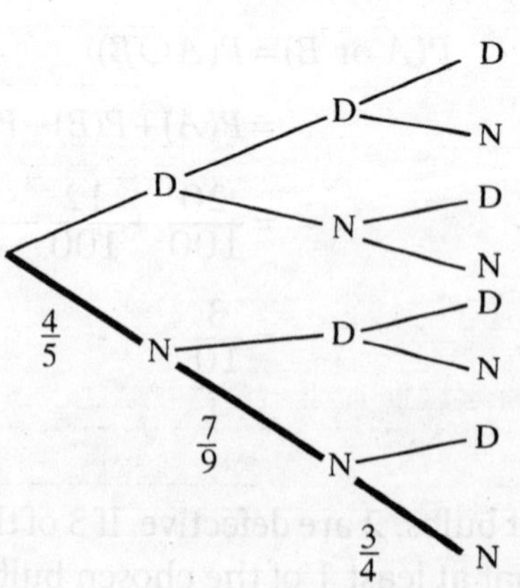

Only one branch leads to an outcome in which none of the bulbs is defective. The probabilities are shown at each stage along this branch: The probability of picking a nondefective bulb the first time is $\dfrac{8}{10} = \dfrac{4}{5}$, since 8 bulbs are not defective. The probability of picking a nondefective bulb the second time is affected by the fact that a nondefective bulb is already gone: there are 9 bulbs left, of which 7 are nondefective. Similarly, at the third stage there are 8 bulbs left, of which 6 are nondefective. Notice that the following are dependent events, since the probabilities at each stage are affected by the result of the previous stage:

Drawing a nondefective bulb at the first stage
Drawing a nondefective bulb at the second stage
Drawing a nondefective bulb at the third stage

In a tree diagram, to find the probability of any branch, multiply the probabilities along the way:

$$P\text{ (no defective bulb)} = \left(\frac{4}{5}\right)\left(\frac{7}{9}\right)\left(\frac{3}{4}\right)=\frac{7}{15}$$

Now use the complement rule, as in the above method of solving:

$$P\text{ (at least 1 defective)} = 1-P\text{ (none defective)}$$
$$=1-\frac{7}{15}=\frac{8}{15}$$

Note: In a tree diagram, if more than one branch leads to a required outcome, add the probabilities for all of the successful branches.

Coaching: *To find the probability that "at least 1 . . ." occurs, it is usually much easier to find 1 – the probability that "none . . ." occurs.*

SEQUENCES AND SERIES 序列和级数

A sequence is a list of numbers that generally follow a pattern, for example, 2, 5, 10, 17, 26, ...

The pattern for the *k*th term is "square *k* and add 1." Thus the next term in the sequence is 37.

Arithmetic and Geometric Sequences and Series
算术序列和级数与几何序列和级数

There are two particular types of sequences that you should know, arithmetic and geometric.

An *arithmetic sequence* generates its next term by adding a *common difference* to the preceding term. For example:

–2, 2, 6, 10, . . . common difference = 4
10, 8, 6, 4, . . . common difference = –2

Notice that the *n*th term of the first sequence is $-2 + (n - 1)4$, and the *n*th term of the second sequence is $10 + (n - 1)(-2)$. The *n*th term of an arithmetic sequence is always the first term plus $(n - 1)$ common differences.

A *geometric sequence* generates its next term by multiplying the preceding term by the same number, called a *common ratio*. For example:

3, 9, 27, 81, . . . common ratio = 3

$4, \frac{4}{3}, \frac{4}{9}, \frac{4}{27}, \ldots$ common ratio = $\frac{1}{3}$

Notice that the *n*th term of the first sequence is $(3)(3)^{n-1}$, and the *n*th term of the second sequence is $(4)\left(\frac{1}{3}\right)^{n-1}$. The *n*th term of a geometric sequence is always the first term multiplied by the $(n - 1)$th power of the common ratio.

Sequences Involving Exponential Growth 幂增长序列

The growth of a geometric sequence is called *exponential growth.* It is illustrated in Example 5.

Example 5 Grid-In

A colony of bacteria numbers 2,000 at 1 P.M. and increases 20 percent per hour. What is the population at 4 P.M. that same day?

Coaching: *High scorers should know that if a number x increases by $\frac{1}{5}$, it becomes $\frac{6}{5}x$.*

Solution: The answer is 3,456.

An increase of 20 percent means that the second term in the sequence is

$$2{,}000 + 20\% \text{ of } 2{,}000$$

$$= 2{,}000 + \left(\frac{1}{5}\right)(2{,}000) = 2{,}000\left(1+\frac{1}{5}\right) = 2{,}000\left(\frac{6}{5}\right)$$

Here is the sequence of population numbers for the colony:

1 P.M.	2 P.M.	3 P.M.	4 P.M.
2,000	$2{,}000\left(\frac{6}{5}\right)$	$2{,}000\left(\frac{6}{5}\right)^2$	$2{,}000\left(\frac{6}{5}\right)^3$

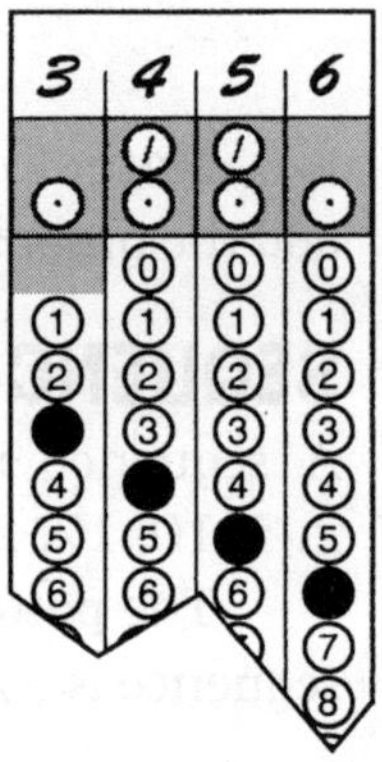

This is a geometric sequence with common ratio $\frac{6}{5}$.

The answer is $2{,}000\left(\frac{6}{5}\right)^3 = 3{,}456$.

Grid-in 3456.

EXPONENTS 指数

The laws of exponents should be second nature to high scorers.

$$a^x \cdot a^y = a^{x+y}$$
$$a^x \div a^y = a^{x-y}$$
$$(a^x)^y = a^{xy}$$
$$a^0 = 1$$

Negative exponents are also fair game on the SAT:

$$a^{-n} = \frac{1}{a^n} \text{ and } a^n = \frac{1}{a^{-n}}$$

So are fractional exponents:

$$a^{\frac{1}{n}} = \sqrt[n]{a}\text{, the } n\text{th root of } a$$

$$a^{\frac{m}{n}} = \sqrt[n]{a^m} = \left(\sqrt[n]{a}\right)^m$$

Example 6

$16^{-\frac{3}{4}}$ is equal to

(A) -8 (B) 8 (C) $-\frac{1}{8}$ (D) $\frac{1}{8}$

Solution: (D)

$$16^{-\frac{3}{4}}=\frac{1}{16^{\frac{3}{4}}}=\frac{1}{\left(\sqrt[4]{16}\right)^3}=\frac{1}{2^3}=\frac{1}{8}$$

Scientific Notation 科学计数法

Scientific notation is a convenient way of representing very small or very large numbers. The number is written as a number between 1 and 10 multiplied by a power of 10. For example,

$6.235 \times 10^6 = 6{,}235{,}000$ (move the decimal point 6 places to the right)
$2.08 \times 10^{-4} = 0.000208$ (move the decimal point 4 places to the left)

Example 7

If $x = 2.4 \times 10^6$ and $y = 6.0 \times 10^{-8}$, express xy in scientific notation.

(A) 1.44×10^{-1} (C) 1.44×10^{-2}

(B) 14.4×10^{-2} (D) 1.44×10^{-3}

Solution: (A)

Method I: Multiplication

$$\begin{aligned} xy &= (2.4\times10^6)(6.0\times10^{-8}) \\ &= (2.4\times6.0)(10^6\times10^{-8}) \\ &= 14.4\times10^{-2} \end{aligned}$$

If you think choice (B) is the correct answer, look again! In scientific notation the number multiplied by the power of 10 must be between 1 and 10. You need to rewrite 14.4×10^{-2} as $(1.44 \times 10^1) \times 10^{-2} = 1.44 \times 10^{-1}$.

Method II: Graphing Calculator

Set the MODE to Sci (Scientific Notation) and type in
2.4 × 10^6 × 6.0 × 10^(–8).

Your calculator will tell you that the answer is 1.44E–1, which means 1.44×10^{-1}. If you don't use Scientific Notation mode, you will need to convert the decimal answer, .144, to scientific notation, namely, 1.44×10^{-1}.

Monomials 单项式

You may need to use the laws of exponents to simplify a *monomial*, an algebraic expression with just one term.

Example 8

If $x^2b^4 = ab^{-1}$, what is a in terms of b and x?

(A) x^2b^3 (B) x^2b^5 (C) x^2b^{-3} (D) x^2b^{-5}

Solution: (B) The question means: Solve for *a*.

$$x^2b^4 = ab^{-1}$$

$$\frac{a}{b} = x^2b^4$$

$$a = x^2b^5 \text{ (Multiply both sides by } b\text{.)}$$

ABSOLUTE VALUE 绝对值

The *absolute value* of a quantity x, denoted as $|x|$, equals x if $x \geq 0$, and $-x$ if $x < 0$. For example, $|-2.3| = 2.3$, and $|10| = 10$. The answer is always positive or zero. You can think of the absolute value of a number as being its distance from 0 on a number line. Also, $|a-b| = |b-a|$ = the distance from a to b.

POINTS, LINES, ANGLES 点、线、角

The SAT distinguishes between geometric objects and their measures. You should be familiar with the following definitions and corresponding notations.

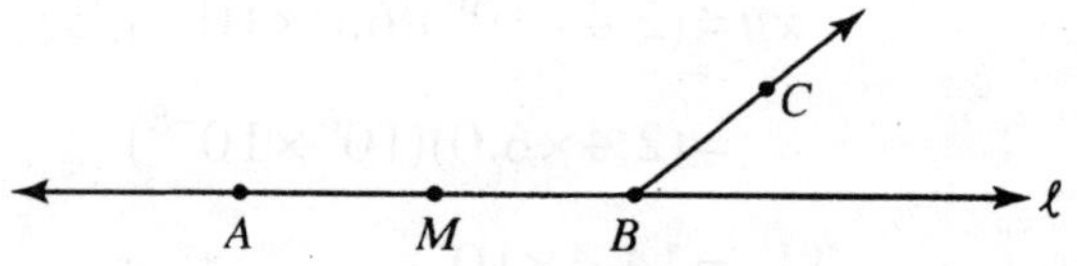

In the figure above:

- $\overleftrightarrow{AB}$, $\overleftrightarrow{MB}$, and $\overleftrightarrow{AM}$ all denote *line* ℓ, the line containing points A, M, and B.
- $\overline{AM}$ is the *line segment* with endpoints A and M. It does not contain point B.
- AM is the length of $\overline{AM}$.
- $\overrightarrow{BC}$ is the *ray* with endpoint B that contains C. Notice that ray MA does not contain B, but ray $\overrightarrow{AM}$ does.
- $\angle CBA$ is the *angle* formed by rays $\overrightarrow{BC}$ and $\overrightarrow{BA}$.
- $m\angle CBA$ is the measure of $\angle CBA$.

- M is the *midpoint* of $\overline{AB}$ if and only if $\overline{AM}$ is congruent to $\overline{BM}$, denoted as $\overline{AM} \cong \overline{BM}$. This implies that $AM = BM$.

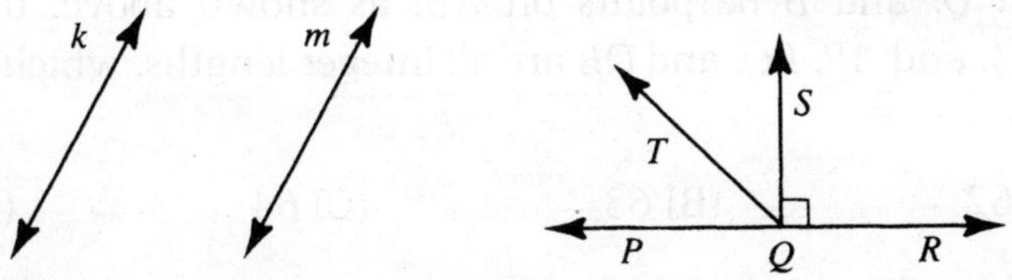

In the figure above:

- Line k is *parallel* to line m. Denote this as $k \parallel m$.
- Line $\overleftrightarrow{PR}$ is *perpendicular* to ray $\overrightarrow{QS}$, denoted as $\overleftrightarrow{PR} \perp \overrightarrow{QS}$. If $\overleftrightarrow{PR} \perp \overrightarrow{QS}$, then $\angle SQR$ and $\angle SQP$ are *right angles*, and $m\angle SQR = m\angle SQP = 90°$.
- $\angle TQP$ is an *acute angle* since $m\angle TQP$ is less than $90°$.
- $\angle TQR$ is an *obtuse angle* since $m\angle TQR$ is between $90°$ and $180°$.
- $\angle TQP$ and $\angle TQS$ are *complementary*, that is, the sum of their measures is $90°$.
- Two angles are *supplementary* if the sum of their measures is $180°$. Two adjacent angles on a line are supplementary. Thus the following pairs of angles are supplementary:

  $\angle PQT$ and $\angle TQR$, $\angle PQS$ and $\angle RQS$

Parallel Lines 平行线

Here are some angle relationships that you should know when parallel lines are cut by a transversal and when two lines intersect.

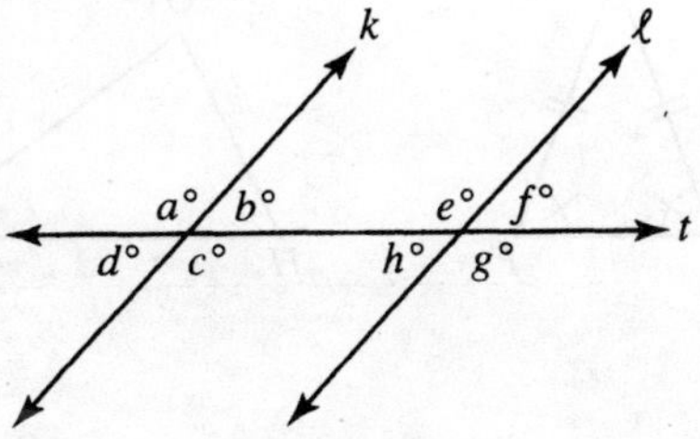

Given $k \parallel \ell$, cut by transversal t, in the figure above:

- *Corresponding angles* are congruent.
  $\therefore a = e, b = f, d = h$, and $c = g$
- *Alternate interior angles* are congruent.
  $\therefore c = e$ and $b = h$
- *Interior angles on the same side of a transversal* are supplementary.
  $\therefore b + e = 180°$ and $c + h = 180°$
- When two lines intersect, *vertical angles* are formed. Vertical angles are congruent.
  $\therefore a = c, b = d, e = g$, and $f = h$

Example 9

Let A, P, Q, and B be points on $\overline{AB}$, as shown above. If $AP : PQ = 1 : 4$, $PQ : QB = 8 : 3$, and AP, PQ, and QB are all integer lengths, which could be the length of AB?

(A) 62 (B) 63 (C) 64 (D) 65

Solution: (D)

Method I: Logical Reasoning

Notice that $AP : PQ : QB = 1 : 4 : 1.5$. Since each length must be an integer, the lengths could be 2, 8, and 3. Total number of parts equals $2 + 8 + 3 = 13$. Of the choices given, only E, 65, is a multiple of 13. Note that $13 \times 5 = 65$, and multiplying each of the lengths 2, 8, and 3 by 5 gives 10, 40, and 15, which add up to 65. Note also that 2, 8, and 3 can be scaled so that their sum is any of answer choices (A)–(D), but only for a multiple of 13 do the lengths have integer values.

Method II: Algebra

The ratio $AP : PQ : QB = 2 : 8 : 3$.

If $AP = 2x$, then $PQ = 8x$, and $QB = 3x$.

$\therefore AB = 13x$

If you set $13x$ equal to any of the answer choices, you notice that $13x = 65$ is the only case that gives integer values for each of the lengths.

TRIANGLES 三角形

Types of Triangles 三角形的类型

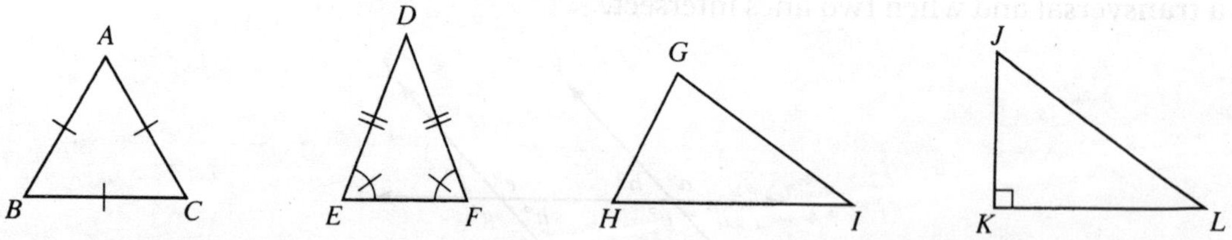

In the figures above:

- $\triangle ABC$ is an *equilateral* triangle. All three sides are congruent, and each of the three angles measures 60°.
- $\triangle DEF$ is an *isosceles* triangle. Two sides, $\overline{DE}$ and $\overline{DF}$, are congruent. The third side, $\overline{EF}$ in the diagram above, is called the *base*. The *base angles*, $\angle E$ and $\angle F$, are congruent.
- $\triangle GHI$ is a *scalene* triangle. All three sides have different lengths, and all three angles have different measures. The angle opposite the longest side has the greatest measure. The angle opposite the shortest side has the smallest measure.
- $\triangle JKL$ is a *right triangle*. $\overline{JK}$ and $\overline{KL}$ are the *legs*. $\overline{JL}$, the side opposite the right angle, is the *hypotenuse*.

Some Triangle Facts 一些三角形的定律

- The triangle inequality theorem: The sum of the lengths of any two sides is greater than the length of the third side.
- The sum of the measures of the three angles in a triangle is 180°.
- The Pythagorean theorem: In any right triangle, the sum of the squares of the legs equals the square of the hypotenuse. In $\triangle ABC$, $a^2 + b^2 = c^2$.

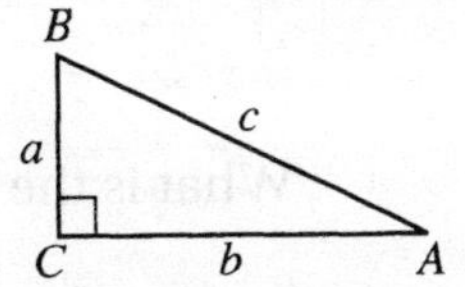

You should memorize the following Pythagorean triangles since they come up often in math problems.

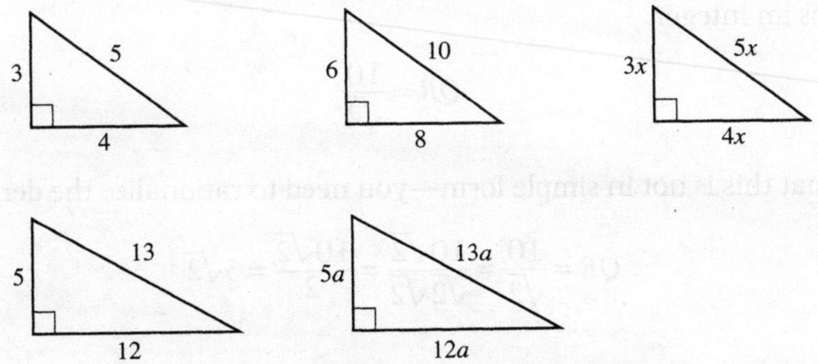

Special Right Triangles 特殊直角三角形

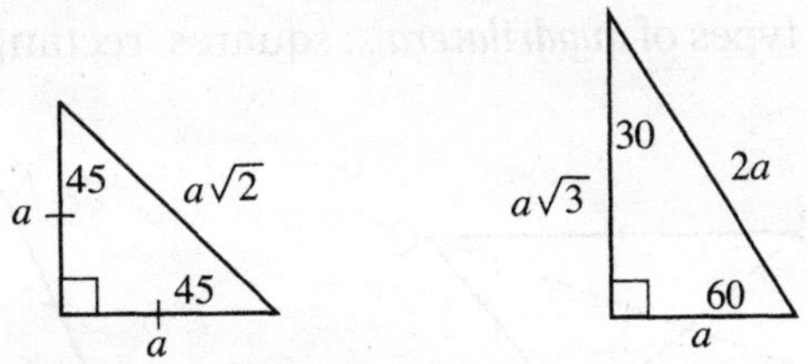

Know the lengths shown above! (But just in case, they are provided at the start of each math section.)

You should also know how to handle 45–45–90° triangles in which the hypotenuse is an integer, and 30–60–90° triangles where the side opposite the 60° angle is an integer.

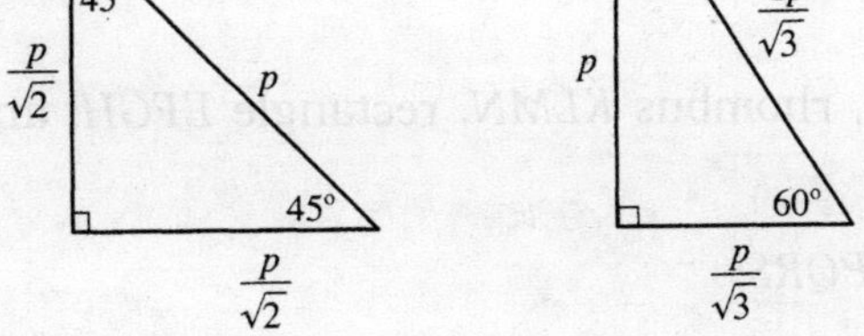

Example 10

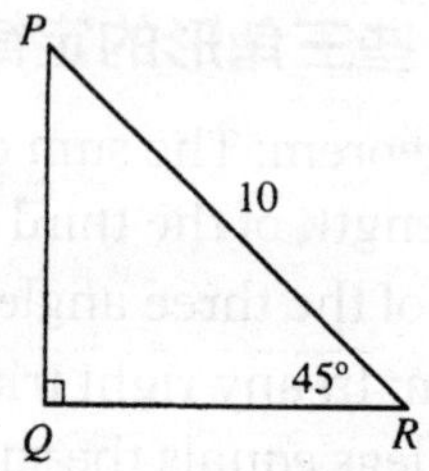

What is the length of $\overline{QR}$?

(A) 5 (B) $\frac{5\sqrt{2}}{2}$ (C) $10\sqrt{2}$ (D) $5\sqrt{2}$

Solution: (D) The figure represents a 45–45–90° triangle where the hypotenuse is an integer.

$$QR = \frac{10}{\sqrt{2}}$$

Note that this is not in simple form—you need to rationalize the denominator:

$$QR = \frac{10}{\sqrt{2}} = \frac{10\sqrt{2}}{\sqrt{2}\sqrt{2}} = \frac{10\sqrt{2}}{2} = 5\sqrt{2}$$

QUADRILATERALS AND POLYGONS 四边形和多边形

Quadrilaterals 四边形

You need to know four types of *quadrilaterals*: squares, rectangles, parallelograms, and rhombi:

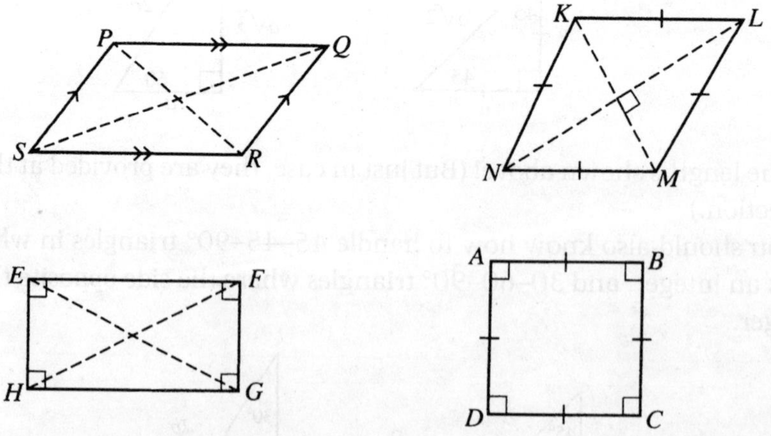

Parallelogram *PQRS*, rhombus *KLMN*, rectangle *EFGH*, and square *ABCD* are shown above.

- In parallelogram *PQRS*:
  1. Opposite sides are parallel and congruent: $\overline{PQ} \parallel \overline{SR}$, $\overline{PS} \parallel \overline{QR}$, $\overline{PQ} \cong \overline{SR}$, and $\overline{PS} \cong \overline{QR}$.
  2. Opposite angles are congruent: $\angle P \cong \angle R$ and $\angle S \cong \angle Q$.
  3. The diagonals bisect each other: $\overline{PO} \cong \overline{RO}$ and $\overline{SO} \cong \overline{QO}$.

- Every rhombus is also a parallelogram. Thus, rhombus *KLMN* has all the properties of a parallelogram. Additionally:
  1. All four sides are congruent.
  2. The diagonals are perpendicular to each other: $\overline{KM} \perp \overline{LN}$.
- Every rectangle is also a parallelogram. Thus, rectangle *EFGH* has all the properties of a parallelogram. Additionally:
  1. All four angles are right angles.
  2. The diagonals are congruent: $\overline{EG} \cong \overline{HF}$.
- Every square is also a rectangle and a rhombus. Therefore, square *ABCD* has all the properties of a rectangle and a rhombus. Additionally:
  1. The length of a diagonal is $x\sqrt{2}$, where x is the length of a side. The reason is that the diagonal splits the square into two isosceles right triangles, each a special 45–45–90° triangle.

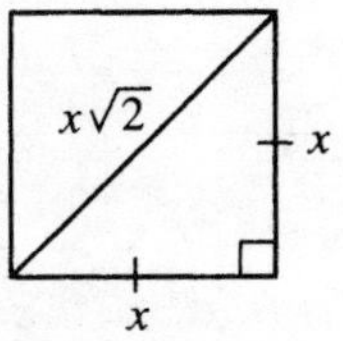

Angles in a Quadrilateral 四边形的角

The sum of the measures of the angles in a quadrilateral is 360°.

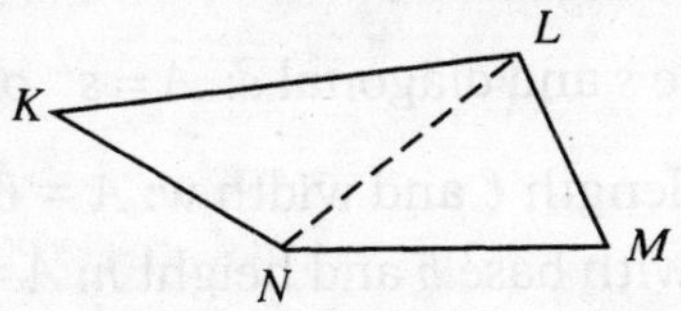

In quadrilateral *KLMN* above, diagonal $\overline{LN}$ divides the figure into two triangles, as shown:

Sum of the angles in $\triangle KLN = 180°$.
Sum of the angles in $\triangle MLN = 180°$.
Sum of the angles in $KLMN = 360°$.

Polygons 多边形

- The sum of the measures of the angles in a polygon is $(n-2)180°$, where n is the number of sides in the polygon. You can see this if you pick any vertex and join it to each of the other vertices of the polygon.

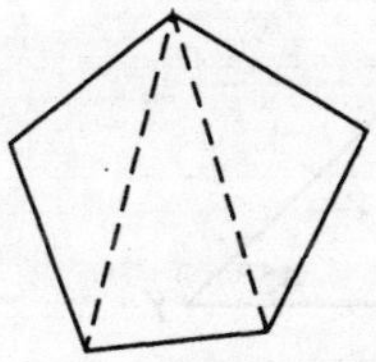

5 sides, 3 triangles

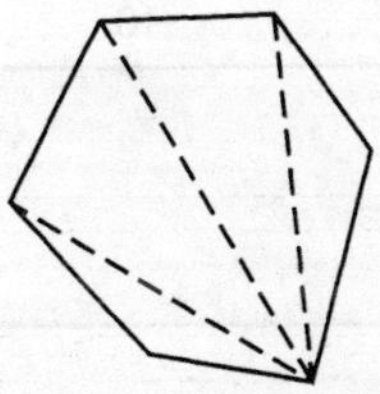

6 sides, 4 triangles

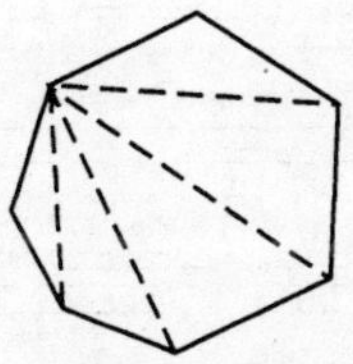

7 sides, 5 triangles

In each of the polygons shown above, the sum of the angle measures in the polygon is the number of triangles multiplied by 180°, namely, $(n-2)180°$, where n is the number of sides of the polygon.

- In a *regular polygon* all the sides are congruent and all the angles are congruent.
- Another useful fact is that the sum of the exterior angles of any polygon is 360°.

AREAS AND PERIMETERS 面积和周长

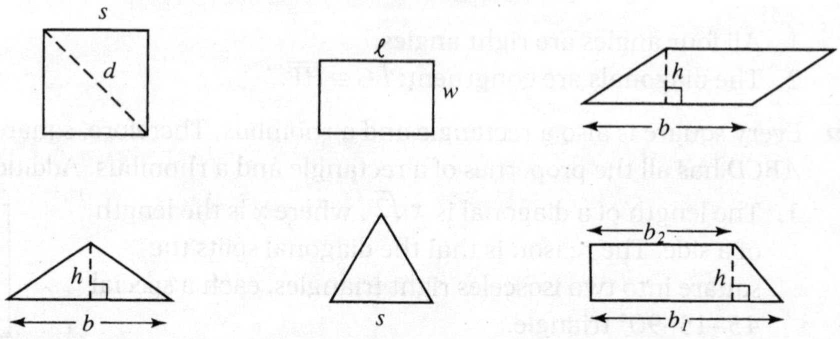

Area 面积

You must know the formulas for the area A of each of the figures shown above:

- A square with side s and diagonal d: $A = s^2$ or $A = \frac{1}{2}d^2$
- A rectangle with length ℓ and width w: $A = \ell w$
- A parallelogram with base b and height h: $A = bh$
- A triangle (which is half a parallelogram) with base b and height h: $A = \frac{1}{2}bh$
- An equilateral triangle with side s: $A = \frac{s^2\sqrt{3}}{4}$
- A trapezoid with bases b_1 and b_2 and height h: $A = \frac{1}{2}h(b_1+b_2)$

Perimeter 周长

The *perimeter* of a polygon is the sum of the lengths of its sides.

Example 11

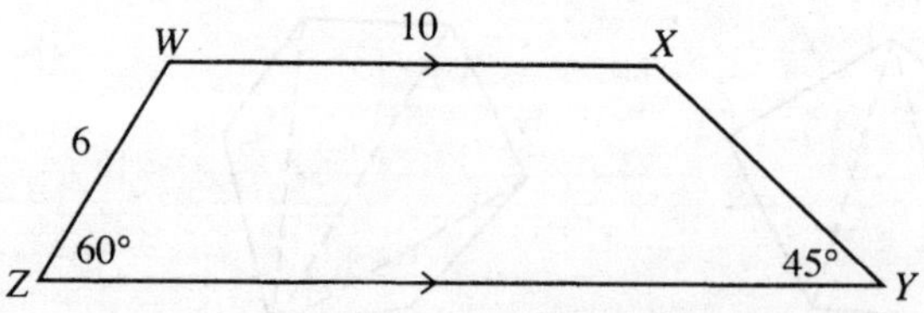

In the figure shown above, $\overline{WX}$ is parallel to $\overline{ZY}$. What is the perimeter of quadrilateral $WXYZ$?

(A) $29+3\sqrt{3}+3\sqrt{6}$

(B) $29+3\sqrt{3}+3\sqrt{2}$

(C) $29+6\sqrt{3}+6\sqrt{6}$

(D) $35+3\sqrt{2}$

Solution: (A)

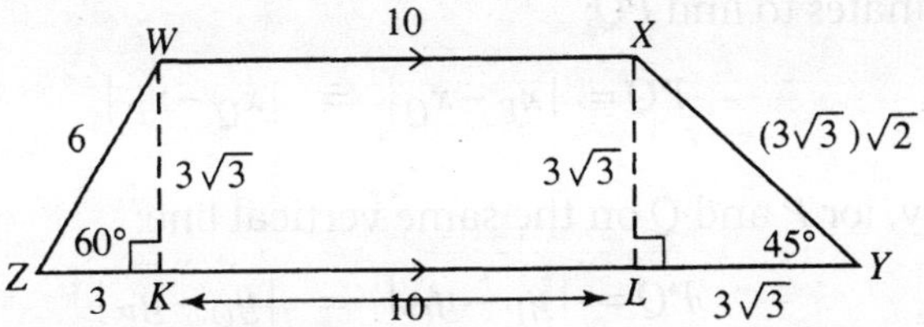

Fill in all the facts you can conclude on the diagram. The picture begs for altitudes; so draw $\overline{WK}$ and $\overline{XL}$. Angles of 60° and 45° are magic numbers on the SAT, and you should direct your energies toward creating special triangles that contain these angles.

$\triangle WZK$ is a 30–60–90° triangle, $\therefore$ leg $ZK = \frac{1}{2}$ hypotenuse $ZW = 3$.

Also, altitude $WK = 3\sqrt{3}$; $\therefore$altitude $XL = 3\sqrt{3}$.

(Notice that quadrilateral $WXLK$ is a rectangle.)

$\triangle XLY$ is a 45–45–90° triangle, $\therefore$leg XL = leg $LY = 3\sqrt{3}$.

$\therefore$ Hypotenuse $XY = LY\sqrt{2} = 3\sqrt{3}\sqrt{2} = 3\sqrt{6}$.

Perimeter of $WXYZ = WX + WZ + ZY + YX$

$= WX + WZ + ZK + KL + LY + YX$

$= 10 + 6 + 3 + 10 + 3\sqrt{3} + 3\sqrt{6}$

$= 29 + 3\sqrt{3} + 3\sqrt{6}$

COORDINATE GEOMETRY 平面几何

High scorers have the following facts at their fingertips. Refer to the diagram below.

Distance 距离

- The *distance* between two points in the plane is

$$PQ = \sqrt{(x_P - x_Q)^2 + (y_P - y_Q)^2}$$

- If P and Q are on the same horizontal line, you can subtract their x-coordinates to find PQ:

$$PQ = |x_P - x_Q| = |x_Q - x_P|$$

- Similarly, for P and Q on the same vertical line:

$$PQ = |y_P - y_Q| = |y_Q - y_P|$$

- The *midpoint* M of $\overline{PQ}$ is $\left(\frac{x_P + x_Q}{2}, \frac{y_P + y_Q}{2}\right)$ (the average of the x-coordinates and the average of the y-coordinates of the endpoints of the given segment).

Geometric Transformations 几何变换

You should be familiar with the following transformations in a plane:

- A *translation* shifts all points of a figure horizontally or vertically. There is no rotation, reflection, or distortion.

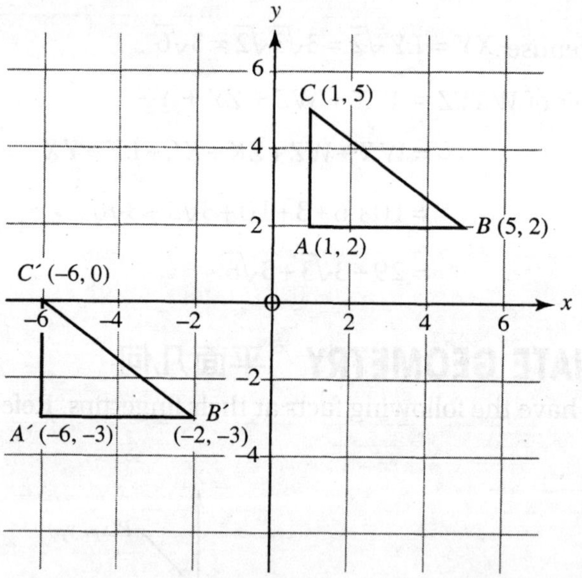

In the diagram, $\triangle ABC$ is translated 7 units to the left and 5 units down. The *image* after translation is $\triangle A'B'C'$.

- A *reflection* produces a mirror image across a line. Every point of the figure is the same distance from the line of reflection as its image.

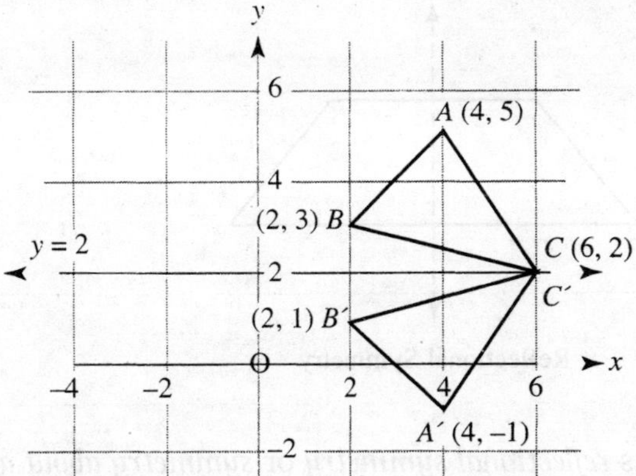

In the diagram, $\triangle A'B'C'$ is the *image* of $\triangle ABC$ reflected across the line $y = 2$.

- A *rotation* rotates a figure about a point, called the center of rotation. After rotation, the image of the point is the same distance from the point of rotation as the original point.

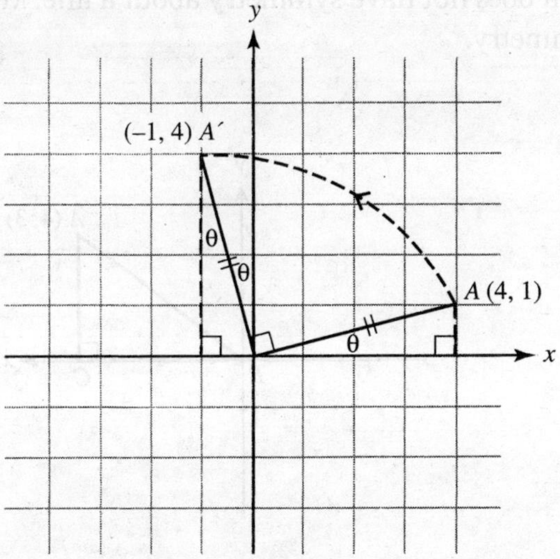

In the diagram, A' is the image of A rotated counterclockwise 90° about the origin.

Symmetry 对称

There are two types of symmetry that you should know:

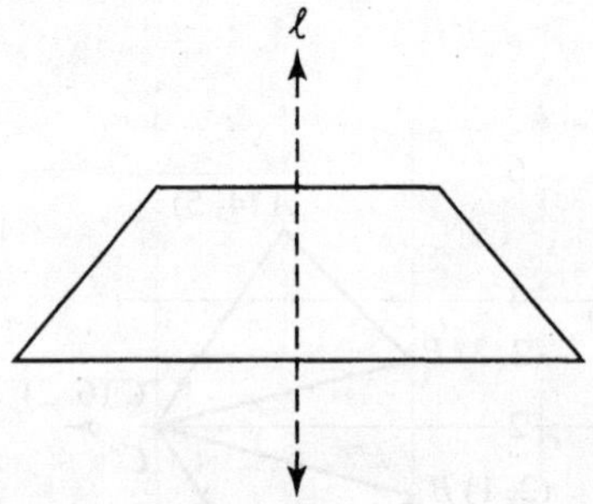

Reflectional Symmetry

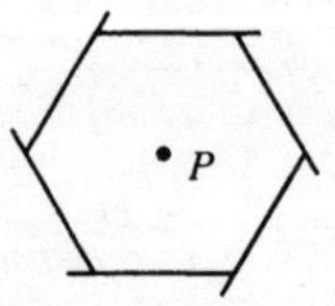

Rotational Symmetry

A figure has *reflectional symmetry* or *symmetry about a line* if reflection across the line produces an identical figure. Line ℓ is a *line of symmetry* for the trapezoid shown above.

A figure has *rotational symmetry* or *symmetry about a point P* if a rotation of k degrees, $0 < k < 360$, clockwise or counterclockwise, about P produces an identical figure. The point P is a *point of symmetry* for the figure. The angle of rotation can be 60°, 120°, 180°, or 240° for the hexagon on the right above.

Note that the figure on the left does not have symmetry about a point, and the figure on the right does not have symmetry about a line. Many figures, however, have both types of symmetry.

Example 12

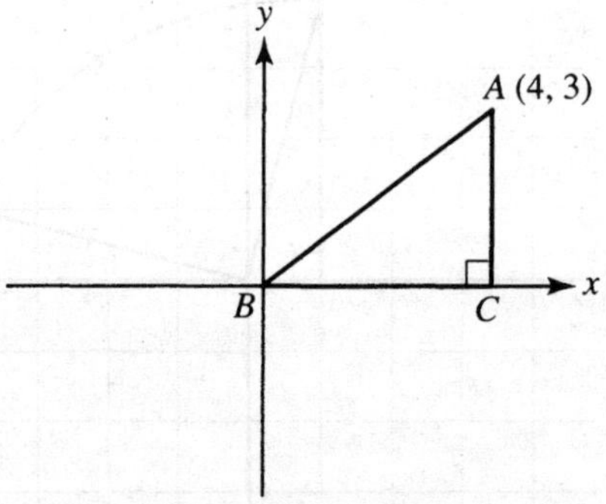

In the figure above, $\triangle ABC$ is rotated counterclockwise through 90° about the origin. Its image is $\triangle A'B'C'$. What is the slope of $\overline{A'B'}$?

(A) $\frac{3}{4}$ (B) $\frac{4}{3}$ (C) $-\frac{3}{4}$ (D) $-\frac{4}{3}$

Solution: (D) Reduce the problem. $\overline{A'B'}$ is the image of the hypotenuse. Therefore the rest of the triangle is irrelevant. You must rotate $\overline{AB}$ and find the slope of its image, $\overline{A'B'}$.

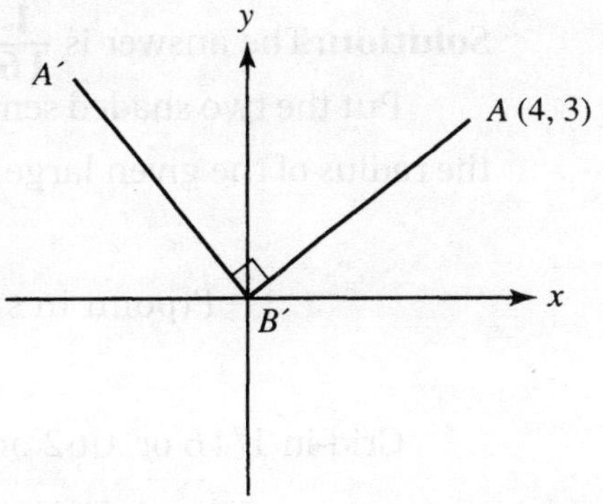

Since $\overline{A'B'} \perp \overline{AB}$, their slopes are negative reciprocals. The slope of $\overline{AB} = \frac{3}{4}$, so the slope of $\overline{A'B'} = -\frac{4}{3}$.

GEOMETRIC PROBABILITY 几何概率

A typical SAT question chooses a point at random in a geometric figure and asks you to find the probability that the point lies in a specified region.

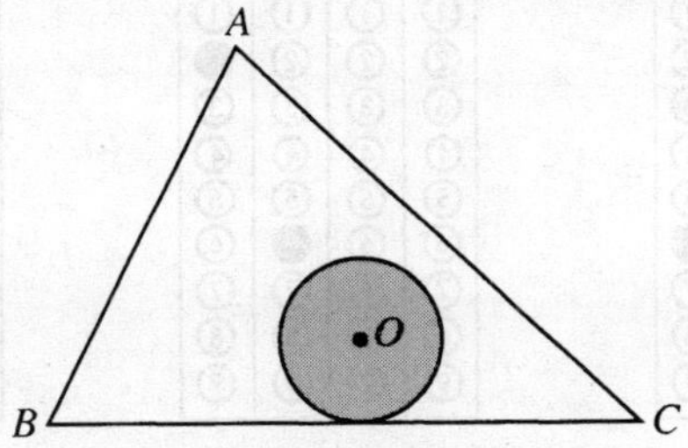

For example, a point is chosen at random in $\triangle ABC$, shown above. What is the probability that the point lands in circle O?

$$P(\text{point in circle}) = \frac{\text{area of circle } O}{\text{area of } \triangle ABC}$$

Example 13 Grid-In

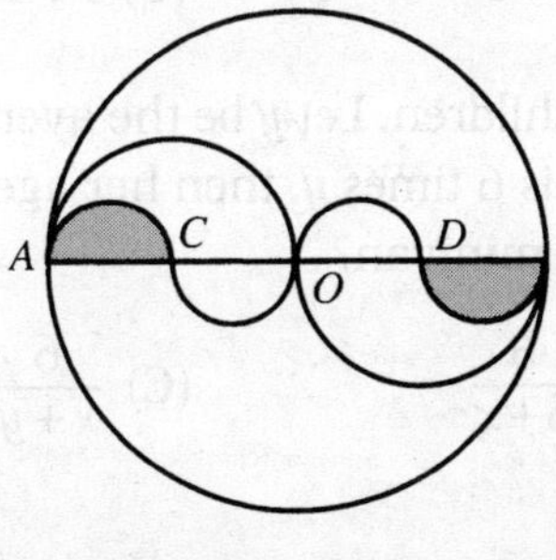

In the circle shown above, O is the center and AB is a diameter. There are two semicircles with diameters $\overline{AO}$ and $\overline{BO}$, and four smaller semicircles with congruent diameters $\overline{AC}$, $\overline{CO}$, $\overline{OD}$, and $\overline{DB}$. A point is picked at random in the large circle. What is the probability that it lands in a shaded region?

Solution: The answer is $\frac{1}{16}$.

Put the two shaded semicircles together to get one small circle whose radius is $\frac{1}{4}$ the radius of the given large circle. Then:

$$P(\text{point in small circle}) = \frac{\text{area of small circle}}{\text{area of large circle}} = \left(\frac{1}{4}\right)^2 = \frac{1}{16}$$

Grid-in 1/16 or .062 or .063.

Coaching:
High scorers save time by remembering this fact:
If $\frac{r_1}{r_2}$ is the ratio of radii for two circles, then $\left(\frac{r_1}{r_2}\right)^2$ is the ratio of the areas of the circles.

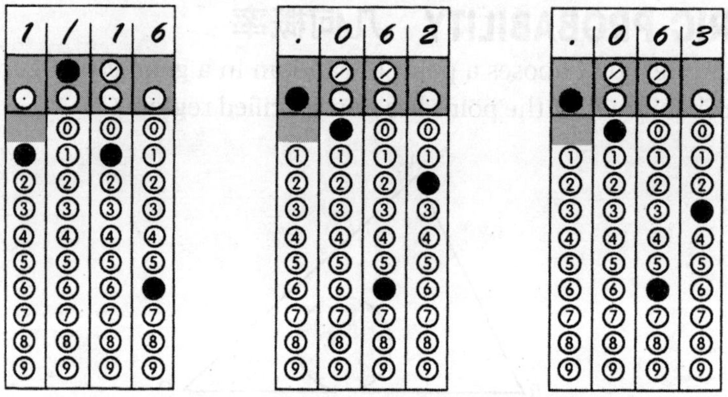

PRACTICE TEST QUESTIONS 练习测试题

1. Points A and B are on the number line in such a way that A corresponds to 0.625 and B corresponds to 0.637. If P is the midpoint of $\overline{AB}$, and Q is on the number line two-thirds of the distance from A to B, what is the ratio of PQ to AQ?

(A) 1 : 4 (B) 1 : 3 (C) 1 : 2 (D) 2 : 3

2. Ali is in a minivan with x children. Let y be the average (arithmetic mean) of the children's ages. If Ali's age is 6 times y, then her age is what fraction of the total ages of all the people in the minivan?

(A) $\frac{6}{6+y}$ (B) $\frac{6}{6+x}$ (C) $\frac{6}{x+y}$ (D) $\frac{x}{6y}$

3. For the expression $x\sqrt{x}$, where x is an integer such that $-100 \leq x \leq 100$, how many x values are there such that the expression is an integer?

(A) 100 (B) 21 (C) 20 (D) 11

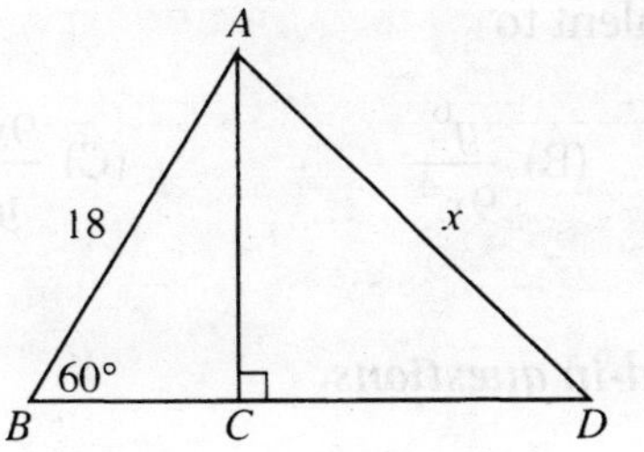

4. In the figure shown above, given that $\overline{AC} \cong \overline{DC}$, the value of x is

(A) $18\sqrt{6}$ (B) $18\sqrt{2}$ (C) $9\sqrt{2}$ (D) $9\sqrt{6}$

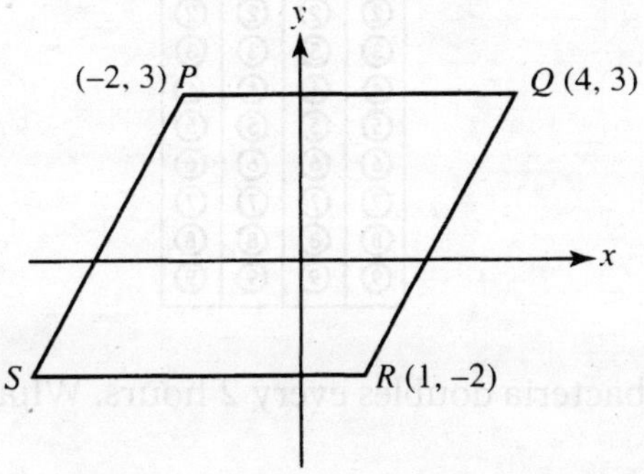

5. In the diagram above, $PQRS$ is a parallelogram. What is the area of $PQRS$?

(A) 15 (B) 18 (C) 30 (D) $3\sqrt{34}$

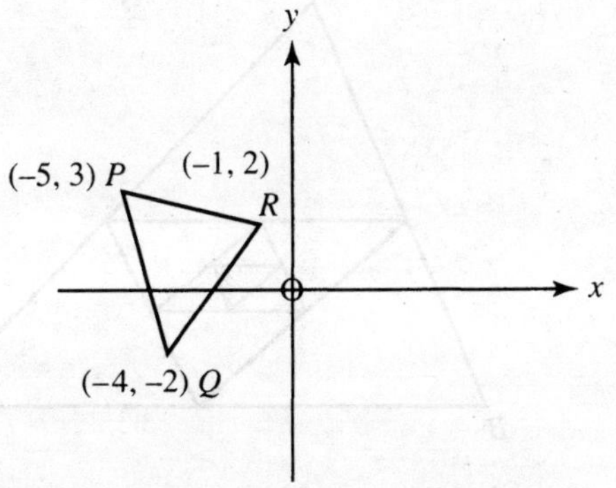

6. Triangle PQR, shown in the diagram above, is translated 4 units to the right and 5 units down. The resulting triangle is then rotated 180° counterclockwise about the origin. What is the final image of point P?

(A) (−1, −2) (B) (1, 2) (C) (2, 1) (D) (−2, 1)

7. A line intersects two parallel lines, forming eight angles. If one of the angles has measure $a°$, how many of the other seven angles are supplementary to it?

(A) 1 (B) 2 (C) 3 (D) 4

8. $(3x^2y^{-3})^{-2}$ is equivalent to

(A) $\dfrac{9}{x^4y^6}$ (B) $\dfrac{y^6}{9x^4}$ (C) $\dfrac{9x^4}{y^6}$ (D) $-\dfrac{9}{x^4y^6}$

Questions 9–11 are grid-in questions.

9.

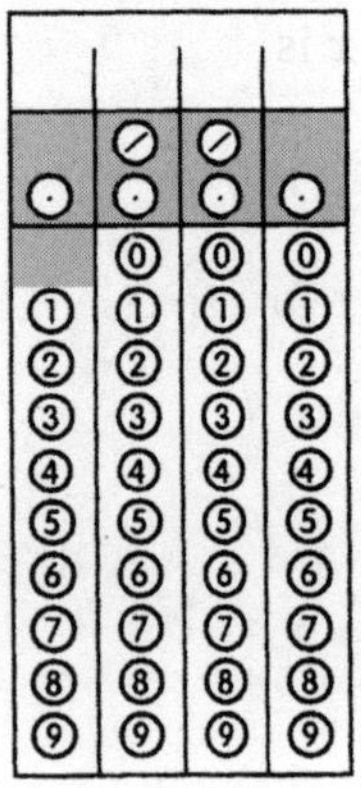

10.

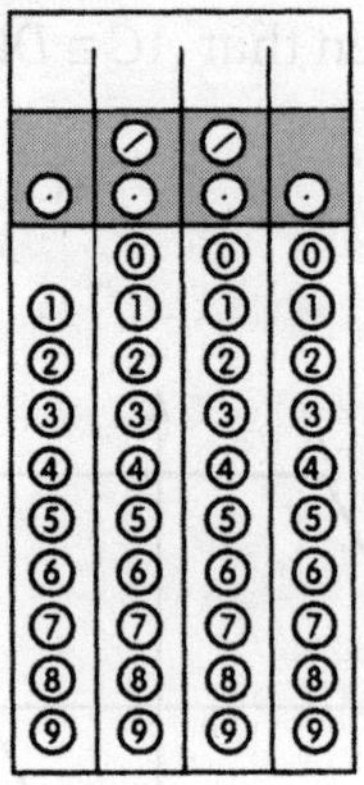

11.

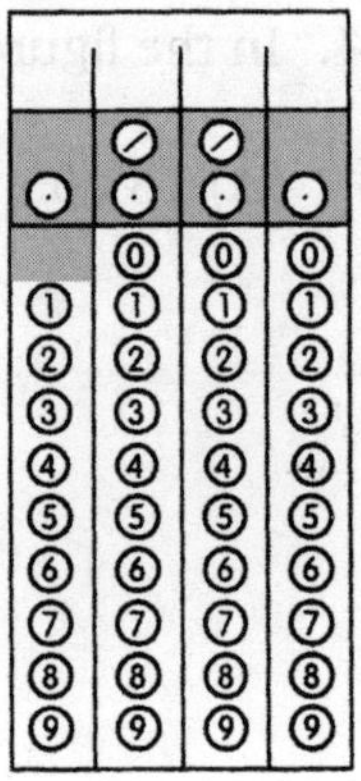

9. A population of bacteria doubles every 2 hours. What is the percent increase after 4 hours?

10. Six chairs are placed in a row to seat six people. How many different seating arrangements are possible if two of the people insist on sitting next to each other?

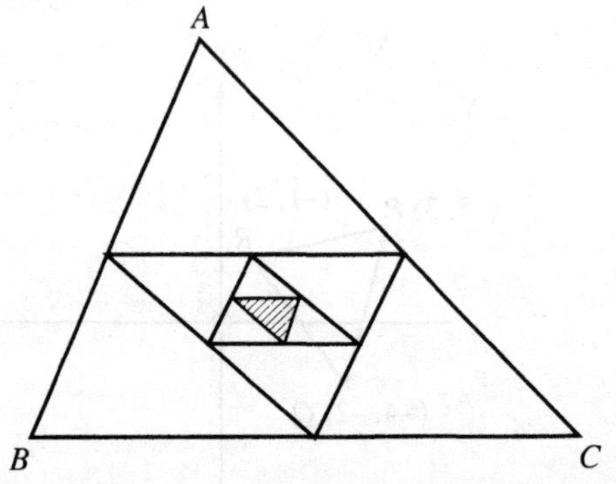

11. The triangles inside $\triangle ABC$, shown above, are formed by joining the midpoints of the sides and then repeating the process. If a point is chosen at random inside $\triangle ABC$, what is the probability that the point lies in the shaded region?

Answers and Explanations 答案与解析

The difficulty level for each question is specified in parentheses: (E) = Easy, (M) = Medium, (H) = Hard.

1. A (M) **4.** D (M) **7.** D (E) **10.** 240 (H)
2. B (H) **5.** C (M) **8.** B (E) **11.** 1/64 (H)
3. D (M) **6.** B (H) **9.** 300 (M)

9.

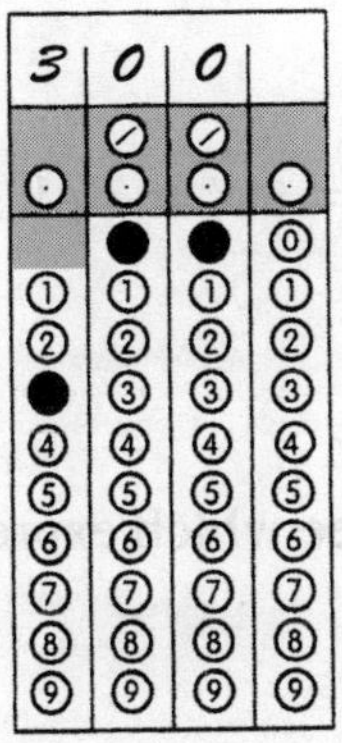

10.

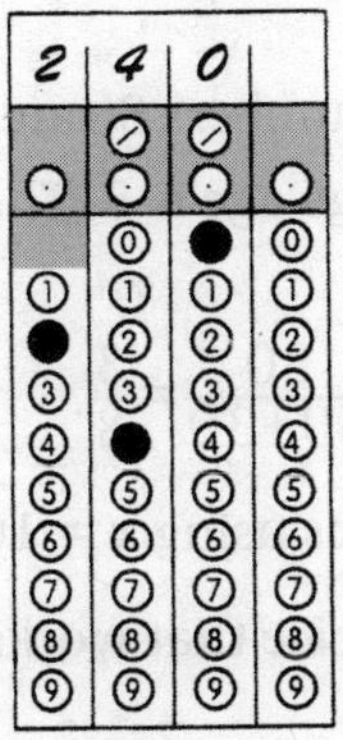

11.

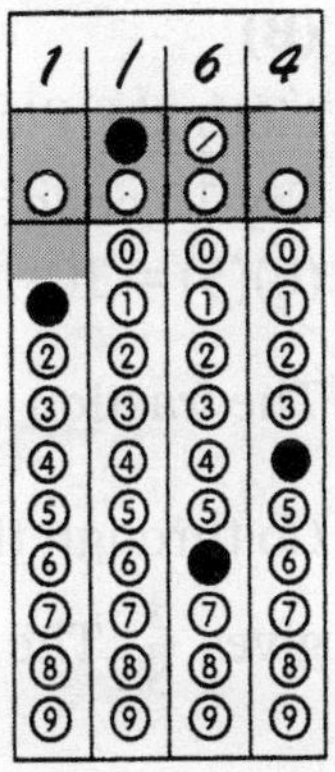

1. (A)

Draw a picture of the points on the number line:

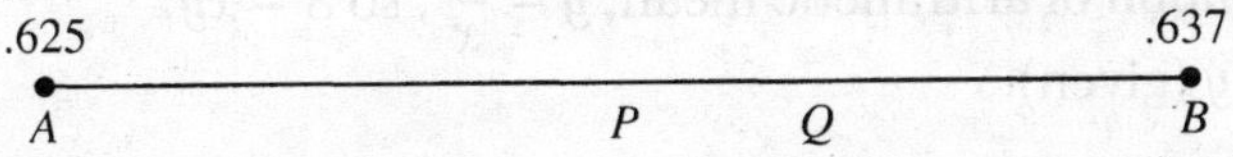

Imagine blowing up the picture so that A is at 625 and B is at 637. Now solve the problem without decimals. The ratios won't change!
P is midway between A and B, so take the average of 625 and 637:

$$\frac{625+637}{2}=631$$

Distance $AB = 637 - 625 = 12$. Point Q is $\frac{2}{3}$ of the distance from A to B, and $\frac{2}{3}$ of 12 is 8. Therefore Q is 8 units from A, at 633.
Here is the picture:

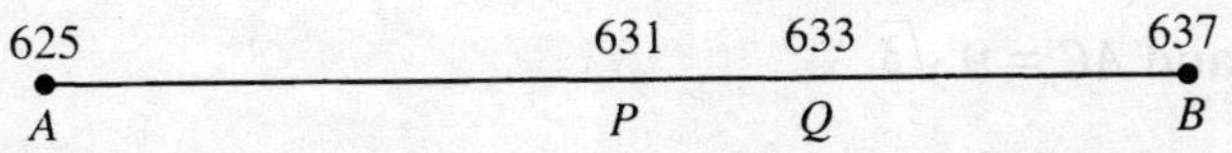

$$\frac{PQ}{AQ}=\frac{2}{8}=\frac{1}{4}\text{, so the ratio is } 1:4.$$

Coaching:
It is always easier to work with whole numbers than with decimals or fractions.

Note that you don't even need the given values:

P is $\frac{1}{2}$ the distance from A to B, and Q is $\frac{2}{3}$ the distance from A to B.

Using common denominators

$$AP : AQ = \frac{3}{6} : \frac{4}{6}$$

$$\therefore PQ : AQ = \frac{1}{6} : \frac{4}{6} = 1:4$$

2. **(B)**

Method I: Pick-Convenient-Numbers Strategy

Try 10 children whose average age is 5. Then, sum of ages = 50, and Ali's age = (6)(5) = 30.

The fraction $\frac{\text{Ali's age}}{\text{total of ages}} = \frac{30}{50+30} = \frac{3}{8}$.

Go through the answer choices using $x = 10$ and $y = 5$ to see which expression gives $\frac{3}{8}$. The only answer choice that works is $\frac{6}{6+x}$.

Method II: Logical Reasoning and Algebra

You have y = average age of children and x = number of children.

Let S = sum of ages of children.

Let A = Ali's age.

By the definition of arithmetic mean, $y = \frac{S}{x}$, so $S = xy$.

Also, $A = 6y$ (given).

$$\text{Ali's age as fraction of total ages} = \frac{A}{S+A}$$

$$= \frac{6y}{xy+6y} = \frac{6y}{(x+6)y} = \frac{6}{6+x}$$

3. **(D)** Recall that the integers are . . . , −3, −2, −1, 0, 1, 2, 3, ...
The expression $x\sqrt{x}$ will be an integer only if x is an integer perfect square. Then x could be 1, 4, 9, 16, 25, . . . ,100. But, of course, you shouldn't forget 0, which gives you 11 possible values of x. Don't even *think* of including negative numbers for x. The square root of a negative number is not a real number.

4. **(D)** $\triangle ABC$ is a 30–60–90° triangle.

$\therefore BC = 9$ and $AC = 9\sqrt{3}$.

$\triangle ADC$ is a 45–45–90° triangle.

$\therefore AD = AC\sqrt{2} = (9\sqrt{3})\sqrt{2} = 9\sqrt{6}$.

The 1600 Club has special right triangles down cold.

5. **(C)** The area of a parallelogram equals base × height. Use $\overline{PQ}$ as base since you have the coordinates of both P and Q. The height of the parallelogram is the distance between horizontal lines $\overline{PQ}$ and $\overline{SR}$.

Notice that *P* and *Q* are on the same horizontal line (same *y*-coordinate), so don't waste your time with the distance formula to get the base. Simply subtract the *x*-coordinates: $PQ = 4 - (-2) = 6$. Similarly, *Q* and *R* are on the same vertical line, so get the height by subtracting the y-coordinates of *Q* and *R*: $3 - (-2) = 5$.

Area $= bh = (6)(5) = 30$

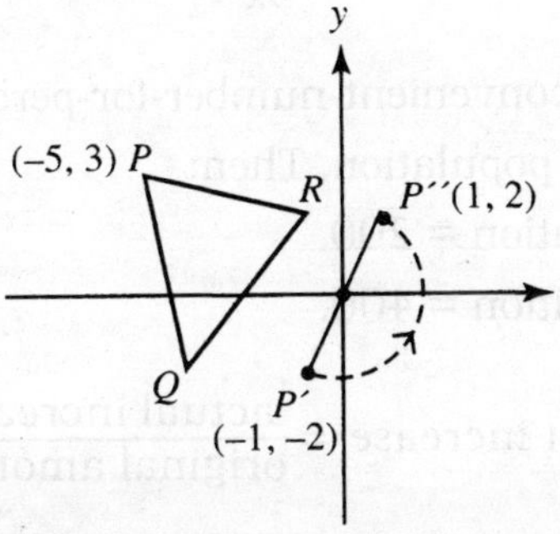

6. **(B)** A careful reading of the problem tells you to reduce it to: Where does point P land? The rest of the figure is irrelevant, so don't waste time on it. $P'(-1, -2)$ is the image of P after translating P 4 units right and 5 units down. $P''(1, 2)$ is where P' lands, that is, it is the final image of P after rotating P' 180° through O.

7. **(D)**

A diagram always helps.

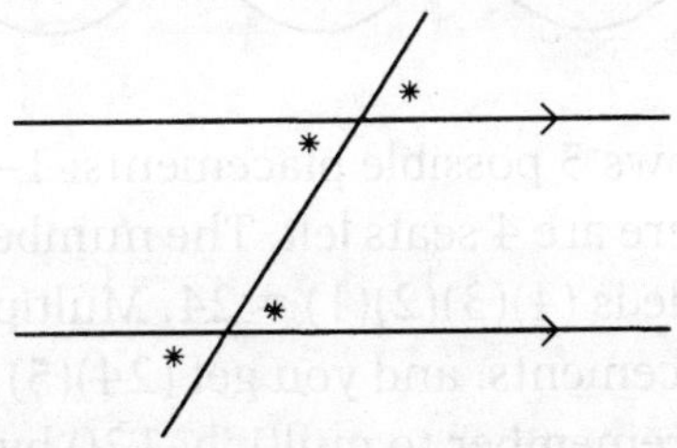

Two angles are supplementary if the sum of their measures is 180°. Either of the angles adjacent to the marked angle is supplementary to it. Mark these adjacent angles (each with an asterisk, say). Now, using the facts that corresponding angles are congruent, and alternate interior angles are congruent, mark all of the angles that are congruent to that "asterisk" angle, as shown. There are four such angles.

8. **(B)** Each factor in the parentheses must be raised to the −2. Also, use the fact that $a^{-n} = \frac{1}{a^n}$.

$$(3x^2y^{-3})^{-2} = 3^{-2} \cdot (x^2)^{-2} \cdot (y^{-3})^{-2}$$

$$= 3^{-2} \cdot x^{-4} \cdot y^6$$

$$= \frac{1}{3^2} \cdot \frac{1}{x^4} \cdot y^6$$

$$= \frac{y^6}{9x^4}$$

9. **300** Use the pick-a-convenient-number-for-percent-problems strategy.
Let 100 be the initial population. Then:
After 2 hours: population = 200.
After 4 hours: population = 400.

$$\text{Percent increase} = \frac{\text{actual increase}}{\text{original amount}} \times 100$$

$$= \frac{400-100}{100} \times 100 = 300\%$$

Grid-in 300.

10. **240**

Draw a picture of the chairs and the possible placements of the two people who must sit together.

The picture above shows 5 possible placements: 1–2, 2–3, 3–4, 4–5, or 5–6. In each of these cases there are 4 seats left. The number of permutations for seating the remaining 4 people is (4)(3)(2)(1) = 24. Multiply this number by the 5 possible two-together placements, and you get (24)(5) = 120. Don't pat yourself on the back yet: did you remember to multiply 120 by 2, because there are 2 ways of arranging the 2 people sitting together? Final answer = (2)(120) = 240.
Grid-in 240.

11. The answer is **1/64**.

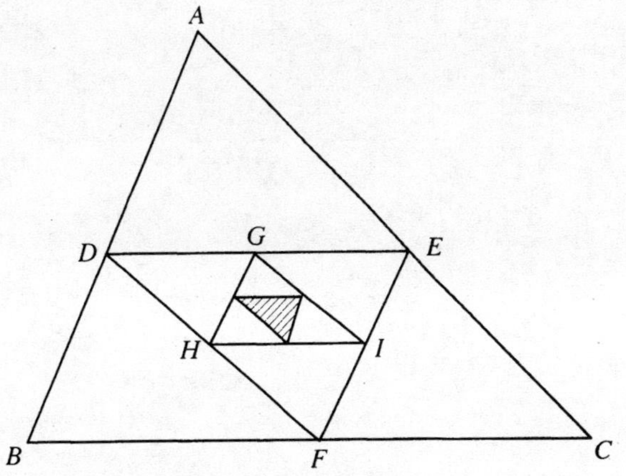

area of $\triangle DEF = \frac{1}{4}$ area of $\triangle ABC$

area of $\triangle GHI = \frac{1}{4}$ area of $\triangle DEF$

$= \frac{1}{16}$ area of $\triangle ABC$

Here is the sequence of areas you get, compared with area $\triangle ABC$:

$$1, \frac{1}{4}, \frac{1}{16}, \frac{1}{64}, \ldots$$

This is a geometric sequence with common ratio $\frac{1}{4}$.

Since area of shaded region $= \frac{1}{64}$ area of $\triangle ABC$, the probability of a random point landing there is $\frac{1}{64}$.

Grid-in 1/64.

第十章 Chapter 10

PROBLEMS IN CONTEXT 应用题

1600 Club Steps for Tackling a Problem in Context
1600分俱乐部应用题解题步骤

CARESS the problem. Yes, really!

Step 1: **C**oncentrate deeply during a first reading of the problem.
Step 2: **A**ctive pencil! Draw diagrams and charts. Assign variables.
Step 3: **R**educe the problem to a concise statement of what you need to find.
Step 4: **E**xpress the problem type so that you can apply a familiar technique.
Step 5: **S**olve the problem.
Step 6: **S**ensible answer? Ask yourself whether your answer makes sense.

WHAT IS IT? 什么是应用题?

What, exactly, is a problem in context? It's a real-life situation that can be translated into math and expressed with an equation or graph—the familiar "word problem" or "function modeling" in your math textbooks. The updated SAT Math Test contains many problems in context. Here are some of the situations you may encounter on the test. Is it cheaper to rent a car or take a train? How much gas must you buy to make it to Los Angeles? How many hours will it take to empty the pool? How many Euros will you get in Spain at the current exchange rate? What will the population be in ten years' time? What does the slope of this graph mean?

In your daily life you are constantly bombarded with situations where you must do the math. Can you make sense of the numerical data that surrounds you?

Additionally, there are the familiar "word problems" that you have seen in your Algebra classes for years.

On the SAT Math Test, you will be given a story and asked to do any of the following:

- Identify a graph that describes the situation.
- Identify an equation that fits the data.
- Identify a term of an equation that solves a problem.
- Make an additional calculation based on the given setup.

As you can see, questions in context involve a lot of reading, focusing, and analyzing.

The bugaboo about problems in context exists because not only must you solve a math problem, but also you must first extricate that problem from statements embedded in a real-world scenario. You must extract the pertinent information from a web of details, some of which are extraneous. This can be a daunting task—but not for the 1600 Club. You are bringing years of math experience to the SAT, plus the ability and confidence to solve any question the test makers may devise.

HOW TO APPROACH A WORD PROBLEM 怎样解答应用题?

When you come to a word problem, especially one that looks tricky, don't flail about and panic. You need to be systematic and to force yourself to go through the following steps. If you need an acronym to help you remember, here's a thought: stay calm and CARESS the problem.

1. **C**oncentrate with 100 percent of your ability as you read the question carefully, beginning to end. This advice sounds trite, but it's important to absorb as much as possible on a first reading.
2.  Use an **A**ctive pencil as you analyze the problem. Start writing things down as you think. Draw a diagram or a chart. Fill in pertinent values. Assign variables. Play with the problem on paper as you mull it over in your head.
3. **R**educe the problem to a concise statement of what must be calculated.
4. **E**xpress the question as a known problem type if at all possible. If you can identify the problem type, often you can apply a familiar technique or formula.
5. **S**olve the problem! By now you should have a pretty good idea how to do this.
6. **S**ensible answer? Ask yourself this question. If you came up with 62 as the average age of kindergartners, you need to reassess. Did you bubble in the quantity asked for? What a tragedy to correctly calculate Fran's current age, when the question actually asks how old she was 10 years ago!

TRANSLATING ENGLISH INTO MATH 将语言转换为数学表达式

Translating English into math should be second nature to high scorers:

- 34 more than x: $x + 34$.
- 16 less than y: $y - 16$.
- The product of two numbers is: $xy =$.
- The cost of an opera ticket and dinner is: $t + d =$.
- Length ℓ is divided in the ratio 3 : 4: $\ell = 3x + 4x$, where x is one part.
- Marvin ate 5 candies for every 2 candies that Raymond ate: $\frac{m}{r} = \frac{5}{2}$.
- The difference between Sarah's salary and Jon's salary is \$100: $|s - j| = 100$.
- The difference between Sarah's salary and Jon's salary is less than \$100: $|s - j| < 100$.
- Peter is 4 years older than Lauren: $p = \ell + 4$.
- The discount is 25 percent off the price: $d = 0.25p$.

SOME FAMILIAR PROBLEM TYPES 一些熟悉的问题类型

This section describes some of the standard problem types alluded to in Step 4 of the "How to Approach a Word Problem" section of this chapter. These are problems that the 1600 Club should easily recognize. The techniques for solving such problems should be at your fingertips.

Age Problems 年龄问题

To represent a past age, subtract from the present age. To represent a future age, add to the present age.

Sample Problem 样例

Barb is 3 times as old as Pat. Six years from now, Barb will be twice as old as Pat will be then. Find the present ages of both Barb and Pat.

Solution: Pat is 6, Barb is 18. Let Pat's present age equal x. (Start with the younger person's age to avoid using fractions!) Then Barb's present age equals $3x$.

It often helps to organize the data for the two time frames in a table, as shown.

Person	Present Age	Age in 6 Years
Pat	x	$x + 6$
Barb	$3x$	$3x + 6$

Now write an equation that translates the following into math:

Barb's age six years from now will be twice Pat's age six years from now.

$$3x + 6 = 2(x + 6)$$

Solving this equation yields $x = 6$. Therefore, Pat's present age is 6, and Barb's present age is $3(6) = 18$.

A related question on the SAT Math Test may be as follows:

Example 1

$$3x + 6 = 2(x + 6)$$

The equation above is used to represent the following situation. Barb is 3 times as old as Pat. Six years from now, Barb will be twice as old as Pat will be then. Suppose Pat is now x years old. What does the expression $3x + 6$ represent in this equation?

(A) Three times Pat's current age
(B) Barb's current age
(C) Pat's age in 6 years' time
(D) Barb's age in 6 years' time

Solution: (D) Based on the analysis in the Sample Problem, Barb's current age is $3x$, so $3x + 6$ represents her age in 6 years' time.

Sale-of-Two-Items Problems 出售两种物品问题

A typical problem has quantities x of Item 1 and y of Item 2, each item with a different sale price. You will be given the total number of items sold and the total amount of money made, leading to two equations in two variables. Solving the equations simultaneously leads to the values of x and y.

Sample Problem 样例

At a school bake sale, muffins are sold for \$1.50 each, and brownies are sold for \$2.25 each. If a total of 68 items are sold, and the amount raised at the bake sale is \$123, how many muffins were sold?

Solution: 40 muffins were sold. This kind of problem is easily solved using two variables, x and y, to represent the numbers of each kind of item sold. Let x be the number of muffins sold. Let y be the number of brownies sold. Organize the data in a table:

	Muffins	Brownies
How many	x	y
Amount of money raised	$1.50x$	$2.25y$

Translate into a math equation: 68 items were sold.

$$x + y = 68$$

Translate into a math equation: Amount of money raised was \$123.

$$1.50x + 2.25y = 123$$

Solving the two equations simultaneously yields $x = 40$ and $y = 28$. Therefore, 40 muffins were sold. (To review solving two equations simultaneously, flip to the "Systems of Linear Equations" section of Chapter 11.)

A similar question on the SAT Math Test may be as follows:

Example 2

At a school bake sale, muffins are sold for \$1.50 each, and brownies are sold for \$2.25 each. If a total of 68 items are sold, and the amount raised at the bake sale is \$123, which of the following is a pair of equations that could be used to find out how many muffins and how many brownies were sold?

(A) $x + y = 68$
$1.50x + 2.25y = 123$

(B) $x + y = 123$
$1.50x + 2.25y = 68$

(C) $x + y = 123$
$2.25x + 1.50y = 68$

(D) $x + y = 68$
$2.25x + 1.50y = 68$

Solution: (A) Refer to the analysis from the sample problem. The total number of items sold is 68, so $x + y = 68$. Eliminate choices (B) and (C). Now eliminate choice (D) because the money raised from muffins is $1.50x$, not $2.25x$. You need look no further than choice (A).

Distance, Speed, and Time Problems 距离、速度与时间问题

Keep in mind the following equations:

$$D = ST \qquad T = \frac{D}{S} \qquad S = \frac{D}{T}$$

D = Distance, S = Speed (or rate) of travel, and T = Time taken for trip. Note that S represents one of the following:

- The uniform speed that stays constant throughout the trip.
- The average speed, which equals the total distance traveled divided by the total time traveled. Thus, a car that traveled 120 miles in 3 hours was traveling at an average speed of $\frac{120}{3}$ or 40 miles per hour.

Sample Problem 样例

Two trains started at the same time from stations that were 360 miles apart and traveled toward each other. The speed of the fast train exceeded the speed of the slow train by 10 mph. At the end of 2 hours, the trains were still 120 miles apart. Find the speed of each train.

Solution: Speed of slow train = 55 mph. Speed of fast train = 65 mph. Let x be the speed of the slow train. Then $x + 10$ is the speed of the fast train. Use a table to fill in the speed, time, and distance for each train.

	Speed (mph)	Time (hr)	Distance (mi)
Slow Train	x	2	$2x$
Fast Train	$x + 10$	2	$2(x + 10)$

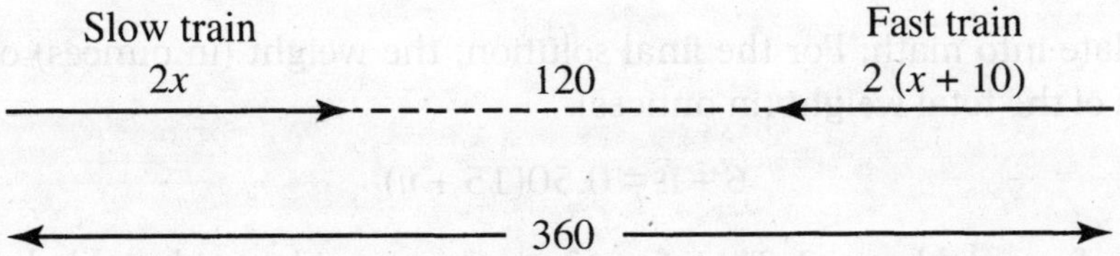

Coaching: *Always use a figure for a distance-speed-time problem.*

Using the figure as a guide, translate into math: The total distance between the stations was 360 miles.

$$2x + 120 + 2(x + 10) = 360$$

Solving yields $x = 55$, so the speeds of the trains were 55 mph and 65 mph.

The Math section of the SAT test may use a problem like this one as a grid-in question, asking for the speed of the faster train. You would need to be careful that you use $x + 10$, namely 65, as your answer, and grid-in 65.

Mixture Problems 混合问题

The first thing to understand is: 25 ounces of a 20 percent solution of salt and water means 20% of 25 oz = 5 oz of pure salt, and the rest, 20 oz, is water. Typically, you will be given a diluted solution and asked how much pure substance must be added to change the percentage dilution.

Sample Problem 样例

How much pure acid must be added to 15 oz of an acid solution that is 40% acid in order to produce a solution that is 50% acid?

Solution: 3 oz of pure acid The number of ounces of pure acid in the given solution is $(0.40)(15) = 6$. Let n equal the number of ounces of pure acid to be added. Then $n + 6$ equals the number of ounces of pure acid in the final solution. The total weight of the new solution equals:

$$\text{(original weight)} + \text{(weight of acid added)} = 15 + n$$

Again, arrange the information in a table:

Kind of Solution	Total Number of Ounces	Part Pure Acid	Number of Ounces of Pure Acid
Original solution	15	0.40 (40%)	6
Pure acid added	n	1.00 (100%)	n
New mixture	$15 + n$	0.50 (50%)	$0.50(15 + n)$

Translate into math: For the final solution, the weight (in ounces) of pure acid equals 50% of the total weight (in ounces).

$$6 + n = 0.50(15 + n)$$

Solving for n yields $n = 3$. Therefore, 3 oz of pure acid must be added.

Here is an alternative, quick solution. If the numbers given are simple whole numbers, it is often easier to focus on the part of the solution that stays constant, in this case the water. Since the amount of pure acid in the original solution is 6 ounces, there are 9 ounces of water $(15 - 6)$. A solution that is 50% (namely half) acid would need 9 ounces of acid in the 9 ounces of water, so you need to add 3 ounces of pure acid.

On the Math section of the SAT, you may be asked the following type of question that uses the Sample Problem:

Example 3

$$6 + n = 0.50(15 + n)$$

The equation above is used to find a solution to the following problem: How much pure acid must be added to 15 ounces of an acid solution that is 40% acid in order to produce a solution that is 50% acid? In the given equation, if n is the number of ounces of pure acid to be added, what does the expression $15 + n$ represent?

(A) The weight of the original solution
(B) The weight of the final solution
(C) The weight of pure acid in the original solution
(D) The weight of pure acid in the final solution

Solution: (B) The problem states that the original solution weighs 15 ounces. After you've added n ounces of acid to this solution, the weight of the final solution is $15 + n$.

Work Problems 工作问题

To solve these types of problems, you need to understand the *rate of work* concept. For example, if Harry can paint a wall in 40 minutes, in one minute, he will complete $\frac{1}{40}$ of the job. The part of a job that can be completed in 1 unit of time (in this case 1 minute) is the *rate of work*. Therefore, $\frac{1}{40}$ is Harry's rate of work. Note that in 2 minutes he'll complete $\frac{2}{40}$ of the job, and in x minutes he'll complete $\frac{x}{40}$ of the job.

Note this formula:

$$\text{Rate of work} \times \text{Time of work} = \text{Part of work done}$$

Suppose Sam's rate of work is $\frac{1}{60}$, and Harry and Sam start painting that same wall together. After 1 minute, they will finish $\frac{1}{40} + \frac{1}{60} = \frac{5}{120}$ of the job. At the end of x minutes, they will finish $\frac{x}{40} + \frac{x}{60} = \frac{5x}{120}$ of the job. Note that if Harry and Sam complete the job, that fraction on the right side, $\frac{5x}{120}$, must equal 1, the whole job. This is the basis of work problems.

***Sample Problem* 样例**

Sam can mow a lawn in 20 minutes, and Bob can mow the same lawn in 30 minutes. If they work together, how long will it take them to complete the job?

Solution: 12 minutes Let x equal the number of minutes to complete the job working together.

$$\text{Sam's rate of work} = \frac{1}{20}$$

$$\text{Sam's fraction of work in } x \text{ minutes} = \frac{x}{20}$$

$$\text{Bob's rate of work} = \frac{1}{30}$$

$$\text{Bob's fraction of work in } x \text{ minutes} = \frac{x}{30}$$

Translate into math:

Sam's fraction of work + Bob's fraction of work = 1

$$\frac{x}{20} + \frac{x}{30} = 1$$

Solving yields $x = 12$. Therefore, they will take 12 minutes to mow the lawn together.

A question on the Math section of the SAT, based on this type of problem, could be as follows:

Example 4

Sam can mow a lawn in 20 minutes, and Bob can mow the same lawn in 30 minutes. If they work together, you are to find the time it will take them to complete the job. Suppose x is the number of minutes taken for Sam and Bob to complete the job. Which of the following is the best equation to solve the problem?

(A) $\frac{20}{x} + \frac{30}{x} = 1$

(B) $\frac{x}{20} + \frac{x}{30} = 1$

(C) $\frac{x}{20} + \frac{x}{30} = \frac{5x}{60}$

(D) $\frac{20}{x} + \frac{30}{x} = \frac{50}{x}$

Solution: (B) The equation to solve this problem must use the principle that Sam's fraction of the work added to Bob's fraction of the work must equal 1, the whole job. Therefore, eliminate choices (C) and (D), which do nothing more than add two fractions together. Since Sam's fraction of work is $\frac{x}{20}$, and Bob's fraction of work is $\frac{x}{30}$, the sum of their fractions is given by $\frac{x}{20}+\frac{x}{30}$, which is the expression used in choice (B).

ADDITIONAL PROBLEM TYPES 其他类型

Here are some additional problem types you may encounter:

- Rate problems, where p is proportional to q. Think: $\frac{p_1}{q_1}=\frac{p_2}{q_2}$
- Inverse variation problems, where a is inversely proportional to b. Think: $a_1b_1 = a_2b_2$. (See "Direct and Indirect Variation" in Chapter 12.)
- Bacterial growth or population growth problems. Think: Geometric sequence and exponential function. (See "Linear, Quadratic, and Exponential Models" in Chapter 12.)
- Percent increase problems. Think:

$$\text{Percent increase} = \frac{\text{new} - \text{original}}{\text{original}} \cdot 100$$

- "Outfit" counting problems. Think: k hats, m shirts, and n slacks means $(k)(m)(n)$ possible outfits.
- "Committee" problems where order isn't important. How many different 3-person committees can be formed from 10 people?

  Think: Slots divided by arrangements of 3 people: $\frac{(10)(9)(8)}{(3)(2)(1)}$. (See "Permutations and Combinations" in Chapter 9.)
- "Committee" problems where order *is* important. How many different ways can you pick a secretary, treasurer, and president from 10 people? Think slots: (10)(9)(8).
- Arithmetic mean of k values, $v_1, v_2, \ldots, v_k$: Think $\frac{v_1+v_2+v_3+\cdots+v_k}{k}$.
- Median of data. Arrange data in order and find the middle value or average of the two middle values.
- Function modeling problems. For a linear function, find an equation of the form $y = mx + b$.
- Shaded areas problems. Think: Subtraction.

SOME ADDITIONAL TIPS 一些补充提示

In translating English into math, pick variable names that suggest what is represented to help you keep track. For example, Wendy's DVDs and Carol's videos should be represented as w and c, not x and y.

The verbiage in a problem that involves a graph can be extensive. Be systematic in examining the header, axes, and individual points.

Occasionally you will encounter a problem that you can't classify, a "no category" problem. Stay calm. High scorers are accustomed to using their brains. Gather your experience and wits, and focus in. Also, be aware that, if a problem is toward the end of a set, it will not be straightforward.

Here is a final thought that you should carry with you to the SAT:

The 1600 Club has the talent to solve every math problem on the SAT.

Example 5

Mrs. Teukolsky gave a test that was so difficult that she decided to scale the grades upward. She raised the lowest score, 42, to 60, and the highest score, 77, to 90. A linear function that gives a fair way to convert any other test score x to the new score y is

(A) $y=-\frac{7}{6}x+11$ (C) $y=\frac{6}{7}x+24$

(B) $y=-\frac{6}{7}x+24$ (D) $y=\frac{7}{6}x+11$

Solution: (C)

Active Pencil: Write 42 → 60 and 77 → 90, or (42, 60) and (77, 90).

Reduce the problem: Identify the linear function that contains (42, 60) and (77, 90).

Express the problem type: Find a linear function that contains two given points.

Solve: The quickest method is the plug-in strategy. Find the equation in the answer choices that works for each ordered pair.

Save time. Don't try the equations with negative slopes: as *x* increases, *y* increases, so the negative-slope choices can't be correct!

When you tried this problem, did you pick choice (D) because (42, 60) works?

$60 = \frac{7}{6}(42) + 11 \Rightarrow 60 = 49 + 11$, yes!

If you did, you got the wrong answer, because *both* ordered pairs must work.

Sensible answer? Choice (C) seems reasonable.

Example 6

A solid white cube with an edge of 8 inches is painted red. The cube is then sliced into 512 1-inch cubes. How many of these cubes have exactly 2 red faces?

(A) 48 (B) 72 (C) 80 (D) 96

Solution: (B)

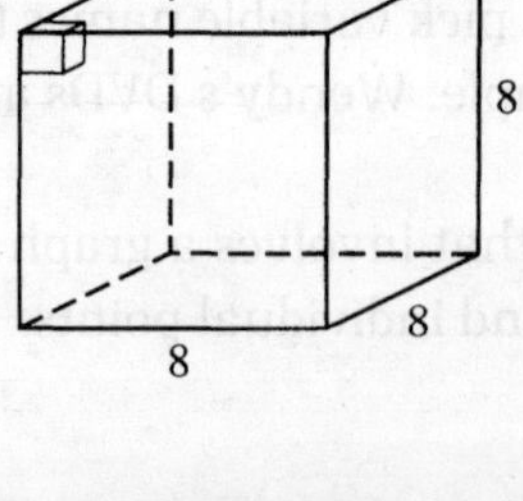

Concentrate! Picture that painted red cube in your mind's eye.

Active Pencil: Draw an 8-inch cube, and label the edges. Then draw in 1 or 2 little 1-inch cubes.

Reduce the problem: Find the number of "little" cubes that have exactly 2 red faces.

Express the problem type: Counting, and visualizing a three-dimensional solid.

Solve: Picture the little 1-inch cubes. Each corner cube will be red on 3 faces: top, side, and front. Now picture the non-corner cubes underneath the corner cube shown. These are the cubes you want. Can you see that there are 6 such cubes on each edge? Since there are 12 edges, there are $(12)(6) = 72$ cubes, each with exactly 2 red faces. The cubes in the "middle" of the faces have exactly 1 red face, and those on the "inside" of the big cube have no red faces, so 72 is the final answer.

Sensible answer? The total number of little cubes, 512, is the volume of the given cube. Most of the little cubes will *not* be red on 2 faces, so 72 is a reasonable answer.

Example 7 Grid-In

Lauren rode her bike from her house to a friend's house $3\frac{1}{2}$ miles away. On the first leg of her trip, she rode uphill at 3 miles per hour. The second part of the trip covered a larger distance but was downhill, and Lauren rode at 5 miles per hour. If the downhill part of the ride took half an hour, how many minutes did the uphill part take?

Solution: 20

Concentrate. Both minutes and hours are mentioned, so units will be an issue.

Active Pencil: Draw a diagram showing the trip.

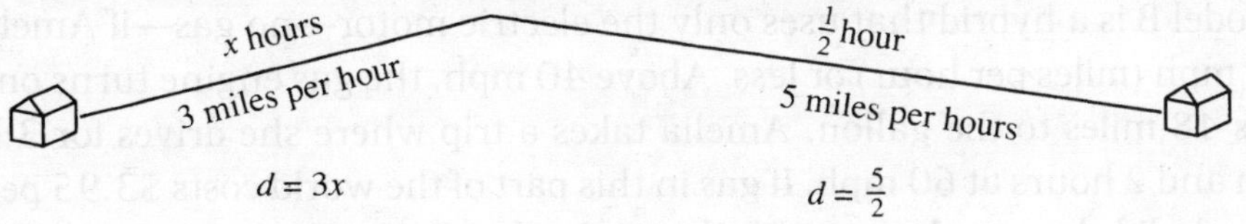

Reduce the problem: You are to find the time *in minutes* for the uphill part of the trip.

Express the problem type: Distance = speed × time.

Solve: Let x be the time for the uphill part of the trip. Work with x in hours, since the speeds are given in miles per *hour*. Write MINUTES in your test booklet to remind yourself to do the conversion at the end.

Distance for first part $= 3x$.

Distance for second part $= (5)\left(\frac{1}{2}\right)$.

Total distance $= 3\frac{1}{2}$ miles.

$\therefore$ Distance for first part = 1 mile.

$\therefore 3x = 1$

$x = \frac{1}{3}$

Sensible answer? Check! Don't blow it by gridding-in $\frac{1}{3}$.

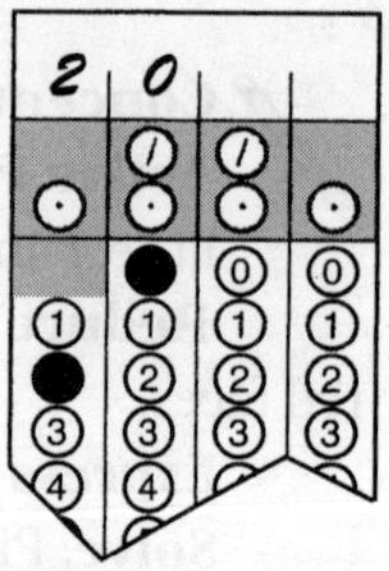

Your answer is in hours, but you are asked for time in minutes. Grid-in 20.

EXTENDED REASONING QUESTIONS 扩展推理问题

In the grid-in part of the calculator section of the SAT Math Test, there will be two extended reasoning questions, each of which is based on the same preamble. Note that the answer to the second question does not depend on the answer to the first question and can be solved independently. Each of these questions is worth 2 points.

Example 8

Amelia wants to buy a bare bones car and has narrowed her choice to two models. Model A sells for \$12,500, gets 25 miles to the gallon, and costs \$350 per year for insurance. Model B sells for \$16,100, gets 48 miles to the gallon and costs \$425 per year for insurance.

Question 1

Suppose Amelia drives 36,000 miles per year and gas costs \$3.50 per gallon. Within how many years, to the nearest hundredth of a year, does it become cheaper for Amelia to own Model B?

Question 2

Model B is a hybrid that uses only the electric motor—no gas—if Amelia drives it at 40 mph (miles per hour) or less. Above 40 mph, the gas engine turns on and the car gets 48 miles to the gallon. Amelia takes a trip where she drives for 3 hours at 40 mph and 2 hours at 60 mph. If gas in this part of the world costs \$3.95 per gallon, how much did she spend on gas for the trip?

Solution to Question 1: 1.54

Concentrate: You need to express the cost of each model in terms of n, the number of years.

Active Pencil: And active calculator!

Cost of each model for n years = price + insurance + cost of gas.

For Model A: Cost $= 12{,}500 + 350n + (36{,}000/25)(3.50n)$

$= 12{,}500 + 5{,}390n$

For Model B: Cost $= 16{,}100 + 425n + (36{,}000/48)(3.50n)$

$= 16{,}100 + 3{,}050n$

Reduce the problem: Find the minimum n for which:

$$16{,}100 + 3{,}050\,n < 12{,}500 + 5{,}390n$$

Express the problem type: Solving a linear inequality.

Solve:

$16{,}100 + 3{,}050\,n < 12{,}500 + 5{,}390n$

$\Rightarrow n > \dfrac{3{,}600}{2{,}340}$

$\Rightarrow n > 1.54$

Grid-in 1.54.

Sensible answer? You can see that it won't take long for Model B to be a cheaper car.

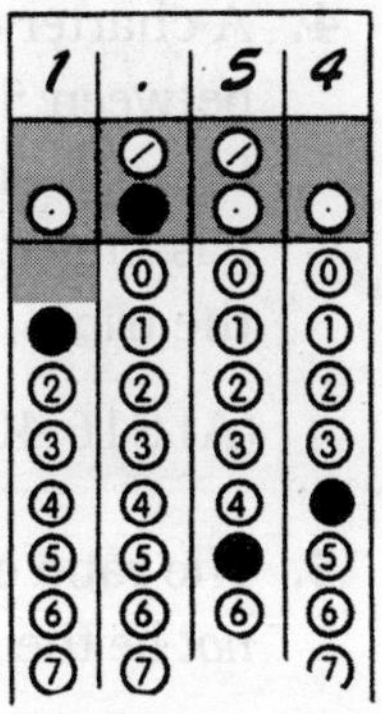

Solution to Question 2: 9.87 or 9.88

Concentrate: Since the 3 hours at 40 mph did not use gas, ignore that piece of information.

Active Pencil: 2 hours at 60 mph = 120 miles that used gas.

Reduce the problem: Number of gallons of gas needed

$= \dfrac{120}{48}$ multiplied by $3.95 cost/gal.

Express the problem type: Arithmetic.

Solve:

$\dfrac{120}{48} \cdot 3.95 \approx 9.875$

Grid-in 9.87 or 9.88.

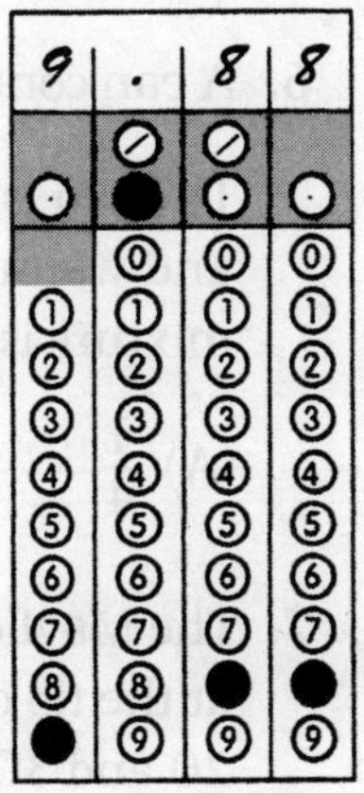

PRACTICE TEST QUESTIONS 练习测试题

1. Mika is doing an experiment with bacteria. She finds that, provided there is enough space and food, the population doubles every 2 hours. The population in hour $y + 10$ will be how many times the population in hour y?

(A) 5 (B) 10 (C) 16 (D) 32

2. Ian has a job that pays him p dollars every day. From this amount he pays out $\frac{p}{5}$ dollars per day for supplies. He also spends an additional $\frac{1}{3}$ of what's left for lunch every day. He saves the rest of the money. In terms of p, how many days will it take Ian to save $1,000?

(A) $\dfrac{3{,}750}{p}$ (B) $\dfrac{1{,}875}{p}$ (C) $1{,}000p$ (D) $\dfrac{800p}{3}$

3. Adam delivered n pizzas on Monday, 5 times as many pizzas on Tuesday as on Monday, 3 fewer pizzas on Wednesday than on Tuesday, and 7 more pizzas on Thursday than on Tuesday. What is the average (arithmetic mean) number of pizzas he delivered per day over the 4 days?

(A) $3n + 1$ (B) $3n + 4$ (C) $4n + 1$ (D) $\dfrac{3n+5}{2}$

4. A charter company will provide a plane for a fare of \$300 per person if there are between 50 and 100 passengers. If there are more than 100 passengers, then, for each additional passenger over 100, the fare will be reduced by \$2 for every passenger. How much revenue will the company make if 120 passengers take the trip?

(A) \$16,400 (B) \$24,000 (C) \$31,200 (D) \$35,200

5. The ratio of girls to boys at a certain school is 4 : 3. Which of the following could *not* be the number of students at the school?

(A) 1,430 (B) 1,477 (C) 1,547 (D) 2,107

6. A can contains $\frac{1}{4}$ pound of cashews.

The can is then filled with a mixture that has equal weights of cashews, pecans, and walnuts. If the final weight is 1 pound, what fraction of the final nut mixture is cashews?

(A) $\frac{1}{4}$ (B) $\frac{1}{3}$ (C) $\frac{1}{2}$ (D) $\frac{2}{3}$

7. The Mayflower Diner has a rule that dessert pies must be sliced so that the angle at the tip of a piece of pie (where the tip is at the center of the pie) lies between 20 and 30 degrees. Which of the following inequalities can be used to determine whether an angle a at the tip of a pie slice satisfies the rule?

(A) $|a-25|<5$

(B) $|a-25|<30$

(C) $|a-25|<20$

(D) $|a|<30$

8. The larger of two pipes can fill a tank twice as fast as the smaller. Together, the two pipes require 20 minutes to fill the tank. You are to find the number of minutes required for the larger pipe, operating alone, to fill the tank. Assuming that x is the number of minutes required for the larger pipe, operating alone, to fill the tank, which of the following is a correct equation for solving the problem?

(A) $\frac{20}{x}+\frac{20}{2x}=20$

(B) $\frac{x}{20}+\frac{2x}{20}=1$

(C) $\frac{20}{x}+\frac{20}{2x}=1$

(D) $\frac{x}{20}+\frac{2x}{20}=20$

9. When an elastic object, such as a coil spring or rubber band, is subjected to a force *f*, an increase in length, called a *strain*, occurs. Hooke's law states that force *f* is directly proportional to strain *s*. Suppose that a coil spring has a natural length of 4 feet and that a force of 60 pounds stretches the length to 6 feet. What magnitude of force, in pounds, would stretch the spring to a length of 7 feet?

(A) 40 (B) $51\frac{3}{7}$ (C) 70 (D) 90

Questions 10 and 11 are grid-in questions.

Questions 10 and 11 refer to the following information.

A house has an old gas furnace that is only 70% efficient. This means that only 70% of the heat produced by the gas goes into heating the house, while 30% of the heat is lost. There is a constant charge per unit of gas, and the owner's gas bill is $1,200 per year.

10. The owner is considering replacing the furnace with a new one that is 90% energy efficient. To the nearest dollar, what would the gas bill be per year, assuming that the same amount of heat is required for the house?

11. Instead of replacing the furnace, the owner keeps the old furnace but doubles the thickness of insulation under the roof, thus cutting the heat loss by a factor of two. Assume that all of the heat supplied by the furnace goes into replacing the heat lost through the roof. If it costs $2,000 to install the insulation, how many years is the payback period, namely, after how many years would the cost of insulation equal the savings on the gas bill? Round your answer to the nearest tenth.

10.

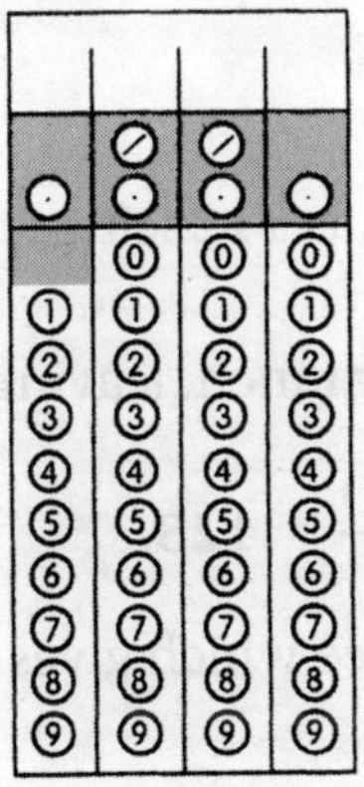

11.

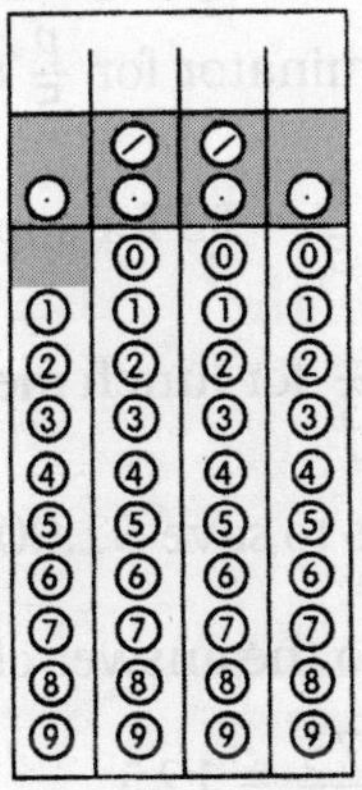

Answers and Explanations 答案与解析

The difficulty level for each question is specified in parentheses.

1. D (H)	**4.** C (H)	**7.** A (M)	**10.** 933 (H)
2. B (H)	**5.** A (M)	**8.** C (H)	**11.** 3.3 (H)
3. C (M)	**6.** C (M)	**9.** D (H)	

10.

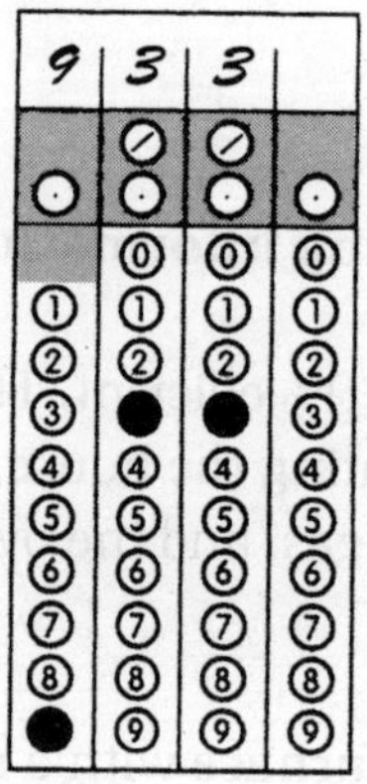

11.

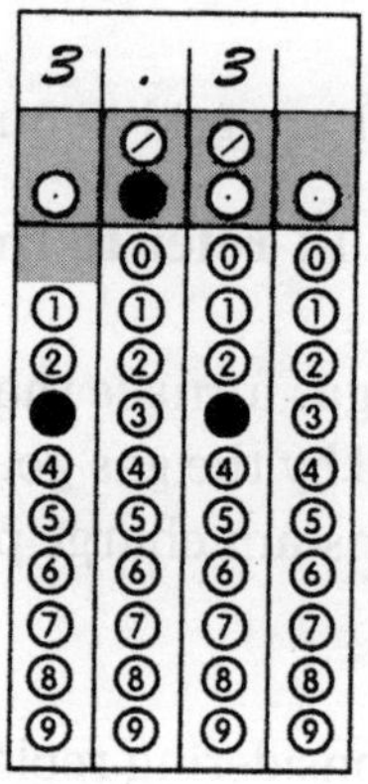

1. **(D)** From time y to time $y + 10$ there are 10 hours, and therefore 5 doublings of population. The bottom row of the table shows the geometric sequence for the population, assuming that the population at time y is p.

Time	y	$y+2$	$y+4$	$y+6$	$y+8$	$y+10$
Population	p	$2p$	$4p$	$8p$	$16p$	$32p$

Thus, the final population is 32 times the original population.

2. **(B)** Use the pick-a-number strategy for fractions. Choose $p = \$15$, the least common denominator for $\frac{p}{5}$ and $\frac{1}{3}$.

After Ian pays $\frac{p}{5} = \$3$ for supplies, he has \$12 left.

An additional $\frac{1}{3}$ for lunch means \$4 for lunch, leaving \$8.

Number of days to save \$1,000 $= \frac{1{,}000}{8} = 125$.

Plug $p = 15$ into the answer choices to see which gives 125.

Choice (B)! $\frac{1{,}875}{p} = 125$.

3. (C)

Method I: Algebra

Make a chart showing the number of pizzas Adam delivered on each day:

Monday	n
Tuesday	$5n$
Wednesday	$5n-3$
Thursday	$5n+7$

$$\text{Arithmetic mean} = \frac{n+(5n)+(5n-3)+(5n+7)}{4} = \frac{16n+4}{4} = 4n+1$$

Method II: Pick-a-Number

Pick a number for n, the number of pizzas Adam delivered on Monday, such as 10.

Then the number of pizzas delivered on each day would be Monday 10, Tuesday 50, Wednesday 47, and Thursday 57. The mean of these is

$$\frac{10+50+47+57}{4} = \frac{164}{4} = 41$$

Now plug $n = 10$ into the answer choices. The choice that gives 41 is the correct answer, in this case, choice (C), since $4n + 1 = 4(10) + 1 = 41$.

4. (C) The key piece of information that you need from the first sentence is that the base price for a ticket is \$300. The rest is fluff, because you are dealing only with the case where there are more than 100 passengers. You need to make sure that you understand *exactly* how the ticket price is being reduced. For 120 passengers, all 120 will pay $(120 - 100)(2) = \$40$ less than \$300 for their tickets: that is, the ticket price for each passenger will be \$260. Revenue $= (120)(260) = \$31{,}200$.

5. (A) If n = number of students, then $4x + 3x = n$, where x is some positive integer:

$$7x = n \Rightarrow x = \frac{n}{7}$$

If n is not divisible by 7, you will end up with a fraction of a student. Realizing this possibility makes the problem go fast: choice (A), 1,430, is not divisible by 7.

6. (C) Amount of mixture added = final weight − original weight $= 1 - \frac{1}{4} = \frac{3}{4}$ pound.

Equal weights of cashews, pecans, and walnuts means that $\frac{1}{4}$ pound of each was added. Since the can already contained $\frac{1}{4}$ pound of cashews,

$$\text{Final weight of cashews} = \frac{1}{4} + \frac{1}{4} = \frac{1}{2} \text{ pound}$$

This is $\frac{1}{2}$ of the final mixture.

7. **(A)** The problem boils down to this: Which of the given inequalities is equivalent to $20 < a < 30$?

Recall that $|x| < k \Rightarrow -k < x < k$.

Notice that choice (A) works:

$$|a - 25| < 5 \Rightarrow -5 < a - 25 < 5$$
$$\Rightarrow 20 < a < 30$$

8. **(C)** This is a work problem. (See "Some Familiar Problem Types" earlier in this chapter.)

Let x equal the number of minutes required for the larger pipe, operating alone, to fill the tank. Then $2x$ is the number of minutes for the smaller pipe, operating alone, to fill the tank.

$$\text{Part of the tank filled by the larger pipe in 1 minute} = \frac{1}{x}$$

$$\text{Part of the tank filled by the smaller pipe in 1 minute} = \frac{1}{2x}$$

Then $\frac{20}{x}$ equals the part of the tank filled by the larger pipe in 20 minutes, and $\frac{20}{2x}$ equals the part of the tank filled by the smaller pipe in 20 minutes. If the tank is filled, the fractional part of the tank filled by the larger pipe added to the fractional part of the tank filled by the smaller pipe must equal 1.

$$\frac{20}{x} + \frac{20}{2x} = 1$$

This matches choice (C).

9. **(D)** Since f is directly proportional to s, $\frac{f_1}{s_1} = \frac{f_2}{s_2}$. Beware! Note that s is defined as an *increase* in length, so

$$s_1 = 6 - 4 = 2 \quad \text{and} \quad s_2 = 7 - 4 = 3$$

The corresponding proportion is

$$\frac{60}{2} = \frac{f_2}{3} \Rightarrow f_2 = 90$$

10. **933**

Method I: Logic

Suppose the old furnace uses 100 units of gas per year. Then 70 units are used to heat the house, while 30 units are wasted. To supply the same amount of heat, the new furnace has to turn the same 70 units of gas into heat. Since the new furnace is 90% efficient, this will require $\frac{70}{0.9}$ total units of gas. Since 100 units of gas cost \$1,200, one unit costs \$12, and $\frac{70}{0.9}$ units cost

$$\frac{70}{0.9} \cdot (12) = \$933.33$$

Grid-in 933.

Method II: Algebra

Let y_1 be the number of gas units used by old furnace.
Let y_2 be the number of gas units used by new furnace.
Same amount of heat to heat house means $0.7y_1 = 0.9y_2$.

Note that $\frac{y_2}{y_1} = \frac{0.7}{0.9}$

The cost of one unit of gas $= \frac{1{,}200}{y_1}$

Therefore, the cost of y_2 units of gas is

$$y_2 \cdot \frac{1{,}200}{y_1} = \frac{y_2}{y_1} \cdot 1{,}200 = \frac{0.7}{0.9} \cdot 1{,}200 = \$933.33$$

Grid-in 933.

11. 3.3

Method I: Logic

Halving the heating requirement means the energy bill is reduced by \$600 per year.

The number of years for the savings to equal \$2000 is $\frac{2{,}000}{600} \approx 3.3$.

Grid-in 3.3.

Method II: Algebra

Let n be the number of years before the savings equals the cost of insulation.
The cost of n years without insulation $= 1{,}200n$.
The cost of n years with insulation $= 2{,}000 + 600n$.
You want to find the value of n such that $2{,}000 + 600n < 1{,}200n$.
Solving for n gives $n > 3.3$.
Grid-in 3.3.

第十一章 Chapter 11

HEART OF ALGEBRA 代数

Linear relationships—functions, equations, inequalities, and graphs—are at the heart of algebra. These are disproportionately important on the SAT Math Test: 35 percent of all math questions will involve something linear, more than any other category. You will receive a subscore for the Heart of Algebra questions.

1600 Club Strategies in the Heart of Algebra
1600分俱乐部代数策略

Strategy 1:	**L**inear functions: know them inside out.
Strategy 2:	**I**n standard form: this is the first step to analyze line graphs.
Strategy 3:	**N**o solution: be aware that sometimes there is no solution to a system of equations.
Strategy 4:	**E**quations and inequalities: get variables on one side, numbers on the other.
Strategy 5:	**A**pplications are key: practice function modeling and problems in context.
Strategy 6:	**R**ecognize algebraic conditions for parallel and perpendicular lines.

FUNCTIONS 函数

Definition 定义

A *function* is a relation in which each x-value corresponds to one and only one y-value. Here are some of the ways in which functions can be represented:

- A set of ordered pairs
- An equation in x and y
- A graph

From the definition you should see that a function cannot have two (or more) ordered pairs that start with the same x-value.

Here are three examples of functions:

(1) $y = x + 4$ (2) 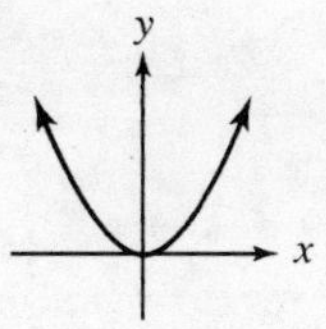

(3) $\{(1, 1), (2, 1), (3, 1), \ldots\}$

Notice that the graph of a function always passes the *vertical line test*: No vertical line cuts the graph in more than one point.

Example 1

Which does *not* represent a function?

(A)

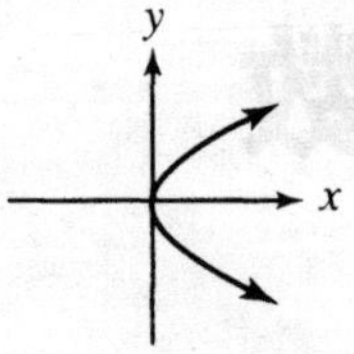

(B)

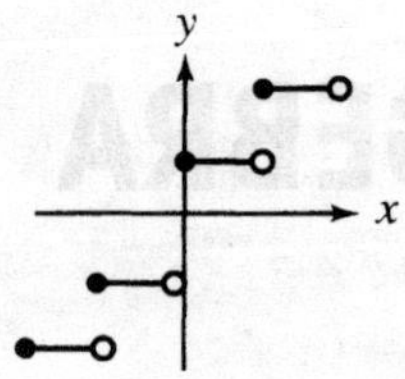

(C)

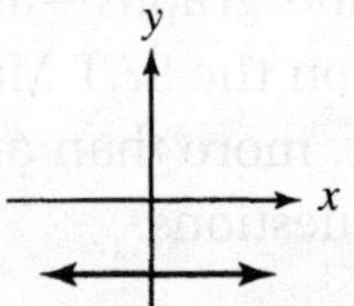

(D)

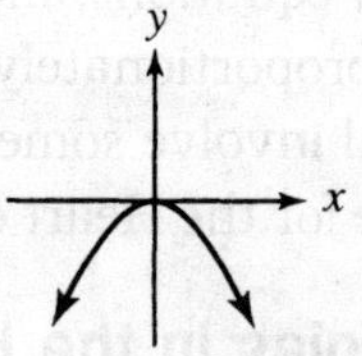

Solution: (A) Choice (A) is the only choice that fails the vertical line test. In the accompanying diagram, line ℓ, for example, cuts the graph in more than one place. In this diagram the given x-value corresponds to both a positive and a negative y-value, thereby violating the definition of a function.

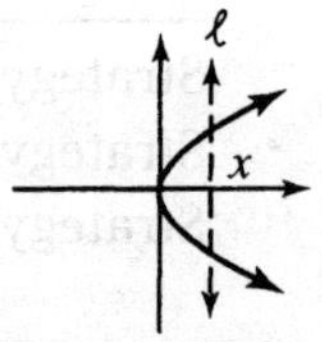

Function Notation 函数符号

A function can be represented with $f(x)$ notation: $f(x) = (x - 3)^2$ is equivalent to $y = (x - 3)^2$. To evaluate $f(5)$, for example, means to find the value of $(x - 3)^2$ when $x = 5$:

$$f(5) = f(5 - 3)^2 = 4$$

Similarly, $f(-1) = (-1 - 3)^2 = 16$, and $f(a) = (a - 3)^2$.

Example 2

If $f(x) = x^2 + 3$ and $g(x) = x - 5$, evaluate $f(g(9))$.

(A) 4 (B) 19 (C) 79 (D) 81

Solution: (B) To find $f(g(9))$, evaluate $g(9)$ first: $g(9) = 9 - 5 = 4$, so:

$$f(g(9)) = f(4) = 4^2 + 3 = 19$$

Example 3

If $f(x)=\frac{ax}{b}$ and $g(x)=\frac{cx^2}{a}$, then $g(f(a))$ equals

(A) $\frac{a^2}{b}$ (B) $\frac{a^2c}{b}$ (C) $\frac{a^2c}{b^2}$ (D) $\frac{ca^3}{b^2}$

Solution: (D) This question is similar to Example 2. Just be careful with the algebraic substitution. To find $g(f(a))$, evaluate $f(a)$ first:

$$f(a)=\frac{a\cdot a}{b}=\frac{a^2}{b}$$

$$g(f(a))=g\left(\frac{a^2}{b}\right)=\frac{c}{a}\left(\frac{a^2}{b}\right)^2=\frac{ca^4}{ab^2}=\frac{ca^3}{b^2}$$

THE LINEAR FUNCTION 线性函数

The linear function is a function whose graph is a straight line: $f(x) = mx + b$, where m is the slope and b is the y-intercept.

Slope 斜率

Slope measures the "steepness" of a line—how quickly it rises (or falls) as you move from left to right. You can think of the slope as the ratio of rise to run:

$$\text{slope} = \frac{\text{rise}}{\text{run}}$$

If you know the coordinates of any two points on a line, (x_1,y_1) and (x_2,y_2), you can find the slope using the slope formula:

$$m=\frac{y_1-y_2}{x_1-x_2}$$

Lines with positive slopes rise to the right as x increases. The greater the slope, the steeper the line.

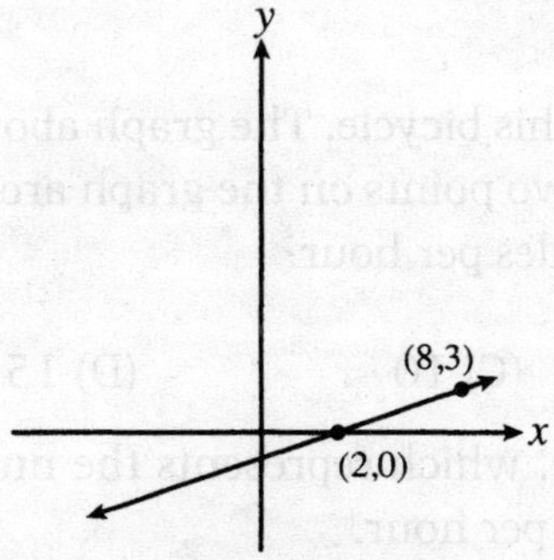

$m=\frac{3-0}{8-2}=\frac{1}{2}$

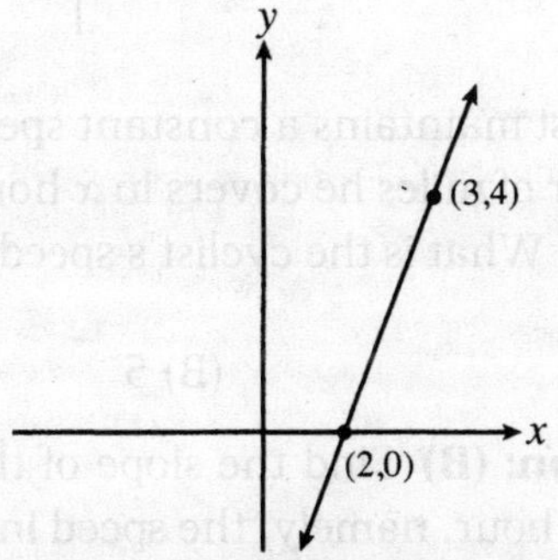

$m=\frac{4-0}{3-2}=4$

Lines with negative slopes go down as x increases. The greater the absolute value of the slope, the steeper the decline.

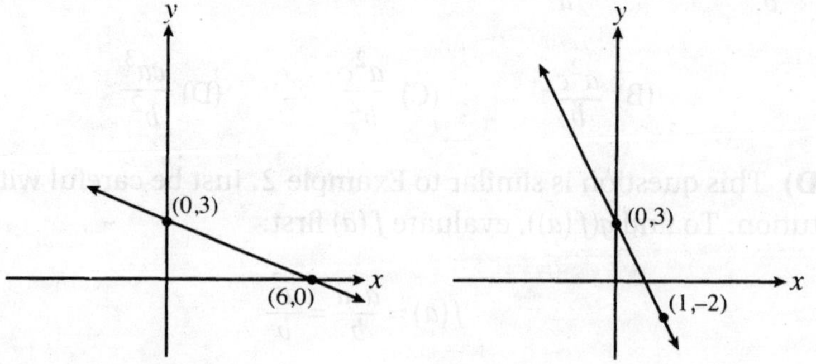

$$m = \frac{3-0}{0-6} = -\frac{1}{2}$$ $$m = \frac{3-(-2)}{0-1} = -5$$

Coaching: *The slope of a line is constant, independent of the two points used to find it.*

A horizontal line has equation $y = k$, where k is constant. The slope of a horizontal line is 0. A vertical line has equation $x = k$, where k is constant. The slope of a vertical line is undefined. Note that a vertical line does not represent a function, since there are infinitely many points on it that have k as the x-coordinate.

Unit Rate 单位比率

Another way to think of slope is as the rate of change in y per unit change in x. For example, if the slope of a line is 5, this means that over a single unit of x, y goes up 5 units.

Example 4

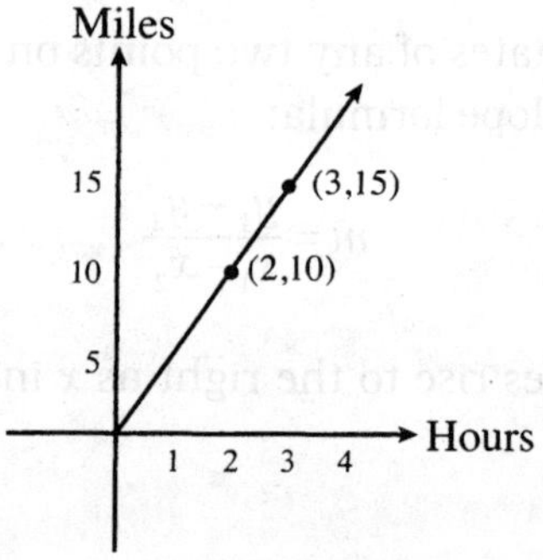

A cyclist maintains a constant speed on his bicycle. The graph above shows the number of miles he covers in x hours. Two points on the graph are (2, 10) and (3, 15). What is the cyclist's speed, in miles per hour?

(A) 1 (B) 5 (C) 10 (D) 15

Solution: (B) Find the slope of the line, which represents the number of miles covered in 1 hour, namely, the speed in miles per hour.

$$\text{Slope} = \frac{15-10}{3-2} = 5$$

Equations of a Line 线性方程式

The Standard Form 标准形式

Any equation of the form $ax + by = c$, where a and b are not both 0, is a linear equation.

The Slope-Intercept Form 斜截式

The slope-intercept form is $y = mx + b$, where m is the slope and b is the y-intercept. This is the most useful form for visualizing and drawing the graph.

The Point-Slope Form 点斜式

If you know the slope, m, of a line, and have one point on the line, (x_1, y_1), you can easily find the equation of the line using the point-slope form:

$$y - y_1 = m(x - x_1)$$

In particular, if you know two points on the line, you can get the slope by using the slope formula and then, using either point, find the equation of the line using the point-slope form.

Parallel and Perpendicular Lines 平行线和垂直线

- Parallel lines have the same slope.
- Perpendicular lines have slopes that are negative reciprocals of each other.

Example 5

The slope of the line with equation $2x - 2y = 7$ is

(A) −1 (B) 1 (C) −2 (D) 2

Solution: (B) Rewrite the equation in slope–intercept form:

$$2x - 2y = 7 \Rightarrow 2y = 2x - 7 \Rightarrow y = x - \frac{7}{2}$$

Then slope = coefficient of x, which equals 1.

Example 6 Grid-In

What is the y-intercept of the line through points (3, −2) and (−1, 6)?

Solution: 4

The slope is

$$m = \frac{6-(-2)}{(-1)-3} = \frac{8}{-4} = -2$$

The slope–intercept form of the equation is $y = -2x + b$, where b is the y-intercept. Plug in one of the points, (−1, 6) say:

$$6 = -2(-1) + b \Rightarrow b = 4$$

Grid-in 4.

Example 7

A line containing point (2, 4) has slope 3. If point P lies on this line, which of the following could be point P?

(A) (3, 7) (B) (2, 6) (C) (2, 7) (D) (3, −1)

Solution: (A) The slope of the line is 3, which means that for every horizontal move to the right of 1 unit, there is a vertical move up of 3 units. Thus, if you start on the line at point (2, 4), and move up the line until $x = 3$, you land on point (3, 7), answer choice (A). You can check this with the slope formula. The slope for (3, 7), choice (A), and (2, 4) is $\frac{7-4}{3-2} = 3$.

You should immediately eliminate choices (B) and (C), since if (2, 4) is on the line, then neither (2, 6) nor (2, 7) can be.

The 1600 Club is always on the lookout for shortcuts.

Example 8

What value of k will make the line containing points (k, 3) and (−2, 1) perpendicular to the line containing (5, k) and (1, 0)?

(A) −4 (B) $-\frac{4}{3}$ (C) −1 (D) $-\frac{3}{4}$

Solution: (B) For the lines to be perpendicular, the product of the slopes must be −1:

$$\left(\frac{3-1}{k+2}\right)\left(\frac{k-0}{5-1}\right)=-1\Rightarrow\left(\frac{2}{k+2}\right)\left(\frac{k}{4}\right)=-1\Rightarrow k=-\frac{4}{3}$$

The straight algebraic solution is quicker here. Plugging in requires you to deal with negative fractions and four different points, two of which contain k.

Coaching: *On the SAT you will need to apply some judgment in choosing the best strategy.*

Example 9 Grid-In

The table of values shown is for some linear function $f(x)$. Find $f(10)$.

x	y
−2	−11
−1	−7
0	−3
1	1

Solution: 37 Whichever method you choose to solve this problem, it will probably involve using the slope-intercept form of the linear equation: $y = mx + b$.

Method I: y-Intercept and Slope

Since $(0, -3)$ is a point on the graph, the y-intercept, b, is -3.

Since the y-values go up 4 units for every 1 unit that x goes up, the slope, m, is 4.

$\therefore$ Equation of $f(x)$ is $y = 4x - 3$

$\therefore f(10) = 4(10) - 3 = 37$

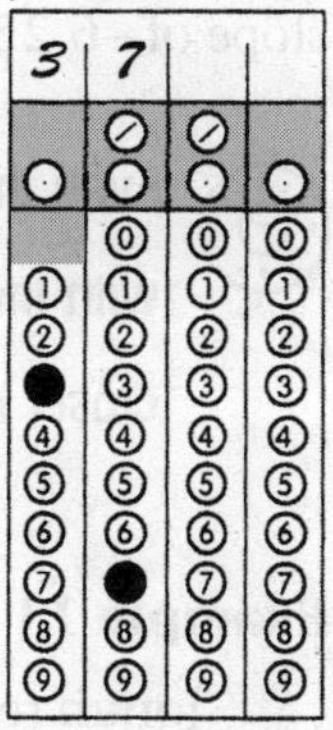

Method II: y-Intercept and Plug-In

Since -3 is the y-intercept, the equation of $f(x)$ is $y = mx - 3$. Now plug in any point from the table to find m. Plugging in $(1, 1)$ gives $1 = m - 3$ or $m = 4$. Therefore, the equation is $y = 4x - 3$, and

$$f(10) = 4(10) - 3 = 37$$

Grid-in 37.

Linear Functions as Models 图像模型的线性函数

On the SAT you are often given a formula for a function and asked about the graph, or vice versa. But, as you know, real-world situations can be modeled using functions. Sometimes, therefore, you will be given the story behind the function and then be asked about the graph or the equation of the function.

The 1600 Club embraces functions that model stories.

Example 10

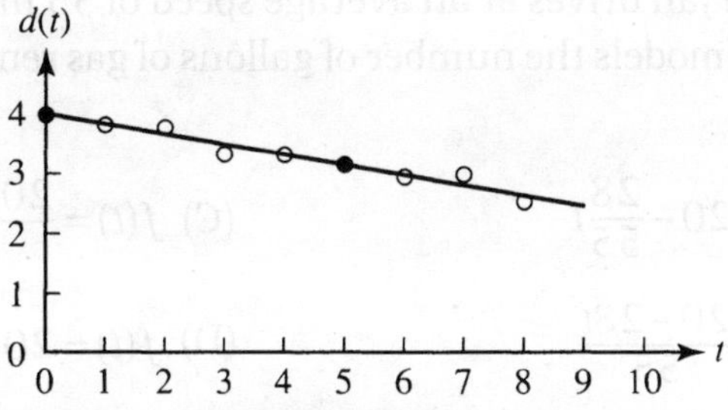

Joe bikes 4 kilometers to school. Because of the traffic and road conditions along the way, his speed varies. The dots on the graph above show his distance from the school at various times, starting at home at $t = 0$ (black dot). After 5 minutes Joe is 3.2 kilometers from the school (second black dot). The data show that his speed is almost constant, and his distance from the school can be approximated by a straight line. The graph of the function that models Joe's distance from school as a function of time, in minutes, is shown as a solid line. Which of the following equations best represents this function?

(A) $d(t) = -0.5t + 4$

(B) $d(t) = -6.25t + 4$

(C) $d(t) = -0.16t + 4$

(D) $d(t) = 0.16t + 4$

Solution: (C) The given function is linear and has the form $d = mt + 4$. The slope m differs in each answer choice. The line shown has negative slope, so eliminate choice (D). Then eliminate choice (B): the slope in the given graph is small, close to 0, so a slope of -6.25 is too steep. You must now choose between choices (A) and (C).

Even though you are given points (0, 4) and (5, 3.2) on the line, don't waste time with the slope formula. Get the answer quickly by noticing that $\frac{\text{rise}}{\text{run}} \approx -\frac{1}{5}$, which is closer to −0.16 than to −0.5.

Example 11

Jonah rented a car for two days and his bill came to \$108.00. The rental company charged \$30 a day and 15¢ for each mile driven. If x is the number of miles that Jonah drove, which equation correctly determines x?

(A) $30x + 15(2) = 108$
(B) $15x + 30(2) = 108$
(C) $0.15x + 30(2) = 108$
(D) $15x + 30(2) = 10{,}800$

Solution: (C) $0.15x$ is the mileage cost at \$0.15 per mile, in dollars.
30(2) is the cost at \$30 per day, also in dollars.
The total cost is \$108. Therefore, $0.15x + 30(2) = 108$.

Example 12

The gas mileage for Jan's car is 28 miles per gallon when the car travels at an average speed of 55 miles per hour. The car's gas tank has 20 gallons of gas at the beginning of a trip. If Jan drives at an average speed of 55 miles per hour, which of the following functions f models the number of gallons of gas remaining in the tank t hours after the trip begins?

(A) $f(t)=20-\frac{28}{55}t$
(B) $f(t)=\frac{20-28t}{55}$
(C) $f(t)=\frac{20-55t}{28}$
(D) $f(t)=20-\frac{55t}{28}$

Solution: (D) If t = number of hours, distance = $55t$ miles.
Number of gallons used in t hours = $\frac{55t}{28}$.
The tank started with 20 gallons.
Therefore, the number of gallons left in the tank after t hours = $20-\frac{55t}{28}$.
Therefore, $f(t)=20-\frac{55t}{28}$.

SOLVING LINEAR EQUATIONS AND INEQUALITIES
解答线性方程式和不等式

Some general rules:

1. The same quantity can be added to both sides of an equation or inequality without changing it. For example, if $x - 4 < 8$, then $x < 12$.
2. Both sides of an equation can be multiplied or divided by the same nonzero quantity. For example, if $-5x = 37$, then $x = -\frac{37}{5}$.
3. If both sides of an inequality are multiplied by a negative quantity, the inequality sign flips around. For example, if $-2x < 12$, then $x > -6$.
4. Fractions can be eliminated by multiplying throughout by the least common denominator (LCD) of the fractions. For example, if $\frac{x}{5} - \frac{2}{3} = 2x + \frac{1}{2}$, multiplying both sides by 30, the LCD, yields $6x - 20 = 60x + 15$.
5. To solve a linear equation or inequality, get the variables on one side, and the numbers on the other.

SYSTEMS OF LINEAR EQUATIONS 线性方程组

You may be asked to solve a system of equations in two variables, for example:

$$2y + x = 22 \quad (1)$$
$$3y - 2x = -2 \quad (2)$$

Eliminate one of the variables. Rewrite equation (1) as $x = 22 - 2y$ and substitute in equation (2).

$$3y - 2(22 - 2y) = -2$$
$$3y - 44 + 4y = -2$$
$$7y = 42$$
$$y = 6$$

Substituting $y = 6$ in equation (1) or (2) gives $x = 10$.

Solution: $x = 10$ and $y = 6$ Sometimes adding or subtracting the equations in parallel is the quickest way to the solution, especially if it eliminates one of the variables.

$$x - 3y = -2 \quad (1)$$
$$2x + 3y = 14 \quad (2)$$

Adding equations (1) and (2) eliminates y:

$$3x = 12$$
$$x = 4$$

Substituting x into either equation gives $y = 2$.

An algebraic solution may not be the quickest way of solving a system of equations on the SAT.

Example 13

The graphs of $y = 2x - 5$ and $x + 3y = -1$ intersect at

(A) $(-1, 2)$ (B) $(-2, -1)$ (C) $(2, -1)$ (D) $(-2, 1)$

Solution: (C)

Method I: Plug-In Strategy

The ordered pair in the answer must satisfy both equations. Plug-in each answer choice until you find one that works. The numbers are easy, so you should be able to reject quickly those that don't pan out. Notice that choice (C) works:

$$-1 = 2(2) - 5 \text{ and } 2 + 3(-1) = -1$$

Method II: Graphing Calculator

Plot $y = 2x - 5$ and $x + 3y = -1$ on the calculator. (Be sure to rewrite the second equation as $y = (-x - 1)/3$.) A quick look at the point of intersection on the graph tells you that choice (C) is the answer.

One Solution, No Solution, Infinite Number of Solutions
唯一解，无解，无穷多解

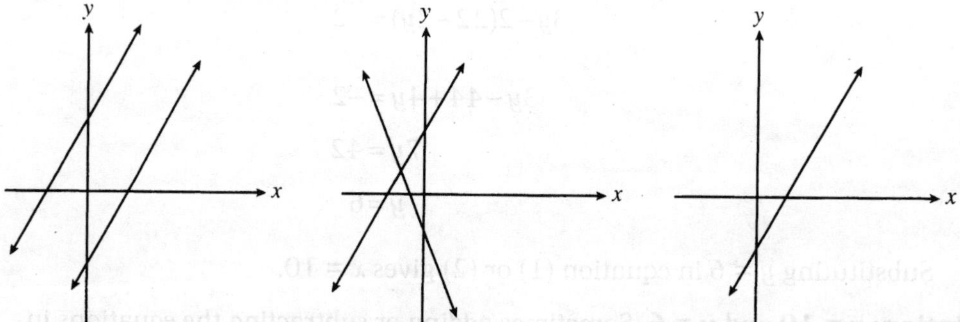

No solution (2 parallel lines) | 1 solution (2 intersecting lines) | Infinite number of solutions (2 lines that are the same)

A system of equations in two variables has no solution if the graphs of the equations are parallel lines, for example,

$$y = 30x + 10$$
$$y = 30x + 5$$

In each case, the coefficient of x gives the slope, provided the equation is in slope–intercept form,

$$y = mx + b$$

Notice that if the two equations represent the same line, then every point on that line is a solution of the system because it satisfies both equations. Thus, suppose the given equations were

$$y = 30x + 10$$
$$-2y = -60x - 20$$

There would be an infinite number of solutions, since the second equation is simply the first multiplied by –2.

Example 14

$$15x + 5y = -8$$
$$y + 4 = -3x$$

How many solutions does the system above have?

(A) 0 (B) 1 (C) 2 (D) An infinite number

Solution: (A)

Method I: Slope–Intercept Form

The first equation can be written as:

$$15x + 5y = -8$$

$$5y = -15x - 8$$

$$y = -3x - \frac{8}{5}$$

The second equation can be written as:

$$y = -3x - 4$$

Since the graphs of the equations have the same slopes but different y-intercepts, the lines are parallel and don't intersect. Therefore, there are 0 solutions.

Of course you didn't need to do all that work! You could have just glanced at the coefficient of *x* for each equation, and then checked that the *y*-intercepts would be different.

Method II: Substitution

From the second equation, $y = -3x - 4$. Substitution in the first equation gives

$$15x + 5(-3x - 4) = -8$$
$$15x - 15x - 20 = -8$$
$$-20 = -8$$

Since there are no values of x for which $-20 = -8$, there are no solutions to the system.

SYSTEM OF LINEAR INEQUALITIES 线性不等式

To solve a *system of linear inequalities* means to find the region on a graph that satisfies both inequalities. There are four steps to a correct solution:

1. Write each inequality in a standard form:

   $$y < mx + b,\ y \leq mx + b,\ y > mx + b, \text{ or } y \geq mx + b$$

2. Sketch the line $y = mx + b$. This line is solid if the inequality is $\leq$ or $\geq$, dotted for $<$ or $>$.
3. Shade the region above the line if the inequality is $>$ or $\geq$, below the line if the inequality is $<$ or $\leq$.
4. The solution set for the system of inequalities is the intersection of the regions (i.e., where the shaded regions overlap).

For example, find the solution set for this system:

$$4 - 2y \leq x \text{ and } 3y - 4x > 12$$

Step 1:	$4-2y\leq x$	$3y-4x>12$
	$-2y\leq x-4$	$3y>4x+12$
	$y\geq -\frac{1}{2}x+2$	$y>\frac{4}{3}x+4$

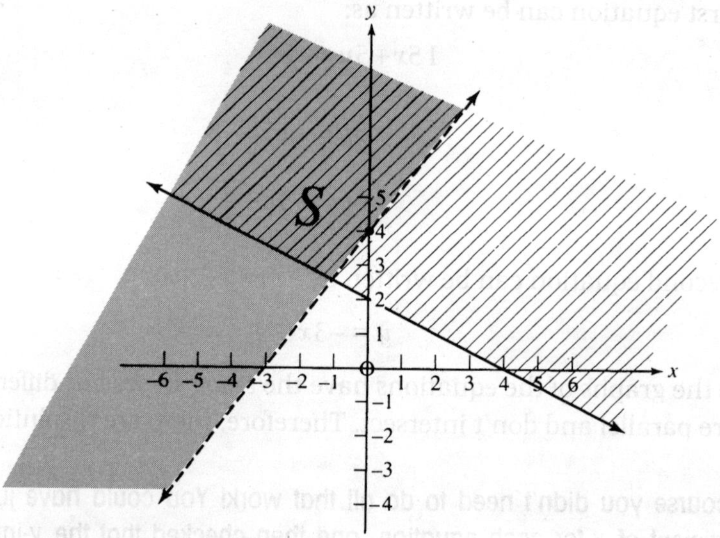

Step 2: Sketch $y=-\frac{1}{2}x+2$ (solid line).

Sketch $y=\frac{4}{3}x+4$ (dotted line).

Step 3: Shade above $y=-\frac{1}{2}x+2$ and above $y=\frac{4}{3}x+4$.

Step 4: Region S, where the two shaded regions overlap, is the solution set.

PRACTICE TEST QUESTIONS 练习测试题

1. The distance d, in miles, that an object travels at a uniform speed is directly proportional to the number of hours t it travels. If the object travels 6 miles in 2 hours, which could be the graph of the relationship between d and t?

(A)

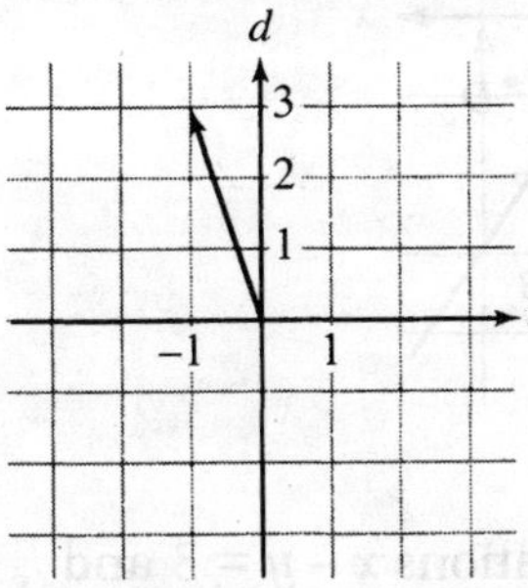

(B)

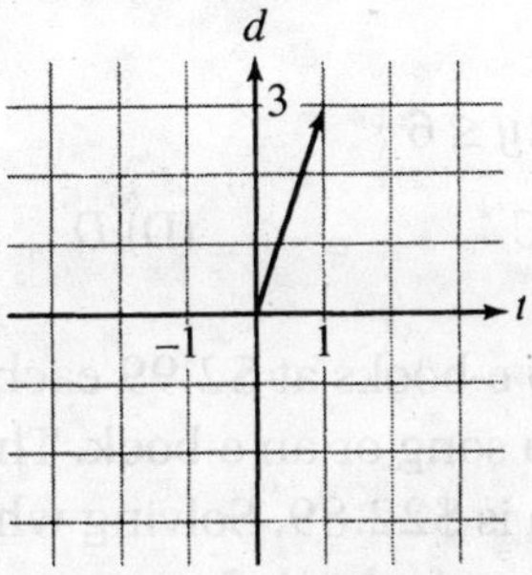

(C)

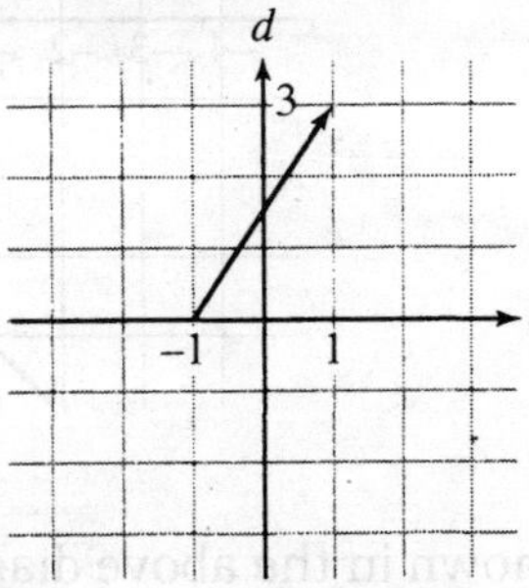

(D)

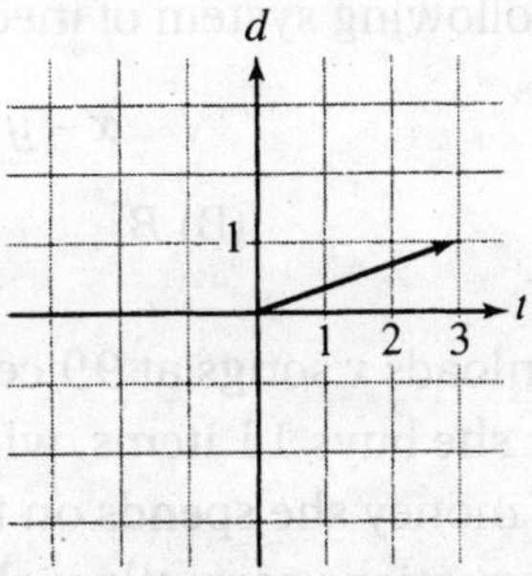

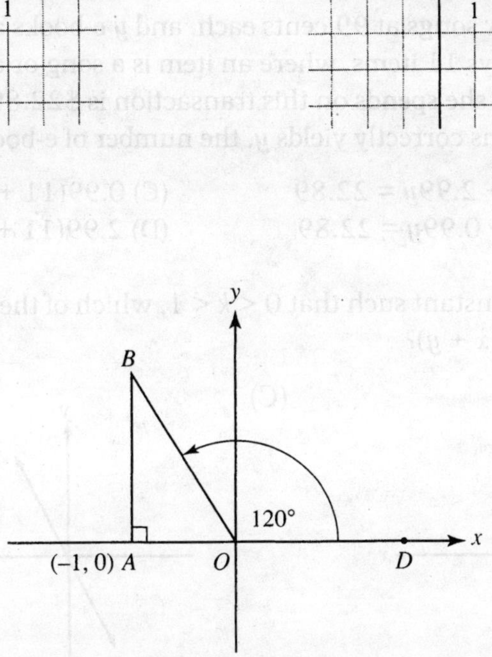

2. In the diagram above, A and D are points on the x-axis. Point A has coordinates $(-1, 0)$, and $\angle BOD$ measures $120°$. What is the slope of line $\overleftrightarrow{BO}$?

(A) $\sqrt{3}$ (B) $\frac{\sqrt{3}}{2}$ (C) $-\frac{\sqrt{3}}{2}$ (D) $-\sqrt{3}$

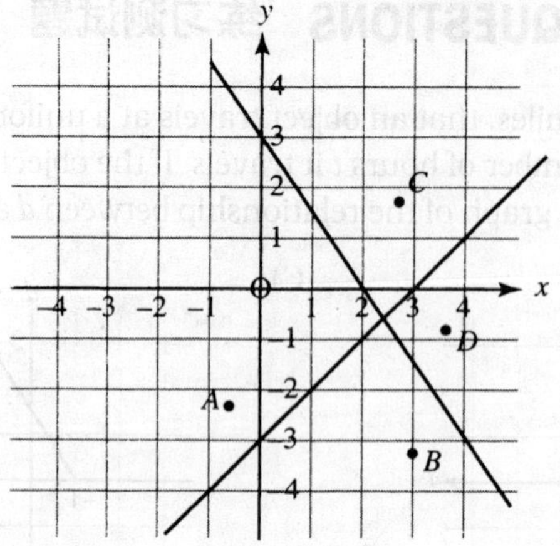

3. The lines shown in the above diagram have equations $x - y = 3$ and $3x + 2y = 6$. Of the four labeled points, *A*–*D*, which one is in the solution set of the following system of inequalities?

$$x - y < 3 \text{ and } 3x + 2y \leq 6$$

(A) *A* (B) *B* (C) *C* (D) *D*

4. Carol downloads *x* songs at 99 cents each, and *y* e-books at \$2.99 each. Altogether she buys 11 items, where an item is a song or an e-book. The total amount of money she spends on this transaction is \$22.89. Solving which of the following equations correctly yields *y*, the number of e-books?

(A) $0.99(11 - y) + 2.99y = 22.89$
(B) $2.99(11 - y) + 0.99y = 22.89$
(C) $0.99(11 + y) + 2.99y = 22.89$
(D) $2.99(11 + y) + 0.99y = 22.89$

5. If *k* is a positive constant such that $0 < k < 1$, which of the following could be the graph of $y - x = k(x + y)$?

(A)

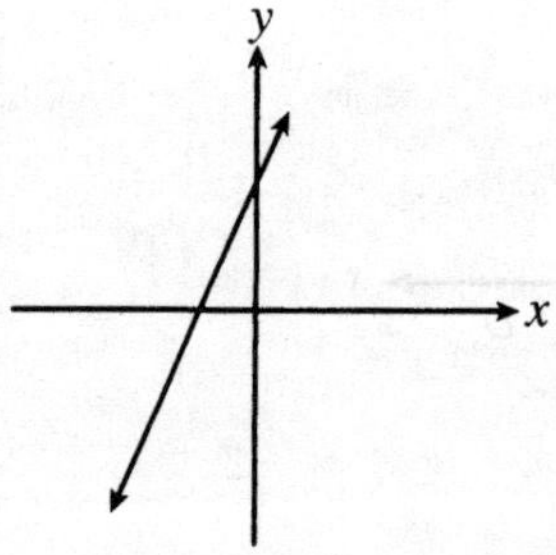

(C)

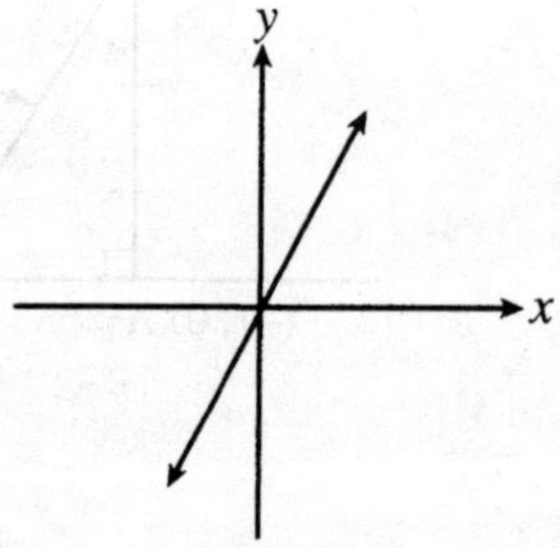

(B)

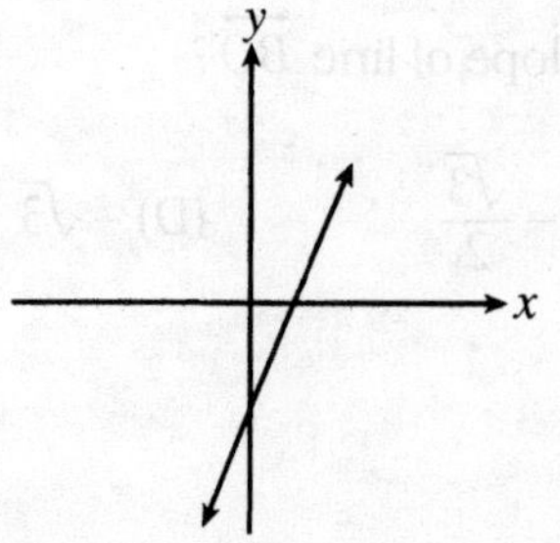

(D)

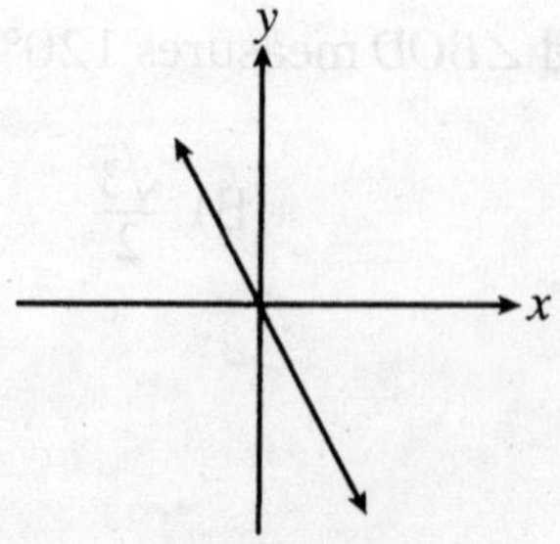

6.

$$\frac{1}{3}x+\frac{1}{2}y=4$$

$$ax+3y=6$$

In the system of linear equations above, a is a constant. If the system has no solutions, what is the value of a?

(A) 6 (B) 2 (C) $\frac{1}{3}$ (D) -2

$$3x + 2y = 6$$
$$y - 2x = 24$$

7. Based on the system of equations above, what is the value of the quotient $\frac{x}{y}$?

(A) 2 (B) $\frac{1}{2}$ (C) $-\frac{1}{2}$ (D) -2

8. Which of the following could be the graph of $2x + 3y + 12 = 0$?

(A)

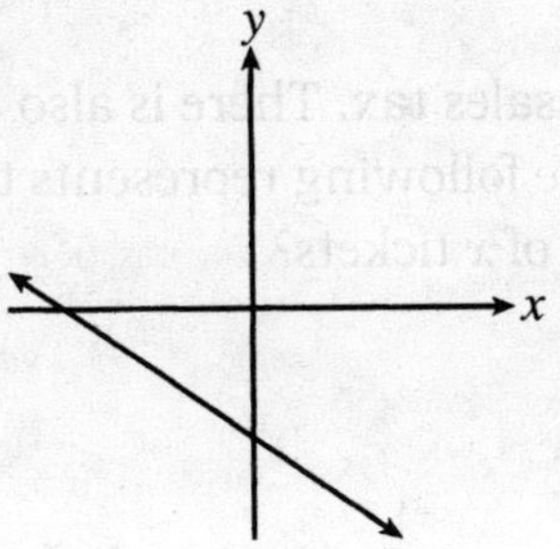

(B)

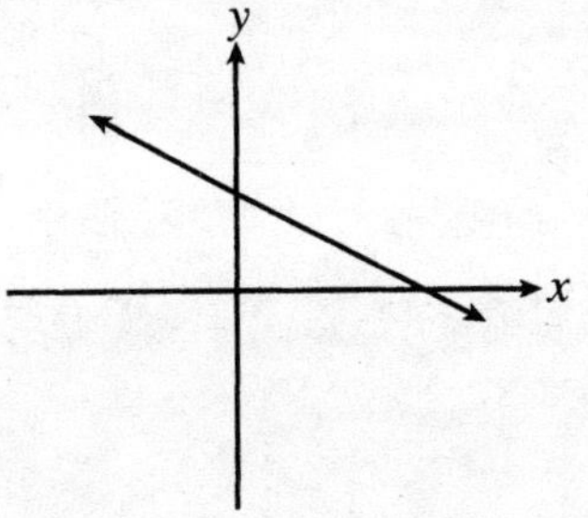

(C)

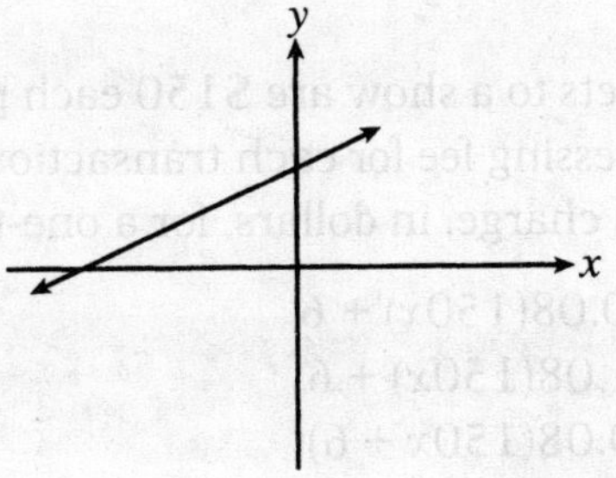

(D)

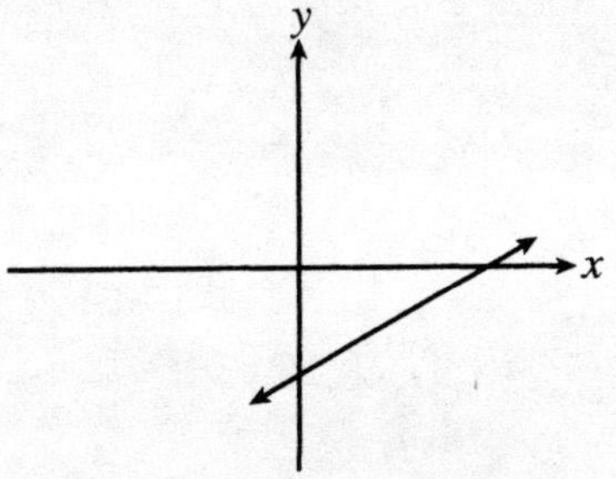

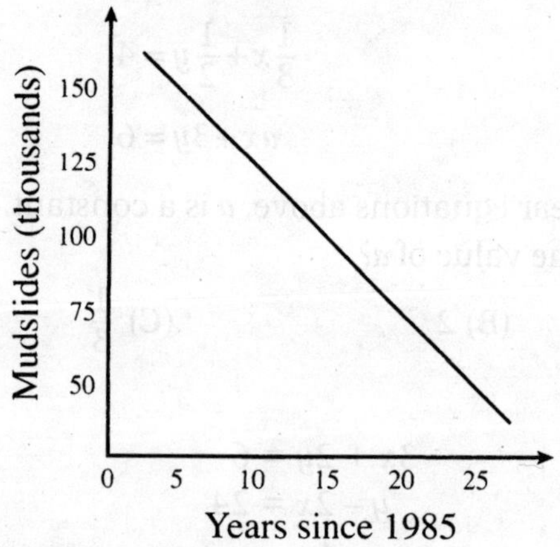

9. The number of mudslides in a certain country for the past 25 years is approximated by the graph shown above. The graph displays the number of mudslides (in thousands) from 1985 to 2010. Based on the graph, which of the following is closest to the average yearly decrease in the number of mudslides?

(A) 1 (B) 5 (C) 10 (D) 25

10. Tickets to a show are $150 each plus 8 percent sales tax. There is also a $6 processing fee for each transaction. Which of the following represents the total charge, in dollars, for a one-time purchase of x tickets?

(A) $0.08(150x) + 6$
(B) $1.08(150x) + 6$
(C) $0.08(150x + 6)$
(D) $1.08(150x + 6)$

Questions 11–14 are grid-in questions.

11.

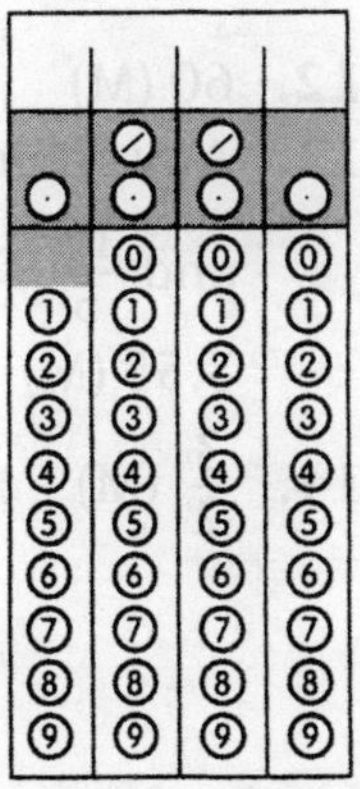

12.

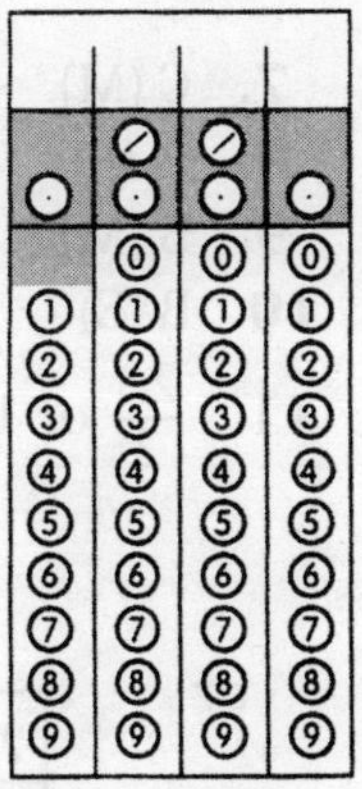

13.

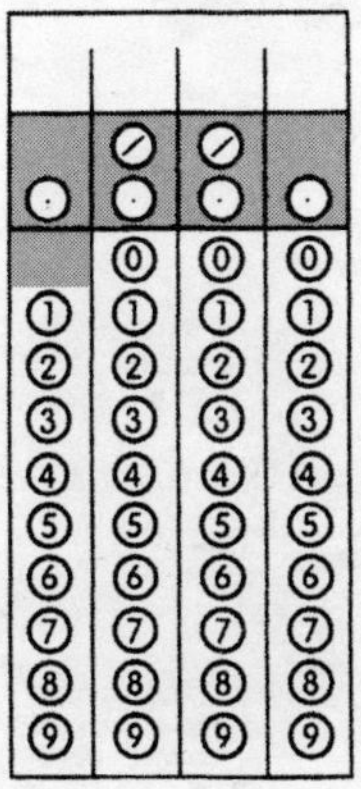

14.

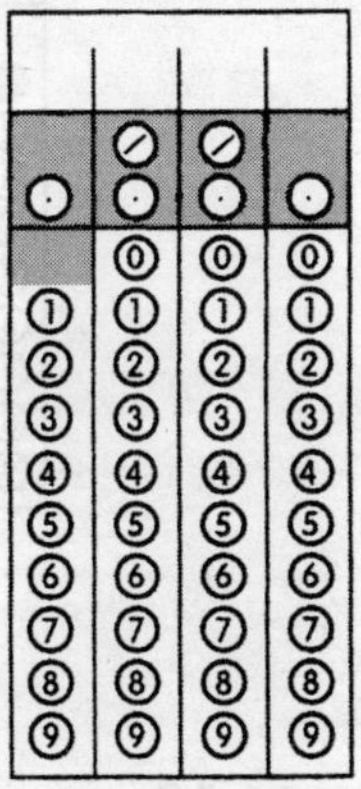

11. $\dfrac{2(p+3)-7}{4}=\dfrac{16-2(3-p)}{6}$

In the equation above, what is the value of p?

12. If $\frac{1}{5}x-\frac{2}{3}y=4$, what is the value of $3x-10y$?

13. If $-\frac{9}{5}<-5t+2<-\frac{7}{4}$, what is one possible value of $10t-4$?

14. The graph of $3x-4y=5$ is perpendicular to the graph of $2x+ky-10=0$. Find k.

Answers and Explanations 答案与解析

The difficulty level for each question is specified in parentheses.

1. B (M)
2. D (M)
3. A (M)
4. A (M)
5. C (M)
6. B (M)
7. C (M)
8. A (E)
9. B (M)
10. B (E)
11. $\frac{23}{2}$ or 11.5 (E)
12. 60 (M)
13. Any value between $\frac{7}{2}$ and $\frac{18}{5}$, for example, 3.55 (M)
14. $\frac{3}{2}$ (M)

11.

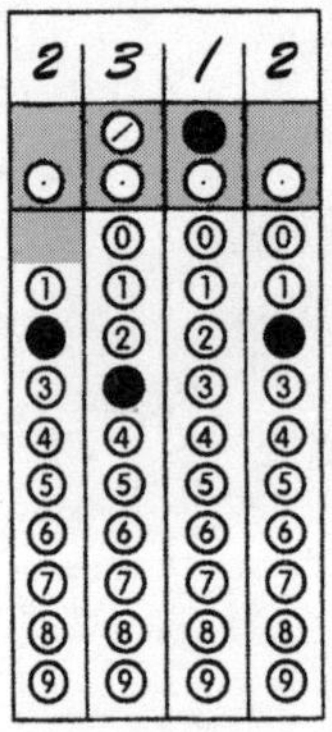

or

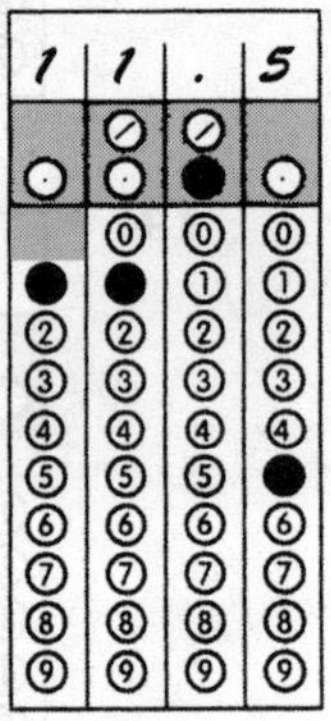

12.

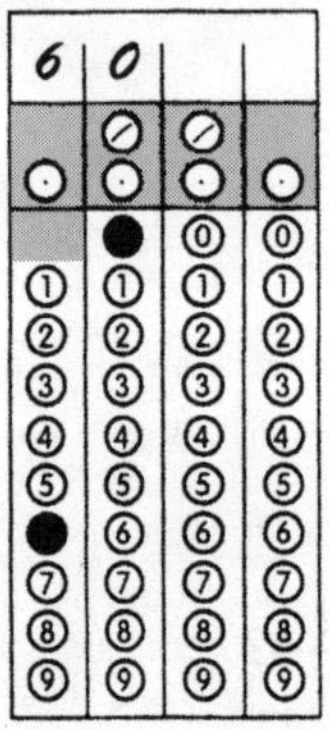

13.

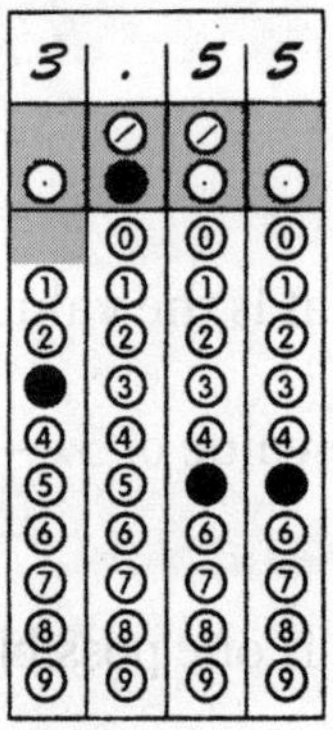

14.

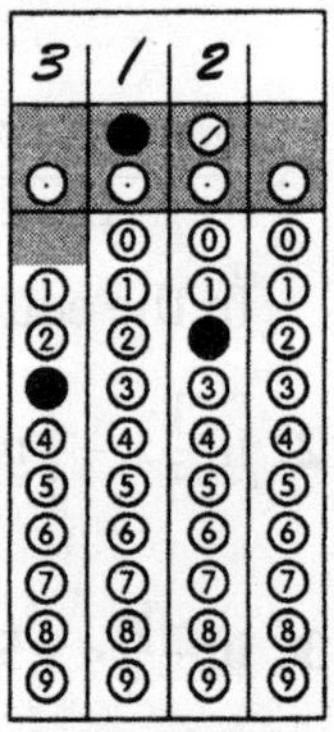

1. **(B)** Since the object travels 6 miles in 2 hours, its speed, which is constant, is $\frac{6}{2} = 3$. The equation of the relationship is therefore $d = 3t$. The graph is a line passing through the origin with slope 3. Eliminate choice (C), which doesn't pass through the origin. Eliminate choice (A) since it has negative slope. Choice (D) is wrong because the line has slope $\frac{1}{3}$ (rise of 1 over 3 horizontal units). The correct answer is therefore choice (B).

2. **(D)** From the given information you can conclude that $AO = 1$, $m\angle BOA = 60°$, and $\triangle BAO$ is a 30–60–90° triangle.
$\therefore$ point B has coordinates $(-1, \sqrt{3})$.
Use the slope formula or inspection to see that the slope of $\overleftrightarrow{BO}$ is $-\sqrt{3}$.

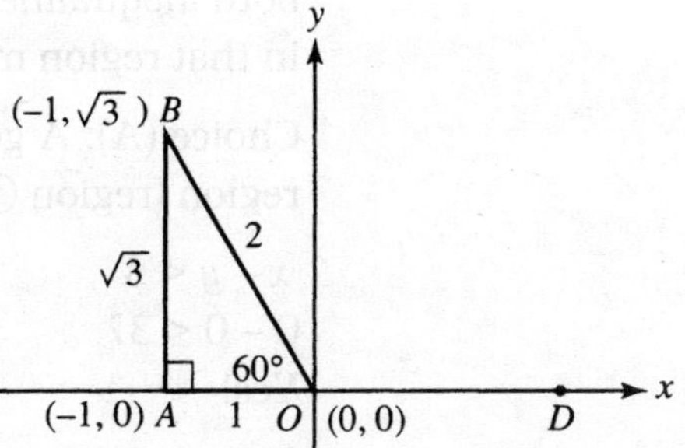

3. **(A)**
Method I: Algebra (Your math teacher would be proud.)
Write the inequalities in standard form:
$y < mx + b$ and $y > mx + b$

$$x - y < 3 \Rightarrow -y < -x + 3 \Rightarrow y > x - 3$$

(Multiply both sides by −1.)
The points that satisfy this inequality are above the line $y = x - 3$, not including the line (dotted line in the graph).

$$3x + 2y \leq 6 \Rightarrow 2y \leq -3x + 6 \Rightarrow y \leq -\frac{3}{2}x + 3$$

The points that satisfy this inequality are below the line $y = -\frac{3}{2}x + 3$, including the line (solid line in the graph).

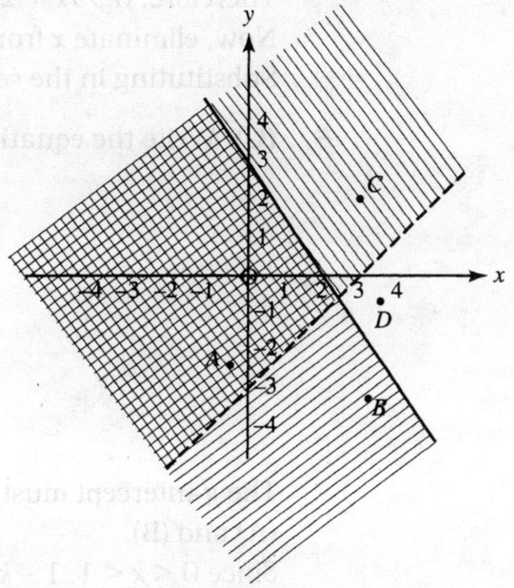

The region that satisfies both inequalities is the double-hatched shaded region on the graph. Point A is the only point in the required region. Notice that point B is not correct because points on the dotted line are not included. If the given inequality had been $y \geq x - 3$, then B would have satisfied the system of inequalities.

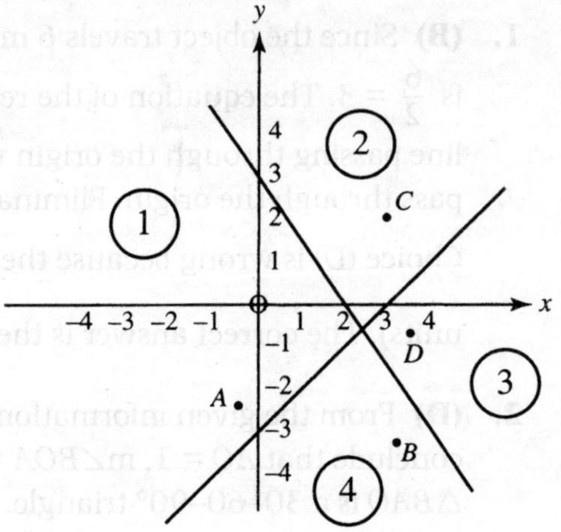

Method II: Plug-In (Faster!)

Notice that the two intersecting lines divide the plane into four regions, numbered as shown, and that each point is in a different region. A fast way to solve this problem is to select an easy point with integer coordinates in each region. If your point satisfies both inequalities, then the given point in that region must be the answer.

Choice (A): A good point to pick in *A*'s region (region ① in the figure) is (0, 0).

$x - y < 3$	$3x + 2y \le 6$
$0 - 0 < 3$?	$0 + 0 \le 6$?
Yes!	Yes!

Therefore point *A* is the correct answer.

4. **(A)** The total number of items is 11, so $x + y = 11$.
Also, total cost = \$22.89, so cost of songs + cost of e-books = 22.89.
Therefore, $0.99x + 2.99y = 22.89$.
Now, eliminate x from the first equation: $x = 11 - y$.
Substituting in the second gives: $0.99(11 - y) + 2.99y = 22.89$

5. **(C)** Write the equation in slope–intercept form:

$$y - x = k(x + y)$$
$$y - x = kx + ky$$
$$y - ky = kx + x$$
$$y(1 - k) = x(k + 1)$$
$$y = \frac{1+k}{1-k}x$$

The y-intercept must be 0, since there's no constant term, so eliminate choices (A) and (B).
Since $0 < k < 1$, $1 - k > 0$. Therefore, the slope is positive, as in choice (C).

6. **(B)** The system has no solution if their graphs are parallel. Notice that multiplying the top equation by 6, the least common denominator of the fractions, yields: $2x + 3y = 24$. The graph of this line will be parallel to the graph of $ax + 3y = 6$ only if their slopes are the same, namely, $a = 2$.

7. **(C)** Solve for x and y and then find the quotient $\frac{x}{y}$.

$$3x + 2y = 6 \quad (1)$$
$$y - 2x = 24 \quad (2)$$

From (2): $y = 2x + 24$ (3)

Substitute y in (1)

$$3x + 2(2x + 24) = 6$$
$$3x + 4x + 48 = 6$$
$$7x = -42$$
$$x = -6$$

Substitute x in (3)

$$y = 2(-6) + 24$$
$$y = 12$$
$$\therefore \frac{x}{y} = \frac{-6}{12} = -\frac{1}{2}$$

8. **(A)** Rewrite $2x + 3y + 12 = 0$ in slope–intercept form:

$$2x + 3y + 12 = 0$$
$$3y = -2x - 12$$
$$y = -\frac{2}{3}x - 4$$

Slope of the line is $-\frac{2}{3}$, and y-intercept is -4.

Choice (A) is the only choice that has both a negative slope and a negative y-intercept.

9. **(B)** The slope of the line is the average decrease in mudslides per year. Using two values along the line (125 after 10 years, 100 after 15 years) the slope is $\frac{25}{-5} = -5$. You should expect the answer to be negative, since the numbers are decreasing as the years increase.

10. **(B)** Cost for x tickets is $150x$.
Tax on x tickets is $0.08(150x)$.
Total charge is

$$150x + 0.08(150x) + 6 = 150x(1 + 0.08) + 6 = 1.08(150x) + 6$$

11. $\mathbf{\frac{23}{2}}$ or **11.5**

$$\frac{2(p+3)-7}{4}=\frac{16-2(3-p)}{6}$$

$$\frac{2p+6-7}{4}=\frac{16-6+2p}{6}$$

$$\frac{2p-1}{4}=\frac{10+2p}{6}$$

Cross-multiplying, $\Rightarrow 12p-6=40+8p$

$$4p=46$$

$$p=\frac{46}{4}=\frac{23}{2}$$

12. 60 Notice that multiplying both sides by 15 clears the fractions and gives you $3x-10y$.

$$\frac{1}{5}x-\frac{2}{3}y=4$$

$$(15)\frac{1}{5}x-(15)\frac{2}{3}y=(15)4$$

$$3x-10y=60$$

13. Any value between $\frac{7}{2}$ and $\frac{18}{5}$, for example, 3.55.

$$-\frac{9}{5}<-5t+2<-\frac{7}{4}$$

$$\frac{18}{5}>10t-4>\frac{7}{2}$$

$$\frac{7}{2}<10t-4<\frac{18}{5}$$

This means you want any value between 3.5 and 3.6.

14. $\mathbf{\frac{3}{2}}$ Write both equations in slope–intercept form:

$$3x-4y=5\Rightarrow y=\frac{3}{4}x-\frac{5}{4} \text{ and } 2x+ky-10=0\Rightarrow y=-\frac{2}{k}x+\frac{10}{k}$$

Since the lines are perpendicular, the product of their slopes is –1.

$$\left(\frac{3}{4}\right)\left(-\frac{2}{k}\right)=-1\Rightarrow\frac{3}{2k}=1\Rightarrow k=\frac{3}{2}$$

Notice that you don't need the *y*-intercepts for this problem; so you could just find the slopes by inspection!

第十二章 Chapter 12

PROBLEM SOLVING AND DATA ANALYSIS 问题解析与数据分析

Take out your high school statistics notes and brush up! This section on data analysis is one of the most important chapters for the 1600 Club to master. As with the Heart of Algebra, these topics are disproportionately important on the SAT Math Test: 28 percent of all math questions will involve data analysis. This becomes a whopping 42 percent of all questions on the calculator section of the test. You will receive a subscore for the Problem Solving and Data Analysis questions.

1600 Club Strategies in Problem Solving and Data Analysis
1600分俱乐部问题解析与数据分析策略

Strategy 1:	**P**roblems on standard deviation: know what it means.
Strategy 2:	**R**ange and outliers: know what these are.
Strategy 3:	**O**wn the data! Learn to read any chart, table, graph, or scatterplot.
Strategy 4:	**B**rush up on your statistics: know the vocabulary.
Strategy 5:	**L**ine graphs, lots of them! State what one point means.
Strategy 6:	**E**xponential functions: distinguish these from linear and quadratic functions.
Strategy 7:	**M**ean, median, and mode: find each "average" from a list of data.
Strategy 8:	**S**et up a proportion for percentage and ratio problems.

Problem solving and data analysis requires you to analyze the evidence or data presented in tables, charts, and graphs. The topics vary—everything from science to social studies to career-related contexts.

The questions for data analysis are all in the calculator section of the SAT Math Test, which doesn't mean you will necessarily require a calculator for the solutions.

Remember, judicious use of the calculator is a time saver for you.

Here are some of the skills you will apply to these problems:

- Set up ratios, percentages, and proportions
- Understand measurement and unit conversion
- Apply statistical analysis to a set of data: mean, median, mode, standard deviation, and range
- Do calculations using standard deviation in a normal distribution
- Interpret a graph and reach conclusions or make predictions
- Understand scatterplots
- Recognize the difference between linear, exponential, and quadratic models
- Compare data in two or more graphs
- Calculate conditional probability from tables

RATIO, PROPORTION, PERCENTS 比，比例，百分比

A *ratio* is a quotient of two quantities. For example, suppose that the ratio of boys to girls at a school is 4 to 5; that is, for every 4 boys there are 5 girls. Another way of expressing this is:

$$\frac{\text{Number of boys}}{\text{Number of girls}} = \frac{4}{5}$$

The ratio can also be denoted as

$$\text{Number of boys} : \text{Number of girls} = 4 : 5$$

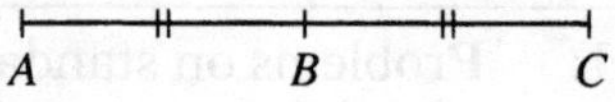

In the picture on the right, $AB = BC$.

The ratio of AC to $AB = \frac{2}{1}$ or 2:1 or 2 to 1.

A *percent* is a ratio in which the second quantity is 100. For example,

$$23\% = \frac{23}{100} = 0.23$$

A *proportion* is an equation that sets two ratios equal to each other. For example,

$$\frac{2}{5} = \frac{6}{15}$$

Proportions are often used in the solution of SAT problems.

Example 1 Grid-In

The price of a toaster was originally x dollars. Later, the toaster went on sale at a 20 percent discount, and was eventually sold for $50.40 after an additional 10 percent discount off the sale price. What was x, the original price, in dollars, of the toaster?

Solution: 70 This is a tricky problem that can be simplified by using the pick-a-number strategy. Instead of working backward from the actual price, note that the problem deals with percents, so start with x = \$100. Now work through the problem to see what percent of the original price, x, was actually paid:

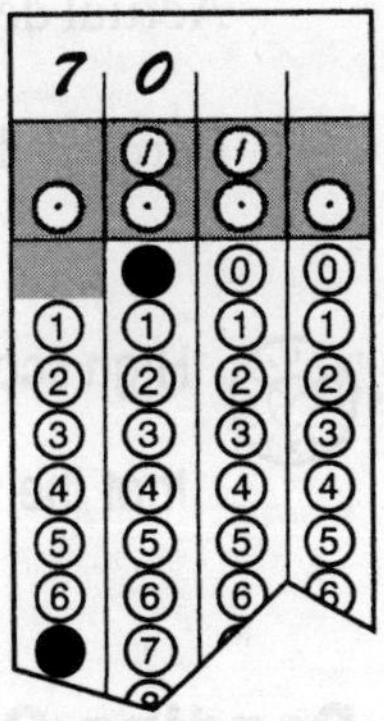

The 20 percent discount gives a sale price of \$80.

The additional 10 percent discount leaves a final price of \$72, which is 72 percent of \$100.

Therefore \$50.40, the actual final price paid, was 72 percent of x, the original price.

Set up the following proportion: $\dfrac{72}{100} = \dfrac{50.40}{x}$

Cross-multiply to solve for x: $x = \dfrac{(50.40)(100)}{72} = 70$

Grid-in 70.

Percent Increase and Decrease 百分比的增加和减少

Some of the more challenging problems on the SAT involve *percent increase* or *percent decrease.*

The percent increase of a quantity equals

$$\frac{\text{amount of increase}}{\text{original amount}} \cdot \frac{100}{1}$$

The percent decrease of a quantity equals

$$\frac{\text{amount of decrease}}{\text{original amount}} \cdot \frac{100}{1}$$

Example 2

The following chart shows the cost of one Roku streaming device at a discount store during each of the first 6 months of the year.

Month	January	February	March	April	May	June
Cost	\$200.99	\$195.99	\$150.00	\$150.00	\$135.99	\$120.85

The percent decrease in the cost of the device from January to June was closest to

(A) 12% (B) 40% (C) 50% (D) 60%

Solution: (B)

Actual decrease = cost in January – cost in June = $200.99 – $120.85 = $80.14.

Percent decrease = $\dfrac{80.14}{200.99} \cdot 100 \approx 40\%$.

High scorers don't waste time using a calculator for the final calculation. You can see that the fraction is approximately $\dfrac{80}{200}$, which is $\dfrac{40}{100}$ or 40%.

Reading Graphs 读图

The 1600 Club learns how to read a graph before answering questions about it.

Four-Step Drill 四步训练

The key to success is to approach each graph with an automatic, disciplined four-step drill. And this is irrespective of whether you are looking at a table, a simple graph, or a complicated spider's web of a figure that gives you fits. See the figure, do the drill. Here are the key words in the routine:

- Read and summarize
- Variables
- Units
- Trends

This drill should become second nature to you. Practice it every time you see a graph in this book or in a textbook at school. Do you read the newspaper? Science articles? When you come to a graph, do the drill! This means that when you get to the actual SAT Math Test, you will ace the graph questions.

Strategies for Reading Simple Graphs 读简单图的策略

- Focus on the graph's header. Also the one or two sentences that describe what's going on. Now jot down what the graph shows.
- What are the variables? You will find them by reading the labels on the axes. The independent variable is the one that's being changed and manipulated. Typically, but not always, the independent variable is represented along the horizontal axis. The dependent variable changes as a result of manipulating the independent variable. These values are usually—but not always—shown along the vertical axis.
- Check out the units. These will always be mentioned somewhere in the statement of the question and will also appear as labels on the axes themselves. Units on the axes may be abbreviated. They may also be weird and unfamiliar. Fear not. If this is the case, the units will be spelled out without their abbreviations.

- By this stage you should have a pretty good idea of what the graph is about. To check that you do, pick a single point and state precisely what it means. For example, "At an ocean depth of 20 meters there are 100 critters per square meter." If you can't do this, go back and reread the description of the graph.
- A graph need not necessarily be a line graph. Whatever it is, though, you need to be able to state what a single component means. In a pie chart, what is one slice of the pie? In a bar graph, what is one bar? For a pictograph, what is one picture?
- Once you understand the nuts and bolts of the scenario, you should look for trends in the numerical data. How are the quantities related? As x increases, does y increase, decrease, or stay the same? Are the points scattered, with no discernible pattern?

Try to analyze the following graph.

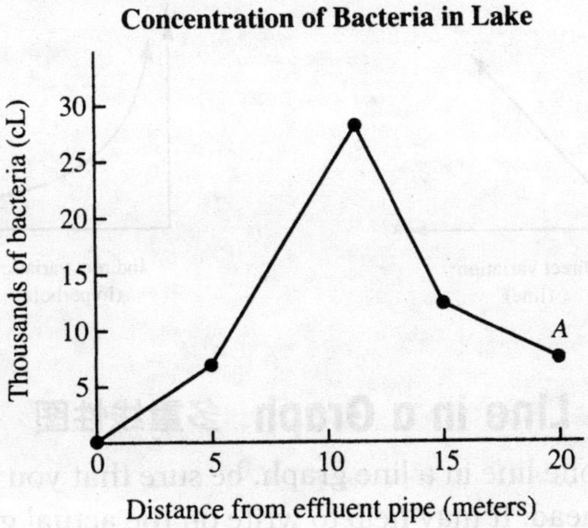

Coaching:
If you look at point A, say, you should be able to say: "At a distance of 20 meters from the pipe, the concentration of bacteria is about 7,500 bacteria per centiliter."

The graph above shows concentration of bacteria in a lake near an industrial meat-processing plant. An effluent pipe empties into the lake and the number of bacteria, in thousands per centiliter (cL), is plotted against distance, in meters (m), from the mouth of the pipe.

Use the checklist to "read" this graph. Here's what you could jot down.

- **Read and summarize:** Graph shows number of bacteria plotted against distance from effluent pipe.
- **Variables:** Independent variable is distance from pipe (horizontal axis), and dependent variable is number of bacteria (vertical axis).
- **Units:** Distance in meters (m) and concentration of bacteria in thousands per centiliter (thousands/cL).
- **Trends:** Concentration increases with distance from pipe, until maximum concentration reached at about 11 meters from pipe. Concentration falls off steeply after that.

Direct and Indirect Variation 正变分和反变分

If $y = kx$, where k is constant, the relationship between x and y is called a *direct variation*, and the graph is a straight line. We also say that *y is directly proportional to x*. If (x_1, y_1) and (x_2, y_2) are two points on the graph, then $y_1 = kx_1$ and $y_2 = kx_2$, from which you should see that $\frac{x_1}{y_1} = \frac{x_2}{y_2}$.

If $y = \frac{a}{x}$, where a is constant, the relationship between x and y is called an *indirect variation* or *inverse variation*, and the graph is a hyperbola. We also say that *y is indirectly proportional to x* or *inversely proportional to x*. If (x_1, y_1) and (x_2, y_2) are two points on the graph, then $y_1 = \frac{a}{x_1}$ and $y_2 = \frac{a}{x_2}$, from which you should see that $x_1y_1 = x_2y_2$.

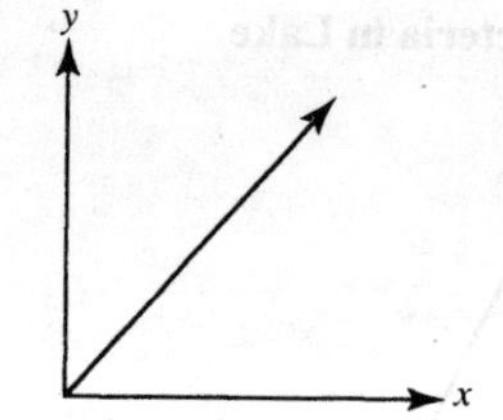

Direct variation
(line)

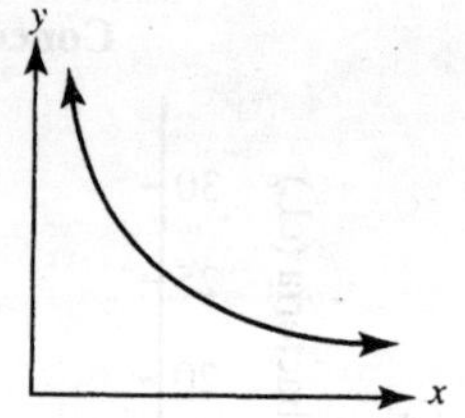

Indirect variation
(hyperbola)

More Than One Line in a Graph 多重线性图

If there is more than one line in a line graph, be sure that you have the different lines nailed down in your head. It may help to write on the actual graph which line stands for what. There's no excuse for getting a question wrong because you got the lines confused. Look at the following graph.

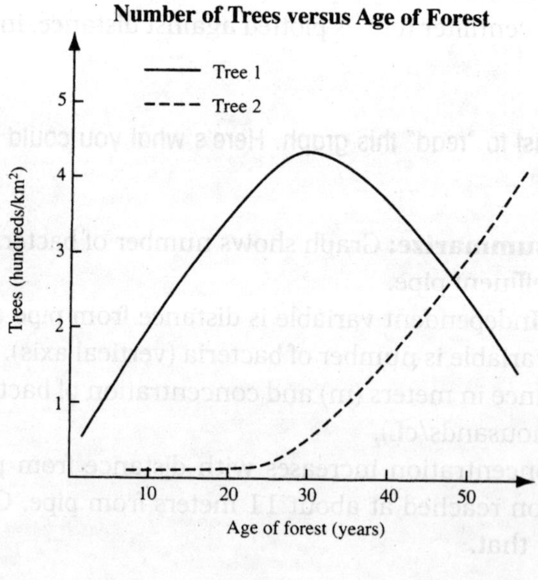

This is not a difficult graph to understand. Just be sure that you write "Tree 1" on the solid line and "Tree 2" on the dotted line, and then refer to the correct line when they ask you questions about the two types of trees!

Refer to the graph shown below for Examples 3 and 4.

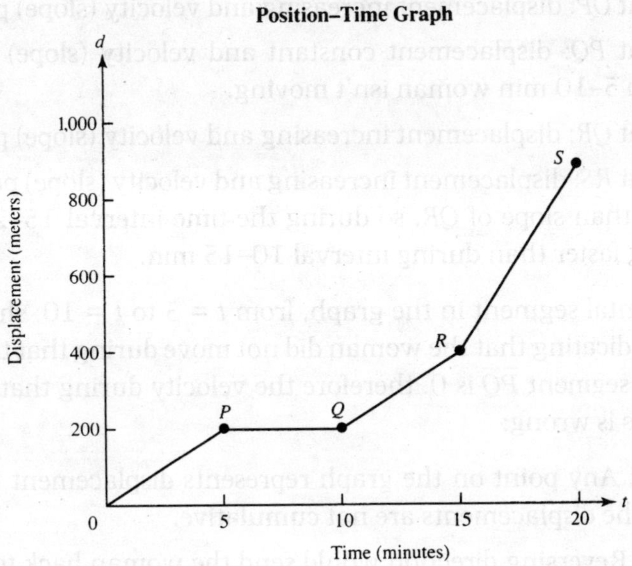

Example 3

A position–time graph for linear motion of an object in one dimension shows the object's displacement d from some origin at any given time t. If the graph is linear, its slope m is given by

$$m = \frac{\text{rise}}{\text{run}} = \frac{\text{change in } d}{\text{change in } t} = \frac{d_1 - d_2}{t_1 - t_2} = \bar{v},$$

where $\bar{v}$ is the average velocity of the object. (t_1, d_1) and (t_2, d_2) are any two points on the line. The graph above is a position–time graph for a person who takes a walk from her house.

Which of the following scenarios is consistent with the graph?

(A) After 20 minutes the displacement of the person from her house is approximately 230 + 230 + 410 + 900 = 1770 m.
(B) The woman reverses direction every 5 minutes during her walk.
(C) After the first 5 minutes of her walk, the woman stops for 5 minutes. She then resumes walking.
(D) The woman stops walking briefly at $t = 5$, $t = 10$, and $t = 15$ minutes.

Solution: (C) Using the drill described earlier:

- **Read and summarize:** Graph shows displacement versus time as woman walks from house. For linear parts of graph, slope is average velocity of woman during that time frame.
- **Variables:** Independent variable is time. Dependent variable is displacement from house.
- **Units:** Time in minutes and displacement in meters.

- **Trends:**

  Segment *OP*: displacement increasing and velocity (slope) positive.

  Segment *PQ*: displacement constant and velocity (slope) zero. So, for time equal to 5–10 min woman isn't moving.

  Segment *QR*: displacement increasing and velocity (slope) positive.

  Segment *RS*: displacement increasing and velocity (slope) positive. Slope of *RS* steeper than slope of *QR*, so during the time interval 15–20 min, woman is walking faster than during interval 10–15 min.

The horizontal segment in the graph, from $t = 5$ to $t = 10$, shows no change in displacement, indicating that the woman did not move during that time interval. Also, the slope of line segment $\overline{PQ}$ is 0, therefore the velocity during that time is 0. Each of the other choices is wrong:

Choice (A): Any point on the graph represents displacement from the origin *at that time*. The displacements are not cumulative.

Choice (B): Reversing direction would send the woman back to her house, causing the displacement to decrease, which is not the case.

Choice (D): If this scenario were true, there would be horizontal line segments starting at each of $t = 5$, $t = 10$, and $t = 15$.

Example 4

Which of the following graphs best describes the velocity of the woman on her walk?

(A)

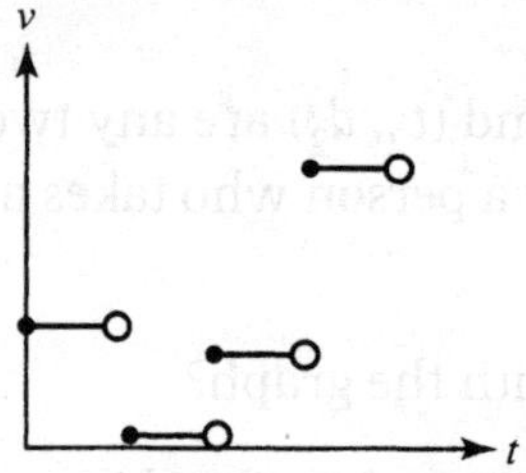

(C)

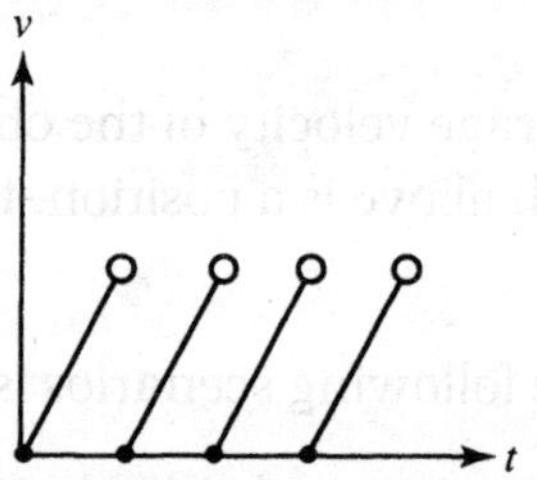

(B)

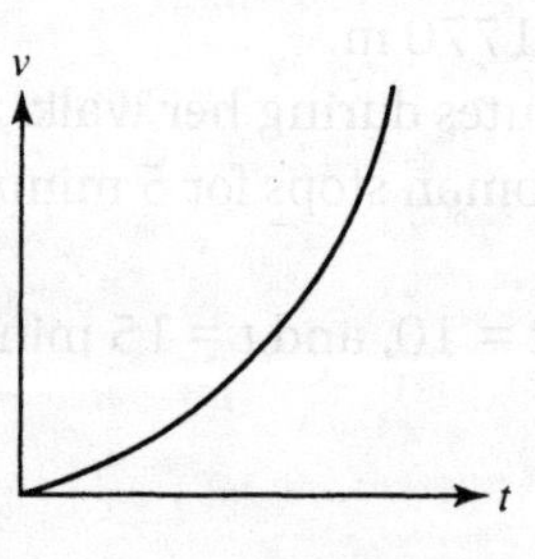

(D)

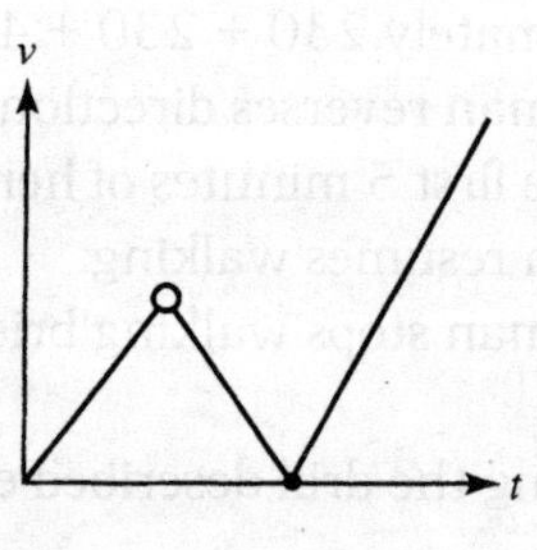

Solution: (A) For each linear segment of the walk in the original position–time graph, the velocity is the slope $\dfrac{\text{change in } d}{\text{change in } t}$. The slope of a line is constant, which means that the graph representing the velocity is a horizontal segment for each part of the walk.

The 1600 Club doesn't forget that the slope of a line is constant.

TYPES OF GRAPHS 图的类型

Circle Graphs 饼形图

In a *circle graph* or *pie chart*, the size of a wedge is proportional to the size of the number it represents.

Example 5

Marital Status of U.S. Citizens over 15 in 2003

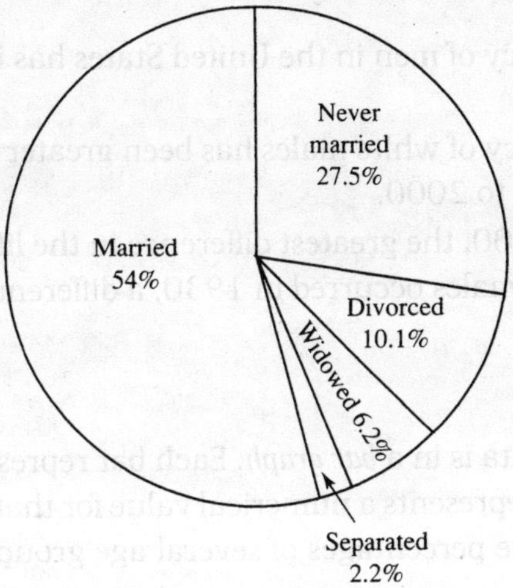

The graph shows the marital statuses of U.S. citizens ages 15 and over in 2003. If the total number of U.S. citizens over 15 was approximately 222 million in 2003, how many, to the nearest million, were divorced or separated?

(A) 3 million (B) 10 million (C) 22 million (D) 27 million

Solution: (D) The pie chart shows that "Divorced" and "Separated" add up to $10.1 + 2.2 = 12.3\%$.

12.3% of 222 million ≈ 27 million.

Don't waste time using your calculator here. Since 10 percent of 222 $\approx$ 22, you should pick the only answer choice that is greater than 22.

Time Plots 线性图

A *line graph* or *time plot* is a good way to examine trends over a given time period. Below is a double-line graph that shows the life expectancies at birth for males born in the United States between 1920 and 2000.

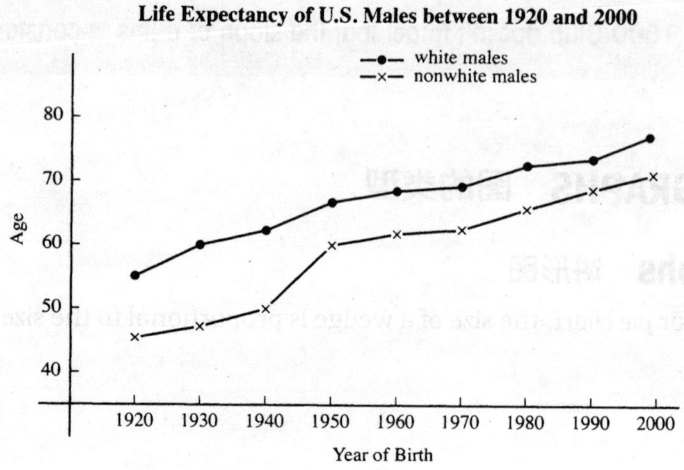

From this graph you can see many trends:

- The life expectancy of men in the United States has increased from 1920 to 2000.
- The life expectancy of white males has been greater than that of nonwhite males from 1920 to 2000.
- From 1920 to 2000, the greatest difference in the life expectancy of white and of nonwhite males occurred in 1930, a difference of about 13 years.

Bar Graphs 柱状图

Another way to display data is in a *bar graph*. Each bar represents a different category, and the height of the bar represents a numerical value for that category. The bar graph shown below compares the percentages of several age groups who have completed 4 or more years of college.

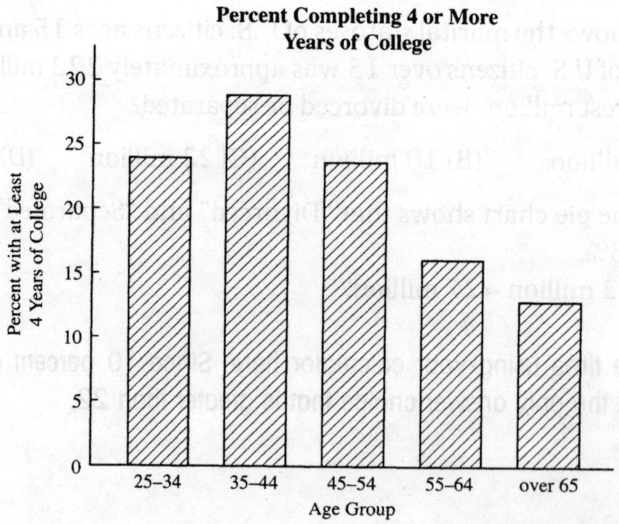

The graph shows that almost 30 percent of people aged 35–44 have completed at least 4 years of college. Also, at a glance you can see that older people are less likely to have achieved this level of education.

Pictographs 象形图

A *pictograph* presents data using pictorial symbols. Typically, one symbol represents a fixed number of items. The pictograph below shows the number of students who graduated each year from a small college.

Number of Students Graduating from a Small College

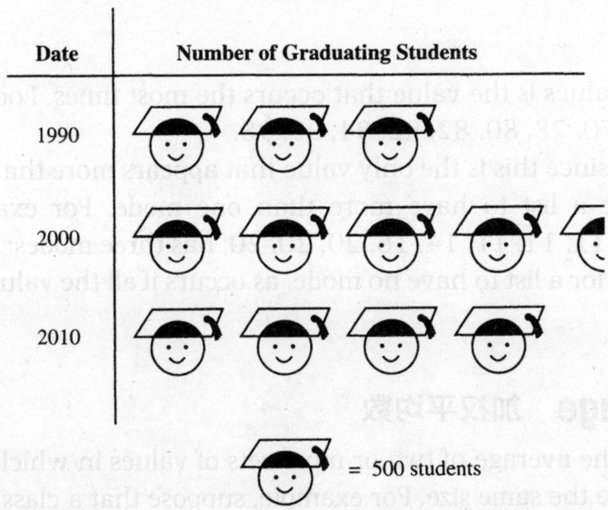

From the graph you can see that about 2,250 students graduated in 2000, but there were only 1,500 graduates in 1990.

CENTERS OF DATA 数据

Arithmetic Mean (Average) 算术平均值

$$\textit{arithmetic mean} \text{ of } n \text{ values} = \frac{\text{sum of } n \text{ values}}{n}$$

For example, a student in the 1600 Club has the following test scores in math (so far): 98, 94, 98, 78, 82, 80, 92. Then:

$$\text{arithmetic mean of her scores} = \frac{98+94+98+78+82+80+92}{7}$$
$$\approx 88.9$$

Median 中位数

To find the *median* of *n* values, *arrange the numbers in order.* If *n* is odd, the median is the middle number. If *n* is even, the median is the arithmetic mean of the two middle numbers. For example, to find the median of the test scores above, arrange them in order: 78, 80, 82, $\boxed{92}$, 94, 98, 98.

The median score is 92.

Now suppose that the same student takes another test and has a *really bad* day, scoring 70. Her scores, in order, are now 70, 78, 80, [82, 92], 94, 98, 98. The number of scores is even, and the median equals $\frac{82+92}{2}=87$.

Note that since the median is literally the middle number in an ordered set of numbers, it could be the lowest number in the set or the highest. For example, the median of 1 1 1 1 2 6 7 is 1. In a "symmetrical" set, where the numbers are equally spaced, the median will be the same as the arithmetic mean of the numbers. For example, the median of 1 3 5 7 9 is the middle number, 5, and the mean is $\frac{1+3+5+7+9}{5}=\frac{25}{5}=5$.

Mode 众数

The *mode* of a list of values is the value that occurs the most times. Look again at the student's test scores: 70, 78, 80, 82, 92, 94, 98, 98.

The mode is 98, since this is the only value that appears more than once.

It is possible for a list to have more than one mode. For example, the list 1, 1, 6, 6, 6, 9, 9, 10, 11, 11, 11, 14, 16, 20, 20, 20, has three modes: 6, 11, and 20.

It is also possible for a list to have no mode, as occurs if all the values appear only once.

Weighted Average 加权平均数

A *weighted average* is the average of two or more sets of values in which both or all of the sets do not all have the same size. For example, suppose that a class is divided into three groups:

Group A, with 10 students, has a test average of 65.
Group B, with 5 students, has a test average of 90.
Group C, with 7 students, has a test average of 80.

To find the class average, high scorers know that what you *can't* do is find $\frac{65+90+80}{3}$. What you must do is weight each score by multiplying by the number of students in that group. This gives the total of scores in that group. Then find the sum of the results and divide by 22, the total number of students.

$$\text{Arithmetic mean of scores} = \frac{(65)(10)+(90)(5)+(80)(7)}{22} \approx 75.5$$

Example 6

The Hadleys took a car trip to visit relatives. Mr. Hadley drove for 2 hours and covered 100 miles. For the last 60 miles, their teenage son, Hank, drove. He took 1 hour to complete this leg of the trip. What was the average speed (arithmetic mean), in miles per hour, for the trip?

(A) 50 (B) $53\frac{1}{3}$ (C) 55 (D) $56\frac{2}{3}$

Solution: (B)

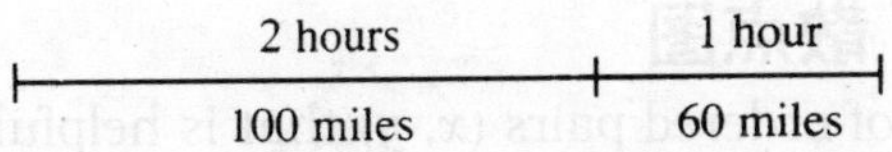

Mr. Hadley drove 2 hours at $\frac{100}{2} = 50$ miles per hour.

Hank drove 1 hour at $\frac{60}{1} = 60$ miles per hour.

$$\text{Average speed} = \frac{\text{total number of miles}}{\text{total number of hours}} = \frac{(50)(2)+(60)(1)}{3} = \frac{160}{3} = 53\tfrac{1}{3} \text{ miles per hour}$$

READING TABLES 读懂表格

On the SAT you will be asked to interpret information that is presented in tables. Sometimes you will be given calculations based on that information.

Example 7

In a certain school district, teachers are allowed to take three personal days, at full pay, during one school year. Here is a summary of the number of personal days taken by teachers in 2013–2014.

Number of Teachers Who Took Personal Days	Number of Personal Days Taken by Those Teachers
Fewer than 10	0
50	1
200	2
85	3

From this table you can accurately find

I. the arithmetic mean of personal days taken
II. the median number of personal days taken
III. the mode of the number of personal days taken

(A) I only (B) II only (C) III only (D) II and III only

Solution: (D) Think of the data as laid out, in order, as shown below:

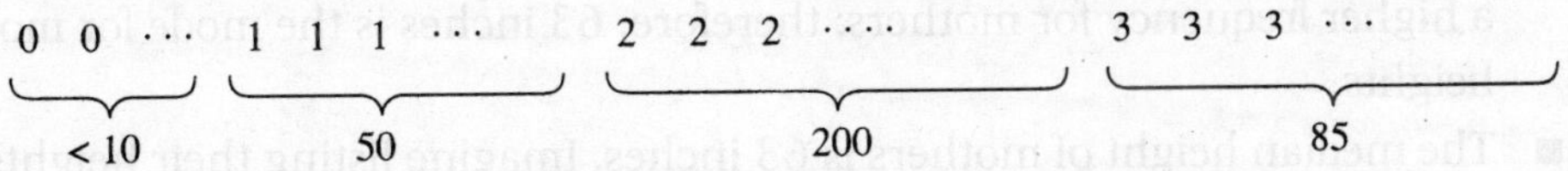

It is not possible to find the arithmetic mean because you don't know how many items are in the list. (What will the denominator be?)

It is possible, however, to see that 2 is the middle number, whether 0 occurs zero or nine times. Therefore the median is 2.

You can also find the mode: 2 occurs more often than the other numbers.

SCATTERPLOTS 散点图

A *scatterplot* is a graph of ordered pairs (x, y) that is helpful in finding a relationship between the variables x and y. Often, but not always, the variable along the x-axis is a predictor for the variable along the y-axis. For example, if the scatterplot shows the heights of people (x-axis), plotted against their weights (y-axis), one might expect taller people to weigh more.

The scatterplot below shows the heights of pairs of parents. In each case, the father's height is plotted on the horizontal axis and the mother's height on the vertical axis.

Heights of Parents

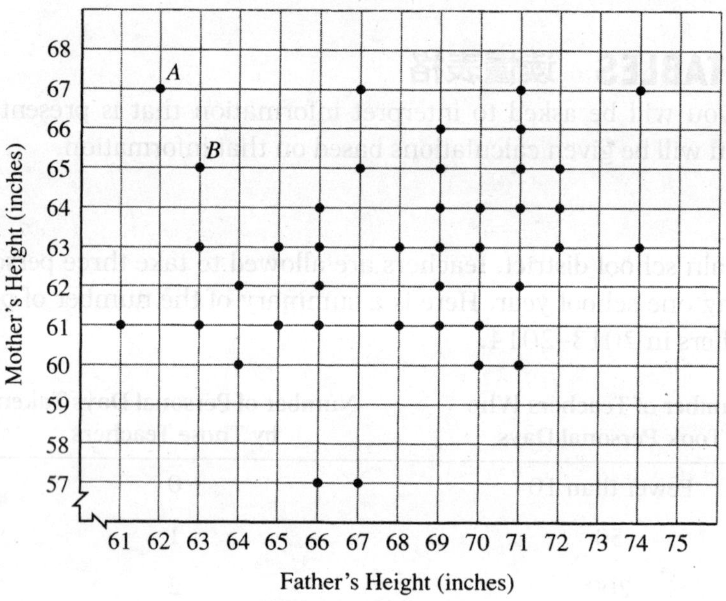

Here are some conclusions you can draw from the graph:

- A point in this plot represents one pair of parents.
- There are 40 such pairs, one per point.
- There are only two pairs in which the mother is taller than the father: a 62-inch father with a 67-inch mother (point *A*), a 63-inch father with a 65-inch mother (point *B*).
- There are six fathers who are 69 inches tall, and six others who are 71 inches tall. These numbers, 69 inches and 71 inches, are the two modes for fathers' heights.
- There are eight mothers who are 63 inches tall. No other height occurs with a higher frequency for mothers; therefore, 63 inches is the mode for mothers' heights.
- The median height of mothers is 63 inches. Imagine listing their heights in order. Start at the bottom of the graph, and move up: 57, 57, 60, 60, 60, ... The number 63 occurs in both the 20th and 21st (middle) slots.
- The middle two heights for fathers are 68 and 69 inches. Therefore, the median height for fathers is 68.5 inches. Again, list the heights in order, starting at the left: 61, 62, 63, 63, 63, ... Just move right until you get to the middle. The 20th and 21st (middle) slots are 68 and 69.

Notice that the relationship between heights of fathers and heights of corresponding mothers seems to be weak, but it is not nonexistent: few tall women have short men as partners.

Line of Best Fit 最佳拟合线

On the SAT you may be asked to find the *line of best fit* for a scatterplot. This is a straight line that passes through the arithmetic means of the x and y variables. Typically, this line has the same number of points on either side of it. Sometimes called the "trend" line, the line of best fit indicates the correlation between the variables. If the slope is positive, there is a *positive correlation*; as one variable increases, so does the other. If the slope is negative, the correlation is negative; as one variable increases, the other decreases.

For example, a scatterplot of GPAs of high school students versus numbers of hours per day spent reading would be expected to show a positive correlation (see the diagram on the left below). On the other hand, a scatterplot of GPAs of high school students versus numbers of hours per day spent on social media would be expected to show a negative correlation, as in the diagram on the right.

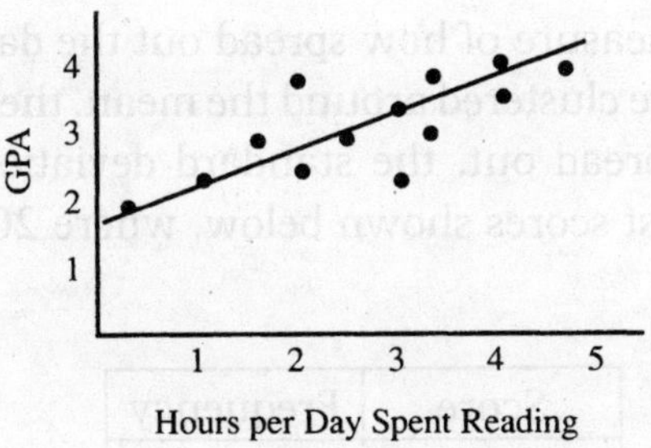

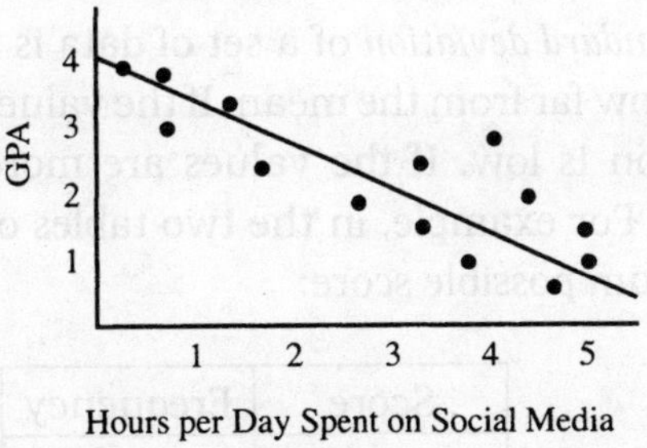

Interpolation and Extrapolation 内插法和外推法

Does it make sense to *interpolate* between two points on a graph? This means connect the points and estimate a y-value that lies between two x-values, based on other known (x, y) pairs. If the points are part of a scatterplot, draw the line of best fit, the line that comes closest to all of the points. Then find the y-value on the line that corresponds to the given x-value. Shown below is an example of a line of best fit in a scatterplot.

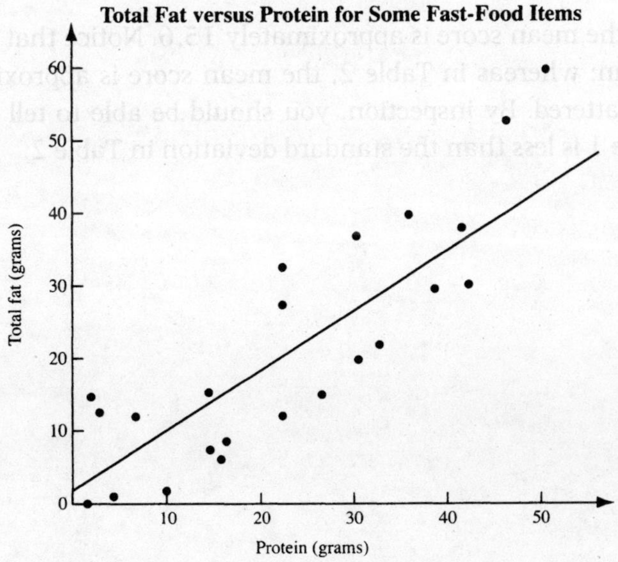

According to the graph, a person who wants to get 35 grams of protein from his fast food lunch can expect to consume about 31 grams of fat. This value was obtained by interpolating between 30 and 40 grams of protein.

Does it make sense to *extrapolate*? This means extend the graph beyond the values on the axes to find a y-value for an x-value that is out of the given range. If the graph is linear, just extend the line in your booklet. If it's a "curved" line, extend it in a way that looks right to you, then estimate the required value.

Correlation 相关性

Are there *correlations* between variables? Correlation measures the strength of the linear association between two numerical variables. For example, you could imagine that for children, age correlates with height: the older the child, the taller he or she is. You could reasonably expect to get a straight line or upward curve with a positive slope when you plot age against height.

STANDARD DEVIATION 标准差

The *standard deviation* of a set of data is a measure of how spread out the data values are—how far from the mean. If the values are clustered around the mean, the standard deviation is low. If the values are more spread out, the standard deviation will be higher. For example, in the two tables of test scores shown below, where 20 was the maximum possible score:

Score	Frequency
10	1
13	2
15	12
18	2
19	1
20	2

Table 1

Score	Frequency
10	4
13	5
15	1
18	2
19	1
20	7

Table 2

In Table 1, the mean score is approximately 15.6. Notice that most of the scores are near the mean; whereas in Table 2, the mean score is approximately 15.8, and the values are scattered. By inspection, you should be able to tell that the standard deviation in Table 1 is less than the standard deviation in Table 2.

NORMAL DISTRIBUTION 正态分布

A *normal distribution* of data is one that has just one mode and is symmetrical about the mean. Its graph is the familiar bell curve.

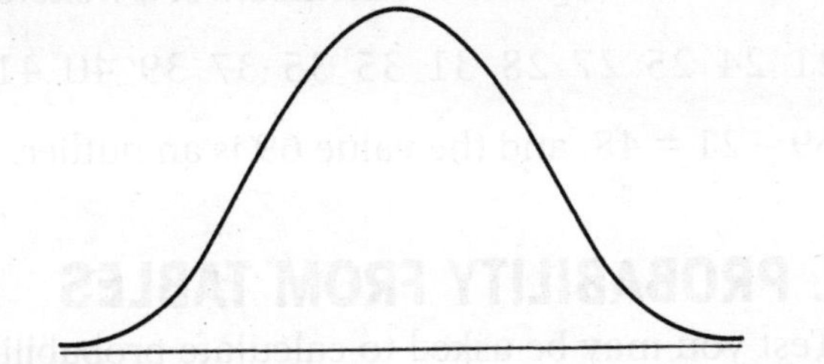

In a normal distribution, about 68 percent of the values fall within 1 standard deviation of the mean, about 95 percent fall within 2 standard deviations of the mean, and about 99.7 percent fall within 3 standard deviations of the mean. This 68–95–99.7 rule corresponds to the proportions of the areas under the bell curve.

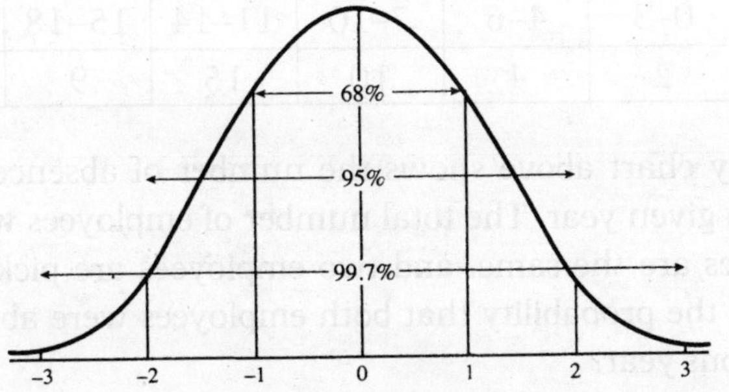

Number of standard deviations from the mean

Example 8

The scores on the SAT Math Test have a normal distribution with an overall mean of about 500 and standard deviation of 100 for all test takers. Jamal earned a score of 600 for his SAT Math Test. Given that about 68 percent of all scores lie within 1 standard deviation of the mean, approximately what percentage of test takers earned a higher score?

(A) 2.5 (B) 5 (C) 16 (D) 32

Solution: (C) Jamal's score is 1 standard deviation above the mean. About 68 percent of those who took the test had scores that fell no more than 1 standard deviation from the mean. Therefore, 100% − 68% = 32% of all students had scores more than 1 standard deviation away. Only half of those, 16 percent, were better than Jamal's.

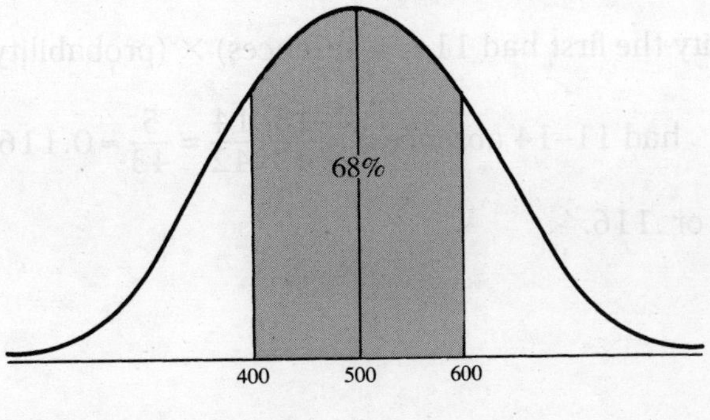

RANGE OF DATA AND OUTLIERS 极差和异常值极差

The *range* of a set of data is the difference between the highest and lowest values.

An *outlier* is a data value that doesn't fit with the rest of the data.

For example, here are the ages of the members of a writers' group:

21 24 25 27 28 31 35 35 37 39 40 41 69

The range is 69 − 21 = 48, and the value 69 is an outlier.

CONDITIONAL PROBABILITY FROM TABLES 条件概率

On the SAT Math Test you may be asked to calculate probabilities that are related to data in a table.

Example 9 Grid-In

							Total
Absences	0–3	4–6	7–10	11–14	15–18	19–22	
Frequency	2	4	10	15	9	3	43

The frequency chart above shows the number of absences for employees in a small business in a given year. The total number of employees was 43. The following year, the employees are the same, and two employees are picked at random for an interview. What is the probability that both employees were absent between 11 and 14 times the previous year?

Solution: 5/43 or .116

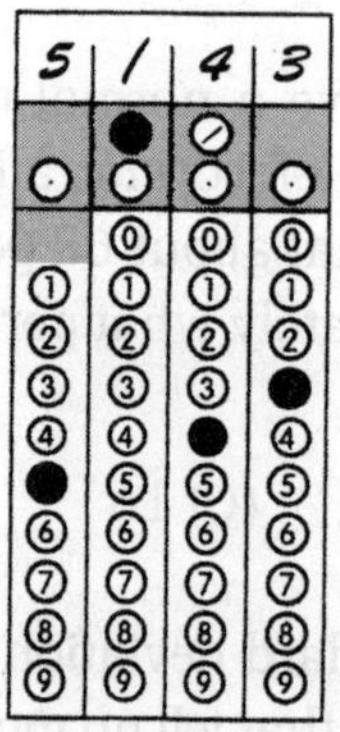

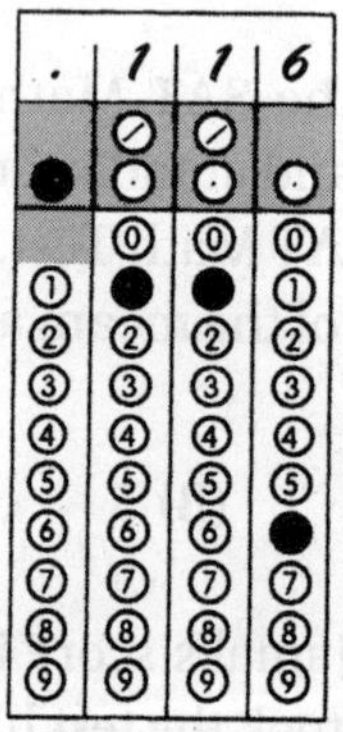

15 out of the 43 employees had 11–14 absences.

The probability that two of those were picked is equal to:

(probability the first had 11–14 absences) × (probability the second

$$\text{had 11–14 absences}) = \frac{15}{43}\cdot\frac{14}{42} = \frac{5}{43} \approx 0.116$$

Grid-in 5/43 or .116.

STATISTICAL SAMPLING 统计抽样

On the SAT Math Test, there may be questions on the validity of surveys and data collection. More often than not, you'll be able to answer these questions using common sense; but there are some general principles you should know.

To examine a feature of the entire population, it is valid to inspect a smaller group of individuals—a *sample*—provided they are randomly selected from the population. A sample that overlooks an important subset of the population is biased. Thus, it's important that chance, rather than human choice, is used to select the sample.

Surveys 调查

Here are some examples of biased samples that will invalidate a survey:

- A voluntary response survey in which a large number of people are invited to respond and only those who respond are counted. For example, call-in shows and people who write letters to Congress.
- Convenience sampling, in which only the people at hand are used for the sample. An example of this would be to sample all the people in a given restaurant on a Saturday night.
- Undercoverage, in which part of the population is excluded from the survey. An example of this would be a telephone poll that excludes cellphone users.
- Nonresponse bias. Most surveys don't get everyone to respond. This becomes a problem if those who don't respond differ from those who do in exactly the feature that's being investigated, such as the amount of free time a person has on a weekday.

Experimental Research 实验研究

Experimental research is used to study a small group of people and generalize the results to a larger population. In order to make a generalization involving cause and effect:

- The population must be well defined.
- The participants must be selected at random.
- The participants must be assigned randomly, either to an experimental group (one that is subjected to the experimental feature) or to a control group (one that is not). An example of an experimental feature is a new medical treatment.

Example 10

A large health club with more than 5,000 members has a swimming pool, weight room, aerobics classes, and a gym, not all of which are used by all of the members. A staff member conducted a survey concerning the temperature of the weight room. For one month, every tenth member who signed in at the club was asked if the weight room temperature was too high, too low, or just right. Which of the following factors is most likely to invalidate the conclusion drawn about the temperature of the weight room?

(A) The membership size
(B) The sample size
(C) The number of people who refused to respond
(D) The composition of the sample

Solution: (D) The population that was sampled was not necessarily a representative sample of members who used the weight room. In order for this survey to be valid, only members who used the weight room should have been surveyed.

Choice (A) is incorrect. The size of the membership is irrelevant in this survey.

Choice (B) is incorrect. Every tenth person would probably provide at least 100 people in the sample, which would have allowed a reasonable conclusion if the sampling population were correct.

Choice (C) is incorrect. People are not forced to respond to surveys. Even if some refused to respond, a reliable conclusion could be reached if a sample of weight room users was randomly selected.

LINEAR, QUADRATIC, AND EXPONENTIAL MODELS
线性，二次函数和指数模型

On the SAT Math Test, you are expected to recognize graphs, equations, and contexts (real-life situations) that represent linear, quadratic, and exponential relationships.

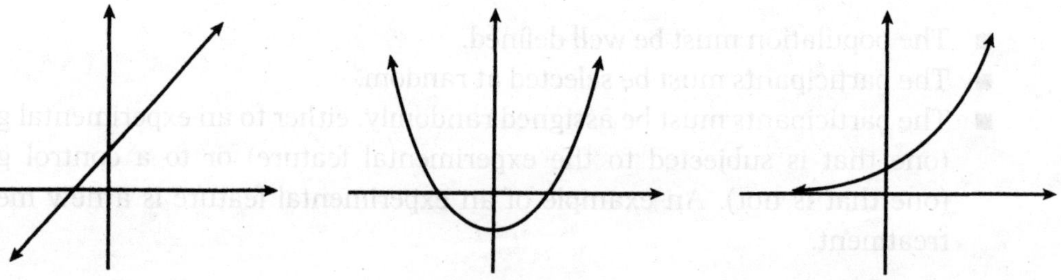

Linear　　Quadratic　　Exponential

A linear relationship is one in which the independent variable is multiplied by a constant. For example, if x is the number of tickets, and each ticket costs \$50, then y, the total cost is a linear function of x. The price per ticket is the constant.

An example of a quadratic function is the area of a plane figure, where x is the measurement of one dimension, and a second dimension is expressed in terms of x. Any situation where x is multiplied by a linear expression in terms of x, is a quadratic function. The graph is a parabola.

An exponential function has the independent variable x as an exponent. Any situation that involves doubling the previous y value, tripling, or halving, and so on, is exponential. Typical situations are bacterial growth (where the number of bacteria doubles every hour, say) or radioactive decay (where the weight of a pure radioactive substance gets halved every five years, say).

Example 11

Which of the following could be the graph of $y = 3^{-2x}$?

(A)

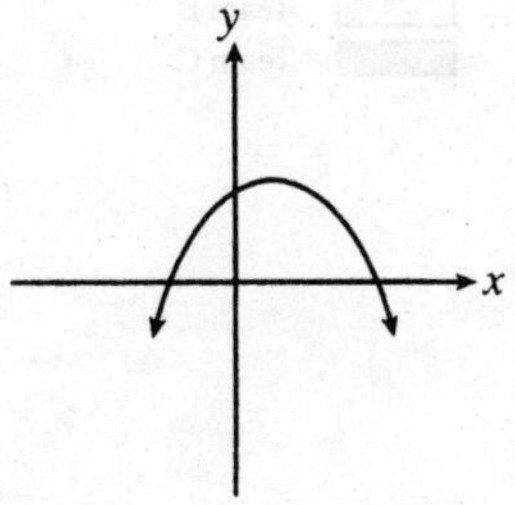

(C)

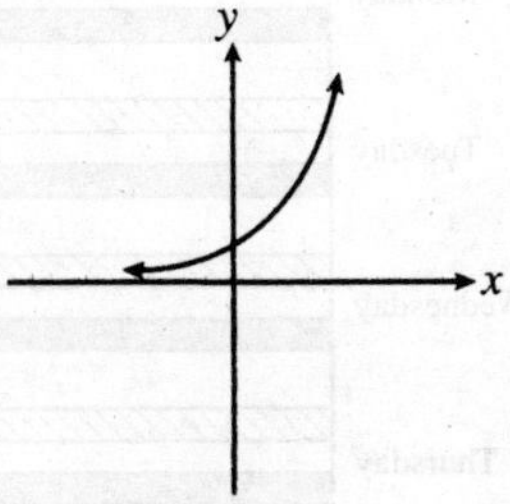

(B)

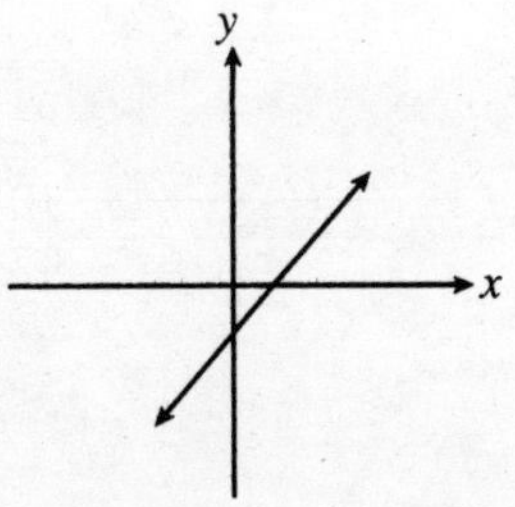

(D)

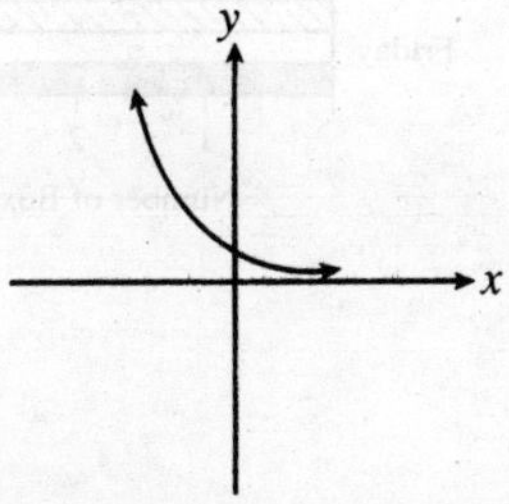

Solution: (D) Eliminate choices (A) and (B), since the function is exponential, with the independent variable, x, as an exponent.

Notice that when $x = 1$, $y = 3^{-2} = \frac{1}{3^2} = \frac{1}{9}$.

When $x = 2$, $y = 3^{-4} = \frac{1}{3^4} = \frac{1}{81}$.

Since the function is decreasing, the graph corresponds to choice (D).

PRACTICE TEST QUESTIONS 练习测试题

1. Marie is an assembly-line supervisor at a plant that packages boxes of chocolates. Each week Marie reviews the production rates for the three teams that work on her assembly line. According to the following bar graph, which team had the highest overall production for week 20?

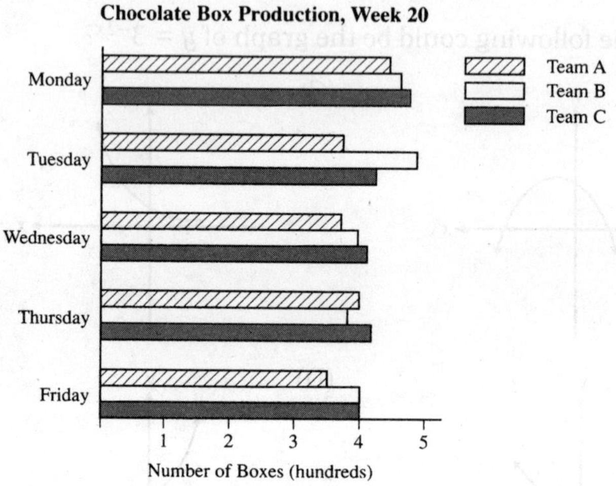

(A) Team A
(B) Team B
(C) Team C
(D) Team A and Team B had the same high production rate

2. The toe shoes of professional ballerinas often wear out in less than a year. At a ballet school there are 20 students, all of whom bought new toe shoes of different brands and at varying prices. They kept track of how long their shoes lasted. Each point on the graph below shows the duration of a ballet student's toe shoes plotted against their price. Of the five labeled points, which one corresponds to the toe shoes that cost the greatest amount per month of use?

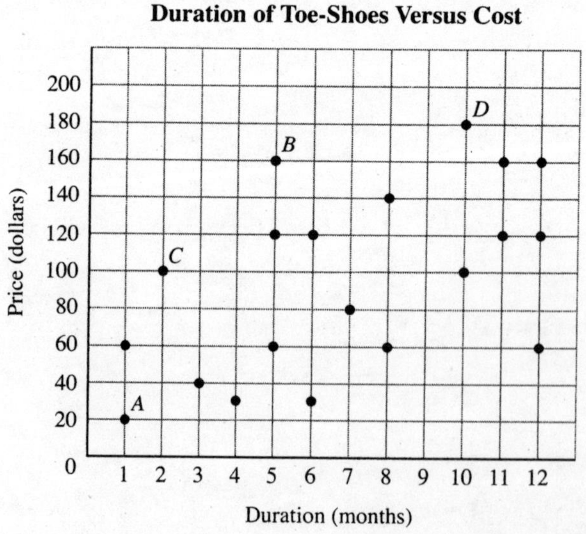

(A) *A*　　(B) *B*　　(C) *C*　　(D) *D*

3. The Math Team and Debate Club at Jackson City High School buy their T-shirts from different stores. The tables below show the numbers of T-shirts ordered by the Math Team and Debate Club, and the costs of medium, large, and extra-large T-shirts.

Numbers of T-shirts Ordered

	Medium	Large	Extra-Large
Math Team	7	18	20
Debate Club	2	20	10

Costs of T-shirts

	Math Team	Debate Club
Medium	\$11	\$9
Large	\$11	\$10
Extra-large	\$11	\$14

Which statement about the costs of T-shirts, as shown in the tables, is true?

I. The Math Team spent more on extra-large T-shirts than the Debate Club spent.
II. On average, the Math Team paid more per T-shirt than the Debate Club paid.
III. Of the three sizes, extra-large T-shirts had the highest median cost.

(A) I only
(B) II only
(C) III only
(D) I, II, and III

Students and Test Scores

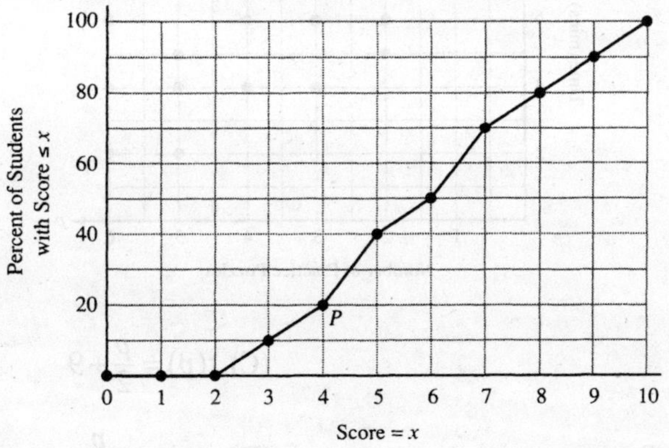

4. When a 10-question true-false quiz was given to 50 students, the number of correct answers ranged from 3 to 10, as shown on the graph above. Each point on the graph shows the percent of students who earned scores less than or equal to x. For example, point P shows that 20 percent of the students received scores of 4 or less. According to the graph, how many students got scores of 6?

(A) 5 (B) 10 (C) 15 (D) 20

5. In the sequence x, $x + d$, $x + 2d$, $x + 3d$, assume that x and d are positive integers. What is the difference between the arithmetic mean and the median of the numbers in the sequence?

(A) $2x + 3d$ (B) $\frac{2x+3d}{2}$ (C) $\frac{x+d}{2}$ (D) 0

6. The table below gives the frequency with which various scores were obtained on a 20-question written section of a drivers' education test.

Score	12	13	14	15	16	17	18	19	20
Frequency	2	3	0	3	3	5	5	6	4

The mode of the data is

(A) 3 (B) 6 (C) 18 (D) 19

7. A psychologist's experiment involved timing 15 small children as they found the solution to a little puzzle. Each child received at least one similar puzzle to play with before being timed. The scatterplot below shows the time each child took to solve the puzzle, and the corresponding number of "practice" puzzles each child received. On the basis of these data, which of the following functions best models the relationship between t, the number of minutes taken to complete the puzzle, and p, the number of practice puzzles?

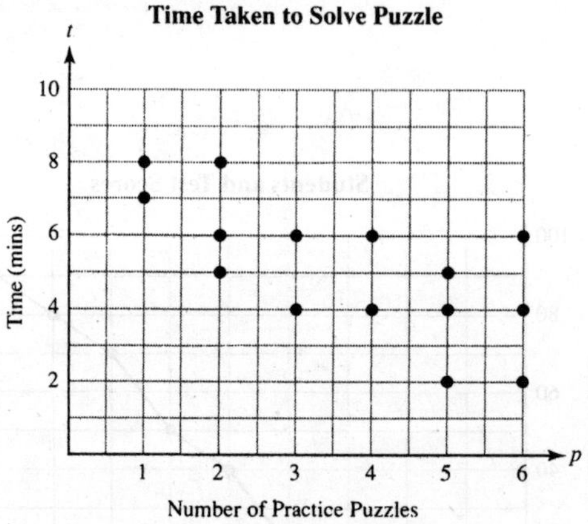

(A) $t(p) = 9$

(B) $t(p) = -\frac{p}{2} + 9$

(C) $t(p) = \frac{p}{2} + 9$

(D) $t(p) = -\frac{p}{2}$

8.

Population in Region *R* by Towns
♀ = 10,000 people

Town *A*	♀♀
Town *B*	♀♀♀♀
Town *C*	♀♀♀♀♀
Town *D*	♀♀♀♀♀♀♀♀♀

If the four towns shown in the graph are the only towns in Region *R*, the combined populations of which two towns account for exactly 45 percent of the population of Region *R*?

(A) *A* and *B*　(B) *B* and *C*　(C) *A* and *C*　(D) *A* and *D*

9. Ali is in a minivan with x children. Let y be the average (arithmetic mean) of the children's ages. If Ali's age is 6 times y, then her age is what fraction of the total ages of all the people in the minivan?

(A) $\frac{6}{6+y}$　(B) $\frac{6}{6+x}$　(C) $\frac{6}{x+y}$　(D) $\frac{x}{6y}$

Number of Pets	Frequency
6	2
5	1
4	3
3	5
2	8
1	14
0	7

10. The numbers of pets owned by children in a sixth grade class are shown in the table above. What is the median of the data?

(A) 1　(B) 2　(C) 3　(D) 5

11. To commute to his office, Mr. Brown can take either the A train or B train. Both train stations are the same distance from his apartment, and both stations claim that on average they run 10 minutes late from the scheduled arrival time. The standard deviation for the A train is 1 minute and for the B train is 5 minutes. Which of the following is a valid conclusion for Mr. Brown?

(A) If he regularly takes the A train, he will arrive at approximately the same time every day.
(B) If he takes the A train, he is less likely to arrive late.
(C) If he takes the A train, he is more likely to be 15 minutes late than with the B train.
(D) If he takes the A train, he is more likely to arrive on time.

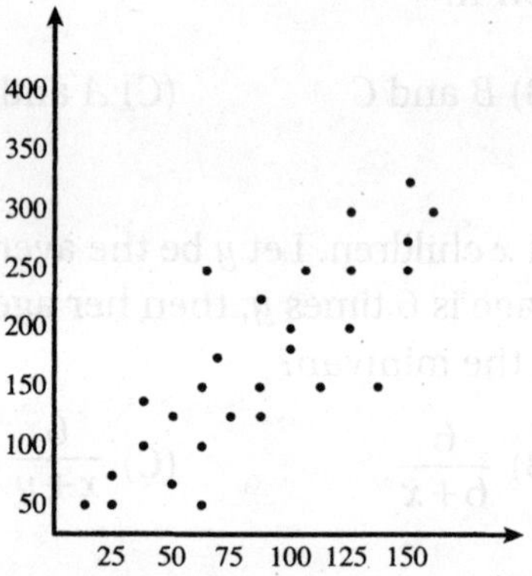

12. For the scatterplot above, which is closest to the slope of the line of best fit?

(A) $\frac{1}{2}$ (B) 1 (C) 2 (D) 3

	Male	Female	Total
Game	279	200	479
Commercials	81	156	237
Won't watch	132	160	292
Total	492	516	1008

13. The table above shows the result of a survey of adults over 18. Each person had to pick one of 3 choices: looking forward to a televised game, looking forward to the commercials, or not planning to watch. Based on the table, if a woman was polled at random, what is the probability, as a percent, that she would respond that she was looking forward to the commercials?

(A) 15 (B) 30 (C) 51 (D) 66

Questions 14–19 are grid-in questions.

14.

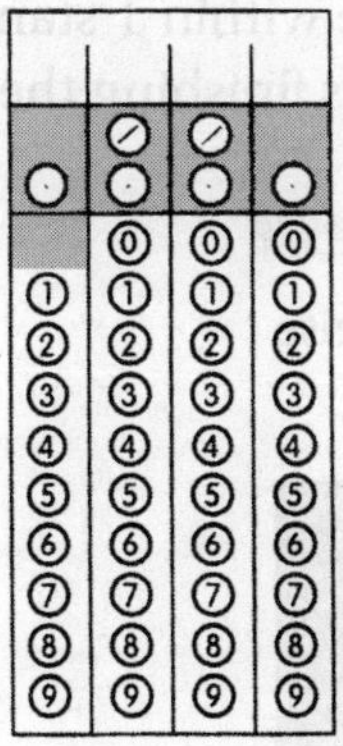

15.

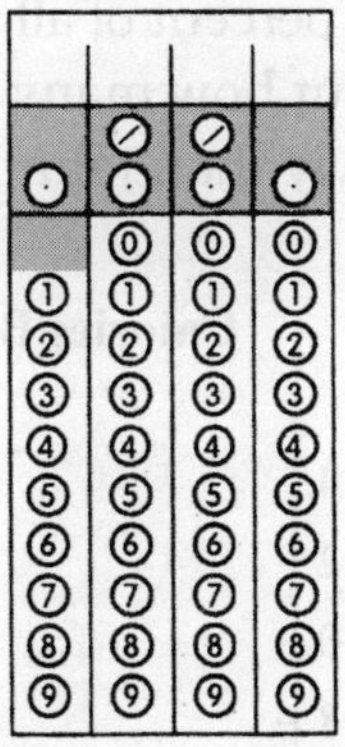

16.

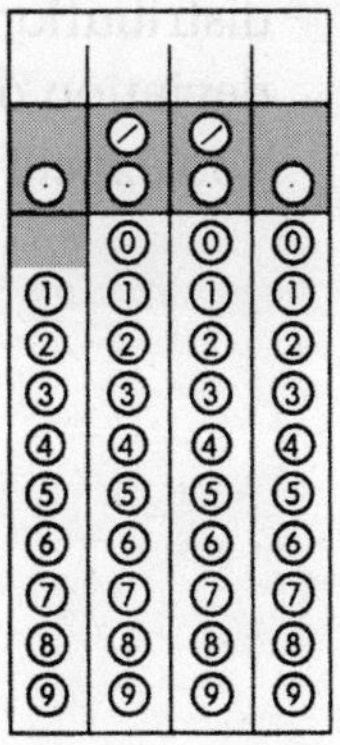

17.

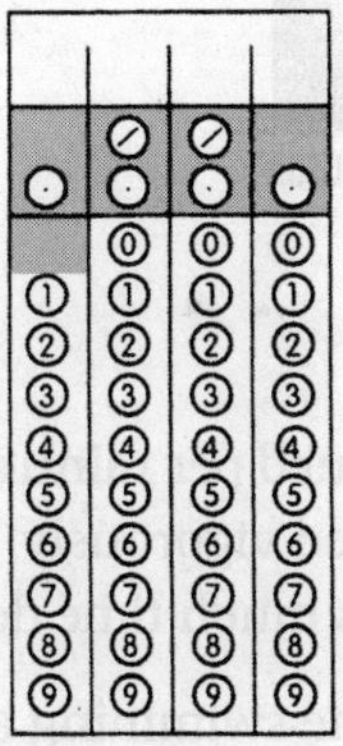

18.

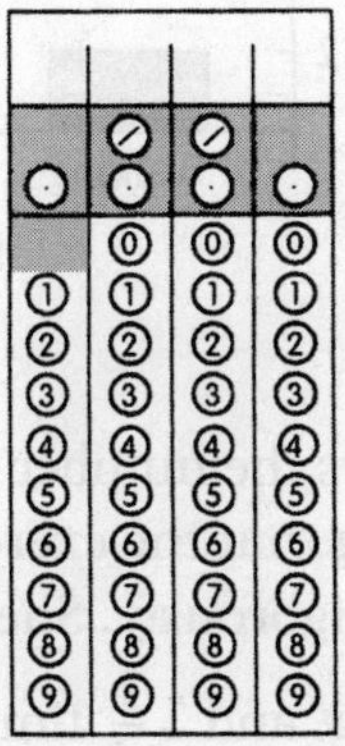

19.

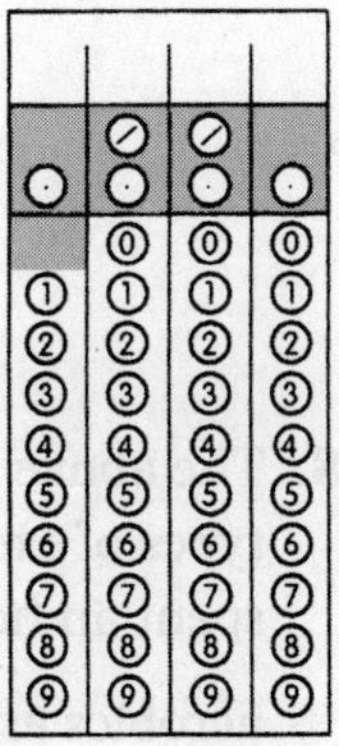

Scores	51–60	61–70	71–80	81–90	91–100	
Frequency	1	6	9	10	5	31

14. The frequency chart shows test scores for a certain class. The total number of students is 31. If a student in the class was picked at random, what is the probability that the student's score was below 71?

15. A population of bacteria doubles every 2 hours. What is the percent increase after 4 hours?

16. Boyle's law states that when a sample of gas is compressed at a constant temperature, the pressure of the gas is inversely proportional to the volume of the gas. If a sample of air occupies $0.106\ m^3$ at 25°C, the pressure is 50 kPa (kilopascals). Find the new pressure, in kPa, if the temperature remains constant and the sample expands to a volume of $0.3\ m^3$.

17. In a men's slalom race, John Li skied in a time of 120.86 seconds for 2 runs, about 1 standard deviation slower than the mean. If skiing times follow a normal distribution, and about 68 percent of all skiing times lie within 1 standard deviation of the mean, about how many of the 48 skiers finishing the race would you expect skied more slowly than John Li?

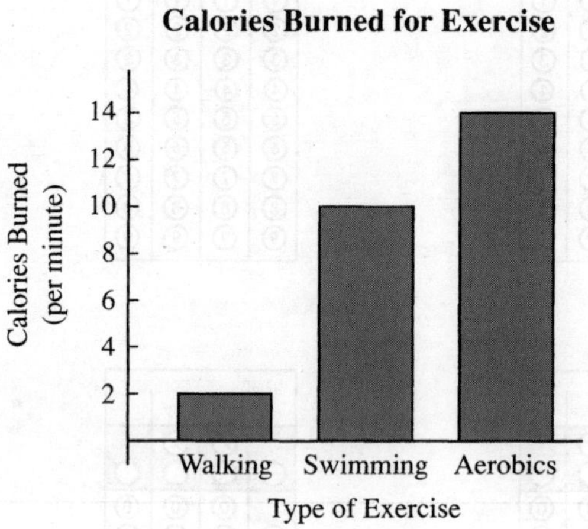

18. The above bar graph shows the number of calories burned per minute for three types of exercise, assuming that the exercise is performed vigorously. Jackie spent an hour exercising vigorously. She spent twice as much time doing aerobics as she did walking, and $1\frac{1}{2}$ times as much time swimming as she did aerobics. According to the graph, how many calories did Jackie expect to burn during that hour of exercise?

19. A typing class in an elementary school is divided into three groups. The Red Robins, with 6 students, has an average typing speed of 60 words per minute; the Blue Wax Bills, with 10 students, has an average typing speed of 45 words per minute; and the Gold Finches, with 16 students, has an average typing speed of 30 words per minute. What is the average (arithmetic mean) of the typing speeds, in words per minute, for the class?

Answers and Explanations 答案与解析

The difficulty level for each question is specified in parentheses.

1. C (H)	**8.** B (M)	**14.** 7/31 or .225 or .226 (E)
2. C (H)	**9.** B (H)	**15.** 300 (H)
3. A (H)	**10.** A (M)	**16.** 17.6 or 17.7 (M)
4. A (H)	**11.** A (H)	**17.** 7 or 8 (M)
5. D (M)	**12.** C (M)	**18.** 600 (H)
6. D (M)	**13.** B (M)	**19.** 40.3 (H)
7. B (M)		

14.

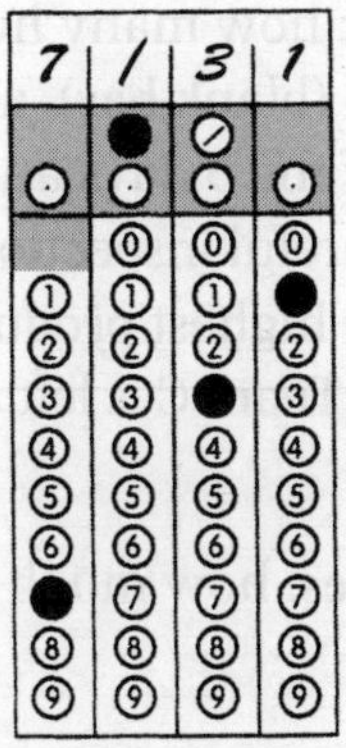

or

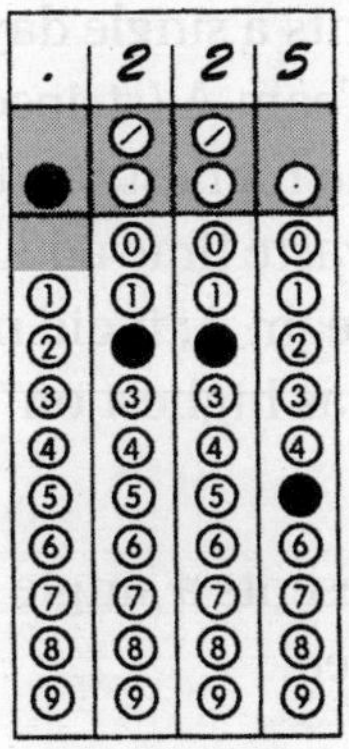

or

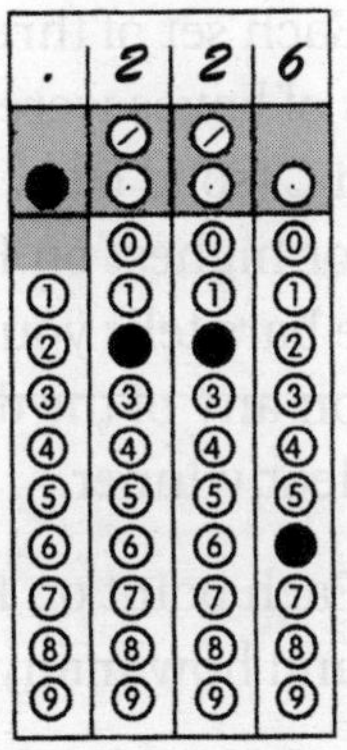

15.

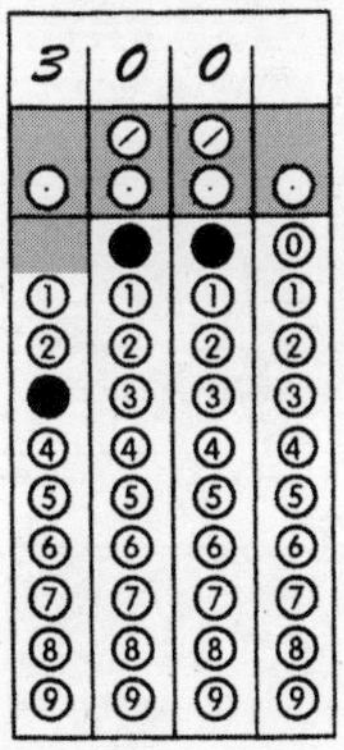

16.

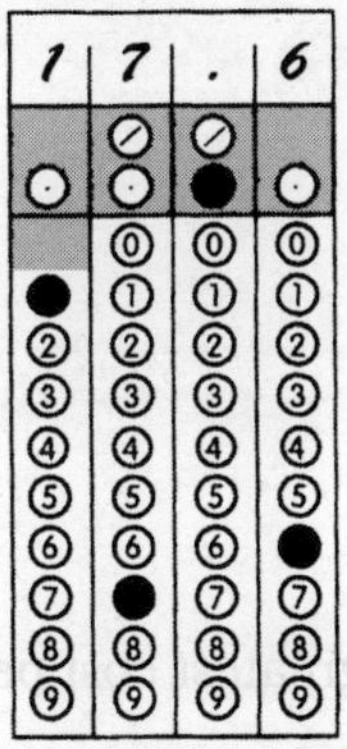

or

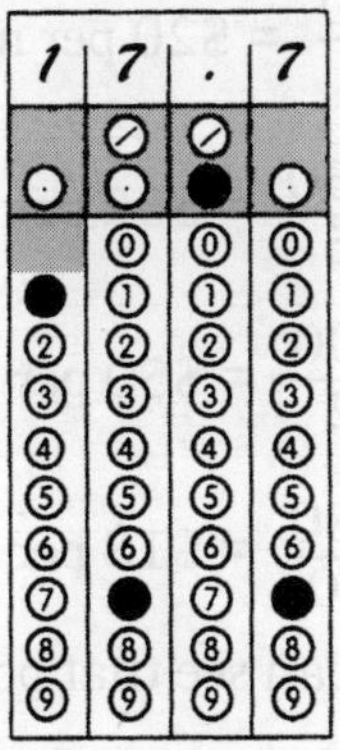

17.

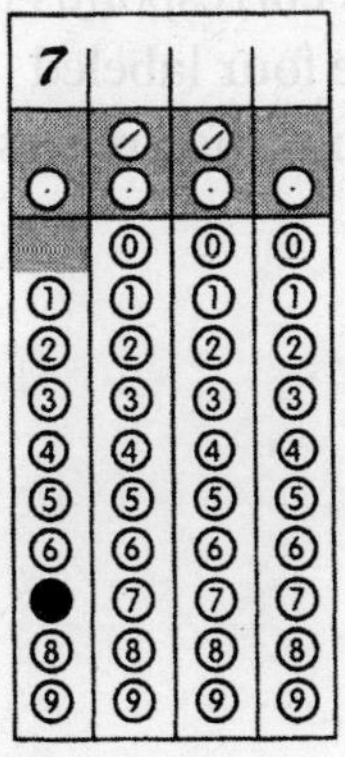

or

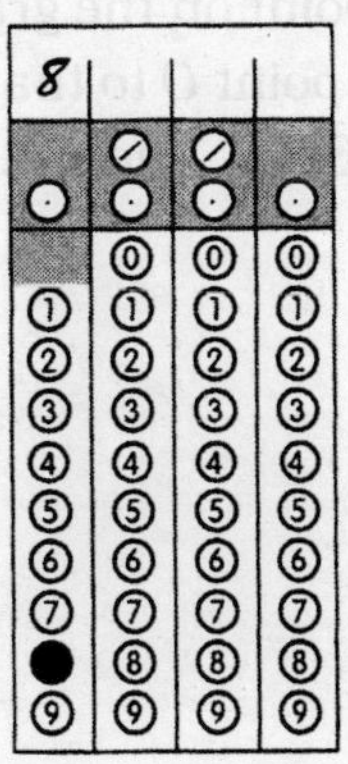

18.

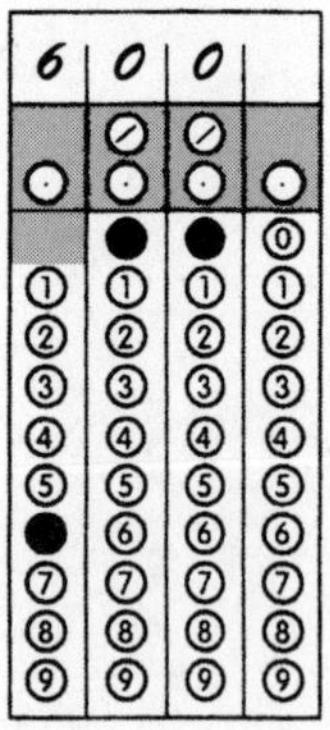

19.

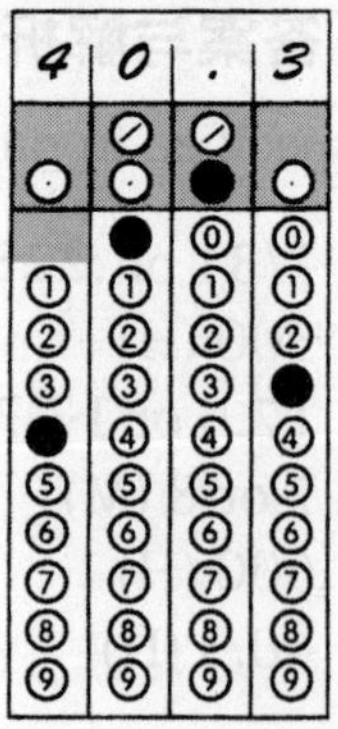

1. **(C)** Each set of three bars represents a single day's production: how many hundreds of boxes were packaged by Team A (striped bar), Team B (blank bar), and Team C (solid bar). Team C had the highest production for 3 of the 5 days and tied for highest on Friday. Don't waste time adding boxes. A careful inspection of the bars tells you to eliminate Team A: it did not achieve the highest production on any of the days. Team B was highest on Tuesday only. Team C is left as the clear winner.

2. **(C)** Each point on the graph represents a single pair of toe shoes: how much it cost and how many months it lasted.

   Method I: Arithmetic
   Find the cost per month for each of the points given as choices.

   A: $\frac{20}{1}$ = \$20 per month.

   B: $\frac{160}{5}$ = \$32 per month.

   C: $\frac{100}{2}$ = \$50 per month.

   D: $\frac{180}{10}$ = \$18 per month.

   You can see that point C had the greatest cost per month.

   Method II: Slope
   For each pair of toe shoes, the cost per month equals the price of the shoes divided by its duration. For each point on the graph, this value corresponds to the slope of the line segment from point O to that point. For the four labeled points, look at the slopes of $\overline{OA}$, $\overline{OB}$, $\overline{OC}$, and $\overline{OD}$. Segment $\overline{OC}$ has the greatest slope, so point C is the answer.

3. (A)

I: The Math Team spent (20)(11) = \$220 on extra-large T-shirts.
The Debate Club spent (10)(14) = \$140 on extra-large T-shirts.
$\therefore$ Statement I is true.

II: The average cost per T-shirt for the Math Team = \$11.
The average cost per T-shirt for the Debate Club

$$= \frac{(2)(9)+(20)(10)+(10)(14)}{32} = \frac{356}{32} > 11$$

$\therefore$ Statement II is false.

III: To find each median cost, list data items in order:

Medium: $\underbrace{9 \quad 9 \quad 11 \quad 11 \cdots 11}_{7}$ Middle term = 11

Large: $\underbrace{10 \quad 10 \cdots 10}_{20} \quad \underbrace{11 \quad 11 \cdots 11}_{18}$ Middle term = 10

Extra-large: $\underbrace{11 \quad 11 \cdots 11}_{20} \quad \underbrace{14 \quad 14 \cdots 14}_{10}$ Middle term = 11

$\therefore$ Statement III is false; the median cost for extra-large was the same as for medium.

4. (A) To answer this question correctly, you must take the time to study the axes and internalize the meaning of a single point: the percentage of students that got *at least* that score. According to the graph, 40 percent received scores of 5 or less, and 50 percent received scores of 6 or less. Therefore, exactly 10 percent received scores of 6, and 10 percent of 50 = 5.

5. (D)

Method I: Pick-Convenient-Numbers Strategy
Take simple values for x and d. For example, $x = 2$ and $d = 3$ gives the sequence 2, 5, 8, 11.

Arithmetic mean $= \frac{26}{4} = 6\frac{1}{2}$

Median $= \frac{5+8}{2} = 6\frac{1}{2}$

$\therefore$ Difference = 0

Method II: Logical Reasoning

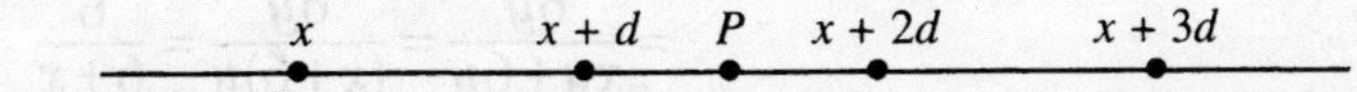

On the line, the numbers are equally spaced, so point P, the point right in the middle, must represent the arithmetic mean. The median is the average of the two middle numbers, which also is point P. Thus the difference between the two quantities is 0.

6. **(D)** The data items are the numbers of questions answered correctly. If you were to list them, they would look like this:

$$12, 12, 13, 13, 13, 15, 15, 15, \ldots$$

The number that would appear the most (six times) would be 19.
$\therefore$ mode = 19.

7. **(B)** The trend in the data shows that the time taken to complete the timed puzzle was lower if the child had more practice. If you placed a "best-fit" line through the points, namely, a line with roughly the same number of points on either side of it, the line would appear to start at roughly 9 on the *t*-axis and slope gently downward. This description represents a line with *t*-intercept around 9 and a negative slope. Of the choices, $t(p) = -\frac{p}{2} + 9$ is the only equation that satisfies these requirements.

8. **(B)** Since each little symbol represents the same number of people, you can reduce the problem: Which combination of two towns accounts for 45 percent of the symbols? You don't need to multiply by 10,000 at any stage! Count the number of symbols: 20; 45% of 20 = 0.45 × 20 = 9. The only two towns that have a total of 9 symbols are *B* and *C*.

9. **(B)**

Method I: Pick-Convenient-Numbers Strategy

Try 10 children whose average age is 5. Then, sum of ages = 50, and Ali's age = (6)(5) = 30.

The fraction $\frac{\text{Ali's age}}{\text{total of ages}} = \frac{30}{50+30} = \frac{3}{8}$.

Go through the answer choices using $x = 10$ and $y = 5$ to see which expression gives $\frac{3}{8}$. The only answer choice that works is $\frac{6}{6+x}$.

Method II: Logical Reasoning and Algebra

You have y = average age of children and x = number of children.

Let S = sum of ages of children.

Let A = Ali's age.

By the definition of arithmetic mean, $y = \frac{S}{x}$, so $S = xy$.

Also, $A = 6y$ (given).

$$\text{Ali's age as fraction of total ages} = \frac{A}{S+A}$$

$$= \frac{6y}{xy+6y} = \frac{6y}{(x+6)y} = \frac{6}{6+x}$$

10. **(A)** There are 40 values in the set of data. The median is the mean of the two middle values. Since there are 21 students who own 1 or fewer pets, both the 20th and 21st data values are 1. Therefore, the median is 1.

11. **(A)** The A train has a 1-minute standard deviation. This means that on most days Mr. Brown will arrive more or less at the same time: 8–12 minutes late (2 standard deviations from the mean, which is 10 minutes late). For the B train, however, with a 5-minute standard deviation, most days he will probably arrive anywhere from 0 to 20 minutes late.

Each of the other choices is false:

Choice (B): With the A train, he is very likely to be 8–12 minutes late. Arriving on time is a real outlier. Since the B train arrival times have more of a spread, it's certainly possible—though unlikely—that he'll not be late.

Choice (C): Again, because of the spread in arrival times, 15 minutes late is more of a possibility for train B.

Choice (D): Since most of the arrival times for the A train are between 8 and 12 minutes late, and most of the arrival times for the B train are between 0 and 20 minutes late, it's much more likely—though rare—that the B train will arrive on time.

12. **(C)** Notice that the scales on the horizontal and vertical axes are different. You should sketch a line that seems to pass through the center of data, as shown.

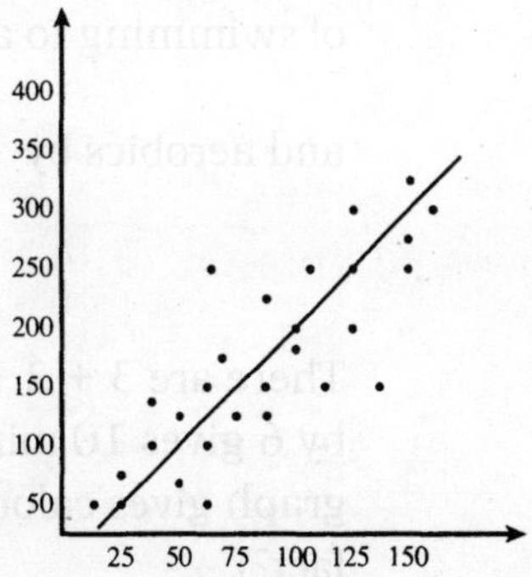

Then pick a couple of points on this line and calculate $\frac{y\text{-distance}}{x\text{-distance}}$ to get the slope. For example, (25, 50) and (100, 200) yield a slope of $\frac{200-50}{100-25} \approx \frac{150}{75} = 2$

13. **(B)** The question asks about women, so ignore the men's column! Out of the 516 women polled, 156 were looking forward to the commercials. Therefore, the required probability as a percentage is $\frac{156}{516} \cdot 100 \approx 30\%$

14. **7/31** or **.225** or **.226** From the chart you can see that 7 out of the 31 students scored less than 71. Therefore, the required probability is $\frac{7}{31}$, which is approximately equal to .226.

Grid-in 7/31 or .225 or .226.

15. **300**

Use the pick-a-convenient-number-for-percent-problems strategy.

Let 100 be the initial population.

After 2 hr: population = 200

After 4 hr: population = 400

$$\text{Percent increase} = \frac{\text{actual increase}}{\text{original amount}} \times 100$$

$$= \frac{400-100}{100} \times 100 = 300\%$$

Grid-in 300.

16. 17.6 or **17.7** Since the pressure P is inversely proportional to the volume V,

$$P_1V_1 = P_2V_2$$

$$(50)(0.106) = P_2(0.3)$$

$$P_2 = \frac{(50)(0.106)}{0.3}$$

$$\approx 17.7$$

Grid-in 17.6 or 17.7.

17. 7 or **8** In a normal distribution, 68 percent of the skiers should be within 1 standard deviation of the mean. Of the remaining 32 percent, half should be on the high end and half on the low end. So, 16 percent of the skiers had slower times than John Li. 16 percent of 48 is 7.7. Grid-in 7 or 8.

18. 600 Say to yourself, "One bar on the graph represents the number of calories burned per minute for the given type of exercise." You need to find the ratio of swimming to aerobics to walking. Multiply walking by 2 to get aerobics, and aerobics by $\frac{3}{2}$ to get swimming. The ratio is

$$\text{swimming : aerobics : walking} = 3 : 2 : 1.$$

There are 3 + 2 + 1 = 6 parts altogether. Dividing the 60 minutes of exercise by 6 gives 10 minutes for each part. (You need to work in minutes, because the graph gives calories burned *per minute.* Did you study the axes and digest this fact?)

Time spent swimming = (3)(10) = 30 minutes.
Time spent on aerobics = (2)(10) = 20 minutes.
Time spent walking = (1)(10) = 10 minutes.

Now, consult the graph to find the number of calories burned for each exercise:

10 minutes of walking = (10)(2) = 20 calories burned.
20 minutes of aerobics = (20)(14) = 280 calories burned.
30 minutes of swimming = (30)(10) = 300 calories burned.
Total = 600 calories burned.

Grid-in 600.

19. 40.3 Recognize this as a weighted average problem. Find the average of these typing speeds:

$$\underbrace{60 \quad 60 \cdots 60}_{6} \quad \underbrace{45 \quad 45 \quad \cdots \quad 45}_{10} \quad \underbrace{30 \quad 30 \quad \cdots \quad 30}_{16}$$

$$\text{average speed} = \frac{\text{sum of speeds}}{\text{number of students}} = \frac{(6)(60)+(10)(45)+(16)(30)}{32} \approx 40.3$$

Grid-in 40.3.

第十三章 Chapter 13

PASSPORT TO ADVANCED MATH 高等数学

Your passport to advanced math is your high school algebra 2 course. The updated SAT Math Test focuses on math content taught in "rigorous high school courses," so take out your high school notes and hone those algebra skills.

As with Heart of Algebra and Problem Solving and Data Analysis, you will receive a separate subscore for your Passport to Advanced Math questions, which make up 27 percent of the SAT test.

1600 Club Strategies in Passport to Advanced Math
1600分俱乐部高等数学策略

Strategy 1:	**P**arabolas: understand the constants in the quadratic function.
Strategy 2:	**A**lgebraic expressions: combine, manipulate, and simplify.
Strategy 3:	**S**olving equations: try plugging-in the answer choices.
Strategy 4:	**S**ystems of equations: the graphing calculator can solve these, too.
Strategy 5:	**P**olynomial functions: remember, the zeros are on the *x*-axis.
Strategy 6:	**O**perations: apply to polynomials and rational expressions.
Strategy 7:	**R**adical equations: solve by isolating the radical.
Strategy 8:	**T**he quadratic formula: solves any quadratic equation.

Here are the topics you'll need to master in order to solve the problems in the Passport to Advanced Math:

- The quadratic function and its graph
- Solving quadratic equations, both by factoring and by using the quadratic formula
- Modeling quadratic functions and solving problems in context
- Solving nonlinear equations: rational, radical, exponential, and quadratic
- Manipulating formulas either to find an equivalent form or to solve for a different variable
- Composition of functions and transformations
- Solving systems of equations where one of the equations is nonlinear

POLYNOMIALS 多项式

A *binomial* has two terms, while a *trinomial* has three. You need to be able to add, subtract, and multiply monomials and binomials.

Factoring 因式分解

You also need to know the following *factored forms* or products:

$x^2 - y^2 = (x + y)(x - y)$ (Difference of perfect squares)

$x^2 + 2xy + y^2 = (x + y)^2$ (Perfect square trinomial)

$x^2 - 2xy + y^2 = (x - y)^2$ (Perfect square trinomial)

You may be expected to factor simple trinomials, for example,

$$x^2 - x - 12 = (x \quad)(x \quad)$$

You must find factors of –12 whose sum equals the middle coefficient, namely, –1.

Answer: $x^2 - x - 12 = (x - 4)(x + 3)$

Example 1

If $x^2 - y^2 = 40$, and $x - y = 4$, then $x^2 + y^2 =$

(A) $2xy$ (B) $-2xy$ (C) $100 + 2xy$ (D) $100 - 2xy$

Solution: (D)

Coaching: *High scorers do not make careless mistakes when factoring. They always check a factored form by taking a minute to mentally multiply the two binomials of their answer. The result must equal the given polynomial.*

Method 1: Algebra

$$x^2 - y^2 = (x + y)(x - y)$$
$$40 = 4(x + y)$$
$$x + y = 10$$

Now square both sides:

$$x^2 + 2xy + y^2 = 100$$
$$x^2 + y^2 = 100 - 2xy$$

Method II: Pick-Some-Numbers Strategy

The numbers are small enough for you to find values of x and y that satisfy the given equations, $x^2 - y^2 = 40$ and $x - y = 4$.

If you take a moment to try some of the perfect squares under 100, you can hit the jackpot with $x = 7$ and $y = 3$. (Check that these numbers work: $49 - 9 = 40$, and $7 - 3 = 4$.) You can now calculate that $x^2 + y^2 = 49 + 9 = 58$. Plugging your x and y values into the choices shows that (D) gives the right value:

$$100 - 2xy = 100 - 2(7)(3) = 100 - 42 = 58$$

Method III: Algebra and Pick-Some-Numbers Strategy

$$x + y = 10 \qquad \text{(See Method I)}$$
$$x - y = 4 \qquad \text{(Given)}$$
$$\therefore 2x = 14 \qquad \text{(Add the equations)}$$
$$\therefore x = 7 \text{ and } y = 3$$

Once you have x and y, proceed with plugging in, as shown in Method II.

RATIONAL EXPRESSIONS 有理式

A *rational expression* is a quotient of two polynomials. Typically, you simplify a rational expression by factoring the numerator and denominator and canceling common factors. For example:

$$\frac{2x^2-98}{x^2+4x-21}=\frac{2(x^2-49)}{(x+7)(x-3)}=\frac{2\cancel{(x+7)}(x-7)}{\cancel{(x+7)}(x-3)}=\frac{2(x-7)}{(x-3)}$$

THE QUADRATIC FUNCTION 一元二次函数

A *quadratic function* is a function whose graph is a parabola. The standard form of the equation is

$$y = ax^2 + bx + c,\ a \neq 0$$

The axis of symmetry of the graph is given by $x=-\frac{b}{2a}$. The constant term c represents the y-intercept. If the coefficient of x^2, a, is positive, the graph is concave up; otherwise it is concave down.

concave up, $a > 0$

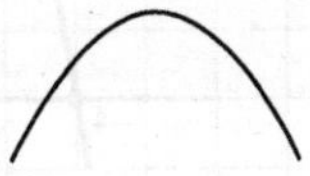

concave down, $a < 0$

Also, a controls the "fatness" of the parabola: the bigger the magnitude of a, the narrower the parabola.

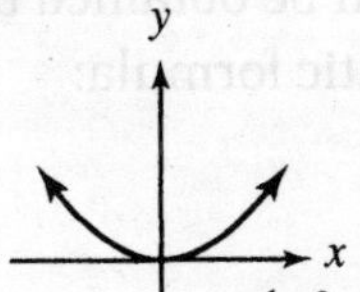

$y = \frac{1}{2}x^2$

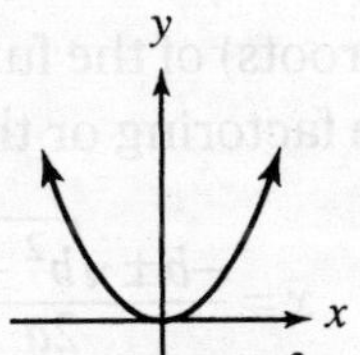

$y = x^2$

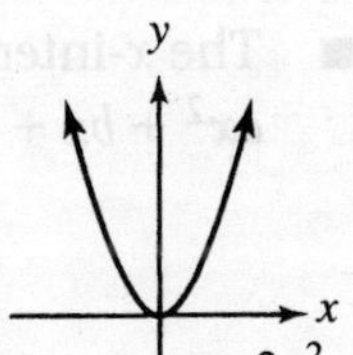

$y = 2x^2$

You should know how to sketch the graph of a quadratic function (parabola) without using your graphing calculator. Here's an example.

Sketch the graph of $y = -x^2 - 2x + 8$.

- Note that $a = -1$, $b = -2$, and $c = 8$.
- The graph is concave down because $a < 0$.
- The y-intercept is 8, since $c = 8$.

- The x-intercepts (roots) are the values of x when $y = 0$. You must solve the equation $-x^2 - 2x + 8 = 0$:

$$-x^2 - 2x + 8 = 0 \Rightarrow x^2 + 2x - 8 = 0 \Rightarrow (x-2)(x+4) = 0$$

Therefore, $x = 2$ or $x = -4$.

- The axis of symmetry is $x = -\frac{b}{2a} = -\frac{-2}{2(-1)} = -1$.
- To find the vertex of the parabola, calculate the y-value on the axis of symmetry; namely, find y when $x = -1$ in the equation $y = -x^2 - 2x + 8$.

$$\begin{aligned} y &= -(-1)^2 - 2(-1) + 8 \\ &= -1 + 2 + 8 \\ &= 9 \end{aligned}$$

Therefore, the vertex is $(-1, 9)$.

The graph is shown below:

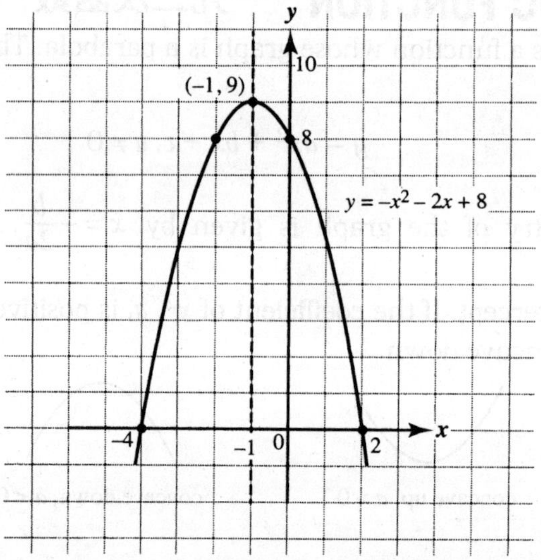

Here are some additional facts you should know about the quadratic function:

- The x-intercepts (or roots) of the function can be obtained by solving $ax^2 + bx + c = 0$. Use factoring or the quadratic formula:

$$x = \frac{-b \pm \sqrt{b^2 - 4ac}}{2a}$$

- The sum of the roots is $-\frac{b}{a}$.
- The product of the roots is $\frac{c}{a}$.
- A quadratic function is often written in the form $y = (x-h)^2 + k$. The axis of symmetry is $x = h$, and the vertex is (h, k).

Example 2

Which could be the graph of $y = x^2 + 3x + k$, where k is an integer?

(A)

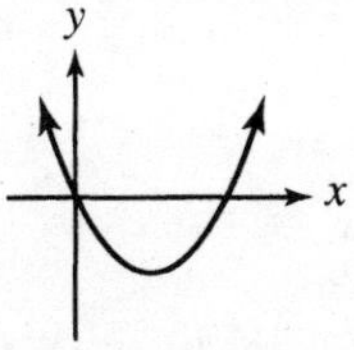

(C)

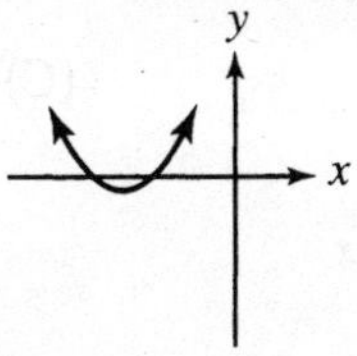

(B)

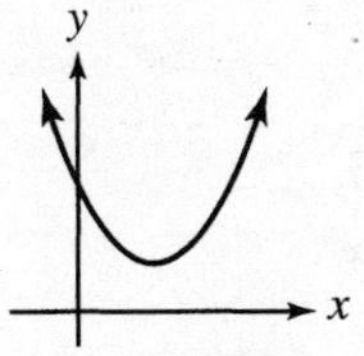

(D)

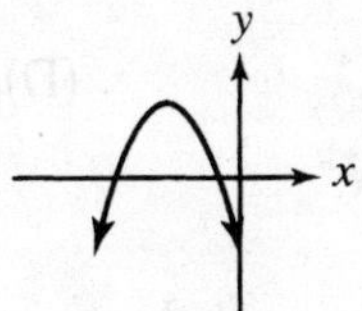

Solution: (C) Since the coefficient of x^2 is positive, the graph must be concave up, so eliminate choice (D). Also, the axis of symmetry is $x = -\dfrac{b}{2a} = -\dfrac{3}{2}$, which is to the left of the y-axis, so eliminate choices (A) and (B). The correct choice is (C).

Example 3

Which function has a double root?

(A) $y = x^2 + 4x - 4$ (C) $y = x^2 + x + 1$

(B) $y = x^2 - 4$ (D) $y = x^2 + 6x + 9$

Solution: (D)

Method I: Perfect Square

To have a double root, the quadratic expression must be a perfect square. Only choice (D), where $y = (x + 3)^2$, satisfies this requirement.

Method II: Graphing Calculator

For the function to have a double root, the parabola must be tangent to the x-axis. Graphing each answer choice will show choice (C) to be the only graph to satisfy this requirement. Using the graphing calculator on this problem, however, is a desperation measure: the method is unnecessarily time-consuming.

Example 4

If $f(x) = ax^2 + bx + c$, $a \neq 0$ and a, b, and c are all negative, which could be the graph of $f(x)$?

(A)

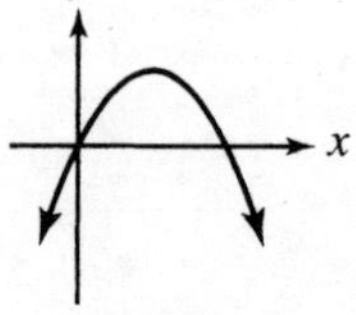

(C)

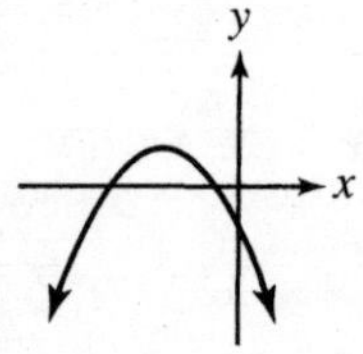

(B)

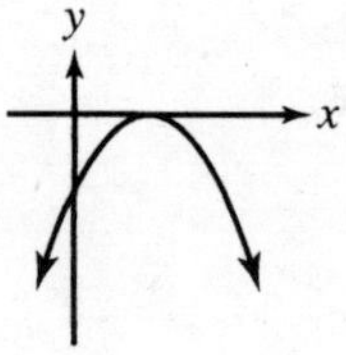

(D)

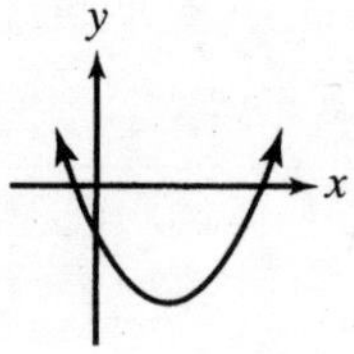

Solution: (C) Since $a < 0$, the graph must be concave down, so eliminate choice (D). Also since $c < 0$, the y-intercept must be negative, so eliminate choice (A). Finally, since $a < 0$ and $b < 0$, the axis of symmetry must be x = (a negative number), since $x = -\frac{b}{2a}$. The only choice that satisfies this requirement is (C).

Example 5

The x-intercepts of a quadratic function are 2 and -4. Which could be the function?

I. $y = x^2 + 2x - 8$
II. $y = -2x^2 - 4x + 16$
III. $y = (x + 1)^2 - 9$

(A) II and III only
(B) I and II only
(C) I and III only
(D) I, II, and III

Solution: (D) A quadratic function with roots 2 and -4 is $y = (x - 2)(x + 4) = x^2 + 2x - 8$, so Function I works. Also, $y = a(x - 2)(x + 4)$ works. Function II is simply function I multiplied by -2, so Function II works also. Multiplying out Function III gives the same expression as in Function I. All three functions work.

Example 6

For the function $f(x) = ax^2 + bx + c$, $a \neq 0$, the sum of the roots is equal to the product of the roots. Which could be $f(x)$?

(A) $x^2 - 4x + 4$
(B) $x^2 - 2x + 1$
(C) $x^2 + x + 2$
(D) $x^2 + 3x - 6$

Solution: (A) Notice the sum of roots = product of roots

$$-\frac{b}{a} = \frac{c}{a}$$

$$-b = c$$

Go through each choice to see which expression has $-b = c$.
Choice (A) is the only one that does.

For problems such as Example 6, don't even *think* of solving each equation and then checking whether the product of the roots equals the sum of the roots.

Example 7

A stone projected vertically upward with an initial velocity of 112 feet per second moves according to the equation

$$s = 112t - 16t^2$$

where s is the distance, in feet, from the ground, and t is time, in seconds. What is the maximum height reached by the stone?

(A) 672 feet (B) 196 feet (C) 112 feet (D) 96 feet

Solution: (B)

Method I: Graphing Calculator

Graph $y = 112x - 16x^2$. Adjust the WINDOW to allow Ymax to be 200. The vertex of the parabola is close to Ymax. Therefore, the answer must be choice B, 196 feet. (You can check using TRACE, but you should not waste the time. None of the other answer choices is close!)

Method II: Axis of Symmetry

The maximum value is on the axis of symmetry, given by

$$t = \frac{-112}{2(-16)} = \frac{7}{2}$$

$$\therefore s = 112\left(\frac{7}{2}\right) - 16\left(\frac{7}{2}\right)^2 = 196$$

Notice that you have enough information to solve the problem without using the initial velocity (it is built into the equation).

The 1600 Club is not sidetracked by extraneous tidbits of information.

SOLVING NONLINEAR EQUATIONS AND INEQUALITIES
解答非线性方程和不等式

Recall that

1. The same quantity can be added to both sides of an equation or inequality without changing it. For example, if $x^2 < 4$, then $x^2 - 4 < 0$.
2. Both sides of an equation can be multiplied or divided by the same nonzero quantity. For example, if $5x^2 = 37$, then $x^2 = \frac{37}{5}$.
3. If both sides of an inequality are multiplied by a negative quantity, the inequality sign flips around. For example, if $-2x^2 < 12$, then $x^2 > -6$.
4. Fractions can be eliminated by multiplying throughout by the least common denominator (LCD) of the fractions. For example, if $\frac{x}{x-1} = \frac{2}{x}$, then multiplying both sides by $x(x-1)$ yields

$$\frac{x}{x-1} \cdot x(x-1) = \frac{2}{x} \cdot x(x-1)$$
$$x^2 = 2(x-1)$$

Quadratic Equations and Inequalities 二次方程和二次不等式

These are solved by inspecting the graph on the graphing calculator, or by factoring, or by using the quadratic formula. For example,

$$x^2 - 6x + 8 = (x-4)(x-2) = 0$$
$$x = 4 \text{ or } 2$$

To solve $x^2 - 6x + 8 > 0$:

$$x^2 - 6x + 8 > 0$$
$$(x-4)(x-2) > 0$$

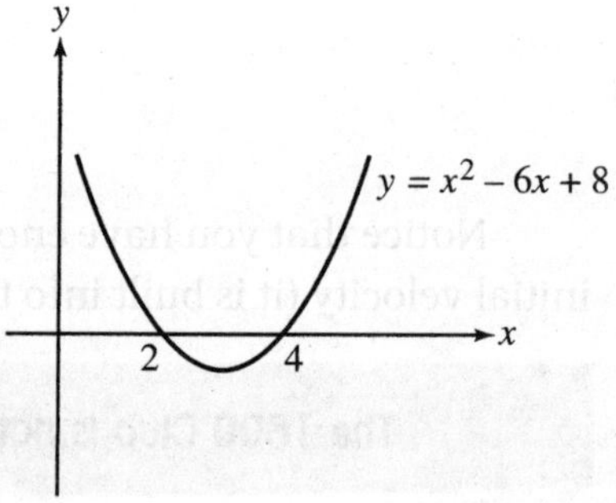

The roots are 2 and 4.

Notice that the y-values in the graph are positive outside the roots. Thus the answer is $x < 2$ or $x > 4$. If asked to solve $x^2 - 6x + 8 < 0$, note that y is negative for x-values between the roots, namely, $2 < x < 4$.

Example 8 Grid-In

Find the larger root of $x^2 - 6x = 10$.

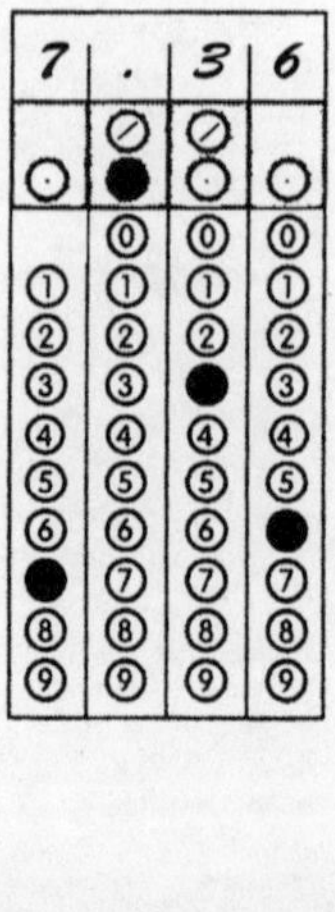

Solution: 7.36 This is a quadratic equation, so put all terms on the left, equal to 0:

$$x^2 - 6x - 10 = 0$$

When you see this doesn't factor, use the quadratic formula

$$x = \frac{-b \pm \sqrt{b^2 - 4ac}}{2a}$$

$$x = \frac{-(-6) \pm \sqrt{(-6)^2 - 4(1)(-10)}}{2(1)}$$

$$= \frac{6 \pm \sqrt{36+40}}{2}$$

$$= \frac{6 \pm \sqrt{76}}{2}$$

You are asked for the larger root, so use your calculator to find $\frac{6+\sqrt{76}}{2}$.
The answer shown is 7.358898 . . .
Grid-in 7.35 or 7.36.

Polynomial Equations of Higher Degree 高次多项式方程

If a function $P(x) = (x - a)(x - b)(x - c)\ldots$, then $a, b, c\ldots$ are *zeros* of the function. They are also *roots* of the equation $(x - a)(x - b)(x - c)\ldots = 0$. A graph of the function would have x-intercepts $a, b, c\ldots$.

Example 9

$$x^3 + 3x^2 - x - 3 = 0$$

If the roots of the equation above are p, q, and r, where $p < q < r$, find the product pq.

(A) 3 (B) −3 (C) 1 (D) −1

Solution: (A)
Method I: Factoring

$$x^3 + 3x^2 - x - 3 = 0$$

$$x^2(x+3) - (x+3) = 0$$

$$(x^2 - 1)(x+3) = 0$$

$$(x+1)(x-1)(x+3) = 0$$

$$x = -1,\ 1,\ \text{or } -3$$

Notice that $-3 < -1 < 1$, so the required product is $(-3)(-1) = 3$.

Method II: Graphing Calculator

On the graphing calculator go to [y =] and enter $y = x^3 + 3x^2 - x - 3$, then [GRAPH].

Inspecting the x-intercepts or using [TRACE] find the roots $x = -1, 1,$ or -3, and the required product, which is 3.

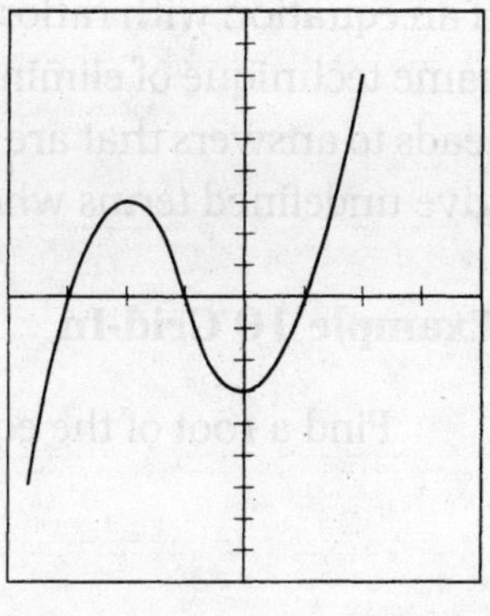

Equations with Radicals 根式方程

To solve equations with radicals, isolate the radical, that is, get it by itself on one side. Then square both sides. For example,

$$\sqrt{x}-5=2 \Rightarrow \sqrt{x}=7 \Rightarrow x=49$$

Equations with x^2 二次方程

To solve equations where x is squared, don't forget the negative root. For example,

$$x^2 = 16 \Rightarrow x = \pm 4$$

Exponential Equations 指数方程

Exponential equations can often be written with the same base b on each side, where $b > 0$ and $b \neq 1$. You can then equate the exponents:

$$b^m = b^n \Rightarrow m = n$$

For example, to solve $3^{2x} = 27^{x-2}$, write both sides with base 3:

$$3^{2x} = 27^{x-2}$$
$$3^{2x} = (3^3)^{x-2}$$
$$3^{2x} = 3^{3x-6}$$
$$2x = 3x-6$$
$$x = 6$$

It goes without saying that high scorers remember the distributive property when multiplying the exponents in the second line!

Equations with Rational Expressions 有理式方程

These equations look a lot easier when you multiply both sides by the least common denominator of the fractions. For example,

$$\frac{x-5}{x+3}=2 \Rightarrow x-5=2(x+3) \Rightarrow x=-11$$

Extraneous Roots 增根

If an equation with rational expressions has more than one rational expression, use the same technique of eliminating the fractions. But be aware that sometimes the solution leads to answers that are *extraneous roots.* These are roots that appear to be correct, but give undefined terms when you plug them back into the original equation.

Example 10 Grid-In

Find a root of the equation $\dfrac{x}{x+2} = \dfrac{3}{x} + \dfrac{4}{x(x+2)}$

Solution: 5

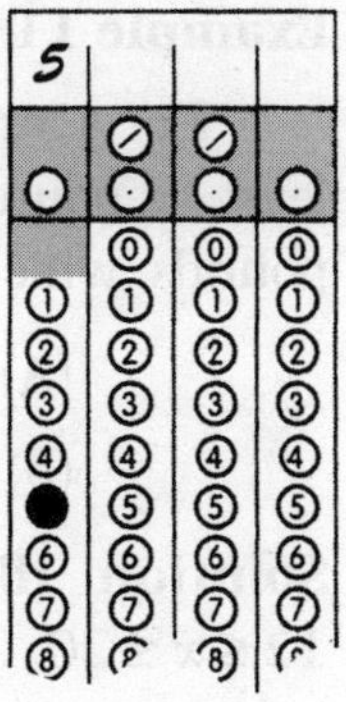

$$\frac{x}{x+2}=\frac{3}{x}+\frac{4}{x(x+2)}$$

$$x(x+2)\left(\frac{x}{x+2}\right)=x(x+2)\left(\frac{3}{x}\right)+x(x+2)\left(\frac{4}{x(x+2)}\right)$$

$$x^2=3x+6+4$$

$$x^2-3x-10=0$$

$$(x-5)(x+2)=0$$

$$x=5 \text{ or } -2$$

$x = 5$ is an actual solution. You can plug it back into the original equation to see that it works.

$x = -2$ is an extraneous solution. Plugging it into the original equation yields

$$\frac{-2}{-2+2}=\frac{3}{-2}+\frac{4}{-2(-2+2)}$$

Since this contains terms that are undefined, $x = -2$ is not a root.
Grid-in 5.

Equations and Inequalities with Absolute Value
含绝对值的方程和不等式

In the examples that follow, visualizing $|x|$ as the distance on the number line from x to 0 can be helpful.

Solve $|x| = 2$. Here, you want values of x whose distance from 0 is 2.

Answer: $x = 2$ or -2, as shown on the number line.

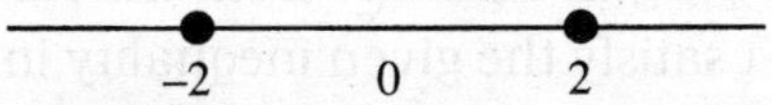

Solve $|x| < 2$. Here, you want x-values whose distance to 0 is less than 2.

Answer: $-2 < x < 2$

Solve $|x| > 2$. Here, you want x-values whose distance to 0 is greater than 2.

Answer: $x < -2$ or $x > 2$

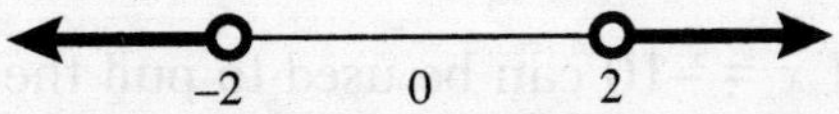

Here is a useful framework to remember for the type of question on absolute value that you will encounter on the SAT:

$$|x-a| = k \Rightarrow x-a=k \text{ or } x-a=-k$$
$$|x-a| < k \Rightarrow -k < x-a < k$$
$$|x-a| > k \Rightarrow x-a > k \text{ or } x-a < -k$$

Example 11

For a large Thanksgiving dinner, Mr. Gonzalez will cook a turkey that weighs at least 12 pounds but no more than 20 pounds. If x represents the weight of a turkey, in pounds, which of the following represents all possible values of x?

(A) $|x-16| \geq 4$
(B) $|x-16| \leq 4$
(C) $|x-12| \leq 20$
(D) $|x-20| \leq 16$

Solution: (B) You need to find which of the given inequalities is equivalent to $12 \leq x \leq 20$. Choice (B) is the one that works:

$$|x-16| \leq 4$$

$$-4 \leq x-16 \leq 4$$

$$12 \leq x \leq 20$$

Inequalities With Rational Expressions 有理不等式

Tricky stuff! What you cannot do is mindlessly multiply both sides by a quantity that may be negative.

Example 12

Which is the solution to $\frac{x-5}{x+3} < -1$?

(A) $x < -3$ or $x > 5$
(B) $-3 < x < 5$
(C) $x < -3$ or $x > 1$
(D) $-3 < x < 1$

Solution: (D)

Method I: Plug-in Strategy

Take some easy-to-plug-in numbers from the range in each answer choice. Just one number that doesn't satisfy the given inequality invalidates that choice.

Choice (A): Try $x = -10$. $\frac{-15}{-7} < -1$. No.

Think about what you're doing here, and notice that any number that produces a negative value in the numerator and denominator will result in a positive quantity, which can't be less than −1. Therefore, you should try a negative number whose magnitude is sufficiently large.

Can you see that $x = -10$ can be used to pull the plug on choice (C) too? You must now choose between choices (B) and (D). Try $x = 4$, which is in (B) but not in (D): $\frac{4-5}{4+3} = -\frac{1}{7}$, which is not less than -1. The answer must be (D).

Method II: Algebra

Beware! You can't just multiply both sides by $x + 3$. If $x + 3$ is negative, the inequality sign must flip. Here is a solution that uses signs analysis.

$$\frac{x-5}{x+3}<-1 \Rightarrow \frac{x-5}{x+3}+1<0$$

$$\frac{x-5}{x+3}+\frac{x+3}{x+3}<0$$

$$\frac{2x-2}{x+3}<0$$

$$\frac{x-1}{x+3}<0 \quad \text{(Divide both sides by 2.)}$$

Use signs analysis, as shown below, to see that the expression is negative when $-3 < x < 1$.

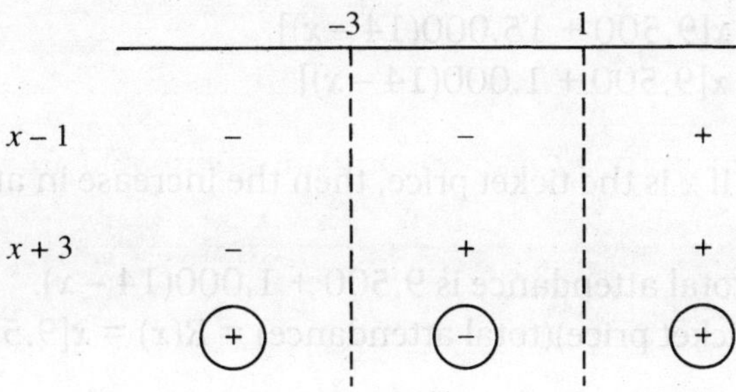

Method I is much better than Method II because it saves time. Wherever possible, use plug-in instead of tricky algebra!

MODELING QUADRATIC FUNCTIONS 二次函数建模

Projectile motion is often modeled with a quadratic function.

Example 13

A ball is thrown in the air from the top of a 50-foot high building. $h(t)$ is a function that gives the height of the ball from the ground, in feet, in terms of t, the time in seconds. You may assume that $t = 0$ corresponds to the time the ball is thrown.

Which of the following equations for h is consistent with the given information?

(A) $h = 50 + 10t + 16t^2$
(B) $h = 50 + 10t - 16t^2$
(C) $h = -50 + 10t - 16t^2$
(D) $h = -50 + 10t + 16t^2$

Solution: (B) When $t = 0$, the height above the ground is 50, so eliminate choices (C) and (D). Since the height of the ball reaches a maximum and then falls, the graph should be a concave down parabola, which means that the coefficient of t^2 must be negative. Therefore, eliminate choice (A).

There are several situations that involve the multiplication of two terms that are linear in x. This leads to a quadratic equation, and a graph that's a parabola.

Example 14

A soccer stadium has a seating capacity of 15,000 spectators. With a ticket price of \$14, the average attendance is 9,500. A survey suggests that for each dollar the ticket price is lowered, the average attendance will increase by 1,000. A function that models revenue in terms of ticket price is:

(A) $R(x) = x[15{,}000 + 1{,}000(14 - x)]$
(B) $R(x) = x[1{,}000 + 9{,}500(14 - x)]$
(C) $R(x) = x[9{,}500 + 15{,}000(14 - x)]$
(D) $R(x) = x[9{,}500 + 1{,}000(14 - x)]$

Solution: (D) If x is the ticket price, then the increase in attendance is $1{,}000(14 - x)$.

Therefore, the total attendance is $9{,}500 + 1{,}000(14 - x)$.

Revenue R is (ticket price)(total attendance) = $R(x) = x[9{,}500 + 1{,}000(14 - x)]$.

Systems of Equations, One Linear and One Quadratic

方程组，一元一次方程和一元二次方程

You may be asked about the solution of a system of equations, where one of the equations is quadratic. In general, you should know that there may be zero, one, or two solutions. A solution is an ordered pair that satisfies both equations, or a point that lies on both graphs.

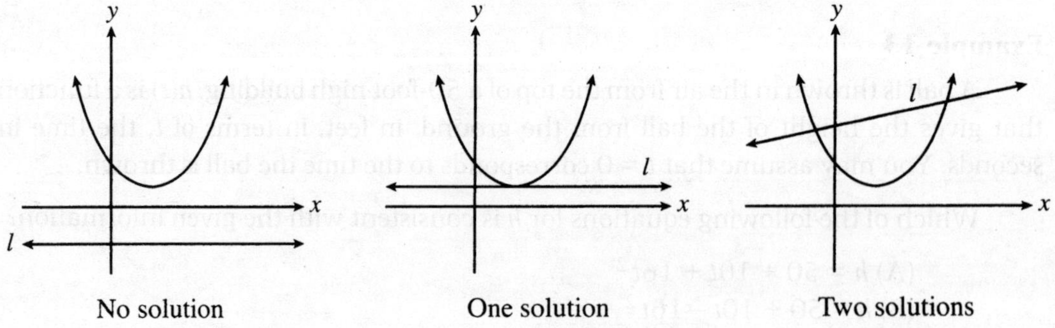

Example 15

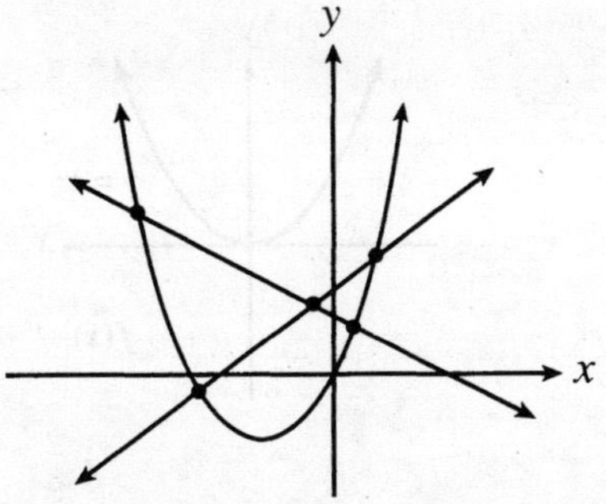

A system of three equations is shown graphically in the xy-plane above. How many solutions does the system have?

(A) 0
(B) 2
(C) 3
(D) 5

Solution: (A) A solution is a point where all three graphs intersect. There is no such point on the graph. Therefore, there are no solutions to the system.

Transformations 变换

Here is a summary of different transformations and their effects on the graph of $f(x)$. Given the graph of $f(x)$, you should know which transformation produces a related graph. In the table, assume $k > 0$ is a constant.

Related Function	Transformation of $f(x)$ That Produces It
$f(x) + k$	Vertical shift, k units up
$f(x) - k$	Vertical shift, k units down
$f(x + k)$	Horizontal shift, k units to the left
$f(x - k)$	Horizontal shift, k units to the right
$-f(x)$	Reflection across the x-axis
$f(-x)$	Reflection across the y-axis
$kf(x)$	Vertical dilation from the x-axis by a factor of k
$f(kx)$	Horizontal dilation from the y-axis by a factor of $\frac{1}{k}$

For example, suppose that $f(x) = x^2$.

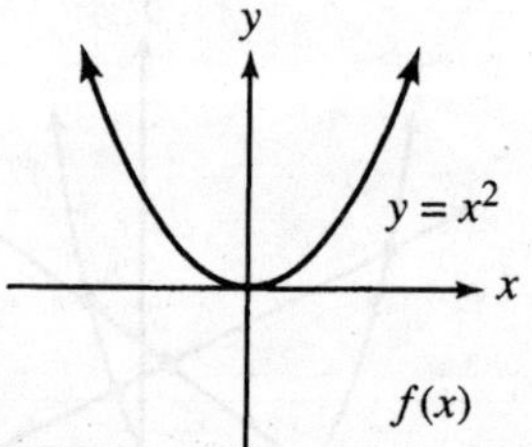

Shown below are the related graphs.

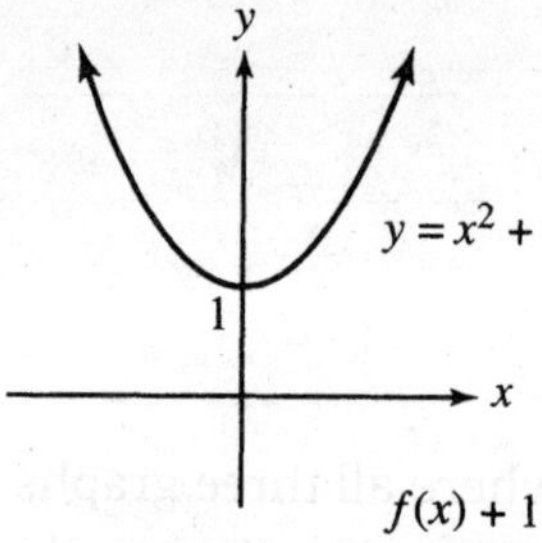

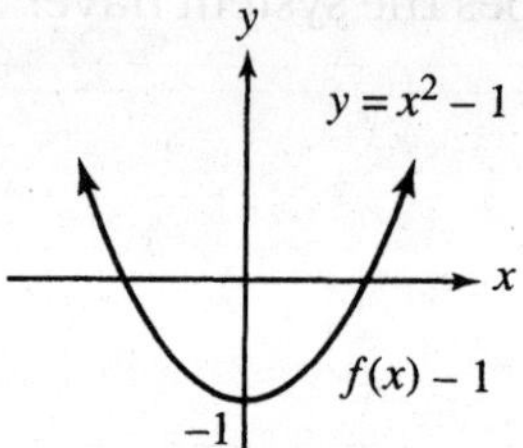

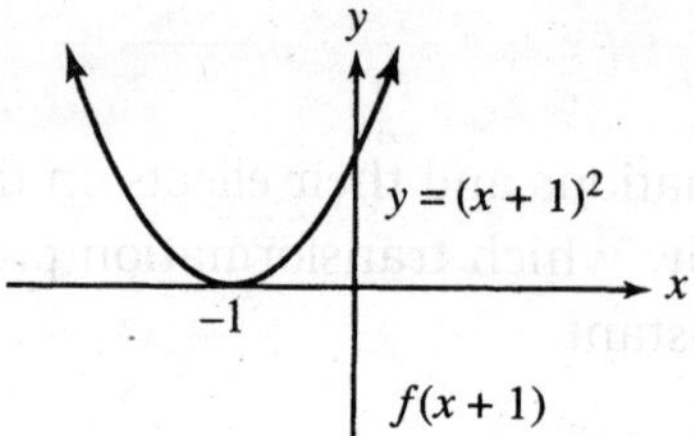

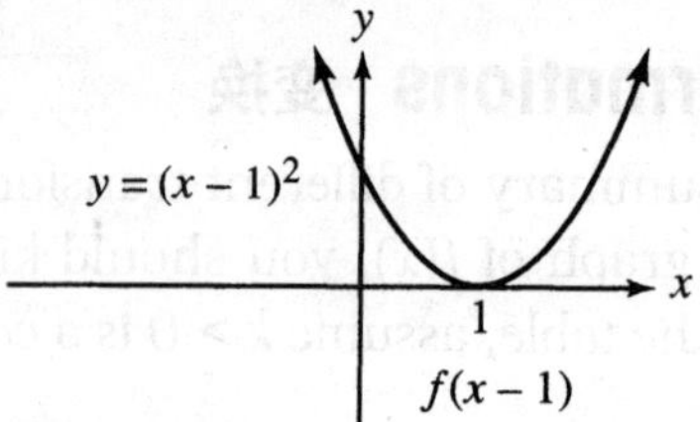

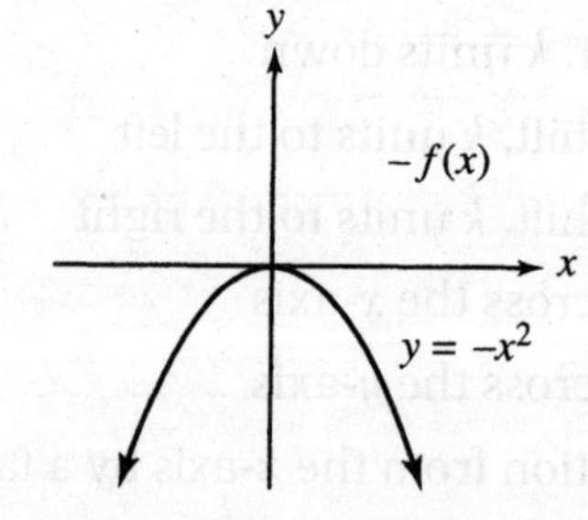

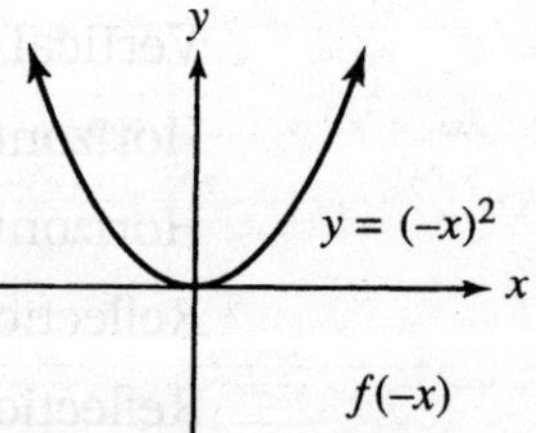

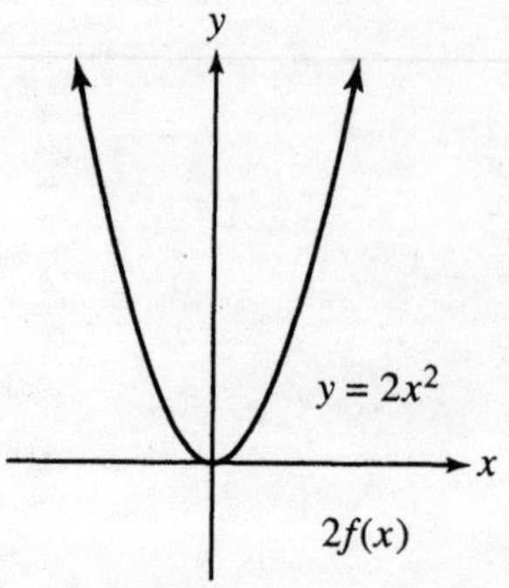

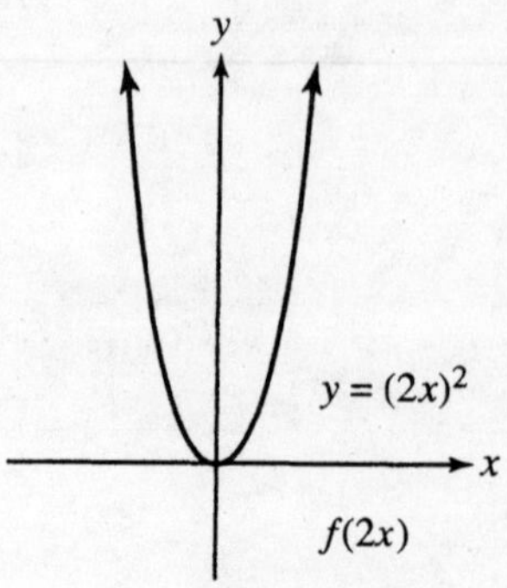

Example 16

If $f(x) = -x^2$, which represents the graph of $f(x) + 3$?

(A)

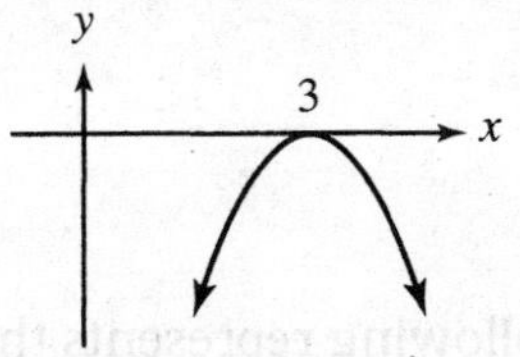

(C)

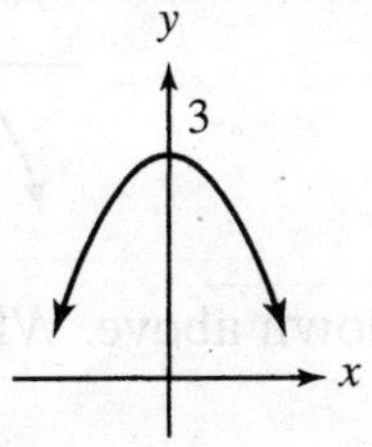

(B)

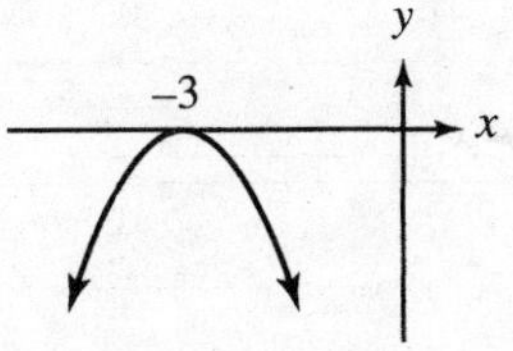

(D)

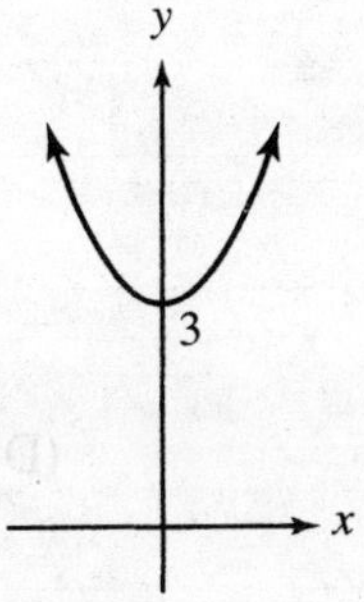

Solution: (C)

Method I: Graphing Calculator

A calculator solution makes the problem trivial. Graph $y = -x^2 + 3$, and note that choice (C) matches the graph shown in the graphing window.

Method II: Transformation of $f(x) = -x^2$

The graph of $f(x) = -x^2$, shown below, is one you've memorized by now.

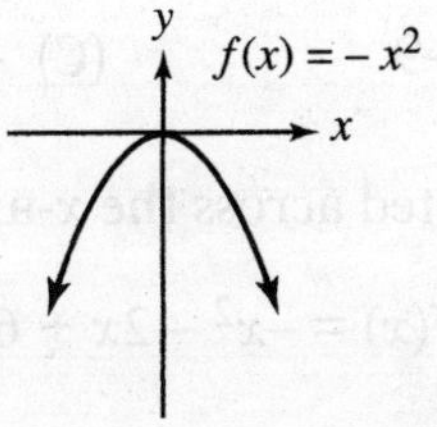

The required graph is the graph of $f(x)$ shifted vertically 3 units up—choice (C).

Example 17

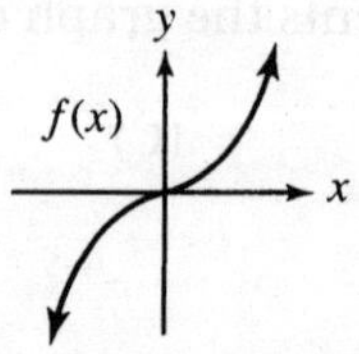

The graph of $f(x)$ is shown above. Which of the following represents the graph of $f(x-3)$?

(A)

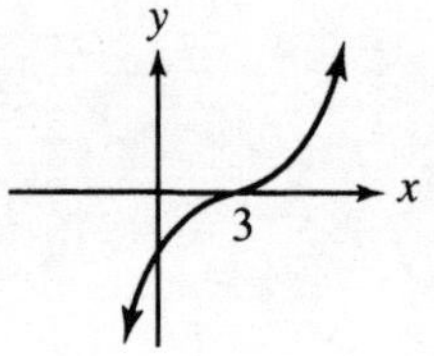

(C)

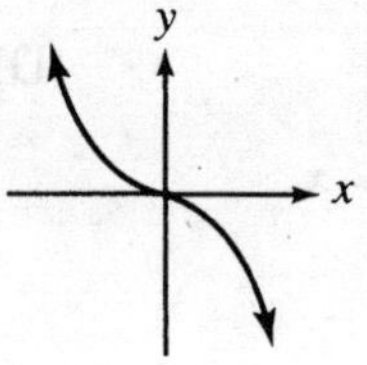

(B)

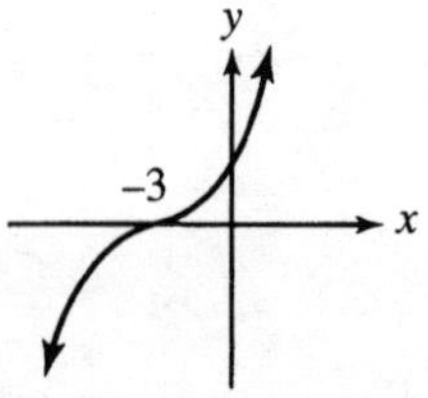

(D)

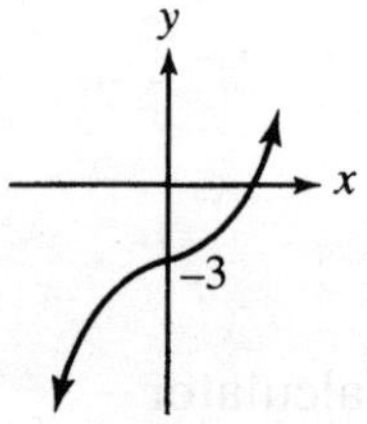

Solution: (A) The graph of $f(x-3)$ is produced when $f(x)$ is shifted horizontally 3 units to the right: choice (A).

Example 18

For the function $f(x) = x^2 + 2x - 6$, if the graph of $f(x)$ is reflected across the x-axis, the graph of a new function, $g(x)$, is produced. Find $g(3)$.

(A) –21 (B) –9 (C) –3 (D) 3

Solution: (B) When $f(x)$ is reflected across the x-axis, the graph of $-f(x)$ is obtained.

$$-f(x) = -x^2 - 2x + 6 = g(x)$$

Then $g(3) = -(3)^2 - 2(3) + 6 = -9$, choice (B).

Composition of Functions 复合函数

A simple way to think about the composition of two functions is as a function of a function. For example, if $f(x) = x^2 + 2$, and $g(x) = x - 5$, then "f composition g," denoted $f \circ g$, equals $f[g(x)]$. This means that in f's formula, replace x with $g(x)$:

$$f \circ g = f[g(x)] = (x-5)^2 + 2 = x^2 - 10x + 27$$

Note that $g \circ f = g[f(x)] = (x^2 + 2) - 5$

Example 19 Grid-In

If $f(x) = x^2 + 1$, and $g(x) = x - 2$, find x such that $f \circ g = g \circ f$.

Solution: 3/2 or **1.5**

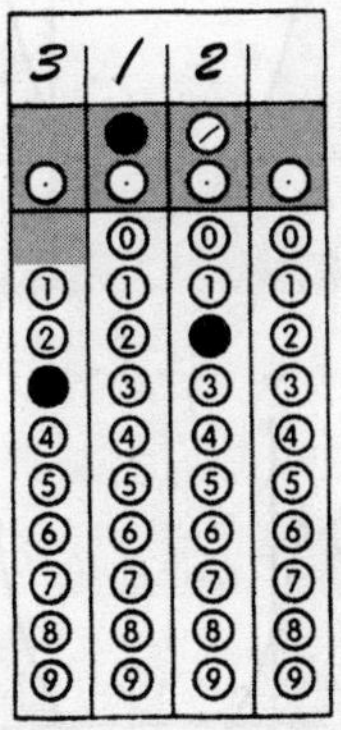

or

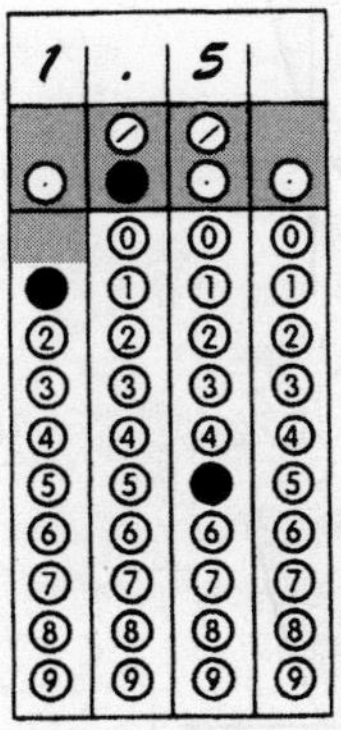

$$f \circ g = g \circ f \Rightarrow f[g(x)] = g[f(x)]$$

$$(x-2)^2 + 1 = (x^2+1) - 2$$

$$x^2 - 4x + 4 + 1 = x^2 - 1$$

$$-4x + 5 = -1$$

$$x = \frac{3}{2}$$

Grid-in 3/2 or 1.5.

PRACTICE TEST QUESTIONS 练习测试题

1. If $p + 2\sqrt{x-1} = q$, and $q > p$, what is $x - 1$ in terms of p and q?

(A) $\frac{\sqrt{q-p}}{2}$ (B) $\sqrt{\frac{q-p}{2}}$ (C) $\frac{(q-p)^2}{2}$ (D) $\frac{(q-p)^2}{4}$

2. The function f is defined by $f(x) = x^4 - 4x^3 - x^2 + cx - 12$, where c is a constant. In the xy-plane, the graph of f intersects the x-axis in the four points $(-2, 0)$, $(1, 0)$, $(p, 0)$, and $(q, 0)$. What is the value of c?

(A) 16 (B) −16 (C) $\frac{p}{q}$ (D) $\frac{q}{p}$

3. Consider the inequality $y \geq ax^2 + bx + c$, where a, b, and c are all positive. Which of the following regions could be the solution set of the inequality?

(A)

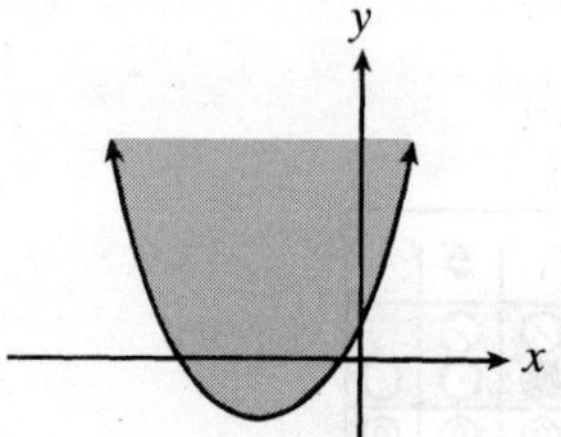

(C)

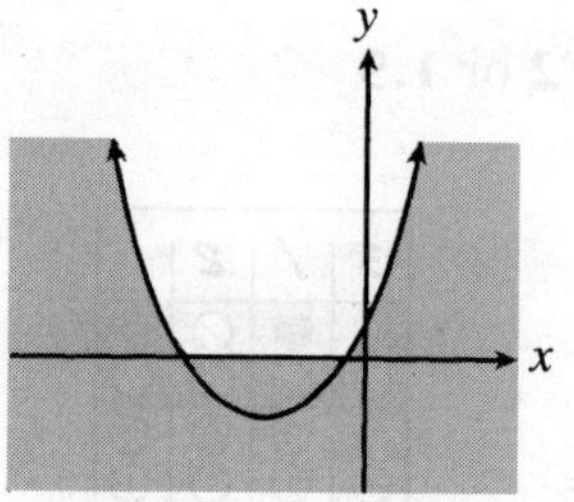

(B)

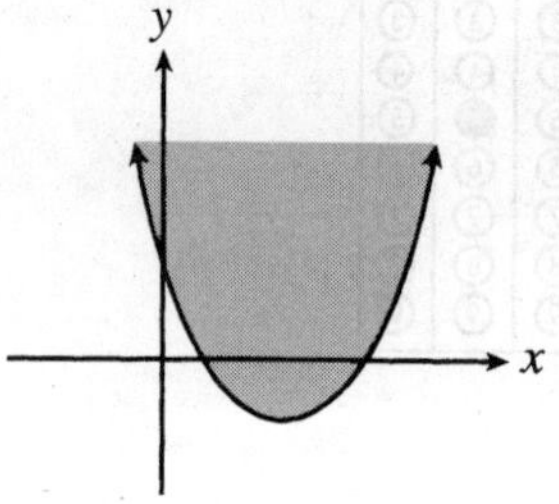

(D)

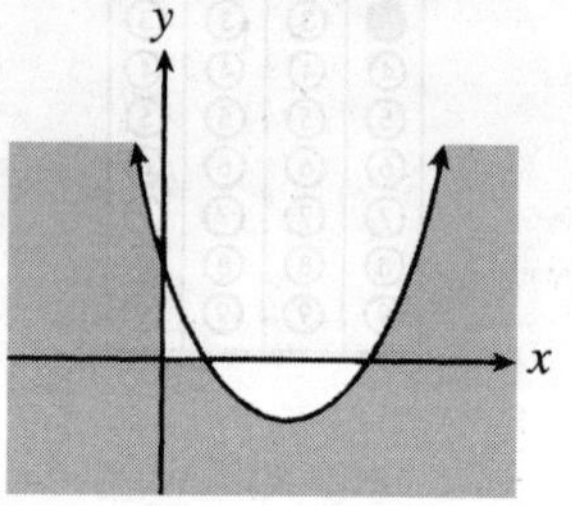

$$y = x^3 - 2x + 1$$
$$y = 2x + 1$$

4. The graphs in the system of equations shown above have three points of intersection, (x_1, y_1), (x_2, y_2), and (x_3, y_3). Find the product $x_1 \cdot x_2 \cdot x_3$.

(A) 4 (B) $\frac{5}{2}$ (C) 1 (D) 0

$$y = x^2 - 4$$
$$x + y = 2$$

5. Based on the system of equations above, what is the minimum value of the product xy?

(A) 2 (B) 0 (C) −5 (D) −15

6. If an object is dropped from a tall building, then the distance it has fallen after t seconds is given by $d(t) = 16t^2$. Find its average speed, in feet per second, between $t = 1$ second and $t = 5$ seconds.

(A) 198 (B) 192 (C) 96 (D) 80

7. A group of students go on a field trip to a play. The cost of the bus is \$450, to be shared equally among the students. The ticket cost is discounted as follows: Tickets usually cost \$50 each, but are reduced by 10 cents per ticket, up to the maximum capacity of the bus. The goal is for the total cost per student to be less than \$54. If x is the number of students in the group, which of the following correctly models the situation described?

(A) $\frac{450}{x}+(0.10)(50)<54$

(B) $\frac{450}{x}+(50-10x)<5{,}400$

(C) $\frac{450}{x}+(50-0.10x)<54$

(D) $\frac{450}{x}+(50)(0.10x)<54$

8. The equation $\left(1+\frac{1}{x}\right)^2-6\left(1+\frac{1}{x}\right)+8=0$ has two roots, a and b. What is $a+b$?

(A) $\frac{2}{3}$ (B) $\frac{4}{3}$ (C) 4 (D) 6

9. If the recommended adult dosage for a drug is D, in milligrams, then to determine the appropriate dosage c for a child of age a, where $a>1$, pharmacists use the equation $c=0.0417D(a+1)$. The formula, rewritten to express a in terms of c and D, is

(A) $a=\frac{c-1}{0.0417D}$

(B) $a=0.0417D(c+1)$

(C) $a=\frac{c}{0.0417D}-1$

(D) $a=0.0417D(c-1)$

10. Which is equivalent to $\left(x-\frac{1}{x}\right)\left(1+\frac{1}{x-1}\right)$?

(A) $x+1$ (B) $x-1$ (C) 1 (D) $\frac{x}{x+1}$

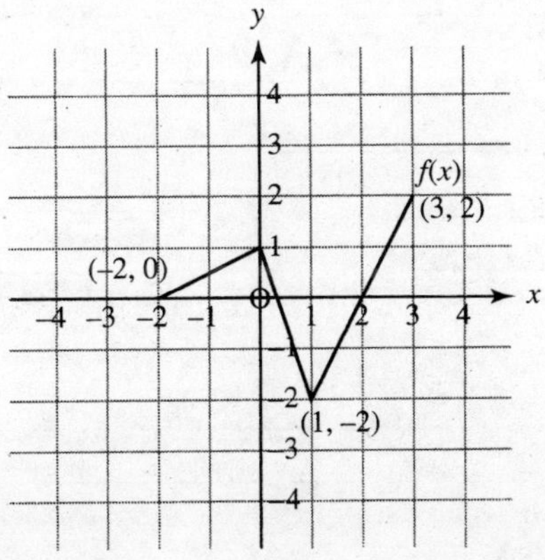

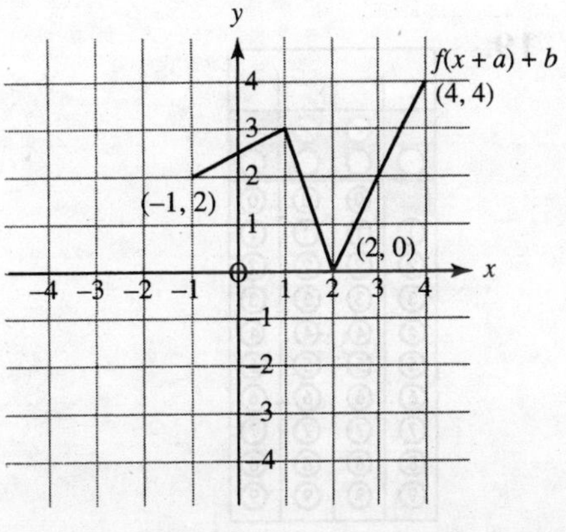

11. The graphs shown above represent $f(x)$ and $f(x+a)+b$, where a and b are constants. Which of the following is the ordered pair (a, b)?

(A) (1, 2) (B) (2, 1) (C) (−1, 2) (D) (2, −1)

12. If $3^{2x}+3^{2x}+3^{2x}=\left(\frac{1}{3}\right)^x$, what is the value of x?

(A) -1 (B) $-\frac{1}{2}$ (C) $-\frac{1}{3}$ (D) $\frac{1}{6}$

Questions 13–19 are grid-in questions.

13.

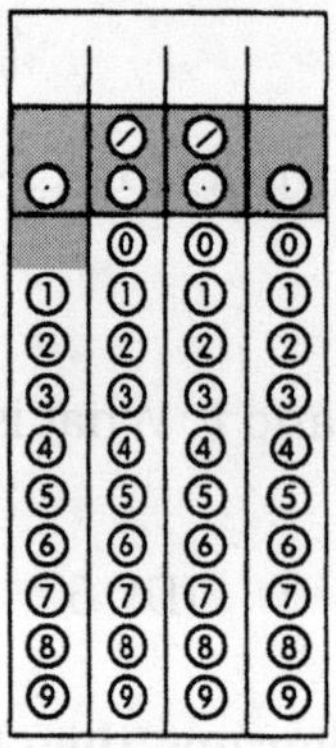

14.

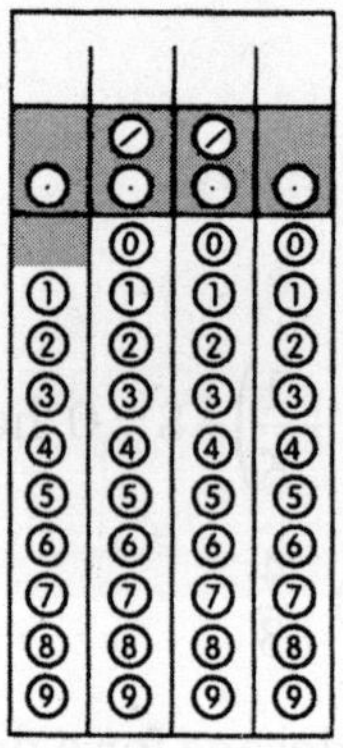

15.

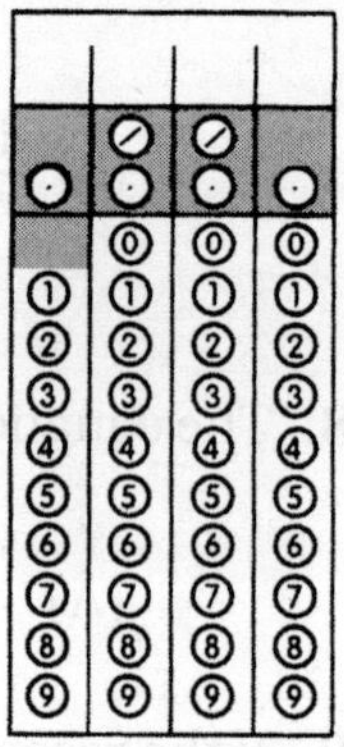

16.

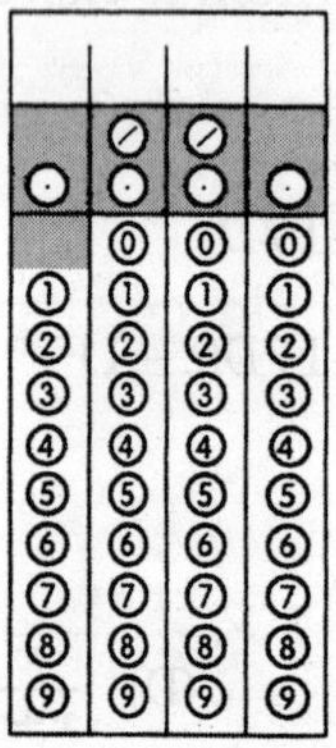

17.

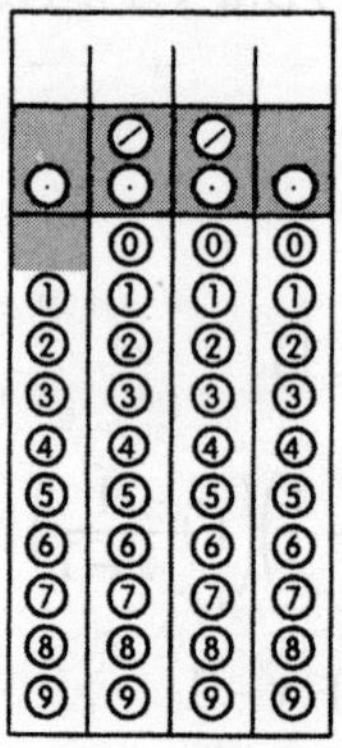

18.

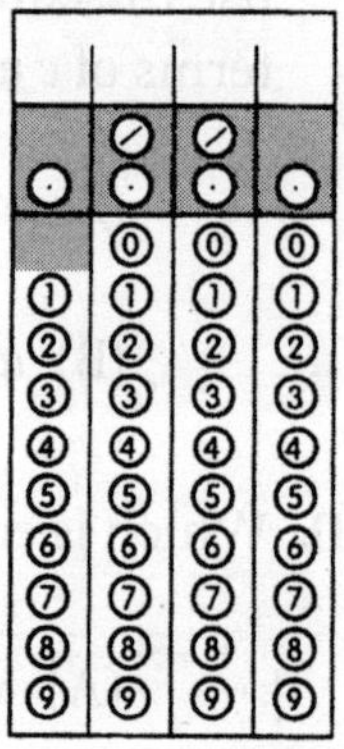

19.

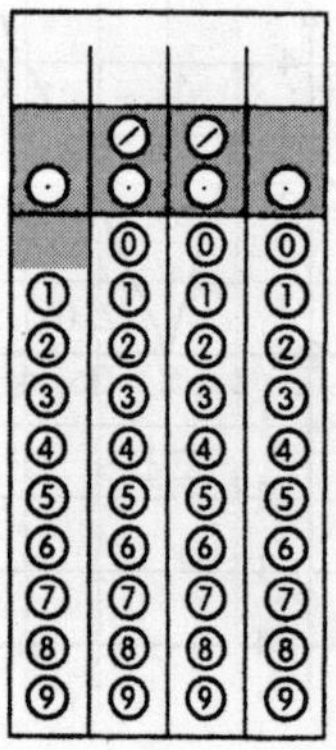

13. Find an integer value of x that satisfies both of the inequalities below:

$$|3x - 5| < 20 \text{ and } |x + 2| > 8$$

14. Let $f(x) = x^2 - 5x + 2$ and $g(x) = f(x - 4)$. Find the positive root of the equation

$$f(x) = g(2)$$

15. A statistics class investigated the cost of cheesecakes at different bakeries around town. Given that $P(x)$ was the cost, in dollars, of a cheesecake with diameter x, the function that best fit the data collected by the class was

$$P(x) = \frac{1}{2}x^2 - 5x + 20$$

According to this model, what was the *least* amount, in dollars, that a town resident could pay for a cheesecake?

16. If $f(x) = x^2 + x - 42$ and $f(p - 1) = 0$, what is a positive value of p?

17. If $\left(\frac{1}{3}\right)^x = (81)^{x-1}$, find the value of x.

18. The height h, in feet, of a ball shot upward from a ground level spring gun is described by the formula $h = -16t^2 + 48t$, where t is the time in seconds. What is the maximum height, in feet, reached by the ball?

19. The drama department at a middle school wants to determine the price to charge for tickets to a show. If the price is too low, there won't be enough money to cover expenses. If it's too high, they may not get a big enough audience. The teacher estimates that the profit, P, in dollars per show, can be represented by $P = -(t - 12)^2 + 100$, where t is the price of a ticket in dollars. When the profit is 0, the drama department breaks even. What is the lowest ticket price for which the department breaks even?

Answers and Explanations 答案与解析

The difficulty level for each question is specified in parentheses.

1. D (M)	**8.** B (H)	**14.** 7 (H)
2. A (M)	**9.** C (M)	**15.** 7.50 or 7.5 or 15/2 (H)
3. A (E)	**10.** A (M)	**16.** 7 (M)
4. D (E)	**11.** C (H)	**17.** 4/5 or .8 (M)
5. D (M)	**12.** C (H)	**18.** 36 (M)
6. C (M)	**13.** 7 or 8 (H)	**19.** 2 (M)
7. C (H)		

13.

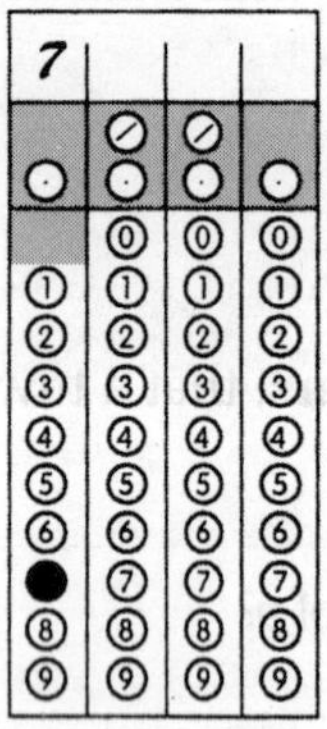

or

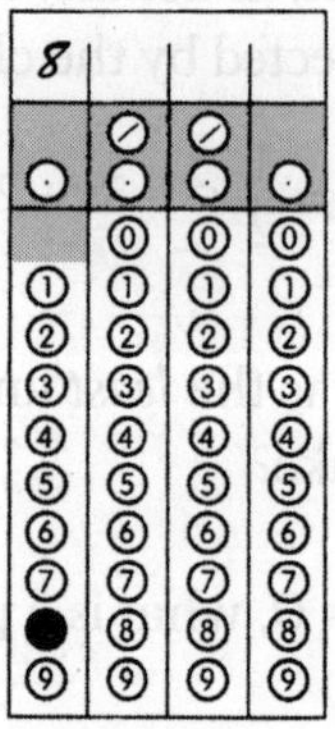

14.

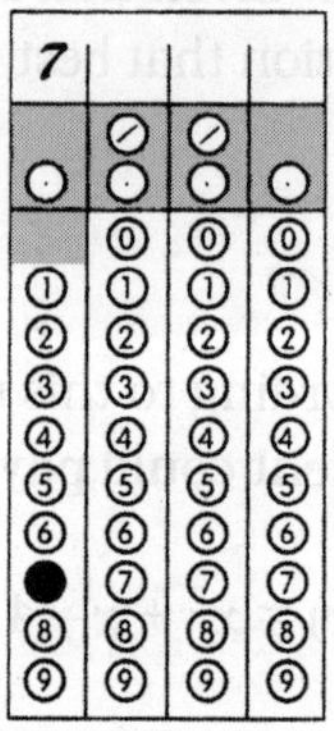

15.

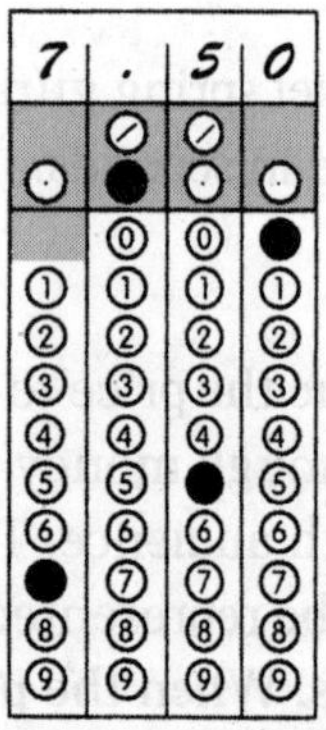

or

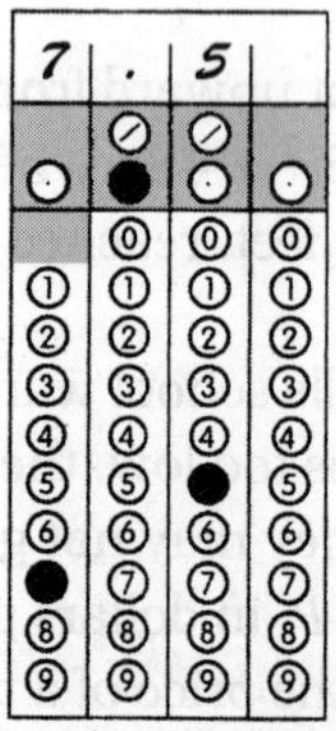

or

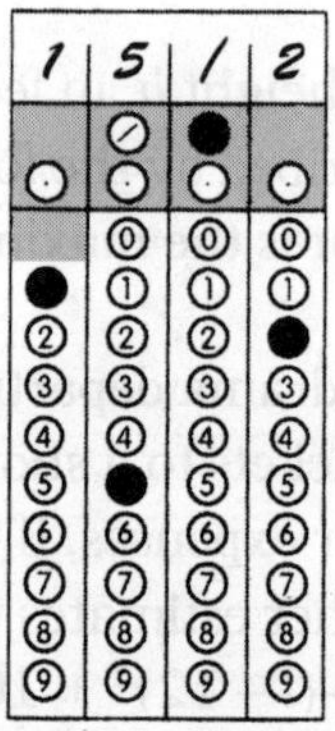

16.

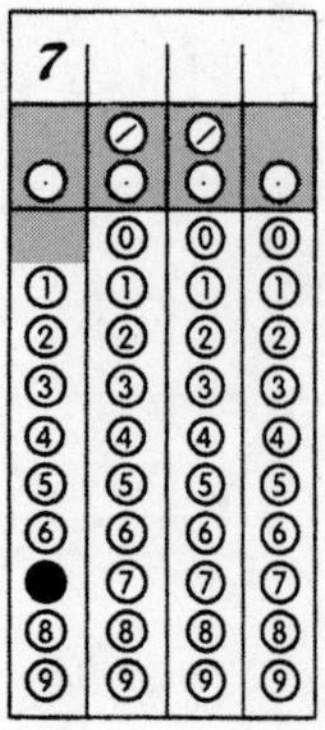

17.

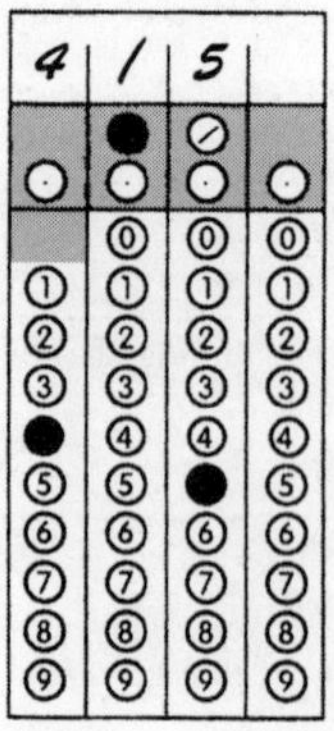

or

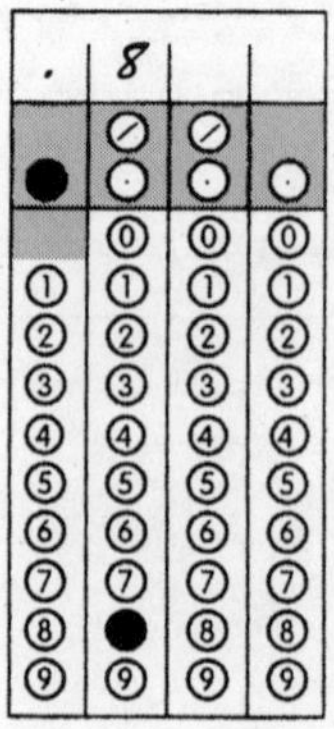

18.

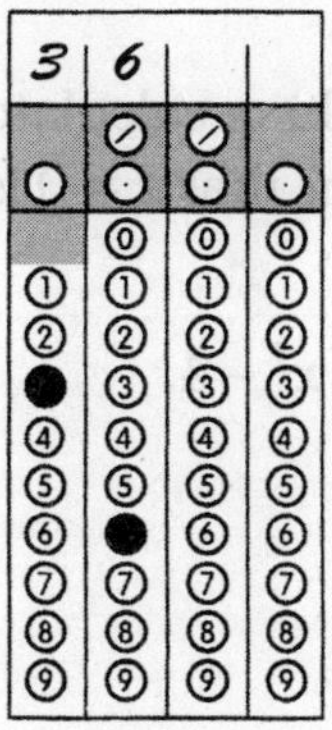

19.

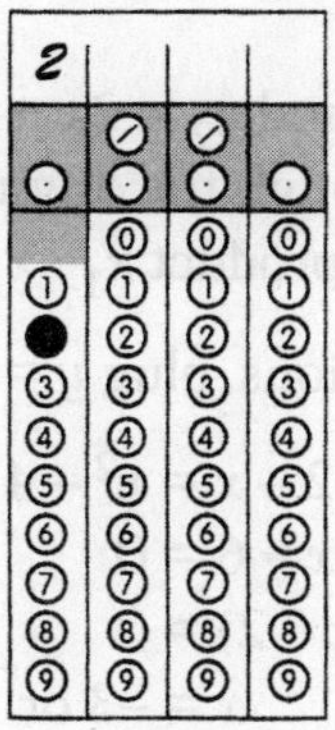

1. **(D)** This is an equation with a radical, so your plan should be to isolate the radical and then square both sides.

$$p+2\sqrt{x-1}=q$$

$$2\sqrt{x-1}=q-p$$

$$\sqrt{x-1}=\frac{q-p}{2}$$

$$x-1=\frac{(q-p)^2}{4}$$

2. **(A)** Given that (1, 0) and (–2, 0) are zeros of *f*, you can plug either one into the equation and solve for *c*. Use (1, 0) because it's easier to plug in 1 than –2:

$$0=(1)^4-4(1)^3-(1)^2+c-12$$

$$0=1-4-1+c-12$$

$$0=c-16$$

$$c=16$$

You weren't taken in by the red herrings (*p*, 0) and (*q*, 0) were you?

3. **(A)** Eliminate choices (C) and (D) because the shaded regions in these choices show the solution to $y \le ax^2+bx+c$, the points *below* the parabola. You want the points above it. Since *a* and *b* are both positive, $-\frac{b}{2a}$, the value for the axis of symmetry, is negative, which eliminates choice (B).

4. **(D)**

Method I: Algebra

$$y=x^3-2x+1 \quad (1)$$

$$y=2x+1 \quad (2)$$

Substitute *y* in (1)

$$2x+1=x^3-2x+1$$

$$x^3-4x=0$$

$$x(x^2-4)=0$$

$x=0$ is one of the required *x* values, which means that the product $x_1 \cdot x_2 \cdot x_3=0$.

Method II: Graphing Calculator

When you plot $y_1 = x^3 - 2x + 1$ and $y_2 = 2x + 1$ on the graphing calculator, notice that both graphs pass through the origin, which means that $x = 0$ is one of the required x values, and the product $x_1 \cdot x_2 \cdot x_3 = 0$.

5. **(D)** To solve the system of equations, plug $y = 2 - x$ into $y = x^2 - 4$.

$$\begin{aligned} 2 - x &= x^2 - 4 \\ x^2 + x - 6 &= 0 \\ (x+3)(x-2) &= 0 \\ x &= -3 \text{ or } 2 \end{aligned}$$

When $x = -3$, $y = 2 - (-3) = 5$, and $xy = -15$.
When $x = 2$, $y = 2 - 2 = 0$, and $xy = 0$.
The minimum value of $xy = -15$.

6. **(C)**

$$\text{speed} = \frac{\text{distance}}{\text{time}}$$

You want the average speed over the 4-second interval.

$$\text{average speed} = \frac{d(5)-d(1)}{5-1} = \frac{16(5)^2-16(1)^2}{4} = \frac{400-16}{4} = 96 \text{ feet/second.}$$

If you make the error of "taking the average" of $d(1)$ and $d(5)$, you will get choice (B), a wrong answer. The average must be taken over the 4-second interval.

7. **(C)** The inequality is formed as follows (Be sure to use dollars in each term.):

bus cost per student + ticket cost per student < 54

$$\frac{450}{x} + (50 - 0.10x) < 54$$

Notice that the ticket price of \$50 is reduced by \$0.10 for each of the x students.

8. **(B)** Notice that the given equation is quadratic in $1+\frac{1}{x}$. If you let $1+\frac{1}{x} = p$, the equation becomes $p^2 - 6p + 8 = 0$. Now solve for p.

$$\begin{aligned} p^2 - 6p + 8 &= 0 \\ (p-4)(p-2) &= 0 \\ p &= 4 \text{ or } 2 \end{aligned}$$

Now substitute back, using $1+\frac{1}{x}$ instead of p.

$$1+\frac{1}{x} = 4 \quad \text{or} \quad 1+\frac{1}{x} = 2$$

$$\frac{1}{x} = 3 \quad \text{or} \quad \frac{1}{x} = 1$$

$$x = \frac{1}{3} \quad \text{or} \quad x = 1$$

Thus, if the roots are a and b, $a + b = \frac{1}{3} + 1 = \frac{4}{3}$.

9. (C) Start by dividing both sides by 0.0417*D*, to get *a* on its own on one side.

$$c=0.0417D(a+1)\Rightarrow a+1=\frac{c}{0.0417D}\Rightarrow a=\frac{c}{0.0417D}-1$$

10. (A) Rewrite each expression in parentheses as a single fraction and then multiply:

$$\left(x-\frac{1}{x}\right)\left(1+\frac{1}{x-1}\right)$$

$$=\left(\frac{x^2-1}{x}\right)\left(\frac{x-1+1}{x-1}\right)$$

$$=\frac{(x+1)(x-1)}{x}\cdot\frac{x}{(x-1)}$$

$$=x+1$$

11. (C) To find the transformation on $f(x)$, simplify the problem by following a single, easily identifiable point of $f(x)$.

For example, the image of (–2, 0) is (–1, 2). From this, you can work out that the graph has been shifted 1 unit to the right and 2 units up. Thus, $f(x + a) + b$ is $f(x - 1) + 2$, and (a, b) is (–1, 2).

12. (C)

Method I: Algebra

$$3^{2x}+3^{2x}+3^{2x}=\left(\frac{1}{3}\right)^x$$

$$3(3^{2x})=(3^{-1})^x$$

$$3^{2x+1}=3^{-x}$$

$$2x+1=-x$$

$$x=-\frac{1}{3}$$

Method II: Plug-In

You can easily eliminate choices (A) and (B).

Choice (A): $3^{-2}+3^{-2}+3^{-2}\overset{?}{=}\left(\frac{1}{3}\right)^{-2}$

$$\frac{1}{9}+\frac{1}{9}+\frac{1}{9}\overset{?}{=}3^2 \text{ No}$$

Choice (B): $3^{-1}+3^{-1}+3^{-1}\overset{?}{=}\left(\frac{1}{3}\right)^{-1}$

$$\frac{1}{3}+\frac{1}{3}+\frac{1}{3}\overset{?}{=}3 \text{ No}$$

Plugging in the negative fractions is somewhat harder, but the laws of exponents don't let you down, and you *can* come up with the answer.

Choice (C): $3^{-\frac{2}{3}}+3^{-\frac{2}{3}}+3^{-\frac{2}{3}} \stackrel{?}{=} \left(\frac{1}{3}\right)^{-\frac{1}{3}}$

$$3\left(3^{-\frac{2}{3}}\right) \stackrel{?}{=} 3^{\frac{1}{3}}$$

$$3^1 \cdot 3^{-\frac{2}{3}} \stackrel{?}{=} 3^{\frac{1}{3}} \quad \text{Yes!}$$

13. 7 or **8**

Method I: Algebra

$\lvert 3x-5 \rvert < 20$	$\lvert x+2 \rvert > 8$
$-20 < 3x-5 < 20$	$x+2>8$ or $x+2<-8$
$-15 < 3x < 25$	$x>6$ or $x<-10$
$-5 < x < 8\frac{1}{3}$	

The only integer values of x that satisfy both inequalities are 7 and 8. Pick either one of these and grid it in.

Your impeccable algebra in Method I just got you a gold star, but you didn't win any kudos on the SAT. You wasted a lot of time. The following time-saving method is far superior.

Method II: Plug-In

Notice that the smallest positive integer that satisfies $\lvert x+2 \rvert > 8$ is $x = 7$. Your plan should be to keep trying integers from 7 on until you find one that works in the other inequality. (**Note:** Since this is a grid-in question, the answer can't be negative.) When you plug in 7, it works: $\lvert 3(7)-5 \rvert < 20$! End of story.

Grid-in 7.

14. 7

$f(x) = x^2 - 5x + 2$ and $g(x) = f(x-4)$

$\therefore g(2) = f(2-4) = f(-2) = (-2)^2 - 5(-2) + 2 = 16$

Solve $f(x) = g(2)$:

$$x^2 - 5x + 2 = 16$$
$$x^2 - 5x - 14 = 0$$
$$(x-7)(x+2) = 0$$
$$x = 7 \text{ or } -2$$

The positive root is 7.

Grid-in 7.

15. 7.50 or **7.5** or **15/2** Reduce the problem: Find the smallest possible value of

$$P(x) = \frac{1}{2}x^2 - 5x + 20$$

Method I: Graphing Calculator

Graph $y = .5x^2 - 5x + 20$.
Use the **Minimum** function in the **CALC** menu. This shows $y = 7.5$ when $x = 4.9999996$.

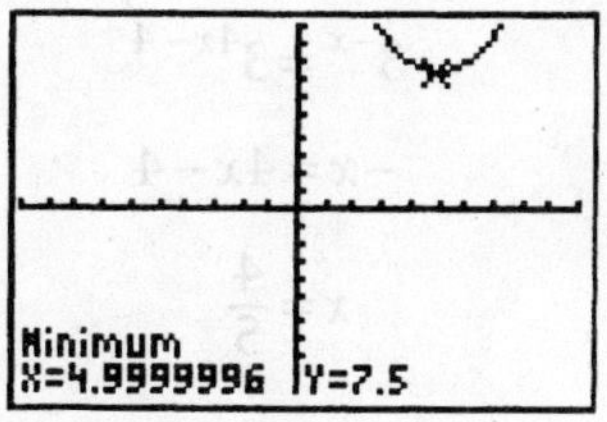

Therefore, the least possible cost is $7.50.

Method II: Algebra

The minimum value of a quadratic function occurs on the axis of symmetry.

$$\text{Axis of symmetry is } x = \frac{-b}{2a} = \frac{-(-5)}{2\left(\frac{1}{2}\right)} = 5$$

$$P(5) = \frac{1}{2}(5)^2 - 5(5) + 20$$

$$= \frac{25}{2} - 25 + 20$$

$$= \frac{15}{2}$$

Grid-in 7.50 or 7.5 or 15/2.

16. 7

Method I: Algebraic Substitution

Let $k = p - 1$. Then

$$f(p-1) = f(k) = k^2 + k - 42 = 0$$
$$(k + 7)(k - 6) = 0$$
$$k = -7 \text{ or } 6$$
$$\therefore p - 1 = -7 \text{ or } p - 1 = 6$$

A positive value for p is 7.

Method II: (Harder) Algebra

$$f(p-1) = 0 \Rightarrow (p-1)^2 + (p-1) - 42 = 0$$
$$p^2 - 2p + 1 + p - 1 - 42 = 0$$
$$p^2 - p - 42 = 0$$
$$(p - 7)(p + 6) = 0$$
$$p = 7 \text{ is the positive root}$$

Grid-in 7.

17. $\frac{4}{5}$ **or .8**

Your goal is to write the left and right sides of the equation with the same base. Remember: if $a^p = a^q$ then $p = q$. The numbers in the equation suggest base 3.

$$\left(\frac{1}{3}\right)^x = (81)^{x-1}$$

$$(3^{-1})^x = (3^4)^{x-1}$$

$$3^{-x} = 3^{4x-4}$$

$$-x = 4x - 4$$

$$x = \frac{4}{5}$$

Grid-in 4/5 or .8.

18. 36

Method I: Algebra

The graph of $h = -16t^2 + 48t$ is a parabola. Maximum h is on the axis of symmetry:

$$t = -\frac{b}{2a} = -\frac{-48}{-32} = \frac{3}{2}$$

$$h = -16\left(\frac{3}{2}\right)^2 + 48\left(\frac{3}{2}\right)$$

$$= -36 + 72$$

$$= 36$$

Method II: Graphing Calculator

Enter $y_1 = -16x^2 + 48x$ and GRAPH. Then 2ND CALC **maximum**. Use the arrow keys to select left and right bounds close to the maximum, and the calculator will tell you that the maximum value of y is 36.

Grid-in 36.

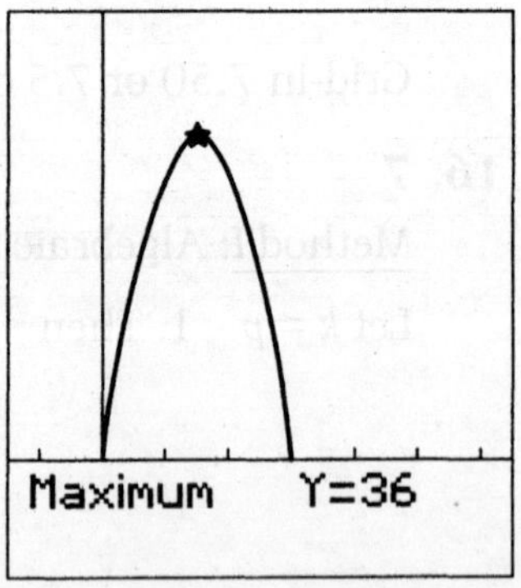

19. 2 To break even,

$$-(t-12)^2 + 100 = 0$$

$$(t-12)^2 = 100$$

$$t - 12 = \pm 10$$

$$t = 2 \text{ or } 22$$

The minimum value is \$2.

Grid-in 2.

第十四章 Chapter 14

ADDITIONAL TOPICS IN MATH 数学部分的其他主题

High scorers know the basic facts. Areas, triangles, trig ratios, solids, and coordinate geometry should be second nature to you.

In the updated SAT Math Test, the four content categories are Heart of Algebra, Problem Solving and Data Analysis, Passport to Advanced Math, and Additional Topics in Math. This fourth category is a catchall of topics: solid geometry, triangle geometry, circle geometry, the equation of a circle in a plane, some trigonometry, and operations on complex numbers.

The Additional Topics comprise 18 percent of the calculator section and 15 percent of the non-calculator section. The 1600 Club must master all of the topics to attain a perfect score.

1600 Club Strategies for Additional Topics
1600分俱乐部其他主题策略

Strategy 1:	**G**eometry: brush up on the background topics in this book.
Strategy 2:	**E**quation of a circle: study the standard form.
Strategy 3:	**O**wn those circles: review the theorems.
Strategy 4:	**M**ake sure you understand volume and surface area of solids.
Strategy 5:	**Tr**ig ratios: know the sine and cosine cofunction relationship.
Strategy 6:	**R**adians: learn the degree-radian conversion formula.
Strategy 7:	**I**n particular: sine and cosine of complementary angles.
Strategy 8:	**G**raphing calculator: learn how to use it for trig functions.

TRIANGLES 三角形

Congruent Triangles 等边三角形

Two triangles are *congruent* if their corresponding sides and angles are congruent. There are four simple cases in which it can be proved that two triangles are congruent:

- All three sides are congruent (SSS).
- Two sides and the included angle are congruent (SAS).
- Two angles and a corresponding side are congruent (ASA).
- In a right triangle, the hypotenuse and a leg are congruent (HL).

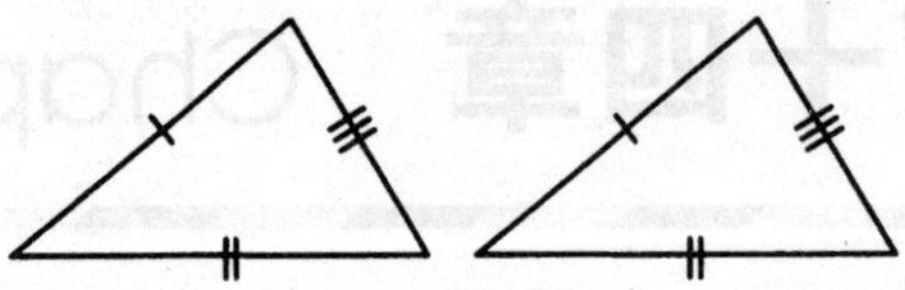

SSS

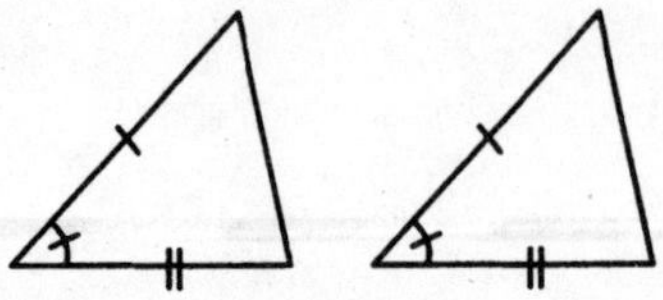

SAS

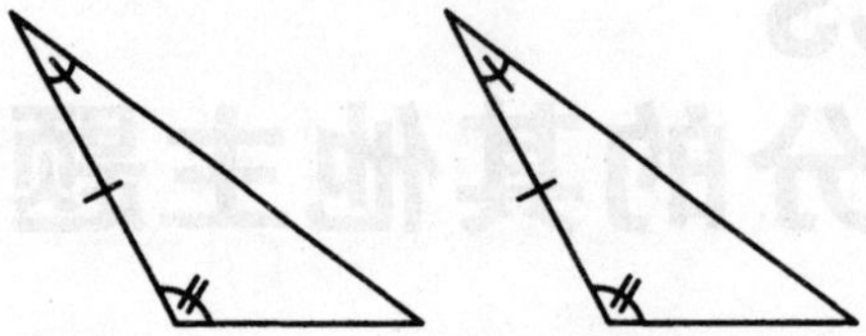

ASA

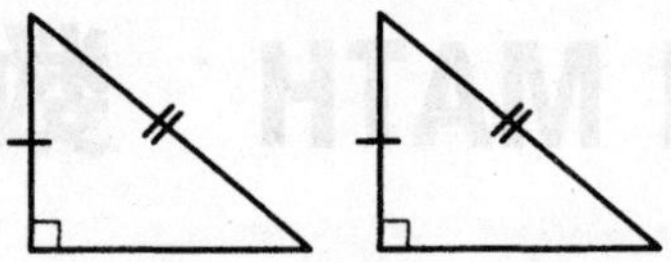

HL

Similar Triangles 相似三角形

- Two triangles are *similar* if their sides are proportional; that is, if the ratios of corresponding sides are equal.

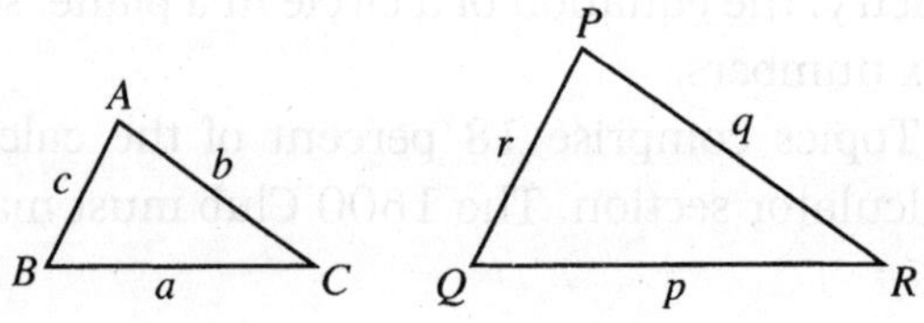

- Given that $\triangle ABC$ above is similar to $\triangle PQR$,

$$\frac{a}{p}=\frac{b}{q}=\frac{c}{r}$$

- The corresponding angles in similar triangles are congruent.
- If two angles of a triangle are congruent to two angles of a second triangle, the triangles are similar.
- If two triangles are similar, and the ratio of a pair of corresponding sides is $\frac{x}{y}$, then, for these triangles, the ratio of their perimeters is $\frac{x}{y}$, the ratio of their altitudes is $\frac{x}{y}$, and the ratio of their areas is $\left(\frac{x}{y}\right)^2$.
For example,

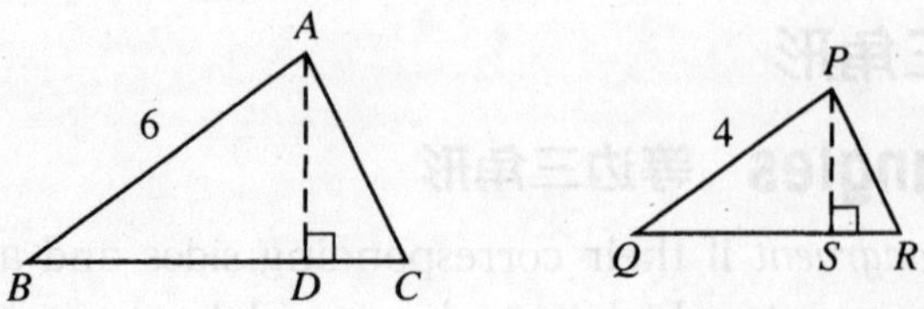

Given that $\triangle ABC$ in the previous example is similar to $\triangle PQR$, then

$$\frac{AB}{PQ}=\frac{6}{4}=\frac{3}{2},\quad \frac{AD}{PS}=\frac{3}{2}$$

$$\frac{\text{Perimeter of }\triangle ABC}{\text{Perimeter of }\triangle PQR}=\frac{3}{2}$$

$$\frac{\text{Area of }\triangle ABC}{\text{Area of }\triangle PQR}=\left(\frac{3}{2}\right)^2=\left(\frac{9}{4}\right)$$

Example 1 Grid-In

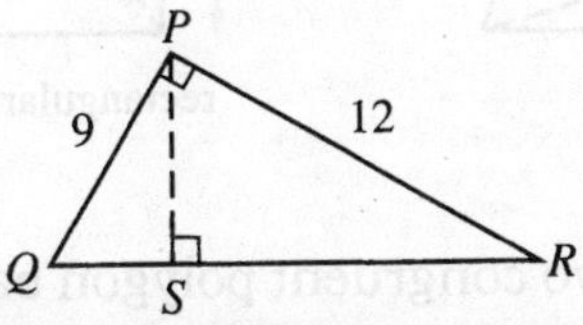

In the above figure, $\triangle PQR$ is a right triangle with the right angle at P. Line segment PS is an altitude, $PQ = 9$, and $PR = 12$. What is the area of $\triangle PQS$?

Solution: 19.4 Here is what this problem boils down to: Find the area of a triangle that is similar to a triangle whose area you know. Each triangle, $\triangle PQR$ and $\triangle PQS$, contains a right angle, and both contain $\angle Q$. Therefore, the triangles are similar. Picture them side by side:

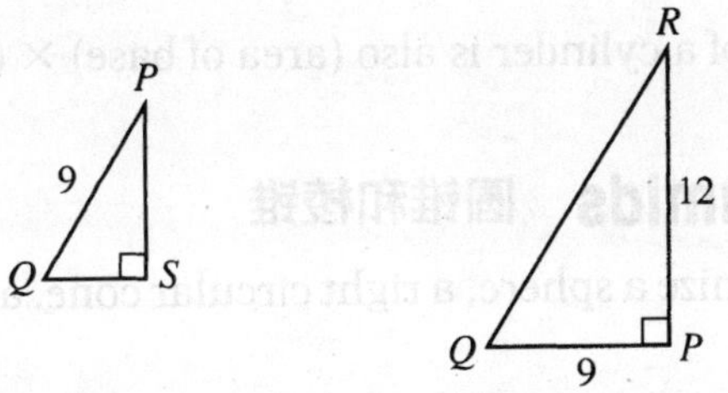

Once you realize that $\triangle PQS$ is similar to $\triangle RQP$, you can find ratio $\frac{PQ}{RQ}$.

By the Pythagorean theorem,

$$RQ=15,\quad \therefore \frac{PQ}{RQ}=\frac{9}{15}=\frac{3}{5}$$

$$\therefore \frac{\text{Area of }\triangle PQS}{\text{Area of }\triangle RQP}=\left(\frac{3}{5}\right)^2$$

$$\therefore \frac{\text{Area of }\triangle PQS}{(\frac{1}{2})(12)(9)}=\left(\frac{9}{25}\right)$$

$$\therefore \text{Area of }\triangle PQS=\frac{(9)(54)}{25}\approx 19.4$$

Grid-in 19.4.

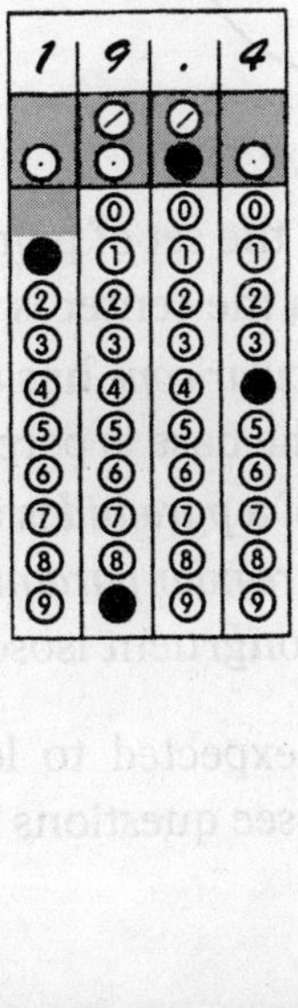

Coaching:

Recognize this picture:

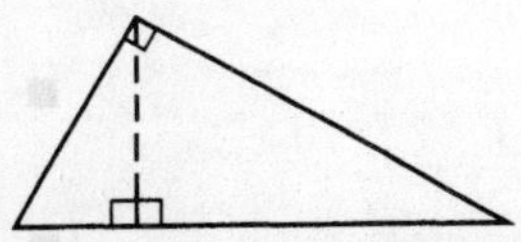

The three right triangles that you see are similar to each other.

SOLID GEOMETRY 立体几何

Prisms and Cylinders 棱柱和圆柱

Recognize the solids shown below. Each is a right prism.

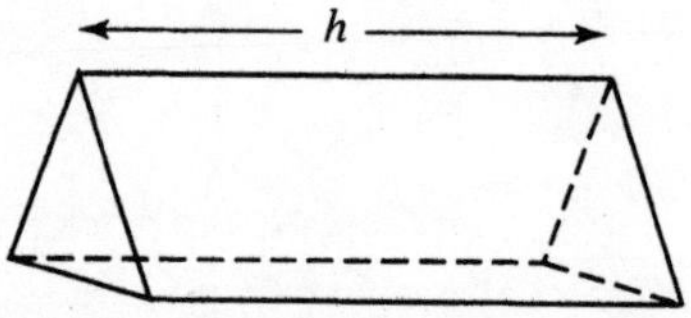

triangular prism

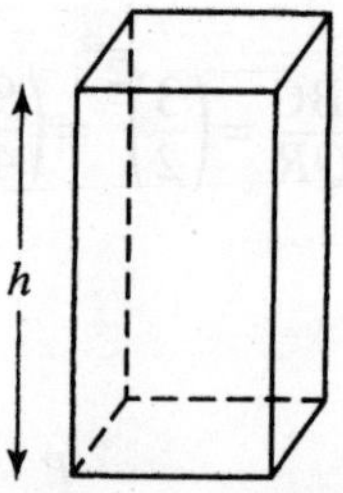

rectangular prism

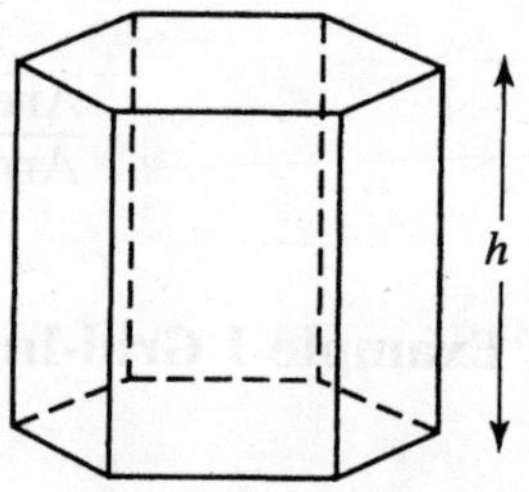

hexagonal prism

- A *right prism* has two congruent polygon bases connected by faces that are perpendicular to the bases. The name of the prism depends on the shape of the base. The height is the distance between the bases.
- The volume of a prism is (area of base) × (height).
- A *right circular cylinder* resembles a right prism: the bases are congruent circles, and the connecting curved surface is perpendicular to the bases. As with a prism, the height of a cylinder is the distance between bases.

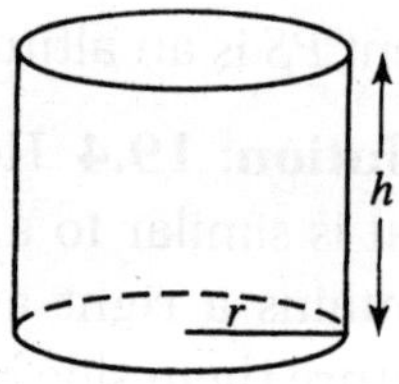

- The volume of a cylinder is also (area of base) × (height) = $\pi r^2 h$.

Cones and Pyramids 圆锥和棱锥

You should also recognize a sphere, a right circular cone, and a pyramid, shown below.

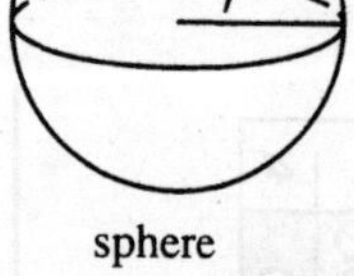

sphere

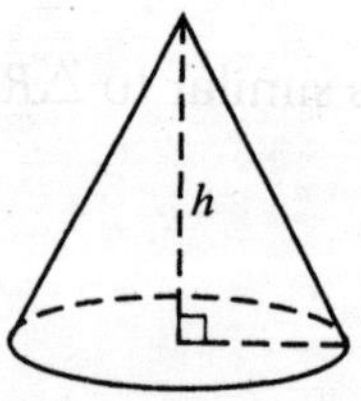

cone

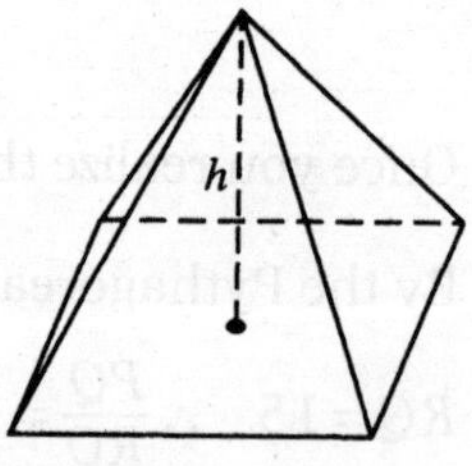

pyramid

- A *sphere* is the set of points in space equidistant from the center. This distance from the center is *r*, the radius.
- A *right circular cone* has a circular base. The line connecting the vertex to the center of the base is perpendicular to the base.
- The base of a *pyramid* is a polygon. It is connected to the vertex by triangular faces. In a *regular pyramid*, the base is a regular polygon, and the triangular faces are congruent isosceles triangles.

You are not expected to learn complicated formulas for the SAT. You can, however, expect to see questions about the various solids.

Questions about the surface areas of solids can sometimes be solved using an "imaginary scissors" technique. Picture the solid as a hollow cardboard container. Now cut it open, and flatten it out to make a plane figure. For example, here is a rectangular solid, flattened out in the plane of the bottom of the box:

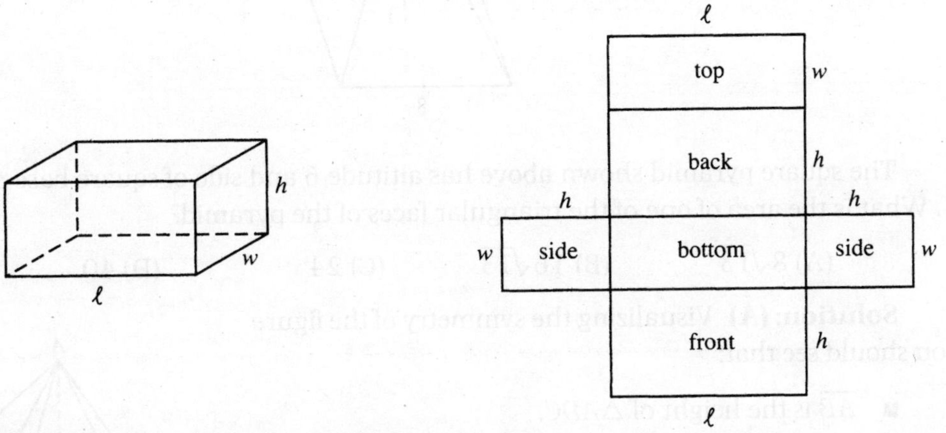

Example 2

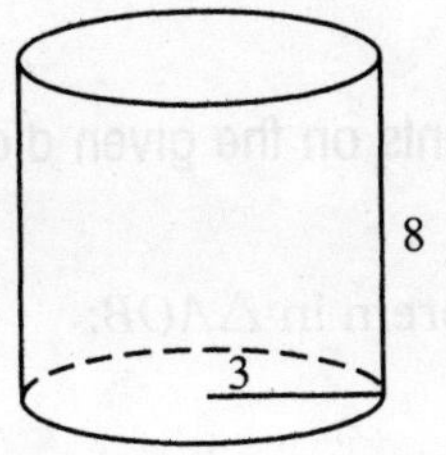

What is the total surface area of the cylindrical can shown above, including its lid?

(A) $18\pi + 64$ (B) $48\pi + 18$ (C) 57π (D) 66π

Solution: (D) Use the imaginary scissors technique. Cut off the lid and base; then cut the rest of the cylinder open, and lay it flat:

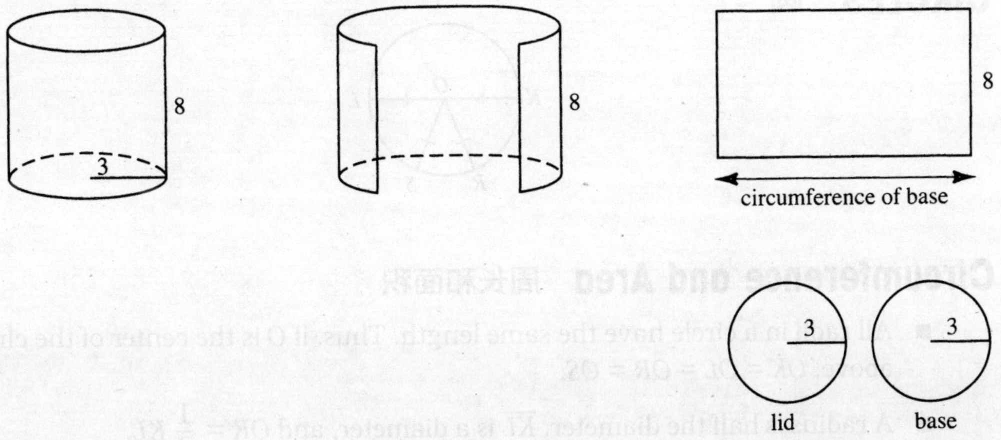

You can now see that the surface area *SA* is the area of two circles plus a rectangle whose length is the circumference of the base:

$$SA = 2\pi r^2 + 2\pi rh = 2\pi(9) + 2\pi(24) = 18\pi + 48\pi = 66\pi$$

Example 3

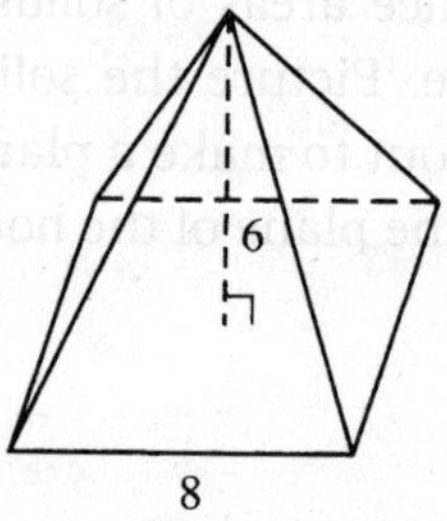

The square pyramid shown above has altitude 6 and side of square base equal to 8. What is the area of one of the triangular faces of the pyramid?

(A) $8\sqrt{13}$ (B) $16\sqrt{13}$ (C) 24 (D) 40

Solution: (A) Visualizing the symmetry of the figure you should see that:

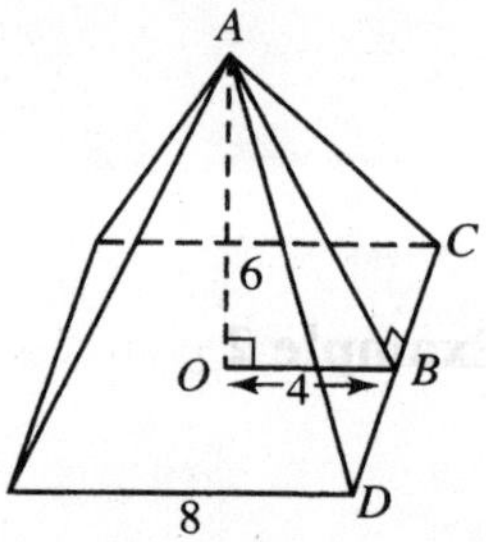

- $\overline{AB}$ is the height of $\triangle ADC$.
- O is the center of the square.
- OB = half the side of the square base, namely, 4.

Draw in some line segments on the given diagram.

Use the Pythagorean theorem in $\triangle AOB$:

$AB^2 = 6^2 + 4^2$

$\therefore AB = \sqrt{52} = 2\sqrt{13}$

$\therefore$ Area of $\triangle ADC = \left(\frac{1}{2}\right)(DC)(AB) = \left(\frac{1}{2}\right)(8)(2\sqrt{13}) = 8\sqrt{13}$

CIRCLES 圆

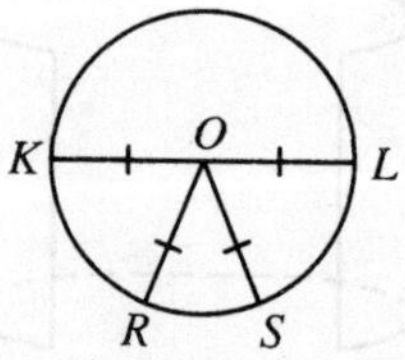

Circumference and Area 周长和面积

- All radii in a circle have the same length. Thus, if O is the center of the circle above, $OK = OL = OR = OS$.
- A radius is half the diameter. $\overline{KL}$ is a diameter, and $OR = \frac{1}{2}KL$.
- The *circumference* of a circle is πd or $2\pi r$, where d is the diameter and r is the radius.
- The *area* of a circle is πr^2.

Arc and Sector 圆弧和扇形

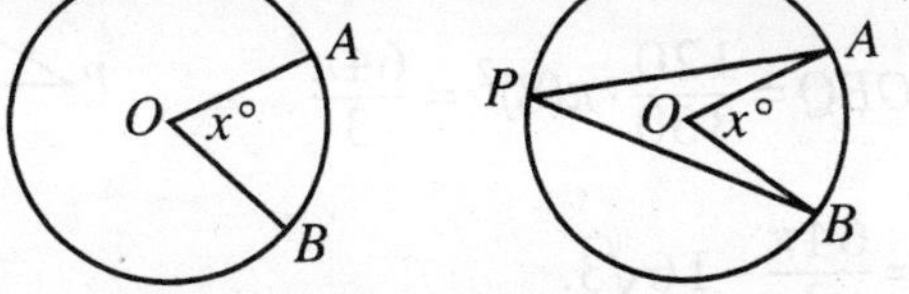

- An angle whose vertex is the center of a circle is a *central angle.*
- In the circles above, central angle AOB intercepts arc AB. The measure of arc AB is the measure of the central angle that intercepts it.
  ∴ Measure arc $AB = m\angle AOB = x°$.
  Also, the measure of an angle whose vertex is on the circumference of the circle is $\frac{1}{2}$ that of the arc cut off by that angle. Therefore, in the circle on the right above:
  Measure of $\angle APB = \frac{1}{2}$ measure of arc $AB = \frac{1}{2}$ measure of $\angle AOB = \frac{x°}{2}$
- High scorers distinguish between the measure of an arc (in degrees) and the *length* of an arc. Since there are 360° in a circle, an arc of $x°$ cuts off $\frac{x}{360}$ of the circumference. Let L be the length of an arc whose measure is x. Then $L = \frac{x}{360} 2\pi r$. (**Note:** L has the same units as r.)
- A *sector* is a region in a circle bounded by a central angle and the arc it intercepts. The area of sector AOB is $\frac{x}{360}\pi r^2$.

Example 4

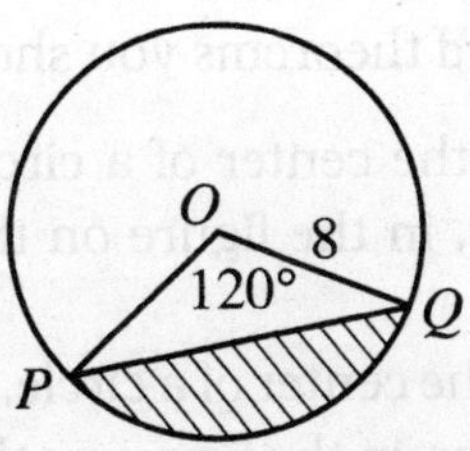

In the figure above, what is the area of the shaded region?

(A) $\frac{16\pi}{3} - 16\sqrt{3}$ (B) $\frac{16\pi}{3} - 16$ (C) $\frac{16\pi}{3} - 64\sqrt{3}$ (D) $\frac{64\pi}{3} - 16\sqrt{3}$

Solution: (D) Finding shaded areas usually involves subtraction, and this problem is no exception.

Shaded area = area of sector OPQ – area of $\triangle OPQ$.

To find the area of $\triangle OPQ$, draw in an altitude and fill in the lengths for the 30–60–90° triangle.

Since $OP = OQ$, $\triangle OPK \cong \triangle OQK$ and $PQ = 8\sqrt{3}$.

Area of $\triangle OPQ = \frac{1}{2}(8\sqrt{3})(4) = 16\sqrt{3}$.

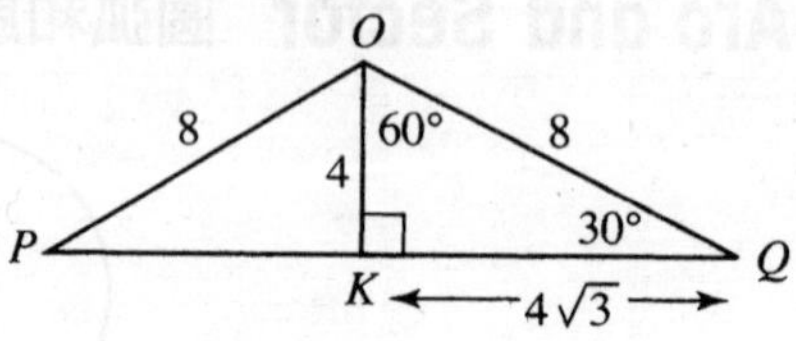

Area of sector $OPQ = \frac{120}{360} \cdot \pi(8)^2 = \frac{64\pi}{3}$.

$\therefore$ Shaded area $= \frac{64\pi}{3} - 16\sqrt{3}$.

Chords 弦

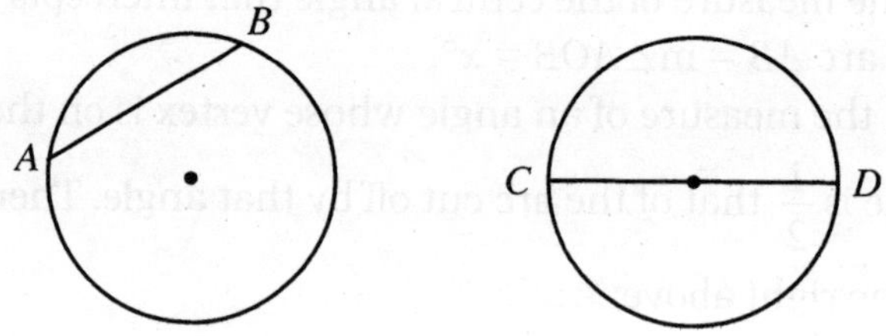

- A *chord* is a line segment connecting any two points on a circle, for example, line segment $\overline{AB}$, shown on the left above.
- A diameter is a chord that contains the center of the circle, for example, line segment CD, shown on the right above.

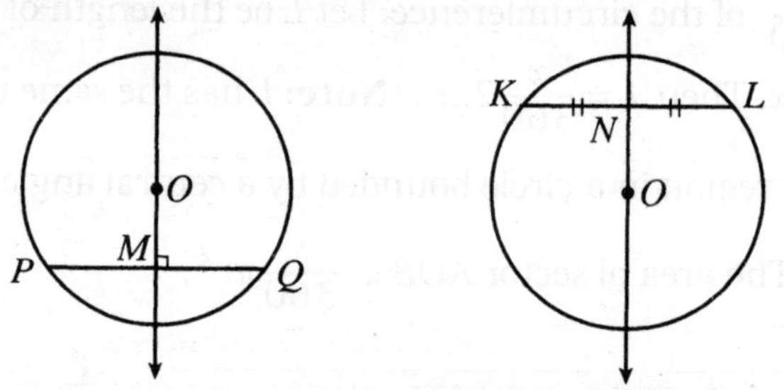

- There are two chord theorems you should know:
  1. A line through the center of a circle, perpendicular to a chord, bisects the chord. Thus, in the figure on the left above, you can conclude that $PM = QM$.
  2. A line through the center of a circle, that bisects a chord, is perpendicular to the chord. Thus, in the figure on the right above, you can conclude that $\overleftrightarrow{ON} \perp \overline{KL}$.

Example 5

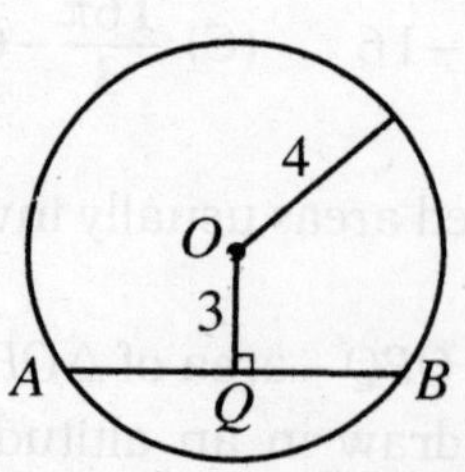

A chord $\overline{AB}$ is 3 cm. from the center of a circle with radius 4. What is the length of chord $\overline{AB}$?

(A) $\sqrt{7}$ (B) $2\sqrt{7}$ (C) 5 (D) 10

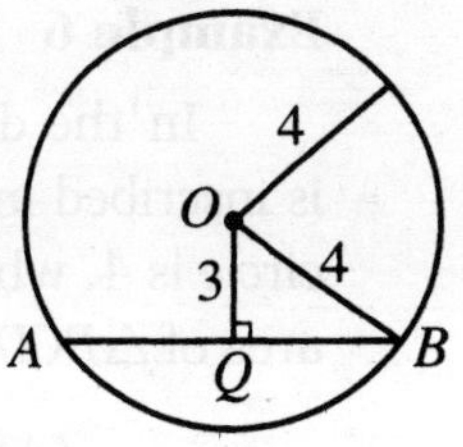

Solution: (B) In the diagram, draw a radius that connects the center of the circle to an endpoint of the chord, $\overline{OB}$, say. Then use the Pythagorean theorem to find QB:

$$QB^2 = OB^2 - OQ^2$$
$$= 4^2 - 3^2$$
$$= 7$$
$$\therefore QB = \sqrt{7}$$

Since $\overline{OQ} \perp \overline{AB}$, $\overline{OQ}$ bisects $\overline{AB}$.

$\therefore AB = 2\sqrt{7}$

Tangents 切线

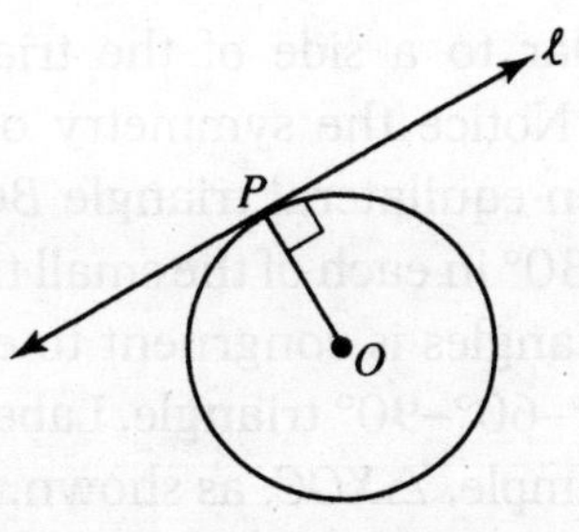

Use subtraction for shaded areas.

In the figure above, line ℓ is *tangent* to the circle with center O at point P, meaning that ℓ intersects the circle in exactly one point, namely, P. By the tangent–radius theorem, a tangent is perpendicular to a radius at the point of contact; therefore, $\ell \perp \overline{OP}$.

Inscribed Circles and Polygons 内切圆和圆内接多边形

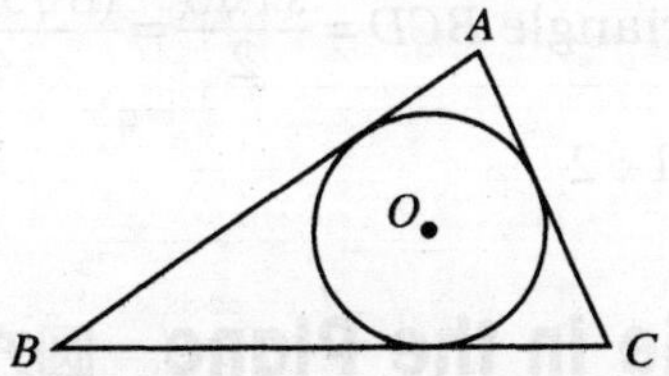

- A circle is *inscribed* in a polygon if each side of the polygon is tangent to the circle. In the figure above, for example, circle O is inscribed in $\triangle ABC$.

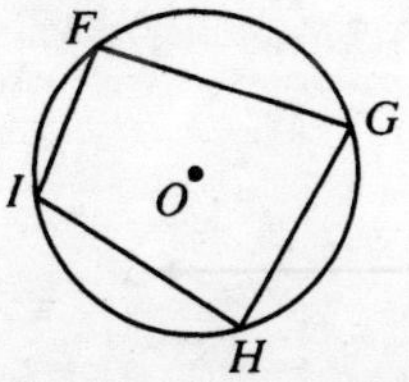

- A polygon is *inscribed* in a circle if each vertex of the polygon is on the circle. In the figure above, for example, quadrilateral $FGHI$ is inscribed in circle O.

Example 6

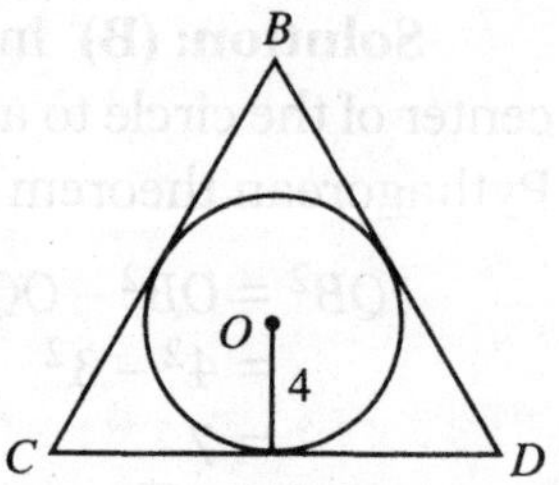

In the diagram to the right, the circle with center O is inscribed in equilateral triangle BCD. If the radius of the circle is 4, what is the ratio of the perimeter of $\triangle BCD$ to the area of $\triangle BCD$?

(A) $1 : 2\sqrt{3}$ (C) $1 : \sqrt{3}$

(B) $1 : 2$ (D) $1 : 4$

Solution: (B)

Draw in some line segments, as shown.

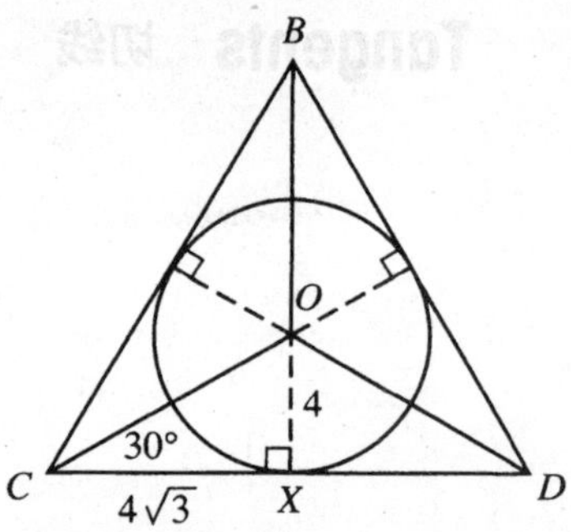

Each radius is perpendicular to a side of the triangle (tangent–radius theorem). Notice the symmetry of the picture. Each vertex of given equilateral triangle BCD is bisected, giving an angle of 30° in each of the small triangles. Each of these small triangles is congruent to every other, and each one is a 30°–60°–90° triangle. Label the sides in one of them, for example, $\triangle XOC$, as shown.

$$\text{perimeter of } \triangle BCD = 6(CX) = 24\sqrt{3}$$

$$\text{area of } \triangle BCD = 6(\text{area of } \triangle XOC) = 6\frac{1}{2}(4\sqrt{3})(4) = 48\sqrt{3}$$

Alternatively:

$$\text{area of equilateral triangle } BCD = \frac{s^2\sqrt{3}}{2} = \frac{(8\sqrt{3})^2\sqrt{3}}{4} = \frac{(64)(3)\sqrt{3}}{4} = 48\sqrt{3}$$

$\therefore$ perimeter : area = 1 : 2

Equation of a Circle in the Plane 圆方程式

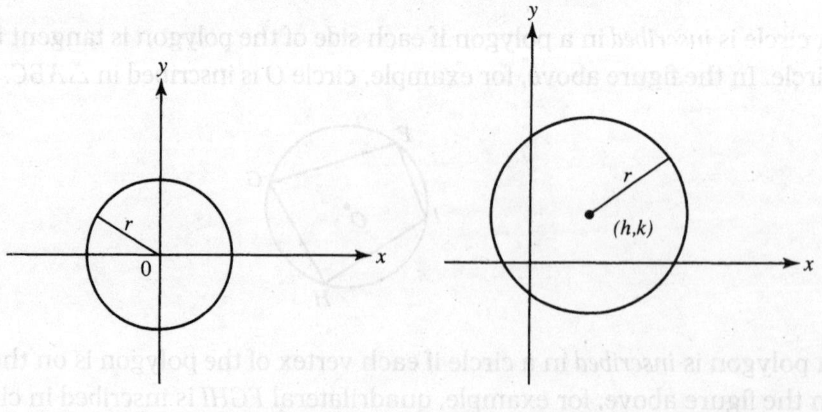

For a circle with radius r centered at the origin, as shown in the circle on the left above, the equation is

$$x^2 + y^2 = r^2$$

If the circle with radius r is centered at (h, k), as shown in the circle on the right on the previous page, the equation is

$$(x-h)^2 + (y-k)^2 = r^2$$

For example, a circle with equation $(x+2)^2 + (y-7)^2 = 36$ is a circle in the (x, y) coordinate plane with center $(-2, 7)$ and radius 6.

Example 7

A circle in the xy-plane is tangent to the x-axis at -10 and the y-axis at 10. Which of the following is an equation of the circle?

(A) $(x-10) + (y+10) = 100$
(B) $(x-10)^2 + (y+10)^2 = 100$
(C) $(x-10)^2 + (y-10)^2 = 100$
(D) $(x+10)^2 + (y-10)^2 = 100$

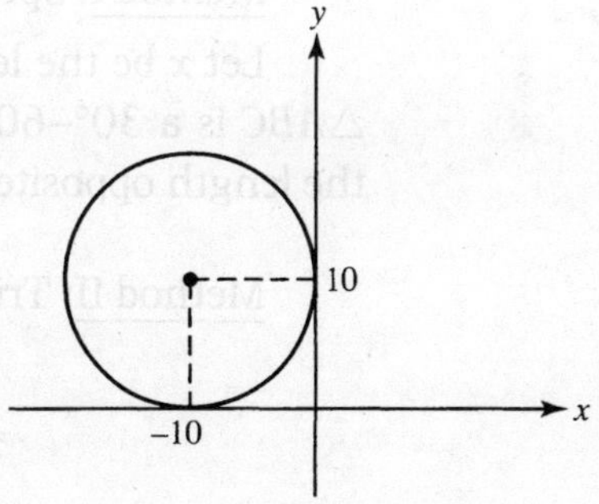

Solution: (D) From the picture, notice that the center of the circle is $(-10, 10)$, and the radius is 10. To find the equation, use the standard form of the circle with center (h, k) and radius r, namely, $(x-h)^2 + (y-k)^2 = r^2$.

$$(x-(-10))^2 + (y-10)^2 = 10^2 \Rightarrow (x+10)^2 + (y-10)^2 = 100$$

A sketch is worth a thousand words.

TRIGONOMETRY 三角学

Even though you probably won't get more than one trig question on the SAT Math Test, the topic is broad. Be sure to brush up on your high school trig course, and, in particular, pay special attention to each of the following topics.

Right Triangle Trigonometry 直角三角形三角函数

Problems that require you to find missing lengths in right triangles can sometimes be solved using special right triangles or the Pythagorean theorem. The following trigonometric ratios are also helpful:

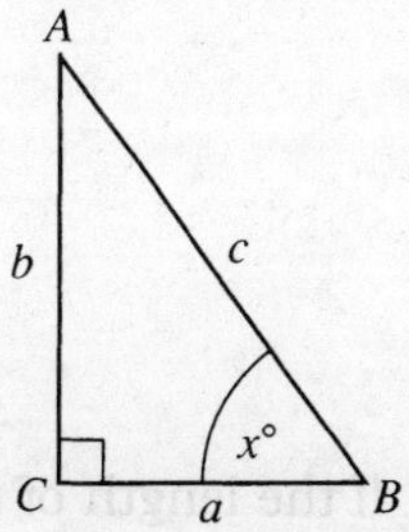

$$\sin x = \frac{\textbf{o}\text{pposite}}{\textbf{h}\text{ypotenuse}} = \frac{b}{c} \quad \text{(soh)}$$

$$\cos x = \frac{\textbf{a}\text{djacent}}{\textbf{h}\text{ypotenuse}} = \frac{a}{c} \quad \text{(cah)}$$

$$\tan x = \frac{\textbf{o}\text{pposite}}{\textbf{a}\text{djacent}} = \frac{b}{a} \quad \text{(toa)}$$

You are probably familiar with the words in parentheses, which provide a simple way of remembering which sides correspond to each ratio.

From the diagram, notice that

$$\frac{\textbf{opposite}}{\textbf{hypotenuse}} = \frac{b}{c} = \sin A = \cos B, \text{ and } B = 90° - A$$

Therefore, in general, $\sin \alpha = \cos(90° - \alpha)$, and $\cos \alpha = \sin(90° - \alpha)$. This is called the *cofunction* relationship.

Example 8

The foot of a ladder leaning against the wall of a house is 4 feet from the base of the wall. If the ladder makes a 30° angle with the wall, what is the length, in feet, of the ladder?

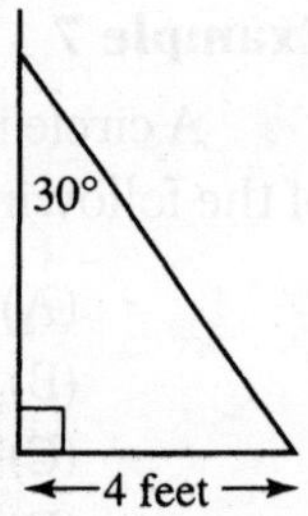

(A) $2\sqrt{3}$ (B) $4\sqrt{3}$ (C) $8\sqrt{3}$ (D) 8

Solution: (D)

Method I: Special Triangles

Let x be the length of the ladder shown at the right. Since $\triangle ABC$ is a 30°–60°–90° triangle, $x = 8$ (hypotenuse is double the length opposite the 30° angle).

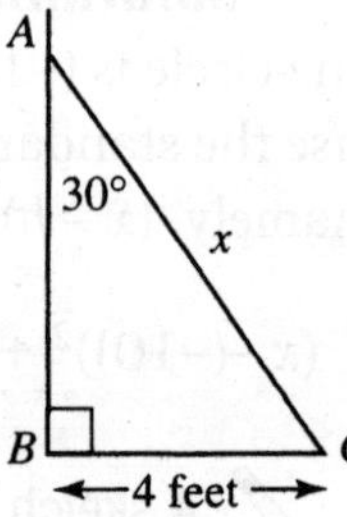

Method II: Trigonometry

$$\frac{4}{x} = \sin 30° = \frac{\text{opposite}}{\text{hypotenuse}}$$

$$x = \frac{4}{\sin 30°} = \frac{4}{0.5} = 8$$

You can use your calculator to find $\frac{4}{\sin 30°}$, but be sure to check that the calculator is in Degree MODE ! (See the section on the graphing calculator in this chapter.)

Radians and Arc Length 弧度和弧长

Picture an angle at the center of a circle:

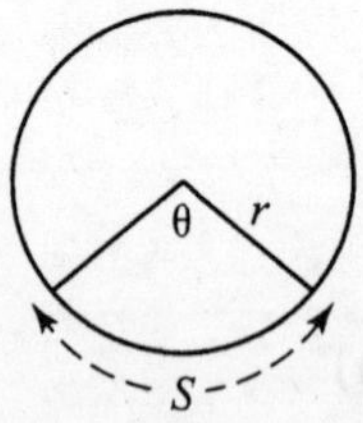

If the length of the arc cut off by the angle is s, and the radius of the circle is r, then the measure of θ in radians is defined as $\theta = \frac{s}{r}$.

If $s = r$, then $\theta = 1$. One radian is approximately 57°.
Notice that if s, the arc length, is equal to the circumference of the circle, then

$$s = 2\pi r \text{ and } \theta = \frac{2\pi r}{r} = 2\pi$$

Another way of saying this is that a rotation through the entire circle, 360°, is equivalent to 2π radians.

The 1600 Club remembers that 180° = π radians.

You should easily be able to convert the familiar angles to radians:

$$90° = \frac{\pi}{2} \text{ radians}$$

$$60° = \frac{\pi}{3} \text{ radians}$$

$$45° = \frac{\pi}{4} \text{ radians}$$

$$30° = \frac{\pi}{6} \text{ radians}$$

Example 9

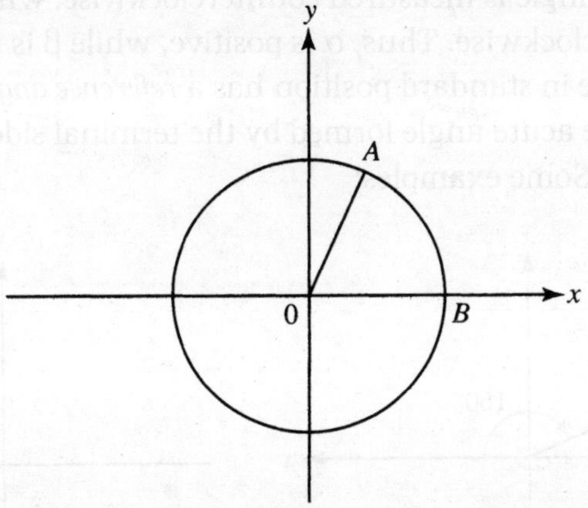

The equation of the circle shown above is $x^2 + y^2 = 36$. If the measure of $\angle AOB$ is 1.2 radians, what is the length of arc AB in coordinate units?

(A) 6 (B) 7.2 (C) 3π (D) 6π

Solution: (B) From the equation of the circle, its radius is $\sqrt{36} = 6$.
Recall the definition of an angle in radians: If the vertex of an angle θ is the center of a circle radius r, then $\theta = \frac{s}{r}$, where s is the length of the arc cut off by the angle.

Therefore, $s = r\theta$.
In the given picture, $s = 6(1.2) = 7.2$.

Trig Ratios in Four Quadrants 四个象限中的三角函数

Angle in Standard Position 标准位置角

In the figures below, angles α and β are in *standard position*:

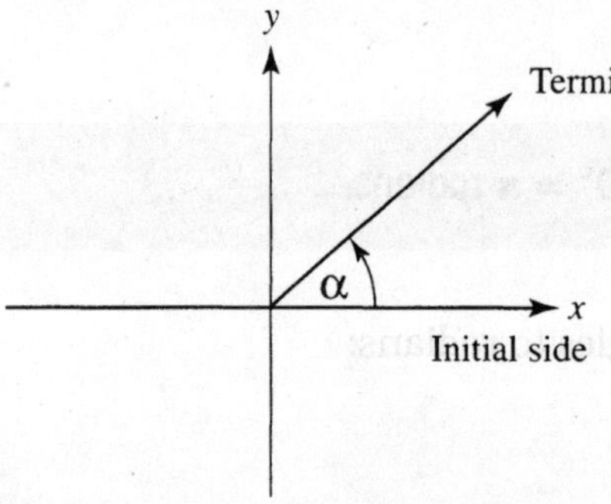

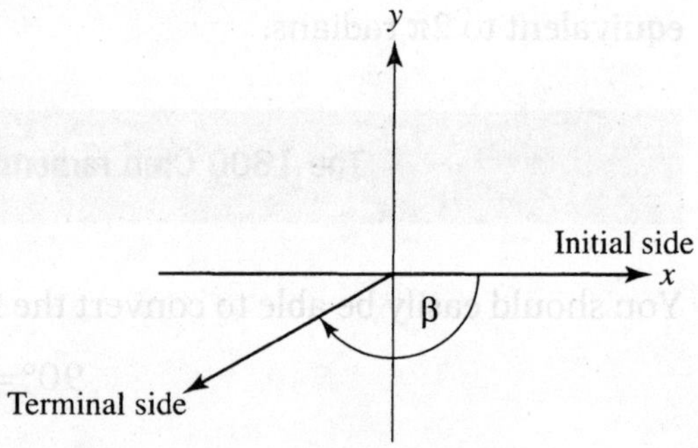

You should know each of the following:

- An angle is in standard position if its initial side is the positive x-axis and its vertex is at the origin.
- The quadrant that contains the terminal side determines the quadrant that the angle lies in. For example, α represents an angle in Quadrant I, while β is in Quadrant III.
- A positive angle is measured counterclockwise, while a negative angle is measured clockwise. Thus, α is positive, while β is negative.
- Every angle in standard position has a *reference angle*. The reference angle is the positive acute angle formed by the terminal side of the given angle and the x-axis. Some examples:

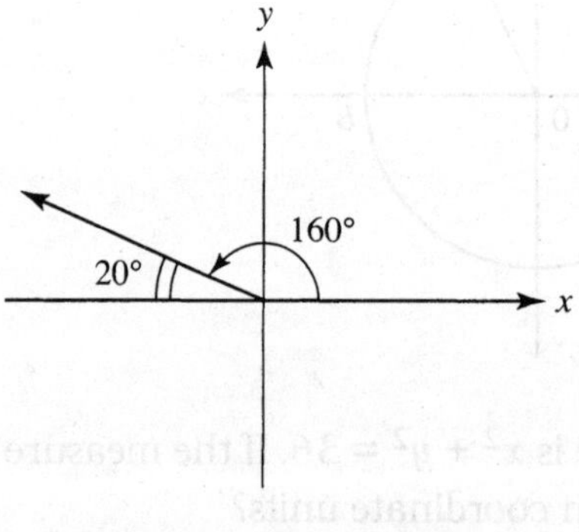

Reference angle = 20°

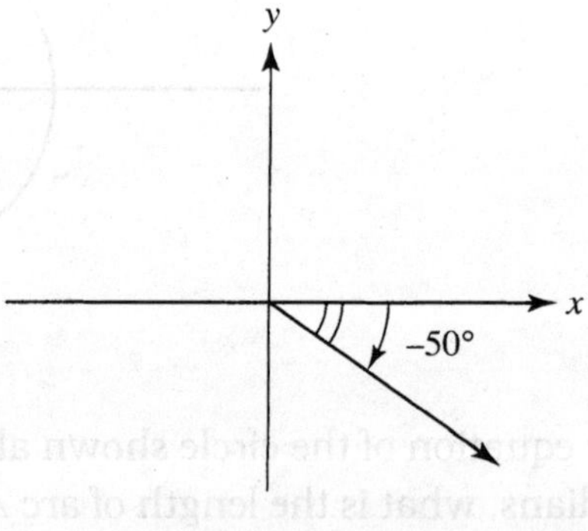

Reference angle = 50°

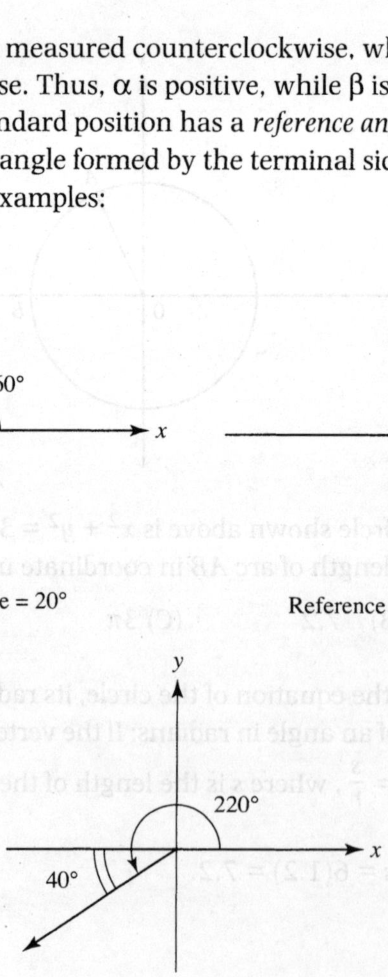

Reference angle = 40°

- If the terminal side of an angle in standard position is one of the axes, the angle is a *quadrantal angle*. For example, 90° and −180° are quadrantal angles.

Trig Ratios 三角比

You can get the trig ratios for any nonquadrantal angle as follows:

- Place the angle in standard position.
- Take any point (x, y) on the terminal side.
- Drop a perpendicular to the x-axis to form a right triangle.
- Label the hypotenuse r.
- Now use the familiar definitions from right triangle trig:

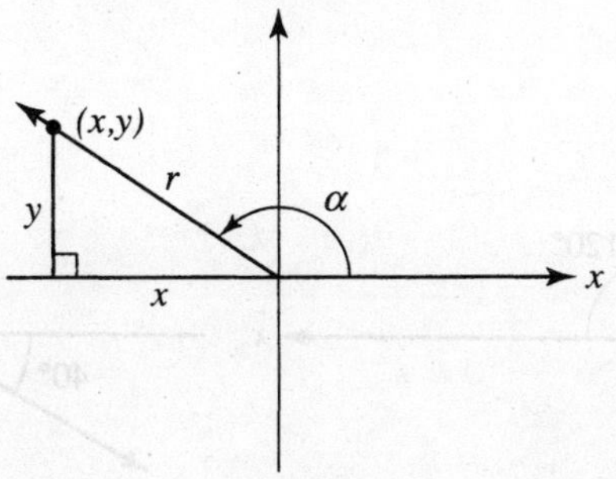

$\sin \alpha = \frac{y}{r}$ $\csc \alpha = \frac{r}{y}$

$\cos \alpha = \frac{x}{r}$ $\sec \alpha = \frac{r}{x}$

$\tan \alpha = \frac{y}{x}$ $\cot \alpha = \frac{x}{y}$

Notice from the diagram that α is in Quadrant II, where $x < 0$ and $y > 0$. (r is always positive.) Therefore, sin α and csc α are the only two ratios that are positive in Quadrant II. All the other ratios are negative. This is true for all second-quadrant angles. The same kind of reasoning can be used to show that all the ratios for a first quadrant angle are positive. Here is something that you've seen before: a summary of which trig ratios are positive in the four quadrants:

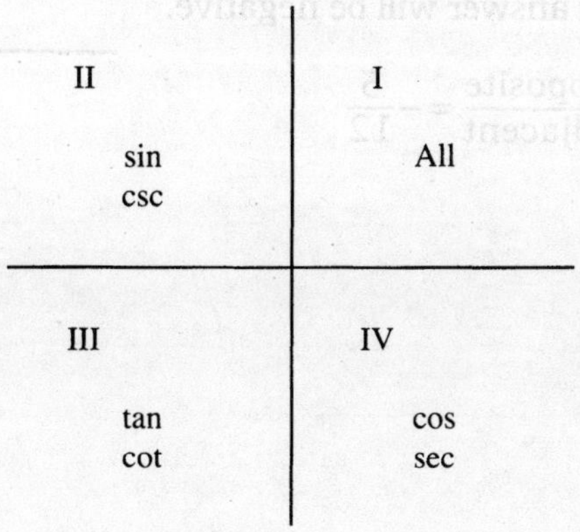

**Here is a mnemonic to help you remember the signs of ratios in the four quadrants. Starting at Quadrant I: All Students Take Courses. ASTC. All, sine, tan, cosine. Note: ASTC tells you which ratios are positive. All other ratios are negative. This means that in Quadrant I, <u>A</u>ll the ratios are positive.
In Quadrant II, <u>S</u>ine and csc are positive.
In Quadrant III, <u>T</u>an and cot are positive.
In Quadrant IV, the <u>C</u>os and sec are positive.**

When you find a trig ratio, figure it out for the reference angle; then affix the correct quadrant sign.

For example, tan 120° = –tan 60° (See figure below left.)
cos 220° = –cos 40° (See figure below right.)

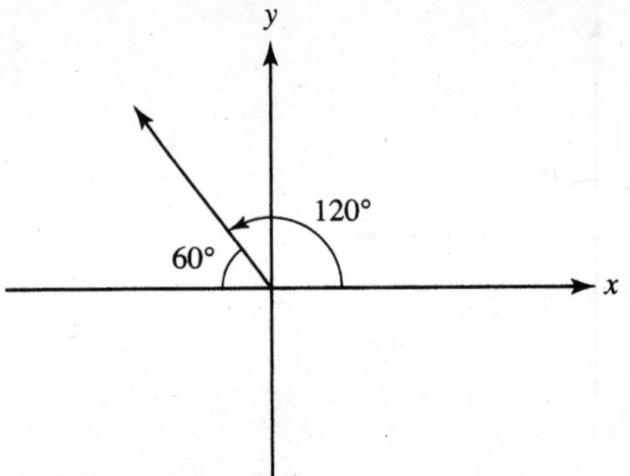

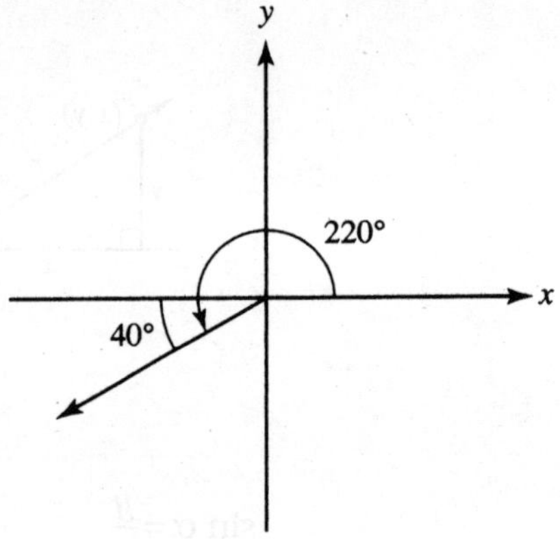

Example 10

If $\cos\theta = \frac{12}{13}$, and $\frac{3\pi}{2} \le \theta < 2\pi$, then $\tan\theta = ?$

(A) $-\frac{5}{13}$ (B) $-\frac{12}{5}$ (C) $-\frac{5}{12}$ (D) $\frac{5}{12}$

Solution: (C) Draw a picture of the angle in standard position, including the right triangle with lengths 12 and 13 correctly marked. Use the Pythagorean theorem to find the missing length, 5. You are required to find the tan of an angle in the fourth quadrant, so your answer will be negative.

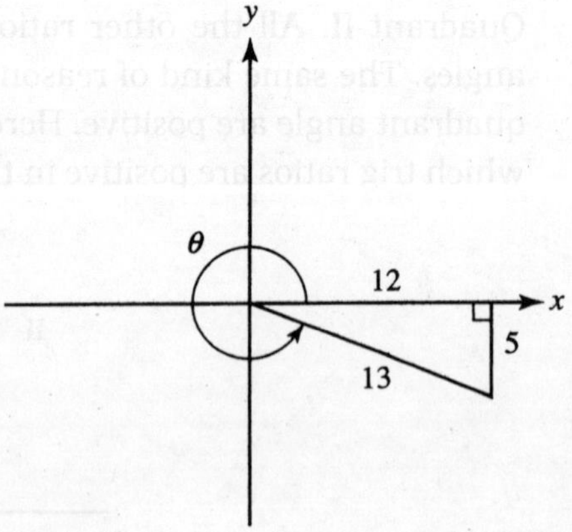

$$\tan\theta = -\frac{\text{opposite}}{\text{adjacent}} = -\frac{5}{12}$$

The Unit Circle 单位圆

The unit circle, which has a radius equal to 1, provides a useful way of finding the sine and cosine of any angle whose vertex is the center of the circle. For example, consider 60°, as shown below in a unit circle.

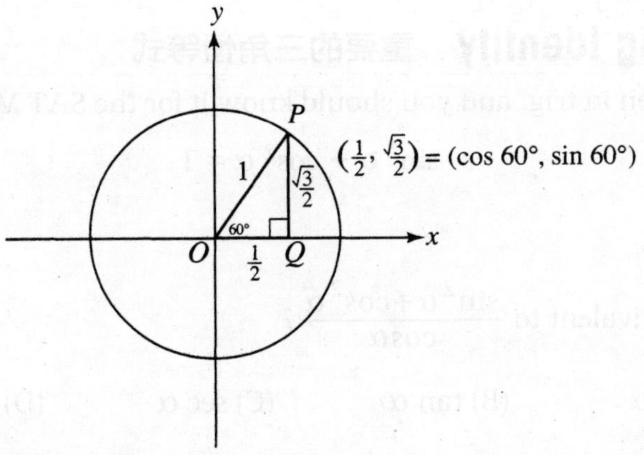

Point P is on the terminal side of the angle and also on the unit circle. $\triangle POQ$ is a 30°–60°–90° triangle, giving the lengths as shown. The x- and y-coordinates provide cos 60° and sin 60°, respectively.

In general, if a point on the terminal side of an angle θ is also on the unit circle, then the coordinates of the point (x, y) are equivalent to $(\cos\theta, \sin\theta)$. This is because $\cos\theta = \frac{x}{1} = x$ and $\sin\theta = \frac{y}{1} = y$. Coordinates on the unit circle, therefore, give a way to see the sine and cosine of an angle at a glance.

Here are some familiar angles, in radians, with their $(\cos\theta, \sin\theta)$ values:

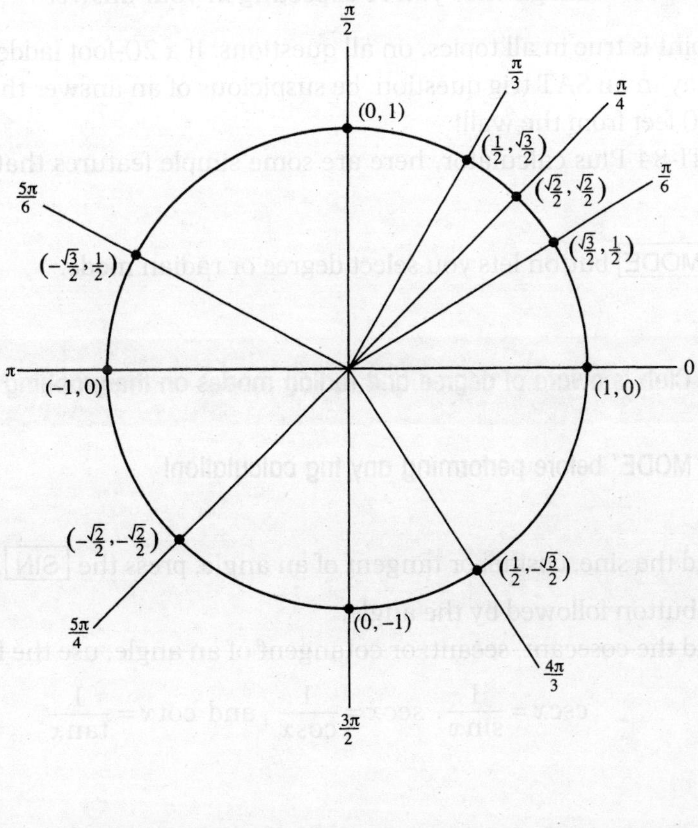

From this unit circle, you can see, for example, that $\cos 0 = 1$, $\sin 0 = 0$, $\cos\frac{\pi}{3} = \frac{1}{2}$, $\sin\frac{\pi}{3} = \frac{\sqrt{3}}{2}$, $\cos\pi = -1$, $\sin\pi = 0$, $\cos\frac{5\pi}{6} = -\frac{\sqrt{3}}{2}$, $\cos\frac{5\pi}{4} = -\frac{\sqrt{2}}{2}$, $\sin\frac{5\pi}{4} = -\frac{\sqrt{2}}{2}$, and so on.

Important Trig Identity 重要的三角恒等式

This comes up often in trig, and you should know it for the SAT Math Test:

$$\sin^2\alpha + \cos^2\alpha = 1$$

Example 11

Which is equivalent to $\dfrac{\sin^2\alpha + \cos^2\alpha}{\cos\alpha}$?

(A) $\sin\alpha$ (B) $\tan\alpha$ (C) $\sec\alpha$ (D) $\csc\alpha$

Solution: (C)

$$\frac{\sin^2\alpha + \cos^2\alpha}{\cos\alpha} = \frac{1}{\cos\alpha} = \sec\alpha$$

Trig and the Graphing Calculator 三角函数和图表计算器

Your graphing calculator allows you to find the values of trig ratios and the angles that correspond to given ratios. At all times you must be aware of

- Whether you're in degree or radian mode
- What order of magnitude you're expecting in your answer

The second point is true in all topics, on all questions. If a 20-foot ladder leans against a wall, as it may in an SAT trig question, be suspicious of an answer that tells you the ladder is 1,000 feet from the wall!

For the TI-84 Plus calculator, here are some simple features that are massively helpful.

- The MODE button lets you select degree or radian mode.

The 1600 Club is aware of degree and radian modes on the graphing calculator.

Think "MODE" before performing any trig calculation!

- To find the sine, cosine, or tangent of an angle, press the SIN, COS, or TAN button followed by the angle.
- To find the cosecant, secant, or cotangent of an angle, use the facts that

$$\csc x = \frac{1}{\sin x},\ \sec x = \frac{1}{\cos x},\ \text{and}\ \cot x = \frac{1}{\tan x}$$

- To find an angle whose sine, cosine, or tangent value is given, you need to use one of the inverse trig functions: $\sin^{-1}$, $\cos^{-1}$, or $\tan^{-1}$, respectively. Think of $\sin^{-1} x$ as "an angle whose sine is x."

Example 12

If the value to the nearest thousandth of $\cos\theta$ is -0.892, which of the following could be true about θ?

(A) $0° \le \theta < 60°$ (C) $120° \le \theta < 180°$
(B) $60° \le \theta < 90°$ (D) $300° \le \theta < 360°$

Solution: (C)

Method I: Logic

Since the cosine is negative, θ must lie in the second or third quadrants. Choice (C) is the only third-quadrant choice.

Method II: Graphing Calculator

Put your calculator in degree mode. You want to find an angle whose cosine is -0.892. Press [2ND] [COS] [(–)] 0.892 [ENTER], and you will get 153.1256519. This is an angle between 120° and 180°, so you should select choice (C).

You didn't waste time using your calculator to find θ, did you?

COMPLEX NUMBERS 复数

Here are some facts about complex numbers that you should know for the SAT Math Test:

- $i = \sqrt{-1}$
- $i^2 = -1$
- $(1 + 1)(1 - i) = 1 - i^2 = 1 - (-1) = 2$
- The standard form of a complex number is $a + bi$, where a and b are real numbers.

When adding or subtracting complex numbers, collect like terms and express the result in standard form.

For example, $(3 - 2i) - (-4 + 5i) = 3 - 2i + 4 - 5i = 7 - 7i$.

When multiplying complex numbers, use the distributive law or binomial multiplication and express the result in standard form.

For example, $(3 - 2i)(-4 + 5i) = -12 + 15i + 8i - 10i^2 = -12 + 23i + 10 = -2 + 23i$.

When dividing complex numbers, you need to get the i term out of the denominator, so you can write the result in standard form.

For example, to simplify $\frac{i}{2-i}$, multiply the fraction by $\frac{2+i}{2+i}$. This produces a difference of perfect squares in the denominator, which eliminates the i term as follows:

$$\frac{i}{2-i}\cdot\frac{2+i}{2+i} = \frac{2i+i^2}{4-i^2} = \frac{-1+2i}{4-(-1)} = \frac{-1+2i}{5} = -\frac{1}{5}+\frac{2}{5}i$$

Example 13

$3i(1-i)$?

(A) $3+3i$ (B) $3-3i$ (C) $6i$ (D) 6

Solution: (A)
Multiply, using the distributive property, then use the fact that $i^2=-1$:

$$3i(1-i)=3i-3i^2$$
$$=3i-3(-1)$$
$$=3i+3 \text{ or } 3+3i$$

PRACTICE TEST QUESTIONS 练习测试题

1. A rectangular box with length 22 inches, width 5 inches, and height 5 inches is to be packed with steel balls of radius 2 inches in such a way that the centers of the balls are collinear. What is the maximum number of balls that can fit into the box, provided that no balls should protrude from the box?

(A) 0 (B) 5 (C) 6 (D) 10

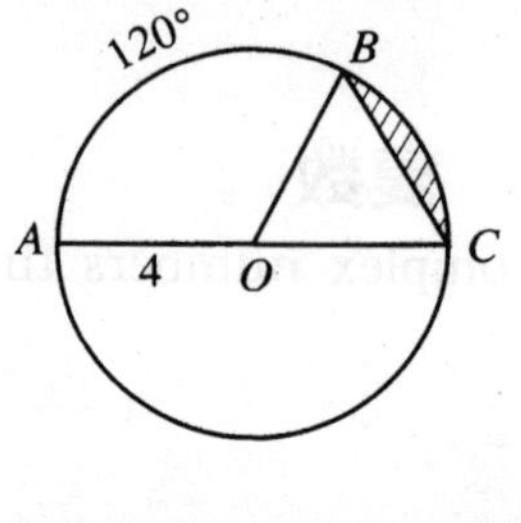

2. In the diagram above, the circle has center O and diameter $\overline{AC}$. The measure of arc AB is 120°, and $AO=4$. What is the area of the shaded region?

(A) $\frac{16\pi}{3}-8\sqrt{3}$ (B) $\frac{8\pi}{3}-2\sqrt{3}$ (C) $\frac{8\pi}{3}-4\sqrt{3}$ (D) $\frac{8\pi}{3}-8\sqrt{3}$

3. In the xy-plane, a circle with center (6, 0) is tangent to the line $y=x$. What is the radius of the circle?

(A) $2\sqrt{6}$ (B) $2\sqrt{3}$ (C) $3\sqrt{2}$ (D) 3

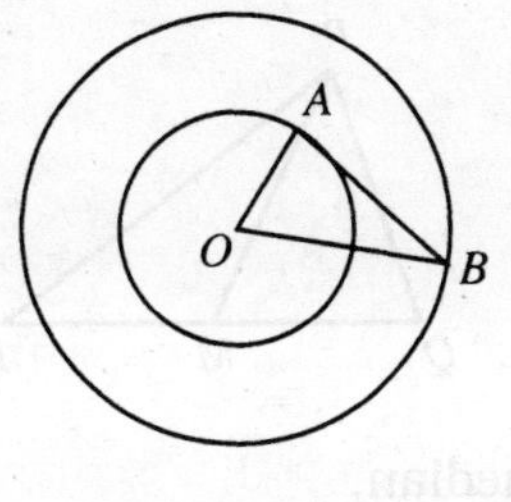

Note: Figure not drawn to scale.

4. The figure above shows two circles, each with center O. Line segment $\overline{AB}$ is tangent to the smaller circle. If $OA = 5$ and $AB = 12$, what is the ratio of the area of the smaller circle to the area of the larger circle?

(A) 5 : 13 (B) 5 : 12 (C) 25 : 169 (D) 25 : 144

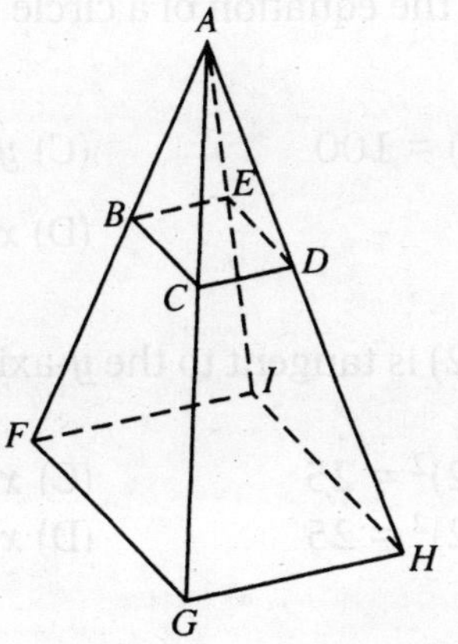

5. The pyramid in the figure above has square base $FGHI$, and all triangular faces are congruent. The base $BCDE$ of the small pyramid is also square, and is parallel to $FGHI$. If the ratio of the area of square $BCDE$ to the area of square $FGHI$ is 1 : 4, what is the ratio of the volume of the small pyramid to the volume of the large pyramid?

(A) 1 : 2 (B) 1 : 3 (C) 1 : 4 (D) 1 : 8

6. $2i^4 - i^6 = ?$

(A) $i - 1$ (B) $i + 1$ (C) -3 (D) 3

7. A rectangular aquarium 3 ft × 2 ft × 1 ft is $\frac{2}{3}$ full of water. In cubic feet, how much water is in the tank?

(A) $14\frac{2}{3}$ (B) 11 (C) $7\frac{1}{3}$ (D) 4

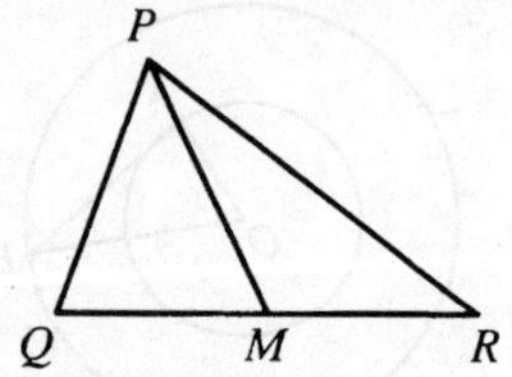

8. In $\triangle PQR$ above, $\overline{PM}$ is a median.

Which of the following assertions is justifiable from the given information?

I. $\angle QPM$ is congruent to $\angle RPM$.
II. perimeter of $\triangle PQM$ equals perimeter of $\triangle PRM$.
III. area of $\triangle PQM$ equals area of $\triangle PRM$.

(A) I only (B) II only (C) III only (D) II and III only

9. Which of the following is the equation of a circle in the standard (x,y) coordinate plane?

(A) $(x-3)+(y+6)=100$
(B) $x^2=y^2+25$
(C) $y=x^2+25$
(D) $x^2=36-y^2$

10. A circle with center $(5,-2)$ is tangent to the y-axis. What is the equation of the circle?

(A) $(x-5)^2+(y+2)^2=25$
(B) $(x+5)^2+(y-2)^2=25$
(C) $x^2+y^2=25$
(D) $x^2+y^2=5$

11. The center pole of a tent is 8 feet tall, and a side of the tent is 12 feet long, as shown below.

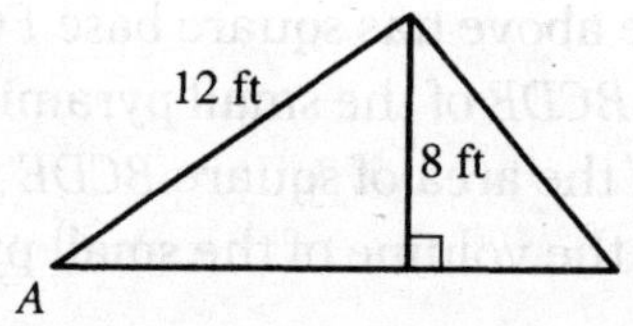

Which of the following expressions could be used to find the measure of $\angle A$?

(A) $\cos A=\frac{8}{12}$ (B) $\sin A=\frac{8}{12}$ (C) $\tan A=\frac{8}{12}$ (D) $\sin A=\frac{4\sqrt{5}}{12}$

12. Which of the following expressions is *not* equal to $\sin(-135°)$?

(A) $\sin 135°$ (B) $\cos 135°$ (C) $-\cos(-45°)$ (D) $\sin 225°$

13. For the angle α shown below, which of the following statements is true?

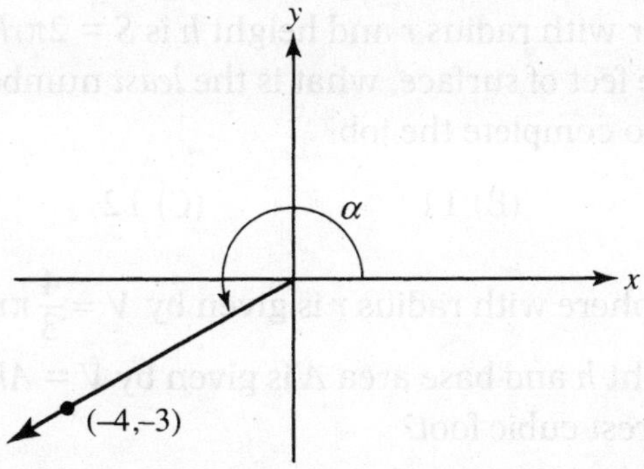

(A) $\sin\alpha = -\frac{3}{5}$ (B) $\cos\alpha = \frac{4}{5}$ (C) $\tan\alpha = -\frac{3}{4}$ (D) $\cot\alpha = -\frac{4}{3}$

14. If $\cos\frac{2\pi}{3} = \sin\alpha$, which could be α?

(A) $\frac{\pi}{6}$ (B) $-\frac{\pi}{6}$ (C) $\frac{2\pi}{3}$ (D) $-\frac{2\pi}{3}$

Use the following information to answer questions 15–17.

A grain silo, shown below, is in the shape of a cylinder with a half sphere on top. The radius of the base of the cylinder is 10 feet, and the height of the cylindrical part is 60 feet, as marked.

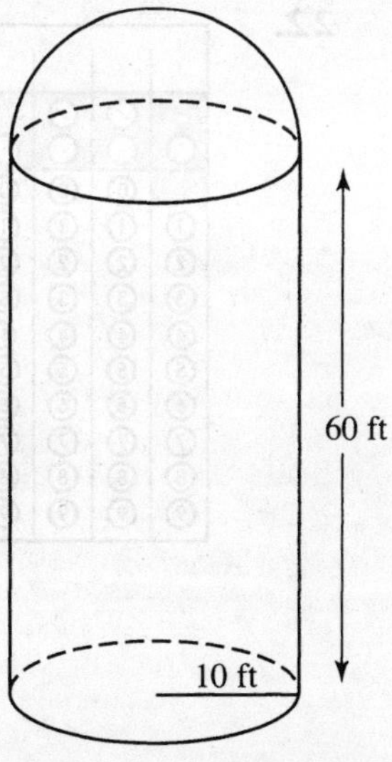

15. The silo, when full, can hold 2,100 bushels of wheat. On each of five consecutive days, the farmer sells 150 bushels from an initially full silo. After these sales, approximately what percent of the silo's capacity is still filled with wheat?

(A) 16 (B) 36 (C) 45 (D) 64

16. The farmer who owns the silo plans to apply a coat of paint to the cylindrical exterior. This does not include the spherical top. A formula for the lateral surface area S of a cylinder with radius r and height h is $S = 2\pi rh$. If one can of paint covers 300 square feet of surface, what is the *least* number of cans that the farmer must buy to complete the job?

(A) 10 (B) 11 (C) 12 (D) 13

17. The volume of a sphere with radius r is given by $V = \frac{4}{3}\pi r^3$, and the volume of a cylinder with height h and base area A is given by $V = Ah$. What is the volume of the silo to the nearest cubic foot?

(A) 5,864 (B) 7,959 (C) 20,944 (D) 23,038

Questions 18–24 are grid-in questions.

18.

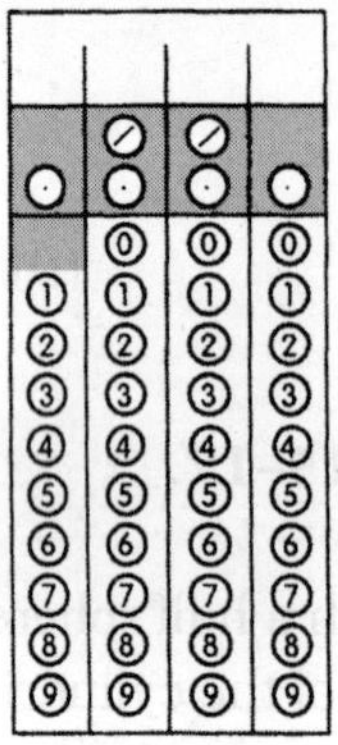

19.

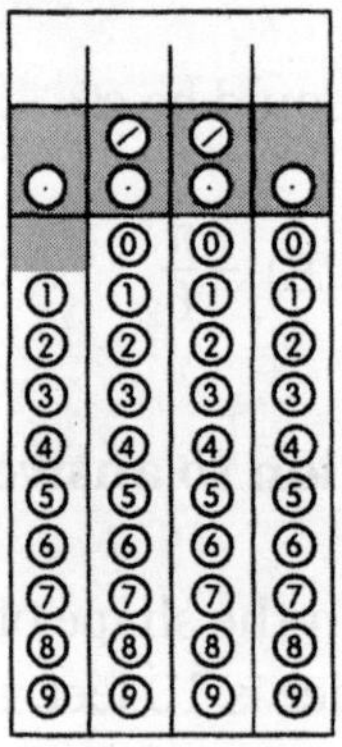

20.

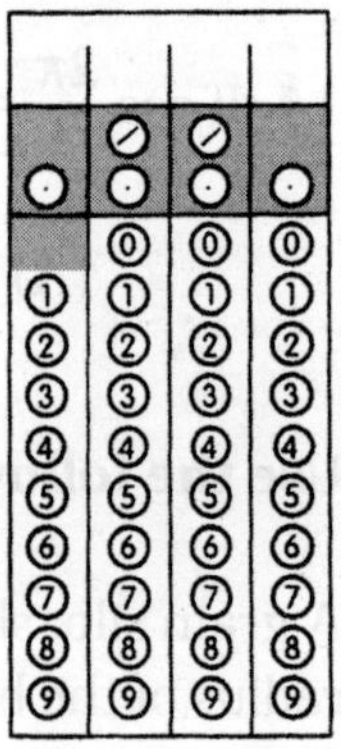

21.

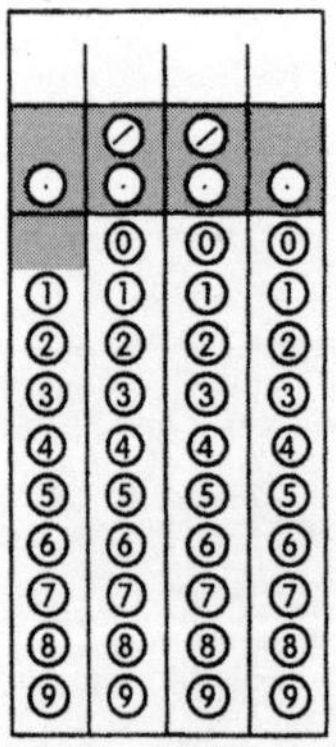

22.

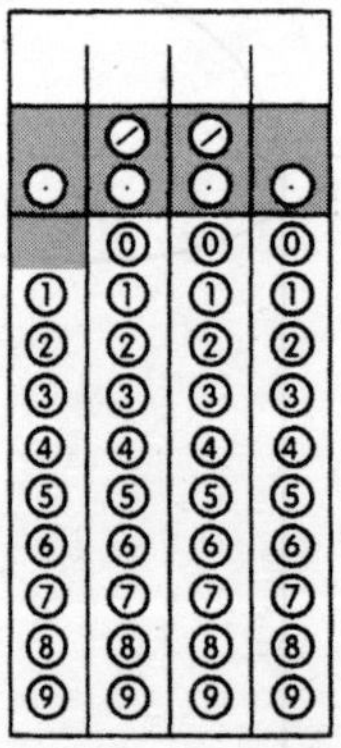

23.

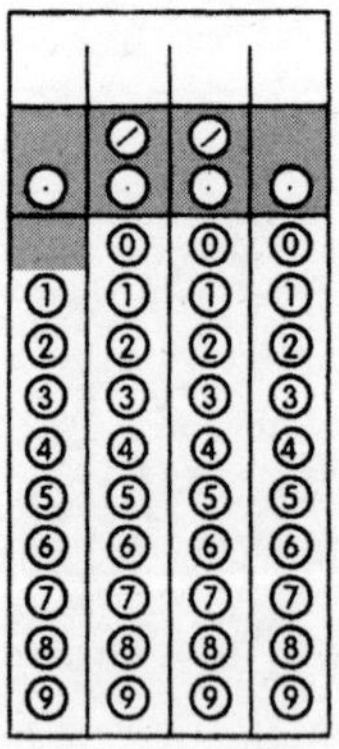

24.

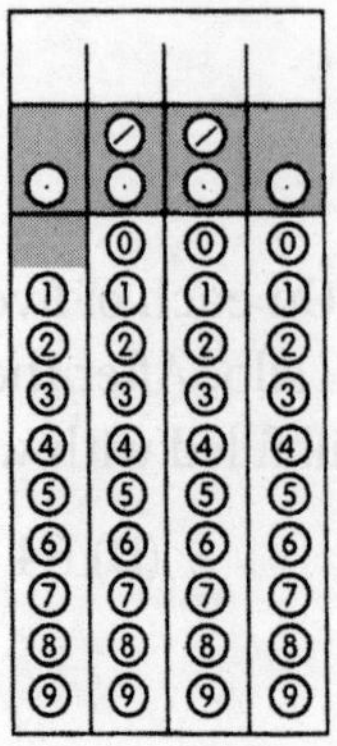

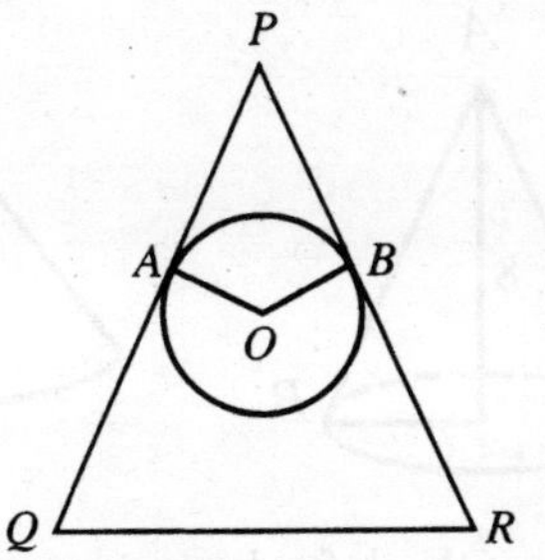

18. In the figure shown above, $\angle Q$ measures 70°, $\overline{PQ} \cong \overline{PR}$, and $\overline{PQ}$ and $\overline{PR}$ are tangent to the circle with center O at points A and B. Find, in degrees, the measure of $\angle AOB$.

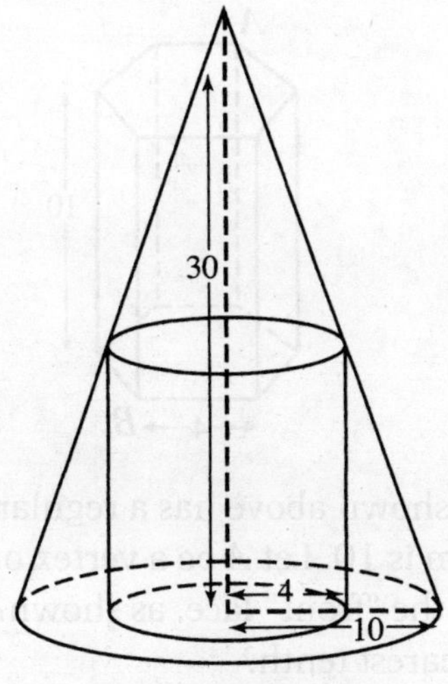

Note: Figure not drawn to scale.

19. A cylinder is inscribed in a cone with height 30 and base radius 10, as shown in the above figure. If the radius of the base of the cylinder is 4, what is the height of the cylinder?

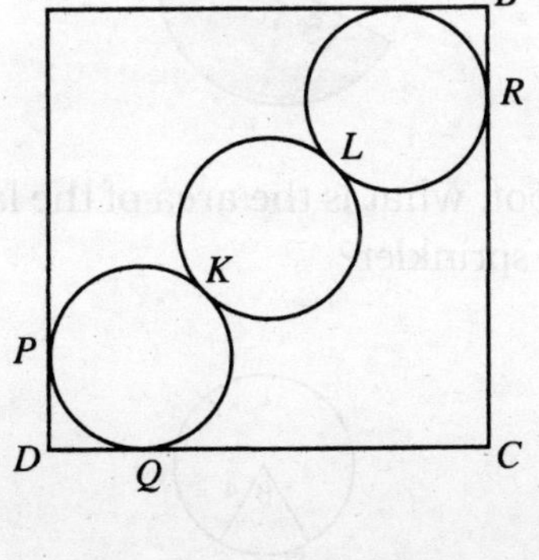

20. In the diagram above, $ABCD$ is a square. The circles, whose centers lie on $\overline{BD}$, are congruent to each other. The sides of the square are tangent to the outer circles at P, Q, R, and S, and the circles are tangent to each other at K and L. If the radius of each circle is 1 inch, what is the area, to the nearest square inch, of the square?

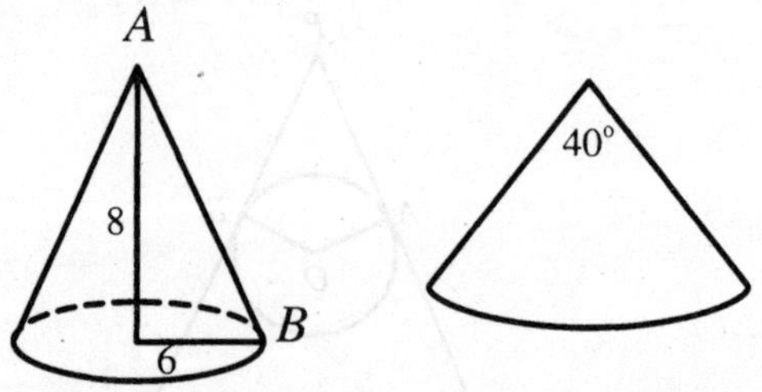

21. When the cone shown on the left above is cut straight up the side along $\overline{AB}$ and laid down flat, the resulting plane figure is shown on the right. The area of this figure represents the lateral surface area of the given cone. What is the lateral surface area of this cone, to the nearest integer?

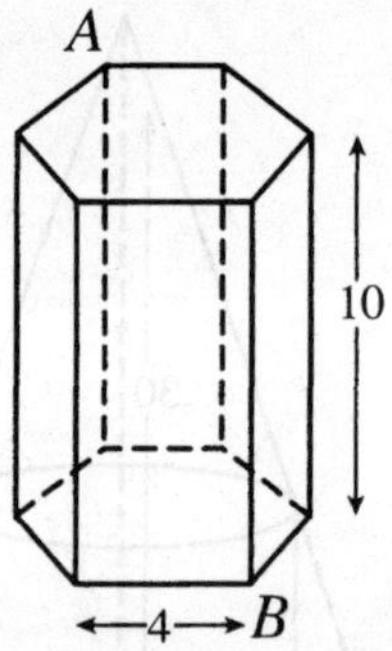

22. The hexagonal prism shown above has a regular hexagon with side 4 as base. The height of the prism is 10. Let A be a vertex on the "back" face of the prism, while B is a vertex on the "front" face, as shown. What is the length of the diagonal $\overline{AB}$, to the nearest tenth?

23. Jack waters his lawn with a sprinkler that sprays water in a circular pattern. The maximum reach of the sprinkler is 15 feet, and the sprinkler head rotates through an angle of 300°, as shown in the diagram below. The sprinkler head is represented at point O.

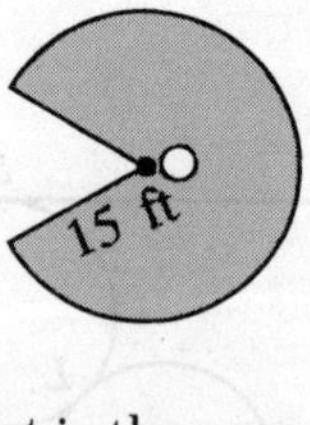

To the nearest square foot, what is the area of the lawn (the shaded area) that receives water from the sprinkler?

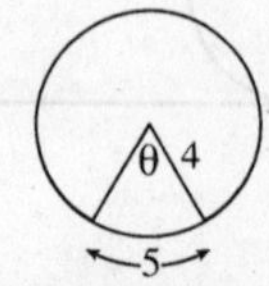

Note: Figure not drawn to scale.

24. In a circle of radius 4, two radii cut off an arc of length 5, as shown above. To the nearest degree, find the acute angle θ formed by the radii.

Answers and Explanations 答案与解析

The difficulty level for each question is specified in parentheses.

1. B (M)	**7.** D (M)	**13.** A (M)	**19.** 18 (H)
2. C (M)	**8.** C (M)	**14.** B (M)	**20.** 23 (H)
3. C (H)	**9.** D (E)	**15.** D (H)	**21.** 35 (H)
4. C (M)	**10.** A (M)	**16.** D (H)	**22.** 12.8 (H)
5. D (H)	**11.** B (M)	**17.** C (H)	**23.** 589 (H)
6. D (M)	**12.** A (M)	**18.** 140 (M)	**24.** 72 (M)

18.

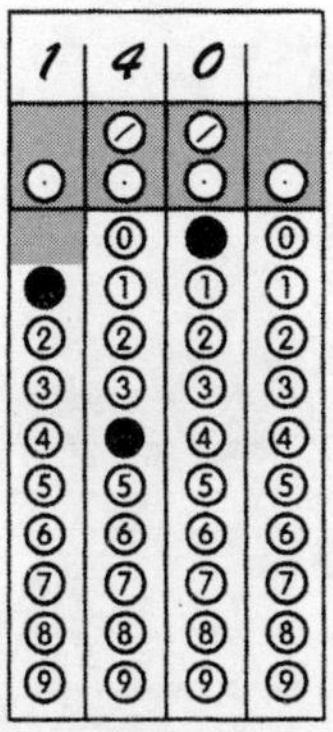

19.

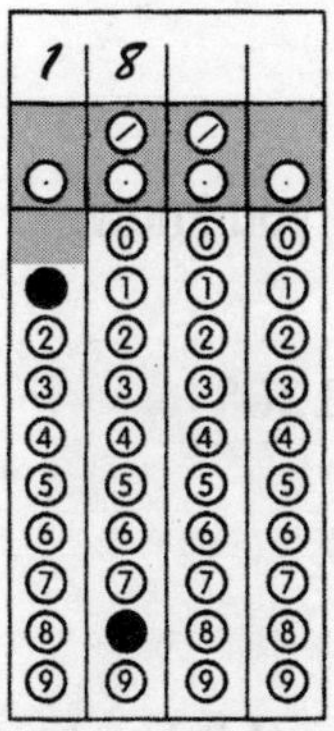

20.

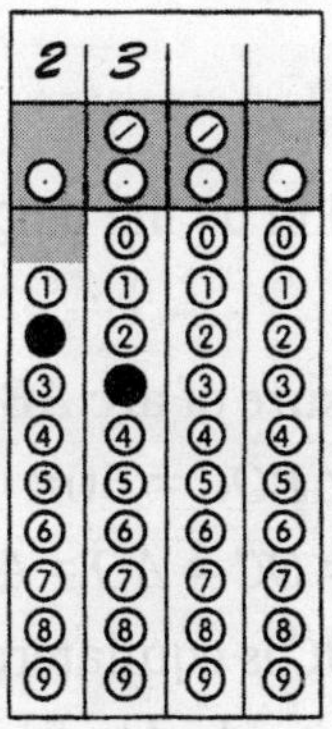

21.

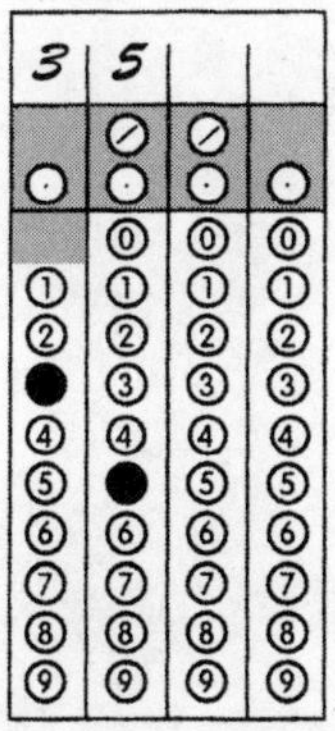

22.

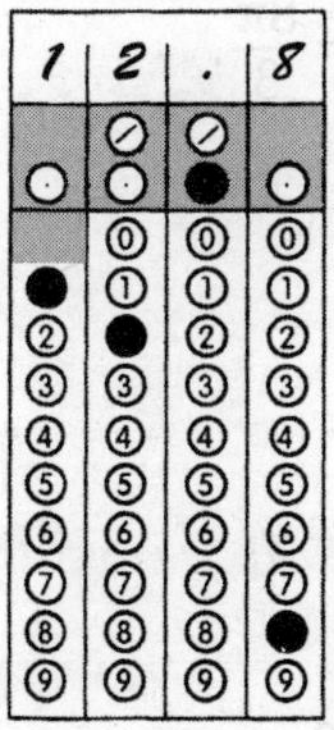

23.

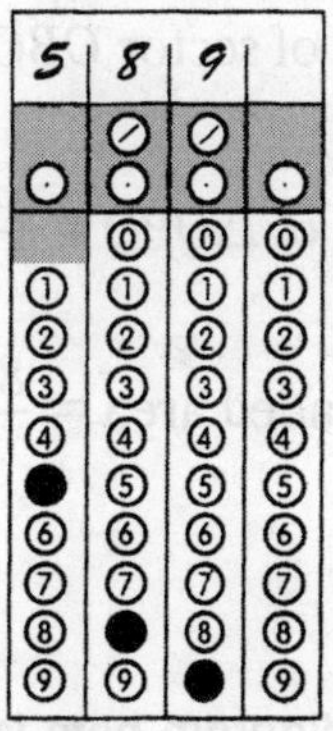

24.

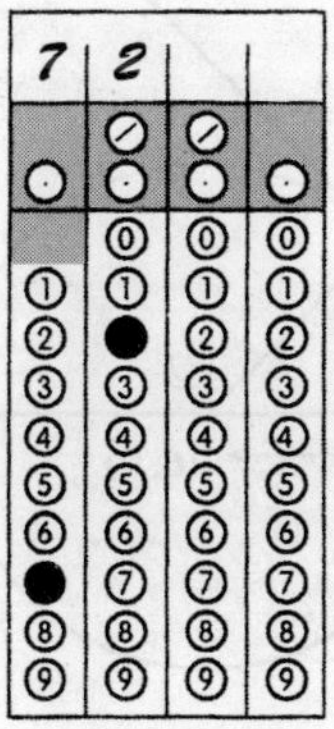

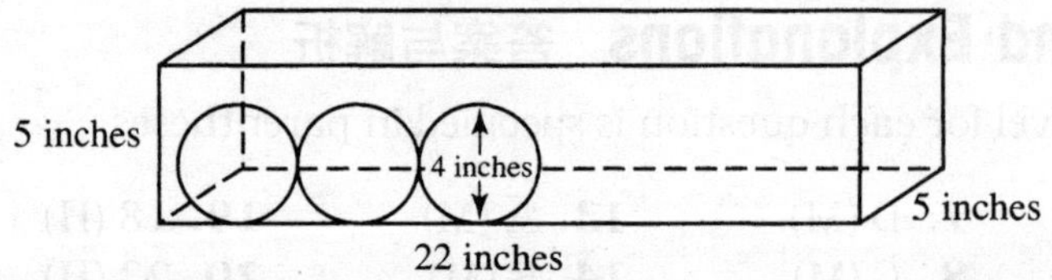

1. **(B)** Some visualization is needed here. This is a long, skinny box, as shown above. The diameter of each ball is 4 inches, so the balls will need to be packed one by one, lengthwise, to fit into the box. Since this is a question about length, not volume, reduce the question to: How many 4-inch diameters will fit into the 22-inch length? The answer is $\frac{22}{4}$ = 5, with a bit left over. There is not enough room to squeeze another ball in, so the answer is 5.

2. **(C)**

Fill in on the diagram everything you know.

Measure of arc $AB = m\angle AOB = 120°$
$\therefore m\angle BOC = 60°$.
$OB = OC = AO = 4$ (radii).
$\triangle OBC$ is equilateral.
When asked to find a shaded area, think subtraction:
Shaded area = area of sector OBC – area $\triangle OBC$.

Area of sector $OBC = \frac{60}{360}\pi(4)^2 = \frac{8\pi}{3}$.

Area of $\triangle OPQ = \frac{s^2\sqrt{3}}{4} = 4\sqrt{3}$.

$\therefore$ Shaded area $= \frac{8\pi}{3} - 4\sqrt{3}$.

3. **(C)**

A diagram here is crucial, and be sure to include the radius to the point of tangency.

The key to this problem is seeing that $\triangle PQO$ is a 45°–45°–90° triangle, since the line $y = x$ makes a 45° angle with each axis.

$\therefore PO = \frac{6}{\sqrt{2}} = 3\sqrt{2}$

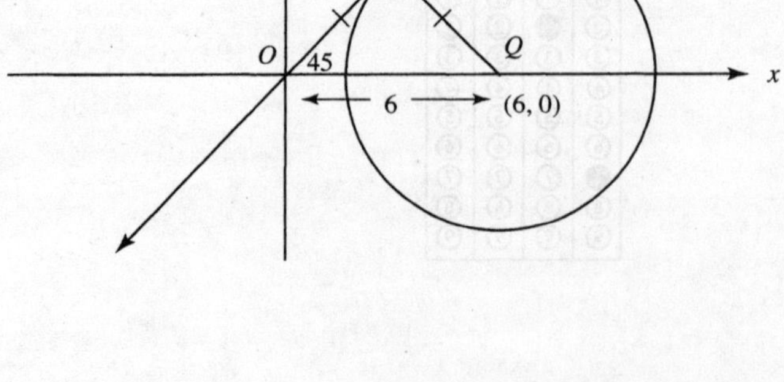

4. (C) By the tangent-radius theorem, $\angle A$ is a right angle.
Using the Pythagorean theorem in $\triangle ABC$ gives $OB = 13$.

$$\frac{\text{Radius of small circle}}{\text{Radius of large circle}} = \frac{5}{13}$$

$$\therefore \frac{\text{Area of small circle}}{\text{Area of large circle}} = \left(\frac{5}{13}\right)^2 = \frac{25}{169} = 25:169$$

5. (D)

$$\frac{\text{Area of small square}}{\text{Area of large square}} = \frac{1}{4}$$

$$\therefore \frac{\text{Side of small square}}{\text{Side of large square}} = \frac{1}{2}$$

$$\therefore \frac{\text{Volume of small pyramid}}{\text{Volume of large pyramid}} = \left(\frac{1}{2}\right)^3 = \frac{1}{8} = 1:8$$

6. (D) Remember that $i^2 = -1$.
Then $i^3 = (i^2)i = -i$ and $i^4 = (i^3)i = (-i)i = -i^2 = -(-1) = 1$

$$\begin{aligned}\therefore 2i^4 - i^6 &= 2(1) - (i^4)(i^2) \\ &= 2 - (1)(-1) \\ &= 3\end{aligned}$$

7. (D) Volume of rectangular prism = $(3)(2)(1) = 6$ cubic feet.

Two-thirds full means that the volume of water = $\frac{2}{3}(6) = 4$ cubic feet.

8. (C) Assertion I is wrong because in general a median does not bisect the angle at its vertex. Assertion II will only work if $PQ = PR$, which is not necessarily true. (Notice that two out of the three sides of the inside triangles are equal: the common median $\overline{PM}$, and the bases $\overline{QM}$ and $\overline{RM}$.) Assertion III is true because the area of each triangle depends only on the base and height for each. Because $\overline{PM}$ is a median, the bases $\overline{QM}$ and $\overline{RM}$ are the same. Also, the altitude from P to $\overleftrightarrow{QR}$ is the same for each triangle. Therefore the areas are the same.

9. (D) The standard form for a circle with radius r and centered at the origin is $x^2 + y^2 = r^2$. If the circle is centered at (h, k), the standard form is $(x-h)^2 + (y-k)^2 = r^2$. The equation in choice (D) can be written as $x^2 + y^2 = 36$. Eliminate choice (A) because it has no squared terms. Eliminate choice (B) because it can be written as $x^2 - y^2 = 25$, which has the wrong sign on the left-hand side (and is the equation of a hyperbola). Eliminate choice (C) because it does not have a y^2 term.

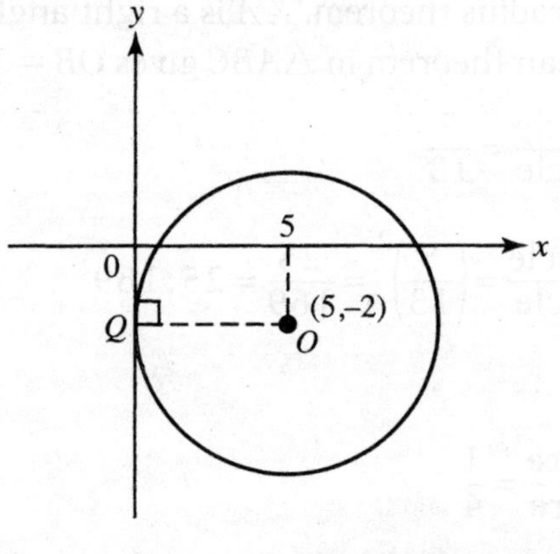

10. (A) $\overline{QO}$ is a radius of the circle, since O is the center and Q is on the circle. The length of $\overline{QO}$ equals 5, the x-coordinate of O. Thus, the radius is 5. The equation of a circle with center (5,–2) and radius 5 is $(x-5)^2 + (y-(-2))^2 = (5)^2$, which equals $(x-5)^2 + (y+2)^2 = 25$.

11. (B) In the diagram, 8 feet is opposite $\angle A$, and 12 feet is the hypotenuse.

$$\sin A = \frac{\text{opposite}}{\text{hypotenuse}} = \frac{8}{12}$$

12. (A) Note that each of the angles in the answer choices has 45° as a reference angle. Also, $\sin 45° = \cos 45° = \frac{1}{\sqrt{2}}$

Therefore, each answer choice is equal to plus or minus $\frac{1}{\sqrt{2}}$.

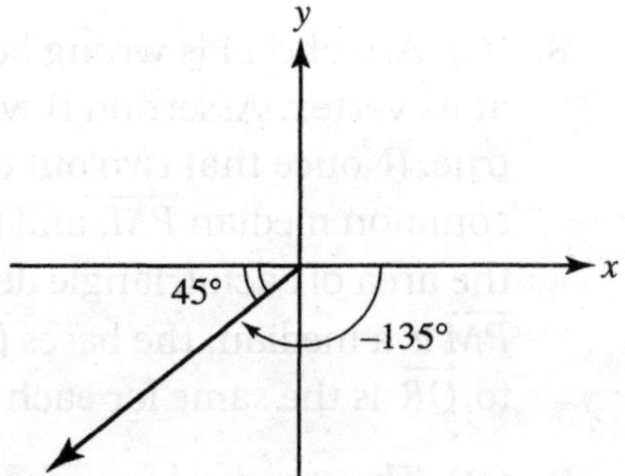

The question boils down to realizing that $\sin(-135°)$ is negative because $-135°$ is in the third quadrant. You must therefore find the answer choice that is positive.
Choice (A), $\sin 135° = \sin 45°$, is positive because 135° is in Quadrant II. This is the correct answer. All of the other answer choices represent a negative number:
(B): $\cos 135° = -\cos 45°$ (cosine in Quadrant II negative)
(C): $-\cos(-45°) = -\cos 45°$ (cosine in Quadrant IV positive)
(D): $\sin 225° = -\sin 45°$ (sine in Quadrant III negative)

13. (A) On the picture that's given, draw the right triangle with reference angle β. Remember, only the tan and cot are positive in the third quadrant (no other trig functions are), so you can eliminate choices (B), (C), and (D).

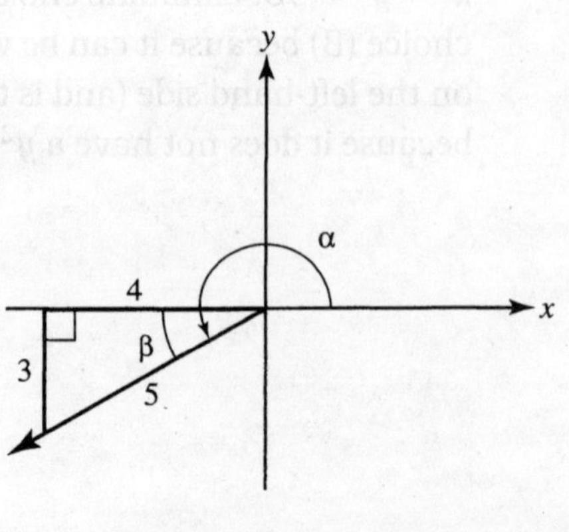

$$\sin\alpha = -\sin\beta = -\frac{\text{opposite}}{\text{hypotenuse}} = -\frac{3}{5}$$

14. (B)

$$\cos\frac{2\pi}{3} = \sin\left(\frac{\pi}{2}-\frac{2\pi}{3}\right) = \sin\left(\frac{3\pi}{6}-\frac{4\pi}{6}\right) = \sin\left(-\frac{\pi}{6}\right)$$

$$\therefore \alpha = -\frac{\pi}{6}$$

15. (D)

Method 1: Arithmetic and Algebra

150 bushels a day for 5 days means that a total of 750 bushels were sold. The amount of wheat remaining is 2,100 – 750 = 1,350 bushels. The problem now boils down to: 1,350 is what percent of 2,100?

$$\frac{1{,}350}{2{,}100}=\frac{x}{100}\Rightarrow x=\frac{135{,}000}{2{,}100}\approx 64$$

Method II: Quick Estimation

750 is a little more than $\frac{1}{3}$ of 2,100. This means that a little less than $\frac{2}{3}$, or $66\frac{2}{3}\%$ is left. The answer closest to this is 64%.

16. (D)

$$\text{Surface area } S = 2\pi rh$$
$$= 2\pi(10)(60)$$
$$= 1{,}200\pi$$

Number of cans needed = $\frac{1{,}200\pi}{300} = 4\pi$, which is approximately 12.5.

Therefore, 13 cans are needed.

Notice that 4π is a little more than $4 \times 3 = 12$. Don't waste your time using a calculator here!

17. (C)

$$\text{Volume of cylinder } = \pi r^2 h$$
$$= \pi(100)(60)$$
$$= 6{,}000\pi$$

For the sphere you need to realize that its radius is equal to the radius of the base of the cylinder, namely, 10.

$$\text{Volume of half sphere } = \frac{2}{3}\pi r^3$$
$$= \frac{2}{3}\pi(1{,}000)$$
$$= \frac{2{,}000}{3}\pi$$

$$\begin{aligned}\text{Total volume } &= \pi\left(6{,}000+\frac{2{,}000}{3}\right)\\ &= \pi\left(\frac{18{,}000}{3}+\frac{2{,}000}{3}\right)\\ &= \frac{20{,}000}{3}\pi\\ &\approx 21{,}000\end{aligned}$$

Notice that when you get as far as $\frac{20{,}000}{3}\pi$, you should see that this is slightly more than 20,000 (because when you are estimating, the 3 and π "cancel"). A glance at the answer choices will then tell you that choice (C), 20,944, is the correct answer.

18. 140

Jot down everything you know on the diagram.

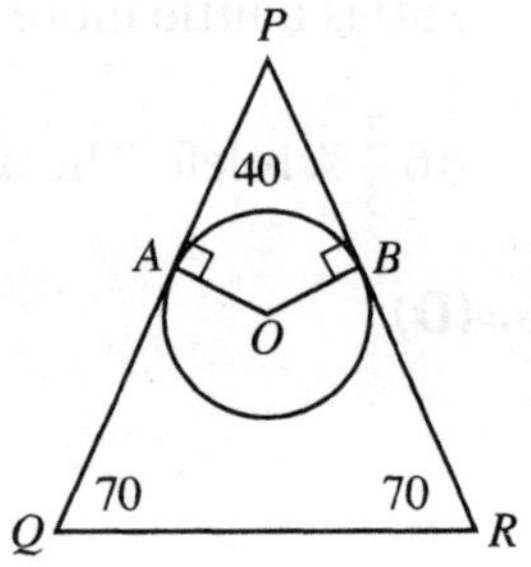

The triangle is isosceles, so the base angles are congruent. Three angles in a triangle are supplementary, so m∠P = 40°. Radii are perpendicular to tangents, so there are right angles at A and B.

The problem is now easy to solve. $PAOB$ is a quadrilateral; therefore the sum of its angles is 360°.

∴ m∠AOB = 360 – (90 + 90 + 40) = 140°.

Grid-in 140.

19. 18 You can reduce this three-dimensional setup to a question about similar triangles in a plane. If you draw in segment $\overline{AB}$, as shown below, you should see that $\triangle PAB$ is similar to $\triangle PQR$ (both contain a right angle and ∠P).

Let h be the height of the cylinder.

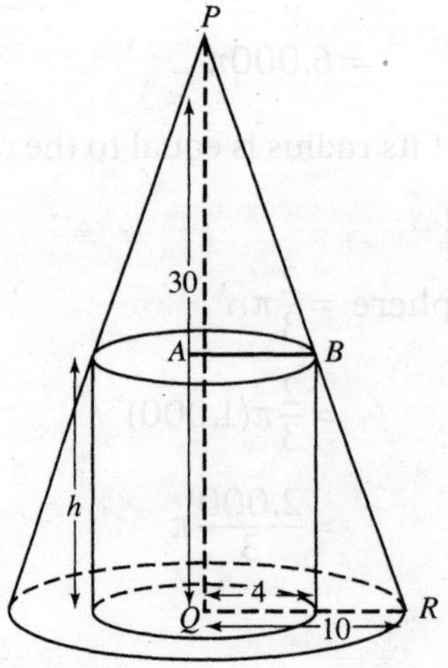

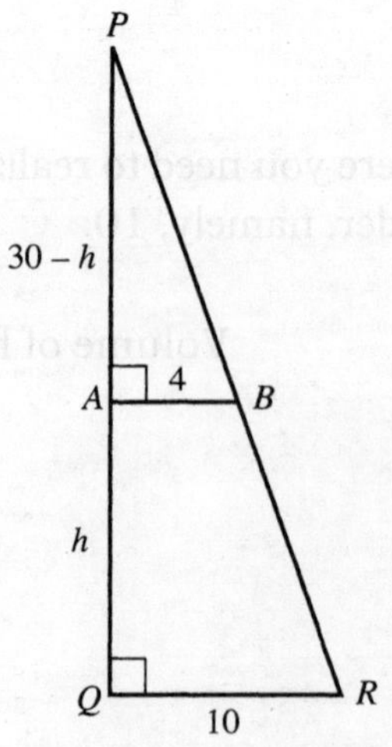

Then:

$$\frac{PA}{PQ}=\frac{AB}{QR}\Rightarrow\frac{30-h}{30}=\frac{4}{10}=\frac{2}{5}$$

Cross-multiply to solve for h:

$$5(30-h)=60\Rightarrow h=18$$

Grid-in 18.

20. 23

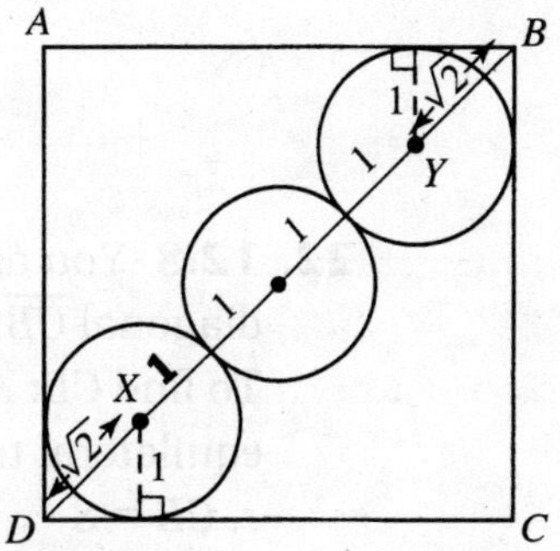

Length of diagonal $\overline{BD}=XY+XD+YB$.
$XY=4\times\text{radius}=4$.
Both $\overline{XD}$ and $\overline{YB}$ are in 45°–45°–90° triangles, and each has length $\sqrt{2}$.
$\therefore BD=4+2\sqrt{2}$.
You are asked for the area of square $ABCD$.

Method I: One-Half Product of Diagonals

$$\text{Area of } ABCD=\left(\frac{1}{2}\right)(4+2\sqrt{2})(4+2\sqrt{2})$$
$$=(2+\sqrt{2})(4+2\sqrt{2})$$
$$=8+8\sqrt{2}+4$$
$$=12+8\sqrt{2}$$
$$\approx 23$$

Method II: Side Squared
$\triangle DBC$ is a 45°–45°–90° triangle.

$$\therefore \text{If } BD=4+2\sqrt{2},\ DC=\frac{4+2\sqrt{2}}{\sqrt{2}}=\frac{4}{\sqrt{2}}+2=2\sqrt{2}+2.$$

$$\text{Area of square }=(2\sqrt{2}+2)^2=8+4+8\sqrt{2}\approx 23.$$

Grid-in 23.

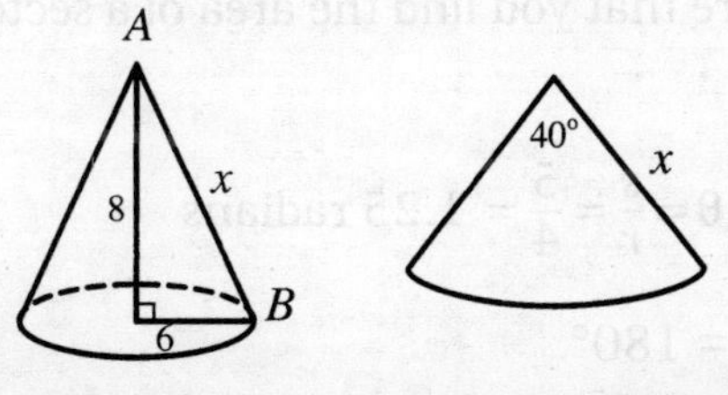

21. 35 First find x. Using the Pythagorean theorem in the right triangle shown, $x=10$. The area is a sector with angle 40°, and radius $x=10$.

$$\text{Area }=\frac{40}{360}\pi(10)^2$$
$$=\frac{100\pi}{9}\approx 35$$

Grid-in 35.

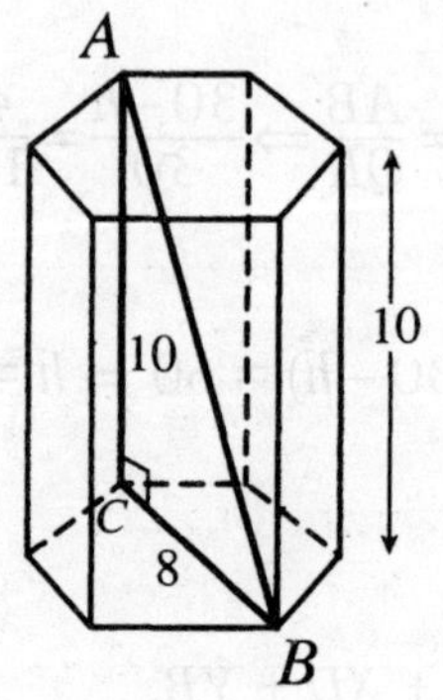

22. 12.8 You are required to find AB. Draw base diagonal $\overline{CB}$, and notice that $\triangle ABC$ is a right triangle.
To find CB: A regular hexagon has 6 congruent equilateral triangles, as shown on the right.
$\therefore CB = 8$
The problem boils down to finding the hypotenuse in $\triangle ABC$.

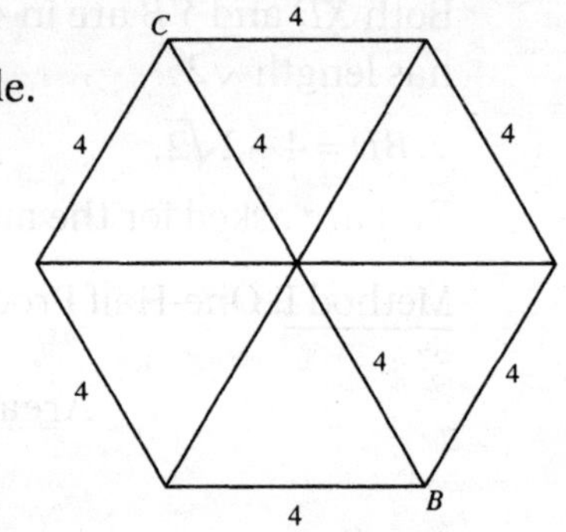

$$AB^2 = 10^2 + 8^2$$
$$= 164$$
$$\therefore AB = \sqrt{164} \approx 12.8$$

Grid-in 12.8.

23. 589

$$\text{Shaded area} = \frac{300}{360}(\text{area of circle})$$
$$= \frac{5}{6}\pi(15)^2$$
$$\approx 589 \text{ sq ft}$$

Grid-in 589.
Compare this problem to question 21. On the face of it, they are quite different. Both, however, require that you find the area of a sector whose angle and radius are given.

24. 72 If θ is in radians, $\theta = \frac{s}{r} = \frac{5}{4} = 1.25$ radians

Recall that π radians = 180°.

$$\therefore 1.25 \text{ radians} = \frac{1.25}{\pi} \cdot 180° = 72°$$

Grid-in 72.

第五部分　PART 5

SAT PRACTICE TEST
SAT练习测试题

ANSWER SHEET
答题纸
Practice Test
练习测试题

Section 1: Reading

1. Ⓐ Ⓑ Ⓒ Ⓓ	14. Ⓐ Ⓑ Ⓒ Ⓓ	27. Ⓐ Ⓑ Ⓒ Ⓓ	40. Ⓐ Ⓑ Ⓒ Ⓓ
2. Ⓐ Ⓑ Ⓒ Ⓓ	15. Ⓐ Ⓑ Ⓒ Ⓓ	28. Ⓐ Ⓑ Ⓒ Ⓓ	41. Ⓐ Ⓑ Ⓒ Ⓓ
3. Ⓐ Ⓑ Ⓒ Ⓓ	16. Ⓐ Ⓑ Ⓒ Ⓓ	29. Ⓐ Ⓑ Ⓒ Ⓓ	42. Ⓐ Ⓑ Ⓒ Ⓓ
4. Ⓐ Ⓑ Ⓒ Ⓓ	17. Ⓐ Ⓑ Ⓒ Ⓓ	30. Ⓐ Ⓑ Ⓒ Ⓓ	43. Ⓐ Ⓑ Ⓒ Ⓓ
5. Ⓐ Ⓑ Ⓒ Ⓓ	18. Ⓐ Ⓑ Ⓒ Ⓓ	31. Ⓐ Ⓑ Ⓒ Ⓓ	44. Ⓐ Ⓑ Ⓒ Ⓓ
6. Ⓐ Ⓑ Ⓒ Ⓓ	19. Ⓐ Ⓑ Ⓒ Ⓓ	32. Ⓐ Ⓑ Ⓒ Ⓓ	45. Ⓐ Ⓑ Ⓒ Ⓓ
7. Ⓐ Ⓑ Ⓒ Ⓓ	20. Ⓐ Ⓑ Ⓒ Ⓓ	33. Ⓐ Ⓑ Ⓒ Ⓓ	46. Ⓐ Ⓑ Ⓒ Ⓓ
8. Ⓐ Ⓑ Ⓒ Ⓓ	21. Ⓐ Ⓑ Ⓒ Ⓓ	34. Ⓐ Ⓑ Ⓒ Ⓓ	47. Ⓐ Ⓑ Ⓒ Ⓓ
9. Ⓐ Ⓑ Ⓒ Ⓓ	22. Ⓐ Ⓑ Ⓒ Ⓓ	35. Ⓐ Ⓑ Ⓒ Ⓓ	48. Ⓐ Ⓑ Ⓒ Ⓓ
10. Ⓐ Ⓑ Ⓒ Ⓓ	23. Ⓐ Ⓑ Ⓒ Ⓓ	36. Ⓐ Ⓑ Ⓒ Ⓓ	49. Ⓐ Ⓑ Ⓒ Ⓓ
11. Ⓐ Ⓑ Ⓒ Ⓓ	24. Ⓐ Ⓑ Ⓒ Ⓓ	37. Ⓐ Ⓑ Ⓒ Ⓓ	50. Ⓐ Ⓑ Ⓒ Ⓓ
12. Ⓐ Ⓑ Ⓒ Ⓓ	25. Ⓐ Ⓑ Ⓒ Ⓓ	38. Ⓐ Ⓑ Ⓒ Ⓓ	51. Ⓐ Ⓑ Ⓒ Ⓓ
13. Ⓐ Ⓑ Ⓒ Ⓓ	26. Ⓐ Ⓑ Ⓒ Ⓓ	39. Ⓐ Ⓑ Ⓒ Ⓓ	52. Ⓐ Ⓑ Ⓒ Ⓓ

Section 2: Writing and Language

1. Ⓐ Ⓑ Ⓒ Ⓓ	12. Ⓐ Ⓑ Ⓒ Ⓓ	23. Ⓐ Ⓑ Ⓒ Ⓓ	34. Ⓐ Ⓑ Ⓒ Ⓓ
2. Ⓐ Ⓑ Ⓒ Ⓓ	13. Ⓐ Ⓑ Ⓒ Ⓓ	24. Ⓐ Ⓑ Ⓒ Ⓓ	35. Ⓐ Ⓑ Ⓒ Ⓓ
3. Ⓐ Ⓑ Ⓒ Ⓓ	14. Ⓐ Ⓑ Ⓒ Ⓓ	25. Ⓐ Ⓑ Ⓒ Ⓓ	36. Ⓐ Ⓑ Ⓒ Ⓓ
4. Ⓐ Ⓑ Ⓒ Ⓓ	15. Ⓐ Ⓑ Ⓒ Ⓓ	26. Ⓐ Ⓑ Ⓒ Ⓓ	37. Ⓐ Ⓑ Ⓒ Ⓓ
5. Ⓐ Ⓑ Ⓒ Ⓓ	16. Ⓐ Ⓑ Ⓒ Ⓓ	27. Ⓐ Ⓑ Ⓒ Ⓓ	38. Ⓐ Ⓑ Ⓒ Ⓓ
6. Ⓐ Ⓑ Ⓒ Ⓓ	17. Ⓐ Ⓑ Ⓒ Ⓓ	28. Ⓐ Ⓑ Ⓒ Ⓓ	39. Ⓐ Ⓑ Ⓒ Ⓓ
7. Ⓐ Ⓑ Ⓒ Ⓓ	18. Ⓐ Ⓑ Ⓒ Ⓓ	29. Ⓐ Ⓑ Ⓒ Ⓓ	40. Ⓐ Ⓑ Ⓒ Ⓓ
8. Ⓐ Ⓑ Ⓒ Ⓓ	19. Ⓐ Ⓑ Ⓒ Ⓓ	30. Ⓐ Ⓑ Ⓒ Ⓓ	41. Ⓐ Ⓑ Ⓒ Ⓓ
9. Ⓐ Ⓑ Ⓒ Ⓓ	20. Ⓐ Ⓑ Ⓒ Ⓓ	31. Ⓐ Ⓑ Ⓒ Ⓓ	42. Ⓐ Ⓑ Ⓒ Ⓓ
10. Ⓐ Ⓑ Ⓒ Ⓓ	21. Ⓐ Ⓑ Ⓒ Ⓓ	32. Ⓐ Ⓑ Ⓒ Ⓓ	43. Ⓐ Ⓑ Ⓒ Ⓓ
11. Ⓐ Ⓑ Ⓒ Ⓓ	22. Ⓐ Ⓑ Ⓒ Ⓓ	33. Ⓐ Ⓑ Ⓒ Ⓓ	44. Ⓐ Ⓑ Ⓒ Ⓓ

ANSWER SHEET
答题纸
Practice Test
练习测试题

Section 3: Math (No Calculator)

1. Ⓐ Ⓑ Ⓒ Ⓓ
2. Ⓐ Ⓑ Ⓒ Ⓓ
3. Ⓐ Ⓑ Ⓒ Ⓓ
4. Ⓐ Ⓑ Ⓒ Ⓓ
5. Ⓐ Ⓑ Ⓒ Ⓓ
6. Ⓐ Ⓑ Ⓒ Ⓓ
7. Ⓐ Ⓑ Ⓒ Ⓓ
8. Ⓐ Ⓑ Ⓒ Ⓓ
9. Ⓐ Ⓑ Ⓒ Ⓓ
10. Ⓐ Ⓑ Ⓒ Ⓓ
11. Ⓐ Ⓑ Ⓒ Ⓓ
12. Ⓐ Ⓑ Ⓒ Ⓓ
13. Ⓐ Ⓑ Ⓒ Ⓓ
14. Ⓐ Ⓑ Ⓒ Ⓓ
15. Ⓐ Ⓑ Ⓒ Ⓓ

16.

17.

18.

19.

20.

ANSWER SHEET
答题纸
Practice Test
练习测试题

Section 4: Math (With Calculator)

1. Ⓐ Ⓑ Ⓒ Ⓓ
2. Ⓐ Ⓑ Ⓒ Ⓓ
3. Ⓐ Ⓑ Ⓒ Ⓓ
4. Ⓐ Ⓑ Ⓒ Ⓓ
5. Ⓐ Ⓑ Ⓒ Ⓓ
6. Ⓐ Ⓑ Ⓒ Ⓓ
7. Ⓐ Ⓑ Ⓒ Ⓓ
8. Ⓐ Ⓑ Ⓒ Ⓓ
9. Ⓐ Ⓑ Ⓒ Ⓓ
10. Ⓐ Ⓑ Ⓒ Ⓓ
11. Ⓐ Ⓑ Ⓒ Ⓓ
12. Ⓐ Ⓑ Ⓒ Ⓓ
13. Ⓐ Ⓑ Ⓒ Ⓓ
14. Ⓐ Ⓑ Ⓒ Ⓓ
15. Ⓐ Ⓑ Ⓒ Ⓓ
16. Ⓐ Ⓑ Ⓒ Ⓓ
17. Ⓐ Ⓑ Ⓒ Ⓓ
18. Ⓐ Ⓑ Ⓒ Ⓓ
19. Ⓐ Ⓑ Ⓒ Ⓓ
20. Ⓐ Ⓑ Ⓒ Ⓓ
21. Ⓐ Ⓑ Ⓒ Ⓓ
22. Ⓐ Ⓑ Ⓒ Ⓓ
23. Ⓐ Ⓑ Ⓒ Ⓓ
24. Ⓐ Ⓑ Ⓒ Ⓓ
25. Ⓐ Ⓑ Ⓒ Ⓓ
26. Ⓐ Ⓑ Ⓒ Ⓓ
27. Ⓐ Ⓑ Ⓒ Ⓓ
28. Ⓐ Ⓑ Ⓒ Ⓓ
29. Ⓐ Ⓑ Ⓒ Ⓓ
30. Ⓐ Ⓑ Ⓒ Ⓓ

31. | | | | |
|---|---|---|---|
| | ⊘ | ⊘ | |
| ⊙ | ⊙ | ⊙ | ⊙ |
| | ⓪ | ⓪ | ⓪ |
| ① | ① | ① | ① |
| ② | ② | ② | ② |
| ③ | ③ | ③ | ③ |
| ④ | ④ | ④ | ④ |
| ⑤ | ⑤ | ⑤ | ⑤ |
| ⑥ | ⑥ | ⑥ | ⑥ |
| ⑦ | ⑦ | ⑦ | ⑦ |
| ⑧ | ⑧ | ⑧ | ⑧ |
| ⑨ | ⑨ | ⑨ | ⑨ |

32. | | | | |
|---|---|---|---|
| | ⊘ | ⊘ | |
| ⊙ | ⊙ | ⊙ | ⊙ |
| | ⓪ | ⓪ | ⓪ |
| ① | ① | ① | ① |
| ② | ② | ② | ② |
| ③ | ③ | ③ | ③ |
| ④ | ④ | ④ | ④ |
| ⑤ | ⑤ | ⑤ | ⑤ |
| ⑥ | ⑥ | ⑥ | ⑥ |
| ⑦ | ⑦ | ⑦ | ⑦ |
| ⑧ | ⑧ | ⑧ | ⑧ |
| ⑨ | ⑨ | ⑨ | ⑨ |

33. | | | | |
|---|---|---|---|
| | ⊘ | ⊘ | |
| ⊙ | ⊙ | ⊙ | ⊙ |
| | ⓪ | ⓪ | ⓪ |
| ① | ① | ① | ① |
| ② | ② | ② | ② |
| ③ | ③ | ③ | ③ |
| ④ | ④ | ④ | ④ |
| ⑤ | ⑤ | ⑤ | ⑤ |
| ⑥ | ⑥ | ⑥ | ⑥ |
| ⑦ | ⑦ | ⑦ | ⑦ |
| ⑧ | ⑧ | ⑧ | ⑧ |
| ⑨ | ⑨ | ⑨ | ⑨ |

34. | | | | |
|---|---|---|---|
| | ⊘ | ⊘ | |
| ⊙ | ⊙ | ⊙ | ⊙ |
| | ⓪ | ⓪ | ⓪ |
| ① | ① | ① | ① |
| ② | ② | ② | ② |
| ③ | ③ | ③ | ③ |
| ④ | ④ | ④ | ④ |
| ⑤ | ⑤ | ⑤ | ⑤ |
| ⑥ | ⑥ | ⑥ | ⑥ |
| ⑦ | ⑦ | ⑦ | ⑦ |
| ⑧ | ⑧ | ⑧ | ⑧ |
| ⑨ | ⑨ | ⑨ | ⑨ |

35. | | | | |
|---|---|---|---|
| | ⊘ | ⊘ | |
| ⊙ | ⊙ | ⊙ | ⊙ |
| | ⓪ | ⓪ | ⓪ |
| ① | ① | ① | ① |
| ② | ② | ② | ② |
| ③ | ③ | ③ | ③ |
| ④ | ④ | ④ | ④ |
| ⑤ | ⑤ | ⑤ | ⑤ |
| ⑥ | ⑥ | ⑥ | ⑥ |
| ⑦ | ⑦ | ⑦ | ⑦ |
| ⑧ | ⑧ | ⑧ | ⑧ |
| ⑨ | ⑨ | ⑨ | ⑨ |

36. | | | | |
|---|---|---|---|
| | ⊘ | ⊘ | |
| ⊙ | ⊙ | ⊙ | ⊙ |
| | ⓪ | ⓪ | ⓪ |
| ① | ① | ① | ① |
| ② | ② | ② | ② |
| ③ | ③ | ③ | ③ |
| ④ | ④ | ④ | ④ |
| ⑤ | ⑤ | ⑤ | ⑤ |
| ⑥ | ⑥ | ⑥ | ⑥ |
| ⑦ | ⑦ | ⑦ | ⑦ |
| ⑧ | ⑧ | ⑧ | ⑧ |
| ⑨ | ⑨ | ⑨ | ⑨ |

37. | | | | |
|---|---|---|---|
| | ⊘ | ⊘ | |
| ⊙ | ⊙ | ⊙ | ⊙ |
| | ⓪ | ⓪ | ⓪ |
| ① | ① | ① | ① |
| ② | ② | ② | ② |
| ③ | ③ | ③ | ③ |
| ④ | ④ | ④ | ④ |
| ⑤ | ⑤ | ⑤ | ⑤ |
| ⑥ | ⑥ | ⑥ | ⑥ |
| ⑦ | ⑦ | ⑦ | ⑦ |
| ⑧ | ⑧ | ⑧ | ⑧ |
| ⑨ | ⑨ | ⑨ | ⑨ |

38. | | | | |
|---|---|---|---|
| | ⊘ | ⊘ | |
| ⊙ | ⊙ | ⊙ | ⊙ |
| | ⓪ | ⓪ | ⓪ |
| ① | ① | ① | ① |
| ② | ② | ② | ② |
| ③ | ③ | ③ | ③ |
| ④ | ④ | ④ | ④ |
| ⑤ | ⑤ | ⑤ | ⑤ |
| ⑥ | ⑥ | ⑥ | ⑥ |
| ⑦ | ⑦ | ⑦ | ⑦ |
| ⑧ | ⑧ | ⑧ | ⑧ |
| ⑨ | ⑨ | ⑨ | ⑨ |

ANSWER SHEET
答题纸
Practice Test
练习测试题

Section 5: Essay

PLANNING PAGE

START YOUR ESSAY HERE

1 1 1

READING TEST 阅读测试

65 MINUTES, 52 QUESTIONS

Directions: Each passage or pair of passages is accompanied by several questions. After reading the passage(s), choose the best answer to each question based on what is indicated explicitly or implicitly in the passage(s) or in the associated graphics.

Questions 1–11 are based on the following passage.

Michael Jan Friedman is the author of 72 books, including I Am The Salamander, *from which the following excerpt is taken. Friedman has written for the* After Earth, Aliens, Predator, Wolf Man, Lois and Clark, DC Super Hero, Marvel Super Hero, *and* Star Trek *licensed book universes. Eleven titles, including the autobiography* Hollywood Hulk Hogan, *have appeared on* The New York Times *primary bestseller list.*

"Tim?" Mom said. She was leaning across the front seat of our sensible, mid-sized sedan, looking up at me. "You there, kiddo?"

I blinked and looked back and gave her a smile, though I couldn't pack much enthusiasm into it. "Yeah."

"Got your lunch?"

"Uh huh."

"That book you were reading?"

"Check."

"Your calculator?"

"That too. And my notebook. And my pens, and my pad. And my student ID, in case anybody in an SS uniform clicks his heels and demands to see my papers."

"You're making fun of me." Mom pushed back a thick lock of red hair, exposing wise blue eyes and an upturned nose.

She was the kind of mother you see on TV, always cheerful, always looking on the bright side. Well, *almost* always. In the last few months, I had caught glimpses of her when she was the *opposite* of cheerful.

"Hey," I said, "you're an easy target. I keep telling you."

I wanted to sound confident so she wouldn't worry. Unfortunately, the best I could do was sound *not too scared.*

"I'll see you at three," Mom assured me.

"In point of fact," I said, "we get out at two-fifty."

"In point of fact" was something my dad used to say. *In point of fact, Dana, I had no choice but to drive the guy home. It was snowing. I couldn't leave him in the* snow, *could I?*

Mom chuckled. "Two-fifty, then."

She wanted to tell me a million things. I could see them crowding each other in the confines of her skull, each one doing its best to squeeze its way out. But she kept from saying them because she knew they wouldn't do either of us any good.

I mean, I wasn't a little kid anymore, even though I *felt* like one as I turned and left the safe haven of our car and started stiff-legged, mechanically across The Lawn. Like I was on a different planet, where the atmosphere was a little thicker and gravity was a little stronger. Where it was an effort to breathe, to put one foot in front of another.

Don't freak out.

All around me, heads turned in my direction. Not everybody was so obvious

GO ON TO THE NEXT PAGE

1 1 1

about it because, you know, some people are just smoother than others. But I could see the eyes sliding toward me, checking me out.

And I didn't have to guess why.

I hadn't gone to a plastic surgeon and gotten my identity changed so I could escape the vengeance of the Russian Mafia. Nothing anywhere near that cinematic. But I also didn't look like the Tim Cruz they remembered.

I was ten pounds thinner, maybe more—it's hard to remember exactly what I weighed back in the fall. And what I laughingly called my hair was still only a stubbly promise that I wouldn't be bald forever.

But it wasn't just my appearance that made people want to turn and eyeball me. It couldn't be. The football team had shaved their heads back around Halloween, so I wasn't the first kid to show up in school that year without a lot of hair.

They were glomming me because I was there *at all* on that sunny day in April. Because for a while, it had looked like a good bet that I wouldn't be.

1. Throughout this fiction excerpt there is a palpable tension between all of the following EXCEPT

(A) poverty and affluence
(B) the spoken and the unspoken
(C) fear and optimism
(D) reality and appearance

2. The author is best described as

(A) a first-person narrator.
(B) an omniscient, third-person narrator.
(C) a detached observer.
(D) an orator delivering a satirical soliloquy.

3. Which of the following contrasts does the author primarily emphasize in this passage?

(A) The difference between the mother's pessimism and her son's optimism
(B) The difference between the mother's internal dialogue and her son's terseness
(C) The attitude of the football team versus that of Tim's mom
(D) The physical appearance of the mother's hair versus that of her son

4. Which rhetorical feature(s) is most prevalent in this fiction passage?

(A) Innuendo and dialogue
(B) Vivid imagery
(C) Juxtaposition
(D) Formal narrative tone

5. Given the evidence and details presented in lines 52–54 ("Where it was an effort to breathe, to put one foot in front of another.") and 69–74 ("I was ten pounds thinner . . . still only a stubbly promise that I wouldn't be bald forever."), which of the following course of events best summarizes what Tim Cruz has experienced?

(A) Loss, recovery, triumph
(B) Fear, anxiety, depression
(C) Sickness, treatment, convalescence
(D) Alienation, socialization, stardom

1 1 1

6. As used in line 59, "smoother" most closely means

   (A) more discreet.
   (B) more refined.
   (C) more lithe.
   (D) more astute.

7. In lines 41–43 ("I could see them crowding each other in the confines of her skull, each one doing its best to squeeze its way out."), the author uses which figurative device?

   (A) Allusion
   (B) Irony
   (C) Simile
   (D) Personification

8. Lines 63–66 ("I hadn't gone to a plastic surgeon and gotten my identity changed so I could escape the vengeance of the Russian Mafia.") most closely relate to which of the following rhetorical devices?

   (A) Hyperbole
   (B) Personification
   (C) Oxymoron
   (D) Epiphany

9. As used in context, "glomming" in line 82 most closely means

   (A) glaring at.
   (B) sad about.
   (C) grabbing.
   (D) staring at.

10. What does the textual evidence in lines 34–38 reveal about Tim's father?

   (A) That he liked to drive in all sorts of weather
   (B) That he was altruistic
   (C) That he had a great many friends
   (D) That he didn't like accepting favors from people

11. What is the author's primary purpose in writing this piece of prose fiction?

   (A) To illustrate the damaging repercussions of prejudice
   (B) To emphasize the indomitable power of the human spirit
   (C) To satirize today's self-centered youth
   (D) To illustrate the strong bond between mother and son

Questions 12–21 are based on the following passage.

Published by the University of Toronto Press, this literary-historical passage is excerpted from Ignazio Silone: Beyond the Tragic Vision, *written by Maria Nicolai Paynter, Professor of Italian Literature in the Department of Romance Language at Hunter College, New York.*

Silone wrote his first three novels in Switzerland, where he was a political refugee from 1930 to the end of World War II. Emerging from the depth of the most severe crisis that he experienced in his life, he found an "emergency exit" in his literary vocation, and went on to become the first Italian writer to denounce the plight of the poor farmers, or *cafoni*. Unlike Verga, he felt that the cycle of oppression that historically held the poor in captivity could and should be broken. But his concern transcended Marxist influence and materialism; his focus was on the dehumanizing power of oppression—on the realization that it deprived the oppressed of the spiritual dimension of human life. Thus, in his work, he went beyond the tragic vision to reveal the liberating power that is within the self.

Of the circumstances and sentiments that compelled him to write his first novel, he states, "I began to write *Fontamara* . . . driven by homesickness and by a passion for politics that could not find any other outlet." Having requested sick leave from the party, Silone could devote all of his energy to this new endeavor, and he composed the novel almost compulsively. Writing to Gabriella Seidenfeld, in July 1930, he speaks of his work in progress and describes his Fontamara *cafoni* as follows: "They are so alive that I speak with them. I believe that they are the first farmers that appear in flesh and blood in Italian literature"; and also, "Some nights I suddenly awake and I have to get up to jot down some notes; at other times I am in the garden and I run to my room to change a paragraph in one of the chapters." Although the end of the preface to the original Italian version bears the notation "Zurigo, estate 1930" above the signature "Ignazio Silone," there is convincing evidence that the novel itself was not entirely finished before 1931. Silone wrote the novel in Italian, but finding it impossible to have it published in that language, he had it translated into German by Nettie Sutro. In this form it reached its first readers in the spring of 1933. Its immediate popularity made it easier for the original Italian version to be published by the end of the same year. American and English editions followed in 1934, and the novel was subsequently translated into twenty-five other languages.

While the readers of other countries read *Fontamara*, and learned about an Italian reality that was totally unlike the one heralded in the Fascist media, at home the book remained exiled along with its author. The historical circumstances that made it impossible for the novel to be released in Italy colored the view of many readers abroad. Some American reviewers tended to stress its political aspect to the point of presenting fiction as fact. Clifton Fadiman, for instance, wrote in *The New Yorker*: "*Fontamara* is a little epic of peasant resistance, based upon an actual event in recent Italian history—the little book exists only on a profoundly political level." A similar view was one forcefully

GO ON TO THE NEXT PAGE

1

expressed by another reviewer, who wrote: "The value of this book as a pamphlet depends on its truth or partial truth . . . if it is even fifty percent true, Italy under Mussolini is worse off than Italy under the Austrians or the Lombards."

12. The stance Paynter takes in the passage is best described as that of

(A) a political upstart.
(B) a scholarly historian.
(C) a rebel scientist.
(D) a disillusioned theologian.

13. The primary rhetorical effect of the author's collective use of the words "compelled," "passion," and "compulsively" in lines 23–30 is to

(A) accentuate Silone's intense feelings toward the subject about which he is writing.
(B) mock Silone's egomaniacal literary tendencies.
(C) shed light on Silone's mental instability.
(D) juxtapose the peasant lifestyle to that of a frantic writer.

14. The passage in its entirety most strongly suggests that Silone espouses or is most closely aligned with which of the following beliefs?

(A) Prose that is translated into multiple languages attests to the talent of the author.
(B) The political and personal lives of an author should not intermingle.
(C) All human beings are inherently dignified and worthy of respect.
(D) The partial truth can be as valuable as the full truth.

15. Which lines provide the best passage-based evidence to support the answer to the previous question?

(A) Lines 4–9 ("Emerging . . . farmers")
(B) Lines 10–21 ("the cycle . . . self")
(C) Lines 27–30 ("Having . . . compulsively")
(D) Lines 65–68 ("The historical . . . abroad")

16. In lines 48–53, what is the most likely purpose for Paynter drawing a distinction between the book's being published in Italian versus being published in German?

(A) To stress how Italy's political climate restricted its readers' personal perspectives
(B) To stress how a German audience would afford the work a more far-reaching global appeal
(C) To stress how Italy's publishing world is less circumscribed compared to that of Germany
(D) To stress how the work loses its essential message in translation

17. In lines 63–65 (". . . at home the book remained exiled along with its author."), which literary device is most analogous to the one that appears here?

(A) Simile
(B) Hyperbole
(C) Personification
(D) Irony

18. As used in line 63, "heralded" most nearly means

(A) popularized.
(B) contradicted.
(C) belittled.
(D) advocated.

19. As used in line 67, the phrase "colored the view" is best represented by which of the following?

(A) How literary contemporaries of Silone shaped their writing after his
(B) How readers abroad interpreted the political circumstances within Italy
(C) How critics of Silone developed prejudices and biases against certain sectors of society
(D) How domestic and overseas readers offered each other insight into their respective, colorful ideas about Italian culture

20. The author mentions Clifton Fadiman in lines 70–71 in order to demonstrate that

(A) some cynics publicized Silone as an unethical propagandist.
(B) some reviewers ascribed too much historical reality to Silone's novel.
(C) some critics found fault with Silone's inaccurate presentation of facts.
(D) some readers saw elements of science fiction in Silone's book that were unintended by him.

21. As used in line 76, "forcefully" most closely means

(A) frantically.
(B) compellingly.
(C) forcibly.
(D) enforceably.

1 1 1

Questions 22–32 are based on the following passage.

This passage, The Preamble to The Bill of Rights and the first ten amendments, makes up part of the Great Global Conversation. The following text is a transcription of the first ten amendments to the Constitution in their original form. These amendments were ratified December 15, 1791, and form what is known as the Bill of Rights. (*Source:* archives.gov)

Congress of the United States begun and held at the City of New York, on Wednesday the fourth of March, one thousand seven hundred and eighty nine.

THE Conventions of a number of the States, having at the time of their adopting the Constitution, expressed a desire, in order to prevent misconstruction or abuse of its powers, that further declaratory and restrictive clauses should be added: And as extending the ground of public confidence in the Government, will best ensure the beneficent ends of its institution.

RESOLVED by the Senate and House of Representatives of the United States of America, in Congress assembled, two thirds of both Houses concurring, that the following Articles be proposed to the Legislatures of the several States, as amendments to the Constitution of the United States, all, or any of which Articles, when ratified by three fourths of the said Legislatures, to be valid to all intents and purposes, as part of the said Constitution.

ARTICLES in addition to, and Amendment of the Constitution of the United States of America, proposed by Congress, and ratified by the Legislatures of the several States, pursuant to the fifth Article of the original Constitution.

Amendment I

Congress shall make no law respecting an establishment of religion, or prohibiting the free exercise thereof; or abridging the freedom of speech, or of the press; or the right of the people peaceably to assemble, and to petition the Government for a redress of grievances.

Amendment II

A well regulated Militia, being necessary to the security of a free State, the right of the people to keep and bear Arms, shall not be infringed.

Amendment III

No Soldier shall, in time of peace be quartered in any house, without the consent of the Owner, nor in time of war, but in a manner to be prescribed by law.

Amendment IV

The right of the people to be secure in their persons, houses, papers, and effects, against unreasonable searches and seizures, shall not be violated, and no Warrants shall issue, but upon probable cause, supported by Oath or affirmation, and particularly describing the place to be searched, and the persons or things to be seized.

Amendment V

No person shall be held to answer for a capital, or otherwise infamous crime, unless on a presentment or indictment of a Grand Jury, except in cases arising in the land or naval forces, or in the Militia, when in actual service in time of War or public danger; nor shall any person be subject for the same offence to be twice put in jeopardy of life or limb; nor shall be compelled in any criminal case to be a witness against

GO ON TO THE NEXT PAGE

1 1 1

himself, nor be deprived of life, liberty, or property, without due process of law; nor shall private property be taken for public use, without just compensation.

Amendment VI

In all criminal prosecutions, the accused shall enjoy the right to a speedy and public trial, by an impartial jury of the State and district wherein the crime shall have been committed, which district shall have been previously ascertained by law, and to be informed of the nature and cause of the accusation; to be confronted with the witnesses against him; to have compulsory process for obtaining witnesses in his favor, and to have the Assistance of Counsel for his defense.

Amendment VII

In Suits at common law, where the value in controversy shall exceed twenty dollars, the right of trial by jury shall be preserved, and no fact tried by a jury, shall be otherwise re-examined in any Court of the United States, than according to the rules of the common law.

Amendment VIII

Excessive bail shall not be required, nor excessive fines imposed, nor cruel and unusual punishments inflicted.

Amendment IX

The enumeration in the Constitution, of certain rights, shall not be construed to deny or disparage others retained by the people.

Amendment X

The powers not delegated to the United States by the Constitution, nor prohibited by it to the States, are reserved to the States respectively, or to the people.

22. The passage most strongly suggests that The Bill of Rights is primarily concerned with

(A) the material possessions and property of an individual.
(B) intangible rights such as privacy, worship, and self-expression.
(C) protection against hostile forces, whether domestic or overseas.
(D) spiritual connections and sympathies shared among all Americans.

23. As used in lines 21–23 "all, or any of which Articles, when ratified by three fourths of the said Legislatures," the word "said" most closely means

(A) understood.
(B) outspoken.
(C) beheld.
(D) outmoded.

24. In lines 14–20 ("Resolved . . . Constitution"), how might the collective effectiveness of these words and phrases—"resolved," "assembled," "two thirds," "both houses," "concurring"—best be described in terms of their collective, or combined, message?

(A) A unified vision and purpose
(B) A stifled but bitter controversy
(C) A perpetual state of inquiry
(D) A delay of tact and diplomacy

25. Within Amendment I (lines 31–38), the adverb "thereof" refers back to which of the following?

(A) Amendment I itself
(B) Congress
(C) Religion
(D) Freedom of speech

1 1 1

26. As used in line 52, "effects" most likely refers to

(A) an individual's emotional state.
(B) an individual's property.
(C) special effects.
(D) sound effects.

27. In line 73, "just compensation" is best paraphrased as

(A) partial recompense.
(B) limited respect.
(C) fair remuneration.
(D) deserved merit.

28. The varying meanings of the words "respecting," as used in line 32, and "respectively," as used in line 108, most accurately mean

(A) revering and respectfully.
(B) with respect to and honorably.
(C) accepting and individually.
(D) with regard to and correspondingly.

29. In lines 35–38 ("the right . . . grievances."), which of the following best expresses the benefit conferred upon Americans as they are granted this "right"?

(A) To contend that the American people have the right to reiterate their frustrations
(B) To request that the government re-express its laws in new ways so that people can clearly understand their rights
(C) To grant Americans the right to ask the government to listen to and address their concerns
(D) To argue for common people's improved roles in local government

30. Which choice provides the best evidence for the answer to the previous question?

(A) Lines 5–13 ("Conventions . . . institution")
(B) Lines 21–24 ("all . . . Constitution")
(C) Lines 50–54 ("The . . . issue")
(D) Lines 90–94 ("right . . . law")

31. The passage most strongly suggests that the authors of The Bill of Rights share which assumption?

(A) Ultimately, it is most beneficial for Americans when final power resides with the government.
(B) The military is the most valuable facet of ensuring American prosperity.
(C) Americans are worthy of a broad spectrum of personal rights and protection.
(D) The tensions between common people and people in power will ultimately erode the scope of human rights, as outlined in The Bill of Rights.

32. As used in line 101, "construed" most closely means

(A) impeded.
(B) constituted.
(C) constrained.
(D) interpreted.

PRACTICE TEST

GO ON TO THE NEXT PAGE

1 1 1

Questions 33–43 are based on the following passage and its supplementary material.

The data for the following article were based on "Production and Evaluation of Black Soldier Fly Larvae and Termites as Protein Supplements for Chickens," by Bui Xuan Men, et al., 2005.

Scientists at an experimental poultry farm carried out three experiments. Two evaluated the feasibility of producing live termites and fly larvae locally. A third tested the use of termites and fly larvae as protein supplements for chickens raised on the farm.

Experiment 1: Production of Termites

Method 1

Shallow holes surrounding termite mounds and under shady trees were filled with bundles of bagasse (residue of processed plants) and dry wood of silk cotton trees. These were covered with jute sacks and sprinkled with water to keep the holes dark and humid. The termites were harvested after 3 weeks.

Method 2

Cartons were filled with bagasse and wood from silk cotton trees. Termite nests containing whole families were collected from different sites and placed into the cartons. Each carton was tightly closed to keep the inside dark and humid. Termites were harvested after 3 to 4 weeks.

Experiment 2: Production of Fly Larvae

Method 1

Small holes were dug and filled with damp rice straw and fresh cow manure in alternating 15-centimeter-thick layers. These were covered with thin layers of rice gruel. About 1 kilogram of spoiled fish was added. To maintain high humidity, 2 to 3 liters of water were poured over the holes when the eggs had been laid. Growing larvae were harvested 5 days after the first observation of larvae.

Method 2

Open rectangular wooden boxes were placed under trees. The boxes were lined with rice straw and then filled with fresh pig manure; 3 to 4 liters of wastewater from a fish shop were sprinkled over the boxes. Fly larvae were harvested 5 days after the first observation of larvae.

Table 1 below shows the yield, in grams per hole or box (g/setup), for termite and fly larvae production.

Table 1

	Termite Yield (g/setup)	Fly Larvae Yield (g/setup)
Method 1	97	negligible
Method 2	133	210

Experiment 3: Termites and Fly Larvae as Protein in Chicken Feed

Sixty 10-day-old chicks were brooded in wire cages under the same conditions of temperature, humidity, lighting, feeding times, and feeding containers. During the brooding stage, before the 10th day, all chicks were fed commercial crumbs, as much food as they wanted.

When they were 10 days old, the chicks were randomly assigned to one of three groups. Each group was then fed one of three diets:

- The control group was fed a commercial diet consisting of approximately 51.6% maize meal, 13% rice bran, 21.3% roasted soybean, 14.2% fish meal, and 0.25% vitamin-mineral premix.
- The "termite" group was fed freshly harvested termites twice daily, in the morning and afternoon. Additionally, they were offered maize meal at all times of day.
- The "fly larvae" group was fed freshly harvested fly larvae that had been cleaned,

1 1 1

Table 2
Chemical Composition of Feed Ingredients

	% of DM						
	DM, %	CP	EE	NFE	CF	Ash	ME (MJ/kg)
Maize meal	85.9	8.2	4.5	82.7	2.4	1.9	16.0
Rice bran	90.0	13.5	12.7	58.5	7.6	7.7	12.6
Soy bean	91.0	43.1	15.4	32.6	4.1	4.8	16.3
Fish meal	81.3	29.7	4.4	18.1	6.0	41.7	8.5
Fresh termites	21.0	70.1	7.0	1.2	13.5	8.3	14.1
Fresh larvae	26.5	59.0	23.0	2.6	8.7	6.6	17.5

drained, and weighed before feeding, also in the morning and afternoon. This group, too, was offered maize meal at all times of day.

All of the feeds were analyzed for their nutrient composition as a percentage of the dry matter (DM) they contained. Table 2 shows the chemical composition of the feed ingredients used in the experiment, including crude protein (CP), ether extract (EE), nitrogen-free extract (NFE), crude fiber (CF), and ash. The metabolizable energy (ME) was calculated based on a chemical analysis and is given in megajoules per kilogram (MJ/kg).

Table 3 below shows the daily intakes, in grams (g), of maize, termites or larvae, dry matter (DM), and crude protein (CP). Metabolizable energy (ME) is shown in megajoules (MJ).

Table 3
Daily Intakes of Ingredients by Chicks

	Control Group	Termite Group	Fly Larvae Group
Maize intake (g)	28.7	26.0	26.2
Termite or larvae intake (g)	0	1.9	2.1
Total DM intake (g)	28.7	27.9	28.3
ME intake (MJ)	0.42	0.44	0.46
CP intake (g)	5.6	3.5	3.4
CP/ME (g/MJ)	13.3	8.0	7.4

Table 4 shows the weight gain data of chicks under the three treatments.

Table 4
Daily Weight Gain and Feed Conversion Ratios of Chicks

	Control Group	Termite Group	Fly Larvae Group
Average daily weight gain (g)	9.1	9.0	10.9
Feed conversion ratio (kg feed/kg gain)	3.2	3.1	2.6
Crude protein per kg gain (g)	615	388	312
Metabolizable energy per kg gain (MJ/kg)	46.1	48.9	42.2

GO ON TO THE NEXT PAGE

33. Based on the information in the passage, which of the following was necessary to produce fly larvae successfully?

    (A) Pig manure
    (B) Cattle manure
    (C) Bagasse
    (D) Silk cotton tree wood

34. According to the information in the passage, which of the following statements is true about termite or fly larvae production?

    (A) Spoiled fish is an essential ingredient in the production of fly larvae.
    (B) Cattle manure alternating with layers of spoiled fish is an effective method of fly larvae production.
    (C) It was not possible to harvest termites if the colonies were not housed in cartons.
    (D) Placing termites into cartons was a more effective method of termite production than cultivating termites in holes in the ground.

35. Scientists speculated as to why Method 2 yielded more termites than Method 1. Which of the following is a plausible explanation?

    (A) The bagasse and silk cotton tree wood rotted in the holes but were preserved in the cartons.
    (B) Termite reproduction was lowered by sunlight. The interiors of the cartons were dark.
    (C) The termites in the holes were exposed to attack by other insects, like ants and small centipedes. Those in the cartons were protected from other insects.
    (D) Termites in the holes, exposed to rain, sun, and wind, were less likely to reproduce than those in the cartons, which were protected from the elements.

36. When researchers analyzed the dry matter in the feed of the chicks, what did they find?

    (A) The amount of ash in the termite and larvae dry matter was lower than that in the fish meal.
    (B) The crude protein content of the dry matter of soybean meal and fish meal was higher than that of the termite and fly larvae dry matter.
    (C) The metabolizable energy content of the larvae was lower than that of soybean meal.
    (D) The fiber content of fresh termites and larvae was comparable to that in the maize, soybean, and fish meal.

GO ON TO THE NEXT PAGE

37. Which of the following is not borne out by the data in the passage? The consumption of metabolizable energy was

    (A) dependent on the quantities of maize meal consumed by the chicks in the three groups.
    (B) independent of the crude protein consumption of the three groups of chicks.
    (C) independent of the concentration of metabolizable energy of the feed of the three groups of chicks.
    (D) relatively constant for the three groups of chicks.

38. Let the three groups of chicks be represented as follows:

    Control Group: CG
    Termite Group: TG
    Fly Larvae Group: FLG

    Which of the following statements is best supported by the information provided in Tables 3 and 4?

    (A) The rates of weight gain were comparable for the CG, TG, and FLG diets.
    (B) Crude protein intake per kilogram of weight gain for FLG was lower than that of CG, but daily weight gains for FLG were higher.
    (C) The dry matter feed conversion ratio was best for the CG diet.
    (D) The chicks in FLG consumed more metabolizable energy per kilogram of weight gain than those in the other two groups.

39. Evidence for all of the following statements is provided by the details as outlined in Experiment 3 EXCEPT that

    (A) maize was a consistent component in the diets offered to CG, TG, and FLG.
    (B) both TG and FLG were offered food several times per day.
    (C) some of the feed ingredients for TG and FLG contained noxious chemical components.
    (D) environmental constants pertaining to all chicks included setting, levels of humidity, as well as brightness or dimness.

40. Which of the following is not a logical deduction, based on the information provided in Experiment 3 and Table 2?

    (A) Scientists involved with the FLG were the most conscientious when it came to maintaining sterile conditions.
    (B) Detailed measurements were an indispensible feature of this research.
    (C) Multiple environmental factors were taken into consideration by the research scientists.
    (D) The ten-day-old chicks were not assigned to a group based on their appearance.

41. Given all of the evidence, as provided in the experiments and accompanying tables, which of the following factors is disregarded as relatively trivial by the researchers?

    (A) Protein intake of the chicks
    (B) Satiation of the chicks' natural impulses of hunger
    (C) Luster and denseness of the chick's plumage
    (D) Weight gain of the chicks

42. Based on Experiment 3 and Table 4, which feed source is of the highest quality in terms of the energy it provides to the chicks?

    (A) Commercial crumbs
    (B) Vitamin-mineral premix
    (C) Freshly harvested fly larvae
    (D) Freshly harvested termites

43. Based on the data presented in Table 4, which of the following is true?

    (A) For all chicks, there is no obvious relationship between the crude protein per kilogram intake and average weight gain.
    (B) Consumption of fly larvae benefits chicks by providing them with the highest levels of ME.
    (C) There is a correlative relationship between weight gain and the feed conversion ratio.
    (D) CG gained the most weight because of the soybean and rice that primarily constituted their daily diet.

1 1 1

Questions 44–52 are based on the following passage and supplemental material.

This excerpt is adapted from a research abstract published by Information Age Publishing, Charlotte, North Carolina, 2014.

Astronomical Measures

Did you ever think about mathematics, astronomy and *folding* as interrelated? Traditional examples of folding that we may come across in our everyday lives may include origami birds, paper party hats, and a fortune cookie game created through folding paper. Folding can be fun or very precise and intricate. Folding that is more serious would include the specific folds required to fold the American flag to result in its iconic triangular shape.

Folding can become even more intricate and serious when the precise folds are the difference between life and death. A parachute goes from being folded in a small bag to expanding into a large size. If the parachute is not folded precisely in the bag, the parachute will not expand correctly when the sky diver pulls the lever, and the air bag apparatus may not release properly. As you can see, folding can decide life or death.

Now let's take a look at folding paper involving math. We will try to find the center of a circle by folding. Two folds are made to find the center of a circle. By making a horizontal and vertical fold along the diameter of the circle, then unfolding it, the point where the two creases meet is the center of the circle. From these examples, you can tell that a slight mistake in the initial fold could have substantially larger effects on the outcome.

Next in this research, we will find the length of the crease made on a 3 × 5 inch index card from the bottom left corner to the top right corner. The first idea that may come to mind is to use a ruler and measure the length of the crease. However, we can also use algebra to solve this problem. This project involves geometry, algebra, and graphing and will seek the answers to these questions: How would the length of the crease change if the length of the index card changed? Does the crease have a maximum or minimum length?

Let's take a look at a graph that represents the measurements we have collected.

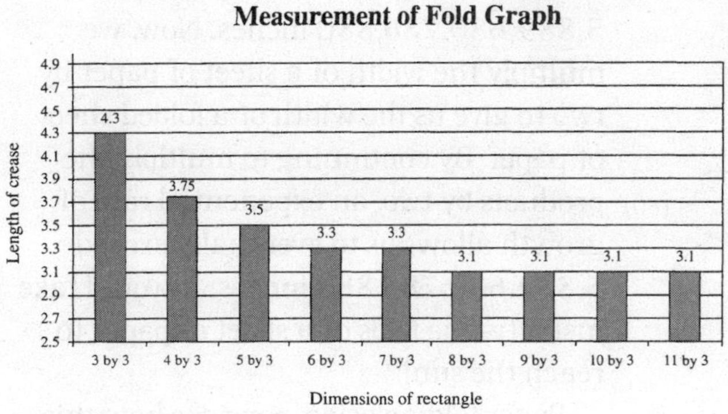

Figure 1. This graph shows the lengths of the folds (inches) of sheets of paper in various widths.

For example, for an 11 by 3 inch rectangle, the length of its crease is 3 and 1/8 inches. The crease for the 3 inch by 3 inch rectangle was the longest, while the length of the creases gradually declined as the length of the sheet of paper increased.

* * *

1 1 1

Furthering the notion of paper folding, did you ever wonder how many folds of paper it would take to reach the sun from Earth? In this research, we will determine the answer to this question. The distance between Earth and the sun is 92,955,820 miles.

A sheet of paper has a width of .003875 of an inch. This is found by measuring the width of a stack of a specific amount of paper (in this case we used a ream of five-hundred sheets) and then dividing by the number of sheets to find the width of a single sheet. Now, we have to convert the distance between Earth and the sun into inches. This converted measurement of the distance between Earth and the sun is 5,889,680,786,880 inches. Now, we multiply the width of a sheet of paper by two to give us the width of a folded sheet of paper. By continuing to multiply the products by two, an exponential rate of growth allows us to eventually exceed 5,889,680,786,880 inches. It would take just fifty-one folds of a sheet of paper to reach the sun!

Paper folding aside, consider how this exponential rate of growth is analogous to the scenario in which one is given a choice to receive one million dollars in one month, or a penny doubled every day for thirty days. Which option would you choose? The scenarios illustrate a huge difference. In the latter scenario, you would get over 5 million dollars with the penny doubled every day for 30 days.

The mathematical calculations speak for themselves:

Day 1: $.01
Day 2: $.02
Day 3: $.04
Day 4: $.08
Day 5: $.16
Day 6: $.32
Day 7: $.64
Day 8: $1.28
Day 9: $2.56
Day 10: $5.12
Day 11: $10.24
Day 12: $20.48
Day 13: $40.96
Day 14: $81.92
Day 15: $163.84
Day 16: $327.68
Day 17: $655.36
Day 18: $1,310.72
Day 19: $2,621.44
Day 20: $5,242.88
Day 21: $10,485.76
Day 22: $20,971.52
Day 23: $41,943.04
Day 24: $83,886.08
Day 25: $167,772.16
Day 26: $335,544.32
Day 27: $671,088.64
Day 28: $1,342,177.28
Day 29: $2,684,354.56
Day 30: $5,368,709.12

1 1 1

44. Throughout the passage, which rhetorical strategy does the speaker use most often?

(A) Repetition of concepts and formulas
(B) Rhetorical questions that intend to engage his audience's attention
(C) Allusions to significant related works
(D) Digressions that stray from his topic

45. According to the author, which of the following lists represents examples of paper folding in decreasing order of intricacy and seriousness?

(A) A circle cut from paper, an index card, a parachute
(B) An airbag, an index card, an origami bird
(C) A parachute, a folded American flag, a fortune cookie made of paper
(D) An index card, an airbag, a paper party hat

46. Which is the primary reason for the author discussing the circle made of paper?

(A) To stress the precision involved in folding
(B) To emphasize the unimportance of paper representations
(C) To distract the reader with simplified ideas
(D) To turn his discussion to the topic of circles and spheres

47. Based on the passage, which choice best describes the relationship between a sheet of paper and measuring the distance to the sun?

(A) Use of the paper is ineffective because its thickness is negligible.
(B) Thickness and distance are mathematically incompatible measurements.
(C) The paper thickness is used as a tool of sorts to measure distance.
(D) The vast differences in paper width and intergalactic distance make them mutually exclusive when considering the problem of measuring the distance from Earth to the sun.

48. The author refers to "the distance between Earth and the sun" (line 62–63) and the width of a sheet of paper (lines 65–66) mainly to

(A) dramatically contrast the staggering difference between these measurements.
(B) humorously explain how particular modes of measurement are counterproductive.
(C) frankly devalue the inadequate nature of fundamental materials.
(D) plainly establish the starting point of his mode of measuring distance to the sun.

PRACTICE TEST

PRACTICE TEST

1

49. According to the Measurement of Fold Graph, which of the following is true?

(A) As paper width increases, so does the measurement of the length of the fold.
(B) There is no correlation between fold length and paper length.
(C) There is an inconsistent relationship between the measurement of the paper and the measurement of the length of the folds.
(D) As paper width increases, the length of the fold line either decreases or remains constant.

50. The primary rhetorical effect of incorporating terms such as "algebra" (line 41), "convert" (line 72), and "products" (line 80) is to

(A) establish his facility or expertise within the discipline of math.
(B) ostracize the reader from an active engagement with the text.
(C) bemuse the reader with extraneous words.
(D) lend an air of authority to his audience.

51. In his investigation of solving the problem of the distance from Earth to the sun, the researcher relies most heavily on which of the following pairs?

(A) Repetition of a process and division
(B) Visualization and multiplication
(C) Mathematical conversions and repetition of a process
(D) Subjective notions and estimation

52. As used in the sentence "It would take just fifty-one folds of a sheet of paper to reach the sun!" (lines 82–84), the word "just" most closely means

(A) justifiably.
(B) about.
(C) less than.
(D) merely.

STOP

If there is still time remaining, you may review your answers.

2 2 2

WRITING AND LANGUAGE TEST 写作和语言测试

35 MINUTES, 44 QUESTIONS

Directions: The passages below are each accompanied by several questions, some of which refer to an underlined portion in the passage and some of which refer to the passage as a whole. For some questions, determine how the expression of ideas can be improved. For other questions, determine the best sentence structure, usage, or punctuation given the context. A passage or question may have an accompanying graphic that you will need to consider as you choose the best answer.

Choose the best answer to each question, considering what will optimize the writing quality and make the writing follow the conventions of standard written English. Some questions have a "NO CHANGE" option that you can pick if you believe the best choice is to leave the underlined portion as is.

Questions 1–11 are based on the following passage and supplementary material.

Case Study

Epidemic keratoconjunctivitis (EKC) is a highly contagious, distinctive clinical entity that **1** affects the both the cornea and the conjunctiva. There are variations in presentation, yet the clinical course is well known. After an incubation period of approximately two to fourteen days post-infection, patients commonly **2** presents with a red eye and combined papillary/follicular conjunctivitis. There may also be mild discharge, conjunctival chemosis, a pseudomembrane in severe cases, and an associated preauricular adenopathy. Symptoms vary and include **3** marked tearing, burning, and foreign body sensation. The presentation is usually unilateral, yet becomes bilateral

1. (A) NO CHANGE
   (B) likewise affects both
   (C) effects both
   (D) affects both

2. (A) NO CHANGE
   (B) present themselves
   (C) present
   (D) are presenting

3. (A) NO CHANGE
   (B) marks
   (C) markers
   (D) manifesting

2 2 2

in the majority of cases. **4** After another seven to sixteen days, a superficial punctuate keratitis develops, with or without more focal epithelial lesions. After approximately eleven **5** upwards til fifteen days from onset, deeper sub epithelial infiltrates (SEIs) develop as the more superficial epithelial lesions regress. SEIs are white, granular opacities that represent antigen-antibody complexes. The viral antigen from the epithelial surface **6** filter through Bowman's membrane and reacts with antibodies in the anterior stroma. These subepithelial infiltrates may persist for months to years and may or may not have an effect on vision. This course of progression is outlined in Table 1, which is featured below.

Adenovirus has been isolated as the virus responsible for EKC. Adenovirus also causes a variety of syndromes including keratoconjunctivitis with upper respiratory tract infection (pharyngoconjunctival fever), and lower respiratory tract illness with pneumonia. There are various serotypes of adenovirus, yet those most commonly associated with EKC include Ad-4, Ad-8, Ad-9, Ad-10, Ad-19, and Ad-37. Diagnosis is **7** generally made upon clinical observation, as lab testing is difficult and can take several days.

There is no accepted treatment for EKC and no effective antiviral therapy. Controversy still exists over the use of topical steroids secondary to increased risk of infection, glaucoma, and cataract formation. Other studies, however, show significant benefit with the addition of steroids in improving patient comfort and decreasing SEIs. Appropriate hygiene and isolation of infected persons **8** is necessary to

4. Which choice best replaces the underlined sentence based on Table 1?
   (A) NO CHANGE
   (B) After about a month, a superficial punctuate keratitis develops, but this time without more focal epithelial lesions.
   (C) After another two weeks to sixteen days, a superficial punctuate keratitis develops, with red eye gradually fading.
   (D) After another seven to sixteen days, a superficial punctuate keratitis develops, consistently presenting with more focal epithelial lesions.

5. (A) NO CHANGE
   (B) toward
   (C) through
   (D) to

6. (A) NO CHANGE
   (B) is filtrating among and through
   (C) filters through
   (D) filtering thru

7. As used in this context, the term "generally" most closely means
   (A) casually.
   (B) domineeringly.
   (C) haphazardly.
   (D) customarily.

8. (A) NO CHANGE
   (B) are necessary
   (C) being necessary
   (D) are of necessity

2 2 2

prevent contraction **9** the disease generally spreads via eye-to-eye, eye-to-hand, or via air and droplet transmission.

CASE REPORT:

[1] **10** A 25-year-old Asian male presented to the University Eye Center on December 16, 2009, with a long history of previous diagnoses and subsequently various past treatments. [2] His symptoms began at the end of a trip to Hong Kong two weeks earlier. [3] The patient was in good general health, denied any allergies, and was not taking any systemic medications. [4] The patient had never worn contact lenses, and reported this was the first time he had suffered from these symptoms. [5] The patient sought treatment while in Hong Kong, and was given a drop for which he didn't know the name. [6] He used this unknown drop for only a few days with some relief, then self discontinued. [7] During this time, the patient reported self-medicating with Robitussin cough syrup for an upper respiratory tract infection which had since resolved. [8] Upon return to the United States, the patient sought care from a primary care physician who prescribed Tobradex to be used every night OD only. [9] The patient reported only minimal use, then self discontinued. [10] The patient reported only a mild decrease in symptoms with residual blur (right worse than left), redness, tearing, mild photophobia, mucous discharge, and irritation. **11**

Table 1 summarizes the three distinct phases of the disease process.

Table 1: Stages of EKC

	Initial Presentation	**Next 8 Days**	**Following 8 days**
Clinical presentation	Red eye, combined papillary/ follicular conjunctivitis	Corneal superficial punctate keratitis	Corneal sub-epithelial infiltrates

9. Which choice most effectively combines the sentences at the underlined portion?
   (A) NO CHANGE
   (B) in consideration that the disease
   (C) as the disease
   (D) given that as the disease

10. Which choice is grammatically sound and most logically and effectively establishes the main topic of the paragraph?
   (A) As it is now
   (B) The University Eye Center seeing thousands of patients each year, who suffer from mild to severe eye health issues.
   (C) Although a 25-year-old Asian male presented to the University Eye Center on December 16, 2009, with complaints of blurriness and redness, there was solid ground to believe he was fabricating his symptoms.
   (D) Accompanied by his visually impaired mother, a 25-year-old Asian male presented to the University Eye Center on December 16, 2009.

11. For the sake of coherence in this paragraph, sentence 4 should be placed
   (A) where it is now
   (B) before sentence 2
   (C) after sentence 5
   (D) after sentence 9

2 2 2

Questions 12–22 are based on the following passage.

Ancient Egypt

Geography influenced the development of Ancient Egypt in **12** quite a many ways. The Nile River, the Mediterranean Sea, **13** the Sahara Desert, and the Red Sea all influenced Ancient Egypt **14** in different and various ways. In particular, the Nile River, which runs south to north and **15** empties out into the Mediterranean Sea, **16** would have affected the development of this civilization. Ancient Egypt developed along the Nile River, which provided **17** them with a valuable source of water. The Nile would often flood, causing the land surrounding it to be fertile and thus a good place for farmers to plant their crops. In addition to providing water for crops and drinking, the Nile River was also a source for food **18** because of fish.

The Mediterranean Sea was a great trade route for Ancient Egypt to access Europe and other foreign countries. Because of this, Ancient Egyptians needed to build boats. Egyptians created this outstanding invention to sail the Nile River and Mediterranean

12. (A) NO CHANGE
    (B) quite ways
    (C) many ways
    (D) many ways, quite so

13. (A) NO CHANGE
    (B) Sahara Desert, as well as Red Sea
    (C) Sahara Desert, and including the Red Sea
    (D) Sahara Desert and along with the Red Sea

14. (A) NO CHANGE
    (B) in differing and a variety of ways
    (C) in divergently various ways
    (D) Delete the underlined portion.

15. (A) NO CHANGE
    (B) empties
    (C) empties on
    (D) emptying

16. (A) NO CHANGE
    (B) affected
    (C) effected
    (D) has been affecting

17. (A) NO CHANGE
    (B) these
    (C) there
    (D) it

18. (A) NO CHANGE
    (B) because of their fish
    (C) because of the fish it provided
    (D) on account of the fish there

2 2 2

Sea. (19) To the east, Egypt traded with Canaan. To the south, Egypt traded with Dubai. And to the west, Egypt traded with Libya. Ancient Egyptians typically imported timber, silver, slaves, horses, copper, tin, and wine. The Mediterranean Sea was of great value to the Ancient Egyptians.

The Sahara Desert acted as a barrier, preventing intruders from entering Egypt from the west. It also limited the space that the Ancient Egyptians could use to the west because of this dry land. Intruders weren't able to sail the Nile because of (20) its six primary cataracts, or shallow rapids. The Ancient Egyptians were protected also by the Red Sea to the east. If intruders wanted to reach Ancient Egypt from the east, they would need to cross the Red Sea. Geography significantly influenced the development of Ancient Egypt. In turn, the Ancient Egyptians contributed to our modern world in many ways. Important innovations we utilize today, such as pyramids, the calendar, astronomy, and dolls, were invented by the Ancient Egyptians. First, The Great Pyramids are still used in contemporary architecture (21) today, as our architectural landscape features pyramid-like structures. Second, the calendar was invented by Ancient Egyptians. They created the calendar by recording the flood cycle of the Nile River. A vital innovation to the modern world, we use it to keep dates, organize our schedules, and record important events. Third, astronomy was a great invention of the Ancient Egyptians. Decans were groups of stars used for telling time. Each group of stars rose forty minutes later each night. By observing the position of a constellation and knowing the day of the year, the Ancient Egyptians could tell (22) what time it was. To do this, Ancient Egyptians needed to know mathematics. In our modern world, we sometimes use the Egyptian's strategy to tell time. Ancient Egyptians bestowed many contributions on today's world.

19. Which of the following most effectively lends concision to this sentence while maintaining clarity?

To the east, Egypt traded with Canaan. To the south, Egypt traded with Dubai.

(A) NO CHANGE
(B) To the east, Egypt traded with Canaan and to the south, Egypt traded with Dubai.
(C) To the east, Egypt traded with Canaan while to the south, Egypt was trading with Dubai.
(D) To the east, Egypt traded with Canaan; to the south, Dubai.

20. (A) NO CHANGE
(B) its'
(C) it's
(D) its having

21. (A) NO CHANGE
(B) meanwhile
(C) nowadays
(D) Delete the underlined portion.

22. (A) NO CHANGE
(B) the time
(C) the time of day
(D) the time using this celestial method

PRACTICE TEST

2 2 2

Questions 23–33 are based on the following passage.

Game Day

The seatbelts clicked, and we were on our way. My five-year-old **23** brother, Luca, and I were heading to the Community Center for his first soccer game of the fall season. I am not foreign to the Community Center, **24** where I spent much of my youth playing travel soccer and baseball with friends I still am close to today. Before Luca stepped **25** on to the field, his cleats had to be tied tightly and his shin guards, **26** they had to be fastened snugly. He seemed somewhat uneasy to meet his teammates and check out the competition, but I knew one thing for **27** sure; he wanted to score a goal.

Luca and I took the field together, holding hands and scouting for players with the same uniform **28** as his was. After I had taken seven or eight steps onto the field (twelve or thirteen steps for Luca), Luca jumped and exclaimed, "Look! There's my team!" I was surprised by his excitement, completely contrary to the uneasy mood **29** he displayed in the car. He darted toward his coach and teammates, stepping in line for the shooting drill. This would be the little bit of

23. (A) NO CHANGE
(B) brother, Luca, and I,
(C) brother Luca and I
(D) brother, Luca, and I, as siblings

24. (A) NO CHANGE
(B) where I had been spending
(C) in which I spent
(D) a location where I spent

25. (A) NO CHANGE
(B) to the field,
(C) onto the field
(D) onto the field,

26. (A) NO CHANGE
(B) would be fastened snugly.
(C) fastened snug.
(D) fastened snugly.

27. (A) NO CHANGE
(B) sure: he wanted to score a goal.
(C) sure: they wanted to score a goal.
(D) sure, in that he certainly wanted to score a goal.

28. (A) NO CHANGE
(B) as his uniform
(C) as his
(D) as his looked

29. (A) NO CHANGE
(B) he had been displaying
(C) displayed, as he did,
(D) he did go on to display

2 2 2

practice he would get before the game. The whistle **30** signing the start of the game blew; the players began to kick and run. They didn't pass; they just hit the ball and ran after it, hoping it would end up in the other team's net.

A mob of eight to ten five-year-olds surrounded the ball until **31** they eventually started in kicking it out of the swarm, only to be swarmed upon again. The first half quickly passed with the score tied at zero. Luca walked over to me on the sideline, expecting some cold water to quench his thirst. His head was down, and he took the water without looking at me. I went to give my brother a high five and he responded, "I didn't score . . ."

I added, ". . . *yet*."

A grin came to his face, and the word gave him just enough confidence to start the second half with zeal. The whistle sounded once again, and the swarm of players continued. Luca ran with a little more spark than he did in the first half. Toward the end of the game, while others were fading, Luca seemed to be picking up speed. Another throng of players formed, and eventually the ball popped out. It was now a footrace. The ball shot out of the cluster of five-year-olds and landed right in front of the opposition's goal with only Luca and a defender from the other team **32** chasing on after it.

First to reach the ball, Luca placed his left foot, and his right foot came swinging through his target. The ball hit the back of the net. He ran to me with both arms straight up, smiling ear to ear. From then on, Luca played every game confidently, with that zest and spark he showed in the second half **33** with the self-confidence given himself with just one word.

30. (A) NO CHANGE
(B) cuing in
(C) announcing
(D) signaling

31. (A) NO CHANGE
(B) it was eventually kicked by the players
(C) it was eventually kicked
(D) ultimately it was eventually kicked

32. (A) NO CHANGE
(B) chasing after it
(C) chasing along after it
(D) chasing them after it

33. (A) NO CHANGE
(B) confidentiality given to him
(C) confidence given to him
(D) Delete the underlined portion.

PRACTICE TEST

PRACTICE TEST

2 2 2

Questions 34–44 are based on the following passage and supplementary material.

An Investigation into Cystic Fibrosis

Cystic fibrosis is a terrible disease (34) in effecting the most innocent people. In fact most individuals with cystic fibrosis succumb to the disease before their twentieth birthday. The disease not only proves to be a very common disease at childbirth (35) but it also presents as an extremely enigmatic disease. Cystic fibrosis causes scarring in the pancreas, serious pneumonia, (36) and disturbs the lungs. What makes (37) it so mysterious is that technically the gene should not be passing on all these generations if the victims of the disease die before they (38) are reproducing.

If society were able to test for cystic fibrosis genes in the American population today, this scientific advancement would be extremely beneficial, as this knowledge could curb the spread of this gene and (39) young children die. For us to do so, the price of DNA testing would have to drastically drop. It is very unlikely for us to see a widespread screening of Americans for the cystic fibrosis gene. As of 1999, genetic testing for cystic fibrosis is still not widely used. Most of the time one will only test for the gene because he or she knows that one of his or her family members (40) has the gene.

34. (A) NO CHANGE
(B) in its affecting
(C) that effects
(D) that affects

35. (A) NO CHANGE
(B) but also presenting
(C) as it also presents as
(D) but it also presents to be

36. (A) NO CHANGE
(B) and disturbing effects on
(C) and disturbing the lungs
(D) while adversely disturbing the lungs

37. (A) NO CHANGE
(B) these ailments and others
(C) sicknesses such as these
(D) this disease

38. (A) NO CHANGE
(B) have reproduced
(C) have underwent reproduction
(D) are of productive age

39. (A) NO CHANGE
(B) young people dying
(C) mortality among the young
(D) deaths among the young people of our society

40. (A) NO CHANGE
(B) harbors
(C) attributes
(D) carries

2 2 2

In our day and age it is not cost friendly to test for (41) cystic fibrosis, however if one day it does become a few dollars per sample, the advantage to a couple at risk far outweighs the struggle and money spent. Why might the cystic fibrosis gene get passed down through generations even if the majority of its victims succumb to the disease before the age of twenty? Dr. Knudsen answers that if people with cystic fibrosis were merely 2% more fertile than people without the gene it would be plausible for the gene to continue to be passed on.

There is also a (42) morality to this story. I don't mean that figuratively either, (43) I mean it literally. Each and every couple with a baby who has a one-fourth risk for cystic fibrosis has a decision to make, and it is extremely difficult. Based on a couple's religion or culture, it may be an easier or harder decision compared to that of others. Cystic fibrosis certainly does live up to (44) it's reputation as brutal and enigmatic.

41. Which choice most effectively combines the sentences at the underlined portions?
(A) As it is now
(B) cystic fibrosis, still
(C) cystic fibrosis; however,
(D) cystic fibrosis, and

42. (A) NO CHANGE
(B) moral
(C) morale
(D) mortality

43. Which choice completes the sentence most accurately, based on the passage evidence and explanation that follow?
(A) NO CHANGE
(B) as I mean it symbolically.
(C) as I mean it in jest.
(D) as I mean it logistically.

44. (A) NO CHANGE
(B) its' reputable
(C) its reputability
(D) its reputation

PRACTICE TEST

STOP

If there is still time remaining, you may review your answers.

3 3

MATH TEST (NO CALCULATOR) 数学测试（不用计算器）

25 MINUTES, 20 QUESTIONS

Directions: For questions 1-15, solve each problem and choose the best answer from the given options. Fill in the corresponding oval on your answer document. For questions 16–20, solve the problem and fill in the answer on the answer sheet grid. Please use scrap paper to work out your answers.

Notes:

- **You CANNOT use a calculator on this section.**
- **All variables and expressions represent real numbers unless indicated otherwise.**
- **All figures are drawn to scale unless indicated otherwise.**
- **All figures are in a plane unless indicated otherwise.**
- **Unless indicated otherwise, the domain of a given function is the set of all real numbers *x* for which the function has real values.**

REFERENCE INFORMATION

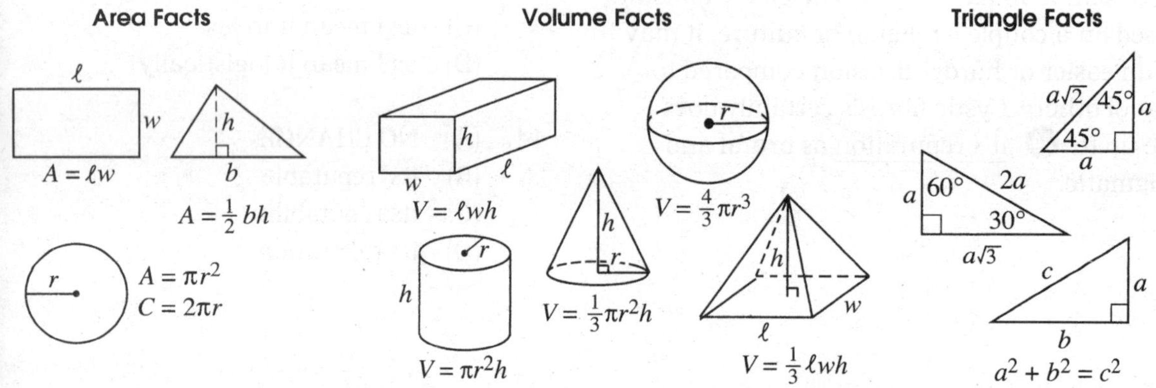

The arc of a circle contains 360°.

The arc of a circle contains 2π radians.

The sum of the measures of the angles in a triangle is 180°.

1. If $3(y-5)=33$, then $y+4=$?

   (A) 6

   (B) $12\frac{2}{3}$

   (C) 16

   (D) 20

2. Consider the following system of equations:

$$x^2+y^2-x-y=10$$

$$x^2+y^2-5x+3y=4$$

   What is the value of $2x-2y$?

   (A) 6

   (B) 5

   (C) 4

   (D) 3

GO ON TO THE NEXT PAGE

3. The length of a rectangle is 2 ft shorter than twice the width. Which of the following graphs represents the area of the rectangle in terms of its width?

(A)

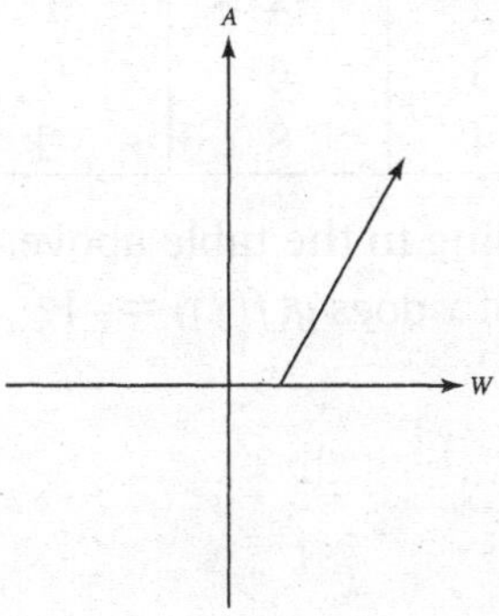

(B)

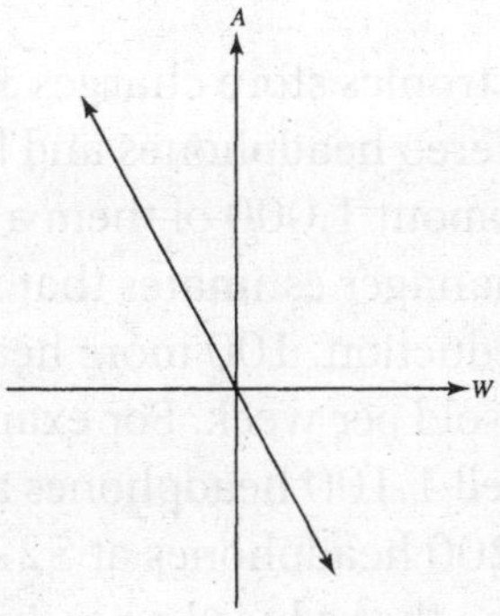

(C)

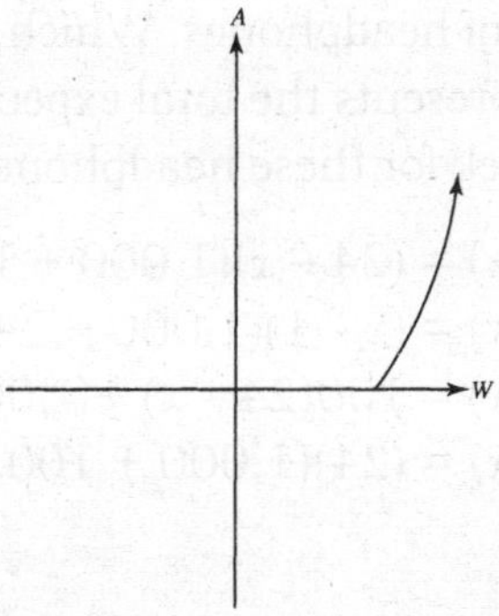

(D)

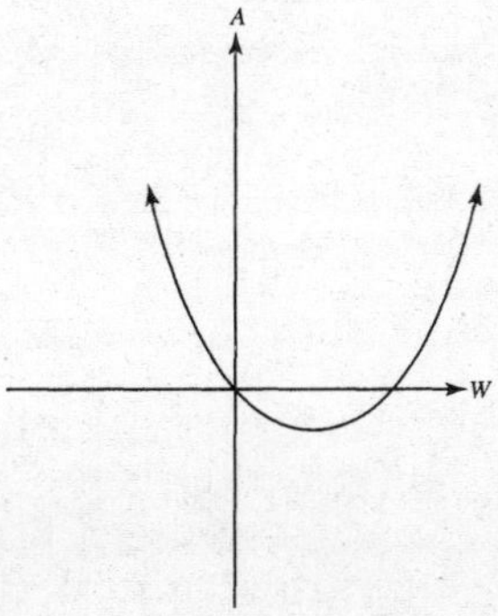

4. Which of the following is *not* equivalent to the equation $\frac{a}{bc}=\frac{d}{ef}$?

(A) $\frac{ae}{db}=\frac{c}{f}$

(B) $\frac{af}{d}=\frac{bc}{e}$

(C) $\frac{a}{d}=\frac{bc}{ef}$

(D) $\frac{ae}{f}=\frac{db}{c}$

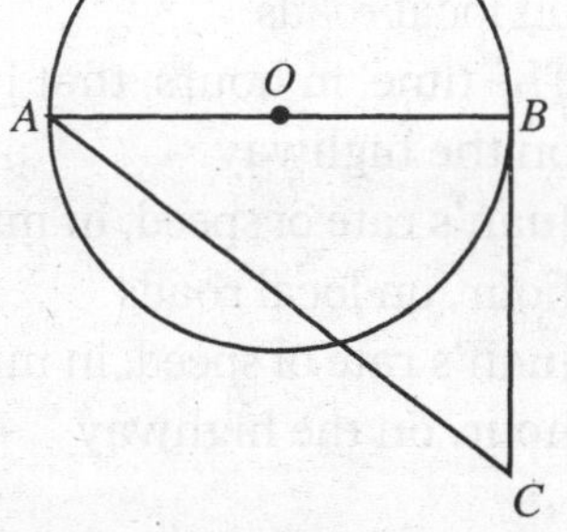

5. The figure above shows a circle with center O, radius 4, and diameter $\overline{AB}$. Line segment $\overline{BC}$ has length 8 and is tangent to the circle at B. What is the length of $\overline{AC}$?

(A) 8
(B) 16
(C) $8\sqrt{2}$
(D) $8\sqrt{3}$

6. For the equation $2x-1=-\sqrt{2-x}$, find the sum of the roots.

(A) $-\frac{1}{4}$

(B) $\frac{1}{2}$

(C) $\frac{3}{4}$

(D) 1

3

3

$$\frac{15}{x}+\frac{90}{x+30}=2$$

7. The equation above represents the following situation. On his way home from college, Juan traveled 15 miles on local roads and 90 miles on the highway. On the highway he traveled 30 miles per hour faster than on local roads. The whole trip took 2 hours. Which of the following describes what the expression $\frac{90}{x+30}$ represents in the equation?

(A) The time, in hours, that Juan drove on local roads
(B) The time, in hours, that Juan drove on the highway
(C) Juan's rate of speed, in miles per hour, on local roads
(D) Juan's rate of speed, in miles per hour, on the highway

8. In the complex numbers, where $i^2 = -1$, $\frac{i-1}{i} = ?$

(A) $-1 - i$
(B) $-1 + i$
(C) $1 + i$
(D) $1 - i$

x	$f(x)$	$g(x)$
−1	−2	4
0	0	3
1	2	2
2	4	1
3	6	0
4	8	−1

9. According to the table above, for what value of x does $g(f(x)) = -1$?

(A) 2
(B) 3
(C) 4
(D) 8

10. An electronics store charges $24 for a set of stereo headphones and has been selling about 1,000 of them a week. The store manager estimates that for every $1 price reduction, 100 more headphones can be sold per week. For example, he could sell 1,100 headphones at $23 each and 1,200 headphones at $22 each. Let $24 - x$ be the reduced price, in dollars, per set of headphones. Which function best represents the total expected revenue in a week for these headphones?

(A) $f(x) = (24 - x)(1{,}000 + 100x)$
(B) $f(x) = (x - 1)(1{,}000 + 24x)$
(C) $f(x) = 100(24 - x) + 1{,}000$
(D) $f(x) = (24)(1{,}000 + 100x) - x$

3

3

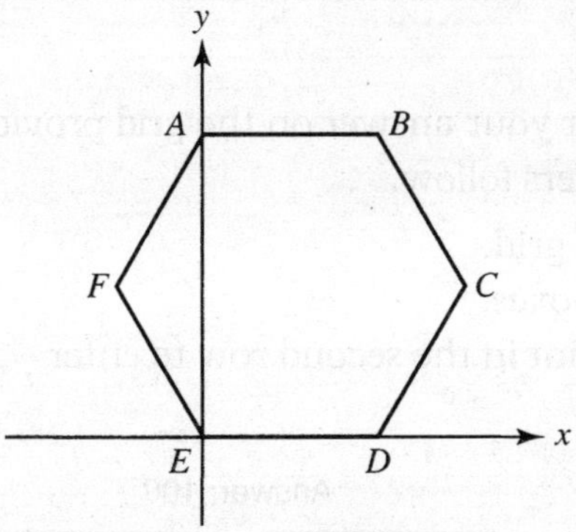

11. *ABCDEF* is a regular hexagon. What is the slope of the line containing $\overline{FE}$?

(A) $-\frac{1}{2}$
(B) $-\sqrt{3}$
(C) $-\sqrt{2}$
(D) $\sqrt{3}$

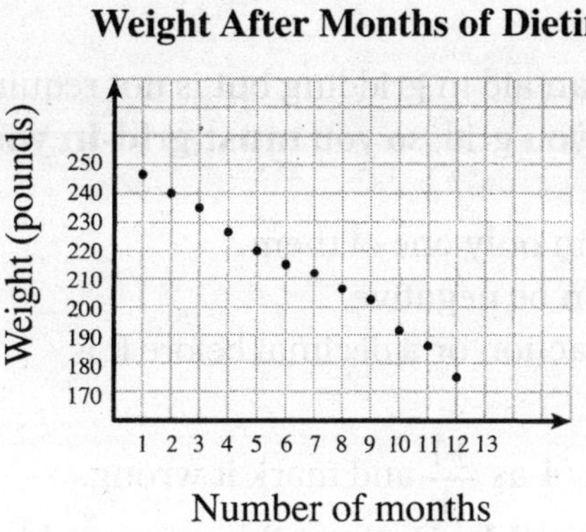

12. John joins a program to lose weight. Each month he records the number of months in the program, x, and his weight at the end of the month, w. The graph of his progress is shown above.

Which of the following could be the equation of the line that best fits this data?

(A) $w = -0.159x + 254.3$
(B) $w = 0.159x + 254.5$
(C) $w = 6.28x + 254.5$
(D) $w = -6.28x + 254.5$

13. Which of the following is a root of the equation $\frac{x}{x+2} = \frac{3}{x} + \frac{4}{x(x+2)}$?

(A) 5
(B) 2
(C) −2
(D) 0

14. The endpoints of the diameter of a circle are $P(6, 1)$ and $Q(-4, -5)$. Which is the equation of the circle?

(A) $x^2 + y^2 + 2x - 4y - 29 = 0$
(B) $x^2 + y^2 + 2x - 4y - 131 = 0$
(C) $x^2 + y^2 - 2x + 4y - 29 = 0$
(D) $x^2 + y^2 - 2x + 4y - 131 = 0$

15. If $12 + 6n$ is 20 percent bigger than k, what is k?

(A) $\frac{12+6n}{5}$
(B) $10 + 5n$
(C) $60 + 30n$
(D) $\frac{6(12+6n)}{5}$

PRACTICE TEST

Grid-in Response Directions

In questions 16–20, first solve the problem, and then enter your answer on the grid provided on the answer sheet. The instructions for entering your answers follow.

- First, write your answer in the boxes at the top of the grid.
- Second, grid your answer in the columns below the boxes.
- Use the fraction bar in the first row or the decimal point in the second row to enter fractions and decimals.

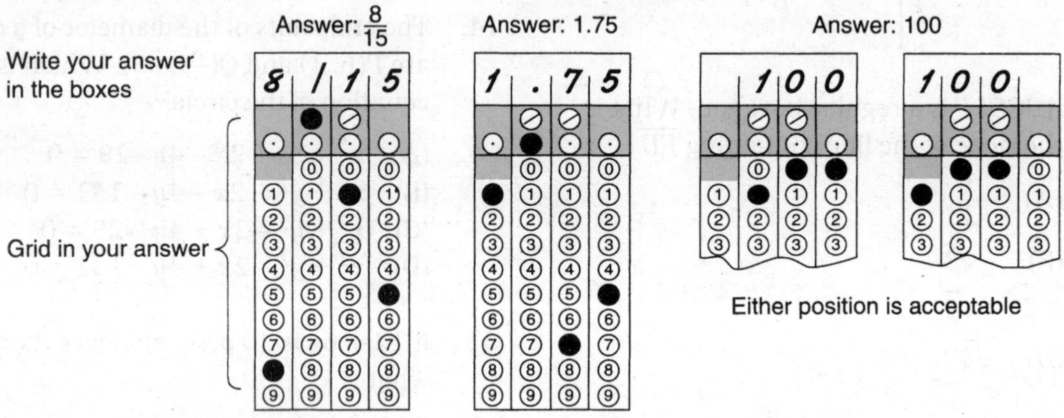

- Grid only one space in each column.
- Entering the answer in the boxes is recommended as an aid in gridding but is not required.
- The machine scoring your exam can read only what you grid, so you **must grid-in your answers correctly to get credit**.
- If a question has more than one correct answer, grid-in only one of them.
- The grid does not have a minus sign; so no answer can be negative.
- A mixed number *must* be converted to an improper fraction or a decimal before it is gridded.

  Enter $1\frac{1}{4}$ as $\frac{5}{4}$ or 1.25; the machine will interpret 11/4 as $\frac{11}{4}$ and mark it wrong.
- **All decimals must be entered as accurately as possible.** Here are three acceptable ways of gridding

$$\frac{3}{11} = 0.272727\ldots$$

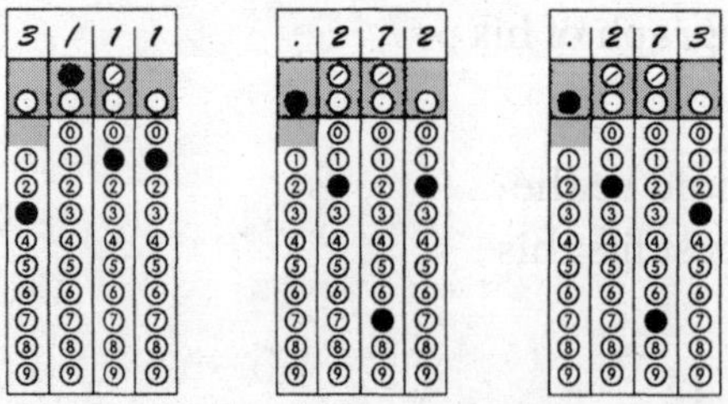

- Note that rounding to .273 is acceptable because you are using the full grid, but you would receive **no credit** for .3 or .27, because they are less accurate.

3 3

16. If $\frac{1}{2}x+\frac{1}{5}y=x+2$, what is the value of $2y-5x$?

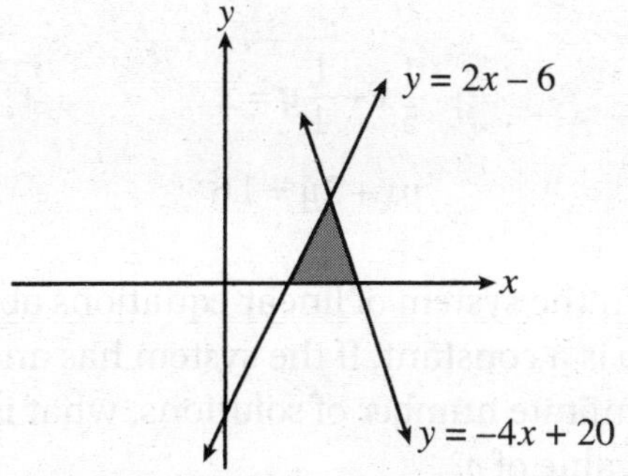

18. Find the area of the triangle that lies in the first quadrant, with its base on the x-axis and that is bounded by the lines $y = 2x - 6$ and $y = -4x + 20$ (the shaded area in the diagram shown above).

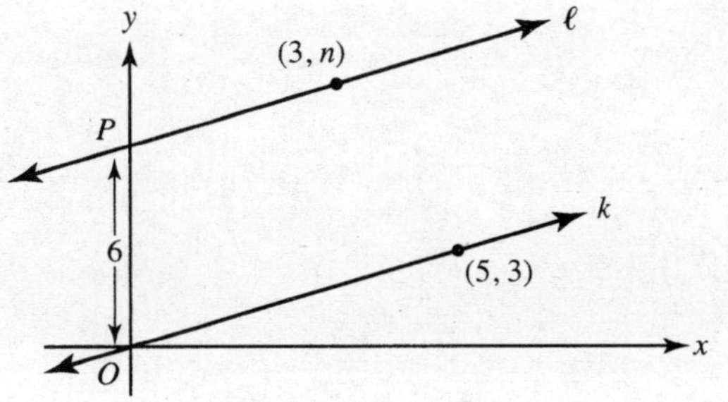

Note: Figure not drawn to scale.

17. In the xy-coordinate system shown above, the lines ℓ and k are parallel, and distance OP is 6. If the point (5, 3) is on line k, and the point $(3, n)$ is on line ℓ, what is the value of n?

3 3

19.

$$\frac{1}{5}x+\frac{1}{4}y=2$$

$$px+2y=16$$

In the system of linear equations above, p is a constant. If the system has an infinite number of solutions, what is the value of p?

20. If $2x + y = 16$, $x + 2z = 14$, and $2y + z = 12$, find the arithmetic mean of x, y, and z.

STOP

If there is still time remaining, you may review your answers.

4 4

MATH TEST (WITH CALCULATOR) 数学测试（使用计算器）

55 MINUTES, 38 QUESTIONS

Directions: For questions 1–30, solve each problem and choose the best answer from the given options. Fill in the corresponding oval on your answer document. For questions 31–38, solve the problem and fill in the answer on the answer sheet grid. Please use scrap paper to work out your answers.

Notes:

- You may use a calculator.
- All variables and expressions represent real numbers unless indicated otherwise.
- All figures are drawn to scale unless indicated otherwise.
- All figures are in a plane unless indicated otherwise.
- Unless indicated otherwise, the domain of a given function is the set of all real numbers x for which the function has real values.

REFERENCE INFORMATION

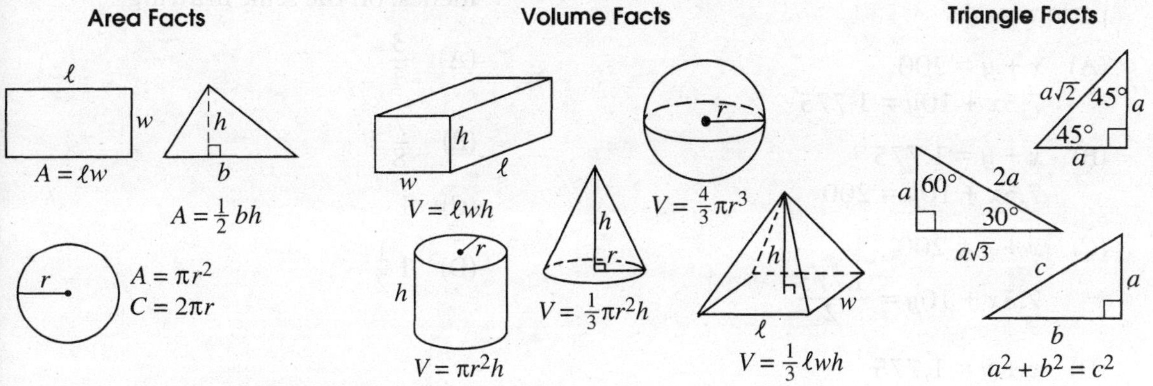

The arc of a circle contains 360°.
The arc of a circle contains 2π radians.
The sum of the measures of the angles in a triangle is 180°.

1. Jake can type 60 words per minute. If the total number of words typed is w and the number of hours that he types is h, which correctly shows the relationship between w and h?

(A) $w = 60h$
(B) $w = 3{,}600h$
(C) $\frac{w}{h} = \frac{1}{60}$
(D) $\frac{w}{h} = \frac{1}{3{,}600}$

2. Which is a solution to the following system of equations?

$$y + x^2 = 6x - 3$$

$$y - x = 1$$

(A) (3, 4)
(B) (4, 5)
(C) (5, 6)
(D) (1, 3)

3. In the junior class of a certain school, there are 24 more girls than boys. If the ratio of girls to boys is 5 : 4, which is the number of girls in the junior class?

(A) 216
(B) 144
(C) 120
(D) 96

4. Ticket prices for a school play are \$7.50 for students and \$10.00 for adults. For a given performance, 200 tickets were sold, and the performance took in \$1,775. Solving which of the following systems of equations yields the number of student tickets, x, and the number of adult tickets, y, that were bought for that performance?

(A) $x + y = 200$
$7.5x + 10y = 1{,}775$

(B) $x + y = 1{,}775$
$7.5x + 10y = 200$

(C) $x + y = 200$
$7.5x + 10y = \frac{1{,}775}{2}$

(D) $x + y = 1{,}775$
$7.5x + 10y = (1{,}775)(2)$

5. Which is equivalent to $x^{-\frac{2}{3}} = 4$?

(A) $x^{\frac{2}{3}} = \frac{1}{4}$

(B) $x^{\frac{2}{3}} = 4$

(C) $x^{-\frac{2}{3}} = -\frac{1}{4}$

(D) $x^{\frac{3}{2}} = \frac{1}{4}$

6. A scale drawing of a new building has $\frac{1}{2}$ inch representing 40 feet. If a conference room has a floor length of 60 feet, what is the floor length. in inches, on the scale drawing?

(A) $\frac{3}{4}$

(B) $\frac{7}{8}$

(C) 1

(D) $1\frac{1}{2}$

7. Which of the following could be the graph of $2x + 3y + 12 = 0$?

(A)

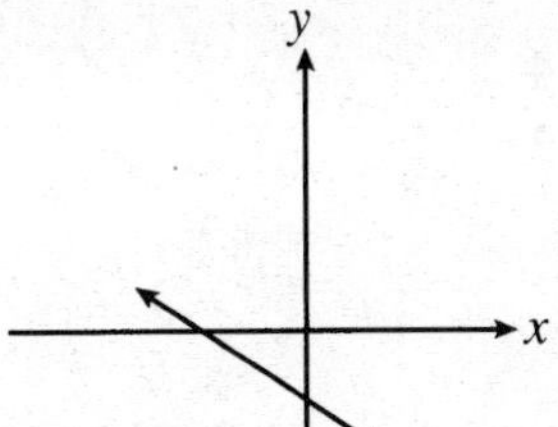

(B)

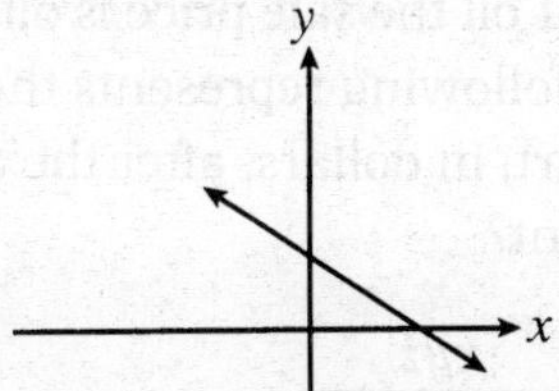

(C)

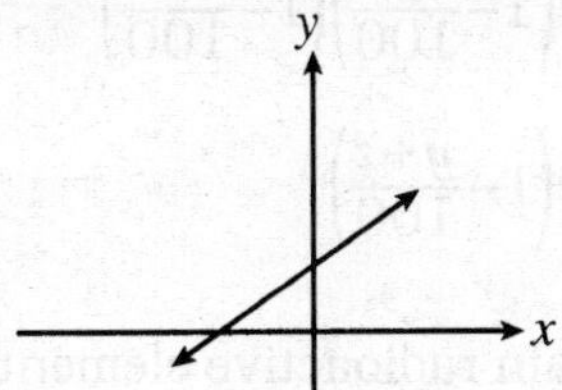

(D)

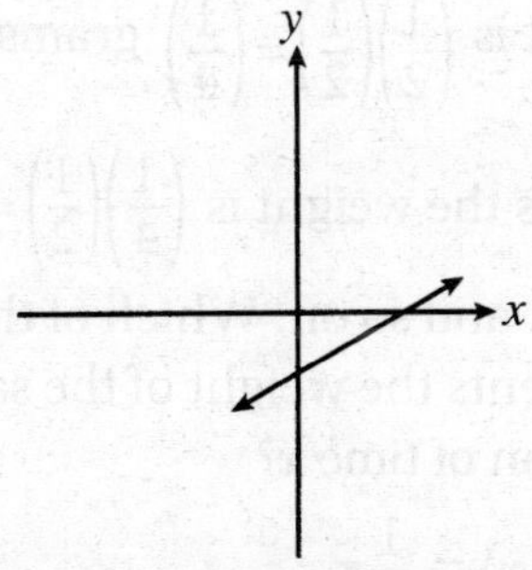

8. The management of a large sports equipment store conducts a survey of its 15 treadmill salespeople. The average number of minutes spent with each potential customer and the number of treadmills sold in a week are recorded for each salesperson. The results are shown in the scatterplot below.

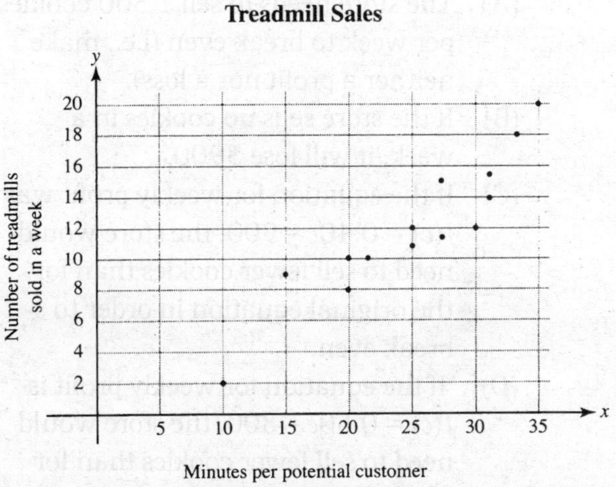

Which could be the line of best fit for this data?

(A) $y = 0.54x + 1.2$
(B) $y = 0.54x + 5$
(C) $y = 0.54x - 3.7$
(D) $y = -0.54x - 3.7$

9. One leg of a right triangle is 1 cm shorter than the other leg and the hypotenuse is 2 cm longer than the longer leg. What is the length of the longer leg?

(A) $2 + 2\sqrt{3}$
(B) $3 + 2\sqrt{3}$
(C) $5 + 2\sqrt{3}$
(D) $3 - 2\sqrt{3}$

4

10. A cookie store's weekly profit is a function of the number of cookies, c, that it sells. The equation approximating the weekly profit, in dollars, is

$$f(c) = 0.60c - 900$$

Which of the following is a false statement about the weekly profits?

(A) The store needs to sell 1,500 cookies per week to break even (i.e., make neither a profit nor a loss).
(B) If the store sells no cookies in a week, it will lose $900.
(C) If the equation for weekly profit was $f(c) = 0.40c - 900$, the store would need to sell fewer cookies than for the original equation in order to break even.
(D) If the equation for weekly profit is $f(c) = 0.60c - 800$, the store would need to sell fewer cookies than for the original equation in order to break even.

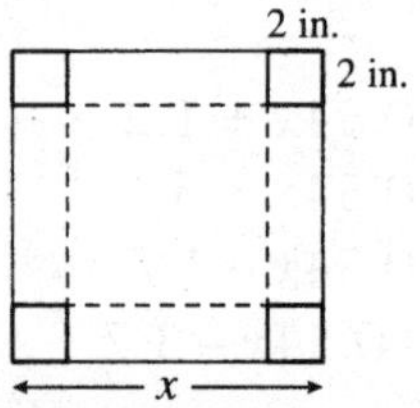

11. A square piece of cardboard measuring x inches by x inches is to be used to form an open box by cutting off 2-inch squares, and then folding the sides up along the dotted lines, as shown in the figure above.
If x is an integer, and the volume of the box must be greater than 128 cubic inches, what is the smallest value of x that can be used?

(A) 6
(B) 8
(C) 10
(D) 13

12. If the line $y + 2x + 3 = 0$ is parallel to the line $2y - px - 4 = 0$, what is the value of p?

(A) −4
(B) −2
(C) 2
(D) 4

13. The original price of a shirt is x dollars. During a sale, the original price is marked down y percent. On the last day of the sale, an additional discount of z percent off the sale price is offered. Which of the following represents the price of the shirt, in dollars, after the additional discount?

(A) $\dfrac{xyz}{(100)(100)}$

(B) $\dfrac{x(1-y)(1-z)}{100}$

(C) $x\left(1-\dfrac{y}{100}\right)\left(1-\dfrac{z}{100}\right)$

(D) $x\left(1-\dfrac{y+z}{100}\right)$

14. A certain radioactive element has a half-life of one year. This means that after 1 year, 1 gram of the element has decayed to $\frac{1}{2}$ gram, after 2 years the weight is $\left(\frac{1}{2}\right)\left(\frac{1}{2}\right)=\left(\frac{1}{4}\right)$ grams, after 3 years the weight is $\left(\frac{1}{4}\right)\left(\frac{1}{2}\right)=\left(\frac{1}{8}\right)$ grams, and so on. Which of the following represents the weight of the sample as a function of time x?

(A) $f(x) = \frac{1}{2}x$
(B) $f(x) = x^{-2}$
(C) $f(x) = 2^x$
(D) $f(x) = 2^{-x}$

4

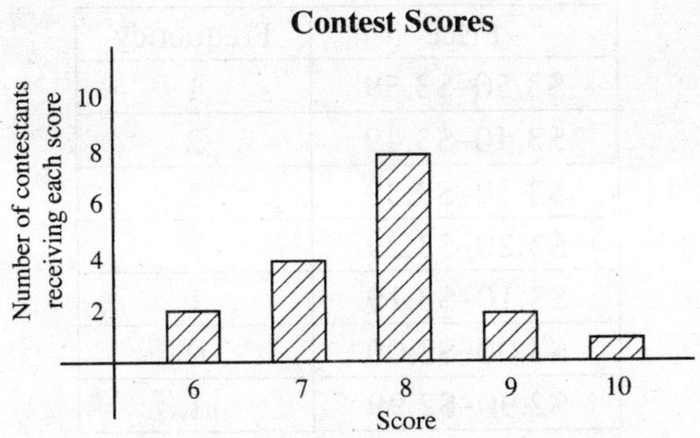

15. In a contest, each contestant could receive a score of 6, 7, 8, 9, or 10. The bar graph above shows how many contestants received each score.

    The score of 8 is described by which of the following measures?

    I. The average (arithmetic mean)
    II. The median
    III. The mode

    (A) I only
    (B) II only
    (C) III only
    (D) II and III only

16. An office buys a photocopier for \$5,800 with a servicing fee of \$25 a month. Each copy costs 3 cents. The office makes about 8,000 copies per month. A formula for the approximate cost *C* of buying and using the copier for *n* months is

    (A) $C = 5{,}800 + 240n$
    (B) $C = 5{,}800 + 265n$
    (C) $C = 5{,}800 + 2{,}400n$
    (D) $C = 5{,}800 + 2{,}425n$

17. Hooke's law states that the force needed to keep a spring stretched beyond its natural length is directly proportional to *x*, the distance the spring is stretched. If a spring has a natural length of 10 cm, and a force of 40 N (newtons) is required to keep the spring stretched to a length of 15 cm, what force, in newtons, will be needed to keep the spring stretched to a length of 14 cm?

    (A) 8
    (B) 32
    (C) 37.3
    (D) 50

18. The monthly cost *C* of driving a car depends on the number of miles driven *d*. Jo found that in November her cost of driving was \$380 for 480 miles, and in December her cost was \$460 for 800 miles. If the relationship between *C* and *d* is linear, what does the slope of the line, with *C* as a function of *d*, represent?

    (A) The cost per mile
    (B) The cost for 320 miles
    (C) The distance driven per dollar
    (D) The distance driven for \$80

4 4

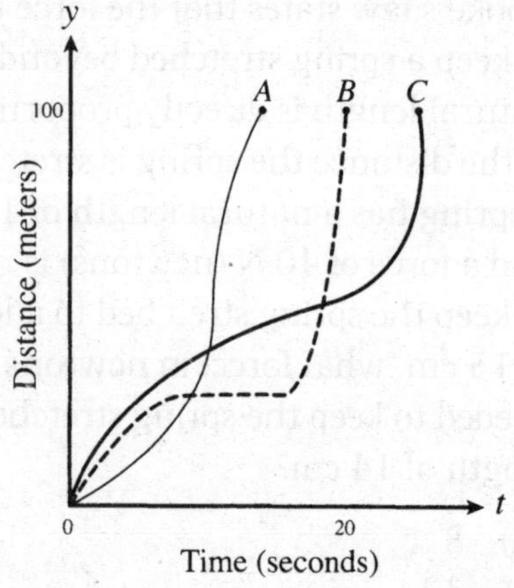

19. Three runners compete in a 100-meter obstacle race. The graph above depicts the distance run as a function of time for each runner. Which is *not* a valid conclusion?

(A) Runner *A* won the race.
(B) Runner *B* fell, then got up and completed the race.
(C) Each of the runners, *A*, *B*, and *C* completed the race.
(D) Runner *C* was ahead of runners *A* and *B* for at least half of the distance run.

Price	Frequency
\$3.50–\$3.59	1
\$3.40–\$3.49	2
\$3.30–\$3.39	3
\$3.20–\$3.29	7
\$3.10–\$3.19	1
\$3.00–\$3.09	0
\$2.90–\$2.99	1

20. The frequency chart above shows the prices of a gallon of milk in 15 stores in Tompkins County in 2010. Which of the following is a true statement about the data?

(A) The mode of the milk prices is \$3.25.
(B) The median price of a gallon of milk is \$3.25.
(C) The median price of a gallon of milk is in the range \$3.20–\$3.29.
(D) The mean price of a gallon of milk is \$3.25.

4 4

21. $0.06x + 0.045(100{,}000 - x) = 5.025$

The equation above represents the following situation: John inherits \$100,000 and invests it in two certificates of deposit. One pays 4.5% simple interest annually, and an investment with higher penalties for early withdrawal pays 6% simple interest annually. John's total interest from these investments is \$5.025 at the end of the first year.

Suppose John invested x dollars at 6%. Which of the following describes what the expression $0.045(100{,}000 - x)$ represents in the equation?

(A) The portion of the inheritance invested at 4.5%
(B) 4.5% of \$100,000
(C) The amount of interest earned from the 6% investment
(D) The amount of interest earned from the 4.5% investment

22. As dry air moves upward, it expands and cools. If the temperature on the ground is 20°C and the temperature at a height of 1 km is 10°C, which of the following linear models best describes the temperature t in degrees C at a height of h km above the ground?

(A) $t = -\frac{1}{10}h + 20$
(B) $t = \frac{1}{10}h + 20$
(C) $t = -10h + 20$
(D) $t = 10h + 20$

23. If the expression $\frac{3x^2}{x+2}$ is written in the equivalent form $\frac{12}{x+2} + A$, what is A in terms of x?

(A) $3x - 6$
(B) $3x + 6$
(C) $3x^2$
(D) $3x^2 - 1$

24. Because of anticipated heavy rain, the water level in a swimming pool must be lowered by 1 foot. Opening drain A lowers the level by 1 foot in 4 hours, whereas opening the smaller drain B does the job in 6 hours. How long will it take to lower the water level by 1 foot if both drains are opened?

Assuming that x is the number of hours to complete the job, an equation that solves the problem is

(A) $\frac{1}{4} + \frac{1}{6} = \frac{1}{x}$
(B) $\frac{4}{x} + \frac{6}{x} = 1$
(C) $\frac{x}{4} + \frac{x}{6} = x - 1$
(D) $\frac{1}{4} + \frac{1}{6} = x$

PRACTICE TEST

Flow Rate (%)	Mosquito Positive Rate (%)
0	22
10	16
40	12
60	11
90	6
100	2

25. The table above shows the relative abundance of mosquitoes (as measured by the mosquito positive rate) versus the flow rate (measured as a percentage of maximum flow) of a river in China.

Which of the following is a valid conclusion from the data?

(A) The faster the river flows, the greater the abundance of mosquitoes.

(B) When the flow rate of the river is about half its maximum, the mosquito positive rate is between 11 and 12 percent.

(C) At minimum flow rate, the mosquito population is close to 0.

(D) At maximum flow rate, just 2 mosquitoes were observed.

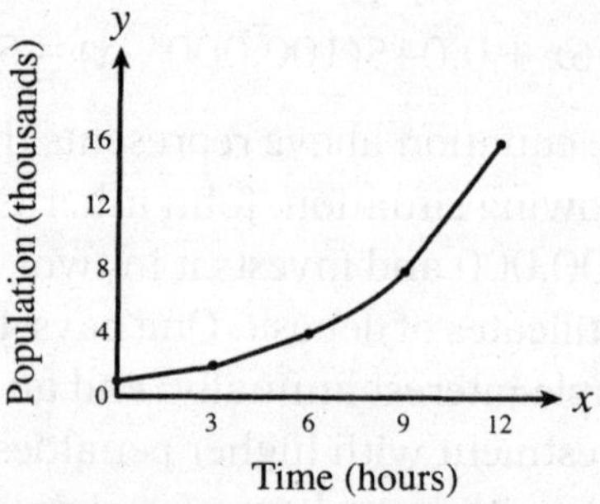

26. The graph above shows the size of a certain population after time t. Which of the following equations correctly shows y as a function of t?

(A) $y=t^3$

(B) $y=1{,}000\cdot 2^{\frac{t}{3}}$

(C) $y=3t^2$

(D) $y=1{,}000t-2{,}000$

27. A circle with center (2, 1) has a tangent to the circle at (3, 6). The equation of the tangent is

(A) $5y-x=27$

(B) $y+5x=21$

(C) $x+5y=21$

(D) $5y+x=33$

4

4

28. A research study was conducted to determine whether a certain electrical implant, I, is successful in improving hearing. From a large population of people with hearing loss, 400 participants were selected at random. Half were randomly selected to receive the implant and the other half did not receive the implant. The resulting data showed that people who received the implant had significantly improved hearing compared to those who did not receive the implant.

Based on the study, which of the following is an appropriate conclusion?

(A) Electrical implant I is likely to improve the hearing of people who have hearing loss.
(B) Electrical implant I is likely to improve the hearing of all people who have the implant.
(C) Electrical implant I is better than other treatments for hearing loss.
(D) Electrical implant I will cause a substantial improvement in hearing.

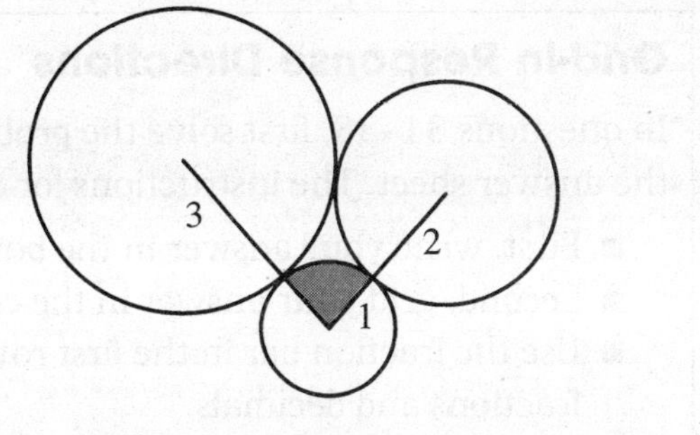

Note: Figure not drawn to scale.

29. Three circles with radii 1, 2, and 3 inches are externally tangent to one another, as shown in the figure above. The area, in square inches, of the sector of the circle of radius 1 that is cut off by the line segments joining the center of that circle to the centers of the other two circles (the shaded area) is

(A) π
(B) $\frac{\pi}{2}$
(C) $\frac{\pi}{3}$
(D) $\frac{\pi}{4}$

30. If the value, to the nearest thousandth, of $\sin\theta$ is 0.747, which of the following must be true?

(A) $\sin\left(\frac{\pi}{2}-\theta\right)\approx 0.747$
(B) $\cos\left(\frac{\pi}{2}-\theta\right)\approx 0.747$
(C) $\cos\left(\frac{\pi}{2}-\theta\right)\approx (1-0.747)$
(D) $\sin\left(\frac{\pi}{2}-\theta\right)\approx (1-0.747)$

PRACTICE TEST

Grid-in Response Directions

In questions 31–38, first solve the problem, and then enter your answer on the grid provided on the answer sheet. The instructions for entering your answers follow.

- First, write your answer in the boxes at the top of the grid.
- Second, grid your answer in the columns below the boxes.
- Use the fraction bar in the first row or the decimal point in the second row to enter fractions and decimals.

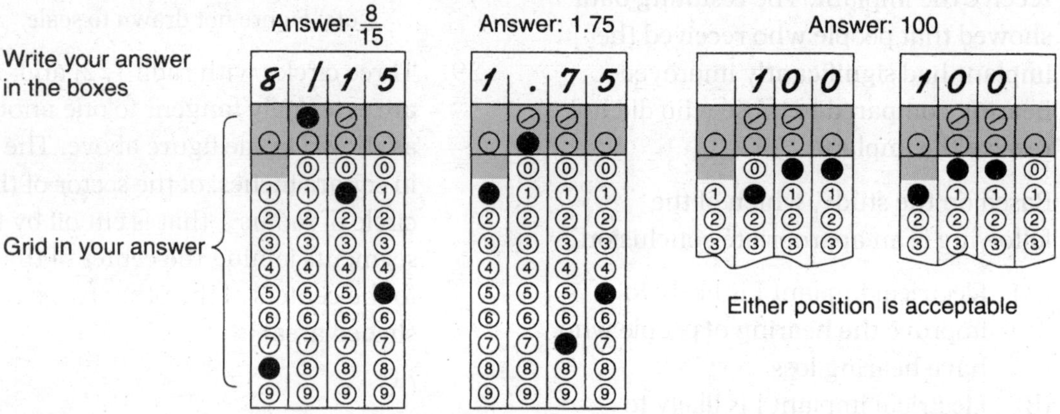

Either position is acceptable

- Grid only one space in each column.
- Entering the answer in the boxes is recommended as an aid in gridding but is not required.
- The machine scoring your exam can read only what you grid, so you **must grid-in your answers correctly to get credit**.
- If a question has more than one correct answer, grid-in only one of them.
- The grid does not have a minus sign; so no answer can be negative.
- A mixed number *must* be converted to an improper fraction or a decimal before it is gridded.

  Enter $1\frac{1}{4}$ as $\frac{5}{4}$ or 1.25; the machine will interpret 11/4 as $\frac{11}{4}$ and mark it wrong.
- **All decimals must be entered as accurately as possible.** Here are three acceptable ways of gridding

$$\frac{3}{11} = 0.272727\ldots$$

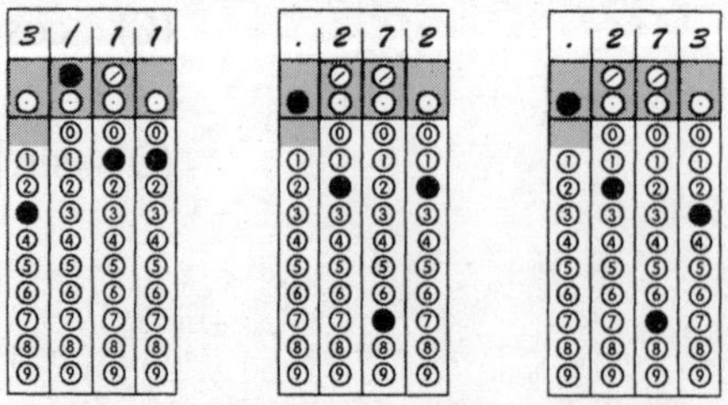

- Note that rounding to .273 is acceptable because you are using the full grid, but you would receive **no credit** for .3 or .27, because they are less accurate.

4

4

31. The weight of an object on or beneath the surface of the moon varies directly as its distance from the center of the moon, assuming that the moon has uniform density. The radius of the moon is approximately 1,080 miles. If an object weighs 60 pounds on the surface of the moon, how far beneath the surface, in miles, would it have to be to weigh 50 pounds?

32. The function f is defined by:

$$f(x)=\frac{1}{3}(x^3+x^2-11x-3)$$

If p_1, p_2, and p_3 are the zeros of $f(x)$, find the product $p_1 p_2 p_3$ to the nearest integer.

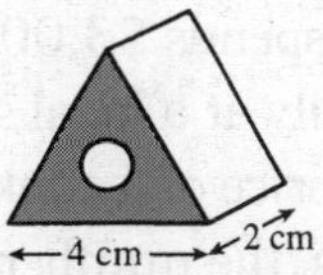

33. The figure above shows a metal triangular solid with two equilateral triangle faces and a thickness of 2 cm. The length of each side of a triangular face is 4 cm. A hole with a diameter of 1 cm is drilled through the solid. The density of the metal is 6 grams per cubic centimeter. What is the mass of this solid to the nearest gram? (Density is mass divided by volume.)

34. For a new car, the gas mileage in terms of its speed x is modeled by the function $G(x)=-\frac{1}{28}x^2+3x-31$, where $15 \le x \le 90$, and x is speed in miles per hour and G is miles per gallon. At what speed, in miles per hour, does the car attain its best gas mileage?

4

4

35. Mrs. Yang spends \$3.00 a day on cookies for her family at a local supermarket. When the price of a cookie increased by 10 cents, the number of cookies she bought decreased by 1. What was the original price, in dollars, of a cookie?

												Total
Absences	10	9	8	7	6	5	4	3	2	1	0	
Frequency	2	1	4	8	5	15	12	18	26	37	12	140

36. The student attendance record for a class in a one-semester course is shown above. If 2 students are chosen at random, what is the probability, to the nearest hundredth, that both students have fewer than 2 absences?

Questions 37 and 38 refer to the following information.

A juice manufacturer advertises its apple drink as "natural," even though it contains only 5% apple juice. A new regulation stipulates that to use "natural" on the label, a drink must contain at least 10% fruit juice.

37. How many gallons of pure apple juice must this manufacturer add to 900 gallons of its apple drink to satisfy the new regulation?

38. The minimum daily requirement of Vitamin C for teenagers is 70 mg. If one ounce of pure apple juice contains 0.31 mg of Vitamin C, what percent of the daily requirement does a teenager get by drinking an 8-ounce cup of the apple drink that contains 10% pure apple juice?

STOP

If there is still time remaining, you may review your answers.

ESSAY 写作

Directions: This is your opportunity to show that you can read and understand a passage and write an analysis of that passage. Be sure your essay demonstrates a clear and logical analysis of the passage, using precise language.

On the actual test, you will write your essay on the lines provided in your answer booklet; for now, write your essay on a lined paper. Remember to write or print legibly so that others can read what you've written.

You have 50 minutes to read the essay and write a response to the prompt provided.

As you read the passage below, consider how the author, Johnson, uses:

- Evidence, such as examples, facts, and/or data, to support claims.
- Reasoning to develop his thoughts and to connect his ideas and claims with evidence.
- Rhetorical (stylistic) or persuasive features, such as diction (word choice) or appeals to emotion, to add power to his expressed ideas.

President Lyndon B. Johnson's
Special Message to the Congress: The American Promise

March 15, 1965

[As delivered in person before a joint session at 9:02 P.M.]

1 Mr. Speaker, Mr. President, Members of the Congress:

2 I speak tonight for the dignity of man and the destiny of democracy.

3 I urge every member of both parties, Americans of all religions and of all colors, from every section of this country, to join me in that cause.

4 At times history and fate meet at a single time in a single place to shape a turning point in man's unending search for freedom. So it was at Lexington and Concord. So it was a century ago at Appomattox. So it was last week in Selma, Alabama.

5 There, long-suffering men and women peacefully protested the denial of their rights as Americans. Many were brutally assaulted. One good man, a man of God, was killed.

6 There is no cause for pride in what has happened in Selma. There is no cause for self-satisfaction in the long denial of equal rights of millions of Americans. But there is cause for hope and for faith in our democracy in what is happening here tonight.

7 For the cries of pain and the hymns and protests of oppressed people have summoned into convocation all the majesty of this great Government—the Government of the greatest Nation on earth.

8 Our mission is at once the oldest and the most basic of this country: to right wrong, to do justice, to serve man.

9 In our time we have come to live with moments of great crisis. Our lives have been marked with debate about great issues; issues of war and peace, issues of prosperity and depression. But rarely in any time does an issue lay bare the secret heart of America itself. Rarely are we met with a challenge, not to our growth or abundance, our welfare or our security, but rather to the values and the purposes and the meaning of our beloved Nation.

10 The issue of equal rights for American Negroes is such an issue. And should we defeat every enemy, should we double our wealth and conquer the stars, and still be unequal to this issue, then we will have failed as a people and as a nation.

11 For with a country as with a person, "What is a man profited, if he shall gain the whole world, and lose his own soul?"

12 There is no Negro problem. There is no Southern problem. There is no Northern problem. There is only an American problem. And we are met here tonight as Americans—not as Democrats or Republicans—we are met here as Americans to solve that problem.

13 This was the first nation in the history of the world to be founded with a purpose. The great phrases of that purpose still sound in every American heart, North and South: "All men are created equal"—"government by consent of the governed"—"give me liberty or give me death." Well, those are not just clever words, or those are not just empty theories. In their name Americans have fought and died for two centuries, and tonight around the world they stand there as guardians of our liberty, risking their lives.

14 Those words are a promise to every citizen that he shall share in the dignity of man. This dignity cannot be found in a man's possessions; it cannot be found in his power, or in his position. It really rests on his right to be treated as a man equal in opportunity to all others. It says that he shall share in freedom, he shall choose his leaders, educate his children, and provide for his family according to his ability and his merits as a human being.

15 To apply any other test—to deny a man his hopes because of his color or race, his religion or the place of his birth—is not only to do injustice, it is to deny America and to dishonor the dead who gave their lives for American freedom.

http://www.lbjlib.utexas.edu/johnson/archives.hom/speeches.hom/650315.asp

Write an essay in which you explain how LBJ structures and presents an argument to persuade Congress that all Americans deserve equal justice and freedom. In your essay, analyze how Johnson uses one or more of the features listed above (or features of your own choice) to strengthen the logic and persuasiveness of his argument. Be sure that your analysis focuses on the most relevant elements of the passage.

Your essay should not explain whether you agree with Johnson's claims, but rather explain how the author builds an argument to persuade his audience.

Now that you've completed this practice test, be sure to take the online test at *barronsbooks.com/TP/SAT/1600/* for additional practice.

STOP

If there is still time remaining, you may review your answers.

ANSWER KEY
答案
Practice Test
练习测试题

Section 1: Reading

1.	A	14.	C	27.	C	40.	A
2.	A	15.	B	28.	D	41.	C
3.	D	16.	A	29.	C	42.	D
4.	A	17.	C	30.	A	43.	A
5.	C	18.	A	31.	C	44.	B
6.	A	19.	B	32.	D	45.	C
7.	D	20.	B	33.	A	46	A
8.	A	21.	B	34.	D	47.	C
9.	D	22.	B	35.	C	48.	D
10.	B	23.	A	36.	A	49.	D
11.	B	24.	A	37.	A	50.	A
12.	B	25.	C	38.	B	51	B
13.	A	26.	B	39.	C	52.	D

Section 2: Writing and Language

1.	D	12.	C	23.	A	34.	D
2.	C	13.	A	24.	A	35.	A
3.	A	14.	D	25.	D	36.	B
4.	A	15.	B	26.	D	37.	D
5.	D	16.	B	27.	B	38.	B
6.	C	17.	D	28.	C	39.	C
7.	D	18.	C	29.	A	40.	D
8.	B	19.	D	30.	D	41.	C
9.	C	20.	A	31.	C	42.	B
10.	A	21.	D	32.	B	43.	A
11.	A	22.	B	33.	D	44.	D

ANSWER SHEET
答案
Practice Test
练习测试题

Section 3: Math (No Calculator)

For the math sections, the letters in brackets refer to the following key: E = Easy, M = Medium, H = Hard, HA = Heart of Algebra, P = Passport to Advanced Math, DA = Data Analysis, AT = Additional Topic.

1. **D** [E; HA]
2. **D** [E; P]
3. **C** [M; P]
4. **D** [E; P]
5. **C** [M; AT]
6. **A** [M; P]
7. **B** [M; P]
8. **C** [M; AT]
9. **A** [H; P]
10. **A** [H; P]
11. **B** [M; HA]
12. **D** [M; HA]
13. **A** [M; P]
14. **C** [H; AT]
15. **B** [H; HA]

16. **20** [M; P]

17. **39/5** or **7.8** or **7.80** [H; HA]

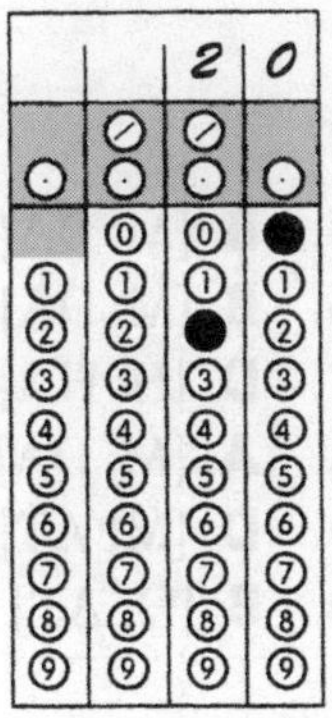

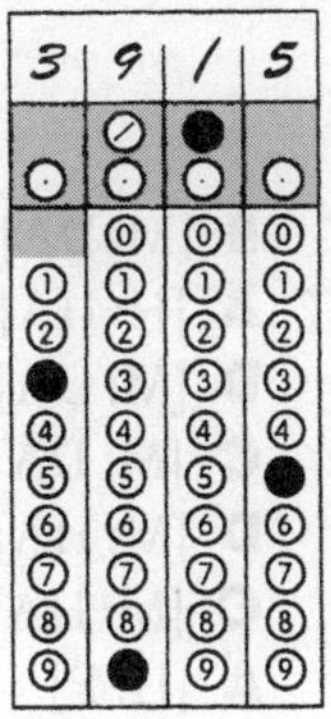

or

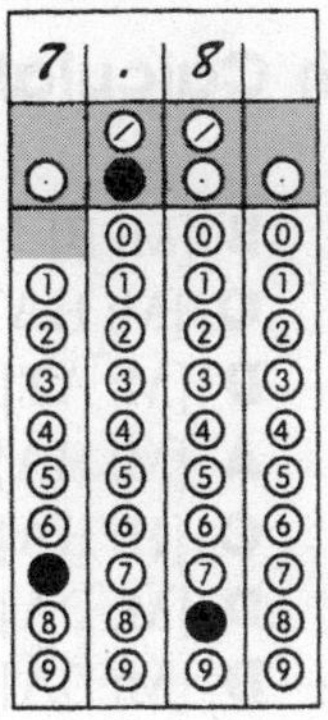

or

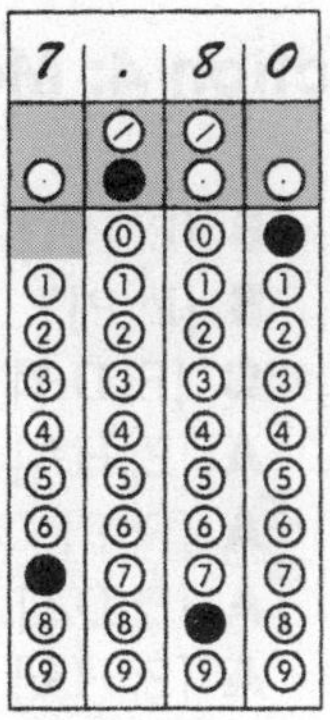

18. **8/3** or **2.67** [M; HA]

19. **8/5** or **1.6** [M; HA]

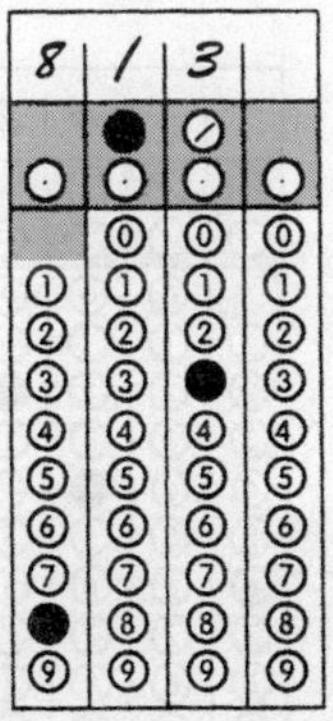

or

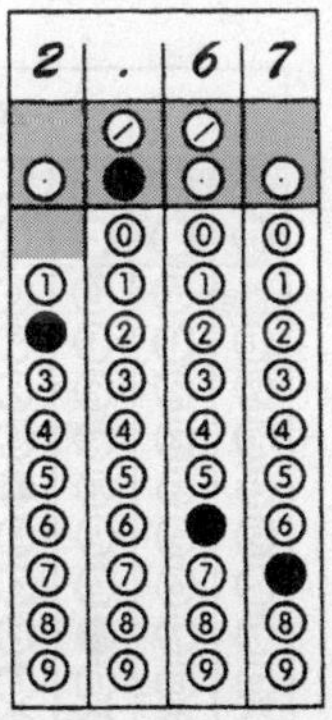

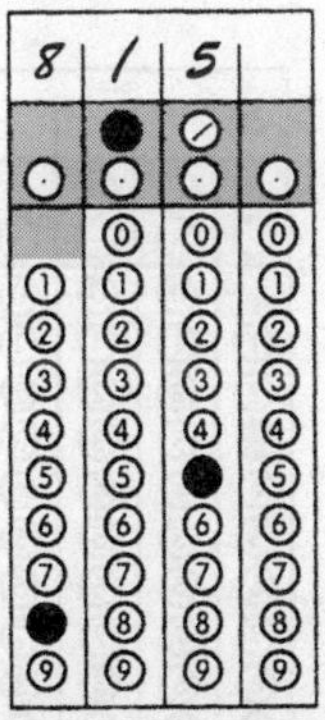

or

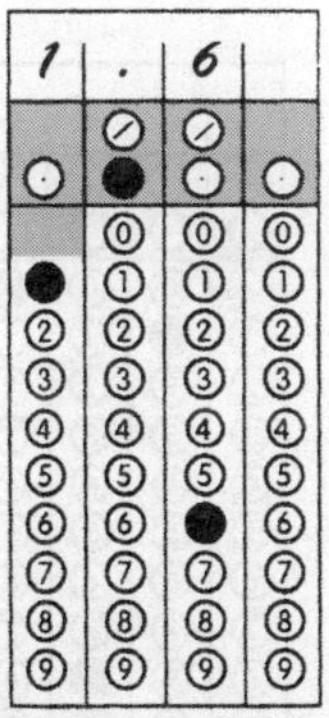

ANSWER SHEET 答案

Practice Test 练习测试题

20. **14/3** or **4.66** or **4.67** [M; HA]

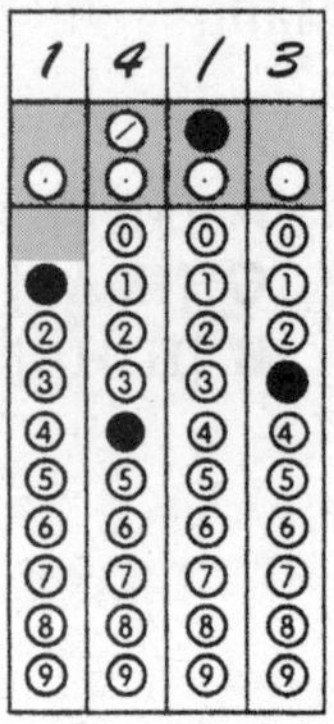

or

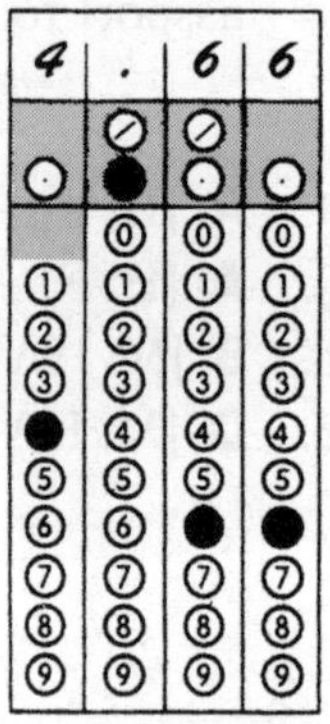

or

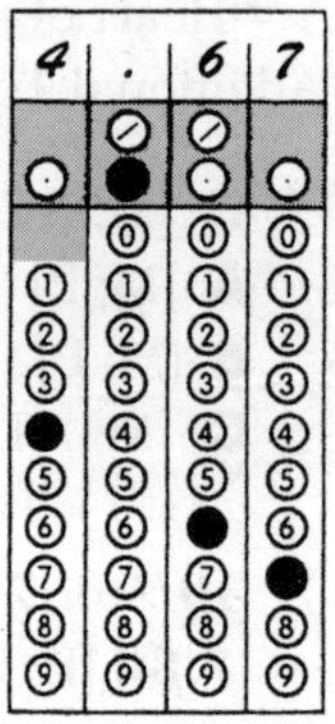

Section 4: Math (With Calculator)

1. **B** [E; HA]
2. **B** [E; P]
3. **C** [E; DA]
4. **A** [E; HA]
5. **A** [E; P]
6. **A** [E; DA]
7. **A** [E; HA]
8. **C** [M; DA]
9. **B** [M; P]
10. **C** [M; HA]
11. **D** [M; AT]
12. **A** [M; HA]
13. **C** [H; HA]
14. **D** [M; DA]
15. **D** [M; DA]
16. **B** [M; HA]
17. **B** [M; DA]
18. **A** [H; HA]
19. **D** [M; DA]
20. **C** [M; DA]
21. **D** [M; HA]
22. **C** [M; HA]
23. **A** [H; P]
24. **A** [M; HA]
25. **B** [M; DA]
26. **B** [M; DA]
27. **D** [H; HA]
28. **A** [M; DA]
29. **D** [M; AT]
30. **B** [H; AT]

31. **180** [H; DA]

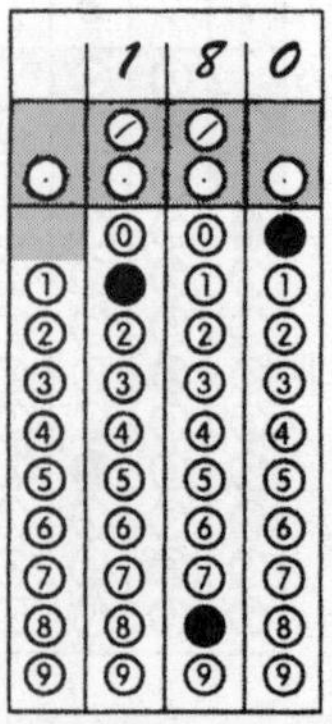

32. **3** [M; P]

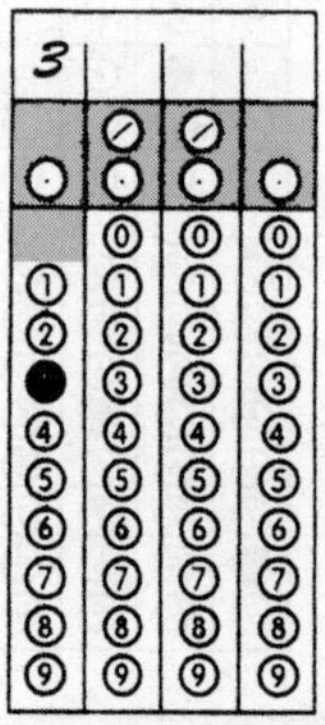

33. **74** [H; AT]

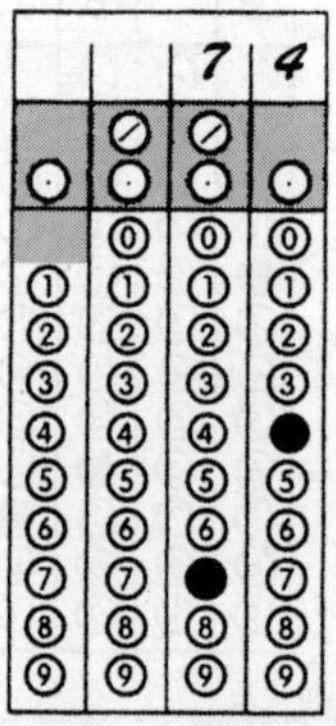

34. **42** [M; P]

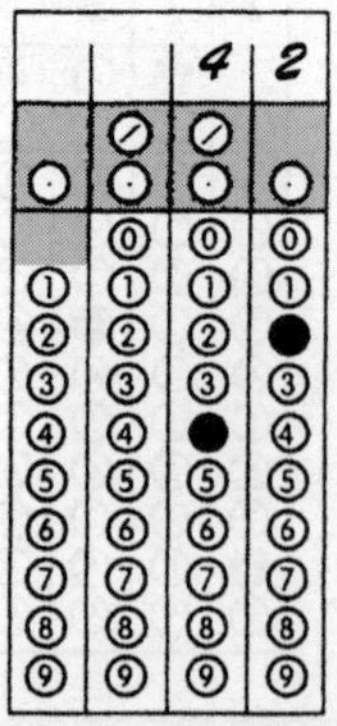

ANSWER SHEET 答案
Practice Test 练习测试题

35. **.5** [H; P]

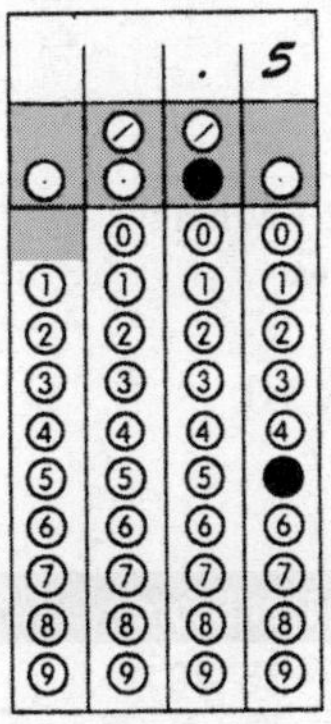

36. **.12** [H; DA]

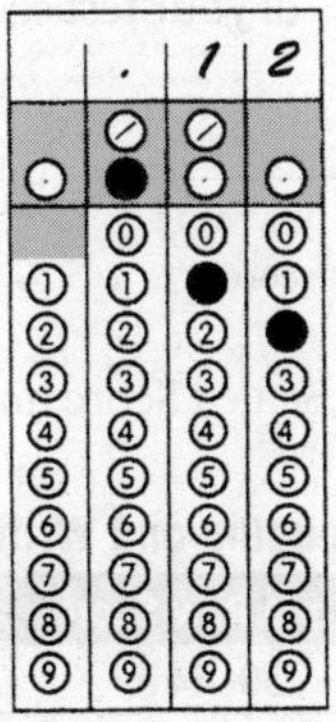

37. **50** [H; DA]

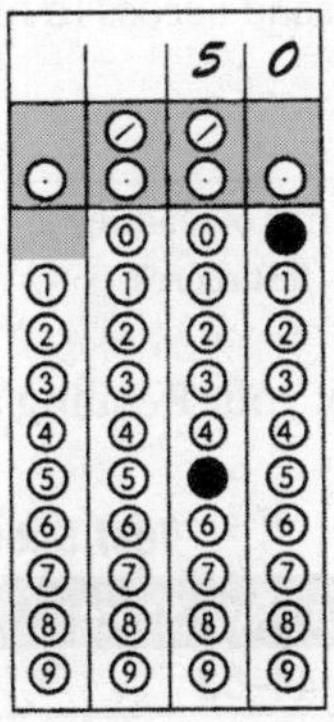

38. **.35** [H; DA]

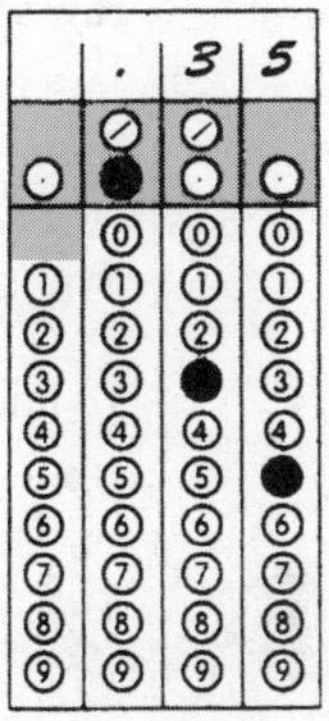

Essay (Optional)

See the Essay Sample Response on page 456.

SCORE ANALYSIS 成绩分析

Reading and Writing Test 阅读和写作测试

Section 1: Reading ____________ = ____________ (A)
correct raw score

Section 2: Writing ____________ = ____________ (B)
correct raw score

To find your Reading and Writing test scores, consult the chart below: find the ranges in which your raw scores lie and read across to find the ranges of your test scores.

____________ + ____________ = ____________ (C)
range of reading test scores / range of writing test scores / range of reading + writing test scores

To find the range of your Reading and Writing Scaled Score, multiply (C) by 10.

Test Scores for the Reading and Writing Sections

Reading Raw Score	Writing Raw Score	Test Score
44–52	39–44	35–40
36–43	33–38	31–34
30–35	28–32	28–30
24–29	22–27	24–27
19–23	17–21	21–23
14–18	13–16	19–20
9–13	9–12	16–18
5–8	5–8	13–15
less than 5	less than 5	10–12

Math Test 数学测试

Section 3: ____________ = ____________ (D)
correct raw score

Section 4: ____________ = ____________ (E)
correct raw score

Total Math raw score: (D) + (E) = ____________

To find your Math Scaled Score, consult the chart below: find the range in which your raw score lies and read across to find the range for your scaled score.

Scaled Scores for the Math Test

Raw Score	Scaled Score
50–58	700–800
44–49	650–690
38–43	600–640
32–37	550–590
26–31	500–540

Raw Score	Scaled Score
20–25	450–490
15–19	400–440
11–14	350–390
7–10	300–340
less than 7	200–290

ANSWERS AND EXPLANATIONS 答案解析

Section 1: Reading Test 第一部分：阅读测试

Note: Some answer explanations provide detail about the type of reading question being posed. This will help you to get a sense of the variety of question types you can expect on test day.

1. **(A)** The contrast that is least accentuated is that between (A) *poverty and affluence*. Throughout the fiction excerpt, dramatic, palpable tensions between the other three pairs of terms can be detected: (B) *the spoken and the unspoken;* (C) *fear and optimism*; and (D) *reality and appearance.*

2. **(A)** The author is best described as (A) *a first-person narrator*. Hint: the use of the first-person personal pronouns "I," "me," and "my" can help the reader detect this narrative point of view. Choice (B) is wrong because *third-person* (he, she, they), *omniscient* (all knowing) narration is not predominant. The narrator is neither (C) *a detached observer* nor (D) *an orator delivering a satirical soliloquy*, as this prose is neither satirical nor a soliloquy (similar to a monologue).

3. **(D)** The contrast that is most accentuated by the author is that between *The physical appearance of the mother's hair versus that of her son.* Choice (A), *The difference between the mother's pessimism and her son's optimism,* does not work because Tim's mother does represent a source of optimism. Choice (B), *The difference between the mother's internal dialogue and her son's terseness,* is less substantiated, as there is little textual evidence to support it as a prevailing contrast. Choice (C), *The attitude of the football team versus that of Tim's mom,* is little stressed, as the football team's attitude is not clearly illustrated.

4. **(A)** The rhetorical features most prevalent (widespread) in this fiction passage are (A) *innuendo and dialogue. Innuendo* refers to that which is suggested or hinted at based on spoken words or gestures. The other devices, such as (B) *vivid imagery*, (C) *juxtaposition*, and (D) *formal narrative tone* are not prevailing features of this text.

5. **(C)** Based on the evidence and details presented in lines 52–54 ("Where it was an effort to breathe, to put one foot in front of another.") and 69–74 ("I was ten pounds ... forever."), Tim has most closely experienced (C), *sickness, treatment, and convalescence* (recovery.) Choice (A) (*loss, recovery, triumph*) is tempting, but not as accurate as choice (C). Choices (B) (*fear, anxiety, depression*) and (D) (*alienation, socialization, stardom*) are partially, but not fully, substantiated by the story so they are both incorrect answers.

6. **(A)** In context, "smoother" (line 59) most closely means *more discreet.* Given their individual meanings, choices (B), (C), and (D) are less fitting. Their definitions are as follows: (B) *more refined* (well mannered, polite, sophisticated); (C) *more lithe* (limber, agile); and (D) *more astute* (smart, wise, shrewd).

7. **(D)** *Personification* (the assigning of human qualities to the nonhuman, such as objects or abstract notions) is illustrated in the given sentence: "I could see them crowding each other in the confines of her skull, each one doing its best to

squeeze its way out." The other figurative devices (*allusion, irony, simile*) are not illustrated in this sentence, so choices (A), (B), and (C) are out. An *allusion* is a reference to a work of literature, art, or an historical event. *Irony* is an unexpected twist or outcome that occurs in the plot of a story; a *simile* is a comparison using "like" or "as."

8. **(A)** The sentence in lines 63–66 (*I hadn't gone to a plastic surgeon and gotten my identity changed so I could escape the vengeance of the Russian Mafia.*) most closely exemplifies the figurative device known as *hyperbole* (exaggeration, a dramatic stretch of the truth). The other figurative devices (*personification, oxymoron, epiphany*) are not featured in this sentence, so choices (B), (C), and (D) are out. An *oxymoron* is a phrase in which two words contradictory in meaning are used together for special effect, such as "jumbo shrimp" or "wise fool." An *epiphany* is a sudden leap of understanding, realization, or insight. Think of it as a "lightbulb moment."
9. **(D)** As used in context, the verb "glomming" most closely means (D) *staring at.* Choices (A) *glaring at,* (B) *sad about,* and (C) *grabbing* neither fit nor flow in context.
10. **(B)** The textual evidence in lines 34–38 reveals that Tim's father was *altruistic,* as he was showing concern for others. Choice (A) (*That he liked to drive in all sorts of weather*) cannot accurately be deduced by these lines. The same reasoning applies to choices (C) (*That he had a great many friends*) and (D) (*That he didn't like accepting favors from people*).
11. **(B)** The author's primary purpose in writing this prose piece is *to emphasize the indomitable power of the human spirit,* choice (B). "Indomitable" means insuperable, or characterized by that which cannot be defeated. The author is not trying *to illustrate the damaging repercussions of prejudice,* choice (A). Likewise, he is not attempting *to satirize today's self-centered youth,* choice (C), or *to illustrate the strong bond between mother and son,* choice (D).
12. **(B)** *A scholarly historian* best describes the author's stance, as Paynter demonstrates a wealth of historical knowledge. The author's position is not so extreme to be that of *a political upstart* (a rebel or maverick), so (A) is out. Likewise, she is not reasonably coming across as *a rebel scientist,* so (C) is also out. There is no evidence to substantiate Paynter's narrative deportment as that of *a disillusioned theologian,* so (D) is also incorrect.
13. **(A)** The primary rhetorical effect of the author's collective use of the words "compelled," "passion," and "compulsively" is to *accentuate* (to stress or emphasize) *Silone's intense feelings toward the subject about which he is writing.* Choices (B) and (C) are out because they contain "red flag" (too extreme based on contextual evidence) words and phrase, "egomaniacal" and "mental instability." Choice (D) is also incorrect because the purpose of these words is not to *juxtapose* (contrast) *the peasant lifestyle to that of a frantic writer.*
14. **(C)** Given the expressed compassion for human life and equality, the best answer is (C), *All human beings are inherently dignified and worthy of respect.* The question

contains the word "espouses," which means believes in or supports. Although Paynter mentions that Silone's work was translated, this does not mean that translation into several languages attests to an author's talent, so (A) is out. The passage never directly states or implies that the author believes that the *political and personal lives of an author should not intermingle*, so choice (B) is also incorrect. Although (D) presents a thought-producing idea, there is no passage evidence to support the author's believing that *the partial truth can be as valuable as the full truth*; (D) is incorrect.

15. **(B)** This question asks you to build on your answer to the previous question by supporting your answer with specific textual references. Lines 10–21 ("the cycle . . . self") best testify to the author's sentiments regarding human life being worthy of respect. Although choices (A), (C), and (D) are directly cited from the passage, they do not substantiate the ideals of human dignity and worth.

16. **(A)** The key word to note in this question is "distinction," which means a difference or discrepancy: In lines 48–53, what is the most likely purpose for Paynter drawing a *distinction* between the book's being published in Italian versus being published in German? Although choices (A) and (B), *To stress how a German audience would afford the work a more far-reaching global appeal*, are close contenders, the correct answer is (A), *To stress how Italy's political climate restricted its readers' personal perspectives.* Choice (C) is incorrect because the context has little to do with the publishing industry and more to do with the consequences based on the book's readership. Choice (D) is wrong because the author does not suggest that the book loses its core message in translation.

17. **(C)** Personification is giving human-like attributes to that which is nonhuman. The reference lines 63–65 ("at home the book remained exiled along with its author.") suggest that the book is like a person who is being exiled, so personification is the literary device used. Choice (A), *simile*, is incorrect because a simile is a comparison using "like" or "as." Choice (B), *hyperbole*, is also out because there is no exaggeration being made. Hyperbole may include phrases like "He is so famished, he could eat a horse" or "It is raining buckets." The figurative device, *irony*, is not expressed in these lines. Irony pertains, in some instances, to sarcasm or to that which is unexpected or paradoxical.

18. **(A)** This word-in-context question requires you to plug in each answer choice for the word "heralded" to see which choice fits and flows the best in the context in which it is used, as follows: "learned about an Italian reality that was totally unlike the one heralded in the Fascist media." Choice (A) is the correct answer because the action verb, *popularized*, fits best. Popularized means "made something widely appreciated and comprehensible to a wide audience." While the two realities alluded to contradicted each other, the term *contradicted* does not flow logically in the context of this sentence; (B) is out. *Belittled*, which means disparaged or made someone feel inferior, does not fit the meaning, so choice (C) is also out. (D), *advocated*, is a tempting choice, but *popularized* is more suited toward media, which refers to newspapers, political journals, radio, and television.

19. **(B)** Revisit the context in which this phrase is used: "The historical circumstances that made it impossible for the novel to be released in Italy colored the view of many readers abroad." Choice (B), *How readers abroad interpreted the political circumstances within Italy*, best paraphrases the intended meaning behind this sentence. In other words, the very fact that the book could not be published in Italy spoke volumes to readers about the political climate of the author's homeland. Choice (A) is off because there is no implied or stated information about Silone influencing or shaping the writing of his literary contemporaries. Choice (C) is incorrect because there is not textual evidence attesting to Silone's critics developing prejudices against specific sectors of society. Choice (D) is an invalid choice because there is no overarching sense of domestic and overseas readers offering each other insight into their colorful views of Italian culture.

20. **(B)** *Some reviewers ascribed too much historical reality to Silone's novel.* Because it is unreasonable, based on passage information and evidence, to conclude that Clifton Fadiman is mentioned by the author to demonstrate any of the following, choices (A), (C), and (D) are out: contrary to choice (A), *some cynics publicized Silone as an unethical propagandist*, passage evidence does not support Silone as unethical or immoral. Passage information that is stated or implied does not support Silone as inaccurately presenting facts, choice (C). Passage details and information do not suggest scientific elements in Silone's book, choice (D).

21. **(B)** (*compellingly*) Consider the context as the adverb "forcefully" is used in the closing sentence: A similar view was one *forcefully* expressed by another reviewer, who wrote: "The value of this book as a pamphlet depends on its truth or partial truth . . . if it is even fifty percent true, Italy under Mussolini is worse off than Italy under the Austrians or the Lombards." Choices (A), *frantically*, and (C), *forcibly*, are too extreme in tone and connotation for this particular sentence. Choice (D), *enforceably*, is out because it is a flawed adverb form and an awkward fit.

22. **(B)** (*Intangible rights such as privacy, worship, and self-expression.*) Holistically, the passage does not suggest that The Bill of Rights is primarily concerned with *material possessions and property* or *protection against hostile forces, whether domestic or overseas*, so choices (A) and (C) are out. Likewise, choice (D) is incorrect. Even though lines 32–36 suggest freedom of religion, "shall make no law respecting an establishment of religion...assemble.", there is no passage evidence to validate the latter part of (D), *shared among all Americans*.

23. **(A)** (*understood*) This word-used-in-context question requires you to read the preceding sentence in order to get a sense of what "said" means. Given the mention of the Senate and House of Representatives in the prior sentence, the legislative bodies or "Legislatures" are "understood" based upon the aforementioned references. A review of the question (As used in lines 21–23 "all, or any of which Articles, when ratified by three fourths of the said Legislatures," the word "said," most closely means . . .) and the definitions of the remaining choices show that *outspoken* (candid, forthright), *beheld* (observed, looked upon), and *outmoded* (outdated, obsolete) neither fit effectively nor flow in context, so the remaining choices—(B), (C), and (D)—are incorrect.

24. **(A)** (*a unified vision and purpose*) This question requires you to determine the overall effectiveness of the given diction (word choice) cluster. The question states: "In lines 14–20 ('Resolved ... Constitution'), how might the collective effectiveness of these words and phrases—'resolved,' 'assembled,' 'two thirds,' 'both houses,' 'concurring'—best be described in terms of their collective, or combined, message?" Taken collectively, these terms and phrases connote *a unified vision and purpose*. Quick vocabulary review: *Resolved* means "determined, decided, and resolute." *Assembled* means "gathered together." *Concurring* means "agreeing, in unison." Given the meanings of these terms, the remaining choices cannot be substantiated by passage evidence, so (B), *a stifled but bitter controversy*, (C), *a perpetual state of inquiry*, and (D), *a delay of tact and diplomacy*, are all out. More vocabulary review: *inquiry* relates to questioning or interrogation; *tact* and *diplomacy* have to do with dealing with people and controversy effectively and peaceably.

25. **(C)** (*religion*) This question requires you to determine the meaning of an adverb, as it is used in a particular context, as follows: "Congress shall make no law respecting an establishment of religion, or prohibiting the free exercise thereof; or abridging the freedom of speech, or of the press; or the right of the people peaceably to assemble, and to petition the Government for a redress of grievances." In most cases, *thereof* means "of that" or "of or about that." Choice (A), *Amendment I itself*, does not make sense because "thereof" is not referencing the Amendment and its various aspects (lawmaking, freedom of speech, petitioning, etc.) in entirety. Even though "Congress" is the subject of the sentence, logically it does not make sense to be the reference for "thereof." Choice (B) is out. Choice (D) is also out because "freedom of speech" is the direct object of the clause that follows "thereof."

26. **(B)** (*an individual's property*) This question asks you to determine the meaning of a plural noun, "effects," as it is used in a particular context, as reproduced as follows: The right of the people to be secure in their persons, houses, papers, and effects, against unreasonable searches and seizures, shall not be violated, and no Warrants shall issue, but upon probable cause, supported by Oath or affirmation, and particularly describing the place to be searched, and the persons or things to be seized." While *an individual's emotional state* is something to be protected and nurtured, it does not fit in line with the nouns that make up the list in which "effects" appears: "persons, houses, papers, and effects." You can think of emotions as "not parallel" to or inconsistent with the other items in this comma series. Cross off choice (A). *Special effects* and *sound effects* are commonly used phrases and these types of *effects* greatly contribute to the entertainment value of movies; however, neither fits in this particular context. Choices (C) and (D) are out.

27. **(C)** (*fair remuneration*) Synonyms for "remuneration" include compensation and payment. In context, the phrase "just compensation" most closely means "fair remuneration: nor shall private property be taken for public use, without just compensation." Even though *recompense* (reimbursement, payment) works, there is no text evidence to substantiate the adjective *partial*, so choice (A) is out. It is illogical to think that individuals would be satisfied with partial payment for their belongings. *Limited respect* does not make logical sense in this sentence, so

cross off choice (B). Likewise, the phrase *deserved merit* does not fit the intended meaning (payment for use of someone's property), so (D) is also incorrect.

28. **(D)** (*with regard to and correspondingly*) Revisit the passage and consider how each similar-looking term (and both formed from the kernel word, "respect") is used differently in its particular context. As used in lines 32–33, "Congress shall make no law respecting an establishment of religion . . ." and as used in lines 105–108, "The powers not delegated to the United States by the Constitution, nor prohibited by it to the States, are reserved to the States respectively, or to the people." Choice (A) is wrong because *revering* means respecting. Although the first part of choice (B) works (*with respect to*), *honorably* is not the intended meaning in line 108. Choice (C) (*accepting and individually*) is also awkward when plugged into these amendments. Although *respecting* and *accepting* sound alike, they are not interchangeable in this usage.

29. **(C)** (*To grant Americans the right to ask the government to listen to and address their concerns*) Essentially, this question requires you to paraphrase a clause within The Bill of Rights, as expressed in lines 35–38: "the right of the people peaceably to assemble, and to petition the Government for a redress of grievances." The question also asks you to identify "the benefit" this clause gives to Americans. Choice (A) is out because these lines do not mention Americans reiterating (repeating themselves). Choice (B), "To request that the government re-express its laws in new ways so that people can clearly understand their rights," would be a considerate gesture, but this re-expression of laws is not described in lines 35–38. Cross off (D) because these lines do not specifically argue or advocate for common people and the roles they play in local government. The references lines advocate for all Americans.

30. **(A)** This evidence-based question requires you to find lines from the text that best support choice (C), *To grant Americans the right to ask the government to listen to and address their concerns*, in the previous question. Choice (A), lines 5–13 ("*Conventions . . . institution*,") does the job. Choice (B) is incorrect because these lines have little or nothing to do with the ideas expressed in Choice (C) of the previous question: Lines 21–24: "all, or any of which Articles, when ratified by three fourths of the said Legislatures, to be valid to all intents and purposes, as part of the said Constitution." Choice (C) is also incorrect because these lines do not pertain to the government listening to Americans' concerns: Lines 50–54: "The . . . issue." Finally, cross off (D), as these lines relate to fair trial: Lines 90–94: "right . . . law."

31. **(C)** Choice (C) is the best choice because the overall message of The Bill of Rights does point to the broad assumption that *Americans are worthy of a broad spectrum of personal rights and protection*. The remaining choices, (A), (B), and (D), are out because the passage does not suggest any of the following assumptions, as held by the authors of The Bill of Rights: (A) *Ultimately, it is most beneficial for Americans when final power resides with the government*; (B) *The military is the most valuable facet of ensuring American prosperity*; or (D) *The tensions between common people and people in power will ultimately erode the scope of human rights, as outlined in The Bill of Rights.*

32. **(D)** (*interpreted*) As used in context, the action verb *construed* most closely means interpreted: "The enumeration in the Constitution, of certain rights, shall not be construed to deny or disparage others retained by people." Given their meanings, none of the other answers fit or flow in this sentence. In choice (A), *impeded* means blocked or prevented. In choice (B), *constituted* means established or amounted to something. Finally, in choice (C), *constrained* means suppressed, held back, or inhibited.

33. **(A)** The successful experiment to produce fly larvae used pig manure. The unsuccessful experiment used cattle manure, so choice (B) is incorrect. Choices (C) and (D) are wrong because bagasse and silk cotton tree wood were used to produce termites.

34. **(D)** From Table 1, you can see that the termite yield from Method 2, the setup that used cartons, was 133 g/carton, versus 97 g/hole for Method 1. Each of the other statements is false.

Choice (A): Since both Methods 1 and 2 used some kind of fish waste (actual fish waste in Method 1 and fish waste water in Method 2), you cannot conclude from the passage that fish waste was an essential ingredient in the production of fly larvae. You would need to do a controlled experiment to make that conclusion.

Choice (B): The experiment that used cattle manure, Method 1, produced a negligible yield of fly larvae. This was therefore an ineffective method.

Choice (C): Method 1 for termites, the holes (no cartons), produced 97 grams of termites per hole (Table 1). Although this was not as effective as Method 2 (with cartons), it is false to say, "It was not possible to harvest termites," if the colonies were not in boxes.

35. **(C)** It is reasonable to assume that other insects were in the ground that could attack the termites in their natural habitat. The carton setup, however, was sealed off from other insects. The explanations in the other choices are implausible.

Choice (A): First, nothing was placed into the boxes to prevent rotting. Second, termites thrive on wood and ate through the wood provided in each setup.

Choice (B): The holes were not exposed to sunlight. They were under shady trees and covered with jute sacks to keep them dark.

Choice (D): Termites in both setups were protected by being covered. Nevertheless, rain was desirable to keep the environments humid. The interiors of the cartons were kept damp and dark.

36. **(A)** All of the numbers for this question are shown in Table 2. Ash values for termite and larvae samples are 8.3% and 6.6%, respectively. These are lower than the 41.7% for the fish meal. The statements in choices (B), (C), and (D) are all directly contradicted by the numbers in Table 2.

37. **(A)** From Table 3, the amounts of daily intake of maize were 28.7 g, 26.0 g, and 26.2 g, which are comparable amounts. The corresponding intakes of metabolizable energy were 0.42 MJ, 0.44 MJ, and 0.46 MJ, which are also comparable amounts. This means that there was no obvious correlation between maize consumed and metabolizable energy consumed. The assertions in the other choices agree with the data presented in Tables 3 and 4. They are therefore wrong answers!

Choice (B): The daily crude protein intake for the control group was 5.6 g, higher than the 3.5 g and 3.4 g for the other two groups; yet the metabolizable energy intake was comparable. This suggests that the metabolizable energy intake was independent of the crude protein consumption.

Choice (C): The consumption of metabolizable energy per kg gain was 46.1 MJ for the control group, 48.9 MJ for the termite group, and 42.2 MJ for the fly larvae group. Yet the corresponding daily consumptions of metabolizable energy were 0.42 MJ, 0.44 MJ, and 0.46 MJ, respectively. This suggests that the energy consumed per kg of weight gain was independent of the daily intake of metabolizable energy.

Choice (D): Irrespective of what they consumed, the energy consumptions of the three groups were comparable.

38. **(B)** From Table 4, protein intake/kg gain was 312 g for FLG and 615 g for CG; yet weight gain for FLG was 10.9 g and weight gain for CG was 9.1 g. So the statement in choice (B) is supported by the table. All of the other choices are contradicted by the table.

Choice (A): Rates of weight gain were higher for FLG than for CG and TG.

Choice (C): To see which feed conversion ratio was "best" means to find the lowest number, the one that represents the smallest amount of feed needed for a 1 kg weight gain. From Table 4, notice that the feed conversion ratio was best for FLG.

Choice (D): The chicks in FLG consumed less metabolizable energy per kilogram of weight gain.

39. **(C)** The information does not indicate if the TG/FLG feed ingredients contained noxious (poisonous or toxic) chemicals. Regarding choice (A), the three bullet points in Experiment 3 clearly say that maize is a consistent component in the diets offered to CG, TG, and FLG. The second and third bullet points indicate the frequency of food offerings to TG and FLG, contradicting choice (B). Environmental constants are indicated in the opening paragraph of Experiment 3 and do not include those offered in choice (D).

40. **(A)** The level of conscientiousness pertaining to the scientists is not only subjective (based on an individual's opinion or bias) but also not implied or directly stated with regard to their maintaining sterile conditions. For choice (B), given the percentages as delineated in Table 2, this research must have relied heavily on detailed measurements of the various feed ingredients. With choice (C), indeed, the scientists considered several environmental factors, as indicated in the opening paragraph of Experiment 3, such as lighting, humidity, and temperature. Finally, choice (D) is a reasonable deduction based on the passage evidence that states (directly before the bullet list), "When they were 10 days old, the chicks were *randomly* assigned to one of three groups."

41. **(C)** The chicks' feathers (plumage) and how full and shiny (lustrous) they are have little to do with this science research in its entirety, so this topic would be most trivial (unimportant or trifling), given the scope and content of the data presented. The following factors were important to the researchers: For choice (A), the protein intake of the chicks was the main point of the termite and fly

larva experiment. For choice (B), satiation (satisfaction) of the chicks' natural impulses of hunger was crucial. TG and FLG were "offered maize meal all times of day" (Experiment 3, bullet point 3) and "During the brooding stage . . . all chicks were fed commercial crumbs, as much food as they wanted" (Experiment 3, opening paragraph). For choice (D), Table 4 presents data on the chicks' average daily weight gain, which is not a trivial piece of the research findings.

42. **(D)** Freshly harvested termites provide the most energy, as evidenced by Table 4, in which TG gains highest (48.9 megajoules) and bullet two of Experiment 3, which says "TG was fed freshly harvested termites twice daily." Choice (A) is ruled out because commercial crumbs were fed to all young chicks; furthermore, their energy yield is not indicated in Table 4. Choice (B) is wrong because only CG (Control Group) was offered vitamin-mineral premix (reference bullet 1 of Experiment 3), and their energy yield was lower than that of TG. Choice (C) is wrong because freshly harvested fly larvae were fed to FLG group, and their energy yield was lower, 42.2 megajoules.

43. **(A)** Based on evidence in Table 4, there is no clear relationship between crude protein per kilogram intake and average weight gain for all chicks. FLG had the lowest crude protein/kg gain and the highest daily weight gain. The control group had the highest crude protein/kg gain and a daily weight gain that was greater than TG but less than FLG. Choice (B) is incorrect because Table 4 data does not substantiate the claim that the consumption of fly larvae benefits chicks by providing them with the highest levels of ME. In choice (C), if anything, the data trend as illustrated in the chart, shows that the relationship between weight gain and the feed conversion ratio is more of an inverse relationship. Based on Table 4 evidence, choice (D) is erroneous. FLG, in fact, gained the most weight.

44. **(B)** Throughout the passage, the rhetorical strategy that the author uses most often are *rhetorical questions that intend to engage his audience's attention.* For passage evidence, refer back to the passage's opening line and to the two consecutive questions at the end of paragraph four. Choice (A) is wrong because he does not tend to repeat concepts and formulas. Likewise, (C) is incorrect because he does not provide allusions (indirect or direct references) to significant related works. Finally, cross off (D), as the text does not contain digressions.

45. **(C)** This question requires you to read the question carefully and to note the underscored key word: "According to the author, which of the following lists represents examples of paper folding in <u>decreasing</u> order of intricacy and seriousness?" Also, you need to analyze the overall argument, as it pertains to seriousness and intricacy when folding. Based on the evidence, as provided by concrete examples in the first two paragraphs, the best answer is (C), *a parachute, a folded American flag, a fortune cookie made of paper*. Choice (A) is wrong because the examples are ordered in increasing level of intricacy and seriousness (*a circle cut from paper, an index card, a parachute*). Choice (B) is also wrong because passage evidence indicates the third example (*origami bird*) as an example from our "everyday lives" (line 4) and is part of a list that includes lighthearted examples such as "party hats" (lines 5–6) and "a . . . game" (line 6). Last, (D), *an index card, an airbag, a paper party hat*, is incorrect because "airbag" is in the middle of the

list but should be at the beginning because the textual evidence introduces the airbag as an illustration of when "folding can decide life or death" (lines 21–22).

46. **(A)** (*To stress the precision involved in folding*) Analyzing the author's argument is central to this rhetorical purpose-based question. In paragraph 3, making folds in a circle of paper is introduced. Choice (B), *To emphasize the unimportance of paper representations*, is illogical, given that passage evidence as provided when the author writes, "a slight mistake . . . outcome" at the end of paragraph three. Choice (C), *To distract the reader with simplified ideas*, is off key and does not maintain the more serious and objective tone of this prose. Choice (D), *To turn his discussion to the topic of circles and spheres*, is also incorrect, as from this point forward, the purpose and point of view are not solely directed toward these specific shapes.

47. **(C)** Based on paragraph 7 ("Furthering the notion...92,955,820 miles."), choice (C), *the paper thickness is used as a tool of sorts to measure distance*, is validated by this evidence. There is no passage, pictorial, or graphical evidence to support the notion that the *use of the paper is ineffective because its thickness is negligible*, so choice (A) is out. Choice (B), likewise, is an unsubstantiated answer choice: *thickness and distance are mathematically incompatible measurements*. The conclusion states, "It would take just fifty-one folds of a sheet of paper to reach the sun." There is no evidence to support the idea of mutual exclusivity as indicated in choice (D), *the vast differences in paper width and intergalactic distance make them mutually exclusive when considering the problem of measuring the distance from Earth to the sun*.

48. **(D)** The author refers to "the distance between Earth and the sun" (lines 62–63) and the width of a sheet of paper (lines 65–66) mainly to *plainly establish the starting point of his mode of measuring distance to the sun* so that he can continue with his explanation. Choice (A) is out because the purpose of these expressions is not to *dramatically contrast the staggering difference between these measurements*. Cross off (B) because there is no tone or undertone of humor in this excerpt. Choice (C) is incorrect because the author is not attempting to "devalue" materials, calculations, or anything else in this context.

49. **(D)** (*As paper width increases, the length of the fold line either decreases or remains constant.*) This type of question requires you to reference a graphical representation of information, which, in this case, is the Measurement of Fold Graph (Figure 1). Choice (B) is wrong because it is inaccurate to say, based on the bar graph, that there is "no correlation" between the two measurements of length. Choice (C) is also incorrect because the graphical depiction is not showing an "inconsistent" or a haphazard, unpredictable relationship between the measurements provided on the horizontal and vertical axes of the graph. Finally, choice (A) is wrong because a visual assessment of the graph clearly shows that the bars steadily lessen in height, which does not evidence that the crease increases as paper width increases. Also, the passage that follows says, "the length of the creases gradually declined as the length of the sheet of paper increased" (lines 55–57).

50. **(A)** (*establish his facility or expertise within the discipline of math*) This type of question requires you to analyze word choice, in this case a cluster of words, to determine the rhetorical effect of the author's choice of diction. Carefully

consider the author's selection of words that he chooses to incorporate in his writing, such as "algebra" (line 41), "convert" (line 72), and "products" (line 80). Choices (B), *ostracize the reader from an active engagement with the text*, and (C), *bemuse the reader with extraneous words*, are poor choices, as the author seeks neither to *ostracize* (alienate, isolate) nor *bemuse* (confuse, obfuscate) his readers. Choice (D), *lend an air of authority to his audience*, is faulty because it is phrased in such a manner as to make it seem like the author is trying to attribute expertise to his readers.

51. **(B)** (*visualization and multiplication*) This question requires you to analyze and determine the author's reasoning as applied to this scientific exposition. The question states, "In his investigation of solving the problem of the distance from Earth to the sun, the researcher relies most heavily on which of the following pairs?" Although choice (A) is tempting, *repetition of a process and division*, it is not the best choice. Furthermore, division is not referenced as often as multiplication. Choice (C), *mathematical conversions and repetition of a process*, lacks passage evidence, as mathematical conversions are not found in the text. Choice (D), *subjective notions and estimation*, is off the mark, as this exposition does not rely on opinions and approximations.

52. **(D)** (*merely*) Words-in-context questions used to mostly feature difficult vocabulary words. In this question, the word asked about is rather simple: "just." Consider the author's use of this relatively simple adverb in the closing sentence: "It would take just fifty-one folds of a sheet of paper to reach the sun!" Even though *justifiably* has "just" built into it, *justifiably* does not make sense in this sentence; cross off choice (A). Choice (B) is incorrect because *about* implies an estimate; in this case, however, a precise number of folds is given (fifty-one folds). Finally, choice (C), *less than*, is wrong because this phrase denatures the original meaning expressed in the concluding line.

Section 2: Writing and Language Test 第二部分：写作和语言测试

1. **(D)** (*affects both*) The other choices use faulty diction (word choice).
2. **(C)** (*present*) Choice (C) illustrates sound subject–verb agreement. A plural or compound subject requires the coordinating plural verb, *present*.
3. **(A)** (*NO CHANGE*) Choice (A) provides the best diction, or most effective word choice, given the meaning and context.
4. **(A)** (NO CHANGE) is the correct answer based on information presented in "Stages of EKG" table. Choice (B) is incorrect because the table does not span a month of time. Nor does it include "red eye gradually fading," choice (C). Choice (D) is incorrect because the table does not evidence a consistent presentation of more focal epithelial lesions.
5. **(D)** (*to*) Choice (D) uses the correct preposition. The prepositions in the other choices ("upwards til," "toward," and "through") create awkward and nonidiomatic constructions.
6. **(C)** (*filters through*) Choice (B) lacks concision (conciseness or succinctness) and the preposition *among* is awkward, as it is used in this context. Choice (A), *NO CHANGE*, is incorrect because there is a lack of agreement between the singular

subject "antigen" and the plural verb "filter." Finally, (D) is not a good choice, as "thru" is considered informal or borderline slang, which is improper for a test that requires standard, written English.

7. **(D)** (*customarily*) The other adverb choices—(A) *casually*, (B) *domineeringly*, and (C) *haphazardly* (which means randomly or without a pattern)—do not effectively fit and flow in the context of this sentence. Effective language is cohesive and expressed according to the conventions of standard written English.

8. **(B)** Choice (B), *are necessary*, illustrates sound subject–verb agreement since the subject is compound (*hygiene and isolation*) and, therefore, plural. Choice (C) results in a sentence fragment. Choice (D) is awkward and not as concise as choice (B). This test has a strong preference for concision. Verbosity does not illustrate writing mastery.

9. **(C)** (*as the disease*) Choices (B) and (D) are verbose (wordy). Choice (A) creates a run-on or a fused sentence, in this case, as the required punctuation is not used. Semicolons can be used to separate the two independent clauses that build a compound sentence.

10. **(A)** Choice (B) is not only a sentence fragment but also too broad to introduce this specific case study of one individual. The latter portion of (C), *solid grounds . . . fabricating his symptoms*, lacks validation, given the contents of the paragraph. Choice (D) mentions the patient's mother, which is an irrelevant detail, given the information in the paragraph. Moreover, there is no implied or stated evidence that the patient's mother has a vision deficit.

11. **(A)** (*where it is now*) To maintain logic and coherence (a sense of organization) within this paragraph, sentence 4 should remain where it is.

12. **(C)** Choice (C) has the most concision (succinctness). Choices (A) and (D) are wordy; (B) is structurally unsound.

13. **(A)** (*NO CHANGE*) Choices (B) and (C) are unnecessarily wordy, and a comma is erroneously placed in choice (B). Choice (D) is very wordy; the SAT has a distaste for diffuse language and phrasing.

14. **(D)** Choices (A), (B), and (C) are redundant (unnecessarily repetitive), given the prior context of the passage.

15. **(B)** Choices (A) and (C) include unnecessary prepositions ("out," "on"). Choice (D) (*emptying*) creates an awkwardly phrased sentence.

16. **(B)** Choice (C) has the wrong verb form ("effect"). Choice (D) is a verbal phrase (*has been affecting*) that is inconsistent with the simple past tense verbs in the previous ("influenced") and following sentence ("developed").

17. **(D)** The singular, inanimate pronoun *it* correctly refers back to its singular antecedent, "Ancient Egypt." Choices (A), (B), and (C) contain pronouns (*them, these, there,* respectively) that do not agree with the geographical place that is being referenced.

18. **(C)** Even though Choice (C) is a bit longer than the others, it has clarity and parallel form, in that it repeats the word "provided," as used in the previous

phrase. Choices (A), (B), and (D) are awkwardly written. Choice (D) is also rather wordy.

19. **(D)** Choice (D) effectively uses a semicolon (;) to create a compound sentences, in which the latter part uses an comma (,) as an omission of parts of the prior sentence that are understood. Choices (A), (B), and (C) lack the concision (conciseness or succinctness) that this question requires. Remember that language economy and precision are preferred on the SAT.

20. **(A)** *NO CHANGE* because "its" correctly expresses singular possessive. Choice (B) is wrong because "its'" is a decoy choice: "its'" does not exist in the English language ("its'" appears as an imposter on this test). Choice (C) is also wrong because "it's" is a contraction that means it is. Choice (D), *its having*, creates a cumbersome construction.

21. **(D)** (*Delete the underlined portion*) Choices (A), (B), and (C) (*today, meanwhile*, and *nowadays*, respectively) contain words that are extraneous, given the context.

22. **(B)** All of the other choices are unfavorably verbose. Choice (D), in particular, drags on. The word "celestial" is not needed, as stars and constellations have been referenced previously.

23. **(A)** (*NO CHANGE*) Choice (B) contains excessive commas. On the other hand, essential commas are missing in (C). Choice (D) is redundant.

24. **(A)** (*NO CHANGE*) Choice (B) is wrong because the verb phrase is unnecessarily long and inconsistent with the verbal phrases used in context. Choice (C) is wrong because "in which" creates awkward phrasing. Choice (D) is redundant or repetitive: the noun "location" is not needed.

25. **(D)** Choices (A) and (B) both show incorrect usage of prepositions (connecting words that show location, direction, and relationship). Choice (C) lacks a comma after "field."

26. **(D)** The original version, (A), contains the unnecessary and potentially ambiguous pronoun, "they." Choice (B) introduces a verb form that is not parallel to the previous verb phrase within the sentence. Choice (C) is wrong because "snug" needs to be in adverb form, "snugly."

27. **(B)** Choice (A) incorrectly uses a semicolon (;). Choice (C) inappropriately uses the pronoun "they," which is unclear or ambiguous. Choice (D) is both redundant ("for sure," "certainly") and verbose.

28. **(C)** The original choice, (A), and choices (B) and (D) are all wordy because words ("was," "uniform," "looked") are unnecessary, given what is made clear to the reader through the context.

29. **(A)** (*NO CHANGE*). Choice (B), *he had been displaying*, uses an unnecessarily long verb phrase, and choice (C), *displayed, as he did*, is cumbersome with commas. Similar to (B), choice (D), *he did go on to display*, is verbose.

30. **(D)** (*signaling*) This question focuses on most effective word choice, or diction. Choice (A), *NO CHANGE*, is awkward. Choices (B), *cuing in*, and (C), *announcing*, do not fit and flow smoothly in context.

31. **(C)** Choice (C), *it was eventually kicked*, is correct because it is most clear and concise. Choice (A), *NO CHANGE*, introduces the preposition "in," which creates nonstandard phrasing. Choice (B), *it was eventually kicked by the players*, is incorrect because the latter part, *by the players*, is understood and, therefore, extraneous. Choice (D), *ultimately it was eventually kicked*, is redundant or repetitive because the adverbs "ultimately" and "eventually" essentially express similar meanings.

32. **(B)** (*chasing after it*) Choice (A), *NO CHANGE*, is awkward. Choices (C), *chasing along after it*, and (D), *chasing them after it*, feature the unnecessary words "along" and "them," respectively.

33. **(D)** Choice (A), *NO CHANGE*, is redundant, given how "confidently" appears earlier in the sentence. Choices (B) and (C) contain redundant expressions as well, and choice (B) contains a diction (word choice and use) error: "confidentiality" is used incorrectly.

34. **(D)** Choice (D), *that affects*, is correct because the relative pronoun *that* is correctly used and the verb "affects" is also correctly used. Choice (A), *NO CHANGE*, is wrong because *in effecting* reads erroneously and awkwardly in context. Choice (B), *in its affecting*, is awkward and wordy. Choice (C), *that effects*, uses the wrong form of the commonly confused action verbs, affects/effects.

35. **(A)** Choice (A), *NO CHANGE*, is correct because it creates balanced or parallel form. Also, the correlative conjunction pair, "not only/but also," is effectively used. Choice (B), *but also presenting*, lacks parallel form. Choices (C), *as it also presents as*, and (D), *but it also presents to be*, are undesirably wordy, and they lack parallel form with the preceding phrasing.

36. **(B)** Choice (B), *and disturbing effects on*, is correct because it creates parallel form in the series comma, which connects three nouns. Choices (A), *NO CHANGE*. and (C), *and disturbing the lungs*, lack parallel form, also known as parallelism. Choice (D), *while adversely disturbing the lungs*, is redundant, as "adversely" and "disturbing" express similar meanings.

37. **(D)** Choice (D), *this disease*, is correct because it is clear and specific. The original choice, *NO CHANGE*, is incorrect because the pronoun "it" is vague and potentially ambiguous. Given the prior sentence, a distracted reader could think that "it" is referring back to the pancreas or even pneumonia. Choices (B) and (C) are both incorrect because the prior sentence discusses cystic fibrosis in the singular; therefore, (B), *these ailments and others*, and (C), *sicknesses such as these*, are inconsistent, given they are plural (*ailments, sicknesses*).

38. **(B)** Choice (B), *have reproduced*, is correct because it is in the correct verb tense. Choice (A), *NO CHANGE*, is wrong because the present tense verb phrase, "are reproducing," does not make sense in context. Both (C), *have underwent reproduction*, and (D), *are of productive age*, are awkward and wordy.

39. **(C)** (*mortality among the young*) The phrasing in choice (C) fits best because the noun "mortality" is parallel in form to the previous noun, "spread." Choice (A), *NO CHANGE*, is awkward and does not flow. Choice (D), *deaths among the young people of our society*, is verbose.

40. **(D)** (*carries*) In terms of diction (word choice), *carries* is most fitting. The remaining choices are either awkward or unfitting verbs in the context of this sentence. Choice (A), *NO CHANGE*, is not the best choice, as it is used in the sentence. Choice (B), *harbors*, means entertains ideas within oneself, and choice (C), *attributes*, means assigns qualities to someone or to something else.

41. **(C)** (*cystic fibrosis; however,*) Choice (C) uses the semicolon to correctly divide independent clauses. Choice (A), *As it is now*, is incorrect because the use of a comma creates a type of run-on sentence called a comma splice. Choice (B), *cystic fibrosis, still*, creates a run-on sentence. Choice (D), *cystic fibrosis, and*, is ineffective because the conjunction *and* does not express the opposite-indicating meaning that the logic of the sentence requires.

42. **(B)** (*moral*) The other choices propose undesirable diction (word choice). Choice (A), *NO CHANGE*, is wrong because the diction is ineffective. Choice (C) is incorrect because *morale* means spirit or level of confidence. Likewise, (D) is wrong because *mortality* means death or rate of death.

43. **(A)** (*NO CHANGE*) Given the passage evidence, which takes the form of an explanation, it is inappropriate to describe the explanation as choice (B), *symbolic*, choice (C), *jesting* (joking around in a lighthearted fashion), or choice (D), *logistic . . .*, which means pertaining to a sequence of actions that need to be managed to produce a desired result), so the best answer is the original, choice (A), "literally."

44. **(D)** (*its reputation*) Choice (D) uses the correct form of the singular possessive, *its*. Choice (A), *NO CHANGE*, is wrong because "it's" is a contraction that stands for *it is*, as used in "*It's* a beautiful day!" Choice (B), *its' reputable*, is incorrect because *its'* does not exist; "its'" is an imposter for a real word in the English language! Choice (C) correctly uses "its," but the noun "reputability" does not fit the context of the sentence: Cystic fibrosis certainly does live up to its reputability as brutal and enigmatic.

Section 3: Math (No Calculator) 第三部分：数学测试（不用计算器）

1. **(D)**

$$3(y-5)=33$$
$$y-5=11$$
$$y=16$$
$$\therefore y+4=20$$

2. **(D)** Number the equations as shown:

$$x^2+y^2-x-y=10 \quad (1)$$
$$x^2+y^2-5x+3y=4 \quad (2)$$

Combine the equations by subtracting equation (2) from equation (1): The $x^2 + y^2$ terms disappear, and the combined equation is: $4x - 4y = 6$, which implies that $2x - 2y = 3$.

3. **(C)** If w is the width of the rectangle, then $2w - 2$ is the length. The area of the rectangle is $w(2w - 2)$, which is $A = 2w^2 - 2w$. This is a quadratic function, whose graph is a parabola, so eliminate choices (A) and (B). The graph should not, however, contain negative values for the width, w, or the area, A, which eliminates choice (D). Thus, the correct answer, choice (C), is the piece of the parabola in the first quadrant, where both w and A are positive.

4. **(D)** You are given $\frac{a}{bc} = \frac{d}{ef}$. Cross-multiplying gives $aef = bcd$. The easiest way to solve this problem is to cross-multiply each of the choices. Only one of these, choice (D), does not give $aef = bcd$.

5. **(C)** $AB = BC = 8$. Also, by the tangent-radius theorem, $\angle B$ is a right angle. Therefore, $\triangle ABC$ is a 90°–45°–45° triangle, and hypotenuse $\overline{AC}$ has length $8\sqrt{2}$.

6. **(A)**

$$2x-1=-\sqrt{2-x}$$

$$(2x-1)^2=2-x$$

$$4x^2-3x-1=0$$

$$(4x+1)(x-1)=0$$

$$x=-\frac{1}{4} \text{ or } 1$$

Checking answers by plugging these x-values into the original equation, shows that $-\frac{1}{4}$ is a solution, but 1 is not. Therefore the sum of the roots is $-\frac{1}{4}$.

7. **(B)** The terms in the equation use the relationship

$$\text{time} = \frac{\text{distance}}{\text{speed}}$$

The equation shows that (time on local roads) + (time on highway) = 2. If x is the speed on local roads, then $\frac{15}{x}$ is the time on local roads, so you can eliminate choice (A). The time on the highway is $\frac{90}{x+30}$. Note that choices (C) and (D) are wrong because the sum of speeds cannot be 2 hours, which is a time quantity.

8. **(C)** You need to eliminate the i in the denominator by multiplying the given fraction by $\frac{i}{i}$.

$$\frac{i-1}{i}=\frac{i-1}{i}\cdot\frac{i}{i}=\frac{i^2-i}{i^2}=\frac{-1-i}{-1}=1+i$$

9. **(A)** $g(4) = -1$ and $f(2) = 4$, $\therefore g(f(2)) = -1$. Since you're asked to find the x value for which $g(f(x)) = -1$, the correct x value is 2.

10. **(A)**

Method I. Pick-a-Number Strategy
Use their example! If $x = 1$ (a \$1 reduction), 1,100 headphones per week can be sold at \$23 each. The revenue will be (23)(1,100) or (24 – 1)(1,000 + 100(1)), which matches only the function given in choice (A).

Method II. Logical Reasoning
Price per headphone $p = (24 - x)$
Number of headphones sold in a week, $n = (1{,}000 + 100x)$
Revenue for a week $= pn$
$\therefore f(x) = (24 - x)(1{,}000 + 100x)$.

11. **(B)** Can you see that the slope of $\overline{FE}$ is independent of the length of the side of the hexagon? The angles at E will be the same, no matter what the length.

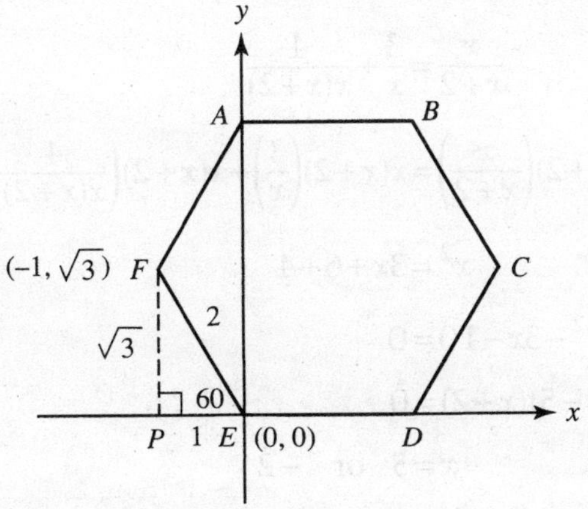

$$\text{Interior angle of a regular hexagon} = \frac{(n-2)180}{n} = \frac{(6-2)180}{6} = 120^\circ$$

The adjacent angle at E measures 60°, $\therefore \Delta FPE$ is a 30°–60°–90° triangle. Suppose $EF = 2$. Then $PE = 1$ and $PF = \sqrt{3}$. $\therefore$ F is the point $(-1, \sqrt{3})$.

$$\therefore \text{slope of } \overline{FE} = \frac{\sqrt{3}-0}{-1-0} = -\sqrt{3}.$$

12. **(D)** A line whose y-values decrease from left to right has a negative slope, so eliminate choices (B) and (C). Examine any two points on the graph to approximately estimate $\dfrac{\text{difference in } y}{\text{difference in } x}$, which is the slope. By inspection you should see that you get a numerical value that is greater than 5. This eliminates choice (A).

13. **(A)**

Method I: Plug-In
This is by far the quickest solution.
You can eliminate choices (C) and (D) at a glance, since these values give you undefined terms, with zeros in the denominator. Here's what you get when you plug in choice (A), $x = 5$:

PRACTICE TEST

$$\frac{5}{5+2} \stackrel{?}{=} \frac{3}{5}+\frac{4}{5(5+2)}$$

$$\frac{5}{7} \stackrel{?}{=} \frac{3}{5}+\frac{4}{35}$$

$$\frac{5}{7} \stackrel{?}{=} \frac{21}{35}+\frac{4}{35}$$

$$\frac{5}{7} \stackrel{?}{=} \frac{25}{35} \text{ Yes!}$$

Look no further—the answer is 5, choice (A).

Method II: Algebra

You can solve the equation by multiplying both sides by $x(x+2)$, the least common denominator of the fractions.

$$\frac{x}{x+2}=\frac{3}{x}+\frac{4}{x(x+2)}$$

$$x(x+2)\left(\frac{x}{x+2}\right)=x(x+2)\left(\frac{3}{x}\right)+x(x+2)\left(\frac{4}{x(x+2)}\right)$$

$$x^2=3x+6+4$$

$$x^2-3x-10=0$$

$$(x-5)(x+2)=0$$

$$x=5 \text{ or } -2$$

$x = 5$ is an actual solution. You can plug it back into the original equation to check that it works. But $x = -2$ is an extraneous solution. Plugging it into the original equation yields a first term of $\frac{-2}{-2+2}$, which is undefined. Therefore $x = -2$ is not a root.

14. **(C)** First find the center of the circle by finding the midpoint of the diameter:

$$\text{Center } M=\left(\frac{6+(-4)}{2}, \frac{1+(-5)}{2}\right)=(1, -2)$$

The radius of the circle is

$$MP=\sqrt{(6-1)^2+(1-(-2))^2}$$
$$=\sqrt{34}$$

Using the center-radius form of the circle with center $(1, -2)$ and radius $\sqrt{34}$,

$$(x-1)^2+(y+2)^2=34$$

Expand this to get the correct form of the equation:

$$(x-1)^2+(y+2)^2=34$$

$$x^2-2x+1+y^2+4y+4=34$$

$$x^2+y^2-2x+4y-29=0$$

Note that you get choice (A) if you mistakenly use $(x+1)^2+(y-2)^2=34$. Choice (B) used the diameter squared instead of the radius squared, and also reversed signs in the parentheses. Choice (D) used the diameter squared instead of the radius squared.

15. **(B)** $12 + 6n$ is 20% bigger than k.

$$12+6n=\left(k+\frac{1}{5}k\right)=\frac{6}{5}k$$

$$k=\frac{5(12+6n)}{6}$$

$$=10+5n$$

16. **20**

$$\frac{1}{2}x+\frac{1}{5}y=x+2$$

$$5x+2y=10x+20$$

$$2y-5x=20$$

17. $\mathbf{\frac{39}{5}}$ or **7.8** or **7.80**

Slope of $k=\frac{3-0}{5-0}=\frac{3}{5}$.

Since $\ell \parallel k$, slope of ℓ = slope of k.
Point P is (0, 6).

$\therefore$ Slope of $\ell=\frac{3}{5}=\frac{n-6}{3-0}\Rightarrow 5n-30=9\Rightarrow n=\frac{39}{5}$.

Grid-in 39/5 or 7.8 or 7.80.

18. $\mathbf{\frac{8}{3}}$ or **2.67**

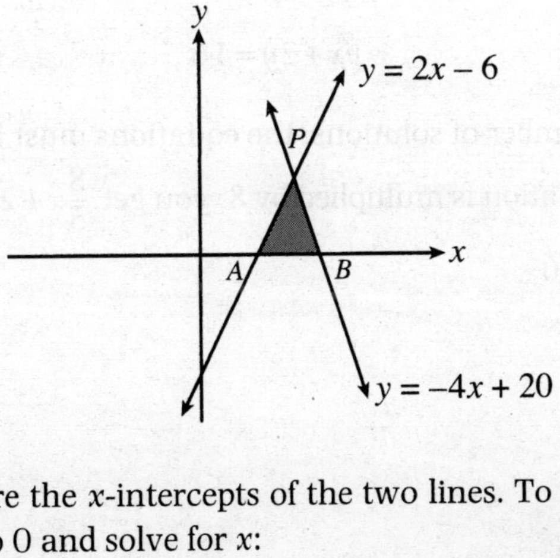

Points A and B are the x-intercepts of the two lines. To find the x-intercept of a line, set y equal to 0 and solve for x:

$$y = -4x + 20$$

$$0 = -4x + 20 \Rightarrow x = 5$$

$$\therefore x\text{-int} = 5$$

$$y = 2x - 6$$

$$0 = 2x - 6 \Rightarrow x = 3$$

$$\therefore x\text{-int} = 3$$

Therefore, the base of $\triangle ABP = 5 - 3 = 2$.
The height of $\triangle ABP$ is the y-value of P, the point of intersection of the two lines:

$$y = 2x - 6 \Rightarrow x = \frac{y}{2} + 3$$

Now substitute x in $y = -4x + 20$

$$y = -4\left(\frac{y}{2} + 3\right) + 20$$

$$y = -2y - 12 + 20$$

$$3y = 8 \Rightarrow y = 2.67$$

Therefore the height of $\triangle ABP$ is $\frac{8}{3}$.

Area of $\triangle ABP = \frac{1}{2}(2)\left(\frac{8}{3}\right) = \frac{8}{3}$ or 2.67

Grid in 8/3 or 2.67.

19. $\mathbf{\frac{8}{5}}$ or **1.6**

$$\frac{1}{5}x + \frac{1}{4}y = 2$$

$$px + 2y = 16$$

For an infinite number of solutions, the equations must be the same. Notice that when the first equation is multiplied by 8, you get $\frac{8}{5}x + 2y = 16$. This means that p must be $\frac{8}{5}$ or 1.6.

Grid-in 8/5 or 1.6.

20. $\frac{\mathbf{14}}{\mathbf{3}}$ or **4.66** or **4.67**

You are given

$$2x+y=16$$

$$x+2z=14$$

$$2y+z=12$$

To find the arithmetic mean of x, y, and z, suggests that you will need the sum of x, y, and z divided by 3. A good place to start is to add the three equations and see where that takes you.

Adding the left sides and setting that equal to the sum of the right sides leaves you with: $3x + 3y + 3z = 42$. Dividing by 3 gives you the sum of x, y, and z that you want: $x + y + z = 14$. Thus, the average of the three numbers is $\frac{14}{3}$.

Grid-in 14/3 or 4.66 or 4.67.

Section 4: Math (With Calculator) 第四部分：数学测试（使用计算器）

1. **(B)** If Jake types 60 words in 1 min, he will type (60)(60) = 3,600 words in 1 hour. Therefore, in h hours he will type $3{,}600h$ words. Therefore, $w = 3{,}600h$.

2. **(B)** To be a solution, the ordered pair must satisfy both equations.

Method I: Plug-In

Try (3, 4) in the nonlinear equation:

$$4+(3)^2 \stackrel{?}{=} 6(3)-3$$

$$13 \stackrel{?}{=} 15 \text{ No}$$

Try (4, 5):

$$5+(4)^2 \stackrel{?}{=} 6(4)-3$$

$$21 \stackrel{?}{=} 21 \text{ Yes!}$$

Notice that (4, 5) also satisfies the linear equation, since $5 - 4 = 1$.

Method II: Graphing Calculator

Rewrite the equations as

$$y=-x^2+6x-3$$

$$y=x+1$$

Then graph the equations on the same set of axes. Inspection of the graph shows (4, 5) is a solution. Alternatively, use the intersect function: [2nd] [CALC] [ENTER] [ENTER] to select both curves. When the calculator asks for a guess, use the arrow keys to move the cursor near one of the intersection points that matches an answer choice, then press [ENTER].

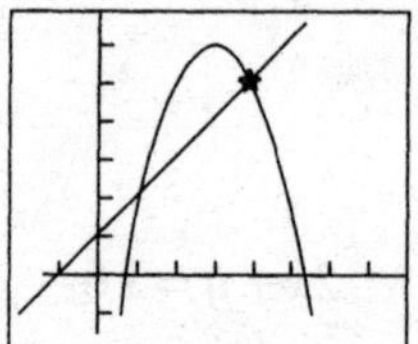

Method III: Algebra
Substitute $y = x + 1$ into $y + x^2 = 6x - 3$:

$$x + 1 + x^2 = 6x - 3$$
$$x^2 - 5x + 4 = 0$$
$$(x-1)(x-4) = 0$$
$$x = 1 \text{ or } 4$$

When you substitute those x values into $y = x + 1$, you get (1, 2) and (4, 5), which is choice (B).

3. **(C)** Let x be the number of girls.
Then $x - 24$ is the number of boys.

$$\frac{x}{x-24} = \frac{5}{4}$$
$$4x = 5x - 120$$
$$x = 120$$

4. **(A)** If x is the number of student tickets and y the number of adult tickets, then $x + y$ represents the total number of tickets. $\therefore x + y = 200$. Eliminate choices (B) and (D). The total amount collected is $7.5x + 10y$.

$$\therefore 7.5x + 10y = 1{,}775$$

5. **(A)** The general rule is: If $x^{-a} = y$, then $x^a = \frac{1}{y}$.

Therefore, given that $x^{-\frac{2}{3}} = 4$, $x^{\frac{2}{3}} = \frac{1}{4}$.

6. **(A)** If $\frac{1}{2}$ inch represents 40 feet, $\frac{1}{4}$ inch represents 20 feet.

Therefore, $\frac{1}{2} + \frac{1}{4} = \frac{3}{4}$ inches represent 60 feet.

More formally:

If $\frac{1}{2}$ inch represents 40 feet, 1 inch represents 80 feet.

$$\frac{80}{1} = \frac{60}{x} \Rightarrow x = \frac{60}{80} = \frac{3}{4}$$

7. **(A)** Rewrite $2x + 3y + 12 = 0$ in slope–intercept form: $y = mx + b$.

$$2x+3y+12=0$$

$$3y=-2x-12$$

$$y=-\frac{2}{3}x-4$$

Slope is $-\frac{2}{3}$ and y-intercept is -4. Choice (A) is the only choice that has both a negative slope and negative y-intercept.

8. **(C)** On your test booklet draw a line that roughly passes through the center of the points. Notice that this line will cut the y-axis below the x-axis, giving a negative y-intercept. So you can eliminate choices (A) and (B). Notice that the line has a positive slope; so the correct answer is choice (C).

Treadmill Sales

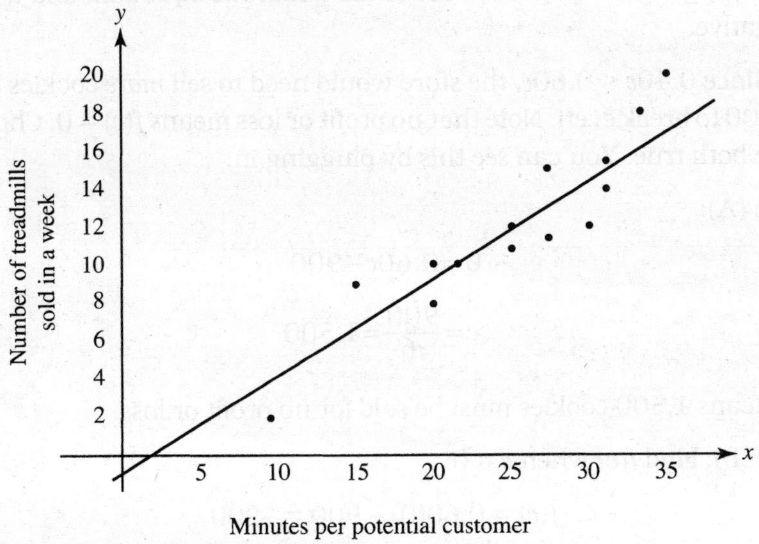

9. **(B)** Let x equal length of longer leg. Then $x - 1$ equals length of shorter leg, and $x + 2$ equals length of hypotenuse.
Using the Pythagorean theorem:

$$x^2+(x-1)^2=(x+2)^2$$

$$x^2+x^2-2x+1=x^2+4x+4$$

$$x^2-6x-3=0$$

Using the quadratic formula:

$$x = \frac{-(-6) \pm \sqrt{(-6)^2 - 4(1)(-3)}}{2(1)}$$

$$= \frac{6 \pm \sqrt{48}}{2}$$

$$= \frac{6 \pm 4\sqrt{3}}{2}$$

$$= 3 \pm 2\sqrt{3}$$

The roots are $3 + 2\sqrt{3}$ and $3 - 2\sqrt{3}$.
Reject the negative root $3 - 2\sqrt{3}$.
Then the length of the longer leg is $3 + 2\sqrt{3}$.
Choice (A) gives the length of the shorter leg.
Choice (C) gives the length of the hypotenuse.
Choice (D) gives the negative root of the quadratic equation, and a length can't be negative.

10. **(C)** Since $0.40c < 0.60c$, the store would need to sell *more* cookies to overcome the -900 to break even. Note that no profit or loss means $f(c) = 0$. Choices (A) and (B) are both true. You can see this by plugging in.

Choice (A):

$$0 = 0.60c - 900$$

$$c = \frac{900}{.6} = 1{,}500$$

This means 1,500 cookies must be sold for no profit or loss.

Choice (B): Find $f(c)$ when $c = 0$:

$$f(c) = 0.60(0) - 900 = -900$$

This represents a loss of $900.

Choice (D) is also true: Compare the equations

$$f(c) = 0.60(0) - 900 \text{ and } f(c) = 0.60(0) = -800$$

A smaller magnitude for the negative constant means a smaller value of c to get $f(c)$ to 0.

11. **(D)** The box is as shown. The volume, V, is the area of the base multiplied by the height:

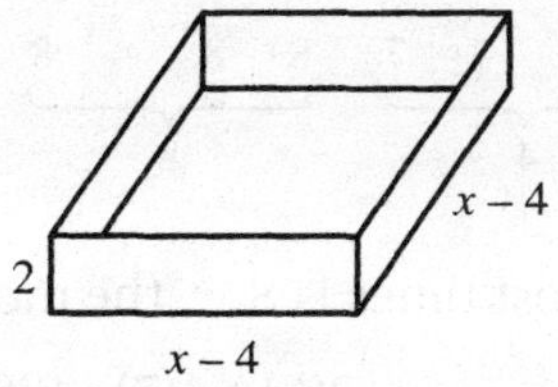

$$V = 2(x-4)^2$$

$$V > 128 \Rightarrow 2(x-4)^2 > 128$$

$$(x-4)^2 > 64$$

$$x-4 > 8 \quad \text{(Ignore negative } x \text{ values)}$$

$$x > 12$$

Since x is an integer, it must be at least 13 inches.

12. **(A)** Parallel lines have the same slope. To get the slope of each line, put it in slope–intercept form: $y = mx + b$. The slope is m, the coefficient of x.
$y + 2x + 3 = 0 \Rightarrow y = -2x - 3$ (The slope for this line is –2.)

$$2y - px - 4 = 0 \Rightarrow 2y = px + 4 \Rightarrow y = \frac{p}{2}x + 2 \quad \text{(The slope for this line is } \frac{p}{2}.)$$

The slopes are equal because the lines are parallel.

$$\therefore \frac{p}{2} = -2$$

$$\therefore p = -4$$

13. **(C)** Use the pick-a-number strategy. Start with $x = 100$ since this is a percent problem. Now take easy numbers for y and z, for example, $y = 10$ and $z = 30$.
Original price = \$100.
Marked down 10% gives a sale price of \$90.
Additional 30% off leaves 70% of 90 = \$63.
Now test each answer choice by plugging in $x = 100$, $y = 10$, $z = 30$, and see which gives an answer of 63.
Choice (C) works:

$$x\left(1-\frac{y}{100}\right)\left(1-\frac{z}{100}\right) = 100(1-0.1)(1-0.3)$$

$$= 100(0.9)(0.7) = 63$$

14. **(D)** The function is exponential, so eliminate choices (A) and (B). Here are the weights for the first three years:

$$\frac{1}{2}, \left(\frac{1}{2}\right)^2, \text{ and } \left(\frac{1}{2}\right)^3, \text{ or } \frac{1}{2^1}, \frac{1}{2^2}, \text{ and } \frac{1}{2^3}, \text{ or } 2^{-1}, 2^{-2}, \text{ and } 2^{-3}$$

The function is $f(x) = 2^{-x}$.

15. **(D)** If you were to list the data in order, you would see that the middle item is 8, $\therefore$ the median is 8.

$$\underbrace{6 \quad 6}_{2} \quad \underbrace{7 \quad 7 \quad 7 \quad 7}_{4} \quad \underbrace{8 \quad 8 \cdots 8}_{8} \quad \underbrace{9 \quad 9}_{2} \quad \underbrace{10}_{1}$$

The item occurring the most times is 8, $\therefore$ the mode is 8.

$$\text{arithmetic mean} = \frac{2(6)+4(7)+8(8)+2(9)+10}{17}$$

Since the numerator is not divisible by 17, the arithmetic mean is not equal to 8.

You don't need to do any calculation at all if you notice from the graph that the size of the bars on either side of 8 will weight the arithmetic mean to the left of 8.

16. **(B)** cost = cost of copier + servicing + 3¢/copy
$= 5{,}800 + 25n + 8{,}000(0.03)n$
$= 5{,}800 + 265n$

17. **(B)** A 5-cm stretch requires 40 N.
Therefore a 4-cm stretch requires $\frac{4}{5}$ of 40, or 32 N.
More formally:
Since F is directly proportional to x, $\frac{F}{x}$ is constant.

$$\therefore \frac{F_1}{x_1} = \frac{F_2}{x_2}$$

Beware! Don't use 15 cm and 14 cm as x_1 and x_2, since you must subtract 10 cm, the natural length of the spring.
x_1 and x_2 are 5 cm and 4 cm, respectively.

$$\frac{F_1}{x_1} = \frac{F_2}{x_2} \Rightarrow \frac{40}{5} = \frac{F_2}{4} \Rightarrow F_2 = \frac{(4)(40)}{5} = 32 \text{ N}$$

18. **(A)** Two ordered pairs on the graph are (480, 380) and (800, 460). This means that in 320 miles \$80 was spent. Therefore in 1 mile \$$\frac{80}{320}$ was spent.

$$\text{slope} = \frac{80}{320} = \frac{\text{difference in cost}}{\text{difference in miles}} = \text{cost per mile}$$

19. **(D)** You can't say that runner *C* was ahead of runner *A*, for example, since the graph shows that runner *A* overtook *C* before the halfway (50-meter) mark.
Each of the other statements is valid:
Choice (A): Runner *A* has the shortest time.
Choice (B): Since *B*'s distance is constant for a period of a few seconds, it looks like he fell and then got up to continue.
Choice (C): Since each runner has a distance of 100 meters for some time *t*, each runner completed the race.

20. **(C)** You can eliminate choices (A), (B), and (D), because if you don't have exact prices you can't precisely find the mean, median, or mode. Choice (C) is correct because the seven values between \$3.20 and \$3.29 fall in the middle of the data; so the median price would land somewhere in that range.

21. **(D)** From the description of the setup, \$5,025 is the total interest earned from both investments. If x is the amount invested at 6%, then $\$(100{,}000 - x)$ is the amount invested at 4.5%. The interest earned on $\$(100{,}000 - x)$ is 4.5% of that amount, or $\$0.045(100{,}000 - x)$.

22. **(C)** When $h = 0$, $t = 20$, and when $h = 1$, $t = 10$. Therefore, (0, 20) and (1, 10) are on the graph.

The slope of the line $= \dfrac{20-10}{0-1} = -10$, and the t-intercept is 20.

Therefore, the equation is $t = -10h + 20$.

23. **(A)**

Method I: Plug-In

Substitute each answer choice for A in the expression $\dfrac{12}{x+2} + A$ to see which one yields $\dfrac{3x^2}{x+2}$. For example, choice (A):

$$\begin{aligned}\frac{12}{x+2}+3x-6 &= \frac{12}{x+2}+\frac{(3x-6)(x+2)}{x+2}\\ &= \frac{12+3x^2-12}{x+2}\\ &= \frac{3x^2}{x+2}\end{aligned}$$

So choice (A), $3x - 6$, works!

Method II: Algebraic Identity

You are given that $\dfrac{3x^2}{x+2} = \dfrac{12}{x+2} + A$.

Notice that this is an identity that should work for all values of x, in particular for $x = 0$.

Substituting $x = 0$ yields:

$$\begin{aligned}\frac{3x^2}{x+2} &= \frac{12}{x+2}+A\\ 0 &= 6+A\\ A &= -6\end{aligned}$$

Now plug $x = 0$ into all the answer choices and see which one equals −6. Bingo! You get the correct answer immediately, with choice (A).

Method III: Algebraic Manipulation

$$\frac{3x^2}{x+2} = \frac{12-12+3x^2}{x+2}$$

$$= \frac{12}{x+2} + \frac{3x^2-12}{x+2}$$

$$= \frac{12}{x+2} + \frac{3(x^2-4)}{x+2}$$

$$= \frac{12}{x+2} + \frac{3(x-2)(x+2)}{x+2}$$

$$= \frac{12}{x+2} + 3(x-2)$$

$$\therefore A = 3x-6$$

Note that in this method, you want to get $\frac{12}{x+2}$ on the right-hand side, so you essentially give it to yourself by introducing 12 – 12!

24. **(A)** Let x be the number of hours to do the job with both drains open. Now set up an equation that shows the fraction of the job that can be done in one hour by each drain.

Drain A does $\frac{1}{4}$ of the job in 1 hour.

Drain B does $\frac{1}{6}$ of the job in 1 hour.

Together they do $\frac{1}{x}$ of the job in 1 hour.

Thus, for 1 hour, (fraction done by A) + (fraction done by B) = (fraction done by both).

So the equation is $\frac{1}{4}+\frac{1}{6}=\frac{1}{x}$.

25. **(B)** For 40 percent of flow rate, the mosquito positive rate is 12, and for 60 percent of flow rate, the mosquito positive rate is 11. So it's valid to interpolate and say that at 50 percent the mosquito positive rate is between 11 and 12 percent.
Choice (A) is false because the faster the river flows, the *smaller* the abundance of mosquitoes.
Choice (C) is false because at minimum flow rate the mosquito population is at 22 percent, the maximum value in the table.
Choice (D) is false because the mosquito positive rate gives no information about actual numbers of mosquitoes.

26. **(B)** The function shows exponential growth. To check that the answer is choice (B), plug in the point (6, 4,000), which lies on the graph:

$$y = 1{,}000 \cdot 2^{\frac{t}{3}}$$

$$4{,}000 \stackrel{?}{=} (1{,}000)2^{\frac{6}{3}}$$

$$4{,}000 \stackrel{?}{=} (1{,}000)2^2 \quad \text{Yes!}$$

The ordered pair (6, 4,000) doesn't satisfy either of the equations in choices (A) and (C). For example, choice (A):

$$y = t^3$$
$$4{,}000 \stackrel{?}{=} 6^3$$
$$4{,}000 \stackrel{?}{=} 216 \text{ No!}$$

Be careful. When you try the ordered pair (6, 4,000) in the equation for choice (D) it works! But choice (D) can't be right because the equation is linear and the given graph is not. When you check the point (3, 2,000) in the equation $y = 1{,}000t - 2{,}000$, it doesn't work:

$$2{,}000 \stackrel{?}{=} (1{,}000)2^{\frac{6}{3}}$$
$$4{,}000 \stackrel{?}{=} (1{,}000)(3) - 2{,}000 \text{ No!}$$

27. **(D)** Let lines l and k be as marked.

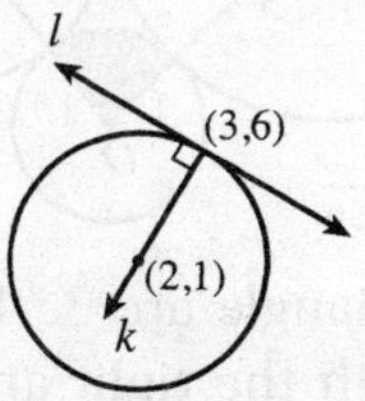

Notice that $l \perp k$, since l is tangent at (3, 6) (tangent–radius theorem).

$$\text{slope of } k = \frac{6-1}{3-2} = 5$$

Since $l \perp k$,

$$\text{slope of } l = -\frac{1}{5} \text{ (negative reciprocal of 5)}$$

The problem now boils down to finding the equation with slope $-\frac{1}{5}$ and containing point (3, 6). Here is the point–slope form of the equation:

$$y - 6 = -\frac{1}{5}(x - 3)$$
$$5y - 30 = -x + 3$$
$$5y + x = 33$$

28. **(A)** The study is well designed because:

- The population is well-defined (people with hearing loss).
- The participants were randomly selected from this population.
- Half the participants were randomly assigned to an experimental group (those who received the implant) and the remaining participants were randomly assigned to a control group (those who did not receive the implant).

One can therefore conclude that the findings are valid: Electrical implant I is likely to improve the hearing of people with hearing loss.
Choice (B) is wrong. The experiment was conducted for people with hearing loss only; so no conclusion can be made about its effectiveness for the general population.
Choice (C) is wrong. The study involved only Electrical implant I; so no conclusion can be made about other treatments for hearing loss.
Choice (D) is wrong. This conclusion is too strong. The study shows that Electrical implant I is likely to improve the hearing of people with hearing loss, but it does not necessarily show that the improvement is substantial.

29. **(D)** The line segments joining the centers pass through the points of tangency, forming $\triangle AOB$, as shown.

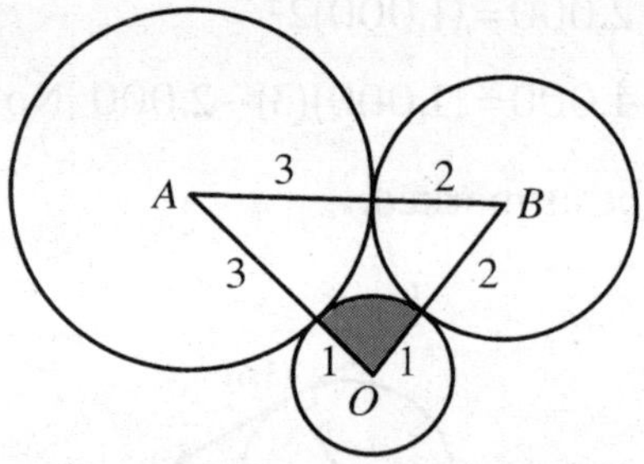

Note that the sides of the triangle are 3, 4, and 5, a Pythagorean triple (i.e., $\triangle AOB$ is a right triangle with the right angle at point O). Thus, the problem is to find the area of a segment of a circle with radius 1 and central angle equal to 90° or $\frac{\pi}{2}$. The required area is $\frac{1}{4}$ the area of the circle, which is $\frac{1}{4}\left[\pi(1)^2\right]=\frac{\pi}{4}$ square inches.

30. **(B)** The cofunction relationship states that $\sin\theta=\cos\left(\frac{\pi}{2}-\theta\right)$.

Therefore, $\sin\theta\approx 0.747\Rightarrow\cos\left(\frac{\pi}{2}-\theta\right)\approx 0.747$.

Don't waste your time with the graphing calculator!

31. **180** How far down is the weight 10 lb less than 60 lb?

10 lb is $\frac{1}{6}$ of 60 lb.

So you need to go down $\frac{1}{6}$ of 1,080 miles, which equals 180 miles.
More formally:
Weight w varies directly as distance d from center.

$$\therefore\frac{w_1}{d_1}=\frac{w_2}{d_2}$$

$$\frac{60}{1{,}080}=\frac{50}{d_2}\Rightarrow d_2=\frac{(50)(1{,}080)}{60}=900\text{ miles}$$

∴ distance beneath surface = 1,080 – 900 = 180 miles.
(You didn't forget the last step, did you?)
Grid-in 180.

32. **3**

Method I: Algebra

Notice that $f(x)=\frac{1}{3}(x^3+x^2-11x-3)$ can be written as

$$f(x)=\frac{1}{3}[(x-p_1)(x-p_2)(x-p_3)]$$

where p_1, p_2, and p_3 are the zeros of the function. If you multiply out the expression in square brackets, the product $-(p_1)(p_2)(p_3)$ is equal to the constant term of the expression $x^3+x^2-11x-3$, namely, –3. Thus, $p_1p_2p_3 = 3$.

Method II: Graphing Calculator

Enter the function into y_1; then inspect the graph.

The zeros look like they're at approximately –3.5, $-\frac{1}{3}$, and 3. You can get the answer quickly by noticing that the product of the negative roots is approximately 1, therefore the required product is 3 to the nearest integer.

For more precise values of the zeros, press 2nd CALC 2 to use the Zero function. To the nearest tenth, you would find that the zeros are –3.7, –.3, and 3. But solving the problem this way is a waste of your precious time!

Grid-in 3.

33. **74**

area of triangular face = $\frac{1}{2}(4)(2\sqrt{3})=4\sqrt{3}$ square cm

volume of solid = (area of triangular face)(thickness)

$= (4\sqrt{3})(2)=8\sqrt{3}$ cubic cm

volume of cylindrical hole = (area of circular base)(thickness)

$=\pi\left(\frac{1}{2}\right)^2(2)=\frac{\pi}{2}$ cubic cm

volume of triangular solid with hole = $8\sqrt{3}-\frac{\pi}{2}$ cubic cm

Density of solid = $\frac{\text{mass}}{\text{volume}}$

Therefore, mass = (density)(volume)

$$= 6(8\sqrt{3}-\frac{\pi}{2}) \approx 74 \text{ grams}$$

Grid-in 74.

34. **42** Notice that the graph of G is a concave down parabola. You want the x-value that makes G a maximum. This corresponds to the x-value of the axis of symmetry:

$$x = -\frac{b}{2a} = \frac{-3}{2\left(-\frac{1}{28}\right)} = 42$$

It's quicker to do the simple calculation above than to type the function into your graphing calculator, then adjust the graphing window to get the graph to fit on the screen.

Grid-in 42.

35. **.5**

Method I: Algebra
Let $x_1 = p$ be the original price per cookie, in cents.
Let $y_1 = n$ be the number of cookies bought at the original price.
Then $x_2 = p + 10$ is the new price per cookie, in cents, and $y_2 = n - 1$ is the number of cookies bought at the increased price.
The total cost of the cookies is fixed, ∴ $x_1y_1 = x_2y_2$

$$pn = (p+10)(n-1)$$

$$pn = pn - p + 10n - 10$$

$$p = 10n - 10$$

Since $pn = 300$,

$$(10n - 10)n = 300$$

$$10n^2 - 10n - 300 = 0$$

$$n^2 - n - 30 = 0$$

$$(n-6)(n+5) = 0$$

$$n = 6 \text{ or } n = -5$$

Reject −5, ∴ $n = 6$.
Solve for p, the original price:

$$p = 10(6) - 10 = 50$$

Required answer is p in dollars: $0.50.

Method II: Guessing

Since the numbers in this problem are easy, you could try integer numbers of cookies that are factors of 300 (cost is 300 cents) and differ by one (one less cookie at the new price), and then check whether the prices would satisfy the 10-cent price difference.

For example, guess that she used to buy 3 cookies and now buys 2: Then old price would be 100 cents each $\left(\frac{300}{3}\right)$, and new price 150 cents. It doesn't work (the price difference is too high). Similarly, the pairs 4 and 3, and 5 and 4, don't work. But the pair 6 and 5 *does* work: $\left(\frac{300}{6}\right) = 50$ and $\left(\frac{300}{5}\right) = 60$, giving a difference of 10 cents in the new and old prices. Therefore, the original price was 50 cents or \$.50.

Grid-in .5.

36. **.12**

Method I: Counting

Number of ways to select 2 students $= \frac{(140)(139)}{2} = 9{,}730$

(Each student can go with every other student, but divide by 2 so you don't count Carol and Amy as being a different pair from Amy and Carol.)

Number of ways to select 2 students from the 49 who have fewer than 2 absences $= \frac{(49)(48)}{2} = 1{,}176$

Probability that both students have fewer than 2 absences $= \frac{1{,}176}{9{,}730} \approx 0.12$.

Method II: Probabilities

Let P be the probability that 2 students chosen at random have fewer than 2 absences.

Then P = [probability(1st student has fewer) × probability(2nd student has fewer)] $= \frac{49}{140} \cdot \frac{48}{139} \approx 0.12$

Grid-in .12.

37. **50** Let x = no. of gals of pure apple juice added to the mixture.

Then the mixture contains $900 + x$ gals of apple drink.

To set up an equation, use the following:

(amt. of apple juice in original mixture) + (amt. of pure juice added)
= (amt of apple juice in final mixture)

Amt. of apple juice in original mixture = 5% of 900 = 45 gal.

Amt. of apple juice in pure juice added = 100% of $x = x$ gal.

Amt. of apple juice in final mixture = 10% of $(900 + x) = 0.1(900 + x)$ gal.

The equation is

$$45+x=0.1(900+x)$$

$$45+x=90+0.1x$$

$$0.9x=45$$

$$x=\frac{45}{0.9}=50$$

Therefore, the manufacturer should add 50 gallons of pure apple juice.
Grid-in 50.

38. **.35** An 8-ounce cup of the drink contains 10% of 8 = 0.8 oz of apple juice. 0.8 oz of apple juice contains (0.8)(0.31) = 0.248 mg of vitamin C. The problem now becomes: What percent of 70 is 0.248?

$$\frac{0.248}{70}=\frac{x}{100}$$

$$x=\frac{24.8}{70}=0.35\%$$

Grid-in .35.

Essay Sample Response 写作范例

This essay is an example of a student response that would, based on the College Board Essay Scoring Rubric, most reasonably score in the Proficient to Advanced range, earning a 3 to 4 in each of the categories of Reading, Analysis, and Writing.

On March 15, 1965, President Lyndon B. Johnson delivered a notably compelling speech to Congress titled "The American Promise." What makes his speech especially vital and worthy of study is its ability to hold the audience's attention and to stir their thoughts and emotions. Johnson achieved this noteworthy historical-political argument by interweaving an effective repertory of rhetorical and stylistic devices. In particular, Johnson created a compelling political discourse by incorporating historical allusion, appealing to democratic ideals, and using strong and formal language.

Throughout his speech, Johnson included historical allusions that not only express pride in America's defense of its ideals but also speak to the widespread seeking of equality among humankind. In paragraph 2, there are allusions to geographical places where battles for such ideals were carried out, such as Lexington, Concord, and Appomattox. Paragraph 8 comprises an expansive historical allusion in which Johnson refers to the founding of America and its founding documents, which he quoted: "All men are created equal" . . . "give me liberty or give me death." He ended this paragraph with a sentence that alludes to the United States at war to defend democracy: "In their name Americans have fought and died . . . risking their lives." Furthering his emphasis on the longstanding struggle and loss of human life that characterizes America's battle for freedom, he dramatically asserted that if we as Americans deny any individual his or her hopes, based on the individual's race, religion, color, or birthplace, we "dishonor the dead who gave their lives for American freedom." Johnson, it would reasonably seem, makes his listeners think—how could we deny anyone freedom now, now that we've been fighting for it for centuries.

President Johnson's speech is emotionally stirring, as it appeals to his listeners' firmly held democratic ideals. Immediately after his greeting to his audience, he mentioned "the dignity of man," which in itself embodies all the freedoms and rights deserving of every man or woman, regardless of gender, race, color, or heritage. In paragraph 3, he defined the American government's mission in upholding the essential beliefs that support democracy: "to right wrong, to do justice, to serve man." He steadfastly tugged at his listeners' emotions as Americans when he stated that the issue of American Negroes' equal rights is the type of issue that "lay[s] bare the secret heart of America itself." This was his way of accentuating how central, unequivocal, and tenderly vital this issue truly was. Johnson masterfully stressed this foundational American ideal, equal rights for all, when he stated in paragraph 5, "And should we defeat every enemy . . . failed as a people and as a nation." Toward the end of this discourse (paragraph 9), Johnson expounded on the ideal of freedom when he itemized all the elements of this great American right to include choosing one's leaders, providing for one's family, educating one's children, and all in alignment with his overall worth as a human being. President Johnson effectively drew upon these founding American tenets of democracy as he pleaded for the rights of American Negroes during this pivotal historical time.

Finally, in his Special Message to the Congress, Johnson used powerful and formal language in numerous places. After his formal greeting to his audience, he spoke on behalf of "the destiny of democracy," which in and of itself is a thought-provoking phrase. He continued with phrases that are similar in their ability to move his listeners in thought and emotion: "shape a turning point in man's unending search for freedom" (paragraph 2) and "the cries and hymns and protests of oppressed people" (paragraph 3). Undeniably, Johnson grabs the attention of his audience with powerful language. Paragraph 4 ends with a rich and potent message: "Rarely are we met with a challenge . . . to the values and the purposes and the meaning of our beloved Nation." His use of diction, in choosing the passion-packed adjective, beloved, to describe his county, speaks to his rhetorical ability in getting his emotional stance across to the members of Congress. An outstanding use of formal and powerful language is illustrated in the rhetorical question he posed in paragraph 6: "What is a man profited, if he shall gain the whole world, and lose his own soul?" Johnson artfully and admirably brought language to a lofty level, thus inspiring elevated thought in his audience.

In this historical speech, President Johnson' political argument is both passionate and persuasive. To effectively express his message to Congress, he incorporated historical allusions, appeals to his audience's democratic ideals, and a formal and powerful writing style. He admirably advocated for all rights for all people in this 1965 speech. The final sentence of this text artfully blends all three predominant aspects of Johnson's rhetorical strategy. His closing sentence merges powerful diction and phrasing (*deny a man his hopes, injustice, deny America, dishonor the dead*), an allusion to American history (latter part of the closing line), and a plea for the values that define democracy. Johnson's speech includes many aspects of language and persuasion to emulate in one's own written or spoken arguments.

附录 Appendix

SAMPLE SOURCE TEXT ADVANCED RESPONSES (CHAPTER 6) 示例范文赏析（第六章）

These essays provide examples of student responses that would, based on the College Board Essay Scoring Rubric, most reasonably score in the proficient to advanced range, earning a 3 to 4 in each of the categories of Reading, Analysis, and Writing.

Source Text 1: Dual Capacity Framework

In expressing his advocacy for the new Dual Capacity Framework, the author's statement, entitled "Department of Education Releases New Parent and Community Engagement Framework," is straightforward and powerful. The passage, however, is unadorned in terms of its more austere style that does not incorporate stylistic or literary elements such as metaphor, personification, hyperbole, and the like. Instead, the author's strong statement is built by his use of facts combined with his references to figures of authority and further sources of information. He also uses repetitive diction to emphasize key ideals behind the framework. Most notably, he includes a current illustrative example that is specific and attention grabbing.

The author's statement is strengthened by his references to facts, figures of authority as well as further sources of information. Facts edify the persuasive aspect of this passage, lending it credibility and a sense of authority. In the opening phrase, several facts are laid out. First, the time frame during which preparations and professional development occur in the educational world is specified: "the fourth quarter of the school year." The opening sentence continues to list specific and factual activities that occur during this time, including budget planning, scheduling, and professional development. In paragraph four, the author presents Secretary of Education, Arne Duncan, as an authority who can provide additional information about the program. As an authority, or expert, on this education-centered subject, Duncan can provide an informational video on the Dual Capacity Framework. The passage also refers readers to the official ed.gov website for updates and further information. All together, these facts and references strengthen the persuasive angle of this education-oriented passage.

Repetitive diction, or word choice, has the effect of emphasizing certain topics or ideals that the author chooses to accentuate. In the case of this prose passage, several words are repeated multiple times. Certain words repeat more often than others and, consequently, serve to lend the essay a highly supportive undertone with regard to this educational program. The title introduces the term "engagement," which repeats in each and every paragraph of the article. Its verb form, "engage," appears numerous times in the body of the passage. Moreover, with the title included, the terms "community" and "communities" are repeated ten times. Additional repeating words are "support," "capacity," "build," and "effective." The phrase "community engagement" appears four times throughout this piece. Collectively, these vocabulary words nuance the essay with an action-oriented, positive bent toward the Department of Education's newly released program. Diction is a powerful persuasive tool that is used in this passage.

Most notably, in paragraph three the author incorporates a real, relevant, and detailed example of the Dual Capacity Framework that was implemented in the Baltimore City Public Schools. This case scenario is particularly effective because, as the author informs his readers, the program was executed in the author's hometown. Given this fact, the author must be impressed by the program's effectiveness; otherwise, he would be unlikely to highlight or elaborate upon it. This illustrative example will arguably draw significant attention in light of Baltimore's recent social unrest and prominent media attention. This illustrative example is enhanced by the author's inclusion of specific facts. For example, he indicates that the Baltimore Schools program benefitted "12,000 pre-kindergarten and kindergarten homes." Also, he explains how, on average, children are exposed to "more than 100 books per year." In portraying the program, the author's inclusion of this example serves to express the author's belief in the program while persuading readers to do the same.

Altogether, this nonfiction passage presents an argument that is solid and firmly supported. By incorporating numerical facts combined with references to figures of authority and sources of information, the author builds a powerful passage on his chosen topic. Additionally, he uses repetitive diction to emphasize central ideals behind the Dual Capacity Framework. Most notably, he includes a contemporary, representative example that is compelling. The author not only effectively describes the literacy and learning program, but he also presents the topic with an overall tone that powerfully conveys his belief in the program.

Source Text 2: Unlocking Our Nation's Wind Potential

In explaining the potential for wind power, writer Mike Carr argues that wind power technology can provide a robust, affordable energy to the United States. In his article "Unlocking Our Nation's Wind Potential," he effectively builds his argument by using inspiring and effective diction, incorporating empirical data and measures, and asserting the economic and environmental benefits of wind power.

Throughout his article, Carr uses powerful and inspiring diction in both individual words and phrases. In the second paragraph, he paraphrases the article's title with an inspiring metaphor, "unlocking wind energy's potential." The words convey a sense of unlocking a door and letting in great possibilities for our nation. In paragraph 3, in describing the new wind towers, Carr's diction stirs a feeling of excitement: "marvels of human ingenuity and engineering savvy." Next he refers to the turbines as "technological wonders." Later, in paragraph 5, the author's diction as used in the expression, "wind energy deployments," effectively creates a visual effect of military troops ready for action. Toward the end of the article, he asserts that wind power will contribute to the United States' "robust clean energy portfolio." Carr's choice of words creates a powerfully persuasive advocacy for, what he calls in the last paragraph, "next-generation wind technology." His diction fortifies his viewpoint through to the very end.

Carr's argument is also furthered by his incorporation of facts and data. Not only is this inclusion compelling but it also establishes Carr's expertise and credibility on this energy topic. From the onset, he establishes wind power's importance using facts and figures: "Wind power supplies nearly five percent of our nation's electricity demand across 39 states." Again using numbers and objective data, he explains how the taller and more powerful turbines that "stand 110 to 140 meters tall . . . and with blades longer than 60 meters" can capture wind potential "across an additional 700,000 square miles—roughly one-fifth" of America's land. Effectively establishing his argument, Carr culminates with more persuasive facts when he writes, "wind energy could support 600,000 American jobs and supply up to thirty-five percent of the nation's power by 2050." Carr's essay reveals that he has done the research, and his thorough use of empirical data provides for a potent persuasive exposition.

Finally, by delineating the numerous benefits of wind power, Carr solidifies his point. Initially, he points out that wind power is both clean and affordable. Then he remarks that it is getting less expensive with each year and alludes to "further improvements" relevant to wind energy. Next Carr emphasizes how this natural energy source is reliable and more efficient than ever before. Building on the benefits, he indicates how the wind energy industry will create jobs, in the Southeastern U.S. states especially. Last but unequivocally not least, Carr concludes by stating how wind energy will become even cheaper for Americans and, as a big benefit to the environment, will reduce emissions of greenhouse gases, earning wind power a "clean energy" accolade.

Writing with a positive-minded and forward-thinking stance, Mike Carr advocates for the benefits of wind energy power in the United States. In doing so, he uses powerful and persuasive diction that creates inspiring phrases and sentences. He also effectively uses facts and figures in his explanation as well as a generous itemization of both the economic and environmental benefits of this energy source. Mike Carr builds his claim compellingly through his use of these persuasive elements working in tandem.

Source Text 3: Statement from EPA Administrator Gina McCarthy on Historic Kigali Agreement

(Remember the importance of annotating. Below, we will show you the most important points that you may have chosen to note when you read Source Text 3 and wrote your essay response.)

In her statement, McCarthy's most notable features include:

1. Diction (the use of words and phrases) that promotes unity among mankind. Examples of diction from the passage include, but are not limited to, the following:

    - "our planet" (paragraph 1), "effort to save the one planet we have" (paragraph 2), and "our collective resolve" (paragraph 2)—all establish a tone of unity for everyone who inhabits Earth
    - "the air we breathe" (paragraph 3)—stresses humanity's common need for clean air

- "our homes . . . our food" (paragraph 4)—accentuates common needs; we are in this together to share in the benefits
- "Together . . . we agreed to take action and get the job done" (paragraph 5)—stresses that together we can make this happen
- "protect ourselves and our children" (paragraph 8)—again, powerfully enforces the idea of humanity, that the children (the future) belong to all of us collectively
- "Our global commitment to protecting our planet brought us to this moment. It's an exciting time for all of us" (paragraph 10)—continues to stress unity with the use of the personal pronouns "our" and "us"

2. The inclusion of several positive steps that have been taken to achieve her goal. Examples of this inclusion include, but are not limited to, the following:

- "This week, nearly 200 nations came together to take a historic step in combatting climate change" (paragraph 1)—demonstrates that 200 nations gathered for a common cause
- "I could not be more delighted with the outcome of the negotiations" (paragraph 2)—emphasizes the positive results of negotiations
- "this week in Rwanda, world leaders took a giant leap forward by agreeing to a global phase-down of these harmful gases" (paragraph 5)—stresses a positive step that was taken for the benefit of everyone in the world

1600 Club Coaching: *Use ellipses (. . .) to condense longer portions of textual evidence that you wish to feature in your essay.*

All of these quotes can be used as evidence to strengthen your argument and compose a well-written essay response. Review your essay response to see if you cited similar supporting evidence from the text.

UPPER-LEVEL VOCABULARY BUILDING 高级词汇的建立

1600 CLUB VOCABULARY IMMERSION
1600分俱乐部词汇表

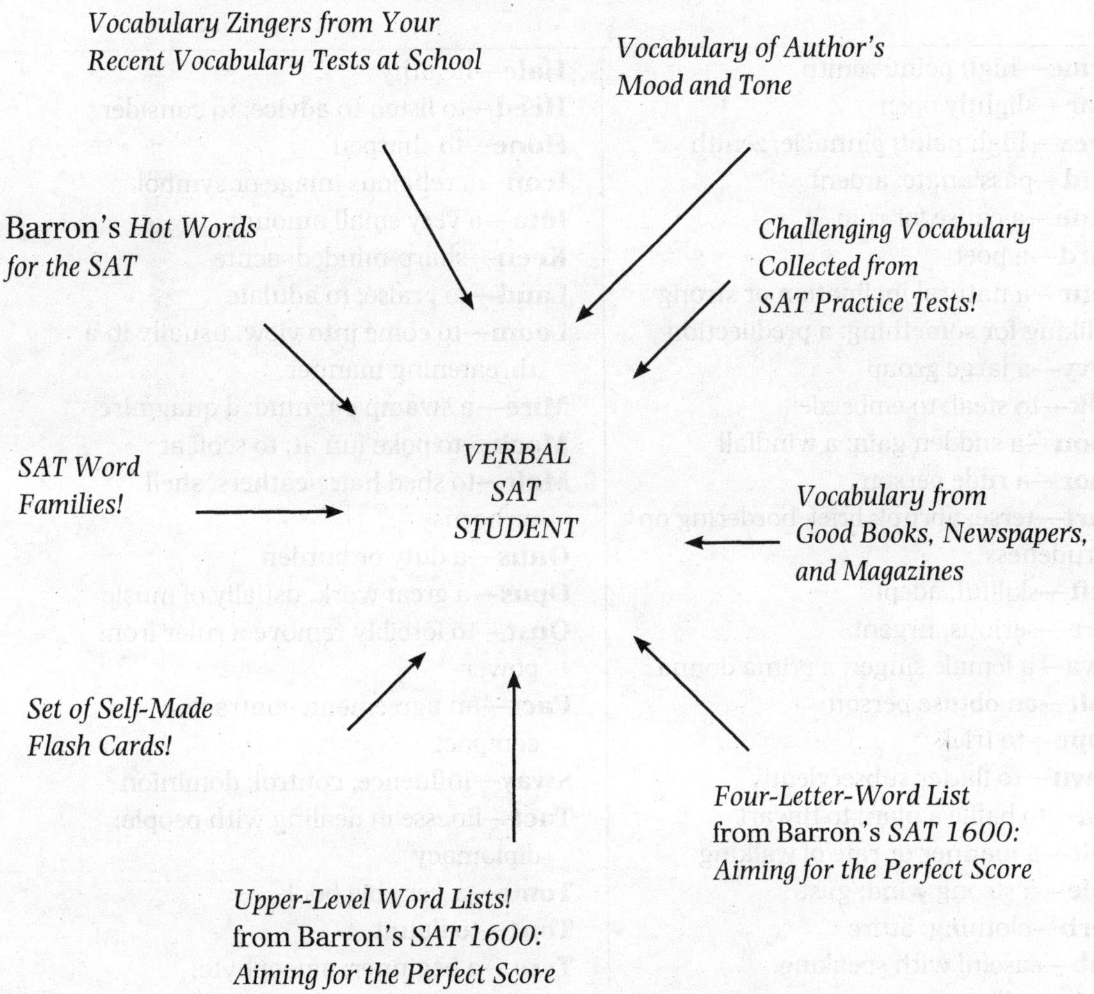

FOUR-LETTER-WORD LIST FOR CLUB MEMBERS
四个字母的词汇表

These are not the four-letter words you may be thinking of—tsk, tsk.

This list could be the very first one of its kind. How exciting! Not all four-letter words are created equal; certainly, not all of them are "bad." In fact, if you're after an added edge, the little words that follow are worth knowing.

Some of these words can be considered part of "core and classic" SAT vocabulary. Others are a bit off the bell curve. Regardless, to a 1600 Club Member, all good words are worth knowing. Enjoy!

Acme—high point; zenith
Ajar—slightly open
Apex—high point; pinnacle; zenith
Avid—passionate; ardent
Bane—a cause for ruin
Bard—a poet
Bent—a natural inclination or strong liking for something; a predilection
Bevy—a large group
Bilk—to steal; to embezzle
Boon—a sudden gain; a windfall
Boor—a rude person
Curt—terse; abrupt; brief, bordering on rudeness
Deft—skillful; adept
Dire—serious, urgent
Diva—a female singer; a prima donna
Dolt—an obtuse person
Dupe—to trick
Fawn—to flatter subserviently
Foil—to baffle a plan; to thwart
Gait—a manner or rate of walking
Gale—a strong wind; gust
Garb—clothing; attire
Glib—easeful with speaking, storytelling
Glut—to oversupply; to stuff
Guru—a learned person who has followers
Hack—hackneyed, trite, stale; to chop
Hail—to praise
Hale—healthy
Heed—to listen to advice; to consider
Hone—to sharpen
Icon—a religious image or symbol
Iota—a very small amount
Keen—sharp-minded; acute
Laud—to praise; to adulate
Loom—to come into view, usually in a threatening manner
Mire—a swamp pit; mud: a quagmire
Mock—to poke fun at; to scoff at
Molt—to shed hair, feathers, shell, or horns
Onus—a duty or burden
Opus—a great work, usually of music
Oust—to forcibly remove a ruler from power
Pact—an agreement, contract; a compact
Sway—influence, control, dominion
Tact—finesse in dealing with people; diplomacy
Tome—a very big book
Tout—to flaunt
Tyro—a beginner; a neophyte; a fledgling
Void—to cancel; to nullify
Wary—cautious; chary
Whet—to sharpen; to stimulate an interest in
Wily—crafty, sly

UPPER-LEVEL WORD LISTS FOR CLUB MEMBERS
高级词汇表

1600 Club members strive to learn more than the core words. You can find "core SAT words" in Barron's *Hot Words for the SAT* and in Barron's *SAT*. If you want the best shot at a 1600, it's foolish not to make every effort to learn these core, high-frequency words. You have a strong work ethic, and you're motivated to go beyond basic test prep, so the lists of hard words that follow have your name on them. You're up for the challenge!

Don't let hard words be stumbling blocks for you as you slog through the tough terrain of the hardest questions. Learn these upper-level words, and you'll move through the sentence-completion and critical reading questions with ease and celerity. Review these words and their definitions often to reinforce and solidify their meanings. The words were taken from *real* tests that the College Board has given over the past several years and from practice tests available through the College Board website. Here's an idea—try using a few of these words in your essay!

1600 Club members do not shy away from big-league vocabulary words. Instead, they tackle them, determined to make these hard words part of their working lexicon. Don't be among the students who self-sabotage by crossing off answer choices just because they contain unfamiliar words. This is a self-defeating approach called "fear of the unknown." Be intrepid; learn these hard words!

One more maxim: A word list a day keeps average scores away!

Word List 1 词汇表1

A–B

Aesthete—one who appreciates and seeks beauty, art, or pleasure
Alacrity—cheerful readiness
Anomalous—rare, unusual, abnormal
Aphorism—a wise saying; an adage; a maxim
Appropriate (v.)—to take another's property as one's own
Arable—able to be cultivated; farmable
Arboreal—relating to trees
Aspersion—misleading or false rumor; gossip
Asylum—a safe place to practice one's religion or follow one's convictions
Auspicious—foretelling well for the future
Austerity—strict economy; relating to asceticism
Avant-garde—cutting-edge; new; experimental
Behemoth—a huge animal; something of great size or power
Bequest—a gift upon one's death
Breadth—a range or scope
Brook (v.)—to endure; to put up with
Bungle—to botch; to mess up
Byzantine—ornate, fancy

Word List 2 词汇表2

C–D

Calumny—slander, defamation
Celerity—cheerful speed
Cerebral—intellectual
Chagrin—embarrassment
Circumscribed—defined or limited; isolated
Cloying—oversweet; saccharine
Confound—to confuse; to perplex; to befuddle
Conjecture—a guess
Constituents—voters
Consummate—complete; perfect
Convoluted—complicated, complex
Crude—rude; lacking refinement
Curtail—to cut short; abridge

Debased—morally low; base
Decorous—having propriety
Denuded—made ineffective or infertile
Desultory—aimless; lacking a plan or purpose
Diaphanous—sheer, gauzy, see-through; transparent
Didactic—relating to instruction, lecturing
Dilatory—lacking goals or purpose; aimless
Din—noise
Dirge—a funeral song
Discomfited—embarrassed; disconcerted
Discretionary—based on personal choice; showing prudence
Disingenuous—dishonest; crafty
Disposed—behaviorally inclined
Divine—heavenly; godly

Word List 3 词汇表3

E–F

Edifice—a building
Effigy—a crude likeness of a loathed person
Egregious—blatantly wrong
Elusive—hard to grasp; escaping; evasive
Emollient—a soothing lotion
Empirical—based on data, evidence, and/or experiments
Enervate—to drain of energy; to weaken
Enfranchise—to free from slavery; to bestow the right to vote
Epitaph—words inscribed on a tomb
Espouse—to support
Expurgate—to delete obscene or other undesirable material from a text
Extant—existing
Fabrication—a lie
Facile—easy
Felicitous—suitable; pleasant
Feral—savage; wild
Flotilla—fleet of ships
Flotsam—wreckage, debris floating around

Word List 4 词汇表4

G–H

Galvanize—to incite; to arouse to action
Gaunt—thin; haggard
Gingerly—carefully
Grovel—to beg or plead; to crawl; to behave subordinately
Hapless—ill fated; unfortunate; unlucky
Harbinger—a messenger; an omen
Hermetic—sealed in an airtight manner
Histrionic—over theatrical; melodramatic
Hubris—excessive pride

Word List 5 词汇表5

I–J

Inanimate—not living
Incantation—a calling out for inspiration or guidance; an invocation
Inchoate—not fully formed
Incisive—harsh; cutting; vitriolic
Incumbent—one who holds political office
Indelible—unable to be erased; permanent
Ineffable—incapable of expression in words
Inexorable—steadfast; resolute
Inflammatory—likely to excite rage or disorder
Insular—isolated; remote
Intemperate—excessive; immoderate
Interlocutor—one who participates in conversation or dialogue
Intractable—hard to manage or control
Jaded—bored from too much pleasure or overindulgence
Jingoism—aggressive touting of one's patriotism
Juggernaut—relentless force
Juxtapose—to place things side by side for the sake of comparing

Word List 6 词汇表6

K–L

Kinetic—relating to motion and energy
Legion—a very large number
Leviathon—a subaquatic, mythological sea creature; something huge
Licentious—morally lax

Word List 7 词汇表7

M–N

Mawkishness—overly sweet sentimentality
Melee—a hand-to-hand fight involving several participants
Mendacity—deceit, dishonesty, fabrication
Milieu—environment
Multifarious—numerous, varied, mixed, diverse, assorted
Munificence—generosity with money, time, compliments; kindness, forgiveness
Myopic—short-sighted
Naivete—lack of experience or sophistication
Nihilism—a philosophical belief involving the rejection of established values and morality
Nondescript—featureless; hard to describe
Nonplussed—confused to the point of being unable to act or speak

Word List 8 词汇表8

O–P

Obfuscate—to obscure the meaning of
Obliged—forced; made to do something because of conscience or obligation
Oblique—indirect; slanted
Obstreperous—unruly, clamorous, boisterous; bad-tempered, argumentative
Olfactory—relating to the sense of smell
Onerous—burdensome
Opprobrium—scorn, contempt
Ostensible—apparent
Panacea—a cure-all
Partisan—biased; opinionated
Pathos—empathy; sympathetic pity
Pedagogic—relating to education; instructive
Pedantic—narrowly or pretentiously learned
Perfidious—disloyal; traitorous
Petulant—irritable
Plaudits—applause; praise
Pontificate—to speak in a supercilious and self-important manner
Pragmatist—a practical person
Precept—a rule of behavior or action
Precipitate—to hurry up; to make happen before planned
Prescience—advance knowledge; foresight; anticipation
Probity—honesty; integrity
Profligate—extravagant to a fault; prodigal
Proliferate—to reproduce or multiply quickly
Promulgate—to make known, formally, a law or set of beliefs
Prose—language ordinarily used in speaking or writing; writing that is *not* poetry
Prototype—a model; an archetype; a first specimen
Prowess—valor, skill
Pundits—erudite (learned, scholarly) persons

Word List 9 词汇表9

Q–R

Qualm—doubt; hesitation; uneasiness
Quibble—to find fault with
Quixotic—romantic or dreamy
Raiment—clothing, apparel, attire
Rectitude—the quality of being right, moral, good
Refractory—stubborn
Relegate—to demote to an inferior position
Reprehensible—worthy of blame
Rescind—to take back; to withdraw
Retrograde—going backward and therefore not progressing
Reverent—respectful; showing deference

Word List 10 词汇表10

S–T

Sanctimonious—pretending to be religious
Sanction (v.)—to approve
Scrupulous—very conscientious
Serendipity—occurring by chance, good fortune
Sophistry—deceptive thinking; invalid arguments
Spate—an outpouring
Specious—false, not authentic; spurious
Steadfastness—loyalty, resolve
Stupefy—to stun
Subterfuge—deception
Supplant—to replace; to substitute for
Surfeit (n.)—a surplus, an oversupply
Sybarite—a pleasure-loving person
Synergistic—working together and having a greater combined effect because of simultaneous operation
Table (v.)—to set aside an issue to be discussed at a later time
Tawdry—cheap-looking; gaudy
Temerity—reckless boldness
Temper (v.)—to lessen the severity of
Threadbare—very worn; shabby
Treachery—disloyalty, perfidy
Treacly or **Treacle**—overly sentimental
Truculent—belligerent
Turgid—swollen; pompous

Word List 11 词汇表11

U–V

Unctuous—inky, oily
Unheralded—unannounced
Unintelligible—unable to decipher, figure out, decode; garbled
Untenable—unable to be defended
Upstart—a rebel, an insurgent; a maverick
Utopian—relating to a perfect society; idealistic
Vaunt—to brag or boast
Venial—forgivable; pardonable
Verdant—green, lush
Verisimilitude—probability; something that has the appearance of truth
Vestigial—extremely small
Victuals—food
Vignette—a brief written description
Virile—manly, strong
Visceral—relating to the abdomen; instinctive rather than reasoned
Vitiate—to impair; to render ineffective
Vitriolic—harsh, biting, caustic
Vocation—a profession to which one feels called to carry out, especially a religious calling

Word List 12 词汇表12

W–Z

Watershed—a defining moment; a turning point
Waylay—to ambush
Wheedle—to cajole or coax
Wily—sly
Windfall—an unexpected gain or boon
Winsome—attractive
Witticism—a clever remark
Xenophobic—fearful of foreigners
Zephyr—a light breeze

EXERCISE: CHOOSE THE CORRECT SYNONYM

习题：选出正确的同义词

As you know, words can be defined in multifarious ways. *Opaque* for example, can mean dark, difficult, or even obscure. *Magnanimous* can mean generous, upright, or even noble. The challenge of this exercise is twofold: First, determine the definition that the group of synonyms shares. Then, select the word that best fits the given sentence completion and, therefore, has a distinct meaning from the others.

> **Directions: Each question in this exercise has two parts. For Part A, select the answer choice that best expresses the shared meaning among the group of synonyms—or fairly close synonyms—that are listed. For Part B, using the sentence (or sentences) provided as a guide, select the word from the list that best fits this particular context and, therefore, has an "exclusive" meaning that the other words do not share.**

Practice Set A 习题A

1. circuitous, meandering, serpentine, sinuous

PART A

(A) joking, jesting
(B) senseless, inane
(C) electrical, dynamic
(D) twisting, bending
(E) strange, exotic

PART B

Which word (or word form) fits the exclusive meaning, as expressed in the sentence below?

"Deceptive Dean speaks in a ______ manner."

2. conviction, credo, doctrine, dogma, tenet

PART A

(A) beliefs
(B) guesses
(C) predictions
(D) rumors
(E) fallacies

PART B

Which word (or word form) fits the exclusive meaning, as expressed in the sentences below?

"After a lengthy trial, ________ was his fate."

"The man on trial was eventually ________."

3. calculated, deliberate, intended, intentional, premeditated

PART A
(A) strong
(B) disgusted
(C) planned
(D) wily
(E) criminal

PART B
Which word (or word form) fits the exclusive meaning, as expressed in the sentence below?

"At first, the trial verdict seemed crystal clear, but then the jurors decided to ___________ over the verdict a bit more."

"I must further ___________ these weighty issues before I make my final decision."

4. acute, astute, keen, penetrating, perspicacious, sagacious, shrewd

PART A
(A) widely traveled
(B) scathingly critical
(C) infinitesimal
(D) mentally sharp; wise
(E) harsh in tone

PART B
Which word (or word form) fits the exclusive meaning, as expressed in the sentences below?

"To the fisherman's distress, the claws of the King Crab are ___________ the dense, bulging fishing net."

"The steel arrow could easily ___________ a wooden board."

Practice Set B 习题B

5. capricious, fickle, impulsive, volatile, whimsical

PART A
(A) relating to chemistry
(B) artistic
(C) lighthearted
(D) changeable
(E) stationary

PART B
Which word (or word form) fits the exclusive meaning, as expressed in the sentences below?

"An avid doodler, Justina loves to sketch ___________ creatures like winged rabbits, ponies bedecked in jewels, and flying puppies!"

"Centaurs and unicorns are ___________ creatures."

6. embroider, equivocate, fabricate, prevaricate

PART A
(A) fib, stretch the truth
(B) deal underhandedly
(C) create by hand
(D) express a strong bias
(E) rehearse

PART B
Which word (or word form) fits the exclusive meaning, as expressed in the sentences below?

"Talented with handicrafts, Nicole can ___________ colorful and intricate butterflies and flowers onto any type of fabric, including linen and cotton."

"I will ___________ this shirt from fine Chinese silk."

7. augur, divine, foresight, foretell, portend, predilection, premonition, prophesize

PART A
(A) associated with mythology
(B) belonging to members of the clergy
(C) pertaining to an early knowledge or prior knowing
(D) relating to Greek gods
(E) of or relating to personal virtue

PART B
Which word (or word form) fits the exclusive meaning, as expressed in the sentence below?

"Immortality and omniscience are traits of entities that are considered to be ________."

8. frugal, miserly, parsimonious, penurious, thrifty

PART A
(A) jaunty
(B) biased
(C) uninspired
(D) dishonest
(E) cheap

PART B
Which word (or word form) fits the exclusive meaning, as expressed in the sentence below?

"The ________ family lived in the impoverished side of town."

Practice Set C 习题C

9. dark, depraved, iniquitous, nefarious, sinister, wicked

PART A
(A) opaque
(B) abandoned
(C) evil
(D) ghost-like
(E) willful

PART B
Which word (or word form) fits the exclusive meaning, as expressed in the sentences below?

"Without streetlights, the long road was ________ and foreboding."

"It is quite ________ outside tonight."

10. embryonic, emerging, germinating, inchoate, incipient, nascent

PART A
(A) developing, at the early stages of
(B) inbred, developmentally impaired
(C) fertile, arable
(D) mentally prepared
(E) childlike, impulsive

PART B
Which word (or word form) fits the exclusive meaning, as expressed in the sentence below?

"The preschoolers are ________ small spider plants from the offshoots of their teacher's large and mature spider plant that she proudly displays on the classroom windowsill."

11. glacial, lethargic, phlegmatic, slothful, sluggish

PART A
(A) reserved
(B) animal-like
(C) jesting
(D) inquisitive
(E) slow-moving

PART B
Which word (or word form) fits the exclusive meaning, as expressed in the sentence below?

"Without an iota of warmth in her rock-hard expression, Clara gave us a ________ stare."

12. concrete, haptic, palpable, tactile, tangible

PART A
(A) subtly sensual
(B) jocular in spirit
(C) introverted
(D) able to be touched
(E) emotionally regressive

PART B
Which word (or word form) fits the exclusive meaning, as expressed in the sentences below?

"John calling Ted a 'jerk' was a ________ insult."

"Shaking like a leaf, Larry felt a ________ fear upon entering the Hall of Horrors!"

Practice Set D 习题D

13. affectionate, amorous, demonstrative, effusive, tender

PART A
(A) showing off
(B) overly sensitive in an insincere manner
(C) showing warmth of emotion
(D) heavy-hearted
(E) ridiculing

PART B
Which word (or word form) fits the exclusive meaning, as expressed in the sentence below?

"The gladiator's wound was very ________ after he was stabbed in the arm."

14. insurgence, mutiny, revolt, revolution, sedition, uprising

PART A
(A) allegiance
(B) rebellion
(C) war
(D) facade
(E) impasse

PART B
Which word (or word form) fits the exclusive meaning, as expressed in the sentence below?

"The ________ of the Earth along its orbit around the sun takes 365 days."

15. economical, financial, fiscal, monetary

PART A

(A) relating to charitable contributions
(B) pertaining to government
(C) pertaining to severe debt
(D) relating to the accumulation of property assets
(E) pertaining to money

PART B

Which word (or word form) fits the exclusive meaning, as expressed in the sentence below?

"Carmen is so ___________ that she only shops at dollar stores."

16. annihilate, devastate, eradicate, raze, ruin

PART A

(A) burden
(B) destroy
(C) detach
(D) bungle
(E) decrease

PART B

Which word (or word form) fits the exclusive meaning, as expressed in the sentence below?

"The ________ of Ancient Rome are quite stunning."

Answer Key 答案

Practice Set A 习题A

1. **A. (D)**
   B. *circuitous*; contextual meaning is deceptive
2. **A. (A)**
   B. *conviction*; contextual meaning is a guilty verdict, jail sentence; second sentence: *convicted*
3. **A. (C)**
   B. *deliberate*; contextual meaning is to contemplate, think over; second sentence: also *deliberate*
4. **A. (D)**
   B. *penetrating*; contextual meaning is piercing, breaking through in a literal sense; second sentence: *penetrate*

Practice Set B 习题B

5. **A. (D)**
   B. *whimsical*; contextual meaning is imaginative, fanciful; second sentence: also *whimsical*
6. **A. (A)**
   B. *embroider*; contextual meaning is to stitch, decoratively, on fabric; do needlework; second sentence: also *embroider*
7. **A. (C)**
   B. *divine*; contextual meaning is relating to gods or omnipotent powers
8. **A. (E)**
   B. *penurious*; contextual meaning is poor, penniless

Practice Set C 习题C

9. **A. (C)**
   B. *dark*; contextual meaning is, literally, without light; second sentence: also *dark*
10. **A. (A)**
    B. *germinating*; contextual meaning is growing
11. **A. (E)**
    B. *glacial*; contextual meaning is cold, lacking a warm spirit
12. **A. (D)**
    B. *palpable*; contextual meaning is blatant, overt, flagrant; second sentence: also *palpable*

Practice Set D 习题D

13. **A. (C)**
    B. *tender*; contextual meaning is tender to the touch, sore
14. **A. (B)**
    B. *revolution*; contextual meaning is one complete circling around
15. **A. (E)**
    B. *economical*; contextual meaning is careful with money, thrifty
16. **A. (B)**
    B. *ruins*; contextual meaning is wreckages, old buildings

USEFUL MATH FORMULAS
有用的数学公式

You can get a perfect score on the Math sections of the SAT without memorizing many formulas. Nevertheless, here are some formulas that may be helpful.

1. Area of a trapezoid with bases b_1 and b_2, and height h:

$$A = \frac{1}{2}h(b_1 + b_2)$$

2. Area of a rhombus with diagonals d_1 and d_2:

$$A = \frac{1}{2}(d_1 d_2)$$

3. Area of an equilateral triangle with side s:

$$A = \frac{s^2\sqrt{3}}{4}$$

4. Sum of angles in a polygon with n sides:

$$S = (n - 2)180°$$

5. Sum of exterior angles in a polygon with n sides:

$$S = 360°$$

6. Area of a sector with radius r and central angle $m°$:

$$A = \frac{m}{360} \cdot \pi r^2$$

7. Arc length of a sector with radius r and central angle $m°$:

$$A = \frac{m}{360} \cdot 2\pi r$$

8. The nth term, a_n, of an arithmetic sequence with first term a and common difference d:

$$a_n = a + (n - 1)d$$

9. The nth term, a_n, of a geometric sequence with first term a and common ratio r:

$$a_n = ar^{n-1}$$

10. The sum of n terms, S_n, of an arithmetic series with first term a and nth term a_n:

$$S_n = \frac{n}{2}(a + a_n)$$

11. The sum of n terms of an arithmetic series with first term a and common difference d:

$$S_n = \frac{n}{2}[2a + (n - 1)d]$$

12. The sum of n terms of a geometric series with first term a and common ratio r:

$$S_n = a \cdot \frac{1 - r^n}{1 - r}$$

13. The sum of the first n positive integers:

$$S_n = \frac{n(n+1)}{2}$$

14. The number of permutations of n objects taken r at a time:

$${}_nP_r = \frac{n!}{(n-r)!}$$

15. The number of combinations of n objects taken r at a time:

$${}_nC_r = \frac{n!}{(n-r)!r!}$$

16. The surface area of a cube with edge e:

$$S = 6e^2$$

17. The surface area of a rectangular prism (box) with edges ℓ, w, and h:

$$S = 2(\ell w + \ell h + wh)$$

18. The surface area of a cylinder with base radius r and height h:

$$S = 2\pi r^2 + 2\pi rh$$

19. The volume of a cone with base radius r and height h:

$$V = \frac{1}{3}\pi r^2 h$$

20. The volume of a pyramid with base area B and height h:

$$V = \frac{1}{3}Bh$$

21. The surface area of a sphere with radius r:

$$S = 4\pi r^2$$

22. The volume of a sphere with radius r:

$$S = \frac{4}{3}\pi r^3$$

USEFUL NUMBERS TO MEMORIZE
记住常用数值

SOME SQUARE ROOTS

$\sqrt{2} \approx 1.41$

$\sqrt{3} \approx 1.73$

$\sqrt{5} \approx 2.24$

$\sqrt{10} \approx 3.16$

SOME PERFECT SQUARES

$11^2 = 121$
$12^2 = 144$
$13^2 = 169$
$14^2 = 196$
$15^2 = 225$
$16^2 = 256$
$17^2 = 289$
$18^2 = 324$
$19^2 = 361$
$20^2 = 400$
$25^2 = 625$

SOME PERFECT CUBES

$2^3 = 8$
$3^3 = 27$
$4^3 = 64$
$5^3 = 125$
$6^3 = 216$
$8^3 = 512$
$10^3 = 1{,}000$

SOME POWERS OF 2

$2^2 = 4$
$2^3 = 8$
$2^4 = 16$
$2^5 = 32$
$2^6 = 64$
$2^7 = 128$
$2^8 = 256$
$2^9 = 512$
$2^{10} = 1{,}024$